# The New Handbook of
# Organizational
# Communication

To the memory of
Frederic M. Jablin,
co-editor, colleague, and good friend
whose hours of labor, passion for teaching,
and research in organizational communication
fostered many of the advances reported in this volume

◆◆◆

# The New Handbook of
# Organizational
# Communication

### Advances in Theory, Research, and Methods

## FREDRIC M. JABLIN
## LINDA L. PUTNAM
*Editors*

Sage Publications, Inc.
*International Educational and Professional Publisher*
Thousand Oaks ▪ London ▪ New Delhi

*For information:*

Sage Publications, Inc.
2455 Teller Road
Thousand Oaks, California 91320
E-mail: order@sagepub.com

Sage Publications Ltd.
1 Oliver's Yard
55 City Road
London EC1Y 1SP
United Kingdom

Sage Publications India Pvt. Ltd.
B-42, Panchsheel Enclave
Post Box 4109
New Delhi 110 017  India

Printed in the United States of America

*Library of Congress Cataloging-in-Publication Data*

Main entry under title:
The new handbook of organizational communication: Advances in theory,
research, and methods / edited by Fredric M. Jablin and Linda L. Putnam.
        p. cm.
Includes bibliographical references and index.
ISBN 0-8039-5503-0
    1. Communication in organizations. I.  Jablin, Fredric M. II.  Putnam, Linda.
HD30.3.H3575 2000
658.4'5—dc21                                    00-010051

                                                    ISBN 1-4129-1525-2

This book is printed on acid-free paper.

04   05   06   07   08   10  9  8  7  6  5  4  3

| | |
|---|---|
| *Acquiring Editor:* | Todd R. Armstrong |
| *Editorial Assistant:* | Deya Saoud |
| *Production Editor:* | Astrid Virding |
| *Editorial Assistant:* | Victoria Cheng |
| *Designer/Typesetter:* | Janelle LeMaster |
| *Cover Designer:* | Ravi Balasuriya |

# Editorial Reviewers

Charles R. Bantz
*Wayne State University*

James R. Barker
*U.S. Air Force Academy*

George Cheney
*University of Montana*

Robin P. Clair
*Purdue University*

Steven R. Corman
*Arizona State University*

Stanley A. Deetz
*University of Colorado at Boulder*

Eric M. Eisenberg
*University of South Florida*

Maha El-Sinnawy
*Texas A&M University*

Gail T. Fairhurst
*University of Cincinnati*

Robert P. Gephart
*University of Alberta. Canada*

Robert Giacalone
*University of North Carolina, Charlotte*

Dennis Gioia
*Pennsylvania State University*

James E. Grunig
*University of Maryland*

Teresa M. Harrison
*Rensselaer Polytechnic Institute*

Robert L. Heath
*University of Houston*

George P. Huber
*University of Texas at Austin*

David Krackhardt
*Carnegie Mellon University*

Joanne Martin
*Stanford University*

Robert D. McPhee
*Arizona State University*

Michael J. Papa
*Ohio University*

Marshall Scott Poole
*Texas A&M University*

Patricia Riley
*University of Southern California*

David R. Seibold
*University of California, Santa Barbara*

Robert Shuter
*Marquette University*

Charles Steinfield
*Michigan State University*

Bryan C. Taylor
*University of Colorado at Boulder*

James R. Taylor
*University of Montreal*

Phillip K. Tompkins
*University of Colorado at Boulder*

Nick Trujillo
*California State University, Sacramento*

John Van Maanen
*Massachusetts Institute of Technology*

Joseph B. Walther
*Rensselaer Polytechnic Institute*

Steve Weiss
*York University, Canada*

Gary Yukl
*State University of New York at Albany*

Robert Zmud
*University of Oklahoma*

Theodore E. Zorn
*University of Waikato, New Zealand*

# Contents

# Part IV. Process: Communication Behavior in Organizations

# Preface

During most of the planning and writing of this book, we referred to it as the "new" *Handbook of Organizational Communication.* There were several reasons for this. In particular, we felt that this volume was more than just a revision of the Jablin, Putnam, Roberts, and Porter *Handbook of Organizational Communication: An Interdisciplinary Perspective* published by Sage in 1987. In the years since the publication of the first handbook, new areas that had developed in the field called for a second edition that expanded the number of issues included in the original volume. Further, we knew that there were important topics not covered in chapters in the first handbook (because of space limitations) that needed to be addressed in any revision. At the same time, we felt that there were a number of chapters written for the first handbook that had "stood the test of time" and did not necessarily require revision. Finally, as the interests of the original editors changed it became apparent that we would not all be involved in the preparation of a follow-up to the original book. Thus, to a considerable extent we felt that this book was not a revision of the original handbook but rather a new volume.

There are some things that are "old" about the book as well. We have retained the same structure in organizing the chapters together in this new handbook as in the original one. Thus, the major parts of the book include discussions of theoretical and conceptual issues, context (internal and external environments), structure (patterns of organizational relationships), and processes (communication behavior in organizations). In addition, our goal in this volume is the same as in the first one: "to pull together many loose threads in the various strands of thinking and research about organizational communication and . . . to point toward new theory and empirical work that can further advance this [still fairly] young and energetic field." Consistent with the original handbook, this new book also maintains a multidisciplinary perspective to understanding organizational communication, explores issues (as relevant) at multiple levels of analysis, and includes numerous suggestions for future research and theory development.

So what exactly is new in this handbook? First, over half of the chapters explore topics that were not included in the original handbook. As a consequence, many new authors contributed to this book, while several of the authors or coauthors of chapters in the first handbook wrote chapters on new topics for this volume. Second, the first part of the book is focused not just on theoretical issues but on methodological ones as well, and chapters

xii ♦ The New Handbook of Organizational Communication

now present discussions of quantitative and qualitative research methods along with various forms of language/discourse analysis that are used in the study of organizational communication. Third, each chapter reviews and updates research in its respective area and also includes, wherever possible, discussions of relevant research and theory from around the world. Fourth, with the rapid diffusion since the 1990s of new information and communication technologies in organizations, we asked authors to develop the known and potential impacts of these technologies on communication phenomena. Finally, chapters in the book were not only reviewed by the editors but also by a distinguished board of outside readers, who provided suggestions for improving initial drafts of the essays.

The handbook now begins with a "prelude" that offers a brief, selective, historical overview of organizational communication as a discipline. Through reviewing and interpreting results of existing reviews of the field over the decades, Tompkins and Wanca-Thibault present a summary of the basic approaches, ideologies, and trends that have shaped the field's identity as it has matured. This discussion suggests that much of our future research will likely focus on developing new perspectives on old processes, relationships, problems, and issues, including the study of communication structures and networks, leader-follower communication, participation, feedback, information flow and the filtering of messages, the creation and interpretation of messages, and communication media and channels. At the same time a set of contemporary research metaphors—"discourse," "voice," and "performance"—that have emerged, guide much work in the field and are moving scholars to ask different kinds of questions and reconsider assumptions about traditional areas of study. These astute observations are clearly reflected in many of the chapters that follow in the handbook.

Part I of the book follows the prelude and explores a variety of issues related to working with and understanding organizational com-

munication theories and research methods. The first two chapters focus on theoretical issues. The Deetz chapter explores conceptual foundations in organizational communication by examining how the concept "organizational communication" is used in the literature. This discussion is framed by consideration of the type of interaction favored by a conceptualization (local/emergent vs. elite/a priori) and the relation of the conceptualization to existing social orders (consensus seeking vs. dissensus seeking). Conrad and Haynes take a different turn in exploring theoretical issues by arguing that various forms of organizational communication theory and research share a common conceptual dilemma: a need to analyze the interconnections between social/organizational structures and symbolic action (the tension between action and structure). They illustrate this notion by identifying clusters of key concepts of organizational communication theory and how they have either tended to privilege one pole of the action-structure dualism over the other or integrate the two together.

The next three chapters in Part I explore methodological issues associated with the study of organizational communication. Putnam and Fairhurst begin by reviewing research and theory related to discourse analysis—the study of words and signifiers—in organizations. They classify approaches to analyzing language as a way of understanding organizational life into eight categories or perspectives: sociolinguistics, conversation analysis, cognitive linguistics, pragmatics, semiotics, literary and rhetorical language analysis, critical language studies, and postmodern language analysis. In the fourth chapter, Miller unpacks the assumptions, practices, and challenges facing quantitative organizational communication research. Among other things, she examines the quantitative elements of experimental, survey, and behavioral observation research methods, and she considers the challenges organizational communication scholars face in the design, collection, analysis and interpretation of quantitative data. The final chapter in this part provides an overview of the use of qualitative research methods in the study of organizational communication and the dilemmas faced by those using this approach. Specifically, Taylor and Trujillo consider the relationship between qualitative and quantitative research, criteria for evaluating qualitative research studies, and issues associated with "representation" and the role of critical theory in qualitative research. In brief, the chapters in this section review and critique existing conceptualizations and research methods associated with the study of organizational communication and suggest ways for improving future work in these areas.

Part II of the book focuses on the contexts of organizations, that is, on the role of internal and external environments in shaping communicative processes. Sutcliffe's chapter centers on organizational environments and organizational information processing, and in particular how organizations gather and interpret environmental information and how, in turn, they direct the flow of information to their environments to achieve organizational goals. Linkages between internal (e.g., employee relations, mission statements) and external (e.g., public relations, marketing) communication and the manner in which organizations attempt to manage issues and their identities are elaborated in Cheney and Christensen's chapter. More specifically, this essay discusses the increasing "fuzziness" of organizational boundaries and what this implies for conceptualizing and studying communication, organizational identity, and issue management. Consistent with many of the themes underlying other chapters in this section of the book, Finet develops a discourse-oriented approach to understanding the complex interactions between organizations and their sociopolitical environments (environmental clusters representing educational institutions, religious organizations, branches of government, charities, and the like). Building on the notions of "enacted environment" and conceptualizing of organizations as "conversations," Finet outlines the rolés of two forms of organizational

discourse—institutional rhetoric and everyday talk—in relations between organizations and their sociopolitical environments.

The final two chapters in Part II focus on issues related to communication and a particular domain of organizational environments: culture. Eisenberg and Riley begin by reviewing how the organizational culture metaphor has been used in communication research, and the basic assumptions on which a communicative view of culture is founded. A variety of frameworks with respect to the role of communication in the organizational culture literature are examined, including culture as symbolism and performance, text, identity, critique, cognition and as climate and effectiveness. Overall, culture is viewed as socially constructed in which organizational members enact, legitimize, and change their environments through their talk and its residue. Subsequently, Stohl examines communication and cultural variability in multinational organizations and the growth of globalization (here globalization refers to the increasingly interconnected global economy and the blurred spatial and temporal boundaries among nations and organizations). Two distinctive models (convergence, the pressures to become similar, and divergence, maintaining differences) to understanding communication, culture, and globalization are identified, and the dynamic tension between them is articulated. Taken together, these last two chapters in Part II suggest that the field of organizational communication is well positioned to lead the organization sciences generally in the study of culture in various organizational forms and at multiple levels of analysis.

The third part of the book considers one of the most traditional areas of study in organizational communication: how patterns of communication produce and are reproduced by organizational structure. In the first chapter in this section, Fairhurst explores hierarchical interdependencies between leaders and followers through an examination of basic dualisms and tensions that characterize the study of leadership communication. Three sets of dualisms (individual and system, cognitive outcomes and conversational practices, and transmission views and meaning-centered views of communication) and their interrelationships are described, and five particular research programs are analyzed to characterize the dualisms and tensions: the study of influence tactics, feedback, charisma and visionary leadership, leader-member exchange, and systems-interaction leadership research. After careful consideration of the issues, Fairhurst concludes that we have more to gain from embracing the complexities of the tensions that she has identified in the literature than in privileging particular poles of the dualisms. In the next chapter, Monge and Contractor review the theoretical mechanisms that have been used to understand the emergence, maintenance, and dissolution of intra- and interorganizational networks. This analysis, which explores ten major families of theories that have been used to explain various aspects of the evolution of networks, lead Monge and Contractor to a number of important conclusions. Among other things, they suggest that we have devoted more attention to studying the emergence of organizational networks than in trying to understand how networks are maintained or dissolved and that we need a more careful conception of communication issues associated with network linkages and the content of messages that produce and reproduce network structures.

In the third chapter in Part III, McPhee and Poole present an analysis of approaches that have been developed to understanding formal structure-communication relationships in organizations. In particular, they discuss relationships between communication and structure in terms of four viewpoints: the dimensional, configurational, multilevel, and "structure as communication" perspectives. As a result of their analysis of the literature, McPhee and Poole argue that future research in this area would benefit from exploring structure-communication relationships in terms of structural configurations and structure as a product of communication. Coincidentally,

the final chapter in this part examines relationships between computer-mediated communication and information systems (CISs) and organizational structuring. In particular, Rice and Gattiker present research related to three basic processes of CIS structuration—adoption/implementation, transformation, and institutionalization—and show how CISs and organizational structures may facilitate or constrain one another with respect to each process. In sum, the chapters in this section highlight the inherent interdependencies that exist between organizational structures and structuring and communication processes in and among organizations.

Part IV develops a number of processes within organizations that are closely associated with communication. These chapters tend to emphasize behavioral issues related to communicating and organizing and promote a dynamic as compared to static view of organizational communication. In the opening essay, Mumby explores relationships among what he considers to be three co-constructed and interdependent phenomena: power, communication, and organization. He also discusses implicit assumptions about communication in noncommunication theories of organizational power, postmodern conceptualizations of power and communication, and the ways in which feminist studies are enhancing our understanding of relations among power, communication, and organizing. Fulk and Jarvis-Collins follow with an analysis of one of the most common activities experienced in organizations: meetings. However, they explore research and theory related to what are becoming increasingly common forms of meetings, those that are mediated through communication technologies, including computer conferencing, teleconferencing, and group support systems. This presentation revolves around three theoretical perspectives on mediated meetings (media capacity theories, input-process-output models, and structuration) and a set of frequently studied communication phenomena in groups (participation, socioemotional expression, conflict and consensus, task efficiency, decision quality, and member satisfaction). Many of the issues discussed in the next chapter, contributed by Seibold and Shea, also concern communication processes in groups. More specifically, they focus attention on the communication characteristics of employee participation programs and the contexts in which they are often implemented, the communication processes through which they work, and the role of communication in moderating their effectiveness. The participation programs they analyze are quality circles, quality-of-work-life programs, employee stock ownership plans, self-directed work teams, and Scanlon gainsharing plans.

To some degree, each of the final three chapters in the book develops issues related to learning and communication in organizations. The essay by Weick and Ashford identifies links between organizational learning and communication and unpacks individual and interpersonal communication processes associated with learning. Although communication-related barriers to organizational learning are also described, suggestions are offered detailing how communication can help ameliorate some of the impediments to learning.

The next chapter is a discussion of communication, vocation, organizational anticipatory socialization, organizational entry and assimilation, and organizational disengagement/exit processes. Unlike the chapter in the first handbook, however, in this review and interpretation of research and theory Jablin discusses organizational entry and assimilation in term of assimilation-communication processes (orienting, socialization, training, mentoring, information seeking, information giving, relationship development, and role negotiation) rather than stages of organizational assimilation, and the chapter focuses on just one aspect of the voluntary turnover process: how leavers and stayers communicate through various stages of the organizational disengagement process.

In the concluding chapter, Jablin and Sias explore selected issues related to learning in their elaboration of research and theory on communication competence and in their developmental-ecological model of organizational communication competence. Potentially problematic assumptions and premises associated with the manner in which communication competence has been conceptualized and investigated in extant research are also outlined, and competence is considered in light of globalization, new information/communication technologies, various organizational forms and managerial philosophies, gender-related expectations and patterns of behavior, and shifts in the employment status (permanent or contingent) of workers. In sum, this last part of the book builds on and expands the set of communication-related organizing processes that was developed in the original handbook.

Although we thought we learned a lot from editing the first handbook that would facilitate preparation of this volume, it actually took longer to complete this book than the earlier one. In light of the delays associated with the completion of the book, we appreciate the patience of all those involved in this project, the many revisions of chapters, and the outstanding group of authors who contributed chapters to the book and with whom it has been a pleasure to work. We also would like to acknowledge the valuable assistance of our colleagues who served on the review board and provided valuable feedback, alternative perspectives, and advice to the contributing authors on early drafts of their essays. We are also indebted to Sophy Craze and Margaret Seawell, who worked with us in planning and preparing various stages of the handbook, and to the other professionals at Sage who assisted in the publication of the book. Without their encouragement and outstanding guidance this project would not have reached fruition. In addition, we would like to express appreciation to Kate Peterson, who worked on copy editing the book, and to Tom Kleiza and Angela Mims, who assisted in checking references and in helping to resolve questions associated with the book manuscript. Gratitude is also due to our respective colleagues at the University of

Richmond and Texas A&M University, whose support helped this book become a reality.

Finally, we would like to express special appreciation to our spouses and families for their support in the pursuit of this project; somehow handbooks seem to take on a life of their own, which results in numerous disruptions in the lives of those closest to the editors. As usual, we are in debt to our loved ones for their ability to endure, with a positive attitude, the projects we initiate. To conclude, we would also like to thank the many readers of the first version of the handbook for their kind comments about that book and their encouragement to prepare this new volume. We hope the final product of the long wait meets your expectations.

—*Fredric M. Jablin*
—*Linda L. Putnam*

# Organizational Communication

## *Prelude and Prospects*

PHILLIP K. TOMPKINS
*University of Colorado at Boulder*

MARYANNE WANCA-THIBAULT
*University of Colorado at Colorado Springs*

Organizational communication as a discipline grew tremendously over the latter part of the 20th century, but accompanying that growth was a struggle to establish a clear identity for the field. And even as we enter a new millennium, the ongoing evolution of complex organizations in an equally complex global environment has scholars continuing to define and redefine the focus, boundaries, and future of the field. This prelude to *The New Handbook of Organizational Communication: Advances in Theory, Research, and Methods* takes a historical approach to assessing where the field has been, as a way of surveying the directions the field is taking. The contributions we discuss here are by no means meant to include all of the paths the field has started down from time to time, nor does it propose to outline all future areas of expansion and development. However, we do believe that the select perspectives we discuss here reflect major past and current approaches and research foci associated with the study of organizational communication.

We concentrate, then, on providing first a brief history of the rubrics, categories, and ideologies that have shaped the identity of the field. We do so by summarizing the findings of major reviews of the field that have been written over the years; in other words, we present a review of the conclusions of previous surveys of the field. Second, we note some trends in the study of organizational communication that we believe demonstrate a certain maturation of the field in that each moves the field in ways that question and deconstruct categories of the past while integrating domains and methods thought to be permanently at odds with each other. Old terministic screens give way to more inclusive ones. Division yields to merger. Mergers are subdivided. The field of organizational communication is enriched.

## REVIEWING THE REVIEWS

Generally speaking, the "modern" study of organizational communication dates from the late 1930s and early 1940s (e.g., Heron, 1942; Jablin, 1990; Redding & Tompkins, 1988). The first major state-of-the-art summaries and theoretical frameworks associated with organizational communication began to appear in the mid-1960s (e.g., Guetzkow, 1965; Thayer, 1968; Tompkins, 1967). Among speech communication scholars, Tompkins's (1967) review represents the first summary of organizational communication research that focused on summarizing solely empirical research studies (about 100 in number). He used the categories of (1) formal and informal channels of communication and (2) superior-subordinate relations to integrate the many different problems and hypotheses pursued in the literature he assessed. As Burke (1966) noted in his famous essay "Terministic Screens," the nomenclature used to define a field not only serves to reflect and select reality, it also *deflects* reality; hence, the vocabulary/language of organizational communication draws attention to certain phenomena, and simultaneously draws it away from others. Thus, while Tompkins's review of the literature found that a downward, top-down management-focus shaped the majority of research about communication in organizations, including that conducted under the rubric of superior-subordinate communication, it is important to note that these labels and concerns deflected attention away from other topics and perspectives that would later be considered by a more mature field (e.g., upward communication, vertical feedback loops, and participation).

The next major summary-integration of organizational communication was published six years later by Redding (1972). This was a massive 538-page "book" in mimeograph form that was influential and highly valued among scholars and practitioners, although not widely available. Therefore, we give some attention to this very rare, out-of-print reference.

Redding's work, unlike Tompkins's much briefer, state-of-the-art paper, placed no empiricist restraints on itself, using even "how-to" literature as stuff for analysis. Redding suggested that while many of the categories Tompkins cited remain useful, "understanding of organizational communication will be enhanced if we go beyond the traditional categories and look at our subject in a frame of reference of basic theoretical concepts" (p. vii). Hence, Redding looked at the internal communication of organizations in terms of ten "postulates" and a set of related "corollaries or extensions" derived from human communication theory and interpreted in terms of the organizational setting. In addition, he discussed the concept of organizational climate and its relationship to effective communication.

The ten postulates presented a way to reframe the relevant research from an organizational communication perspective, and in doing so, to point to potential future areas of study. By discussing the research around these principles of human communication, Redding privileged the process and in some cases put a new spin on research findings (much of which were extrapolated from other social scientific fields). This, in turn, provided future leads or directions for communication researchers. Redding also extended Tompkins's discussion of the topics the field examined at the time: concepts such as feedback, redundancy, communication overload, and serial transmission effects.

Redding's first postulate positioned *meaning* in the interpretive processes of receivers

—not in the transmission (in contrast to the typical communication model of earlier eras). The failure to interpret messages correctly resulted in what Redding (1972) called the *content fallacy:*

> What happens all too often is that we keep tinkering with the content of the message-sender's message, rather than trying to find more ways of making sure that the message-receiver's responses are appropriate. This content fallacy leads us to believe that we are "getting through" to our audience, merely because we are getting through to ourselves. (p. 29)

Next, Redding claimed that in an organization "anything is a potential message" (p. ix). He proposed that the role of both verbal and nonverbal communication had yet to be sufficiently explored in organized settings. The third postulate he discussed was the importance of input/listening, suggesting that much of the "how to manage" literature was in reality targeting good listening skills. With a considerable amount of prescience, he noted that a key behavioral characteristic of a

> participative manager is his [*sic*] ability to listen to his associates, especially his subordinates. Moreover, such listening is generally described as "empathic"—which should be differentiated from other kinds of listening, e.g., listening in order to comprehend and retain information, listening in order to analyze logically, and listening in order to refute. (p. 34)

The fourth postulate proposed that the message received (versus the one sent or intended) is what a receiver will act upon. He used the psychological concept of selective perception to make the case that individuals in organizations will respond to messages based on their personal frames of reference. The fifth postulate supported the importance of feedback in organizations. He made an important distinction between *feedback receptiveness* (the extent to which managers are open to subordinate feedback) and *feedback responsiveness* (the extent to which managers give feedback to subordinates). In brief, he recognized that being an open, receptive receiver of feedback and being a responsive receiver, that is, appropriately responding to the feedback (doing something about the information provided by followers), are not the same things.

Redding's sixth postulate addressed the "cost factor," or efficiency, of communication interactions in organizations. Communication always entails the expenditure of energy. More communication is not necessarily better as he expressed in this simple formula: efficiency = effectiveness/cost. His seventh postulate suggested that the social need for *redundancy* must be balanced by the economic need of efficiency. Too much can evoke boredom; too little makes some messages incomprehensible, particularly if there is "noise" in the system. The eighth postulate, *communication overload,* described the problems associated with an individual's "channel capacity," or the individual's limits of message processing. Redding recommended the further investigation of such concepts as "uncertainty absorption" (how message senders and receivers absorb ambiguity and clarify and make sense of messages as they communicate them upward in the organization hierarchy; e.g., March & Simon, 1958) and the "exception principle" that organizations seemed to use in trying to cope with communication overload.

The ninth postulate dealt with the "serial transmission effect," or the changes of meaning—due to filtering and distortion—as messages are passed from individual to individual in a hierarchy or informal network. Redding again recommended research on this topic to gain a better understanding of the optimal number of "relays" in serial transmissions. And again, the emphasis is on the fidelity of reception—shared meanings. Finally, in the tenth postulate, Redding suggested that the organization's "climate" for communication was more important than communication skills and techniques. After summarizing the work of many researchers and theorists, Redding articulated a trend or a growing consensus; he called it the ideal managerial climate, the components of which are (1) supportiveness; (2) participative decision making; (3) trust, confidence, and credibility; (4) openness and candor; and (5) emphasis on high performance goals (pp. 139-416). The strength of the model was its comprehensive synthesis of research (representing work conducted in many fields).

In summary, Redding tried to connect his conception of communication theory to the study of organizations. This was necessary because many of the early studies were done in cognate disciplines with implicit and superficial notions about the communication process. Redding's communication theory in retrospect is interesting and penetrating in its own right, and also interesting for its degree of self-consciousness of the transition from the *transmission-orientation* of the speech field into a *reception-orientation* of the communication field. Postulate four—"message received in the only one that counts"—perfectly illustrates his awareness of the major changes then under way. In fact, the first five postulates all express in one way or another the new reception-orientation.

Postulate eight turned contemporary assumptions upside down by conceiving of organizations as devices that *restrict* the flow of information. Curiously, Redding felt the need to put the word *networks* in quotation marks to indicate that he was talking about serial communication systems rather than about the broadcasting variety that most people thought of when hearing the word at that time. Moreover, in his discussion of ten major research topics/extensions in the final section of the book, Redding concluded with an attempt to see the future via "the role of communication in an open-system, dynamic organization (a matrix of networks)," an expression that was prescient then and fresh today. Redding had linked the theoretical and empirical nomenclatures for the first time.

Building on and consistent with much of Redding's review, Jablin (1978) summarized

research conducted during the 1940s-1970s in terms of the predominant research questions associated with each era (see Table P.1). His analysis suggested that during each decade, scholars tended to explore many similar research topics and issues: characteristics of superior-subordinate communication, emergent communication networks and channels, and components and correlates of communication climates. As we shall see, many of these research questions continued as major foci of organizational communication research during the 1980s-1990s, although often packaged in terms of "new" research issues and problems associated with communicating and organizing. The late 1970s and early 1980s also saw several, more focused, reviews of research related to organizational communication, including summaries of studies in organizational/industrial psychology (Porter & Roberts, 1976), communication networks (Monge, Edwards, & Kirste, 1978), superior-subordinate communication (Jablin, 1979), organizational group communication (Jablin & Sussman, 1983), and feedback and task performance (Downs, Johnson, & Barge, 1984), among other topics. As Tompkins (1967) observed about the studies conducted in the 1960s, the study of organizational communication relied almost exclusively on "objective means of measuring the operation and consequences of an organizational communication system" (pp. 17-18). Thus, to a considerable degree, the field in its infancy and early adolescence was rather unquestioning about the nomenclature and assumptions of logical positivism (see also Redding & Tompkins, 1988).

Twelve years after Redding's review and 17 years after his first state-of-the-art paper, Tompkins (1984) again surveyed the field of organizational communication. In this analysis, he challenged what he described as the prevailing paradigm by arguing that the field was dominated by the "rational model," that the epistemological-methodological stance of most scholarship was positivistic, and that most research questions emanated from a managerial bias. He developed four overlap-

**TABLE P.1**   Past Priorities in Organizational Communication Research: 1940s-1970s

| Era | Predominant Research Questions |
| --- | --- |
| 1940s | - What effects do downward directed mass media communications have on employees? |
| | - Is an informed employee a productive employee? |
| 1950s | - How do small-group communication networks affect organizational performance and member attitudes and behaviors? |
| | - How can emergent communication networks in organizations be measured? |
| | - What are the relationships between organizational members' attitudes and perceptions of their communication behavior (primarily upward and downward) and their on-the-job performance? |
| | - What is the relationship between the attitudes and performance of workers and the feedback they receive? |
| | - Is a well-informed employee a satisfied employee? |
| 1960s | - What do organizational members perceive to be the communication correlates of "good" supervision? |
| | - To what degree is superior-subordinate semantic-information distance a problem in organizations? |
| | - What is the relationship between subordinates' job-related attitudes and productivity and the extent to which they perceive they participate in decision making? |
| | - In what ways do the actual and perceived communication behaviors of liaison and nonliaison roles within organizational communication networks differ? |
| 1970s | - What are the components and correlates of superior-subordinate, work-group, and overall organizational communication climates? |
| | - What are the characteristics of work-group and organizational communication networks (and in particular, the distribution of "key" communication roles)? |

SOURCE: Adapted from Jablin (1978).

ping challenges to the paradigm: action, power, levels, and process. Central to Tompkins's challenge or critique was the fallacy of reification, the idea that organizations are entities where communication is situated. Instead, Tompkins (1984) asserted that "communication *constitutes* organization" (p. 660, emphasis in the original), an idea inferred from Barnard (1938). From this standpoint, he suggested that organizations might be viewed as "systems of interacting individuals," who through communication are actively involved in the process of creating and re-creating their unique social order. In retrospect, we can say that this was a call for theoretical development

of the notion of communication as *both figure and ground* (see Putnam, Phillips, & Chapman, 1996).

Tompkins then surveyed the literature with the four challenges or critiques as terministic screens, developing four categories that supported the prevailing paradigm yet had potential for opening the field to other perspectives. Studies on the first two categories, formal and informal channels of communication, were characterized as "variable analysis" and as presenting merely a "slice of the organization." As a result, such an approach gave no account of how organizational systems are related to each other. Studies dealing with the third category, systems and holistic research, attempted to remedy that shortcoming by encouraging an understanding of communication-as-social-order. Finally, the fourth category moved beyond the intraorganizational communication issues and highlighted organizational environments and interorganizational research in expanding the domain of the discipline. Tompkins noted that much of the environment of an organization is other organizations, an idea first advanced again by Barnard (1938). As these interorganizational networks become more and more complex (and more and more global) and defined by technological change, organizational boundaries become less formal and rigid. Research in this area was said to have the potential for expanding the exploration of networks outside the defined boundaries of the organization, as well as "lining a profile of the organizational society itself" (p. 706).

In conclusion, Tompkins suggested that the then-current model or paradigm did not pay sufficient attention to the root metaphors of its concepts and approaches. Tompkins encouraged a shift from a mechanistic to an organic root metaphor, one that refuses to conceive organizational actors as cogs or nodes, and one that would have the advantage of framing organizations from an idiographic perspective rather than the ideal of the mechanistic root metaphor. And as such, this perspective had the potential to address the four critiques of the rational model by refocusing on (1) the importance of the actions of organizational members in creating and negotiating organizational reality; (2) power as an overarching force and organizational rhetoric as the system of persuasion; (3) the variability of levels or boundaries and the impact of interorganizational interaction on the system; and (4) process as the ongoing negotiation of organizational order, topics that have been sufficiently explored since then to warrant detailed attention in this handbook.

In 1983, an important "turn" came in the field with the publication of *Communication and Organizations: An Interpretive Approach*,[1] edited by Putnam and Pacanowsky, a volume that grew out of papers given at the First Conference on Interpretive Approaches to Organizational Communication at Alta, Utah, in 1981. The impact of the essays in this book was not so much in defining the boundaries, concepts, and research problems for the field—it was an anthology, not an integrative literature review—as it was in questioning what counted as knowledge in organizational communication. As explained in the introduction, the purposes of the book were (1) to explain the interpretive approach as it might apply to organizational communication, (2) to divide the interpretive approach into naturalistic and critical studies, and (3) to provide exemplar studies using the naturalistic and critical approaches. Thus, essays in the book suggested that the interpretive approach would enrich extant methodologies, which, as indicated above, were mainly "objective," quantitative in nature, and based on functionalist assumptions. In brief, the book reflected some new approaches to studying organizational communication by the use of a new terministic screen (albeit one based on the analytic framework of Burrell and Morgan, 1979, which was developed to explore sociological paradigms evident in organizational analysis generally; see Deetz, 1986, and Chapter 1, this volume).

A couple of years later, Putnam and Cheney (1985) took a slightly different approach by taking into account disciplinary roots of the field. They saw four general categories in previous analyses: channels, climate, network analysis, and superior-subordinate communication. In addition, they identified several trends or directions for future research, including information processing; political perspectives to communicating in organizations; organizational rhetoric, communication and organizational culture; the extension of Weick's (1979) work on enactment or meaning (cf. Redding's first postulate considered above); and research seeking to depict multiple perspectives on organization communication, not just that of management.

The most definitive *history* of the field of organizational communication was written by

Redding in 1985. This book chapter suggested a multitude of influences, both practical and academic, on the creation and development of the field and its emergence as a central area of study in the speech communication discipline. He gave three explanations to suggest why speech communication scholars assumed the organizational communication banner. The first was that other social scientists had abdicated responsibility, regarding communication problems as mere symptoms of deeper conditions. The second was that the speech field was well suited to fill this void because of its traditions, including the rhetorical perspective. The third explanation was given over to identifying persons in the speech field who had provided the leadership necessary to develop the new field (and characteristically, Redding modestly excluded himself from the group).

In 1988, Redding and Tompkins extended Redding's (1985) longitudinal perspective in commenting on the evolution of organizational communication theory, practice, and research methods. The period from 1900 to 1970 was divided into three approaches: *formulary-prescriptive, empirical-prescriptive,* and the *applied scientific.* The formulary-prescriptive position relied primarily on the development of sets of rules or commonsense prescriptions (based on traditional rhetorical theory) for effective business communication. This body of literature bore such titles as "business English," "business and professional speaking," and "winning friends and influencing people." The empirical-prescriptive phase was noted by a dependence on anecdotal and case study data, with a how-to perspective. The final position, applied scientific, was closely identified with traditional forms of scientific measurement used to explore organizational issues "objectively."

Redding and Tompkins (1988) divided the work done after 1970 as *modernistic, naturalistic,* and *critical,* spelling out in a matrix the main assumptions, methodologies, epistemologies, and ontologies used in each of the three. The modernistic (emerging postmodern perspectives at the time began to create a perspective on what it was assumed to be supplanting) approach assumed that organizations were natural, objective forms and, as such, subject to prediction and control. The modernists' mode is nomothetic, the discovery of lawlike regularities that can be applied across organizational contexts. The naturalistic orientation attempts an understanding and anticipation of communicative interactions through an ethnographic lens, a picture of "Gestalt-like knowledge of wholes, or a hermeneutic understanding of part-to-whole and vice versa" (p. 24). At the heart of this approach is the assumption that organizations are subjective forms that are socially constructed by their members. Finally, the critical approach is described by the authors as "a type of consciousness-raising, if not emancipation for, organizational members themselves" (p. 23). Today we could say that the critical theorists substituted for the previous identification with management—the management bias—an identification with other organizational stakeholders, often the lower-ranking members and workers. Redding and Tompkins articulated the primary goal of critical theorists as the critique and exposure of organizations and their practices in the hope of changing them from oppressive to empowering sites.

The publication in the late 1980s of two handbooks focused on compiling and interpreting organizational communication research and theory (Goldhaber & Barnett, 1988; Jablin, Putnam, Roberts, & Porter, 1987) represented a major milestone in the field's development. However, given that the editors of these two volumes did not join together to produce one handbook, the publication of two handbooks may suggest a lack of consensus among scholars with respect to the "stuff" of organizational communication, and as a consequence each of these efforts may reflect and deflect unique categories and approaches to defining the field.

The Jablin et al. (1987) volume clearly reflects a view of the study of organizational communication as (1) a phenomenon occurring at multiple, interrelated levels of analysis (dyadic, group, organizational, and extraorganizational); and (2) a multi-/interdisciplinary research enterprise, as evident in the volume's title, *Handbook of Organizational Communication: An Interdisciplinary Perspective,* as well as the various backgrounds of the editors and contributors to the book. As stated in the book's preface, the editors view organizational communication as a field "intersecting" many areas that had grown so rapidly in recent years that the problem in putting together a handbook was what to exclude versus what to include (a far cry from the task that faced Guetzkow, 1965, and Tompkins, 1967, in earlier reviews). In the end, they organized the book into four terministic "screens" or parts: (1) Theoretical Issues, (2) Context: Internal and External Environments, (3) Structure: Patterns of Organizational Relationships, and (4) Process: Communication Behavior in Organizations. Consistent with earlier reviews of the literature, the editors suggested that the last two parts of the book, *structure* (emergent communication networks, formal organization structure, superior-subordinate communication, and information technologies) and *process* (message exchange processes, power, politics and influence, conflict and negotiation, message flow and decision making, feedback, motivation and performance, and organizational entry, assimilation, and exit) "constitute what is ordinarily regarded as the central core of organizational communication" (Jablin et al., p. 8).

Goldhaber and Barnett (1988) parsed the field in a somewhat different manner. Their handbook is organized into three sections: (1) Theoretical Perspectives and Conceptual Advances in Organizational Communication, (2) Methodological Approaches, and (3) Organizational Communication in the Information Age. While these are merely section labels, and there is overlap in content among chapters included in Jablin et al. (1987) and Goldhaber and Barnett (1988), the lack of congruence in nomenclature between the two books in cate-

gorizing the field is noteworthy and indicative of distinct views on the centrality of various topics to the study of organizational communication. For example, Goldhaber and Barnett's book includes a section "Methodological Approaches," which draws attention to specific research methods the editors perceive as associated with the study of organizational communication. The methods discussed in this section (e.g., network analysis, gradient analysis) tend to focus on quantitative research methodologies associated with the study of communication and formal organizational structures. The methods section of the book does not include any chapters that specifically focus on qualitative, interpretive, or critical research methodologies, although in the foreword to the book the editors acknowledge that these approaches have grown in popularity among researchers (p. 2). Thus, while Jablin et al. (1987) deflect attention away from organizational communication research methods generally (perhaps because of the breadth of methodologies associated with a multi-/interdisciplinary perspective), Goldhaber and Barnett deflect attention away from interpretive methodologies in particular. In turn, whereas Jablin et al. draw attention to the information-communication contexts or environments of organizations by devoting a section of their book to these issues, Goldhaber and Barnett devote an entire section of their book to a more focused topic: organizational communication and new information technologies. Further, both volumes deflect attention away from ethical issues associated with the study and practice of organizational communication (e.g., Conrad, 1993; Redding, 1992), in that there are no chapters or even index entries related to this topic. While the above stances may reflect the preferences of the editors of the two books, they also may suggest that in the late 1980s the field was still in the process of conceptualizing its traditional domain and grappling with ways of approaching emerging areas of study.

Applying the Redding and Tompkins (1988) matrix to organizational communication articles published in 15 communication journals, Wert-Gray, Center, Brashers, and Meyers (1991) categorized research conducted in the field during the decade 1979-1989. They found that during that decade five topics accounted for over 65% of the research: (1) climate and culture; (2) superior-subordinate communication; (3) power, conflict, and politics; (4) information flow; and (5) public organizational communication. Methodologically, 57.8% of the research articles were modernistic (or positivistic) in orientation, 26% used a naturalistic approach, and only 2.1% manifested the critical approach. Although the sample of journals that Wert-Gray et al. included in their study is not inclusive of all the major outlets in which organizational communication research is published, their findings, along with the foci of chapter topics included in the two handbooks noted above, suggest that the so-called interpretive-critical revolution of the early 1980s was not quite as complete as many believed. Modernism was fairly well entrenched during the decade studied—even though the percentages may have changed in the years since the study was conducted.

In what the authors describe as a "reference index" of articles published in 61 journals, Allen, Gotcher, and Seibert (1993) identified the most heavily researched organizational communication topics from 1980 through 1991. Their typology (see Table P.2) emerged as a by-product of analyzing the articles, although the researchers suggest that the areas they used to categorize research are similar to those used in past reviews. According to their study, interpersonal relations, and in particular superior-subordinate communication, was the most researched topic, followed by communication skills, and organizational culture and symbolism. Deetz (1992) suggests that the review shows across topics significant growth in the "social construction of organizations and reality" (p. xiii) during the ten-year period reviewed. Although fairly comprehensive, this review has been criticized for what the researchers left out of their analysis

(e.g., handbooks, yearbook chapters, selected studies) and the manner in which they classified particular articles into topical areas, among other things (DeWine & Daniels, 1993).

The most recent major review and compilation of organizational communication research and theory was completed by Putnam et al. (1996). They approached the process of reviewing and interpreting the literature in a manner distinct from those discussed above: by identifying perspectives, in the form of metaphor clusters, that they believed characterize conceptualizations and approaches to the study of organizational communication. Each of the seven metaphor clusters they identified—conduit, lens, linkage, performance, symbol, voice, and discourse—can be considered a terministic screen/perspective, and as such "researchers can examine any organizational topic from one of these clusters" (Putnam et al., 1996, p. 394). However, it is important to note that since each metaphor varies in complexity and completeness with respect to the study of organizational communication (see Table P.3), it also reflects—as well as neglects—key elements of organizational communication phenomena.

For example, they illustrate the ways boundaries are part of organizational metaphors and how alternative ways of conceiving of organizations remove boundary as a central element. In addition, Putnam et al. (1996) suggest that "the criteria for choosing a particular metaphor are the researcher's goals, the ontological basis of both communication and organization, and the phenomenon that is most central to the organizing process" (p. 394).

In looking back at their analysis of the literature, Putnam et al. (1996) drew three conclusions about organizational communication research:

1. Despite limitations with respect to the completeness and complexity of the perspectives, "the conduit and the lens metaphors are the primary ways that organizational scholars treat communication" (p. 396).

**TABLE P.2**   Frequency of Publication of Organizational Communication Journal Articles by Topical Areas: 1980-1991

| Frequency (total = 889) | Topic/Sample Subtopics |
| --- | --- |
| 233 | Interpersonal relations: includes superior-subordinate relations; interpersonal communication and conflict, stress, race and gender; and interviewing |
| 120 | Communication skills and strategies: includes persuasion, influence strategies, self-presentation, listening, feedback seeking and giving, supervisory communication skills, interviewing, and associations between skill proficiency and outcomes |
| 99 | Organizational culture and symbolism: includes rites and rituals, communication rules/norms, metaphors, organizational texts, stories, images, and myths |
| 74 | Information flow and channels: includes factors affecting information flow, information transmission, direction of communication, media preferences, and innovation |
| 67 | Power and influence: includes power and influence tactics, social construction of power, politics and games, language use, negotiation, bargaining, and argumentation |
| 67 | Positive outcomes associated with communication: includes studies that link communication outcomes such as commitment, performance, satisfaction, productivity, and burnout |
| 67 | Decision making and problem solving: includes participative decision making, factors influencing how decisions are made, and constraints on decision making |
| 57 | Communication networks: includes antecedents and outcomes associated with network membership, network measurement, network roles, and interorganizational networks |
| 57 | Cognitive, communication, and management styles: includes identification of styles and their relationships to outcomes, and relations between styles and behavior |
| 53 | Organization-environment communication interface: includes image-related communication, boundary spanning, information flows, and corporate discourse |
| 45 | Technology |
| 42 | Structure |
| 41 | Language and message content |
| 41 | Groups and organizational effectiveness |
| 40 | Uncertainty and information adequacy |
| 28 | Ethics |
| 24 | Cross-cultural |
| 18 | Climate |

SOURCE: Adapted from a descriptive review of organizational communication articles published in 61 journals from 1980 to 1991 by Allen, Gotcher, and Seibert (1993). Articles may be included in more than one topical category.

**TABLE P.3**   Metaphors of Organizational Communication Research

| Metaphor Cluster | Orientation to Organization/ Communication Perspective/Examples of Research Foci |
|---|---|
| Conduit | - Organization viewed as *containers* or channels of information flow<br>- Communication equated with *transmission;* functions as a *tool*<br>- Examples of research foci: formal and informal channels; comparisons among communication media; organizational structure and information overload, capacity, and adequacy |
| Lens | - Organization viewed as an eye that scans, sifts, and relays information<br>- Communication equated with a *filtering* process, reception and perception processes<br>- Examples of research foci: message distortion and ambiguity, information acquisition and decision making, gatekeeping, media richness |
| Linkage | - Organization viewed as *networks* of multiple, overlapping relationships<br>- Communication equated with *connections* and interdependence<br>- Examples of research foci: intra- and interorganizational network roles, patterns and structures, characteristics of ties/linkages |
| Performance | - Organization viewed as *coordinated actions* that enact their own rules, structures, and environment through social interaction<br>- Communication equated with *social interaction,* dynamic processes of interlocking behaviors, reflexivity, collaboration, and sensemaking<br>- Examples of research foci: enactment cycles, storytelling, symbolic convergence, jamming, co-constructing improvisations |
| Symbol | - Organization viewed as a *novel* or *literary text,* a symbolic milieu in which organizing is accomplished<br>- Communication equated with *interpretation* and representation through the creation, maintenance, and transformation of meanings<br>- Examples of research foci: narratives, organizational metaphors, rites, rituals, ceremonies, paradoxes and ironies, culture and language |
| Voice | - Organization viewed as a *chorus* of diverse voices<br>- Communication equated with the *expression, suppression,* and *distortion* of the voices of organizational members<br>- Examples of research foci: hegemony, power, ideology, marginalization of voices, empowerment, legitimation, unobtrusive control |
| Discourse | - Organization viewed as *texts,* ritualized patterns of interaction that transcend immediate conversations<br>- Communication equated with *conversation,* as both process and structure/ context, intertwining both action and meaning<br>- Examples of research foci: discourse as artifact/codes, structure and process, discursive practices, communication genres |

SOURCE: Adapted from Putnam, Phillips, and Chapman (1996).

2. Examination of the metaphors provides strong support for the notion that "communication and organization are equivalent" (p. 396).

3. As evident in the growing popularity of metaphors of organizations as voice, texts, and discourse, it is possible that organizational communication "no longer mirrors or reflects reality, rather it is formative in that it creates and represents the process of organizing" (p. 396).

In other words, "figure and ground" are becoming more difficult to isolate in organizational communication research.

## PROSPECTS AND CONCLUDING COMMENTS

In this section, we consider the implications of our review of reviews for future research and theory development in the field of organizational communication. Our conclusions are not meant to be comprehensive in nature, but reflect just a handful of themes we perceive are evident in our history and perhaps in the field's future.

First, examination of the topical reviews of literature suggests that a good part of our future research will continue to extend past research by developing "new" perspectives on "old" issues and problems associated with communication and organization. Thus, the field's traditional focus on leader-follower communication; communication networks and structures; the creation, sensing, and routing of information; information flow and participation in decision making; filtering and distortion of messages; communication channels; feedback processing; and the like will remain significant areas of study (see Tables P.1 and P.2). To a large extent, these topics tend to focus on the sorts of communication structures and processes that Jablin et al. (1987) suggested are frequently "regarded at the central core of organizational communication"

(p. 8). Thus, while the specific research questions will vary (e.g., the effects of a new communication technology on the processing of feedback, or communication patterns and roles in "new" organizational forms), much of our research will be expanding on topics that have a long history of study in organizational communication. However, since researchers who explored these topics in the past have tended to conceptualize and operationalize them in terms of the metaphors of "conduit," "lens," "linkages," and more recently "symbols" (Putnam et al., 1996), there is considerable room for advancement of knowledge through the investigation of these topics through (1) other appropriate metaphors and representations (ones that don't confound related assumptions about communication and organization), and (2) the chaining of "threads" of related metaphor clusters together to reveal interrelationships and possibly new metaphors.

Second, we see the emergence of research traditions founded on the metaphors of "voice," "discourse," and "performance" as part of a maturation of the field in that each moves the field in ways that question and deconstruct metaphors and categories of the past while integrating domains and methods thought to be permanently at odds with one another. For example, recent research exploring a construct central to the history of the field (see Redding, 1972)—participation—has enriched our understanding of this notion via consideration from a number of voice-based perspectives including concertive control (e.g., Barker, 1993; Tompkins & Cheney, 1985) and critical theory (e.g., Deetz, 1992), as well as in terms of "discourse" (e.g., Taylor, 1993, 1995) and network metaphors (e.g., Stohl, 1995). Another area of study that has been a focus of interest since the beginning of the field—communication networks—has also benefited from consideration via voice, discourse, and performance perspectives. For example, Taylor (1993) has suggested that networks themselves might be viewed as texts in that they represent relatively ritualized, structured patterns of interaction that "transcend" immediate conversations (see also recent research exploring "semantic" networks in organizations [e.g., Contractor, Eisenberg, & Monge, 1992] and recent studies of networks, meaning, and solidarity [e.g., Kiianmaa, 1997] ). Reflective of the voice metaphor he adds that communication networks practically guarantee "that some influences remain unheard, and hence that some of the accounts which all organizations spontaneously develop are attended to regularly, and others are ignored" (p. 90). Alternatively, based on Tompkins and Cheney's (1985) work on control, Stohl (1995) posits that participation in networks can blur distinctions among individuals and groups in organizations and thereby "further an organization's ability to control unobtrusively individuals" (p. 147). These are important issues to consider and we believe demonstrate how traditional areas of organizational communication research can be enriched through analysis via the discourse, performance, and voice metaphors. They give us a richer nomenclature than we had in the past with which to select and reflect reality for analysis.

Finally, our analysis suggests that the field is now focusing more on communicational theorizing about organizing than in the recent past. In particular, Taylor's (1993, 1995; Taylor, Cooren, Giroux, & Robichard, 1996) work is noteworthy in that it attempts to "reconstruct" a communication-based theory of organization. In brief, he argues that conversations are the stuff of organizations, conversations lead to narratives or texts meaningful to the conversationalists, and organization is a communication system—"an ecology of conversation" (p. 244). Thus, he moves from a metaphor of communication as both the figure and ground, the paint and the canvas of an organization, to one of a "text produced by a set of authors, through conversation" (Taylor, 1993, p. 96). Recent contributions such as Taylor's as well as those of other scholars (e.g., Stohl's, 1995, effort to link relational theories of interpersonal communication with

network explanations of organizational functioning), like Redding's (1972) little-known attempt decades earlier, ground organizational studies in communication theory. Thus, they facilitate a view of organizations as communicational in nature, a perspective that we expect will be central to understanding the more fluid, fragmented, and chaotic forms of organizations and organizing that are expected in the future (e.g., Bergquist, 1993; McPhee & Poole, Chapter 13, this volume). In these contexts communication and organization are equivalent, discourse is organizing; it is the paint and the canvas, the figure and ground.

## NOTE

1. Although Tompkins's summary chapter in the Arnold and Bowers handbook was published in 1984 and the Putnam and Pacanowsky book in 1983, we reverse the apparent chronological order because the Tompkins chapter was submitted in early 1980, some time before the Putnam-Pacanowsky book went to press. In fact, Putnam (1983) refers to the chapter as "(Tompkins, in press)" in her chapter on the interpretive perspective.

## REFERENCES

Allen, M. W., Gotcher, J. M., & Seibert, J. H. (1993). A decade of organizational communication research: Journal articles 1980-1991. In S. A. Deetz (Ed.), *Communication yearbook 16* (pp. 252-330). Newbury Park, CA: Sage.

Barker, J. (1993). Tightening the iron cage: Concertive control in self-managing teams. *Administrative Science Quarterly, 38,* 408-437.

Barnard, C. (1938). *The functions of the executive.* Cambridge, MA: Harvard University Press.

Bergquist, W. (1993). *The postmodern organization: Mastering the art of irreversible change.* San Francisco: Jossey-Bass.

Burke, K. (1966). *Language as symbolic action.* Berkeley: University of California Press.

Burrell, G., & Morgan, G. (1979). *Sociological paradigms and organizational analysis.* London: Heinemann.

Conrad, C. (Ed.). (1993). *The ethical nexus.* Norwood, NJ: Ablex.

Contractor, N., Eisenberg, E., & Monge, P. (1992). *Antecedents and outcomes of interpretive diversity in or-*

*ganizations.* Unpublished manuscript, University of Illinois, Urbana-Champaign.

Deetz, S. (1986). Describing differences in approaches to organization science: Rethinking Burrell and Morgan and their legacy. *Organization Science, 7,* 191-207.

Deetz, S. A. (1992). *Democracy in an age of corporate colonization.* Albany: State University of New York Press.

DeWine, S., & Daniels, T. (1993). Beyond the snapshot: Setting a research agenda in organizational communication. In S. A. Deetz (Ed.), *Communication yearbook 16* (pp. 331-346). Newbury Park, CA: Sage.

Downs, C. W., Johnson, K. M., & Barge, J. K. (1984). Communication feedback and task performance in organizations: A review of the literature. In H. H. Greenbaum, R. L. Falcione, S. A. Hellweg, & Associates (Eds.), *Organizational communication: Abstracts, analysis, and overview* (Vol. 9, pp. 13-48). Beverly Hills, CA: Sage.

Goldhaber, G. M., & Barnett, G. A. (Eds.). (1988). *Handbook of organizational communication.* Norwood, NJ: Ablex.

Guetzkow, H. (1965). Communication in organizations. In J. G. March (Ed.), *Handbook of organizations* (pp. 534-573). Chicago: Rand McNally.

Heron, A. R. (1942). *Sharing information with employees.* Palo Alto, CA: Stanford University Press.

Jablin, F. M. (1978, November). *Research priorities in organizational communication.* Paper presented at the annual meeting of the Speech Communication Association, Minneapolis.

Jablin, F. M. (1979). Superior-subordinate communication: The state-of-the-art. *Psychological Bulletin, 86,* 1201-1222.

Jablin, F. M. (1990). Organizational communication. In G. L. Dahnke & G. W. Clatterbuck (Eds.), *Human communication: Theory and research* (pp. 156-182). Belmont, CA: Wadsworth.

Jablin, F. M., Putnam, L. L., Roberts, K. H., & Porter, L. W. (Eds.). (1987). *Handbook of organizational communication: An interdisciplinary perspective.* Newbury Park, CA: Sage.

Jablin, F. M., & Sussman, L. (1983). Organizational group communication: A review of the literature and a model of the process. In H. H. Greenbaum, R. L. Falcione, S. A. Hellweg, & Associates (Eds.), *Organizational communication: Abstracts, analysis, and overview* (Vol. 8, pp. 11-50). Beverly Hills, CA: Sage.

Kiianmaa, A. (1997). *Moderni totemismi: Tutkimustyoelämästä, solidaarisuudesta ja sosiaalisista verkostoista keskiuokkaistuvassa Suomessa.* Helsinki, Finland: Jyvasklyla.

March, J. G., & Simon, H. A. (1958). *Organizations.* New York: John Wiley.

Monge, P. R., Edwards, J. A., & Kirste, K. K. (1978). The determinants of communication and structure in large organizations: A review of research. In B. D. Ruben (Ed.), *Communication yearbook 2* (pp. 311-331). New Brunswick, NJ: Transaction.

Porter, L. W., & Roberts, K. H. (1976). Communication in organizations. In M. D. Dunnette (Ed.), *Handbook of industrial and organizational psychology* (pp. 1553-1589). Chicago: Rand McNally.

Putnam, L. (1983). The interpretive perspective: An alternative to functionalism. In L. L. Putnam & M. E. Pacanowsky (Eds.), *Communication and organizations: An interpretive approach* (pp. 31-54). Beverly Hills, CA: Sage.

Putnam, L., & Cheney, G. (1985). Organizational communication: Historical developments and future directions. In T. Benson (Ed.), *Speech communication in the 20th century* (pp. 130-156). Carbondale: Southern Illinois University Press.

Putnam, L. L., & Pacanowsky, M. E. (Eds.). (1983). *Communication and organizations: An interpretive approach.* Beverly Hills, CA: Sage.

Putnam, L. L., Phillips, N., & Chapman, P. (1996). Metaphors of communication and organization. In S. R. Clegg, C. Hardy, & W. R. Nord (Eds.), *Handbook of organization studies* (pp. 375-408). Thousand Oaks, CA: Sage.

Redding, W. C. (1972). *Communication within the organization: An interpretive review of theory and research.* New York: Industrial Communication Council.

Redding, W. C. (1985). Stumbling toward an identity: The emergence of organizational communication as a field of study. In R. D. McPhee & P. K. Tompkins (Eds.), *Organizational communication: Traditional themes and new directions* (pp. 15-54). Newbury Park, CA: Sage.

Redding, W. C. (1992). *Ethics and the study of organizational communication: When will we wake up?* Paper presented at the Center for the Study of Ethics in Society, Western Michigan University, Kalamazoo.

Redding, W. C., & Tompkins, P. K. (1988). Organizational communication: Past and present tenses. In G. Goldhaber & G. Barnett (Eds.), *Handbook of organizational communication* (pp. 5-34). Norwood, NJ: Ablex.

Stohl, C. (1995). *Organizational communication: Connectedness in action.* Thousand Oaks, CA: Sage.

Taylor, J. (1993). *Rethinking the theory of organizational communication: How to read an organization.* Norwood, NJ: Ablex.

Taylor, J. (1995). Shifting from a heteronomous to an autonomous worldview of organizational communication: Communication theory on the cusp. *Communication Theory, 5,* 1-35.

Taylor, J., Cooren, F., Giroux, N., & Robichard, D. (1996). The communicational basis of organization: Between the conversation and the text. *Communication Theory, 6,* 1-39.

Thayer, L. (1968). *Communication and communication systems.* Homewood, IL: Irwin.

Tompkins, P. K. (1967). Organizational communication: A state-of-the-art review. In G. Richetto (Ed.), *Conference on organizational communication* (pp. 4-26). Huntsville, AL: National Aeronautics and Space Administration.

Tompkins, P. K. (1984). The functions of communication in organizations. In C. Arnold & J. Bowers (Eds.), *Handbook of rhetorical and communication theory* (pp. 659-719). New York: Allyn & Bacon.

Tompkins, P. K., & Cheney, G. (1985). Communication and unobtrusive control in contemporary organizations. In R. D. McPhee & P. K. Tompkins (Eds.), *Organizational communication: Traditional themes and new directions* (pp. 179-210). Newbury Park, CA: Sage.

Weick, K. E. (1979). *The social psychology of organizing* (2nd ed.). Reading, MA: Addison-Wesley.

Wert-Gray, S., Center, C., Brashers, D., & Meyers, R. (1991). Research topics and methodological orientations in organizational communication: A decade in review. *Communication Studies, 42,* 141-154.

# PART I

# Theoretical and Methodological Issues

# 1

# Conceptual Foundations

STANLEY DEETZ
*University of Colorado at Boulder*

For all of recorded history, people have studied and discussed communication processes within their dominant organizations. In many respects, these discussions differ little from those present during the past three decades of institutional organizational communication study. They have been concerned with the systematic manners by which communication practices can be used to help coordinate and control the activities of organizational members and relations with external constituencies. Our current situation is one of rapid social and organizational change putting great pressure on researchers today to continually develop useful concepts and studies to match the complex interactions characteristic of contemporary workplaces.

Organizational communication research is itself a rich communicative process. Researchers have developed and used their theories and research activities for many positive organizational outcomes. But their work also accomplishes a variety of intertwined life purposes, including the distinction of the researcher and the development and advancement of specific group interests. Fundamental assumptions about the nature of the world, methods of producing knowledge, and values are developed and advanced in the discourse of researchers. Such assumptions are necessary to produce any kind of understanding and knowledge and are usually most contested during periods of rapid change. While fundamental assumptions themselves are not open to refutation, they are to exploration. Scholars rightfully ask of any research program, "To solve what problems?" "To what ends?" "Whose meanings?" "Whose knowledge?"

This essay hopes to foster useful discussions regarding how different scholars construct knowledge and justify practices about organizations, and also about the values, hopes, and groups' interest that they support. To that end, I begin with an overview of how the term *organizational communication* is used—what it delimits, organizes, or draws our attention to. Following this introduction, the central part of the chapter will develop a two-dimensional scheme for directing attention to similarities and differences among research programs. I will argue that the most interesting differences among social research programs can be displayed through looking at (1) the type of interaction particular researchers favor with other groups, characterized as *local/emergent* versus *elite/a priori* conceptions; and (2) the moves the research activity and report make toward closure or indeterminacy in that interaction, characterized as *consensus* seeking versus *dissensus* seeking. These two dimensions when put together provide a two by two matrix characterizing differences in research programs. I will discuss each of four "ideal type" research programs produced in this grid. Finally, I will conclude by looking at the researcher's choice processes in the contemporary context and looking at future research agenda.

## ORGANIZATIONAL COMMUNICATION

What is organizational communication? The possibility of a shared answer to that question seems to be implied in producing a handbook of organizational communication or in detailing conceptual foundations for organizational communication studies. Clear and simple answers can be given. I could just provide a definition, compare it with alternative definitions, and get on with a review. Defini-

tions are nice; they set clear boundaries and justify my looking at the things I am interested in, and excluding the rest. But such definitions are inevitably arbitrary, usually provide political advantage for some group, and can as easily produce blinders as insight. Not only is debate possible over alternative definitions but also over the act of defining (Deetz, 1992, chap. 3; Smith, 1993; Taylor, 1993). Ultimately, the question "What is organizational communication?" is misleading. A more interesting question is, "What do we see or what are we able to do if we think of organizational communication in one way versus another?" Unlike a definition, the attempt here is not to get it right, but to understand our choices. Rather than killing the bird ("definition" definitio, to kill or make final) and getting on with the dissection, perhaps we should watch it fly for a while.

Three very different ways of conceptualizing "organizational communication" are available. Each of these provides different "attentions" and different boundaries regarding what should be covered in this volume and this chapter. Such conceptions guide research and teaching as well as provide an identity to a group of scholars. First, the focus could be on the development of organizational communication as a speciality in departments of communication and communication associations. Organizational communication study is whatever anyone does who is a member of these divisions or publishes in particular journals (see, e.g., Smeltzer, 1993). Like with other "sociologies of fields," time can be spent looking at the history of this development, what members of these divisions have studied and published, how many students major or achieve advanced degrees in this speciality, and how many jobs are available (see Redding, 1979). These are not unimportant concerns and such a conception either explicitly or implicitly has been used to determine what is or is not an organizational communication study in many if not most literature reviews (see Krone, Jablin, & Putnam, 1987; Meyers, Seibert, & Allen, 1993; Putnam & Cheney, 1985; Redding & Tompkins, 1988;

Richetto, 1977; Wert-Gray, Center, Brashers, & Meyers, 1991).[1] From these reviews we often gain more understanding of people, their relations, careers, and university politics than we do about the underlying conceptions of organizations and communication. Moving from reviews of studies to examining alternative theories in organizational communication studies and the social problems such studies address is often difficult. It is not surprising that these reviews often contain laments about the disunity of the field. This may well be an artifact of the organizing principle used.

A second approach to conceptualizing organizational communication focuses on communication as a phenomenon that exists in organizations. If such an object can be defined, then anyone who looks at or talks about that object is studying organizational communication. This is the logic behind many textbook definitions of organizational communication. Within this logic, any number of individuals from different academic units might study this phenomenon. In such a case, interdisciplinarity might be expected. With this focus one might ask what is "communication" in the organization and what is something else, what are the ways the phenomenon can be usefully subdivided, what are the variables that affect it or it affects, and what theories adequately explain it. Handbooks like this one usually work from this type of conception (see Krone et al., 1987). They assume that a unified phenomenon exists, and they form chapters based on subdivisions of the phenomenon or alternative sites where it appears. Introductory chapters like this one typically focus on the variety of ways that the same phenomenon has been examined.

Unfortunately for such a tack, many of the contemporary theories of organizations and communication deny that a unitary phenomenon exists out there. Thus, the phenomenon —organizational communication—is different for different theories. "Organizational communication" is not one phenomenon with many explanations; each form of explanation may conceptualize and explain a different

phenomenon. Fixed subdivisions are always a kind of theoretical hegemony (where one theory's "organizational communication" is privileged over undiscussed others). When this happens, theory debate is reduced to methodological perspectivalism. When thought of as a distinct phenomenon, the conception of "organization" is often reduced to a "site" and the conception of "communication" often becomes narrow with social interaction conceptually reduced to empirical acts of information transfer, often the lowest common denominator (or dominator) in organizational communication (for discussion, see Axley, 1984; Putnam, Phillips, & Chapman, 1996; Smith, 1993; Taylor, 1993).

A third way to approach the issue is to think of communication as a way to describe and explain organizations. In the same way that psychology, sociology, or economics can be thought of as capable of explaining organizations' processes, communication might also be thought of as a distinct mode of explanation or way of thinking about organizations (see Deetz, 1994a; Pearce, 1989). Communication theory can be used to explain the production of social structures, psychological states, member categories, knowledge, and so forth rather than being conceptualized as simply one phenomenon among these others in organizations. The focus would be on the process of organizing through symbolic interaction rather than on "communication" within an "organization" (Hawes, 1974). From such a perspective the interest is not in theories of organizational communication but in producing a communication theory of organizations (Deetz, 1994a). Historically, few scholars in the academic units of organizational communication have approached the issue this way. Until recently, psychological or social-cultural explanations have been more often used in most studies. Gradually, since the early 1980s, scholars in communication departments as well as a large number of non-U.S. scholars and some scholars from other academic units have focused on organizations as complex discursive formations where discursive practices are both "in" organizations and productive of them. Because of the tendency to delimit organizational communication as a professional unit or a distinct phenomenon, until recently non-U.S. and non-communication scholars were often absent from reviews (e.g., the various works of Knights, Willmott, Hollway, Cooper, Burrell, Gergen, Power, Townley, and Alvesson).

In this review, I will accept this third way of thinking about organizational communication. The recursiveness of this position means that the production of the field as an academic unit and organizational communication as a distinct phenomenon are themselves discursive accomplishments. My analysis will thus work at a metalevel from which conceptions of organizations and processes in them by researchers and "organizational members" can themselves be seen "communicationally." This view allows a deeper analysis that can display how study results are produced rather than just providing here another review of results from different research programs. The duality of studying human interaction in a specific location and the assumption that human interaction is a core formative feature of world construction complicates analysis much but also greatly enriches it.

Largely I follow the instruction given by Bourdieu (1991):

> The social sciences deal with prenamed, preclassified realities which bear proper nouns and common nouns, titles, signs and acronyms. At the risk of unwittingly assuming responsibility for the acts of constitution of whose logic and necessity they are unaware, the social sciences must take as their object of study the social operations of *naming* and the rites of institution through which they are accomplished. (p. 106)

Attention can be drawn to how both they who study and they who participate "in" organizations produce phenomena in the world such as "organizations," "communication," "needs," "motivations," "information," "profits," and various personal and social divisions such as "men" and "women," "workers" and "management." Following this tack requires some understanding of a nonrepresentational or constitutive view of language that cannot be developed here at any length but ought to be familiar enough to most readers that a short development will suffice (see Deetz, 1992, chap. 5).

In line with modern discourse theory, conceptions are always contests for meaning (see Epstein, 1988; Weedon, 1987). Language does not name objects in the world; it is core to the process of constituting the indeterminant and ambiguous external world into specific objects. The appearance of labeling or categorizing existing objects is derived from this more fundamental act of object constitution through language. The world thus can be constituted in many ways depending on alternative systems of valuing. The most significant part of this contest for object constitution is the capacity to enact the lines of distinction producing some things as alike and others as different. Only secondarily is the contest over the positive or negative valance ascribed to the produced things. For example, feminist writers for years have shown how male dominance is maintained by the dominant group's ability to define the dimensions of difference and position themselves at the positive end of each dimension (see Treichler, 1989; Weedon, 1987). Marginalized groups, following this analysis, are defined as "the other" thus acquiring an identity and valued functions but only as given by the opposition pole in the dominant group's conceptual map (e.g., "emotionally supportive" rather than "rational" or "private" rather than "public"). They acquire a type of autonomy but only in a language/conceptual game not of their own choosing. In accepting the state of "other," they have little self-definition and the game is stacked (see Bourdieu, 1977, 1991).

From the communicative metaperspective taken here, the core process in understanding alternative research programs is to understand their discourse—how they perceive, think, and talk about organizational life. Understanding a discourse includes identification of the object distinctions they make, whose language is used in making those object distinctions, what and whose values and interests are carried with those distinctions, and how the conflicting descriptions of the world are handled as well as exploring their processes of self-justification and distinction from alternative research programs. Further, research programs differ in the extent to which they recognize and make explicit their own constitutive activities. Many researchers assume that they are merely discovering and naming real-world objects. To the extent that this is done much of the micropractice of research is missed.

## MAPPING APPROACHES TO ORGANIZATIONAL COMMUNICATION STUDIES

Trying to produce any organizing scheme of these discourses accounting for different theoretical conceptions, methodological preferences, and value commitments is filled with difficulties. Each research program might well use different ways of comparing and contrasting itself with other programs. In fact a primary way that any research program establishes itself is in its means of distinction, both in the sense of producing a difference and giving itself the positive terms (see Bourdieu, 1991).

Many schemes have been proposed for organizing and thinking about alternative research programs. Most of these classify studies based on subdivisions of the organizational communication phenomenon or differences in research methods. For example, Wert-Gray et al. (1991) suggest three dominant areas of work: (1) information flow and channels, (2) climate, and (3) superior/subordinate. And Redding and Tompkins (1988) divide the work into (1) formal channels, (2) superior/subordinate communication, (3) informal channels, and (4) measuring and data collection. Putnam and Cheney (1985) suggest (1) channels, (2) communication climate, (3) superior/subordinate, (4) network analy-

sis, and (5) communication media with additional emerging perspectives. And in perhaps the most exhaustive study, Allen, Gotcher, and Seibert (1993) review 17 areas of work: (1) interpersonal relations, (2) communication skills, (3) culture and symbolism, (4) information flow and channels, (5) power and influence, (6) decision making and problem solving, (7) communication networks, (8) communication and management styles, (9) organization-environment interface, (10) technology, (11) language and messages, (12) structure, (13) uncertainty and information adequacy, (14) groups, (15) ethics, (16) crosscultural, and (17) climate. These divisions and study counts are interesting and represent ways of thinking about the field that are fairly common. But such approaches tend to reify topical divisions that are the constructed outcomes of discursive processes thus treating them as natural rather than produced, hiding values and assumptions, and disowning the way these divisions preference particular studies of communication. Let us consider for a moment these preferences.

First, the topical orientation is itself not a neutral classification tool. It assumes and reproduces a particular view of communication and organizations. For example, it assumes an atomistic orientation to the world like the 19th-century natural science model and advantages studies that follow that model. Studies based in holistic assumptions, such as ethnographic approaches, may get put in a category like "culture" or "climate." This makes "culture" into one phenomenon among others in organizations that can be studied. Not only do cultural studies deny that culture is one thing among many *in* organizations, the classification buries the important things that ethnographic researchers said about organizations' structures and activities like channels and interpersonal relations. Only studies that explicitly study channels and interpersonal relations as isolated phenomena appear in those categories. Ethnographic researchers rarely study a topic, they study a particular site. What would we learn if we classified by site, the social problem considered, group allegiance, or the moral stance rather than topic? Topical divisions probably made sense when the vast majority of researchers believed that the elements of organizations were atomistic rather than holistic, that organizations were primarily a thing rather than a process, and that communication was a phenomenon among others rather than an approach one takes to organization studies. As these change so must our ways of accounting for similarities and differences in organization studies.

Second, the devices of data collection shape the review in further ways. In some of these reviews, the data pool is limited to *studies* published in *"communication" journals* and the manner of display is usually the *number* of essays. The classifying processes match assumptions of the natural science model thus both normalizing its preferred manner of report and overemphasizing its impact. The "field" looks different in reviews that consider scholarly book chapters, scholarly books, and/or unpublished research reports to companies instead of journal articles. Further, the concept of "studies" itself tends to get defined in terms of data collection, thus analytic and conceptual work, which often have great impact on the field and its practices, tend to be left out. And further yet, the concept of the "communication field" has often led to the omission of non-North American studies that organize "fields" differently and important "communication studies" on topics that are definitionally excluded. For example, the discursive studies in such journals as *Organization* or *Organization Studies,* communication-based studies in *Accounting, Organizations and Society,* and interaction studies in "sociology" are left out, and works by authors in management schools in such journals as *Management Communication Quarterly* are included. The tendency is to bias the counts toward studies from a psychological and managerial perspective. And finally, *quantity of studies* as a measure favors narrow quantitative analyses. What if we measured significance of impact, transformative

potential, or applicability to wider stakeholder interests? Each of these would provide different pictures of "our" studies and contribution and pressure the field's development in different ways.

I think we get further if we look at the practice of research and researcher commitments rather than looking at topics as if they could be freed from the researcher's orientation. As we become more diverse as a people and as researchers, a consideration of general research assumptions becomes more instructive. Reviewers looking at research assumptions and orientations have tended to focus more on methodological/epistemological differences than study topics. And rarely have they gone beyond methodological choices to a full consideration of the way theoretical and value commitments are carried with them.

Reviews that have considered research orientations have fairly high agreement in categories of classification. Putnam (1982; Putnam & Pacanowsky, 1983), for example, describes studies as functionalist, interpretive, and critical. Redding and Tompkins (1988) describe them in a parallel fashion as modernist, naturalistic, and critical (a scheme followed by Wert-Gray et al., 1991, in their methodological orientations). These authors would probably add "postmodernist" if they were writing these essays today. I suspect that these divisions are largely a result of the influence of Burrell and Morgan's (1979) popular discussion of sociological paradigms as functionalist, interpretive, radical humanist, and radical structuralist. Their paradigm descriptions have been very influential in management and communication studies, and the influence is well deserved. While I believe fundamentally flawed, their approach serves as a useful point of departure for further development (see Deetz, 1996).

Importantly, Burrell and Morgan's discussion of paradigmatic differences in the late 1970s gave legitimacy to fundamentally different research programs and enabled the development of different criteria for the evaluation of research. Their exhaustive review was not only valuable in itself, but they were able to provide an analysis that probed deeply into the assumptions on which different research programs were based. But harms were also created. I believe that there are reasons for this significant influence beyond the clarity of presentation and exhaustive compilation of literature. When the grid and discussion were published in 1979, those of us doing alternative work readily embraced the grid for it gave each of us a kind of asylum. While some of us were uncomfortable with the dimensions and philosophical analysis, we happily accepted the new-found capacity to present ourselves to mainstream critics as doing fundamentally different, but legitimate, kinds of research and began to work on concepts and evaluation criteria within our now produced as different and unitary communities. Many of those doing more mainstream work also found it appealing since, as I will argue, the conceptual distinctions Burrell and Morgan used to produce the grid were the same distinctions the mainstream tradition had used to discuss different research agendas. Thus, they reaffirm that tradition's conceptual map and provide a "safe" understanding of the developing alternatives. Further, the conception of paradigms as distinct schools of thought with their own problem statements and evaluative criteria could be used by the dominant "functionalists" to protect themselves from growing criticism (the isolationist strategy noted by Reed, 1985). They too would have a safe and separate place (see Rodríguez & Cai, 1994).

But as organization science and organizational communication research have continued to evolve, problems with the Burrell and Morgan grid and its adaptations have become more pressing. While not primarily a result of the original analysis, the four-paradigm solution has often led to quick categorizations and to debates around paradigm commensurability and appropriate use of the different paradigms (Hassard, 1991; Jackson & Carter, 1991; Parker & McHugh, 1991; Willmott, 1993). Some of these problems and debates arise from the tendency to reify concepts, es-

pecially in educational programs and materials. The Burrell and Morgan grid can easily produce four unitary paradigms, rather than provide two lines of differentiation that draw attention to important differences in research programs. Burrell and Morgan invite reification by claims of paradigmatic incommensurability, by staying at the level of theory and reconstructed science, and by accepting Kuhn's loose conception of paradigms. The dimensions of contrast can be used as a way of focusing attention to differences that make a difference rather than as a means of classification, but few writers and teachers have done so.

But my main concern is not paradigm commensurability or reification but rather the dimensions of contrast themselves. A deeper and more interesting understanding of contemporary research practices and debates is possible by focusing on other contrastive dimensions. The question is not: Are these the right categories or who fits in each? but: Are these differences that make a difference? Do these dimensions provide insight into genuine differences in research programs? I hope to aid rethinking the differences and similarities among different research approaches, with the aim of making our conflicts and discussions more productive rather than simply replacing four boxes with four different boxes. In many ways, the various adaptations of Burrell and Morgan have hampered the development of new research agenda and led to less than productive conceptions in the field.

Burrell and Morgan, and subsequently many organizational communication scholars, largely accepted the conceptual distinctions from sociological functionalism and its supporting philosophy of science. Burrell and Morgan performed a political intervention as they spoke on behalf of the oppositions, the negative terms, the "others" in "sociological functionalism's" conceptual map. For example, they accepted the traditional functionalist "subjective/objective" distinction but provided a careful development of "subjective" research. Thus, using the dominant conceptions, they merely asked, "Who is 'other'?" and "In what ways are they 'other'?" But they never questioned whether distinctions based on such conceptions as "subjective/objective" were useful at all (see Deetz, 1994a). In contrast to their analysis, each "other" (each marginalized paradigmatic group like "interpretivists" or "radical humanists") would have defined its difference from the dominant functionalist conceptions differently, that is, if they accepted their "groupness" at all (see Bernstein, 1983; Natter, Schatzki, & Jones, 1995). This positioning, as I have suggested, partly accounts for the rapid acceptance of the Burrell and Morgan's grid into the mainstream of management science and organizational communication discussions.

Further, this move protected functionalist researchers from the most damning critiques (and ones they would not understand, e.g., the "artifactual" quality of their "facts") in favor of their preferred battles (e.g., between their "objectivity" and others' "subjectivity"). At the same time, the most innovative of the new researchers found it now even more difficult to express what they did since they had to use a language in which their meanings did not fit (e.g., critical theorists and phenomenologists who did not accept "subject/object" dualism had to accept the classification as "subjective humanists" if they were to have a home at all). They had to choose between misrepresenting themselves clearly through Burrell and Morgan or representing themselves well but being considered obscure or bad writers. Thus, the effect was to normalize the emerging research paradigms favoring rather traditional directions even within them. For example, when Burrell and Morgan, and subsequently Putnam and others, provided "interpretive" work with the "subjective" ascription (even if now positively valued) they, perhaps unwittingly, tended to favor cultural studies that focused on member's meanings that were more subject to cultural management and managerial control. At the same time the "objective" ascription protected "functionalist" studies

from a thorough analysis of their hidden values and sources of subjectivity, as if they might be too objective—a preferred flaw—rather than too subjective—a flaw they would not understand. Similarly, the many critical theorists with strong suspicions of humanist philosophies suddenly found themselves either conceptualized as radical humanists or invisible (lost in some hole in paradigmatic space). The Frankfurt school's attack on the subjective domination in science all too often got lost in the radical humanist conception. My point is not that Burrell and Morgan and their followers were representationally wrong in the presentation of organization and organizational communication studies (for there are many representationally "right" schemes and surely the nearly 20 years since their work has led to many changes), but their conceptions continue to foster less interesting and productive conflicts and developments than are possible. The processes of differentiation in mainstream functionalist sociology must be abandoned before more challenging differentiations are possible and alternative research programs can be given a full complementary role.

By focusing on the constitutive moves of discourse in organizational research and organizational practice rather than in psychological, sociological, or economic theories of organizational behavior, more interesting differences can be displayed. In my development below, I will privilege programmatic differentiations rooted in what I will develop as a "dialogic" perspective. What Burrell and Morgan called "functionalist" research will thus be implicitly represented as an "other." In doing so, both the lines of division and the arguments that extend from this can be redrawn. "Functionalist" style work can be reclaimed as legitimate and useful (though neither cumulative or "true") in specifiable ways as reunderstood from dialogic conceptions. Nondialogic research programs will not be seen as alternative routes to truth, but as specific discourses that specify and provide answers to specific types of problems. By setting

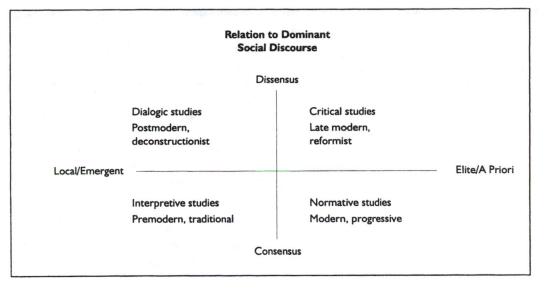

**Figure 1.1.** Contrasting Dimensions From the Metatheory of Representational Practices
SOURCE: Adapted from Deetz (1994d).

aside typical research claims of universality and/or certainty, different research traditions can provide productively complementary and conflictual insights into organizational life. The test of my suggested differentiations is not whether they provide a better map, but whether they provide an interesting (or what Rorty, 1989, developed as "edifying") way to talk about what is happening in research programs.

## ALTERNATIVES FROM A COMMUNICATION PERSPECTIVE[2]

A more contemporary look at alternative communication research programs can be gained by locating research differences in what was conceptualized earlier as "discourses"—that is, the linguistic systems of distinction, the values enacted in those distinctions, the orientations to conflict and relations to other groups. Two dimensions of contrast will be developed here. Later in the essay, four prototypical discourses or research approaches—*normative, interpretive,*

*critical,* and *dialogic*—will be developed from these conceptions. See Figure 1.1.

First, differences among research orientations can be shown by contrasting "local/emergent" research conceptions with "elite/a priori" ones. This dimension focuses on the origin of concepts and problem statements as part of the constitutive process in research.

Second, research orientations can be contrasted in the extent to which they work within a dominant set of structurings of knowledge, social relations, and identities (a reproductive practice), called here "consensus" discourse, and the extent to which they work to disrupt these structurings (a productive practice), called here "dissensus" discourse. This dimension focuses on the relation of research practices to the dominant social discourses within the organization studied, the research community, and/or wider community. I see these dimensions as analytic ideal types in Weber's sense mapping out two distinct continua. While categories of research programs are derivatively produced by the dimensions, the intent here is to aid attention to meaningful differences and similarities among different research activities rather than classification.

**TABLE 1.1**   Characterizations of the Local/Emergent–Elite/A Priori Dimension

| Local/Emergent | Elite/A Priori |
| --- | --- |
| Comparative communities | Privileged community |
| Multiple language games | Fixed language game |
| Particularistic | Universalistic |
| Systematic philosophy as ethnocentric | Grounded in hoped for systematic philosophy |
| Atheoretical | Theory driven |
| Situationally or structural determinism | Methodological determinism |
| Nonfoundational | Foundational |
| Local narratives | Grand narrative of progress and emancipation |
| Sensuality and meaning as central concerns | Rationality and truth as central concerns |
| Situated, practical knowledge | Generalizable, theoretical knowledge |
| Tends to be feminine in attitude | Tends to be masculine in attitude |
| Sees the strange | Sees the familiar |
| Proceeds from the other | Proceeds from the self |
| Ontology of "otherness" over method | Epistemological and procedural issues rule over substantive assumptions |

## The Local/Emergent– Elite/A Priori Dimension

The key questions this dimension addresses are, where and how do research concepts arise, and thus, implicitly *whose* conceptions are used? In the two extremes, either concepts are developed in relation with organizational members and transformed in the research process or they are brought to the research "interaction" by the researcher and held static through the research process—concepts can be developed *with* or applied *to* the organizational members and activities being studied. This dimension can be characterized by a set of paired conceptions that flesh out contrasts embedded in the two poles. Table 1.1 presents an array of these contrasts. The choice of and stability of the language system are of central importance since the linguistic/conceptual system directs the statement of problems, the observational process itself in producing objects and highlighting and hiding potential experiences, the type of claims made, the report to external groups, and the

likely generalizations (whether appropriate or not) readers will make.

The local/emergent pole draws attention to researchers who work with an open language system and produce a form of knowledge characterized more by insight into empirical events than large-scale empirical generalizations. Central to their work is the situated nature of the research enterprise. Problem statements, the researcher's attention, and descriptions are worked out as a play between communities. The theoretical vocabulary carried into the research activity is often considered by the researcher as sensitizing or a guide to getting started constantly open to new meanings, translations, and redifferentiation based on interactions in the research process. Produced insights into organization processes may be particularistic regarding both time and place even though the emerging analytic frame is designed to aid in the deeper understanding of other particular settings. Cumulative understanding happens in providing stories or accounts that may provide insight into other sites rather than cumulative universal aspiring claims. The research attends to the feelings, intuitions, and multiple forms of rationality of both the researched and researcher rather than using a single logic of objectification or purified rationality. The study is guided more by concept formation than concept application. Distantiation and the "otherness" of the other (the way people and events exceed categories and classifications of them) are sought by the researcher to force reconception and linguistic change. This is considered more valuable than the identification and naming of preconceived traits, attributes, or groupings. Objectivity, to the extent that it is considered at all, arises out of the interplay and the constant ability of the researched to object and correct. The researcher is more a skilled collaborator in knowledge production than an expert observer.

The elite/a priori pole draws attention to the tendency in some types of research programs to privilege the particular language system of the researcher and the expertise of the research community as well as hold that language system constant throughout the research process. Such research tends to be heavily theory driven with careful attention to definitions prior to the research process. The experiences of the researched become coded into the researcher's language system. Demands of consistency and/or reliability require changes in the conceptual system to take place outside of rather than in the research process.

Whether intentional or not, the conceptual system of the researcher is considered better or more clearly represents what "really" is the case than that of everyday people and seeks generality beyond the various local systems of meaning. In privileging a language system, there is further a tendency to universalize and justify such moves by appeals to foundations or essentialist assumptions. Research claims, thus, are seen as freed from their local and temporal conditions of production. In most cases, these research approaches follow an enlightenment hope for producing rational knowledge not constrained by tradition or particular belief systems of the researcher or researched. The produced knowledge is treated as progressive or reformist in conception leading to increased capacities or well-being. The more "normative" versions openly proclaim "objectivity" and value neutrality based on the shared-language game and research methods, and tend to overlook the positions of their own community or alliances with other groups. The more "critical" versions quickly note the presence of values and distortions in normative work, and hold out the hope for a better, purer form of knowledge based in processes that include more interests and means of analysis in the work.

Focusing on the origin of concepts and problems using a dimension of "local/emergent–elite/a priori" allows three important gains. First, it acknowledges linguistic/social constructionism in all research positions and directs attention to whose concepts are used in object production and determination of what is problematic (see Deetz, 1973). Second, the focus on the origin of concepts helps distinguish fundamentally different kinds of knowledge. Elite/a priori conceptions lead more to the development of "theoretical codified" knowledge, a kind of "book" knowledge or "knowing about." Local/emergent conceptions lead more to the development of "practical" knowledge, a kind of "street wisdom" or a "knowing how." Third, this dimension helps us remember that both the application and discovery of concepts can demonstrate implicit or explicit political alliances with different groups in the organization or larger society. For example, to the extent that organizational researchers' concepts align with managerial conceptions and problem statements and are applied a priori in studies, the knowledge claims are intrinsically biased toward these interests as they are applied within the site community (Mumby, 1988). The knowledge claims become part of the same processes that are being studied, reproducing worldviews and personal identities and fostering particular interests within the organization (see Knights, 1992).

**TABLE 1.2**  Characterizations of the Consensus-Dissensus Dimension

| Consensus | Dissensus |
|---|---|
| Trust | Suspicion |
| Hegemonic order as natural state | Conflicts over order as natural state |
| Naturalization of present | Present order is historicized and politicized |
| Integration and harmony are possible | Order indicates domination and suppressed conflicts |
| Research focuses on representation | Research focuses on challenge and reconsideration (representation) |
| Mirror (reflecting) dominant metaphor | Lens (seeing/reading as) dominant metaphor |
| Validity central concern | Insight and praxis central concern |
| Theory as abstraction | Theory as way of seeing |
| Unified science and triangulation | Positional complementarity |
| Science is neutral | Science is political |
| Life is discovery | Life is struggle and creation |
| Researcher anonymous and out of time and space | Researcher named and positioned |
| Autonomous/free agent | Historically/socially situated agent |

## The Consensus–Dissensus Dimension

The "consensus–dissensus" dimension draws attention to the relation of research to existing social orders. Consensus or dissensus should not be understood as agreement and disagreement but rather as presentation of unity or of difference, the continuation or disruption of any prevailing discourse. See Table 1.2 for conceptualization of this dimension. This dimension is similar to Burrell and Morgan's use of the traditional sociological distinction between an interest in "change" and "regulation," but enables some advantages. Rather than being class based, contemporary concerns with conflict and power focus on the ways predominant discourses (though often disorganized and disjunct) place limitations on people in general including managers and limit the successful functioning of organizations in meeting human needs. The focus is more on the suppression of diverse values and the presence of destructive control processes than on conflict among groups. The processes of domination today are less often seen as

macrosociological and more often seen as arising in normative or unobtrusive controls (see Barker, 1993; Etzioni, 1961; Tompkins & Cheney, 1985) and instantiated as routine micropractices in the work site itself (Ashcraft & Pacanowsky, 1996; Deetz, 1994b, 1994c, 1998; Knights & Willmott, 1989). The focus on discursive rather than group relations aids the understanding of domination and the various ways important organizational stakeholders are left out of discussions as well as the ways such forms of decisional skewing are reproduced.

The consensus pole draws attention to the way some research programs both seek order and treat order production as the dominant feature of natural and social systems. With such a conception, the primary goal of the research is to display a discovered order with a high degree of fidelity or verisimilitude. The descriptions hope to "mirror" entities and relations that exist out there in a relatively fixed state reflecting their "real" character. In the "normative" version this reality is treated like the natural world while in "interpretive" work it is a social world. Language is treated as a system of representations, to be neutralized and made transparent, used only to display the presumed shared world. Existing orders are largely treated as natural and unproblematic. To a large extent through the highlighting of ordering principles, such orders are perpetuated. Random events and deviance are downplayed in significance in looking at norms and the normal, and attention is usually to processes reducing deviance, uncertainty, and dissonance. In most cases where deviance is itself of attention, it tends to be normalized through looking at the production of deviant groups (i.e., other orders). Conflict and fragmentation are usually treated as system problems and attention is given to how orders deal with them in attempts at maintenance.

The dissensus pole draws attention to research programs that consider struggle, conflict, and tensions to be the natural state. Research itself is seen as inevitably a move in a conflictual site. The existing orders indicate the suppression of basic conflicts and along with that the domination of people and their full variety of interests. Research aims at challenging mechanisms of order maintenance to reclaim conflicts and tension. The nonnormative aspects of human conduct and extraordinary responses are emphasized along with the importance of largely random and chance events. Rather than language naming and describing, researcher conceptions are seen as striking a difference, de- and redifferentiating experience (Cooper, 1989; Cooper & Burrell, 1988; Deetz, 1992; Martin, 1990; Weedon, 1987). The "mirror" gives way to the "lens" as the dominant metaphor for language and theory noting the shifting analytic attempt to see what could not be seen before and showing the researcher as positioned and active (Deetz, 1992, chap. 3; Rorty, 1979). For dissensus style research, the generative capacity (the ability to challenge guiding assumptions, values, social practices, and routines) of an observation is more important than representational validity (see Gergen, 1978). The research is, in Knights's (1992) sense, "antipositive." Dissensus work does not deny

the significance of an ordered observed world, rather it takes it as a powerful (power filled) product and works to break reifications and objectifications to show fuller potential and variety than is immediately apparent. For example, consensus orientations in cultural studies seek to discover the organizational culture or cultures. Dissensus orientations show the fragmentation inherent in any claim of culture and the work required for site subjects to maintain coherence in the face of this as well as subjects' own forms of resistance (see Calás & Smircich, 1991; Holmer-Nadesan, 1996; Martin, 1990, 1992; Smircich & Calás, 1987; Trethewey, 1997). Consensus orientations apply role and identity classifications and relate them to other variables; dissensus orientations see identity as multiple, conflictual, and in process.

While these differences can be characterized clearly in abstraction, in continuous time every consensus arises out of and falls to dissensus, and every dissensus gives away to emerging (if temporary) consensus. The issue is not the ultimate outcome desired nor likely but rather which part of this flow through time is claimed in the research process. For example, while critical theorists clearly seek a social consensus that is more rational, their research tries to produce this through the creation of dissensus in place of dominant orders. For example, ideological critique in the critical theory conception of the negative dialectic is to reclaim conflict and destroy a false order rather than produce a new one. Thus, I place them on the dissensus end. Critical theories differ from many dialogic or "postmodern" positions in the production of dissensus. In critical theories, dissensus is produced by the use of elite understandings and procedures (as in Habermas, 1984, 1987; Kunda, 1992; Mumby, 1987; or several essays in Alvesson & Willmott, 1992). While in dialogic research, deconstructive processes are used to unmask elite conceptions thereby allowing organizational activities to be given new, multiple, and conflicting descriptions (Calás & Smircich, 1991; Kilduff, 1993; Laclau &

Mouffe, 1985; Linstead, 1993; Martin, 1990). The dialogic outcome requires a constant dedifferentiation and redifferentiation for the sake of demythologizing and enriching natural language and consequently opening to reconsideration the most basic and certain experiences of everyday work life.

## PARADIGMS LOST, ORIENTATIONS STILL

The grid produced from these two dimensions provides a spatially and visually convenient, discursive four-space solution (hence we should always be easily reminded of its arbitrary and fictive character). I will describe these as different discourses to note a way of articulating arguments and engaging in research practices rather than a means of reconstructive self-naming. Each discourse provides an orientation to organizations, a way of constituting people and events in them, and a way of reporting on them. I hope that this also leads us to think about which discourse is being used or how it is joined with others rather than pigeonholing specific authors. Table 1.3 provides sketchy prototypical descriptions of each research orientation related to a dozen dimensions of interest shaping organizational communication research programs.

Calling these discourses "paradigms" would be a mistake for several reasons. First, each of these four discourses, which are provisionally held apart for viewing, is filled with internal conflict and strife—including theory debates, moments of incommensurability, dilettantes, and tyrants. Second, the edges are not demarcated. Most researchers and teachers do not cluster around a prototype of each, but gather at the crossroads, mix metaphors, and borrow lines from other discourses, dodging criticism by co-optation. Often practicing researchers happily move from one discourse to another without accounting for their own location. They operate like other organizational members borrowing on discourses that

suit their immediate purposes and the fashions of the moment (see Deetz, 1994b). There are certainly more and less serious plays across the lines, but the issue is not crossing but the seriousness of the play. Third, the discourses are not themselves sealed off from each other. They pose problems for each other and steal insights across the lines. For example, the philosophical fights between Habermas and Gadamer, Habermas and Lyotard, Habermas and Luhmann, and Foucault and everybody have left their traces in each one's work. From these struggles, the various organizational communication research programs based in these works have gained enriched conceptions of power, knowledge, agency, and political action (see, e.g., Mumby & Putnam, 1992).

Provisional ordering of discourses is not to police the lines, but to provide a view of the social resources from which researchers draw and an understanding of the stock arguments used in developing and justifying research activities and claims. The ideal types aid the understanding of differences that matter that are hard to see in the flow of research activity. Clarifying the tendencies in specific types of research positions helps clarify debates and the relation of different groups to them. For example, the interpretive, critical, and dialogic critiques of normative research are quite different. Normative researchers who are accustomed to making arguments against subjectivity and traditionalism simply miss the point of each of these critiques; they often reduce them to abstract and confused presentations of what they think "opponents" should be saying rather than concrete but different arguments from what they expected.

Further, while most researchers are not purists, their work carries assumptions and responsibilities that are central to understanding and evaluating their work, but are rarely explicit in study reports. For example, many feminists' writings carry a general sympathy with the conceptual and analytic power of *dialogic* research programs, while they still wish to have a political agenda that requires *critical* preconceptions that assume social di-

**TABLE 1.3**   Prototypical Discursive Features

| Issue | Discourse | | | |
| --- | --- | --- | --- | --- |
| | *Normative* | *Interpretive* | *Critical* | *Dialogic* |
| Basic goal | Lawlike relations among objects | Display unified culture | Unmask domination | Reclaim conflict |
| Method | Nomothetic science | Hermeneutics, ethnography | Cultural criticism, ideology critique | Deconstruction, genealogy |
| Hope | Progressive emancipation | Recovery of integrative values | Reformation of social order | Claim a space for lost voices |
| Metaphor of social relations | Economic | Social | Political | Mass |
| Organization metaphor | Marketplace | Community | Polity | Carnival |
| Problems addressed | Inefficiency, disorder | Meaninglessness, illegitimacy | Domination, consent | Marginalization, conflict suppression |
| Concern with communication | Fidelity, influence, information needs | Social acculturation, group affirmation | Misrecognition, systematic distortion | Discursive closure |
| Narrative style | Scientific/technical, strategic | Romantic, embracing | Therapeutic, directive | Ironic, ambivalent |
| Time identity | Modern | Premodern | Late modern | Postmodern |
| Organizational benefits | Control, expertise | Commitment, quality work life | Participation, expanded knowledge | Diversity, creativity |
| Mood | Optimistic | Friendly | Suspicious | Playful |
| Social fear | Disorder | Depersonalization | Authority | Totalization, normalization |

visions and gender-based domination to be general (see Flax, 1990; Fraser & Nicholson, 1988; Mumby, 1996). Such works (e.g., Martin, 1990, 1992) can be classified as dialogic, but the ethical and political character of many of these studies cannot be justified easily with dialogic conceptions alone. The distinctions developed in this essay can help display the tensions and the resources from which such researchers draw to conduct and justify their work.

This can further be shown using my own work as an example. I often draw on conceptions from critical and dialogic writings. For me, critical theory conceptions of ideology and distorted communication provide useful sensitizing concepts and an analytic framework for looking for micropractices of unwarranted control, discursive closure, ideology, and skewed representation in organizational sites. But rarely are these conceptions closely tied to the full critical theory agenda. They require considerable reworking in specific sites, and the results of my studies aim more at finding and giving suppressed positions a means of expression than realizing an ideal speech situation or reaching a purer consensus (see Deetz, 1995b, 1998). What is important is not whether I am a late-modern critical theorist or a dialogic postmodernist, but rather the meaning and implications of concepts that I draw from these two competitive research orientations. My degree of consistency is of less interest than how I handle the tension and whether the two conceptual resources provide an interesting analysis or intervention. Some clarity and general understanding in alternative research orientations provide guidance and accountability or at least a common stock of material for building and evaluating new arguments in these cases. Further, exploring general orientations can help reveal assumptions hidden in one's own way of working since they remain unproblematic in one's own research community.

In an ideal research program, we might identify a complementary relation among research orientations with each asking different questions at different moments and each, at the appropriate moment, answering to the specific criteria of a particular orientation. This might operate in a rotation among incompatible orientations without any orientation being privileged or any orientation being reduced to a preliminary or supplementary role. For example, my work relies much on a conception of discursive closure, a conception that draws attention to places where cooperative decision making is hampered by arbitrary limits enacted in the discussion (see Deetz, 1992, pp. 187ff.). As a *critical* researcher I must show how these closures are intrusions of power relations usually based in or supporting social divisions that lead to distorted communication and a false consensus. My study appeals to reason, logical analyses, and a coherent demonstration. As a *dialogic* researcher I see these closures as the suppression of conflicts and see my own concerns with consensus and appeals to reason as simply different acts of

privilege and potential closure. My analysis is now judged by the way indeterminacy is allowed to reemerge and the compelling quality of recovered claims and voices. But at another moment yet, I may well pose *normative* questions: Which means of closure are used most often? Who uses them? When are they used? Can people be taught to avoid them? A study designed to answer such questions now appeals to standards of definition, measurement, sampling, and quantitative data analysis. And further yet, there are *interpretive* concerns: What sense do these discursive moves have in a community? To what ends are they used? How are they self-understood and justified? What are their actual consequences in specific circumstances? Interpretive research standards are now relevant.

One can easily see how such a rotation through orientations might be constant and productive without losing the separation and tension among them. Such tensions could help enrich work from each orientation. Yet, to be honest, few research programs are treated this way and most researchers, like myself, follow their own lines of interest, commitments, and training, which either leads to an eclipse of questions and concerns from other orientations or at least leaves them for someone else who is interested in those problems. Taking seriously other works does not mean that we find other groups' issues and procedures as necessarily interesting or helpful nor should we naively believe that all of them are. But our claims and the relation between our claims and study procedures should be clear so that objections and conflicts can be on those grounds rather than on imposed traditional problem statements and methods. The point is for the researcher to be clear about what type of questions or claims drives the work at any particular time and how the work addresses the standards and criteria appropriate to it.

A basic understanding of alternative research orientations enables shorthand accounts and helps distinguish intentional and/or productive ambiguities from careless and/or unproductive ones. As a reviewer, I am often frustrated by nonreflective mixing of metaphors and conceptions in submitted essays. Often the claims made would require a different kind of study based on different assumptions and research activities. Partly, I think this arises from authors trying to anticipate reviewer needs for normative type generalizations while being committed to a nonnormative research orientation, but it also comes from inattention to what makes different kinds of research different. Clearly, a balance must be struck between (1) reifying research orientations through simplistic grids and subsequent overcharacterizations and rigid standards and (2) having each study try to be totally self-justifying and cut loose from any community. While I do not think there is any easy way out of this tension, having good dimensions of contrast and good characterizations helps. A very brief sketch of the four orientations aids further in highlighting differences and similarities in these community discourses along the suggested dimensions of difference.

## The Discourse of Normative Studies

Normative research tends to accept organizations as naturally existing objects open to description, prediction, and control. Goals established by some specific group, usually upper management, are largely accepted as the goals of the organization and most often the research either implicitly or explicitly supports more efficient accomplishment of these goals. Because of this, commercial corporations are usually discussed in economic terms with issues discussed in relation to "rational" economic goals. The researchers producing this discourse have been described as functionalists, covering-law theorists, or simply practicing the variable analytic tradition. I describe this discourse as "normative" to emphasize the centrality of codification, the search for regularity and normalization, and the implied prescriptive claims (see Deetz, 1973; Hollway, 1984). This discourse is largely dominant in North America and in applied organizational research everywhere. Articles published by U.S. researchers employed by communication departments and published in "communication" journals have been mostly of this sort, though the mix is changing. Most textbooks are written in this discourse emphasizing topical divisions and research findings even when they review research established in other traditions.

The discourse is decisively modern in Gergen's (1992) sense and the knowledge is considered positive, cumulative, and progressive. A grand narrative of progressive emancipation from disease, disorder, and material deprivation is shaped by a commitment to make a better world through discovery of fundamental processes and increased production (Lyotard, 1984). While the organization is usually treated as an existing object produced for instrumental ends, usually making money, some conception of the invisible hand makes that goal well-integrated with other social goals of development and widespread availability of goods and services. Generally, the research is expressly apolitical and value neutral, but as already shown, values reside in elite conceptions, choice of problems to study, and relation to other groups.

Most of this work has implicitly supported an orderly, well-integrated world, with compliant members and regulated conflicts, and has accepted without examination existing organizational goals and member positions. They represent communication primarily in information and administration terms (see Beniger, 1986). Much of the discussion of communication in "information" terms assumes a control orientation and theories of persuasion and information transfer dominate much of the concern with most frequently studied topics such as supervisor/subordinate communication, compliance gaining, networks, power, and relations with the public. Normative works appear in three basic varieties each with distinct assumptions and goals of their own—covering laws, systems theory, and skill development.

## Covering Laws

Research modeled on the search for lawlike generalizations in organizations until fairly recently has dominated organizational communication study. Research of this type was most explicitly defended in communication studies by Berger (1977) and reconstructed and well justified in Donaldson (1985; see also Barley & Kunda, 1992; DiMaggio, 1995; O'Keefe, 1976). The research practices mirror 19th-century conceptions of the natural sciences often involving the most recent advances in operationalization, hypothesization, statistical data reduction, and pattern "recognition" processes. Conceptions of operationalization, "objectivity," and lawlike relations are merely the most obvious form of practice. Conventional practices and methodological ("as if") determinism have in most cases replaced any strong allegiance to the positivist philosophy of science that grounds many of the methods and assumptions.

The "objects" constructed by the practices of this science are given qualities of constancy and permanence (universal across time and place), as if nature endowed them with specific attributes. The combination of a priori conceptions and the focus on consensus leads the artifacts of these research practices to be described as facts. This discourse typifies the development of many data retrieval systems and information technologies since information can be treated as fixed truth claims freed from the time, place, and procedures of production. Facts become commodities and communication can be reduced to a transmission/retrieval process (for discussion of consequences, see Boland, 1987; Coombs, Knights, & Willmott, 1992; Lyytinen & Hirschheim, 1988).

Theory and theory testing are central to the logic of the research and many of the statistical procedures of data reduction. Normative studies of this type are explicitly dependent on theory, though in practice the theoretical concerns may be reduced to a mere reference list of prior studies and theory testing to merely adding to a list of relations among variables of interest. One characteristic self-criticism is the lament over the lack of development or use of theory. Most of the studies work *as if* they were in a deductive theory testing mode even when their theoretical commitments are less than clear. Recently, Sutton and Staw (1995) demonstrated how references, data, variables, diagrams, and hypotheses are often used to cover up the lack of theory and actual theory testing.

This discourse is exemplified in studies of compliance gaining (e.g., Sullivan & Taylor, 1991), strategic message design and persuasion (e.g., Alexander, Penley, & Jernigan, 1991), supervision/subordinate interaction (Infante, Anderson, Martin, Herington, & Kim, 1993; Jablin, 1979; Sias & Jablin, 1995), and other places more completely described by Burrell and Morgan (1979) in their discussion of "functionalist." But it is also clearly present in those advocating the management of culture (e.g., Deal & Kennedy, 1982; Schein, 1992) through their conception of culture as an object to be strategically deployed (as Barley, Meyer, & Gash, 1988, have shown, this became very common in the 1980s). Most of the work on culture, climate, or varieties of total quality management (TQM) in organizational communication are more normative than interpretive owing to the way culture is treated as a variable or objective outcome within a larger strategic move of cultural management (see Shockley-Zalabak & Morley, 1994). Many of those working with new conceptions of organizations as "postmodern" (rather than post-modern approaches; Parker, 1992) have a discourse primarily structured in a normative fashion (e.g., Bergquist, 1993; Peters, 1987). Many Marxist studies, especially those done in contexts of Marxist domination of social discourse, use normative themes, but the elite group that gives rise to the concepts differs from those supporting most European and North American studies. Lenin's embracing of scientific management was in no way inconsistent. Strategic management in virtually every way is highly dependent on this discourse (Knights, 1992; Knights

& Morgan, 1991). Often team, quality, and participation programs are assessed using research procedures grounded in this perspective (e.g., Gordon, Infante, & Graham, 1988; Miller & Monge, 1985).

Studying communication in the organizational context poses some unique problems for this approach. The complexity and interdependence of organizational relationships challenge the rather atomistic and unidirectional models of both the theories and methods. And such relations are hard to duplicate in laboratory settings and control for numerous "extraneous" factors. Researchers have responded to this with much more sophisticated modeling and statistical analysis. Unfortunately, the outcomes of this are fairly abstract relations that lead to questions of validity and usefulness. Further, much of the research has turned to data collection from self-report interviews and survey questionnaires rather than direct observation (see Knapp, Putnam, & Davis, 1988). This has led to a preoccupation with measurement devices and with many studies that are more instrument than theory driven leaving the results difficult to understand or use in any systematic way.

Finally, most researchers conduct such studies primarily for generalization and use statistical significance tests, which allow generalization from the research sample to some population. But the question is often raised as to what is the appropriate "population" for the generalization. Many of the studies draw a sample from a single organization; presumably, this would indicate that this particular organization is the population about which the generalization is proposed. But most researchers want to generalize their findings to organizations in general. There the sample/population relation does not hold. Rarely has any program of work drawn a sample of enough organizations to warrant the type of generalizations made allowable within the assumptions of the studies themselves. Perhaps the Aston studies and the "communication audit" sponsored by the International Communication Association modeled after the Aston studies are partly used exceptions. The important point is that many normative style studies use the rhetorical power of the natural science model and principles of generalization and verification, but often cannot support their studies in organizations based on it. The discourse often conceals this (see Sutton & Staw, 1995). Many attempts have been made to summarize findings across studies, often using meta-analysis. Such studies are often contradictory and inconclusive and even further remove findings from theoretical commitments and specific site characteristics (see Baker, 1991; Miller & Monge, 1985; Wagner & Gooding, 1987; Wilkins & Anderson, 1991).

### Systems Theory

During 1970s and 1980s, much theoretical attention was given to developing "systems" thinking in organizations, especially regarding the organization-environment relation spawned in part by the influence of Lawrence and Lorsch's (1967) work and the development of contingency theory (see Katz & Kahn, 1978; Monge, 1977, 1982; Monge, Farace, Eisenberg, Miller, & White, 1984). More recently, this work has become theoretically more sophisticated through conceptions of self-organizing systems and chaos theory (see Bellman & Roosta, 1987; Contractor, 1994; Senge, 1990; Weick, 1979).

While systems approaches continue the search for order and regularity and ultimately increased control by advantaged groups, they tend to emphasize holism over atomism and dynamic mutual causality over lawlike unidirectional causality. Rather than seeking surface-level, predictive variables the focus is on the deep processes of transformation that produce and interpret overt patterns of behavior—the processes of organizing rather than organizations. As Pettigrew (1990) described: "What is critical is not just events, but the underlying logics that give events meaning and significance . . . logics which may explain how and why these patterns occur in particular chronological sequence" (p. 273). In some cases, in Weick's work, for example, the focus is so strongly on emergent properties, the particular setting, and interpretive processes that the research begins to sound much like *interpretive* studies (see Daft & Weick, 1984). But still, the work is heavily guided by researcher conceptions, the search for regularities anticipated by the researcher, the interpretation of patterns in the researcher's logic, the view from the outside, the hope for enduring regularities, and the assumption of managerial goals. The assumptions and regularities sought differ, however, from those sought by covering laws and even early systems theories.

Contractor (1994) has done an excellent job of making these differences clear. Five conceptions are important.

1. Dynamic inferences: Covering-law theorists develop hypotheses that posit a direct or indirect casual link between variables. These can be tested using rather standard statistical packages (SPSS). Dynamic hypotheses, however, posit an underlying logic or relational mathematical rather than quantitative connection. Similar hypotheses developed by covering-law and systems theorists are the same only when one of two central covering-law assumptions are empirically present (or methodologically produced): (a) There is no change in the two variables over time, or (b) the change is exactly equal.

2. Mutual causality: While covering-law theories posit unidirectional causality, systems theory suggests that many variables exist in mutual or circular causal relations. In such cases, there can be no separation between independent and dependent variables since the casual relation between the variables runs both ways.

3. Historicity: Systems theory suggests that the relation between variables is often time dependent, hence universalizing claims or even generalizations cannot be assumed across time and place. Thus, variable relations (e.g., between trust and compliance) present early in the history of an organiza-

tion can become quite different as the organization ages. A generalization about organizational communication must always reference the time in the organization's history during which it was true.

4. Time irreversibility: Most covering-law models assume that social systems work like closed mechanical systems, hence if an increase in the quantity of a variable leads to an expected outcome then decreasing the quality of that variable will lead to less outcome. Rarely, however, are organizational relations simply transitive or stable like this.

5. Discontinuity: Covering-law theories assume that changes are usually quantitative and incremental. Systems theorists display the presence of sudden qualitative changes at certain thresholds.

Systems conceptions have clearly changed the way people and scholars think about organizations. Much theoretical writing is present. But generally, the empirical research has been more disappointing. Part of this arises from the dominance covering-law conceptions have had on defining the nature of "empirical" research. Frequently, process conceptions in systems theory are reduced to conceptions where covering-law data gathering and statistical analysis are applicable (see Everett, 1994; Monge, Cozzens, & Contractor, 1992). In many respects, systems conceptions are more productive in providing interesting and useful conceptions of complex organizational processes and interventions into them than they are in generating studies that result in journal publications (see Cecchin & Stratton, 1991). The conception of useful empirical work may well be biased in favor of covering-law style studies.

## Communication Skills

The normative orientation not only guides much organizational communication research but also teaching and consulting activities. Arguably, much of the work going on under the title "organizational communication" is more skill development than research directed. Included is everything from interpersonal and basic management skills to public speaking and public relation skills. While it is not my intent to provide any review of this work, I think that it is important to show how textbooks as well as training and development programs have traditionally been connected with the normative approach to organization studies.

In most cases, the implied pedagogy in the writings has been didactic and reliant on the presumption of an expert body of knowledge. And most of the research on skills has used covering-law style assumptions to test hypotheses and measure effectiveness. Further, while there is a directive quality to this work, the skills and the knowledge base from which they are drawn are usually treated as value neutral and as equally available and valuable for different organizational members. In doing so, the influence and control orientation of this work are treated as natural and self-evident, and other human goals and communication purposes are rarely considered. Usually, upper management's goals for the organization are accepted as given and legitimate. Even when the skills are promoted primarily for self-interests, generally those interests are seen as well integrated with upper management's organizational goals. Recently, as teams, stakeholder participation, and organizational creativity and learning have become of greater concern there is increasingly critical attention to understanding skill needs culturally, to the power relations in teaching and textbooks, and to the needs and perspectives of alternative organizational stakeholders (Argyris, 1994; Eisenberg & Goodall, 1993; Grunig & Hunt, 1984; Sprague, 1992).

## The Discourse of Interpretive Studies

The number and importance of interpretive studies grew rapidly during the 1980s. For most interpretive researchers, the organization is a social site, a special type of community that shares important characteristics with other types of communities. The emphasis is on a social rather than economic view of organizational activities. Traditional methods of studying communities are seen as especially useful. The expressed goal of many interpretive studies is to show how particular realities are socially produced and maintained through ordinary talk, stories, rites, rituals, and other daily activities. Most of the early attention for organizational communication researchers was derived from interest in the work of anthropologists such as Geertz (1973; see Pacanowsky & O'Donnell-Trujillo, 1982), phenomenological and symbolic interactionist-inspired work in sociology (Bantz, 1983; Bormann, 1983; Douglas, 1970; Strauss, 1978), and the growing interest in hermeneutics and qualitative research methods (Trujillo, 1987).

While theoretical tensions and competitive traditions have grown along with this work, like these sources, much of the writings have a clear preservationist, naturalistic tone. Allow me to start with the more "naturalistic" assumptions held by interpretive researchers in their studies of organizational culture before turning to some of the tensions that have developed. Like many of the more naturalistic anthropological studies, interpretive research often appears motivated to save or record a life form with its complexity and creativity before it is lost to modern, instrumental life. The concern with community is often connected with the maintenance of a traditional sense of shared values and common practices and the presumed simple harmonious inner life of people who lived in such communities. Gergen (1992) described the romantic sense of this discourse with its depth and connection to the inner life bordering on sentimentality at times. Because of this I refer to the time frame as premodern in Table 1.3. This suggests more a concern with those aspects of life that have not yet been systematized, instrumentalized, and brought under the control of modernism logics and sciences than a focus on the past.

Cultural studies in organizations are interpretive to the extent that they have not been captured by normative, modernist co-optations. Most interpretivists have taken culture to be an evocative metaphor for organizational life rather than a variable or thing that an organization has (Frost, Moore, Louis, Lundberg, & Martin, 1985, 1992; Smircich, 1983). Culture draws attention to what organizational members must know, believe, or be able to do in order to operate in a manner that is understandable and acceptable to other members and the means by which this knowledge, belief, and action routines are produced and reproduced. The interest in communication processes is far richer than that of meaning transmission present in normative work. Communication is considered to be a central means by which the meaning of organizational events is produced and sustained (Donnellon, Gray, & Bougon, 1986).

The basic function of interpretive work is "to translate the interests and concerns of one people into the interests and concerns of another" (Putnam, Bantz, Deetz, Mumby, & Van Maanen, 1993). The needs of translation require both a careful understanding of the other and an ability to present that understanding to one's own culture. A double hermeneutic (an interpretation of an interpreted world) and complex communicative process (metacommunication to the culturally different) is thus central to interpretive work and largely accounts for the situated and emergent nature of the understanding present in its texts (Barley, 1990).

The interpretive researcher often engages in some type of participant observation or other personal contact to collect material and work out understanding with the site community. Studies are usually done in the field and are based on a prolonged period of observation and/or depth interviewing. The interest is in the full person in the organization, thus social and life functions beyond the relation to the job are considered. The goals are much more open and emergent than in normative

work and much less connected to issues of efficiency and productivity. The workplace is seen as a site of human activity, one of those activities being "work" proper. The organization of the entire social community is of interest. While some writing might be somewhat impressionistic and focus on the surface feelings and meanings of either the cultural member or the researcher, generally, these would be considered weak and shallow studies. The point more often is to understand the social conditions of life giving rise to such feelings and meanings—the *deep* cultural read. Analytic attention is thus often directed to symbolism, metaphors, stories, jokes, advice and reason giving, narrative forms, rites and rituals, and the social functions of these activities (see, for examples and reviews, Brown, 1985; Browning, 1992; Goodall, 1990; Knuf, 1993; Smith & Eisenberg, 1987; Trujillo, 1987).

Interpretive studies accept much of the representational and consensual view of science seen in normative writings, but shift the relation between theoretical conceptions and the talk of the subjects under study. People are not considered to be objects like other objects, but are active sense makers like the researcher. Theory is given a far weaker role here. While theory may provide important sensitizing conceptions, it not a device of classification or tested in any simple and direct manner. The key conceptions and understandings must be worked out with the subjects under study. Research subjects can collaborate in displaying key features of their world. But like normative research, the pressure is to get it right, to display unified, consensual culture in the way that it "actually" exists. The report is to display convincingly a unified way of life with all its complexities and contradictions (Goodall, 1990; Pacanowsky & O'Donnell-Trujillo, 1982; Van Maanen, 1988). In DiMaggio's (1995) conceptions, theory in interpretive work is often a narrative account of social processes "with emphasis on empirical tests of the plausibility of the narrative as well as careful attention to the scope of the account" (p. 391).

One gets a sense in tracking this work over time that it is becoming less productive in itself and more treated as a supplement to other kinds of work. Barley et al. (1988) represented well how the early naturalistic and anthropological interest in organizational cultures gradually was eclipsed by a managerial interest in managing culture. Hence, much of the discussion of culture has been reduced to "cultural variables," and the studies became more normative and like the climate studies that preceded them. Data collection techniques and conceptions emergent in the field have been borrowed and then accepted a priori in coding and counting studies, for example, those correlating cultural characteristics with productivity measure or adaptation to change (e.g., Bastien, 1992; Fairhurst, 1993). And critical researchers often reinterpret interpretive studies adding critiques of meaning formations (Martin, 1992; Mumby, 1987). Still, interpretive work is an active and viable research orientation as it continues to evolve. A number of research approaches have been used to help sort out hidden meanings, often hidden as well from the site community participants owing to surface familiarity, and to organize the research process and the presentation of the study itself.

This essay will make no attempt to sort out the diverse ways that interpretive researchers have collected, analyzed, and reported the observations on which their work is based. Ethnography and similar conceptions of "naturalistic" inquiry already discussed remain the purest form of interpretive work. Specific site studies have been analyzed focusing on metaphors, symbols, and themes (Pacanowsky & O'Donnell-Trujillo, 1982; Smith & Eisenberg, 1987; Smith & Turner, 1995; Trujillo, 1987). Other studies have followed other traditions including dramaturgy (Goodall, 1990; Manning, 1992), negotiated order (Geist, 1995), structuration (Bastien, McPhee, & Bolton, 1995; Poole & McPhee, 1983), and rules theory (Schall, 1983). During the past 15 to 20 years, a rich array of studies has been completed. Together these have displayed how organizational cultures develop and change, how social groups conceive and han-

dle conflict, how institutional structures are challenged and/or reinstated, how cultures differ across national settings and management practices, and so forth (see Pepper, 1995).

Interpretive studies are also still evolving. Gradually, many researchers doing interpretive work have began to question the logic of displaying a consensual unified culture and have attended more to its fragmentation, tensions, and processes of conflict suppression (Frost et al., 1992; Marcus & Fischer, 1986; Martin, 1992). In this sense the work has become more dialogic in character. And works following structuration theory have become more critical than interpretive in character (Banks & Riley, 1993; Howard & Geist, 1995; Riley, 1983).

Since the mid-1980s, much of the self-reflection in interpretive work has focused on the relation of the research to the site community and the "voice" taken in the research report. Of importance are both the politics of representation and the role of the report author (Clifford & Marcus, 1986; Conquergood, 1991; Kauffman, 1992). Van Maanen (1988) summarized these relations as alternative tales. Further with greater attention to the relation to the community and action potential in research, interpretive work has become more participatory (Whyte, 1991). Reason (1994) described different types of participatory inquiry. These changes have continued to move much interpretative work to be more dialogic and critical in its account of itself and the type of work done.

## The Discourse of Critical Studies

Critical researchers see organizations in general as social historical creations accomplished in conditions of struggle and power relations. Organizations are largely described as political sites, thus general social theories and especially theories of decision making in the public sphere are seen as appropriate.

While organizations could be positive social institutions providing forums for the articulation and resolution of important group conflicts over the use of natural resources, distribution of income, production of desirable goods and services, the development of personal qualities, and the direction of society, various forms of power and domination have led to skewed decision making and fostered social harms and significant waste and inefficiency. Either explicit or implicit in their presentation is a goal to demonstrate and critique forms of domination, asymmetry, and distorted communication through showing how reality can become obscured and misrecognized. Such insights help produce forums where the conflicts can be reclaimed, openly discussed, and resolved with fairness and justice.

Critical research aims at producing dissensus and providing forums for and models of discussion to aid in the building of more open consensus. Of special concern are forms of false consciousness, consent, systematically distorted communication, routines, and normalizations that produce partial interests and keep people' from genuinely understanding or acting on their own interests. Of the four orientations, critical studies have the most explicitly stated value commitments and the most explicit attention to moral and ethical issues. With this, much of the discourse has a suspicious and therapeutic tone, but also a theory of agency that provides an activist tone, a sense that people can and should act on these conditions and that improved understanding as well as access to communication forums is core to positive action. Theory development in critical theory often has an "enlightenment" quality, in DiMaggio's (1995) sense, whereby euphemisms are developed or exposed "clearing away conventional notions to make room for artful and exciting insights" (p. 391; see also Bourdieu, 1991, for the power of renaming).

The central goal of critical theory in organizational communication studies has been to create a society and workplaces that are free from domination and where all members can contribute equally to produce systems that meet human needs and lead to the progressive development of all. Studies have focused both on the relation of organizations to the wider society and their possible social effects of colonization (rationalization of society) and domination or destruction of the public sphere (Deetz, 1992; DuGay, 1997), and on internal processes in terms of the domination by instrumental reasoning, discursive closures, and consent processes (e.g., Alvesson, 1993; Clair, 1993a, 1993b; Forester, 1989; Mumby, 1987, 1988). As indicated they tend to enter their studies with a priori theoretical commitments, which aid them analytically to ferret out situations of domination and distortion. Critical studies include a large group of researchers who are different in theory and conception but who share important discursive features in their writing. They include Frankfurt school critical theorists (see Alvesson & Willmott, 1992, 1996; Czarniawska-Joerges, 1988; Mumby, 1988), conflict theorists (Benson, 1977; Dahrendorf, 1959), some structurationists (Banks & Riley, 1993; Giddens, 1984, 1991; Howard & Geist, 1995), some versions of feminist work (e.g., Allen, 1996, 1998; Benhabib, 1992; Ferguson, 1984, 1994), some Burkeans (Barker & Cheney, 1994; Tompkins & Cheney, 1985), and most doing labor process theory (Braverman, 1974; Burawoy, 1979, 1985; Knights & Willmott, 1990).

Critical theorists sometimes have a clear political agenda focused on the interests of specific identifiable groups such as women, workers, or people of color, but usually address general issues of goals, values, forms of consciousness, and communicative distortions within corporations. Their interest in ideologies considers disadvantaged groups difficulties in understanding their own political interest, but is usually addressed to people in general, challenging consumerism, careerism, and exclusive concern with economic growth (Allen, 1998; DuGay, 1997). Compared to Marxism, critical theory is not antimanagement per se, even though one tends to treat management as institutionalized and ideologies and practices of management as expressions of contemporary forms of domination. Two principal types of critical studies can be identified in organization studies: Ideological critique and communicative action.

## Ideology Critique

Most of the critical work has focused on ideology critique. Analyses of ideologies show how specific interests fail to be realized because of people's inability to understand or act on their own interests. Some identified ideologies are group specific and others are held by people in technological-capitalist society in general. Ideological critique is guided by a priori researcher conceptions and aims at producing dissensus with the hope that the recovered conflicts and explicit concern with values will enable people to choose more clearly in their own interests.

The earliest ideological critiques of the workplace were offered by Marx. In his analyses of work processes, he focused primarily on practices of economic exploitation through direct coercion and structural differences in work relations between the owners of capital and the owners of their own labor. However, Marx also describes the manner in which the exploitative relation is disguised and made to appear legitimate. This is the origin of ideology critique. Clearly, the themes of domination and exploitation by owners and later by managers have been central to ideology critique of the workplace in this century (see works as varied as Braverman, 1974; Clegg & Dunkerley, 1980; Edwards, 1979). These later analyses became less concerned with class-based coercion and economic explanations through focusing on why coercion was so rarely necessary and on how systemic processes produce active consent (e.g., Burawoy, 1979, 1985; Czarniawska-Joerges, 1988; Deetz & Mumby, 1990; Gramsci, 1929-1935/

1971; Kunda, 1992; Vallas, 1993). Ideology produced in the workplace would supplement ideology present in the media and the growth of the consumer culture and the welfare state as accounting for workers' and other stakeholders' failure to act on their own interests.

Four themes recur in the numerous and varied writings about organizations working from such a perspective: (1) concern with reification, or the way a socially/historically constructed world would be treated as necessary, natural, and self-evident; (2) the suppression of conflicting interests and universalization of managerial interest; (3) the eclipse of reason and domination by instrumental reasoning processes; and (4) the evidence of consent.

In *reification,* a social formation is abstracted from the ongoing conflictual site of its origin and treated as a concrete, relatively fixed entity. The illusion that organizations and their processes are "natural" objects protects them from examination as produced under specific historical conditions (which are potentially passing) and out of specific power relations. Ideological critique is enabled by the elite-driven search for reifications in everyday life. The resultant critique demonstrates the arbitrary nature of "natural objects" and the power relations that result and sustain these forms for the sake of producing dissensus and discovering the remaining places of possible choice.

Lukács (1971), among many others (see Giddens, 1979), has shown that particular sectional interests are often *universalized* and treated as if they were everyone's interests, thus producing a false consensus. In contemporary corporate practices, managerial groups are privileged in decision making and research. *The* interests of the corporation are frequently equated with management's interests. For example, worker, supplier, or host community interests can be interpreted in terms of their effect on corporate—that is, universalized managerial—interests. As such they are exercised only occasionally and usually reactively and are often represented as

simply economic commodities or "costs"—
for example, the price the "corporation" must
pay for labor, supplies, or environmental
cleanup (Deetz, 1995b). Central to the universalization of managerial interest is the reduction of the multiple claims of ownership to financial ownership. In ideological critique,
managerial advantages can be seen as produced historically and actively reproduced
through ideological discursive practices in society and in corporations themselves (see
Bullis & Tompkins, 1989; Deetz, 1992;
Mumby, 1987). Critical theory joins other recent theories in arguing for the representation
of the full variety of organizational stakeholders (see Carroll, 1989; Freeman &
Liedtka, 1991).

Habermas (1971, 1984, 1987) has traced
the social/historical emergence of *technical
rationality* over competing forms of reason.
Habermas described *technical reasoning* as
instrumental, tending to be governed by the
theoretical and hypothetical, and focusing on
control through the development of means-
ends chains. The natural opposite to this,
Habermas conceptualizes as a *practical interest*. Practical reasoning focuses on the process
of understanding and mutual determination of
the ends to be sought rather than control and
development of means of goal accomplishment. But in the contemporary social situation, the form and content of modern social
science and the social constitution of expertise
align with organizational structures to produce the domination of technical reasoning
(see Alvesson, 1987a; Fischer, 1990; Mumby,
1988; Stablein & Nord, 1985). To the extent
that technical reasoning dominates, it lays
claim to the entire concept of rationality, and
alternative forms of reason appear irrational.
To a large extent, studies of the "human" side
of organizations (climate, job enrichment,
quality of work life, worker participation programs, and culture) have each been transformed from alternative ends into new means
to be brought under technical control for extending the dominant group interests of the
corporation (Alvesson, 1987a; Barker, 1993;

Wendt, 1994). The productive tension between the two becomes submerged to the
efficient accomplishment of often unknown
but surely "rational" and "legitimate" corporate goals (Carter & Jackson, 1987).

Early critical theorists focused primarily
on bureaucracies and other forms of direct
control and domination. As the work has developed and these forms have declined, more
sophisticated conceptions of power have
arisen. Various forms of indirect control have
become of greater concern (see Edwards,
1979; Lukes, 1974). Many of the these forms
of indirect control involve active "consent" of
those controlled. *Consent* processes occur
through the variety of situations and activities
in which someone actively, though often unknowingly, accomplishes the interests of others in the faulty attempt to fulfill his or her
own. People are oppressed but are also en-
ticed into activities that create complicity in
their own victimization (for examples, see
Brunsson, 1989; Clair, 1993a; Pringle, 1989).
As a result, rather than having open discussions, discussions are foreclosed or there appears to be no need for discussion. The interaction processes reproduce fixed identities,
relations, and knowledge, and the variety of
possible differences are lost. Thus, important
discussions do not take place because there
appears to be no reason for them. Consent often appears in direct forms as members actively subordinate themselves to obtain
money, security, meaning, or identity; things
that should result from the work process
rather than subordination. In fact, both the
subordination and requirement of it hamper
the accomplishment of these work goals. Critical organizational communication research
during the 1980s and 1990s includes a rather
wide body of studies showing where culture
and cultural engineering may be described as
hegemonic (e.g., Alvesson, 1987b; Knights &
Willmott, 1987; Mumby, 1988, 1997; Rosen,
1985). Other researchers have shown how
normative, unobtrusive, or concertive control
processes develop in organizations and subvert employee participation programs (see

Barker, 1993; Barker & Cheney, 1994; Barker, Melville, & Pacanowsky, 1993; Barley & Kunda, 1992; Bullis, 1991; Bullis & Tompkins, 1989; Etzioni, 1961; Kunda, 1992; Lazega, 1992; Schwartzman, 1989).

Several limitations of ideology critique have been demonstrated. Three criticisms appear most common. First, ideology critique appears ad hoc and reactive. It largely explains after the fact why something didn't happen. Second, the elitist is often criticized. Common concepts like false needs and false consciousness presume a basic weakness in insight and reasoning processes in the very same people it hopes to empower. The irony of an advocate of greater equality pronouncing what others should want or how they should perceive the world "better" is apparent to both dominant and dominated groups. Third, some accounts from ideology critique appear far too simplistic. These studies appear to claim a single dominant group that has intentionally worked out a system whereby domination through control of ideas could occur and its interest could be secured. Clearly, domination is not so simple. Certainly the power of ideology critique can be maintained without falling to these criticisms, and most studies today carefully avoid each problem. Largely this has been aided by the development of Habermas's theory of communicative action.

*Communicative Action*

While earlier critical studies focused on distortions of consciousness, thought, and meanings, Habermas's work since the late 1970s has concentrated on distortions in communication processes (Habermas, 1984, 1987). This project retains many of the features of ideology critique, including the ideal of sorting out constraining social ideas from those grounded in reason, but it envisages procedural ideals rather than substantive critique and thus becomes quite different from traditional ideology critique. It also introduces an affirmative agenda, not based on a utopia, but still on a hope of how we might reform institutions along the lines of morally driven discourse in situations approximating an "ideal speech situation" (see Mumby, 1988). Organizational communication scholars have developed these ideas to support more participatory communication and decision making in organizations and to display power-based limitations on organizational democratization (Cheney, 1995; Deetz, 1992, 1995b; Forester, 1989, 1993; Harrison, 1994). From a participation perspective, communication difficulties arise from communication practices that preclude value debate and conflict, that substitute images and imaginary relations for self-presentation and truth claims, that arbitrarily limit access to communication channels and forums, and that then lead to decisions based on arbitrary authority relations (see Deetz, 1992, for development).

Basically, Habermas argued that every speech act can function in communication by virtue of common presumptions made by speaker and listener. Even when these presumptions are not fulfilled in an actual situation, they serve as a base of appeal as failed conversation turns to argumentation regarding the disputed validity claims. The basic presumptions and validity claims arise out of four shared domains of reality: language, the external world, human relations, and the individual's internal world. The claims raised in each realm are, respectively: intelligibility, truth, correctness, and sincerity. Each competent, communicative act makes four types of claims: (1) presenting an available understandable expression, (2) asserting a knowledge proposition, (3) establishing legitimate social relations, and (4) disclosing the speaker's positioned experience. Any of these claims that cannot be brought to open dispute serves as the basis for systematically distorted communication. The ideal speech situation is to be recovered to avoid or overcome such distortions.

The ideal speech situation, thus, describes four basic guiding conditions as necessary for free and open participation in the resolution of conflicting claims. First, the attempt to reach understanding presupposes a symmetrical distribution of the chances to choose and apply speech acts that can be heard and understood. This would specify the minimal conditions of skills and opportunities for expression including access to meaningful forums, media, and channels of communication. Second, the understanding and representation of the external world needs to be freed from privileged preconceptions in the social development of "truth." Ideally, participants have the opportunity to express interpretations and explanations with conflicts resolved in reciprocal claims and counterclaims without privileging particular epistemologies or forms of data. The freedom from preconception implies an examination of any ideology that would privilege one form of discourse, disqualify certain possible participants, and universalize any particular sectional interest. Third, participants need to have the opportunity to establish legitimate social relations and norms for conduct and interaction. The rights and responsibilities of people are not given in advance by nature or by a privileged, universal value structure, but are negotiated through interaction. The reification of organizational structures and their maintenance without possible dispute and the presence of managerial prerogatives are examples of potential immorality in corporate discourse. Finally, interactants need to be able to express their own authentic interests, needs, and feelings. This would require freedom from various coercive and hegemonic processes by which the individual is unable to form experience openly, to develop and sustain competing identities, and to form expressions presenting them.

The most frequent objection to Habermas, and those who have followed this work, is that he has overemphasized reason and consensus and has only a negative view of power, which hampers both the conception of social change and seeing the possible positivity of power (see Benhabib, 1990; Lyotard, 1984). What Habermas does well is to give an arguable

standard for normative guidance to communication as a critique of domination, even if his position is distinctly Western, intellectual, and male (Fraser, 1987; see Benhabib, 1992, for a discussion of these problems and ways of recovering the critical thrust of his work). The participative conception of communication describes the possibility and conditions for mutual decision making and also provides a description of communication problems and inadequacies. In general, most strategic or instrumental communicative acts have the potential of asserting the speaker's opinion over the attempt to reach a more representative consensus. In such cases, an apparent agreement precludes the conflict that could lead to a new position of open mutual assent. In cases where the one-sidedness is apparent, usually the processes of assertion/counter-assertion and questions/answers reclaim a situation approximating participation.

Critical theorists have been very effective in showing the invisible constraints to mutual decision making in organizations. In many workplaces today, strategy and manipulation are disguised and control is exercised through manipulations of the natural, neutral, and self-evident. Critical work has both demonstrated the presence of ideological domination and processes of "discursive closure" and "systematically distorted communication" (see Deetz, 1992, chap. 7). While Habermas has been criticized for focusing too much on consensus at the expense of conflict and dissensus, implicit in his analyses is the recovery of conflict as an essential precursor to a new consensus and the perpetual critique of each new consensus as interaction continues.

### The Discourse of Dialogic Studies

I have chosen the term *dialogic* rather than the more obvious *postmodernist* to organize this discourse because it attends to key features of this work and because of the growing commercial use of the term *postmodern*, resulting in increased difficulty in distinguishing realist assumptions about a changing world (a postmodern world) and a postmodern discourse, which denies realist claims about the world (Jones, 1992; Parker, 1992). The term also makes it easier to include older theorists such as Bakhtin for whom the term *postmodern* seems inappropriate (see Shotter, 1993). Dialogic perspectives are based in a recent set of philosophical writings originating most often in France. Of greatest interest are the writings emphasizing political issues and conceptions of fragmentation, textuality, and resistance. These philosophically based approaches to organization studies have emerged out of works of Bourdieu, Derrida, Lyotard, Kristiva, Foucault, Baudrillard, Deleuze and Guattari, and Laclau and Mouffe. Organizational researchers following the general themes of this work include Hawes (1991), Martin (1990), Calás and Smircich (1991), Mumby and Putnam (1992), Knights (1992), Burrell (1988), Bhabha (1990), Barker and Cheney (1994), Holmer-Nadesan (1997), Ashcraft (1998), and several of the essays in Hassard and Parker (1993). As with critical writings, this is a wide group of writers and positions with their own disputes, but their work shares features and moves that can be highlighted in treating them together.

Like critical studies, the concern is often with asymmetry and domination in organizational decision making, but unlike the critical studies' predefinition of groups and types of domination, dialogic studies focus more on micropolitical processes and the joined nature of power and resistance. Domination is seen as fluid, situational, and without place or origin. Even group and personal identities cannot be seen as fixed or unitary. The attention is to reclaim conflicts suppressed in everyday experiences, meaning systems, and self-conceptions. Rather than a reformation of the world, dialogic studies hope to show the partiality (the incompletion and one-sidedness) of reality and the hidden points of resistance and complexity. In place of an active political agenda and utopian ideals, attention centers on the space for a continually transforming world through recovery of marginalized and suppressed peoples and aspects of people.

Dialogic research emphasizes dissensus production and the local/situated nature of understanding. Many of the conceptions on which this is based are difficult and not terribly well known by organizational communication scholars. Owing to this I will provide some greater detail here. Seven themes will be highlighted: (1) *the centrality of discourse,* emphasizing language as systems of distinctions that are central to social construction processes; (2) *fragmented identities,* demonstrating the problem of an autonomous, self-determining individual as the origin of meaning; (3) *the critique of the philosophy of presence,* focusing on object indeterminacy and the constructed nature of people and reality; (4) *the loss of foundations and master narratives,* arguing against integrative metanarratives and large-scale theoretical systems such as Marxism or functionalism; (5) *the knowledge/power connection,* examining the role of claims of expertise and truth in systems of domination; (6) *hyperreality,* emphasizing the fluid and hyperreal nature of the contemporary world and role of mass media and information technologies; and (7) *research as resistance and indeterminacy,* stressing research as important to change processes and providing voice to that which is lost or covered up in everyday life. Each of these has an impact on conceptions of quality communication, processes of decision making, and research directions.

## The Centrality of Discourse

Most current dialogic studies grew out of French structuralism by taking seriously the "linguistic turn" in philosophy. In this sense, dialogic studies developed the French tradition by making the same move on structuralist thought that Habermas and others in critical studies did on ideological critique in the development of communicative action in the German tradition. Language replaces consciousness as central to experience. Textual/

discursive fields replaced the structure of the unconscious and/or cultural structures claimed as universal. Both critical and dialogic theorists used these to fight a two-front war; first, against normative researchers and other objectivists with their science aimed at controlling nature and people, and second, against interpretive researchers and other humanists with their privileging of individual experience, unique human rights, and naive versions of human freedom. As discussed later, the linguistic turn enabled a critique of normative research's claim of objectivity through examining the processes by which objects are socially constituted and the role of language in that process and simultaneously a critique of interpretive research through demonstrating the fragmentation of cultures and personal identities and removing the psychological subject from the center of experience. Focusing on language allowed a conception of social constructionism that denied the normative claim of certainty and objective truth and the interpretivists' reliance on experience and neutral cultural claims that led them to miss the social/linguistic politics of experience. Communication thus becomes a mode of explanation of organizations and activities associated with them rather than a phenomenon to be explained within them.

Many organizational researchers have used this insight to produce discursive, communication-centered analyses of organizations. Many of the more empirical dialogic studies, but not all, have followed Foucault's conception of discourse. For example, Knights and Willmott (1989) and Mills (1994) demonstrated the way being subjected led to particular forms of subjugation; Knights and Morgan (1991) used Foucault's discursive practices to show the construction of person and world in the discourse of strategy; Townley (1993) applied it to the discourse of human resource management; and I (Deetz, 1998) have shown how self-surveillance and self-subordination replace explicit control systems in knowledge-intensive companies. Works following other related philosophical perspectives on discourse have tended to be somewhat more theoretical (e.g., Burrell, 1988; Cooper, 1989; Deetz, 1994d; Hawes, 1991).

### Fragmented Identities

The position on the person follows directly from the conception of discourse. Enlightenment thought centered knowledge and understanding in a conception of an autonomous and coherent subject. This conception leads to an emphasis on—what was developed in this essay as—a consensus discourse in science and society. Dialogic studies reject the notion of the autonomous, self-determining individual as the center of the social universe and in its place suggest the complex, conflictual subject with an emphasis on fundamental dissensus (see Garsten & Grey, 1997; Henriques, Hollway, Urwin, Venn, & Walkerdine, 1984; Mills, 1994; Nukala, 1996).

There are two versions of this critique of a secure unitary identity. The first suggests that the Western conception of *man* as a centered subject has always been a myth. Freud's work is used to show the growing awareness in Western thought of the difficulties with it. People have always been filled with conflicts. The conception of a unitary autonomous self was a fiction used to suppress those conflicts and privilege masculinity, rationality, vision, and control. To the extent that dominant discourses spoke the person, the person gained a secure identity but participated in the reproduction of domination marginalizing the other parts of the self and other groups. The sense of autonomy served to cover this subservience and to give conflict a negative connotation. The privileging of consensus and naturalization of a constructed world tended to hide basic conflicts and conceptualize the ones that did arise as based on misunderstandings, incomplete knowledge, or prejudice.

The other dialogic critique suggests that identity was relatively stable in homogeneous societies and their organizations with few available discourses. In contemporary, heterogeneous, global, teleconnected societies and globalization the available discourses expand greatly. Since identity is a discursive production, in this new situation the individual acquires so many simultaneous identities through different competing discourses that fragmentation is virtually inevitable (see Deetz, 1995b; Gergen, 1991). As society becomes more fragmented and/or virtual, the identity-stabilizing forces for organizations as well as people are lost. Such a position suggests the possibility of tremendous freedom and opportunity for marginalized groups and suppressed aspects of each person to be conceptualized and discussed in more heterogeneous societies and chaotic organizations. But the multiplicity of discourses can also lead to what Giddens (1991) called "ontological insecurities." Such insecurities regarding identity can lead to strategies that aim to secure a "normal" identity (see Knights & Morgan, 1991; Knights & Willmott, 1985, 1989). This loose self is open to manipulation (since the stable background of a dominant reproductive discourse is weakened) and can be "jerked" about in the system, leading to a sense of excitement and even "ecstasy" but also can be conversion prone and easily controlled by system forces (as in Baudrillard's conception of simulation, 1988; Deetz, 1994d).

The conception of a fluid conflictual identity, however, creates difficulties in developing political action. Flax (1990), for example, shows the awkward position it leaves women in. If gender is treated as a social construction, one can show that the dominant discourse in modern organizations has produced women and their experience as marginal and "other"—that is, taking all the negative terms in the linguistic system and discourse. Ridding society of strong gender ascriptions and gendered identities—making gender irrelevant to work—is a meaningful activity to provide opportunities for women. But to accomplish such a move in the contemporary situation requires women to organize and show that gender is an issue across nearly all social situations—that is, to fix a centered identity. The dilemma is heightened regarding their experience, for if women's experiences arise out of an essential difference, they cannot be denied as important and needing to be taken into account, but to make the essentialist argument of distinct female experiences denies social constructionism and can easily be used to further stigmatize women as "other" in a society where men have more resources. Ironically, however, this is the type of deep tension and inability to develop a single coherent position that, rather than weakening dialogic work, gives it its reason for being.

## The Critique of the Philosophy of Presence

Normative social science, as well as most of us in everyday life, treats the presence of objects as unproblematic and believes that language is to represent (re-present) these things. When asked what something is, we try to define it and list its essential attributes. Dialogic studies find such a position to be illusionary. Rather, the "elements" of the world are fundamentally indeterminant and can become many different determinant "objects" through different ways of attending to or encountering them. Linguistic and nonlinguistic practices direct attention and means of encountering the "elements" of organizations, thus are central to "object" production. Since the "elements" of organizations may be constructed/expressed as many different "objects," limited only by human creativity and reconfiguration of past understandings, meaning can never be final; objects and meanings are always incomplete and open to redetermination. Many different, and fundamentally irresolvable, "objectivities" thus exist in organizational life and research. The appearance of completeness and closure leads us to overlook the politics in and of construction and the possibilities for understandings hidden behind the apparent and obvious, thus a particular objectivity may be privileged.

Language is central to the production of objects in that it provides the social/historical distinctions that provide unity and difference. Language does not mirror the reality "out there" or people's mental states, but rather is a way of attending to both the insiders and outsiders providing them shape and character (Shotter, 1993; Shotter & Gergen, 1994). Further, the systems of differences or distinctions historically held by language are not fixed but metaphorical, full of contradictions and inconsistencies (Brown, 1990; Cooper & Burrell, 1988). Meaning, thus, is not universal and fixed, but precarious, fragmented, and situated. Since the research community, like others, can only escape this situation through distortion and closures, the conceptual base of research must also be, also already suggested, local and emergent.

Organizational communication researchers have used these conceptions to deconstruct objects of organizational life including the bounded concept of an organization and organizational rationality itself (Mumby & Putnam, 1992). Perhaps among the most productive have been those studying accounting practices. The bottom line, profit and loss, expenses, and so forth have no reality without specific practices creating them (Miller & O'Leary, 1987; Power, 1994). Others have looked at knowledge and information (Boland, 1987; Coombs et al., 1992). And others yet report practices (Sless, 1988) and categories of people (Epstein, 1988). Each of these shows the conditions necessary for objects to exist in organizational life and opens these objects to redetermination through initiating discussions and negotiations of reality that were not possible as long as hidden dominance held sway.

### The Loss of Foundations and Master Narratives

Traditionally, the power of any social position has been gathered from its grounding or foundation. This grounding could either be to a metaphysical foundation—such as an external world in empiricism, mental structures in rationalism, human nature in humanism, or God in religion—or a narrative, a story of history—such as Marxism's class struggle, social Darwinism's survival of the fittest, or market economy's invisible hand. Positions based on such foundations and narratives are made to seem secure and inevitable and not opportunistic or driven by advantage. Certainly, much normative organizational research has been based on appeals to an "object" world, human nature, or laws of conduct. Critical research has a different foundational appeal to qualities of speech communities in its morally guided communicative action. Dialogic researchers are distinctly non- or antifoundational.

Again, like in the case of identity, dialogic researchers take two different but compatible stances in their critique of groundings. First, some argue that foundations and legitimating narratives have always been a hoax. Appeals to foundations have been used (usually unknowingly) to support a dominant view of the world and its order. As feminists, for example, argue following this position, the historical narrative has always been *his*tory. Empiricists' appeal to the nature of the external world covered up the force of their own concepts (and those borrowed from elite groups), methods, instruments, activities, and reports in constructing that world (Harding, 1991). Second, dialogic researchers note the growing social incredulity toward narratives and foundational moves. Lyotard (1984) showed the decline of *grand* narratives of "spirit" and "emancipation." The proliferation of options and growing political cynicism (or astuteness) of the public leads to a suspicion of legitimating moves. In Lyotard's sense perhaps all that is left is *local* narratives—that is, ad hoc and situated attempts at justification without appealing to themes that organize the whole of life.

The concern with integrative narratives has led to sensitive treatments of how stories in organizations connect to grand narratives and how different ones have a more local, situational character (see Martin, 1990). Other researchers have used this opening to display the false certainty in the master narratives in management (Calás & Smircich, 1991; Ingersoll & Adams, 1986). Jehenson (1984), for example, showed how narratives of "effectiveness," "expertise," and "excellence" were used to legitimize managerial control systems. In one of my own studies (Deetz, 1998), I show how narratives of "consultancy" and "integrated solutions" enabled a dominant coalition to maintain control through a financial crisis in a professional service company.

Dialogic researchers do not see the decline of foundations as necessarily leading to positive outcomes. Certainly, the decline of foundations and grand narratives removes the primary prop of security and certainty that dominant groups trade for subordination. But the replacement is not necessarily freedom and political possibility for marginalized groups. Lyotard demonstrated the rise of "performativity," which while developed as a measure of means toward social ends becomes an end in itself. The performativity standard provides new forms of control not directed by a vision of society and social good but simply more production and consumption (see Carter & Jackson, 1987). Many "quality" programs evidence this. Certainly, the loss of grand integrative narratives has not been missed by management groups. One could easily say that the common conceptions of corporate "visions" and "cultures" are strategic local narrative constructions to provide the integration and motivation in a pluralistic society formerly provided by the wider social narratives that have passed away.

A difficulty in dialogic research with the loss of foundations, as in the concept of fragmented identities, is how to generate a political stance in regard to these developments. Women have confronted this most directly in debates over whether men and women have distinctly different experiences grounded in biological sex. Without a grounding, the basis for large-scale political action is lacking, and resistance to domination, even general domination, becomes local and situational. If one rejects an essentialist foundation and believes that more than local resistance is needed, critical theory may well provide the best remaining option, but not without costs (see Fraser & Nicholson, 1988).

## The Knowledge/Power Connection

Within dialogic writings, power is treated far differently from most other writings on organizations. Foucault (1977, 1980, 1988) has led many in suggesting that the "power" of interest is not that which one possesses or acquires (Clegg, 1989; Jermier, Knights, & Nord, 1994). Such power is an outcome of more fundamental power relations. Power resides in the discursive practices and formations themselves. For example, the discourse that produces a "worker" both empowers and disempowers the group of individuals produced through this representation. In particular historical discourses, "workers" and "managers" are produced out of the open "elements" of organizational life and simultaneously provided with solidarity and interests as well as conflicts, material and symbolic resources, and self-understandings. Power thus resides in the demarcations and the systems of discourse that produce and sustain such groupings. Unions and managers mutually sustain the other in their conflicts. It is not the relative power of each that is of interest but how the distinction is reproduced.

One of the most useful terms entering into organization studies from Foucault's work on the knowledge/power connection has been his concept of "discipline." The demarcations developed in discourse provide forms of normative behavior. The combination of training, routines, self-surveillance, and experts provides resources for normalization, then discipline (Deetz, 1998; Knights & Collinson, 1987; Townley, 1993). From such a conception, normative research and the expertise produced from it are considered to provide resources for normalization and a veneer of truth for arbitrary and advantaging discursive practices (Hollway, 1984, 1991). The emphasis on dissensus discourse in dialogic research is aimed at disrupting normalization and provides competing power relations (Holmer-Nadesan, 1997; Knights, 1992; Trethewey, 1997).

### Hyperreality

In dialogic conceptions, linguistic and nonlinguistic practices are considered to open a relation to external elements (people and world) and produce these elements in specific ways. As discussed earlier, the referent ("elements" of the world) has no specific character; it is always determinable in more ways than all the determinations or objects that have been made of it through various historical practices. To the extent that this "indeterminacy" is known (the "otherness" of elements shows), the domination present in any system can be disrupted and objects de- and redifferentiated. To the extent that indeterminacy is recognized, the possibility of self-referentiality in a textual system is avoided. Otherwise, the determinant object produced by the practices is referenced by the practices and the system remains closed.

The presence of media and information systems increases the possibility of such closure and the lack of connection to the external indeterminacy. The referent can disappear as anything more than another sign—a produced object. Thus properly signs would only reference other signs; images would be images of images. The system then becomes purely self-referential or what Baudrillard calls a *simulation* (see Deetz, 1994d, for an example). In such a world, in Baudrillard's analysis, signs, rather than connecting us to the outside world and providing a temporary determination, reference only linguistically already determined objects—the "map" leads us only to earlier "maps" of the world. The "model" is seen as the thing and "model" behavior replaces responsive action. Signs reach the structural limit of representation by referencing only themselves with little relation to any outside or interior. In such a situation, a particular fiction is not produced by a subject in opposition to reality, but positions an imaginary world and subject in place of any real; it has no opposite, no outside. Baudrillard (1983) used the example of the difference between feigning and simulating an illness to show the character of this dialogic representation: "Feigning or dissimulation leaves the reality principle intact; the difference is always clear, it is only masked; whereas simulation threatens the difference between 'true' and 'false,' between 'real' and 'imaginary.' Since the simulator produces 'true' symptoms, is he ill or not? He cannot be treated objectively either as ill, or not ill" (p. 5).

Hochschild (1983) provided an organizational example of this (though from a theoretically different position) in her description of the appropriateness of flight attendants' emotions. Our traditional conceptions allow a fairly simple distinction between "real" spontaneous emotions that arise in response to perceived situations and "acting" where an employee fakes the managerially desired emotion. Hochschild shows, however, that the presence of "deep acting" makes this distinction misleading. In deep acting, the flight attendants in her studies learn to perceive or attend to the situation in such a way that the managerially desired emotion spontaneously arises in the employee. Is it fake or not? In the concepts here, it is self-referential. The system appears open and environmentally adaptive but closes or manipulates the environment in ways that the system adapts to the system reproduced environment. This is not unlike normative research constructing the world using the concepts of the same theory it hopes to test.

### Research as Resistance and Indeterminacy

The role of dialogic research is very different from more traditional roles assigned to social science in both its emphasis on dissensus production and the local forms of knowledge. It primarily serves to attempt to open up the indeterminacy that modern social science, everyday conceptions, routines, and practices have closed off. The result is a kind of antipositive (or positivist) knowledge that Knights (1992) described. The primary methods are deconstruction, resistance readings, and genealogy.

Deconstruction works primarily to critique the philosophy of presence by recalling the suppressed terms that have become devalued in dominant systems of distinction. When the suppressed term is given value, the dependency of the positive term on the negative is revealed and a third term is recovered that shows a way of thinking or attending to the world that is not dependent on the opposition of the first two (see Calás & Smircich, 1991; Martin, 1990; Mumby, 1996; Mumby & Putnam, 1992). The resistance reading demonstrates the construction activity and problematizes any fixed relationship. The positive and the polar constructions are both displayed as acts of domination. Conflicts that were suppressed by the positive are brought back to redecision (see Westenholz, 1991). The conflictual field out of which objects are formed is recovered for creative redetermination—constant dedifferentiation and redifferentiation. Given the power of common sense and organizational routines, such rereads require rigor and imagination. The rereadings are formed out of a keen sense of irony, a serious playfulness, and are often guided by the pleasure one has in being freed from the dull compulsions of a world made too easy and too constraining. The point of research in this sense is not to get it right but to challenge guiding assumptions, fixed meanings and relations, and reopen the formative capacity of human beings in relation to others and the world.

## A LOOK TO THE FUTURE

In looking at different organizational communication research programs, clearly different programs have different goals and assumptions and provide different forms of evaluation. I hope to have displayed differences that give insights into the diverse discourses in organizational communication studies today, displaying some of the ways that they are alike and different. The relation among these alternatives is not addressed well in exclusionary, pluralistic, supplementary, or integrative terms. Each orientation creates a vision of social problems and tries to address them. Different orientations have specific ways of answering the types of questions they pose and do not work terribly well in answering the questions of others.

I, like many others, sometimes wish we were all multilingual, that we could move across orientations with grace and ease, but this type of Teflon-coated, multiperspectival cosmopolitan envisioned by Morgan (1986) or Hassard (1991) is both illusionary and weak (see Parker & McHugh, 1991). Good scholars have deep commitments. Multiperspectivalism often leads to shallow readings and invites unexamined basic assumptions. Some scholars are more multilingual than others, but doing good work within an orientation still must be prized first. Ideally, alternative research programs can complement each other. Consensus without dissensus is stifling and finally maladaptive. Elite/a priori concepts are necessary and probably inevitable, but we can make them more temporary and open to reconfiguration.

Without a doubt, most organizational communication scholars are becoming both more knowledgeable about alternatives and more appreciative of the differences. This development allows us to get beyond relatively unproductive theoretical and methodological arguments to more basic and serious questions. The choice of orientation, to the extent that it can be freed from training and department/discipline politics, can probably be reduced to alternative conceptions of social good and preferred ways of living. This acceptance grounds theory and method debate in a moral debate that has been neither terribly common nor explicit in organizational communication studies. I agree with Gergen (1992) that organizational research and theory need to be evaluated as much by a question of "how shall we live?" as by verisimilitude and methodological rigor. Studies need to be understood and evaluated on their own terms, but should also appeal to the larger social concerns in which both the needs and means of accomplishment are contested.

Discussions of responsibility and value are still relatively infrequent in organizational communication research, but present (see various essays in Conrad, 1993; Deetz, 1995a; Deetz, Cohen, & Edley, 1997). Certainly, we have lagged behind moral and ethical discussions of organization available other places (e.g., Frederick, 1986; Freeman, 1991; Freeman & Liedtka, 1991; Gergen, 1995; Jackell, 1988; MacIntyre, 1984; Mangham, 1995). The justification for much organizational communication research has been aimed at improving the functioning of organizations and management as if they were value-neutral tools without regarding how these tools are applied or whose values are advanced. With such a conception, our research has often focused on the perfectibility of the tool rather than the ends it is used to advance. To the extent that this conception has been useful, organization studies have enhanced the effective use of resources and fulfillment of certain human needs. But many researchers now question this "tool" version of organizations and research, claiming that researchers paid insufficient attention to alternative needs and goals, and the numerous social and political consequences of organizational activities (see Marsden, 1993). Until recently, most organizational communication researchers accepted a managerial bias in their conceptions of organizations and articulations of organizational goals.

The business environment has changed in fundamental ways in the past two decades. These changes require rethinking decision making in corporations: Who should make the decisions? How should they be made? What criteria should be used to evaluate them? If companies are to stay economically viable and their host societies healthy, corporate decisions must be more responsive to rapidly changing environments and human needs. Understanding new values and the rights and capacities of other organizational members is initiating reforms of organizational communication research that are as sweeping as many contemporary changes in organizational life. Certainly, this is seen to some extent in the growth of teams, other participation programs, customer focus, and increased discussion of environmental and social responsibility.

More important than these new programs, in my mind however, is a growing shift in the conception of organizations themselves. This shift offers the greatest challenge and opportunity for organizational communication researchers. Generally, the conceptual shift can be characterized as moving from an "owner/manager" model to a "stakeholder" model of organizations (see Carroll, 1989; Deetz, 1995b; Freeman & Gilbert, 1988; Grunig & Hunt, 1984; Osigweh, 1994). In this model, a variety of groups in addition to stockholders and managers are seen as having made an investment and thus having a stake in corporate decisions. Proponents of such a view argue that in a democratic society all those affected by the activities of corporations (all *stakeholders*) have some representation rights. But beyond the question of rights, direct decisional influence by both internal and external constituencies can lead to greater effectiveness in meeting the diverse social and economic goals. A stakeholder model recognizes multiple forms of ownership and enables widespread participation and thus helps initiate important value debates.

In traditional models of organizations, the core processes in organizations were conceived as economic. Communication aided economic accomplishment, but wherever possible stakeholder representation was limited to economic representation. If communication-based decision making could be reduced to an economic calculation, it was. In a stakeholder model, the core processes involve several simultaneous goals. The interaction among stakeholders can be conceived as a negotiative process aiding mutual goal accomplishment. Communication is the means by which such negotiation takes place. Conceptions of human interaction, negotiation, and rationality developed by communication theorists are uniquely suited to these new needs. To make a full contribution, organizational communication researchers would need to use communication conceptions aimed at increasing genuine participation rather than increased influence and control. This change is still incomplete.

Many organization managers understand the need to attend to stakeholders today but have not accepted a stakeholder model. New communication and decision-making conceptions are often used to increase the number of *forums* in which stakeholder representation and debate could occur, but few have increased stakeholder *voice* (Deetz, 1995b; Deetz et al., 1997; Gordon, 1988). Attention to stakeholders in these cases is a strategic attempt to increase loyalty and commitment and decrease resistance rather than seeking genuine decisional input. The lack of voice results from constrained decisional contexts, inadequate or distorted information, socialization and colonization activities, and the solicitation of "consent" where stakeholders "choose" to suppress their own needs and internal value conflicts. Gradually, we are learning that the problem with traditional organizations was not simply bureaucracy, but control systems in a variety of forms. To overcome these problems, new conceptions of interaction can improve collaborative decision making within corporations. The critical and dialogic scholars were somewhat earlier in fully appreciating these changes while managers and managerial-biased researchers have been more ambivalent—often both advocating new conceptions and programs and subverting their full implementation. But both normative and interpretive researchers can design studies that enhance the functioning of the organization as a site of stakeholder coordination rather than a site of control. Finding new ways of organizing becomes everyone's job.

Understanding our alternatives requires understanding both the relation of conceptions to the various social stakeholders and the relation of research discourse to dominant social theories. Thinking through these relations provides an opening for discussion. We are learning the positive effects of human diversity as organizational members—beyond "separate but equal" and integration—and organizational communication research can benefit from better conceptual discussions of research diversity. In doing so, the ultimate point is not in arguing it out to get it right, but to reclaim the suppressed tensions and conflicts among the many contemporary stakeholders to negotiate a life together based in appreciation of difference and responsive decision making.

## NOTES

1. Citations are selective throughout this essay. Rather than try to be exhaustive and produce a cluttered text with hundreds of references, I will reference what I consider to be well illustrative or especially useful developments and will bias the selection toward authors who work in communication departments. This essay was completed in 1996. Citations to literature published after that time are more limited.

2. Much of this discussion is adapted from Deetz (1996).

## REFERENCES

Alexander, E., III, Penley, L., & Jernigan, I. E. (1991). The effect of individual differences on manager media choice. *Management Communication Quarterly, 5*, 155-173.

Allen, B. J. (1996). Feminist standpoint theory: A black woman's (re)view of organizational socialization. *Communication Studies, 47*, 257-271.

Allen, B. J. (1998). Black womanhood and feminist standpoints. *Management Communication Quarterly, 11,* 575-586.

Allen, M. W., Gotcher, J. M., & Seibert, J. H. (1993). A decade of organizational communication research: Journal articles 1980-1991. In S. A. Deetz (Ed.), *Communication yearbook 16* (pp. 252-330). Newbury Park, CA: Sage.

Alvesson, M. (1987a). *Organizational theory and technocratic consciousness: Rationality, ideology, and quality of work.* New York: Aldine de Gruyter.

Alvesson, M. (1987b). Organizations, culture and ideology. *International Studies of Management and Organizations, 17,* 4-18.

Alvesson, M. (1993). Cultural-ideological modes of management control. In S. A. Deetz (Ed.), *Communication yearbook 16* (pp. 3-42). Newbury Park, CA: Sage.

Alvesson, M., & Willmott, H. (Eds.). (1992). *Critical management studies.* London: Sage.

Alvesson, M., & Willmott, H. (1996). *Making sense of management: A critical introduction.* London: Sage.

Argyris, C. (1994, July-August). Good communication that blocks learning. *Harvard Business Review, 72,* 77-85.

Ashcraft, K. L. (1998). "I wouldn't say I'm a feminist, but . . . ": Organizational micropractice and gender identity. *Management Communication Quarterly, 11,* 587-597.

Ashcraft, K. L., & Pacanowsky, M. E. (1996). "A woman's worst enemy": Reflections on a narrative of organizational life and female identity. *Journal of Applied Communication Research, 24,* 217-239.

Axley, S. (1984). Managerial and organizational communication in terms of the conduit metaphor. *Academy of Management Review, 9,* 428-437.

Baker, M. (1991). Gender and verbal communication in professional settings: A review of the literature. *Management Communication Quarterly, 5,* 36-63.

Banks, S., & Riley, P. (1993). Structuration theory as an ontology for communication research. In S. A. Deetz (Ed.), *Communication yearbook 16* (pp. 167-196). Newbury Park, CA: Sage.

Bantz, C. (1983). Naturalistic research traditions. In L. L. Putnam & M. E. Pacanowsky (Eds.), *Communication and organizations: An interpretive approach* (pp. 55-72). Beverly Hills, CA: Sage.

Barker, J. (1993). Tightening the iron cage—Concertive control in self-managing teams. *Administrative Science Quarterly, 38,* 408-437.

Barker, J., & Cheney, G. (1994). The concept and the practice of discipline in contemporary organizational life. *Communication Monographs, 61,* 19-43.

Barker, J., Melville, C., & Pacanowsky, M. (1993). Self-directed teams at XEL: Changes in communication practices during a program of cultural transformation. *Journal of Applied Communication Research, 21,* 297-312.

Barley, S. (1990). Images of imaging: Notes on doing longitudinal field work. *Organization Science, 1,* 220-247.

Barley, S., & Kunda, G. (1992). Design and devotion: Surges of rational and normative ideologies of control in managerial discourse. *Administrative Science Quarterly, 37,* 363-399.

Barley, S., Meyer, G., & Gash, D. (1988). Cultures of culture: Academics, practitioners and the pragmatics of normative control. *Administrative Science Quarterly, 33,* 24-60.

Bastien, D. (1992). Change in organizational culture: The use of linguistic methods in a corporate acquisition. *Management Communication Quarterly, 5,* 403-442.

Bastien, D., McPhee, R., & Bolton, K. (1995). A study and extended theory of the structuration of climate. *Communication Monographs, 62,* 87-109.

Baudrillard, J. (1983). *Simulations.* New York: Semiotext(e).

Baudrillard, J. (1988). Simulacra and simulations. In M. Poster (Ed.), *Jean Baudrillard: Selected writings* (pp. 166-184). Stanford, CA: Stanford University Press.

Bellman, R., & Roosta, R. (1987). On a class of self-organizing communication networks. In F. Yates (Ed.), *Self-organizing systems.* New York: Plenum.

Benhabib, S. (1990). Afterward: Communicative ethics and current controversies in practical philosophy. In S. Benhabib & F. Dallmayr (Eds.), *The communicative ethics controversy* (pp. 330-369). Cambridge, MA: MIT Press.

Benhabib, S. (1992). *Situating the self: Gender, community and postmodernism in contemporary ethics.* Cambridge, UK: Polity.

Beniger, J. (1986). *The control revolution.* Cambridge, MA: Harvard University Press.

Benson, K. (1977). Organizations: A dialectical view. *Administrative Science Quarterly, 22,* 1-21.

Berger, C. R. (1977). The covering law perspective as a theoretical basis for the study of human communication. *Communication Quarterly, 25,* 7-18.

Bergquist, W. (1993). *The postmodern organization: Mastering the art of irreversible change.* San Francisco: Jossey-Bass.

Bernstein, R. (1983). *Beyond objectivism and relativism.* Philadelphia: University of Pennsylvania Press.

Bhabha, H. (1990). The other question: Difference, discrimination and the discourse of colonialism. In R. Ferguson, M. Gever, & T. Minh-Ha, with C. West (Eds.), *Out there: Marginalization and contemporary culture.* Cambridge, MA: MIT Press.

Boland, R. (1987). The information of information systems. In R. Boland & R. Hirschheim (Eds.), *Critical issues in information systems research* (pp. 363-379). New York: John Wiley.

Bormann, E. (1983). Symbolic convergence: Organizational communication and culture. In L. L. Putnam &

M. E. Pacanowsky (Eds.), *Communication and organizations: An interpretive approach* (pp. 99-122). Beverly Hills, CA: Sage.

Bourdieu, P. (1977). *Outline of a theory of practice.* Cambridge, UK: Cambridge University Press.

Bourdieu, P. (1991). *Language and symbolic power.* Cambridge, UK: Polity.

Braverman, H. (1974). *Labor and monopoly capital.* New York: Monthly Review Press.

Brown, M. H. (1985). That reminds me of a story: Speech action in organizational socialization. *Western Journal of Speech Communication, 49,* 27-42.

Brown, R. H. (1990). Rhetoric, textuality, and the postmodern turn in sociological theory. *Sociological Theory, 8,* 188-197.

Browning, L. (1992). Lists and stories as organizational communication. *Communication Theory, 2,* 281-302.

Brunsson, N. (1989). *The organization of hypocrisy: Talk, decisions and action in organizations.* New York: John Wiley.

Bullis, C. (1991). Communication practices as unobtrusive control: An observational study. *Communication Studies, 42,* 254-271.

Bullis, C., & Tompkins, P. (1989). The forest ranger revisited: A study of control processes and identification. *Communication Monographs, 56,* 287-306.

Burawoy, M. (1979). *Manufacturing consent.* Chicago: University of Chicago Press.

Burawoy, M. (1985). *The politics of production: Factory regimes under capitalism and socialism.* London: Verso.

Burrell, G. (1988). Modernism, postmodernism and organisational analysis 2: The contribution of Michel Foucault. *Organisation Studies, 9,* 221-235.

Burrell, G., & Morgan, G. (1979). *Sociological paradigms and organizational analysis.* London: Heinemann.

Calás, M., & Smircich, L. (1991). Voicing seduction to silence leadership. *Organization Studies, 12,* 567-602.

Carroll, A. (1989). *Business and society: Ethics and stakeholder management.* Cincinnati, OH: South-Western.

Carter, P., & Jackson, N. (1987). Management, myth, and metatheory—From scarcity to post scarcity. *International Studies of Management and Organizations, 17,* 64-89.

Cecchin, G., & Stratton, P. (1991). Extending systemic consultation from families to management. *Human Systems: The Journal of Systemic Consultation and Management, 2,* 3-13.

Cheney, G. (1995). Democracy in the workplace: Theory and practice from the perspective of communication. *Journal of Applied Communication Research, 23,* 167-200.

Clair, R. (1993a). The bureaucratization, commodification, and privatization of sexual harassment through institutional discourse. *Management Communication Quarterly, 7,* 123-157.

Clair, R. (1993b). The use of framing devices to sequester organizational narratives: Hegemony and harassment. *Communication Monographs, 60,* 113-136.

Clegg, S. (1989). *Frameworks of power.* Newbury Park, CA: Sage.

Clegg, S., & Dunkerley, D. (1980). *Organizations, class and control.* Boston: Routledge and Kegan Paul.

Clifford, J., & Marcus, G. E. (Eds.). (1986). *Writing culture.* Berkeley: University of California Press.

Conquergood, D. (1991). Rethinking ethnography: Toward a critical cultural politics. *Communication Monographs, 58,* 179-194.

Conrad, C. (Ed.). (1993). *Ethical nexus.* Norwood, NJ: Ablex.

Contractor, N. (1994). Self-organizing systems perspective in the study of organizational communication. In B. Kovacic (Ed.), *New approaches to organizational communication* (pp. 39-66). Albany: State University of New York Press.

Coombs, R., Knights, D., & Willmott, H. (1992). Culture, control, and competition: Towards a conceptual framework for the study of information technology in organizations. *Organization Studies, 13,* 51-72.

Cooper, R. (1989). Modernism, postmodernism and organisational analysis 3: The contribution of Jacques Derrida. *Organisation Studies, 10,* 479-502.

Cooper, R., & Burrell, G. (1988). Modernism, postmodernism and organisational analysis. *Organization Studies, 9,* 91-112.

Czarniawska-Joerges, B. (1988). *Ideological control in nonideological organizations.* New York: Praeger.

Daft, R., & Weick, K. (1984). Toward a model of organizations as interpretive systems. *Academy of Management Review, 9,* 284-295.

Dahrendorf, R. (1959). *Class and class conflict in industrial society.* Stanford, CA: Stanford University Press.

Deal, T., & Kennedy, A. (1982). *Corporate cultures.* Reading, MA: Addison-Wesley.

Deetz, S. (1973). An understanding of science and a hermeneutic science of understanding. *Journal of Communication, 23,* 139-159.

Deetz, S. (1992). *Democracy in the age of corporate colonization: Developments in communication and the politics of everyday life.* Albany: State University of New York Press.

Deetz, S. (1994a). The future of the discipline: The challenges, the research, and the social contribution. In S. A. Deetz (Ed.), *Communication yearbook 17* (pp. 565-600). Thousand Oaks, CA: Sage.

Deetz, S. (1994b). The micropolitics of identity formation in the workplace: The case of a knowledge intensive firm. *Human Studies, 17,* 1-22.

Deetz, S. (1994c). The new politics of the workplace: Ideology and other unobtrusive controls. In H. Simons & M. Billig (Eds.), *After postmodernism:*

*Reconstructing ideology critique* (pp. 172-199). Thousand Oaks, CA: Sage.

Deetz, S. (1994d). Representative practices and the political analysis of corporations. In B. Kovacic (Ed.), *Organizational communication: New perspectives* (pp. 209-242). Albany: State University of New York Press.

Deetz, S. (1995a). Character, corporate responsibility and the dialogic in the postmodern context. *Organization, 3,* 217-225.

Deetz, S. (1995b). *Transforming communication, transforming business: Building responsive and responsible workplaces.* Cresskill, NJ: Hampton.

Deetz, S. (1996). Describing differences in approaches to organizational science: Rethinking Burrell and Morgan and their legacy. *Organization Science, 7,* 191-207.

Deetz, S. (1998). Discursive formations, strategized subordination, and self-surveillance: An empirical case. In A. McKinlay & K. Starkey (Eds.), *Foucault, management and organization theory* (pp. 151-172). London: Sage.

Deetz, S., Cohen, D., & Edley, P. (1997). Toward a dialogic ethics in the context of international business organization. In F. Casmir (Ed.), *Ethics in intercultural and international communication* (pp. 183-226). Hillsdale, NJ: Lawrence Erlbaum.

Deetz, S., & Mumby, D. (1990). Power, discourse, and the workplace: Reclaiming the critical tradition in communication studies in organizations. In J. A. Anderson (Ed.), *Communication yearbook 13* (pp. 18-47). Newbury Park, CA: Sage.

DiMaggio, P. (1995). Comments on what theory is not. *Administrative Science Quarterly, 40,* 391-397.

Donaldson, L. (1985). *In defense of organizational theory: A reply to critics.* Cambridge, UK: Cambridge University Press.

Donnellon, A., Gray, B., & Bougon, M. (1986). Communication, meaning, and organized action. *Administrative Science Quarterly, 31,* 43-55.

Douglas, J. D. (Ed.). (1970). *Understanding everyday life.* Chicago: Aldine.

DuGay, P. (1997). *Production of culture, cultures of production.* London: Sage.

Edwards, R. (1979). *Contested terrain: The transformation of the workplace in the twentieth century.* New York: Basic Books.

Eisenberg, E., & Goodall, H. L., Jr. (1993). *Organizational communication: Balancing creativity and constraint.* New York: St. Martin's.

Epstein, C. (1988). *Deceptive distinctions.* New Haven, CT: Yale University Press.

Etzioni, A. (1961). *A comparative analysis of complex organizations.* New York: Free Press.

Everett, J. (1994). Communication and sociocultural evolution in organizations and organizational populations. *Communication Theory, 4,* 93-110.

Fairhurst, G. (1993). Echoes of the vision: When the rest of the organization talks quality. *Management Communication Quarterly, 6,* 331-371.

Ferguson, K. (1984). *The feminist case against bureaucracy.* Philadelphia: Temple University Press.

Ferguson, K. (1994). On bringing more theory, more voices and more politics to the study of organizations. *Organization, 1,* 81-100.

Fischer, F. (1990). *Technocracy and the politics of expertise.* Newbury Park, CA: Sage.

Flax, J. (1990). *Thinking fragments: Psychoanalysis, feminism and postmodernism in the contemporary west.* Berkeley: University of California Press.

Forester, J. (1989). *Planning in the face of power.* Berkeley: University of California Press.

Forester, J. (1993). *Critical theory, public policy, and planning practice.* Albany: State University of New York Press.

Foucault, M. (1977). *Discipline and punish: The birth of the prison* (A. Sheridan, Trans.). New York: Pantheon.

Foucault, M. (1980). *The history of sexuality* (R. Hurley, Trans.). New York: Pantheon.

Foucault, M. (1988). Technologies of the self. In L. Martin, H. Gutman, & P. Hutton (Eds.), *Technologies of the self* (pp. 16-49). Amherst: University of Massachusetts Press.

Fraser, N. (1987). What's critical about critical theory? The case of Habermas and gender. In S. Benhabib & D. Cornell (Eds.), *Feminism as critique* (pp. 31-55). Cambridge, UK: Polity.

Fraser, N., & Nicholson, L. (1988). Social criticism without philosophy: An encounter between feminism and postmodernism. *Theory, Culture, & Society, 5,* 373-394.

Frederick, W. C. (1986). Toward CSR3: Why ethical analysis is indispensable and unavoidable in corporate affairs. *California Management Review, 28,* 126-141.

Freeman, R. E. (Ed.). (1991). *Business ethics: The state of the art.* New York: Oxford University Press.

Freeman, R. E., & Gilbert, D. (1988). *Corporate strategy and the search for ethics.* Englewood Cliffs, NJ: Prentice Hall.

Freeman, R. E., & Liedtka, J. (1991). Corporate social responsibility: A critical approach. *Business Horizons, 34,* 92-101.

Frost, P., Moore, L., Louis, M., Lundberg, C., & Martin, J. (Eds.). (1985). *Organizational culture.* Beverly Hills, CA: Sage.

Frost, P., Moore, L., Louis, M., Lundberg, C., & Martin, J. (Eds.). (1992). *Rethinking culture.* Newbury Park, CA: Sage.

Garsten, C., & Grey, C. (1997). How to become oneself: Discourses of subjectivity in post-bureaucratic organizations. *Organization, 4,* 211-228.

Geertz, C. (1973). *The interpretation of cultures.* New York: Basic Books.

Geist, P. (1995). Negotiating whose order? Communicating to negotiate identities and revise organizational structures. In A. Nicotera (Ed.), *Conflict in organizations: Communicative processes.* Albany: State University of New York Press.

Gergen, K. (1978). Toward generative theory. *Journal of Personality and Social Psychology, 36,* 1344-1360.

Gergen, K. (1991). *The saturated self: Dilemmas of identity in contemporary life.* New York: Basic Books.

Gergen, K. (1992). Organizational theory in the postmodern era. In M. Reed & M. Hughes (Eds.), *Rethinking organization* (pp. 207-226). London: Sage.

Gergen, K. (1995). Global organization: From imperialism to ethical vision. *Organization, 2,* 519-532.

Giddens, A. (1979). *Control problems in social theory.* Berkeley: University of California Press.

Giddens, A. (1984). *The constitution of society.* Berkeley: University of California Press.

Giddens, A. (1991). *Modernity and self-identity: Self and society in the late modern age.* Stanford, CA: Stanford University Press.

Goodall, H. L. (1990). A theatre of motives and the "meaningful orders of persons and things." In J. A. Anderson (Ed.), *Communication yearbook 13* (pp. 69-94). Newbury Park, CA: Sage.

Gordon, W. (1988). Range of employee voice. *Employee Responsibilities and Rights Journal, 1,* 283-299.

Gordon, W., Infante, D., & Graham, E. (1988). Corporate conditions conductive to employee voice: A subordinate perspective. *Employee Responsibilities and Rights Journal, 1,* 101-110.

Gramsci, A. (1971). *Selections from the prison notebooks* (Q. Hoare & G. N. Smith, Trans.). New York: International. (Original work published 1929-1935)

Grunig, J., & Hunt, T. (1984). *Managing public relations.* New York: Holt, Rinehart & Winston.

Habermas, J. (1971). *Knowledge and human interests* (J. Shapiro, Trans.). Boston: Beacon.

Habermas, J. (1984). *The theory of communicative action: Vol. 1. Reason and the rationalization of society* (T. McCarthy, Trans.). Boston: Beacon.

Habermas, J. (1987). *The theory of communicative action: Vol. 2. Lifeworld and system* (T. McCarthy, Trans.). Boston: Beacon.

Harding, S. (1991). *Whose science? Whose knowledge?* Ithaca, NY: Cornell University Press.

Harrison, T. (1994). Communication and interdependence in democratic organizations. In S. A. Deetz (Ed.), *Communication yearbook 17* (pp. 247-274). Thousand Oaks, CA: Sage.

Hassard, J. (1991). Multiple paradigms and organizational analysis: A case study. *Organization Studies, 12,* 275-299.

Hassard, J., & Parker, M. (Eds.). (1993). *Postmodernism and organizations.* London: Sage.

Hawes, L. (1974). Social collectivities as communication: Perspectives on organizational behavior. *Quarterly Journal of Speech, 60,* 497-502.

Hawes, L. (1991). Organising narratives/codes/poetics. *Journal of Organizational Change Management, 4,* 45-51.

Henriques, J., Hollway, W., Urwin, C., Venn, C., & Walkerdine, V. (Eds.). (1984). *Changing the subject.* New York: Methuen.

Hochschild, A. (1983). *The managed heart.* Berkeley: University of California Press.

Hollway, W. (1984). Fitting work: Psychological assessment in organizations. In J. Henriques, W. Hollway, C. Urwin, C. Venn, & V. Walkerdine. (Eds.), *Changing the subject* (pp. 26-59). New York: Methuen.

Hollway, W. (1991). *Work psychology and organizational behavior.* London: Sage.

Holmer-Nadesan, M. (1996). Organizational identity and space of action. *Organization Studies, 17,* 49-81.

Holmer-Nadesan, M. (1997). Constructing paper dolls: The discourse of personality testing in organizational practices. *Communication Theory, 7,* 189-218.

Howard, L., & Geist, P. (1995). Ideological positioning in organizational change: The dialectic of control in a merging organization. *Communication Monographs, 62,* 110-131.

Infante, D., Anderson, C., Martin, M., Herington, A., & Kim, J. (1993). Subordinates' satisfaction and perceptions of superiors' compliance gaining tactics, argumentativeness, verbal aggressiveness, and style. *Management Communication Quarterly, 6,* 307-326.

Ingersoll, V., & Adams, G. (1986). Beyond organizational boundaries: Exploring the managerial myth. *Administration and Society, 18,* 360-381.

Jablin, F. M. (1979). Superior-subordinate communication: The state of the art. *Psychological Bulletin, 86,* 1201-1222.

Jackell, R. (1988). *Moral mazes: The world of corporate managers.* New York: Oxford University Press.

Jackson, N., & Carter, P. (1991). In defense of paradigm incommensurability. *Organization Studies, 12,* 109-127.

Jehenson, R. (1984). Effectiveness, expertise and excellence as ideological fictions: A contribution to a critical phenomenology of the formal organization. *Human Studies, 7,* 3-21.

Jermier, J., Knights, D., & Nord, W. (Eds.). (1994). *Resistance and power in organizations.* London: Routledge.

Jones, D. (1992). Postmodern perspectives on organisational communication. *Australian Journal of Communication, 19,* 30-37.

Katz, D., & Kahn, R. (1978). *The social psychology of organizations* (2nd ed.). New York: John Wiley.

Kauffman, B. (1992). Feminist facts: Interview strategies and political subjects in ethnography. *Communication Theory, 2,* 187-206.

Kilduff, M. (1993). Deconstructing organizations. *Academy of Management Review, 18,* 13-31.

Knapp, M., Putnam, L., & Davis, L. (1988). Measuring interpersonal conflict in organizations. *Management Communication Quarterly, 1,* 414-429.

Knights, D. (1992). Changing spaces: The disruptive impact of a new epistemological location for the study of management. *Academy of Management Review, 17,* 514-536.

Knights, D., & Collinson, D. (1987). Disciplining the shop floor: A comparison of the disciplinary effects of managerial psychology and financial accounting. *Accounting, Organizations and Society, 12,* 457-477.

Knights, D., & Morgan, G. (1991). Corporate strategy, organizations, and subjectivity: A critique. *Organization Studies, 12,* 251-273.

Knights, D., & Willmott, H. (1985). Power and identity in theory and practice. *Sociological Review, 33,* 22-46.

Knights, D., & Willmott, H. (1987). Organisational culture as management strategy. *International Studies of Management and Organization, 17,* 40-63.

Knights, D., & Willmott, H. (1989). Power and subjectivity at work: From degradation to subjugation in social relations. *Sociology, 23,* 535-558.

Knights, D., & Willmott, H. (Eds.). (1990). *Labour process theory.* London: Macmillan.

Knuf, J. (1993). "Ritual" in organizational culture theory: Some theoretical reflections and a plea for greater terminological rigor. In S. A. Deetz (Ed.), *Communication yearbook 16* (pp. 43-53). Newbury Park, CA: Sage.

Krone, K. J., Jablin, F. M., & Putnam, L. L. (1987). Communication theory and organizational communication: Multiple perspectives. In F. M. Jablin, L. L. Putnam, K. H. Roberts, & L. W. Porter (Eds.), *Handbook of organizational communication: An interdisciplinary perspective* (pp. 18-40). Newbury Park, CA: Sage.

Kunda, G. (1992). *Engineering culture: Control and commitment in a high-tech corporation.* Philadelphia: Temple University Press.

Laclau, E., & Mouffe, C. (1985). *Hegemony and socialist strategy* (W. Moore & P. Cammack, Trans.). London: Verso.

Lawrence, P., & Lorsch, J. (1967). Differentiation and integration in complex organizations. *Administrative Science Quarterly, 12,* 147.

Lazega, E. (1992). *Micropolitics of knowledge: Communication and indirect control in workgroups.* New York: Aldine de Gruyter.

Linstead, S. (1993). Deconstruction in the study of organizations. In J. Hassard & M. Parker (Eds.), *Postmodernism and organizations* (pp. 49-70). London: Sage.

Lukács, G. (1971). *History and class consciousness* (R. Livingstone, Trans.). London: Merlin.

Lukes, S. (1974). *Power: A radical view.* London: Macmillan.

Lyotard, J.-F. (1984). *The postmodern condition: A report on knowledge* (G. Bennington & B. Massumi, Trans.). Minneapolis: University of Minnesota Press.

Lyytinen, K., & Hirschheim, R. (1988). Information systems as rational discourse: An application of Habermas's theory of communicative action. *Scandinavian Journal of Management, 4,* 19-30.

MacIntyre, A. (1984). *After virtue: A study in moral theory* (2nd ed.). Notre Dame, IN: University of Notre Dame Press.

Mangham, I. (1995). MacIntyre and managers. *Organization, 3,* 181-204.

Manning, P. (1992). *Organizational communication.* New York: Aldine de Gruyter.

Marcus, G., & Fischer, M. (1986). *Anthropology as cultural critique.* Chicago: University of Chicago Press.

Marsden, R. (1993). The politics of organizational analysis. *Organization Studies, 14,* 93-124.

Martin, J. (1990). Deconstructing organizational taboos: The suppression of gender conflict in organizations. *Organization Science, 1,* 339-359.

Martin, J. (1992). *Cultures in organizations: Three perspectives.* New York: Oxford University Press.

Meyers, R., Seibert, J., & Allen, M. (1993). A decade of organizational communication research: Journal articles 1980-1991. In S. A. Deetz (Ed.), *Communication yearbook 16* (pp. 252-330). Newbury Park, CA: Sage.

Miller, K., & Monge, P. (1985). Participation, satisfaction, and productivity: A meta-analytic review. *Academy of Management Journal, 29,* 727-753.

Miller, P., & O'Leary, T. (1987). Accounting and the construction of the governable person. *Accounting, Organizations and Society, 12,* 235-265.

Mills, A. (1994). Man/aging subjectivity, silencing diversity. *Organization, 2,* 243-269.

Monge, P. (1977). The systems perspective as a theoretical basis for the study of human communication. *Communication Quarterly, 25,* 19-29.

Monge, P. (1982). Systems theory and research in the study of organizational communication: The correspondence problem. *Human Communication Research, 8,* 245-261.

Monge, P., Cozzens, J., & Contractor, N. (1992). Communication and motivation predictors of the dynamics of innovation. *Organization Science, 2,* 1-25.

Monge, P., Farace, E., Eisenberg, E., Miller, K., & White, K. (1984). The process of studying process in organizational communication. *Journal of Communication, 34,* 22-34.

Morgan, G. (1986). *Images of organization.* Beverly Hills, CA: Sage.

Mumby, D. (1987). The political function of narrative in organizations. *Communication Monographs, 54,* 113-127.

Mumby, D. (1988). *Communication and power in organizations: Discourse, ideology, and domination.* Norwood, NJ: Ablex.

Mumby, D., & Putnam, L. (1992). The politics of emotion: A feminist reading of bounded rationality. *Academy of Management Review, 17,* 465-486.

Mumby, D. K. (1996). Feminism, postmodernism, and organizational communication: A critical reading. *Management Communication Quarterly, 9,* 259-295.

Mumby, D. K. (1997). The problem of hegemony: Rereading Gramsci for organizational communication studies. *Western Journal of Communication, 61,* 343-375.

Nukala, S. (1996). *The discursive construction of Asian-American employees.* Unpublished doctoral dissertation, Rutgers University, New Brunswick, NJ.

Natter, W., Schatzki, T., & Jones, J. P., III. (1995). *Objectivity and its other.* New York: Guilford.

O'Keefe, D. (1976). Logical empiricism and the study of human communication. *Speech Monographs, 42,* 169-183.

Osigweh, C. (1994). A stakeholder perspective of employee responsibilities and rights. *Employee Responsibilities and Rights Journal, 7,* 279-296.

Pacanowsky, M., & O'Donnell-Trujillo, N. (1982). Communication and organizational cultures. *Western Journal of Speech Communication, 46,* 115-130.

Parker, M. (1992). Postmodern organizations or postmodern organization theory? *Organization Studies, 13,* 1-17.

Parker, M., & McHugh, G. (1991). Five tests in search of an author: A response to John Hassard's "Multiple paradigms and organizational analysis." *Organization Studies, 12,* 451-456.

Pearce, W. B. (1989). *Communication and the human condition.* Carbondale: Southern Illinois University Press.

Pepper, S. (1995). *Communicating in organizations: A cultural approach.* New York: McGraw-Hill.

Peters, T. (1987). *Thriving on chaos.* New York: Knopf.

Pettigrew, A. (1973). *The politics of organizational decision making.* London: Tavistock.

Pettigrew, A. (1990). Longitudinal field research on change. *Organization Science, 1,* 267-292.

Poole, M. S., & McPhee, R. (1983). A structurational analysis of organizational climate. In L. L. Putnam & M. E. Pacanowsky (Eds.), *Communication and organizations: An interpretive approach* (pp. 195-220). Beverly Hills, CA: Sage.

Power, M. (1994). The audit society. In A. Hopwood & P. Miller (Eds.), *Accounting as social and institutional practice* (pp. 299-316). Cambridge, UK: Cambridge University Press.

Pringle, R. (1989). *Secretaries talk.* London: Verso.

Putnam, L. (1982). Paradigms for organizational communication research. *Western Journal of Speech Communication, 46,* 192-206.

Putnam, L., & Cheney, G. (1985). Organizational communication: Historical development and future directions. In T. Benson (Ed.), *Speech communication in the 20th century* (pp. 130-156). Carbondale: Southern Illinois University Press.

Putnam, L. L., & Pacanowsky, M. E. (Eds.). (1983). *Communication and organizations: An interpretive approach.* Beverly Hills, CA: Sage.

Putnam, L. L., Phillips, N., & Chapman, P. (1996). Metaphors of communication and organization. In S. R. Clegg, C. Hardy, & W. J. Nord (Eds.), *Handbook of organization studies* (pp. 375-408). London: Sage.

Putnam, L., Bantz, C., Deetz, S., Mumby, D., & Van Maanen, J. (1993). Ethnography versus critical theory: Debating organizational research. *Journal of Management Inquiry, 2,* 221-235.

Reason, P. (1994). Three approaches to participatory inquiry. In N. Denzin & Y. Lincoln (Eds.), *Handbook of qualitative research* (pp. 324-339). Thousand Oaks, CA: Sage.

Redding, W. C. (1979). Organizational communication theory and ideology: An overview. In D. Nimmo (Ed.), *Communication yearbook 3* (pp. 309-341). New Brunswick, NJ: Transaction.

Redding, C., & Tompkins, P. (1988). Organizational communication—Past and future tenses. In G. Goldhaber & G. Barnett (Eds.), *Handbook of organizational communication* (pp. 5-34). Norwood, NJ: Ablex.

Reed, M. (1985). *New directions in organizational analysis.* London: Tavistock.

Richetto, G. (1977). Organizational communication theory and research. In B. Ruben (Ed.), *Communication yearbook 1* (pp. 331-346). New Brunswick, NJ: Transaction.

Riley, P. (1983). A structurationist account of political cultures. *Administrative Science Quarterly, 28,* 414-438.

Rodríguez, J., & Cai, D. (1994). When your epistemology gets in the way. *Communication Education, 43,* 263-272.

Rorty, R. (1979). *Philosophy and the mirror of nature.* Princeton, NJ: Princeton University Press.

Rorty, R. (1989). *Contingency, irony and solidarity.* Cambridge, UK: Cambridge University Press.

Rosen, M. (1985). Breakfast at Spiro's: Dramaturgy and dominance. *Journal of Management, 11*(2), 31-48.

Schall, M. (1983). A communication-rules approach to organizational culture. *Administrative Science Quarterly, 28,* 557-581.

Schein, E. (1992). *Organizational culture and leadership* (2nd ed.). San Francisco: Jossey-Bass.

Schwartzman, H. B. (1989). *The meeting.* New York: Plenum.

Senge, P. (1990). *The fifth discipline: The art and practice of the learning organization.* New York: Doubleday.

Shockley-Zalabak, P., & Morley, D. (1994). Creating a culture: A longitudinal examination of the influence of management and employee values on communication rule stability and emergence. *Human Communication Research, 20,* 334-355.

Shotter, J. (1993). *Conversational realities: The construction of life through language.* Newbury Park, CA: Sage.

Shotter, J., & Gergen, K. (1994). Social construction: Knowledge, self, others, and continuing the conversation. In S. A. Deetz (Ed.), *Communication yearbook 17* (pp. 3-33). Thousand Oaks, CA: Sage.

Sias, P., & Jablin, F. (1995). Differential superior-subordinate relations, perceptions of fairness, and coworker communication. *Human Communication Research, 22,* 5-38.

Sless, D. (1988). Forms of control. *Australian Journal of Communication, 14,* 57-69.

Smeltzer, L. (1993). A de facto definition and focus of managerial communication. *Management Communication Quarterly, 6,* 428-440.

Smircich, L. (1983). Concepts of culture and organizational analysis. *Administrative Science Quarterly, 28,* 339-358.

Smircich, L., & Calás, M. B. (1987). Organizational culture: A critical assessment. In F. M. Jablin, L. L. Putnam, K. H. Roberts, & L. W. Porter (Eds.), *Handbook of organizational communication: An interdisciplinary perspective* (pp. 228-263). Newbury Park, CA: Sage.

Smith, R. (1993, May). *Images of organizational communication: Root-metaphors of the organization-communication relation.* Paper presented at the annual meeting of the International Communication Association, Washington, D.C.

Smith, R., & Eisenberg, E. (1987). Conflict at Disneyland: A root-metaphor analysis. *Communication Monographs, 54,* 367-380.

Smith, R., & Turner, P. (1995). A social constructionist reconfiguration of metaphor analysis: An application of "SCMA" to organizational socialization theorizing. *Communication Monographs, 62,* 152-181.

Sprague, J. (1992). Expanding the research agenda for instructional communication: Raising some unanswered questions. *Communication Education, 41,* 1-25.

Stablein, R., & Nord, W. (1985). Practical and emancipatory interests in organizational symbolism. *Journal of Management, 11*(2), 13-28.

Strauss, A. (1978). *Negotiations: Varieties, contexts, processes, and social order.* San Francisco: Jossey-Bass.

Sullivan, J., & Taylor, S. (1991). A cross-cultural test of compliance-gaining theory. *Management Communication Quarterly, 5,* 220-239.

Sutton, R., & Staw, B. (1995). What theory is not. *Administrative Science Quarterly, 40,* 371-384.

Taylor, J. (1993). *Rethinking the theory of organizational communication: How to read an organization.* Norwood, NJ: Ablex.

Tompkins, P., & Cheney, G. (1985). Communication and unobtrusive control in contemporary organizations. In R. McPhee & P. Tompkins (Eds.), *Organizational communication: Traditional themes and new directions* (pp. 179-210). Beverly Hills, CA: Sage.

Townley, B. (1993). Foucault, power/knowledge, and its relevance for human resource management. *Academy of Management Review, 18,* 518-545.

Treichler, P. (1989). What definitions do: Childbirth, cultural crisis, and the challenge to medical discourse. In B. Dervin, L. Grossberg, B. O'Keefe, & E. Wartella (Eds.), *Rethinking communication* (pp. 424-453). Newbury Park, CA: Sage.

Trethewey, A. (1997). Resistance, identity, and empowerment: A postmodern feminist analysis of clients in a human service organization. *Communication Monographs, 64,* 281-301.

Trujillo, N. (1987). Implication of interpretive approaches for organizational communication research and practice. In L. Thayer (Ed.), *Organization ↔ communication: Emerging perspectives II* (pp. 46-63). Norwood, NJ: Ablex.

Vallas, S. (1993). *Power in the workplace: The politics of production at AT&T.* Albany: State University of New York Press.

Van Maanen, J. (1988). *Tales from the field.* Chicago: University of Chicago Press.

Wagner, J., III, & Gooding, R. (1987). Effects of societal trends on participation research. *Administrative Science Quarterly, 32,* 241-262.

Weedon, C. (1987). *Feminist practice and poststructuralist theory.* Oxford, UK: Basil Blackwell.

Weick, K. E. (1979). *The social psychology of organizing* (2nd ed.). Reading, MA: Addison-Wesley.

Wendt, R. (1994). Learning to "walk the talk": A critical tale of the micropolitics at a total quality university. *Management Communication Quarterly, 8,* 5-45.

Wert-Gray, S., Center, C., Brashers, D., & Meyers, R. (1991). Research topics and methodological orientations in organizational communication: A decade in review. *Communication Studies, 42,* 141-154.

Westenholz, A. (1991). Democracy as "organizational divorce" and how postmodern democracy is stifled by unity and majority. *Economic and Industrial Democracy, 12,* 173-186.

Whyte, W. (Ed.). (1991). *Participatory action research.* Newbury Park, CA: Sage.

Willmott, H. (1993). Breaking the paradigm mentality. *Organization Studies, 14,* 681-719.

Wilkins, B., & Anderson, P. (1991). Gender differences and similarities in management communication. *Management Communication Quarterly, 5,* 6-35.

# 2

# Development of Key Constructs

CHARLES CONRAD
*Texas A&M University*

JULIE HAYNES
*Rowan University*

Our goal in this chapter is to explore the key constructs of contemporary organizational communication theory. In doing so, we shall define the term *construct* quite literally, as a symbolic creation that enacts the worldview(s) of a language community. As such, constructs are the products of rhetorical processes through which groups of social actors—including groups of scholars—attribute meaning to actions and situations. Constructs come in at least three forms. Some constructs provide means of linking scholarly propositions to empirical observations. Others address conceptual problems that exist within theoretical frames. For instance, many of the key constructs of psychoanalytic theory are derived from and their character determined by problematic features of Freud's construction of unconscious motivation (Burke, 1941/1984). Still other constructs provide links among theoretical perspectives, just as the theory of relativity links chemistry and quantum mechanics. Of course, the notion that the humanities and the social sciences are rhetorical constructions is not new (Simons, 1989, 1990), but as far as we know it has not been used to examine the discourse of organizational communication.

Some commentators view organizational communication as an amalgam of disparate research traditions, each with its own core constructs, epistemological assumptions, and methodological commitments. These traditions are connected by a common subject matter (communication within or among organizations) and unified by a commitment to eclecticism (Goldhaber & Barnett, 1988b; Krone, Jablin, & Putnam, 1987; Leipzig & Moore, 1982). Definitional, conceptual, and methodological problems exist, but they are capable of being worked out within the research perspectives in which they arise. Since these disparate research orientations operate independently of one another, *problems* within one of them do not handicap the development of "normal science" within the others. Nor do these problems raise questions about the fundamental assumptions of different research orientations or threaten the notion of comfortable eclecticism.

We offer an alternative reading. On the one hand, we argue that the various threads of organizational communication research/theory are connected by a common conceptual problem—the need to analyze the interrelationship between symbolic action and social/organizational structures. Although each research orientation is defined by differing choices about how to deal with the action-structure problematic, they are unified by that common problem. Second, we suggest that the development of organizational communication and its component strains of research between 1985 and 1995 can informatively be read as an effort to grapple with problematic elements of a dualism between action and structure.[1]

## ANALYZING KEY CONSTRUCTS

The analytical process used in this essay is drawn from the work of Kenneth Burke (1941/1984, 1970). Throughout his work Burke argues that criticism must be empirical; that is, it must be grounded in the details of texts. He suggests that critics can "chart" the essential concepts present in a text and the interrelationships among those concepts (Berthold, 1976). Critics begin by isolating the key constructs in the text and represent

those concepts in a series of key terms. Some terms coalesce to form the unifying and central principles present in the text; some clusters represent competing principles. The relationships among these equated and contrasted clusters surface through structural configurations that lead critics from one construct to others. Then, through an iterative process, critics use that initial structural configuration to reexamine the text(s), searching for constructs that were not represented in their initial analysis (Conrad, 1984). The process continues until no significant residual constructs are left unaccounted for.

The critics' goal is to construct a *summation* of the core principles and their interrelationships, not to *summarize* every element of the text. This process does not mean that every construct in the text will emerge from the analysis. Indeed, many constructs are so closely interrelated that the principle underlying them can be represented by any one of them. Eventually, a hierarchy will emerge among the clusters of key terms, one that encapsulates the interrelationships among clusters of terms. This hierarchy will culminate in a central tension, an "agon" that "logically contains" (Burke, 1945/1969) the interrelationships among the clusters of terms.

Texts are not composed of seamless webs of associations. Indeed, they are made of constructs that are dialectically related to one another. Key constructs simultaneously reinforce and contradict one another—they merge and divide in complex webs of associations and contrasts. For example, Burke (1970) argues that the first three chapters of *Genesis* are defined by the constructs "God as author/creator" and "God as legislator/disciplinarian." These two senses of "authority" coalesce to define "God" as a multifaceted construct, and thereby articulate the tensions and contradictions implicit in Judeo-Christian notions of divinity. Each of the subordinate constructs in Judeo-Christian theology—guilt and catharsis, mortification and victimage, reward and retribution—are logically contained in this core tension.

Once critics extract a pattern of concepts and concept interrelationships from a text, they must articulate their interpretations of that pattern. Typically, critics will reverse the analytical process in their presentation of the outcome of the analysis, beginning with a discussion of the central construct/relationship and subsequently explaining how it is individuated in the component constructs and their interrelationships.

Our analysis of organizational communication research reveals six clusters of key constructs and construct interrelationships. No cluster is independent of the other clusters, although their interrelationships change as the decade progresses. No cluster is a seamless web of connections, and the conceptual tensions that exist within each construct system became articulated as they develop. Both the interrelationships among the clusters and the developmental processes of each cluster are understandable through an action-structure dialectic.

## The Dialectic Between Action and Structure

It is not especially surprising that the "action-structure" pair emerges as the central tension in organizational communication research and theory. A number of commentators have argued that an action-structure dualism is the defining characteristic of modern Western social and organizational theory (see, e.g., Clegg, 1989, 1990; Dawe, 1970, 1978; Giddens, 1979, 1984; Reed, 1985). Historically, social theorists set forth two conflicting views of human action—one focusing on the myriad factors that determine human action and one concentrating on the processes through which social actors create and sustain social realities. These perspectives differ in their assumptions about the nature of human actors, the sources of action, and the key problematics faced by social theorists.

On the one hand is the doctrine of "social system" that focuses on structural configura-

tions and is articulated through a language of objectivity and externality (Dawe, 1978).[2] Although actors are viewed as choice-making beings, their choices are circumscribed by the characteristics of their "situations" (Dawe, 1978, p. 367). Through communicating with others in a society, individuals learn to accept the values and norms of their society and construct a self-identity that is appropriate to the roles they play. The result is a complex set of constraints that determines individuals' actions. Although the doctrine of social system does not necessarily exclude constructs like "choice" and "symbolic action," it severely restricts their scope and significance.

The central element of this doctrine is the "problem of order," the concern that individuals, "if left to their own devices, can and will create self-and-socially destructive anarchy and chaos" (Dawe, 1978, p. 370). Constraint is necessary for society to exist at all. Constraints exist outside of actors' immediate interpretations and choices. They are self-generating and self-maintaining (Dawe, 1970). The central challenge facing the doctrine of social system is maintaining a view of action as guided and constrained by "external" pressures while not slipping into situational determinism. "Constraint" is not the same thing as "determinism." The latter speaks of determination of individuals' thoughts and actions by forces that are exterior to them. The former speaks of the way social properties influence the choices and actions of members of social collectives (Giddens, 1984, pp. 96-107). But pressure to substitute determinism for constraint is inherent in the doctrine of social system, for the "problem of order" disappears in a determined social/organizational world.

On the other hand, a "doctrine of social action" focuses on subjective experience and voluntary/creative action (Dawe, 1978). Human beings are autonomous agents whose ongoing actions create and re-create both their own selves and their societies. The social world emerges through the actions and interactions of its members. This does not mean that social actors are not constrained by their societies. Indeed, actors create meaning systems that, in turn, constrain their actions. But constraint is not external to and superordinate over people. It is located in actors' actions and interactions, in humanly constructed and humanly reinforced structures of power and domination (Dawe, 1978).

The central element of the doctrine of social action is the "problem of control." In short, how can a view of humans as individual, choice-making beings account for similarities in patterns of action; in other words, how can actionist perspectives avoid slipping into the extreme of voluntarism/subjectivism? A doctrine of social action that omits or fails to explain social/cultural constraint is just as problematic as a doctrine of social system that denies or does not explain individual volition (Bhaskar, 1979). If actions are to be meaningful, people must act in accordance with the rules and resources available in their sociocultural situations. Even though rules and resources are created, re-created, or modified through social action, they are relatively stable within each episode of symbolic interaction. Thus, social/cultural rules and resources serve as guidelines and constraints on action.

However, how can actionist perspectives introduce a conception of constraint without sliding into determinism? According to actionist orientations, action and choice reside between the extremes of fate (determinism) and freedom (voluntarism). The challenge facing actionist perspectives is to remain between these two extremes. Eventually, advocates of the doctrine of social action attempted to solve this problem by constructing the concept of "internalization." External forces do not determine actors' choices, but they create ideas that social actors incorporate into their choices. For example, one's biological sex does not determine one's career choices, but the division of labor in a society leads to patterns of behavior that are codified in ideas (constructs) such as "gender roles" and "femininity/masculinity." Social actors still choose their gender identifications, but their choices (and thus their identifications and related behaviors) are patterned and predictable because

they have internalized social/cultural constraints. Different people internalize social "norms" to different degrees and in different ways, so variations in choices do occur— action is not determined by external factors. The concept of internalization allows actionist researchers to treat the structural guidelines and constraints present in a society as dimensions of social actors' perceptions and interpretations, rather than as external determinants of action. Through "internalization," actionist social theorists avoid both the problem of determinism and a slide toward pure voluntarism.

But "internalization" provides an illusory escape. Substituting internalization (or any of its relatives—"tacit knowledge," for example) for externality accepts the basic logic of the doctrine of social system. "Internalization" may expand the conception of how structural constraint is achieved and may broaden the range of options from which a social actor may "choose," but does not alter the locus of constraint itself—the conditions of action still are external to the actor (Dawe, 1970; Harris, 1980).

In addition, the "internalization" construct has three paradoxical effects. First, internalization elevates social norms to become *constitutive* of persons' identities, not just *regulative* of them. Societal constraint thus can be total—resistance is possible only when processes of internalization are flawed or incomplete. Thus, instead of moving social theory away from an oversocialized view of action (Granovetter, 1985), "internalization" expands and *reinforces* the notion of external constraint (Dawe, 1970, p. 209). Second, the internalization construct explains inaction much better than it explains action (Harris, 1980, p. 27). Any observed variability in social actors' choices within the same social context is explained in terms of the "degree" to which they have internalized cultural values and role definitions. Explaining positive choices in this way makes the whole concept of internalization/role circular (Harris, 1980, pp. 28-29). Actions still are either determined by social/cultural pressures or they are unintelligible (Dawe, 1978). Finally, "internaliza-tion" renders the concept of subjective mean-ing insignificant. If meaning is a function of a social self knowledgeably applying learned interpretive processes to learned definitions of situations, internalization is the only process that needs to be explained (Dawe, 1970, p. 209). Subjectivity/meaning is submerged in internalization and internalization reduces to socialization. Thus, with the addition of "in-ternalization," the doctrine of social action "avoids" the problem of voluntarism/subjec-tivity by incorporating determinism-by-an-other- name.

The two doctrines are dialectically related to one another. Theorists working within the doctrine of social system will simultaneously be pulled toward determinism by a need to confront the problem of order and toward the doctrine of social action by the need to con-struct a human actor capable of choice and vo-lition. Conversely, theorists working within the doctrine of social action will be pulled to-ward voluntarism by the need to avoid deter-minism, and toward concepts of social sys-tems by the need to explain *patterns* of action (the problem of control). In the remainder of this essay, we suggest that the way in which the key constructs of organizational commu-nication theory have developed can be under-stood in terms of this dialectical relationship between the doctrines of social system and so-cial action.

## Clusters That Privilege Structure Over Action

First, we examine three clusters of con-structs that enact the two poles of the action-structure dualism. Two clusters, labeled "in-formation exchange" and "superior-subordi-nate relationship," form the doctrine of social system, while a third, labeled "meaning cre-ation," articulates an actionist doctrine. We then examine the development of three clus-ters of constructs that aim to integrate structure and action: structuration, identification/unob-trusive control, and critical theory.[3] Finally,

we briefly examine construct systems that challenge the action-structure dialectic itself.

### An Information Exchange Cluster

One primary cluster of constructs in orga-nizational communication research included six key terms: *information, networks, uncer-tainty, message, load,* and especially later in the era, *technology.* The central term was *in-formation.* In fact, communication was de-fined as the flow of information through net-works of "conduits" (Axley, 1984; Monge & Miller, 1988; O'Connell, 1988; Wigand, 1988, p. 321). Information exists in "chunks" (Fulk & Mani, 1986; Krone et al., 1987; Rob-erts & O'Reilly, 1978) that often are called "messages." Information, in this mechanistic perspective, moves from one point in an orga-nization to another; varies in quality; may be embedded in messages that are unclear or equivocal; influences the uncertainties that employees face; may be distorted by employ-ees who are motivated to do so; may not arrive at the appropriate point(s) in organizational networks or may arrive at a time or in such a volume that it cannot be used efficiently. As the 1985-1995 era progressed, electronic technologies played an important part in con-ceptualizations of information flow. Different kinds of communication technologies produce different conduits that influence information flow in different ways, but the nature of *infor-mation* itself is constant, regardless of the kind of conduit or network involved.

In much information-exchange research, the concept of organizational "actors" is either absent or marginalized. When analyses in-clude the concept, actors are defined as the us-ers or processors of information, not as active agents involved in the cocreation of meanings and meaning systems (Huber & Daft, 1987). Typically, information-exchange research fo-cuses on how employees' processes of search-ing for information lead them to process a flawed sample of the information that is theo-retically available (Greenbaum, Hellweg, & Falcione, 1988; O'Connell, 1988, pp. 474-

475; O'Reilly, Chatman, & Anderson, 1987, pp. 604-618). Once information arrives (or is obtained, depending on the particular version of this term being used), it is processed—interpreted, integrated with other information, and remembered—processes that "distort" its "real" or "intended" meaning (O'Reilly et al., 1987, especially Figures 17.2, 17.3, and 17.4).[4]

Consistent with the doctrine of social systems, this research attempts to isolate the situational, task-oriented, and personality-related determinants of employees' attitudes, behaviors, or communicative acts, usually in complex, multivariable models. Topical summaries of this research are available in Allen, Gotcher, and Seibert (1993); Wert-Gray, Center, Brashers, and Meyers (1991); and Sutcliffe, Chapter 6, this volume.

Communication technology is treated as a determinant of information exchange, and technology use is seen as the outcome of various external determinants, for example, organizational design (Allen & Hauptman, 1990; Culnan & Markus, 1987; Huber, 1990); organizational structure, including centralization (Contractor & Eisenberg, 1991; Fulk & Dutton, 1985; Fulk, Schmitz, & Steinfield, 1991; Olson, 1982); information flow and "distortion" (Zmud, 1990); and processes of decision making and communication flow (O'Reilly et al., 1987; Sambamurthy & Poole, 1993).

In short, a "structure determines information exchange" construct system remains an important part of organizational communication research and theory, in spite of the extended critiques of functionalist research that emerged during the 1980s. Interrelationships among variables become more complex as the 1985-1995 era progresses, especially after advanced statistical techniques become available (Poole & McPhee, 1994), but the logic of the doctrine of social systems remains intact.

However, even as early as the mid-1980s a second strain of social-systems-oriented research emerges, one that introduces conceptions of social action into the orientation. The initial move comes through suggestions that information has a "symbolic" dimension that explains why people exchange different infor-

mation than economic exchange models predict (see Eisenberg & Riley's, 1988, p. 136, summary of research by Feldman and March and by Larkey and Sproull). Information and processes of information exchange fulfill personal goals of organizational actors, regardless of the intentions of the individual who originally produced the information—goals like legitimating one's self, one's actions, or one's organization (see Eisenberg & Riley's, 1988, p. 136, summary of legitimation theory). Even behavioral decision theory (after Simon's pioneering work) defines messages as "things" that stimulate inferences, not transfer information (Euske & Roberts, 1987).

Efforts to incorporate actionist constructs into systems-oriented research also emerge in research on communication technology and communication networks. Some communication technology research begins to focus on the interrelationships between technology and meaning creation (e.g., Alexander, Penley, & Jernigan, 1991; Fulk et al., 1991; Keen, 1990; Trevino, Daft, & Lengel, 1990), and some studies employ "integrative" perspectives like structuration (DeSanctis & Poole, 1994; Poole & DeSanctis, 1990; Poole & Holmes, 1995). Reconceptualizations of communication networks, initiated at least as early as Monge and Eisenberg's (1987) and Danowski's (1988) analyses of emergent, meaning-centered networks, culminate in Stohl's (1995) conceptualization of networks as "connectedness in action." Networks extend beyond organizational "boundaries," now conceptualized as always permeable and never stable, to include the complex, multidimensional set of connections that each organizational member negotiates in her or his own life. In this expanded sense, "networks" not only "carry" meaning, they are composed of complex, constantly emerging systems of meaning and interpretation (Danowski, 1980). They "contain" organizational actors' relational histories and anticipations of future interactions (Putnam & Stohl, 1990) and "blur" traditional distinctions between "senders" and "receivers" of messages.

At first glance, these changes appear to constitute a major shift away from the doctrine of social system. The "symbolism" construct redefines "information" from a technical "measure of uncertainty" to more of an everyday notion of "symbols and other stimuli that affect our awareness" (Huber & Daft, 1987, p. 157, fn. 1). Organizational actors and their motives and needs move to a more central place in researchers' conceptualizations, creating more of a "receiver orientation" toward processes of information flow. Members of organizations play active roles in the communication process, and meaning is located in context-bound *uses* of information, not in information itself.

In important ways the shift to a receiver orientation inserts actionist constructs into structure-oriented research. However, these additions do not fundamentally change the definition of the information/uncertainty/message/load cluster of constructs. Information remains something that exists independent of perceivers, and is still some*thing* that social actors use and process, that is, obtain, interpret, distribute, and thus potentially distort. Information load still is defined in terms of the quantity of information received, the degree of uncertainty it contains (the extent to which the information can be interpreted differently by different actors), and its *variety*. The latter term is the composite of a number of factors that are external to organizational actors (diversity, independence of sources, turbulence, unpredictability, and instability). Thus, it is easily distorted by their processes of interpreting and exchanging it with others. It is contained in messages characterized by varying degrees of clarity/uncertainty that place different loads on receiver/interpreters. Information is the central construct embedded in a deeply articulated structural language of information exchange.

## *A Supervisor-Subordinate Relationship Cluster*

Research on supervisor-subordinate relationships has been a central focus of organizational communication since the mid-1970s (see Jablin, 1979). This line of research continues to follow the doctrine of social system,

although, like information-exchange research, some moves have been made to incorporate actionist concepts. The key terms of this cluster are *supervisory communication, motivation, performance,* and *situation* (Cusella, 1987; Downs, Clampitt, & Pfeiffer, 1988). Communicating is something that supervisors do to accomplish something else—lead, motivate, influence, control (Thayer, 1988), evaluate, or direct (Cusella, 1987, p. 626). Although subordinates are tacit elements of supervisor-subordinate interactions, they typically are conceptualized as "passive information receptacles" (Cusella, 1987, p. 642). Research on organizational socialization casts subordinates in more active roles—as actors who make attributions about others' behaviors, negotiate role requirements, and influence their supervisors (Jablin, 1987b). Even in this context, supervisors are the "key communicators" because they possess the information that subordinates need to become socialized into their organizations (Falcione & Wilson, 1988).

The fourth key term in this cluster is *situation,* as in "situational determinants." A variety of personal and situational factors are cast as determinants of superior-subordinate communication. Frequently examined personal variables include gender, communicator style, and argumentativeness. Differences in supervisors' and subordinates' interpretive frames are said to create "semantic-informational distance," which contributes to distortion of information and to misunderstandings about what information really means (Dansereau & Markham, 1987). Inadequate organizational socialization increases these differences (Falcione & Wilson, 1988). Situational factors include many of the core constructs of the information exchange cluster (e.g., information flow, communication networks, and communication technology). These factors are cast as determinants of the effectiveness of superior-subordinate exchanges (Dansereau & Markham, 1987). This does not mean that researchers are conceptualizing superior-subordinate communication relationships as *embedded* in "the larger organizational context" (Dansereau & Markham, 1987), only that they construct a number of situational determinants of supervisor-subordinate communication (Cusella, 1987).

However, as the era progresses, a number of studies espouse a "receiver orientation" toward supervisor-subordinate communication. Subordinates are conceptualized as agents who actively seek out a variety of information, and who simultaneously process information from multiple, differing sources (Cusella, 1987; Falcione & Wilson, 1988). Employees' perceptions play a central role in research, as either dependent or independent variables (e.g., Chiles & Zorn, 1995; Eaves & Leathers, 1991; Husband, 1985; Marshall & Stohl, 1993; Sias & Jablin, 1995). Taking more of a receiver orientation in turn necessitates taking a process or "interactional" perspective on supervisor-subordinate exchanges (and vice versa). Jablin's "life-cycle" orientation toward processes of assimilation (Dansereau & Markham, 1987; Jablin, 1987b) and Fairhurst, Green, and Snavely's (1984a, 1984b) longitudinal studies of episodes in "chains" of control episodes are exemplars of this shift.

Discussions of organizational socialization and assimilation also introduce "internalization" as a core communicative process, and move the construct "control" to a central place in supervisor-subordinate research (Cusella, 1987). Some structure-oriented researchers respond to Stohl and Redding's (1987) call for message-centered research and outline factors that guide/constrain organizational actors' choices of communicative/message strategies (e.g., Gayle, 1991; Waldron, 1991). Others cast organizational actors in active "interpretive" roles, by examining the ways in which existing organizational meaning *systems* influence and/or constrain employees' interpretations of organizational actions (e.g., Bach, 1989; Morrill & Thomas, 1992; Stohl, 1993).

Each of these moves extends the systems doctrine by depicting organizational actors as active participants in organizational communication processes. They also lead to ways of substituting the construct "constraint" for situational "determinant." For example, Morrill and Thomas (1992) use longitudinal studies of superior-subordinate conflicts to examine processes of relational development. Their interpretations of a very rich data set focus on emergent contextual constraints rather than a priori situational determinants, but their foci remain on "*behavioral processes embedded in larger social systems*" (p. 400, emphasis in original).

In other cases, the merger of constraints and determinants surfaces in temporal terms, as recursive processes. Albrecht and Hall (1991a) call on structure-oriented researchers to recognize that employees' choices create and maintain communication networks while they focus on ways in which network type and centrality influence perceptions and commitments. Corman and Scott (1994) provide a detailed discussion of the recursive relationship between communicative action and network development. Similarly, Seibold and Contractor (1993) examine the recursive relationship that exists between the use of communication technologies and the creation and reproduction of organizational structures. By defining employees as receivers and interpreters of information, structure-oriented researchers incorporate actionist constructions. By substituting constraint for determinant, they reduce the likelihood that organizational communication research would slip into determinism. But neither shift changes the logic of the doctrine of organizational communication systems, and the continued publication of a sizable amount of research that does not incorporate these integrative constructs suggests that structure-oriented research continues to be a significant part of organizational communication.[5]

## A Cluster That Privileges Action Over Structure

By the mid-1980s, a great deal of effort had been expended articulating the underlying assumptions of "interpretive" perspectives toward organizational communication. Although advocates often extolled the rich potential of these perspectives (Eisenberg & Riley, 1988; Putnam & Poole, 1987), organizational communication scholars produced relatively little actual interpretive, message-oriented, meaning-creation-centered research prior to 1985 (Deetz, 1992a; Huber & Daft, 1987; Stohl & Redding, 1987; Tompkins, 1987). But by the end of the 1980s, a rapidly growing body of action-oriented research had emerged. Initially, a number of scholars examined symbolic forms—stories, myths, rituals, and metaphors—as expressions or reflections of employees' taken-for-granted assumptions, or as strategies for maintaining organizational control (see Brown, 1990; Trice & Beyer, 1993, especially chaps. 3 and 5, for summaries). As the era progressed, relevant research often called for taking a performative perspective on organizational symbolism (Pacanowsky & O'Donnell-Trujillo, 1983), for examining story-*telling* as well as organizational stories, narrative *action* in addition to organizational narratives, the *enactment* of rituals as well as their meanings, and so on (Brown, 1990; Czarniawska-Joerges, 1994; Goodall, Wilson, & Waagen, 1986; Knuf, 1993).

The core constructs of this actionist cluster are *culture, meanings/messages, symbolism,* and *ambiguity*. Some applications of this cluster focus on the ways in which organizational communication practices and cultural artifacts articulate and reflect the shared meanings of a social collective (Cheney & Vibbert, 1987; Smircich & Calás, 1987; Triandis & Albert, 1987). Others examine the processes through which meanings become shared and cultures and subcultures are formed and sustained through symbolic action (Eisenberg & Riley, 1988; Huber & Daft, 1987; Krone et al., 1987; Tompkins, 1987). Still others examine the processes through which ambiguity is managed symbolically. Additional uses of this cluster linked the meaning-symbolism-ambiguity nexus to a number of other constructs—for example, power (Frost, 1987), communication rules (Cushman, Sanderson-King, & Smith, 1988; Monge & Eisenberg, 1987), socialization (Eisenberg & Riley, 1988; Falcione & Wilson, 1988; Jablin, 1987b), and rhetoric (Tompkins, 1987).[6]

The core problematic for actionist perspectives is a tendency to slide toward a subjectiv-ist/actionist extreme. Actions are divorced from the societal and organizational contexts within which they occur. Organizational symbolism is "romanticized"; that is, its meaning is interpreted/constructed without a systematic analysis of the structural configurations surrounding its creation and enactment (Turner, 1992, p. 61; see also Burke, 1991; Deetz, 1994; Ebers, 1985). Organizational texts are treated as self-referential entities rather than as dynamic processes that emerge and develop within particular socioeconomic-organizational contexts through interactional, intersubjective processes. Voluntarist/subjectivist/romanticized analyses generate partial depictions of human symbolic action. For example, recognizing that a society or organization is constituted by a symbolic network does not in itself explain why a particular system of symbols was chosen, what these symbols convey or signify, or why and how the symbol system managed to become relatively autonomous (Ash, 1990; Baudrillard, 1988; Castoriadis, 1987; Turner, 1992). In short, "although institutions are unavoidably symbolic, they cannot be *reduced* to the symbolic" (Turner, 1992, p. 52) without a retreat into relativism; if resistance and transformation are to be possible, constraint cannot be reduced to ideation.

Actionist organizational communication researchers have avoided these subjectivist tendencies by incorporating some concept of situational "constraint" into their analysis, much as structure-oriented researchers avoided determinist extremes by incorporating actionist constructs. The operant "meaning systems" and dominant interpretive processes of organizational cultures/subcultures are depicted as strong influences on organizational action. As a result, the range of "choice" available to organizational actors in actionist research is limited; voluntarism/subjectivism is avoided. However, this adjustment also makes it difficult to maintain a distinction between external "determinants" and situational "constraints" (see Alvesson, 1987, for a critique of this type of "organizational culture" research). Of course, constraint is not the same thing as determinant. But once actionist researchers introduce pressures that are external to immediate communicative interactions into their research, it is difficult for them to avoid introducing other structure-oriented constructs.

### Assessing the Development of the Key Constructs

In many ways, organizational communication evidences the developmental processes that Dawe and others have outlined for social theory in general. Two differing strains of research coexist, one focusing on systems and one concentrating on action. Both strains move toward incorporating key constructs of the other strain, thereby avoiding the extremes of voluntarism and determinism. However, the development of organizational communication construct systems has differed in two ways from the trajectory Dave described for social theory as a whole. First, a substantial amount of "pure" systems-oriented research continues to be produced, in spite of frequent critiques of functionalist research and in spite of efforts by some structure-oriented researchers to incorporate actionist constructs into the doctrine. Second, there has been little or no tendency for actionist-oriented organizational communication researchers to slide toward a voluntarist/subjectivist extreme. The early introduction of "constraint" into actionist research seems to have prevented any tendency to romanticize the symbolic, to divorce symbolic action from systemic pressures, although the pressures to do so continue to exist because they are inherent in the logic of the doctrine of social action.

### Three Clusters That Strive to Integrate Action and Structure

The dialectical relationship between action and structure means that tensions will exist in any effort to explain social or organizational action. One way of managing these tensions is to introduce modifying constructs into each doctrine. Another is to construct perspectives that explicitly integrate action and structure within the same construct system. Paradoxi-

cally, the dialectical tensions between action and structure are especially visible, and especially complicated, in efforts to develop truly integrative perspectives. The challenge faced by integrative perspectives is to retain a balance in the dialectical relationship between action and structure. Only then is it possible to deal simultaneously with the problem of order and the problem of consent. Three differing integrative frameworks were proposed by organizational communication researchers between 1985 and 1995: structuration, identification/unobtrusive control, and critical theory. Each of these perspectives developed in ways that were influenced by the action-structure dialectic.

### Structuration

Applying structuration theory to organizational communication generates a new cluster of key constructs, all linked to an overall construct labeled the "duality of structure." This is the notion that action both produces/reproduces/transforms structure and is possible only because of the existence of structural conditions—the interactional rules and the material and communicative resources that are available to members of a particular society at a particular place and time. Like structure, action also is multidimensional, with component constructs labeled "agency," "symbolic interaction," "subjectivity/ intersubjectivity," and "knowledgeability." These two clusters are linked together by a third cluster, composed of the constructs "power," "production/reproduction," and "resistance/ transformation."

Giddens's conception of the duality of structure is a particularly appropriate vehicle for dealing with the action-structure dialectic because it is grounded in both an extensive critique of the doctrine of social system and the doctrine of social action (see Giddens, 1976, 1979). Giddens rejects the determinism of the doctrine of social system, but also argues that actionist perspectives tend to collapse structural factors into attributes of action. Material conditions are reduced to ideation. The strength of structuration is its ability to avoid both sets of problems; the difficulty of applying structuration is to maintain this kind of balance. The probative force of structuration is lost if the perspective is reduced to either determinism or voluntarism. Structurationist organizational communication research has avoided the temptations of determinism; the attractions of voluntarism have been more difficult to resist.

Structurationist organizational communication originated during an era of extensive criticism of social-system-oriented organizational communication research. For example, Riley (1983) explicitly casts her use of structuration as a rejection of functionalism and an affirmation of interpretive studies of organizational cultures (pp. 414-415). Poole and McPhee's (1983) initial application of structuration to organizational climate begins with an extended critique of systems-oriented research. Monge and Eisenberg (1987) argue that Giddens's notions of "provinces of meaning" would provide a corrective for the problems facing systems-oriented network analysis (pp. 332-333). Eisenberg and Riley (1988) contend that structuration provides a potentially valuable perspective for studying organizational symbolism. Symbolic acts are central to the constitution of organizational "reality," a dynamic revealed in processes of socializing newcomers, legitimizing activities, creating and sustaining power relationships, and managing organizational change (pp. 136-142; see also Eisenberg & Riley, Chapter 9, this volume).[7] For each of these authors, structuration promises a communication-centered (or at least a language-centered), process-oriented perspective for analyzing social action in institutional and institutionalized settings. In particular, Giddens's duality of structure provides a process-oriented framework for scholars to explore the emergence, reproduction, and transformation of meaning systems and communicative interaction. In short, structuration includes constructs that integrate the key terms of the doctrine of social action and those of the doctrine of social system. The resulting perspective serves as a corrective to

deterministic tendencies while not ignoring social structure or reducing it to ideation.

But structuration was introduced into organizational communication amid multiple calls for an "interpretive" turn. Because the central claim of this intellectual climate was an affirmation of actionist social science, the context made it difficult for researchers to maintain a balance between action and structure and resist pressures to reduce the perspective to a version of actionism. We suggest that as structurationist organizational communication research developed, two different "schools" emerged. In one, pressures to reduce this integrative perspective to actionism were more influential than in the other.

*Actionist structuration.* Actionist structuration focuses on how structure influences action while de-emphasizing the processes through which action influences structure. For example, Banks and Riley (1993) examine the ways in which tensions between two cultural assumptions—Americans' focus on individual advancement combined with American engineers' commitments to their profession, on the one hand, and Japanese managers' commitment to "community" combined with the practice of staying with the same firm throughout their career, on the other hand—are managed and reproduced through a language game of control. Banks and Riley effectively describe structural constraints on action—existing rules/resources, temporal and spatial contexts (p. 174), institutionalized practices (p. 177), and actors' ontological insecurities (p. 172) and reflexive self-monitoring (p. 171)—as does similar research by Fairhurst (1993), Fairhurst and Chandler (1989), Harrison (1994), and Shockley- Zalabak and Morley (1994). Each of these studies provides (1) sophisticated analyses of the ways in which situational constraints guide communicative acts, and (2) brief treatments of how action reproduces structural constraint, but (3) little systematic analysis of the origins or possible transformation of these structural constraints. Of course, there is nothing in the underlying assumptions of structuration that would preclude a focus on the construction or transformation of constraint. In fact, at least one actionist structuration study has done so (Keough & Lake, 1993). But our reading of this strain of structurationist research indicates that the tendency has been to move toward the actionist pole of the action-structure continuum and that reversing that tendency will require a reformulation of this interpretation of structuration.

*Integrated structuration.* A second "school" of structurationist organizational communication research was developed by Poole, McPhee, and their associates. This perspective differed from actionist structuration in two ways. First, although it initially evidenced an actionist bias, it eventually included an explicit critique of social actionism. Second, it developed an extended distinction between the concept of the duality of structure and a dualism between action and structure. In the initial articulation of this version of structuration, neither of these differentiating constructs was developed in any detail (Poole & McPhee, 1983). In addition, there were a number of internal tensions within their application of structuration to such topics as organizational climate. At times they discuss the action-structure problematic at a conceptual level, but subsequently reduced it to methodological/ aggregational issues (see, e.g., p. 197). And like actionist structuration, their analysis sometimes slid into a social action perspective that de-emphasized structure (see, e.g., Poole and McPhee's, 1983, reinterpretation of Johnson's climate research, p. 101).

However, as this school of structuration developed, it moved toward an integrative version of structuration. This shift started in Poole's (1985) expanded critique of social-system-oriented perspectives on organizational climate and McPhee's (1985) discussion of formal organizational structure. Poole provides a structurationist interpretation of the ongoing debate about "objective" versus "subjective" measurement of the climate construct and offers an explicit critique of social

action views (p. 97). McPhee extends Giddens's concept of the duality of structure to argue that structure infuses communicative action in three ways: as an indirect constraint on communication, through its involvement in technical languages, and as a legitimizing process. Action cannot be wholly voluntary/subjective because structure (1) "binds" it to a particular place and time ("distanciation"), and (2) limits actors' strategic choices to options that are meaningful in their society ("reflexive monitoring"). But action is not *determined* by structure because some form of resistance always is possible. All actors retain some capacity to act and are knowledgeable about their capacities—they know how to "penetrate" social structures (the "dialectic of resistance and control"). Consequently, individual actions and interpretive frames are integrated with processes of producing/reproducing/transforming structure (pp. 168-171).

Poole, Seibold, and McPhee (1985) move even farther toward an integrative view of structuration by explicitly rejecting a dualism between social structure and social action (pp. 74-75, 81-82), by examining the problem of subjectivity in social action perspectives (p. 90), and by expanding their analysis of the situatedness of action (pp. 77-79) and the ways in which structure infuses action (pp. 79-80). Subsequently, they redefine traditional conceptions of "rules" to include structure (p. 98) and strategic choice-making (p. 90). Thus, like Giddens, they critique both social-structure-oriented research as the language of social action and perspectives that separate action and structure.

The advantages of this integrative model of structuration have become progressively more clear as this school developed. The most important advantage involves the ability to simultaneously examine the ways in which action is guided and constrained by structural processes and the ways in which action reproduces and/or transforms those guidelines and constraints. Some integrated structuration research has examined action-structure transformation in general (Laird-Brenton, 1993), some has examined the impact of action on (structural) rules and resources (Bastien, McPhee, & Bolton, 1995), while others have examined the dialectic between ideological positioning and changing organizational structures (Howard & Geist, 1995). These extensions of structuration focused increasing attention on the ways in which symbolic action reproduces, and potentially transforms, structural constraints. For example, Bastien et al. (1995) explain how municipal employees were able to draw on the protections of civil service systems as a basis for resisting changes being imposed by a newly elected administration, while employing discourse that reinterpreted upper management's penchant for secrecy about coming organizational changes. Consequently, their actions simultaneously reproduced/sedimented some elements of the structure they faced while creating new, and in many ways unintended, rules and resources that subsequently guided and constrained action.

When read together, these two versions of structuration (1) suggest a perspective through which the information, relationship, and meaning-creation clusters might be integrated, and (2) indicate how easily integrative perspectives might slide into an actionist extreme.

## Unobtrusive Control and Identification

The constructs "unobtrusive control" and "identification" proposed by Tompkins, Cheney, and their associates provided a different approach to integrating action and structure. Subordinate constructs/terms include *power/control, internalization, meaning systems,* and *symbolic interaction.* Tompkins and Cheney (1983) contended that organizational life is inherently a decision-making (choice-making) process,

> *a means of tapping the mutual influences of people and organizations.* As stated above, organizations (as well as the various units within

them) communicate decisional premises to their members; members, in turn, make decisions. The decisions themselves also communicate to the organization (i.e., the managers) and to other members something about decisional premises. Members, while engaged in decision-making activity, may echo the premises propounded by the organization, modify them, or communicate premises obtained from another source. The organization may then respond to these decisions as favorable or unfavorable in light of its interests. The decision-making process is thus continually being re-created by both the organization and its members. (p. 124)

Identification enters into the process of unobtrusive control in two ways. First, it enables organizational actors to cope with the multiple, overlapping, and often incongruent demands that make up organizational situations. Second, and conversely, identification opens actors up to persuasive communication from "the organization," making it easier to inculcate the decision premises embedded in the organization's dominant ideology. The former function allows employees to engage in action that is individually meaningful, including action that resists social/organizational control. But paradoxically, the second function restricts actors' freedom and volition by embedding processes of social/organizational control in processes of internalization, identification, and identity formation. Like structuration, the key contribution of the unobtrusive control/identification construct is its ability to simultaneously confront both the problem of control and the problem of consent. And like structuration, the key challenge facing researchers who use the construct system is to maintain a balance between the actionist and the structural dimensions of the construct.

*Developing the identification/unobtrusive control construct.* In subsequent essays, Cheney and Tompkins extend and refine their analysis of unobtrusive control and identification in two ways. One extension links the constructs more explicitly to processes of individual identity formation and transformation. The other extension situates the construct within the broader socioeconomic-political context of Western capitalist democracies.

Identification is an active process by which individuals define themselves in terms of their social/organizational scene (Cheney, 1983a, 1983b). Identification processes are ongoing and in flux because interpretations/evaluations of our experiences affirm or disconfirm our identifications with organizations (1983a). Identity is grounded in processes of negotiating a unique and constantly changing combination of partially conflicting corporate "we's" (1983a; Cheney & Christensen, Chapter 7, this volume).

Tompkins and Cheney provide a deeper analysis of the broader societal context surrounding processes of identification, identity formation, and unobtrusive control in a 1985 essay. They argue that traditional neo-positivist research is incapable of analyzing social/organizational "power" or acts of achieving control. They discuss the way in which imbalances of power favor institutional actors over individuals and examine changes in the way that power is exercised within Western organizations. By extending Karl Weick's (1979) work on "double interacts" to encompass control, they provide a way to analyze the *processes* through which social/organizational structures are "reproduced" through interaction.

The unobtrusive control/identification construct is important for two reasons. First, in their brief critique of the doctrine of social action, Cheney and Tompkins introduce concepts of structural constraint into a process-oriented perspective on power and control. As Dawe (1970, 1978) noted, the challenge faced by perspectives that attempt to integrate action and structure is to maintain a balanced, dialectical relationship between the two. Only then is it possible to avoid the problems of determinism and explain how ac-

tion can transform social and organizational structures.

Tompkins and Cheney avoid both sets of problems. First, they build an analysis of the historical-material constraints that have affected the development of modern organizations into the theory of unobtrusive control. Meanings and meaning systems are contextualized as historical constructions that develop and are sustained through action within social/organizational structures. Consequently, the problems of voluntarism and subjectivism that characterize traditional actionist perspectives are minimized.

Second, the focus on tensions among multiple identifications included in later versions of the perspective avoids some of the problems of the doctrine of social system. Tompkins and Cheney construct social/organizational actors as persons who constantly are involved in managing multiple, incongruent selves. This view of identification shifts the "internalization" construct away from an ideational version of determinism to become an aspect of the dynamic relationship between structure and action. Without the concept of multiple identifications, identification could easily be reduced to internalization, a construct that tends to totalize social and organizational control and explains inaction and consent but not action and resistance.

*Managing tensions of/in unobtrusive control/identification.* Unfortunately, some applications of Tompkins and Cheney's perspective do tend to reduce the concept of organizational "identification" to "internalization." In some studies, identification is treated as an outcome of being socialized to internalize new roles and role constraints (Barge & Musambria, 1992); in others, it entails internalizing organizational beliefs and values or becoming acculturated to mindlessly enact organizational practices (Bullis, 1993b; Czarniawska-Joerges, 1994; Ferraris, Carveth, & Parrish-Sprowl, 1993; Treadwell & Harrison, 1994).

Fortunately, other identification research has been able to maintain the probative force of the model by focusing on the processes through which tensions among actors' multiple identifications are managed. For example, Bullis and Tompkins (1989) examine the ways in which hiring employees with different kinds of occupational socialization has complicated unobtrusive control in the U.S. Forest Service (for additional examples, see Trice & Beyer, 1993, chap. 5). Baxter (1994) provides a rich analysis of the ways in which the tension between individuality and social control that characterizes Anglo-American culture is individuated in the discourse of two academic subcultures. She also examines the ways in which that discourse reproduces personal and cultural identities. Barker and Tompkins (1994) employ the concept of identification as the "management" of multiple, sometimes conflicting identities to examine the tensions that exist between identifying with one's work group (team) and identifying with one's organization. Different modes of managing multiple identities explain observed differences in the level of identification between organizational newcomers and seasoned veterans.

Scott (1996) examines the impact that a "structural" factor—the extent to which workers and work groups are geographically dispersed—has on identification processes. Four factors influence degree of organizational identification: the extent to which the identification pressures from different organizational "targets" (work group, regional office, state office, etc.) are congruent with one another, the extent to which employees have had similar occupational socialization experiences, tenure in the organization, and the "immediacy" (work group/team vs. other sources) of identification pressures. Barker, Melville, and Pacanowsky (1993) find that two sources of tension influence identification processes: the "stage" of a change from traditional forms of control to concertive/team/identification strategies, and the incongruities that are created

when management imposes an "antihierarchical" system on employees. The integrative potential of the unobtrusive control/identification construct system is illustrated most effectively in Barker's (1993) study of how bureaucratic structures were modified, transformed, and reproduced during an organization's shift to a "team" system. Bureaucratic practices guide and constrain actors' interpretations and strategic responses to teams. But those interpretations/responses also led to a number of unintended consequences, transformations of structure and action, and new forms of self-and-other surveillance and discipline.

Taken together, these studies enact the tensions implicit in the unobtrusive control/identification perspective. Many locate "constraint" in the ideas/selves/interpretive processes of organizational actors and illustrate the tendency to reduce the perspective to ideation/internalization. Others retain the concept of multiple identifications, and thus are able to construct identity formation as a contingent, complex, and fragile process. Ideational constraints constantly are being negotiated, but the negotiation is sustained by an integrated and constrained organizational self. By controlling reductionist tendencies, these applications illustrate the integrative potential of the identification/unobtrusive control construct system.[8]

### Critical Theory

A final integrating framework emerges from applications of differing variations of *critical theory* (see, e.g., Alvesson, 1993; Clair, 1993b; Mumby, 1987, 1993a; Taylor, 1992, 1993; Taylor & Conrad, 1992; Wood, 1992).[9] Like other actionist perspectives, critical theory emerged as a response to structural determinism. While the target of traditional doctrines of social action was the determinism of neo-positivist social science, the target of critical theory was the determinism of orthodox (or "vulgar") Marxism (Held, 1980). If language and symbolic action were mere reflections of the material structure of industrial capitalism, as Marx and Engels seem to argue, how could symbolic action influence that structure (Aune, 1994; Coward & Ellis, 1977)? If "capitalism is indeed governed by lawful regularities that doom it to be supplanted by a new socialist society . . . why then stress that 'the point is to change it'? . . . . Why must persons be mobilized and exhorted to discipline themselves to behave in conformity with necessary laws by which, it would seem, they would in any event be bound?" (Gouldner, 1980, p. 32). In short, there is a fundamental contradiction within orthodox Marxism, an inherent tension between structure and struggle: How is struggle (action) even possible, and how can it possibly succeed if material conditions are determining?

Critical theorists confront this contradiction by rejecting the structural determinism of orthodox Marxism and foregrounding a theory of action/communication. They cannot abandon concepts of structural constraint, but seek to avoid determinism by integrating constraint into the beliefs/ideas/ideologies of social and organizational actors. It is through ideas that constraint is actualized, and through action that constraints are created and transformed. Of course, like the other frameworks discussed in this section, the challenge facing critical theorists is to integrate action and structure without merely substituting ideational determinism for structural determinism.

Two variants of critical organizational communication theory have accepted this challenge. The central construct of the first version is "ideology," and its constituent terms are *consent, agency,* and *interests.* The latter term differentiates the two versions of critical theory. An ideological view of interests argues that members of some sectors of a society/economic/culture use ideological communication to dominate the interests of other sectors. Communicative processes encourage members of a society to *reify* its key characteristics, to view existing arrangements as natural (inevitable) and normal (expected and morally correct) (Deetz, 1995; Therborn,

1980).[10] Abercrombie (1980) has labeled this perspective the "dominant ideology thesis." This perspective assumes that the interests of members of various sectors of an economy/society are knowable, both to researcher-theorists who study the society/economy and potentially to the groups of individuals who occupy each sector of it. Emancipation begins when all members of the society/economy are made aware of the communicative practices that privilege one set of interests over others (Papa, Arwal, & Singhal, 1995).

Of course, ideological definitions of interests are problematic in many ways. They fail to explain how the ideology of the dominant class became dominant in the first place or how oppositional ideas emerge or get heard at all. Consequently, they cannot explain either resistance or transformation except as the result of failed communication by the dominant class. In addition, they provide an overly simplistic, almost information-theory-oriented, view of messages as seamless, coherent, and univocal (Abercrombie, 1980; Elster, 1984).

An alternative version of critical theory focuses on "communicative action," a construct whose constituent terms include *participation/democracy* (Cheney, 1995; Harrison, 1994; Witten, 1993), *discursive closure* (processes through which the voices of some persons and groups are distorted or muted and some kinds of claims are trivialized or defined out of possibility) (Deetz, 1992b, 1995), *power* (Conrad & Ryan, 1985; Deetz & Mumby, 1990; Mumby, 1987, 1988), *meaning* (Mumby, 1989), *practices* (Howard & Geist, 1995; Huspek & Kendall, 1991), and *symbolism,* as well as *interests.* Unlike ideological definitions of interests, the communicative action cluster defines interests as processes through which all members of a society/economy are dominated by its modes of rationality. Interests, so defined, underlie a wide range of inequities that affect different groups of people in different ways (Alvesson, 1987; Habermas, 1979, 1984, 1987; Mumby, 1988).

"Symbolism" is an inherently power-laden process. Organizational stories (Ehrenhaus, 1993; Helmer, 1993), narratives (Mumby, 1993a; Witten, 1993), metaphors (McMillan

& Cheney, 1996; Salvador & Markham, 1995), and texts (Banks, 1994; Laird-Brenton, 1993) obscure differing interests, short-circuit participation/democracy by closing off legitimate communication, and reproduce existing patterns of power and domination. Symbolic action, and the modes of rationality created by it, are hegemonic, encouraging persons to consent to the circumstances of their domination (Alvesson, 1993; Clair, 1993a, 1993b; Condit, 1994; Conrad, 1988; Mumby, 1987, 1988). Neither researcher-theorists nor members of dominant groups are immune to the effects of these hegemonic processes (MacIntyre, 1981).

This perspective has been criticized on a number of grounds, one of which is particularly relevant to organizational communication research/theory. The "actor" that is constructed by and in communicative action with critical theory is a unified, rational, autonomous subject who is either alienated by patriarchal, capitalistic work organizations or is "ensnared in contemporary illusions" about them (Alvesson & Willmott, 1992). In extreme versions of the perspective, social/organizational actors are unaware of and incapable of critically analyzing the "totally administered" societies/organizations of which they are a part. Societies (and organizations) are so "dominated by the ideological apparatuses of the state or by omnipresent powers symbolized by Bentham's Panopticon" that "actors," as well as "agents" of change, disappear (Touraine, 1985, p. 767). As in some versions of internalization/identification, problems related to structural determinism are merely replaced by the problems of ideational determinism. In neither case is the action-structure problematic managed successfully.

Critical theorists, particularly those who focus on "communicative action," go to great lengths to avoid suggesting that socialization is totally effective, or that hegemonic domination is complete, but the logic of their position provides little alternative. The only kind of consciousness that is available to members of society/organizations is a false consciousness, an interpretation of "reality" that treats patterns of domination as natural and normal.

Resistance to domination leads only to increased alienation or further domination; the dialectical relationships between action and social structure that might provide grounds for transformation disappear. Because these tensions are central to critical theory, they also are present in critical-theory-oriented organizational communication research.

### Assessing the Development of Integrative Perspectives

Integrative perspectives simultaneously confront the action-structure dialectic and illustrate its component pressures. The key problem facing integrative frameworks is to maintain a balance between structural and actional pressures. For all three of the perspectives surveyed in this chapter, the key threat is the tendency to reduce their construct systems to ideation/action. Structurationist research may focus so completely on the "taken for granted" assumptions of a culture/organization that structural rules, resources, and constraints are slighted or ignored. "Identification" can be so total that the opportunities for resistance embedded in broad sociocultural practices disappear. Critical theorists can become so concerned with avoiding structural determinism that they become trapped in doctrines of "false consciousness." In all three instances, ideational/ideological constraint is totalized. Social actors have no more freedom of choice and social structures have no more possibility for being transformed than they do in deterministic doctrines of social system.

## CHALLENGING KEY CONSTRUCTS

A number of perspectives recently have emerged in organizational communication theory and research to challenge the construct system that developed during the 1980s and early 1990s. Some of these alternatives challenge by foregrounding concepts of resistance and transformation and de-emphasizing notions of constraint. Other alternatives launch a more fundamental challenge by rejecting the dualism between action and structure that underlies the entire construct system.

## Creating Space for Resistance and Transformation

Perhaps the most important construct in contemporary organizational communication theory is "constraint." Incorporating it helps social systems researchers at least appear to avoid the excessive determinism of functionalist social science. Conversely, locating social and organizational constraint in the selves and ideas (beliefs, values, and frames of reference) of organizational members allows actionist researchers to at least appear to avoid sliding into pure voluntarism/subjectivism. However, as we suggest throughout this chapter, the construct "constraint" may not achieve either of these objectives. On the one hand, the distinction between determinant and constraint can easily be blurred, particularly through constructs like internalization or hegemony. On the other hand, "constraint" can be so de-emphasized that even integrative perspectives can be transformed into actionism, a move that is especially easy in an intellectual context suspicious of determinism.

Some organizational communication scholars have extended this critique, arguing that "constraint" must be fundamentally reconceptualized before organizational communication research and theory can fully represent the dynamic interplay between consent and resistance or explain how social/organizational constraints are transformed. One reformulation of "constraint" develops and highlights two additional constructs, the *knowledgeability* of organizational actors, and the *unintended consequences* of action (Giddens, 1984). Organizational actors understand the "material" conditions they face, indeed they can act meaningfully only because they are knowledgeable about the rules and resources that exist in particular situations (Bhaskar, 1979, p. 43). But being knowledgeable about

constraints and the likely effects of different courses of action does not imply that organizational members are able to control the effects of their actions. All acts, whether they seem to be compliant or resistant, have both intended and unintended consequences. It is through these unintended consequences that social and organizational structures are modified by actors whose knowledge is socially constrained (Bhaskar, 1979, pp. 44-45). Examples of research that foreground these constructs are Browning's (1992) discussion of the multivocality of organizational discourse, the progressiveness/historicity of story interpretations, and the difference between local and distant knowledge; Corman and Scott's (1994) and Banks and Riley's (1993) treatments of the unintended consequences of action; McPhee and Corman's (1995) analysis of the "hierarchicalization" of networking processes; and Clair's (1993a, 1993b, 1994) analyses of "reframing" and resistance.

Another reformulation of "constraint" has emerged via versions of critical theory that focus on communicative action (Carnegie, 1996; Scott, 1993). This work critiques views of constraint, identification, and identity formation that overestimate the power of socialization processes and underestimate organizational actors' abilities to engage in strategic resistance (Cheney & Christensen, 1994; see also Cheney & Christensen, Chapter 7, this volume). By doing so, they challenge traditional conceptions of constraint and provide conceptual space within which concepts of resistance and transformation can be developed. Examples include Huspek's (1993) critique/synthesis of the work of Bourdieu and Giddens, Mumby's (1988) extension of Habermas and Foucault, and recent reinterpretations of the "unobtrusive control" construct. Drawing heavily on Foucault, Barker and Cheney (1994) substitute "discipline" for "constraint," thereby foregrounding resistance, while Cheney and Stohl (1991) examine the recursive processes through which recent changes in European economic systems and communicative action are mutually transformative. This alternative conceptualization is important because it undermines the modifications made in both actionist and structure-oriented research to deal with the action-structure problematic. Without those modifications, tensions within the overall construct system are magnified once more, and the potential for sliding into determinist or actionist extremes reappears.

## Postmodernist Challenges

A second challenge comes from perspectives that reject the action-structure dualism itself. Although a number of recently emerging perspectives do so, the most visible one among organizational communication theorists is *postmodernism*.[11] Of course, it is impossible to provide a comprehensive summary of the many versions of postmodernist thought (see Deetz, Chapter 1, and Mumby, Chapter 15, this volume). Instead we briefly sketch postmodernist social/organizational theory and discuss the implications that it holds for organizational communication theory.[12]

Postmodernity (the era) is characterized by a rejection of the modernist notion that it is possible to find rational solutions to social/organizational problems. The modern era is defined by faith in human beings' ability to discover broad explanations of all of human experience, to construct "grand narratives" that explain the sources, origins, perpetuation, and solutions to (or escapes from) social/organizational problems. Embedded in this project are efforts to describe *the* relationship between communicative action and social structure. Postmodernity is characterized by the "death" of all of these assumptions.[13] The postmodern world is simply too complex, too unstable, and too fragmented to be adequately explained by *any* grand narrative or totalizing theory. Consequently, postmodernist social/organizational theory abandons the central goal of modernist science—constructing universal conclusions through the accumulation of "data"—and the key distinctions of modern social science—between science and fiction, reality and unreality. The goal of postmodernist social science is to develop new questions, not to stipulate "answers" to old ones.

Insight comes through the *deconstruction* of texts, not through *constructing* social theories grounded in *reconstructions* of subjects' experiences.

In postmodernist approaches, symbolic action is merged with social/organizational structure. But the action-structure nexus is replete with fissures, tensions, and contradictions. Social/organizational life is a process of negotiating these tensions and contradictions in a particular configuration of time and space. It should be viewed as recurring, routinized "practices" that simultaneously are both symbolic action and social/organizational structure. "Identity" is a tenuous, emergent process. Social actors are enmeshed in multiple, conflicting identifications, where selves and relationships are fragmented, where the knowledge/meaning systems of modernism are meaningless. Organizations are sites where members subject themselves and one another to various practices, where discourse sustains mutually reinforcing patterns of power and powerlessness, and where language obscures the politics of organizational experience. "Power" resides in these discursive/linguistic practices, including the formation of organizational "knowledge" and claims about it.[14] Because power exists at the intersection of multiple, conflicting pressures, it is fluid and fragmented. It emerges as people continually define themselves through practices localized in particular time-space configurations.

Postmodernists argue that modernist constructions separate power/constraint from action/resistance by locating the former in social/organizational structures or internalized ideas and locating the latter in action. As a result, modernists find it difficult to explain how action/resistance might transform structure, power, or constraint. These difficulties are unnecessary because they result from modernists' arbitrary decision to separate action and structure (Clegg, 1989; Fielding, 1988). By refusing to separate structure/constraint/power from action/resistance, postmodernist theory avoids these difficulties. Every disciplinary practice has resistance embedded within it: "With every 'positive' move in disciplinary practices, there is an oppositional one" (Deetz, 1992a, p. 366, 1992b). For example, the symbols of traditional hierarchical organizations simultaneously accent differences in status and authority and draw attention to the arbitrary and political nature of organizational hierarchies, thus undermining the potency of those symbols (Kunda, 1991). Even covert, inactive, seemingly neutral practices such as absence can function as resistance (Barker & Cheney, 1994). As a result, transformation is an inherent part of ongoing practices. It can be explained without having to construct additional concepts to link action and structure (Baudrillard, 1983; Collinson, 1988; Deetz, Chapter 1, this volume; Gergen, 1992; Harris, 1980).

Of course, postmodernist assumptions have been widely criticized. Two criticisms are especially relevant to this chapter. First, some critics argue that postmodernist social/organizational theory neither *eliminates* nor *avoids* the action-structure problematic, it merely *elides* it by collapsing social structure into discursive/linguistic practices (Anderson, 1984; Eagleton, 1983; Rosenau, 1992).[15] However, this move creates its own problems. Language is not like other social/organizational structures—it is much slower to change than economic, political, or religious structures; it has no material constraints (e.g., no scarcity); and it is axiomatically linked to *individuals*. Thus, collapsing social/organizational structure into language/practices does not *integrate* structure into action, it merely defines it out of existence. With no concept of structure, action is no longer tied to material conditions or the practices of social *collectives*. In postmodernist theory,

> power loses any historical determination: there are no longer specific holders of power, nor any specific goals which its exercise serves. (Anderson, 1984, p. 51)

The adoption of the language model as the "key to all mythologies," far from clarifying or decoding the relations between structure and subject, led from a rhetorical absolutism of the

first to a fragmented fetishism of the second, without ever advancing a theory of their *relations*. Such a theory, historically determinate and sectorally differentiated, could only be developed in a dialectical respect for their interdependence. (p. 55)

As a result, postmodernist social theory is unable to integrate its analysis of institutions (i.e., social collectives) with its treatment of the individual self (Best, 1994; Ritzer, 1997, p. 250).

A second and related criticism of most postmodernist social theory is that it lacks a theory of agency (Best, 1994; O'Neill, 1995; Ritzer, 1997, pp. 248-251). While deconstruction can *destroy* (Deleuze & Guattari, 1977/1983, p. 311), it cannot *create* a vision of what society/organizations ought to be like (Coles, 1991; Gitlin, 1988) nor does it provide a theory of praxis to influence societal/organizational change (Giddens, 1990; Habermas, 1981, 1986, 1991).[16]

However, postmodernist social/organizational theory does force organizational communication theorists to reconsider the dominant action-structure dualism, both as a representation of social/organizational life and as an explanation of organizational texts. And whether or not organizational communication theorists choose to embrace postmodernist theories, we must find ways to explain the multiplicity of organizational forms that are rapidly emerging in the world economy (Eisenberg & Goodall, 1997; Ritzer, 1997).

## SUMMARY AND CONCLUSIONS

In this chapter, we have constructed "organizational communication research" as a rhetorical act, a set of symbolic strategies that forms and is informed by a particular discourse community. Our focus has been on processes of emergence and change in part because organizational communication is so

diverse and has developed so rapidly during the past 15 years, and in part because understanding a language community always entails examining processes of symbolic transformation (Frye, 1957; Shils, 1968).

Some transformative pressures are intrinsic to language communities themselves—tensions and incongruities that must be managed communicatively if the community is to continue. The decade between 1985 and 1995 witnessed a marked increase in both the amount of organizational communication research being conducted and the diversity of theoretical frames employed in that research. On the one hand, structure-oriented research, dominant at the beginning of the era, has continued to play a significant role, although concepts of "perception" and "interpretation" are more visible in structure-oriented research and the deterministic assumptions underlying this perspective are "softened" by substituting "constraint" for "determinant." For the rest of organizational communication theory and research, the decade was characterized by substantial theoretical ferment. The two most important trends seemed to be the elevation of complex models of "constraint" and the articulation of a number of challenging perspectives. The resulting diversity of views, often based on conflicting or contradictory core assumptions, has been accompanied by the growth of an ideology of "comfortable eclecticism" (see Goldhaber & Barnett, 1988a, p. 2, for an early articulation of this ideology).

A doctrine of "eclecticism" has the advantage of allowing a discourse community to avoid fragmentation by encouraging the creation of multiple closed paradigms that coexist peacefully (Ackroyd, 1992). It may produce rapid (albeit "normal") scientific "progress," defined both in terms of the generation of substantial amounts of research and the progressive refinement and elaboration of each paradigm. But as Deetz (1992a) has noted, a rhetoric of eclecticism also precludes meaningful critique of fundamental assumptions and undermines the kinds of dialogue that facilitates further transformation (also see Feyerabend, 1975/1993; Gergen, 1982).

Other transformative pressures are extrinsic to language communities—changes in the surrounding intellectual climate and/or socioeconomic milieu (Cheney, 1995; Deetz, 1995; Finet, Chapter 8, this volume). Just as intrinsic pressures generated fundamental changes in organizational communication theory during the past decade, these extrinsic pressures promise to have a profound effect on what we do, how we think, and what kind of community we will become.

## NOTES

1. We chose 1985 as a starting point because by that date the critical and interpretive turns in organizational communication scholarship that began in the late 1970s had solidified sufficiently to allow the publication of a number of coherent summary volumes (e.g., Goldhaber & Barnett, 1988b; Jablin, Putnam, Roberts, & Porter, 1987; McPhee & Tompkins, 1985). We then surveyed essays in the journals published by the Speech Communication Association and International Communication Association between 1985 and 1995 (focusing on *Communication Monographs, Human Communication Research, Quarterly Journal of Speech, Journal of Applied Communication Research, Communication Theory,* and the *Communication Yearbooks*), and added sources that were cited frequently by relevant articles in these publications (articles in *Communication Research* and *Management Communication Quarterly* were frequently added to the survey during this phase). Complete citations are included in the references.

2. Dawe prefers the term *doctrine* to the more common terms *paradigm* or *theory* because it is a way of viewing social action and social theory: "the judgments of value, a social philosophy as well as a system of concepts or of general propositions" (citing Aron, 1968, p. v; cited in Dawe, 1970, p. 208). Following Dawe, we will first present the two doctrines as more distinct and antithetical than they actually are, eventually arguing that attempts to mediate the different doctrines are the core of contemporary social theory.

3. We use the term *theory* (in both critical theory and systems theory) solely because the term is commonly used by organizational communication scholars. Our concern in this chapter is with broad conceptual frameworks, which are defined by a particular set of epistemic assumptions, each of which encompasses a variety of what often are called theories.

4. Our survey of recent organizational communication research identified many studies that operate within an information-exchange construct system. In addition to those cited in the text of this chapter, see Adams and

Parrott (1994); Albrecht and Hall (1991b); Franz and Jin (1995); Holowitz and Wilson (1993); Jablin (1987a); Johnson (1988); Kramer (1993); Miller, Johnstone, and Grau (1994); Plax, Beatty, and Feingold (1991); Poole and DeSanctis (1992); Ralston (1993); and Rogers (1988).

5. Additional related sources include Corman (1990); Cushman and Sanderson-King (1993); Drecksel (1991); Ellis and Miller (1993); Everett (1994); Fairhurst (1988); Fairhurst and Chandler (1989); Fairhurst, Rogers, and Sarr (1987); Falcione, Sussman, and Herden (1987); Fink and Chen (1995); Franz and Jin (1995); Gayle (1991); Hammer and Martin (1992); Hirokawa, Mickey, and Miura (1991); Miller and Monge (1987); Monge and Miller (1988); Monge, Cozzens, and Contractor (1992); Morrill and Thomas (1992); Peterson and Sorenson (1991); Putnam and Sorenson (1992); Richmond and Roach (1992); Stewart, Gudykunst, and Ting-Toomey (1982); Stohl (1986); and Waldron (1991).

6. Actionist organizational communication research not cited in this section includes Alvesson (1993); Banks and Banks (1991); Barge and Musambria (1992); Barker et al. (1993); Barker and Tompkins (1994); Bastien et al. (1995); Baxter (1994); Bingham and Burelson (1989); Bullis (1993a); Cheney and Christensen (1994); Coffman (1992); Cragan and Shields (1992); Ferraris et al. (1993); Goodall (1990); Hess (1993); Hogan (1989); Howard and Geist (1995); Huspek (1993); Jablonski (1988); Laird-Brenton (1993); Levitt and Nass (1994); McPhee (1993); Mumby (1987); Peterson and Sorenson (1991); Ralston and Kirkwood (1995); Shockley-Zalabak and Morely (1994); Smith and Turner (1995); Stohl (1993); Strine (1992); Sypher (1991); Taylor and Conrad (1992); Tracy and Baratz (1993); Treadwell and Harrison (1994); and Wood (1992).

7. Eisenberg and Riley's summary of issues facing organizational symbolism researchers—the extent to which meaning systems can be treated as shared by multiple organizational members, the degree to which symbolic action is conscious or unconscious, and the potential limitations of social constructionist views of organizations—are remarkably similar to existing critiques of the language of social action, particularly those presented in Giddens's (1976, 1979) early work. But they treated these issues as problems in the application of the doctrine of social action in organizational communication research rather than as problematic elements of the perspective itself.

8. Some identification/concertive control research takes a "postmodernist" perspective. It will be considered later in this chapter.

9. Because other chapters in this volume deal at great length with this strain of research (in particular, those chapters by Deetz, by Mumby, by Putnam and Fairhurst, and by Eisenberg and Riley), we will describe its key constructs only briefly. We also accept Deetz's and Mumby's decision to differentiate "critical theory" and "postmodernist/dissensus" perspectives. Interestingly, a very early precursor to the development of criti-

cal theories was introduced in Thayer's (1988) examination of "leadership" as a social construction. Thayer begins by asserting that organizational communication researchers have largely ignored leadership because of their excessively narrow definition of communication as a process of conveying information or ideas (for a similar analysis, see Deetz, 1992b, 1994). He subsequently argues that leadership is a distinctively Western construction, one that functions to create feelings of control over events, outcomes, and so on (1992b, pp. 233-234).

10. This construction separates "leadership" from organizational contexts and legitimizes the empirically questionable assumption that leaders cause organizational outcomes. Recent shifts in orientation from leadership "traits" and "styles" to leadership as adaptation to situational contingencies merely serve to insert researchers further into the dominant ideology (Thayer, 1988, p. 238).

11. Three other perspectives are relevant. Two approaches combine action and structure conceptually but separate them temporally or spatially. Temporally oriented models hold action constant during one time period and structure constant during another. One dimension (action or structure) may create or influence the conditions under which the other operates, or the two may influence one another mutually over time with "swings" from the dominance of one to the dominance of the other (Archer, 1982; Poole & Van de Ven, 1989). Temporal approaches include Tushman and Romanelli's (1985) punctuated equilibrium model in organizational theory and self-organizing systems theory in organizational communication (Baldwin-Leveque & Poole, 1996). Spatially oriented models focus on processes through which action and structure are intertwined across organizational levels, for example, linking action at the microlevel of analysis with structure at a macrolevel (Coleman, 1986; Poole & Van de Ven, 1989; Van de Ven & Poole, 1988). The key to this approach is treating both micro- and macrolevels simultaneously, as in Buckley's "morphogenesis" perspective (Archer, 1982). A third perspective that has explicitly rejected the action-structure dualism has been labeled "flexible structuration theory" (Barnett & Thayer, 1997; Poole, 1994; Seibold & Contractor, 1993).

Space limitations preclude our describing these perspectives in detail, and it is too early in their development to be able to predict the extent to which they will be accepted by organizational communication theorists or to assess the degree to which they actually do avoid the action-structure problematic. But each is a promising alternative to the dominant construct system.

12. More detailed treatments are provided in the chapters by Deetz, Mumby, Cheney and Christensen, Taylor and Trujillo, and Putnam and Fairhurst in this volume, and extended analyses of the implications of postmodernism to social/organizational theory and to social science are available in Boje, Gephart, and Thatchenkery (1996); Calás and Smircich (1991); Clegg (1994); Ritzer (1997); and Rosenau (1992). Examples of feminist postmodernist organizational communication

research include Bingham (1994); Blair, Brown, and Baxter (1994); Bullis (1993a); Buzzanell (1994); Calás and Smircich (1992); Clair (1993a, 1993b, 1994); Gregg (1993); Marshall (1993); Mumby (1993b, this volume); Mumby and Putnam (1992); Strine (1992); and West and Zimmerman (1987).

13. Postmodern theorists differ in their views of the relationship between the modern and postmodern eras. Some posit a dramatic rupture, an end to the modern era and a beginning of the postmodern one (e.g., Baudrillard and Virilio). Others see a continuity in which postmodernity has grown out of modernity (Jameson, Laclau and Mouffe, and some postmodern feminists such as Nancy Fraser and Donna Haraway). Others suggest that "we can see *modernity and postmodernity as engaged in a long-running relationship with one another*, with postmodernity continually pointing out the limitations of modernity (for example, Lyotard)" (Ritzer, 1997, p. 8).

14. Unlike critical theories that focus on revealing conflicting "interests," postmodernist perspectives focus on the ways in which discourse sustains mutually reinforcing patterns of power and powerlessness. Postmodernists argue that actionist perspectives privilege individual experience, linguistic action, integrated selves, and voluntarism. Doing so creates a set of discourse practices that obscure the politics of organizational experience (see Salaman, 1986, and Reed, 1985, for a more detailed explanation; see Deetz, Chapter 1, this volume).

15. Some postmodernists, notably Foucault and Laclau and Mouffe, confront this problem by including both material practices and language within their construction of "discourse." For example, the physical structure of a prison and the medical practices of treating insanity are nonlinguistic "discourse."

16. Ritzer (1997) argues that this is, ironically, most true of Marxian postmodernists like Jameson, and less so of Baudrillard. It is less true of Deleuze and Guattari, Laclau and Mouffe, and feminists such as Donna Haraway, all of whom offer theories of social change and views of "good" societies.

# REFERENCES

Abercrombie, N. (1980). *The dominant ideology thesis*. London: Allen and Unwin.

Ackroyd, S. (1992). Paradigms lost: Paradise regained? In M. Reed & M. Hughes (Eds.), *Rethinking organization: New directions in organization theory and analysis* (pp. 102-119). London: Sage.

Adams, R., & Parrott, R. (1994). Pediatric nurses' communication of role expectations of parents to hospitalized children. *Journal of Applied Communication Research, 22,* 36-47.

Albrecht, T., & Hall, B. (1991a). Facilitating talk about new ideas: The role of personal relationships in organizational innovation. *Communication Monographs, 58,* 273-289.

Albrecht, T., & Hall, B. (1991b). Relationship and content differences between elites and outsiders in innovation networks. *Human Communication Research, 17,* 535-562.

Alexander, E., III, Penley, L., & Jernigan, I. E. (1991). The effects of individual differences on manager media choice. *Management Communication Quarterly, 5,* 155-173.

Allen, M., Gotcher, J. M., & Seibert, J. (1993). A decade of organizational communication research: 1980-1991. In S. A. Deetz (Ed.), *Communication yearbook 16* (pp. 252-330). Newbury Park, CA: Sage.

Allen, T. J., & Hauptman, O. (1990). The substitution of communication technologies for organizational structure in research and development. In J. Fulk & C. Steinfield (Eds.), *Organizations and communication technology* (pp. 237-274). Newbury Park, CA: Sage.

Alvesson, M. (1987). *Organizational theory and technocratic consciousness*. New York: Aldine de Gruyter.

Alvesson, M. (1993). Cultural-ideological modes of management control. In S. A. Deetz (Ed.), *Communication yearbook 16* (pp. 3-42). Newbury Park, CA: Sage.

Alvesson, M., & Willmott, H. (1992). On the idea of emancipation in management and organization studies. *Academy of Management Review, 17,* 432-464.

Anderson, P. (1984). *In the tracks of historical materialism*. Chicago: University of Chicago Press.

Archer, M. (1982). Morphogenesis versus structuration. *British Journal of Sociology, 33,* 455-483.

Aron, R. (1968). *Main currents in sociological thought* (Vol. 2). New York: Weidenfeld & Nicholson.

Ash, M. (1990). *Journey into the eye of a needle*. Devon, UK: Green.

Aune, J. (1994). *Rhetoric and Marxism*. Boulder, CO: Westview.

Axley, S. R. (1984). Managerial and organizational communication in terms of the conduit metaphor. *Academy of Management Review, 9,* 428-437.

Bach, B. W. (1989). The effect of multiplex relationships upon innovation adaptation. *Communication Monographs, 56,* 133-151.

Baldwin-Leveque, C., & Poole, M. S. (1996). Systems thinking in organizational communication inquiry. In P. Salem (Ed.), *Organizational communication and change*. Creskill, NJ: Hampton.

Banks, S. (1994). Performing flight announcements: The case of flight attendants' work discourse. *Text and Performance Quarterly, 14,* 253-267.

Banks, S., & Banks, A. (1991). Translation as problematic discourse in organizations. *Journal of Applied Communication Research, 19,* 223-241.

Banks, S., & Riley, P. (1993). Structuration theory as an ontology for communication research. In S. A. Deetz

(Ed.), *Communication yearbook 17* (pp. 167-196). Newbury Park: Sage.

Barge, K., & Musambria, G. (1992). Turning points in chair-faculty relations. *Journal of Applied Communication Research, 20*, 54-71.

Barker, J. R. (1993). Tightening the iron cage: Concertive control in self-managing teams. *Administrative Science Quarterly, 38*, 408-437.

Barker, J. R., & Cheney, G. (1994). The concept and practices of discipline in contemporary organizational life. *Communication Monographs, 61*, 20-43.

Barker, J. R., Melville, C. W., & Pacanowsky, M. E. (1993). Self-directed teams at Xel. *Journal of Applied Communication Research, 21*, 297-312.

Barker, J. R., & Tompkins, P. (1994). Identification in the self-managing organization. *Human Communication Research, 21*, 223-240.

Barnett, G. A., & Thayer, L. (Eds.). (1997). *Communication—Organization 6*. Norwood, NJ: Ablex.

Bastien, D. T., McPhee, R. D., & Bolton, K. A. (1995). A study and extended theory of the structuration of climate. *Communication Monographs, 62*, 87-109.

Baudrillard, J. (1983). *Simulations*. New York: Semiotext(e).

Baudrillard, J. (1988). *Selected writings* (M. Poster, Ed.). Cambridge, UK: Polity.

Baxter, L. (1994). "Talking things through" and "putting it in writing." *Journal of Applied Communication Research, 21*, 313-326.

Berthold, C. (1976). Kenneth Burke's cluster-agon method: Its development and an application. *Central States Speech Journal, 27*, 302-309.

Best, S. (1994). Foucault, postmodernism, and social theory. In D. R. Dickens & A. Fontana (Eds.), *Postmodernism and social inquiry* (pp. 25-52). New York: Guilford.

Bhaskar, R. (1979). *The possibility of naturalism*. Atlantic Highlands, NJ: Humanities Press.

Bingham, S. (Ed.). (1994). *Conceptualizing sexual harassment as discursive practice*. Westport, CT: Greenwood.

Bingham, S., & Burleson, B. R. (1989). Multiple effects of messages with multiple goals. *Human Communication Research, 16*, 184-216.

Blair, C., Brown, J. R., & Baxter, L. A. (1994). Disciplining the feminine. *Quarterly Journal of Speech, 80*, 383-409.

Boje, D., Gephart, R. P., & Thatchenkery, T. J. (1996). *Postmodern management and organizational theory*. Thousand Oaks, CA: Sage.

Brown, M. H. (1990). Defining stories in organizations: Characteristics and functions. In J. A. Anderson (Ed.), *Communication yearbook 13* (pp. 162-190). Newbury Park, CA: Sage.

Browning, L. D. (1992). Lists and stories as organizational communication. *Communication Theory, 2*, 281-302.

Bullis, C. (1993a). At least it's a start. In S. A. Deetz (Ed.), *Communication yearbook 16* (pp. 144-154). Newbury Park, CA: Sage.

Bullis, C. (1993b). Organizational socialization research. *Communication Monographs, 60*, 10-17.

Bullis, C., & Tompkins, P. (1989). The forest ranger revisited: A study of control practices and identification. *Communication Monographs, 56*, 287-306.

Burke, K. (1969). *A grammar of motives*. Berkeley: University of California Press. (Original work published 1945)

Burke, K. (1970). *Rhetoric of religion*. Berkeley: University of California Press.

Burke, K. (1984). *The philosophy of literary form* (3rd ed.). Berkeley: University of California Press. (Original work published 1941)

Burke, K. (1991). Auscultation, creation, and revision. In J. Chesebro (Ed.), *Extensions of the Burkeian system* (pp. 42-172). Tuscaloosa: University of Alabama Press.

Buzzanell, P. (1994). Gaining a voice: Feminist organizational communication theorizing. *Management Communication Quarterly, 7*, 339-383.

Calás, M., & Smircich, L. (1991). Voicing seduction to silence leadership. *Organization Studies, 12*, 567-602.

Calás, M., & Smircich, L. (1992). Rewriting gender into organizational theorizing: Directions from feminist perspectives. In M. Reed & M. Hughes (Eds.), *Rethinking organization: New directions in organizational theory and analysis* (pp. 227-253). London: Sage.

Carnegie, S. (1996). *The hidden emotions of tourism*. Unpublished master's thesis, Texas A&M University, College Station.

Castoriadis, C. (1987). *The imaginary institution of society* (K. Blamey, Trans.). Cambridge, UK: Polity.

Cheney, G. (1983a). On the various and changing meanings of organizational membership: A field study of organizational identification. *Communication Monographs, 50*, 343-363.

Cheney, G. (1983b). The rhetoric of identification and the study of organizational communication. *Quarterly Journal of Speech, 69*, 143-158.

Cheney, G. (1995). Democracy in the workplace. *Journal of Applied Communication Research, 23*, 167-200.

Cheney, G., & Christensen, L. T. (1994). Articulating identity in an organizational age. In S. A. Deetz (Ed.), *Communication yearbook 17* (pp. 222-235). Thousand Oaks, CA: Sage.

Cheney, G., & Stohl, C. (1991). European transformations and their communicative implications. *Journal of Applied Communication Research, 19*, 330-339.

Cheney, G., & Vibbert, S. L. (1987). Corporate discourse: Public relations and issue management. In F. M. Jablin, L. L. Putnam, K. H. Robert, & L. W. Porter (Eds.), *Handbook of organizational communica-*

tion: An interdisciplinary perspective (pp. 165-194). Newbury Park, CA: Sage.

Chiles, A. M., & Zorn, T. (1995). Empowerment in organizations: Employees' perceptions of the influences on empowerment. *Journal of Applied Communication Research, 23,* 1-25.

Clair, R. P. (1993a). The bureaucratization, commodification, and privatization of sexual harassment through institutional discourse. *Management Communication Quarterly, 7,* 123-157.

Clair, R. P. (1993b). The use of framing devises to sequester organizational narratives. *Communication Monographs, 60,* 113-136.

Clair, R. P. (1994). Hegemony and harassment: A discursive practice. In S. Bingham (Ed.), *Conceptualizing sexual harassment as discursive practice* (pp. 59-70). Westport, CT: Greenwood.

Clegg, S. (1989). *Frameworks of power.* Newbury Park, CA: Sage.

Clegg, S. (1990). *Modern organizations: Organizations in a postmodern world.* Newbury Park, CA: Sage.

Clegg, S. (1994). Power relations and the constitution of the resistant subject. In J. M. Jermier, D. Knights, & W. R. Nord (Eds.), *Resistance and power in organizations* (pp. 274-325). London: Routledge.

Coffman, S. L. (1992). Staff problems with geriatric care in two types of health care organizations. *Journal of Applied Communication Research, 20,* 292-307.

Coleman, J. S. (1986). Social theory, social research, and a theory of action. *American Journal of Sociology, 16,* 1309-1335.

Coles, R. (1991). Foucault's dialogical artistic ethos. *Theory, Culture and Society, 8,* 99-120.

Collinson, D. (1988). "Engineering humor": Masculinity, joking and conflict in shop-floor relations. *Organization Studies, 9,* 181-199.

Condit, C. (1994). Hegemony in mass mediated society. *Critical Studies in Mass Communication, 11,* 205-230.

Conrad, C. (1984). Phases, pentads, and dramatistic critical process. *Central States Speech Journal, 35,* 94-104.

Conrad, C. (1988). Work songs, hegemony, and illusions of self. *Critical Studies in Mass Communication, 5,* 179-194.

Conrad, C., & Ryan, M. (1985). Power, praxis, and self in organizational communication theory. In R. McPhee & P. Tompkins (Eds.), *Organizational communication: Traditional themes and new directions* (pp. 235-258). Beverly Hills, CA: Sage.

Contractor, N. S., & Eisenberg, E. (1991). Communication networks and new media in organizations. In J. Fulk & C. Steinfield (Eds.), *Organizations and communication technology* (pp. 145-174). Newbury Park, CA: Sage.

Corman, S. R. (1990). A model of perceived communication in collective networks. *Human Communication Research, 16,* 582-602.

Corman, S. R., & Scott, C. R. (1994). Perceived networks, activity foci, and observable communication in social collectives. *Communication Theory, 4,* 171-190.

Coward, R., & Ellis, J. (1977). *Language and materialism.* Boston: Routledge and Kegan Paul.

Cragan, J., & Shields, D. (1992). The use of symbolic convergence theory in corporate strategic planning. *Journal of Applied Communication Research, 20,* 199-218.

Culnan, M. J., & Markus, M. L. (1987). Information technologies. In F. M. Jablin, L. L. Putnam, K. H. Roberts, & L. W. Porter (Eds.), *Handbook of organizational communication: An interdisciplinary perspective* (pp. 420-444). Newbury Park, CA: Sage.

Cushman, D., & Sanderson-King, S. (1993). High-speed management. In S. A. Deetz (Ed.), *Communication yearbook 16* (pp. 209-236). Newbury Park, CA: Sage.

Cushman, D. P., Sanderson-King, S., & Smith, T., III. (1988). The rules perspective on organizational communication research. In G. Goldhaber & G. Barnett (Eds.), *Handbook of organizational communication* (pp. 55-94). Norwood, NJ: Ablex.

Cusella, L. P. (1987). Feedback, motivation, and performance. In F. M. Jablin, L. L. Putnam, K. H. Roberts, & L. W. Porter (Eds.), *Handbook of organizational communication: An interdisciplinary perspective* (pp. 624-678). Newbury Park, CA: Sage.

Czarniawska-Joerges, B. (1994). Narratives of individual and organizational identities. In S. A. Deetz (Ed.), *Communication yearbook 17* (pp. 190-210). Thousand Oaks, CA: Sage.

Danowski, J. A. (1980). Group attitude uniformity and connectivity of organizational communication networks for production, innovation, and maintenance content. *Human Communication Research, 6,* 299-308.

Danowski, J. A. (1988). Organizational infographics and automated auditing: Using computers to unobtrusively gather as well as analyze communication. In G. Goldhaber & G. Barnett (Eds.), *Handbook of organizational communication* (pp. 385-434). Norwood, NJ: Ablex.

Dansereau, F., & Markham, S. E. (1987). Superior-subordinate communication: Multiple levels of analysis. In F. M. Jablin, L. L. Putnam, K. H. Roberts, & L. W. Porter (Eds.), *Handbook of organizational communication: An interdisciplinary perspective* (pp. 343-388). Newbury Park, CA: Sage.

Dawe, A. (1970). The two sociologies. *British Journal of Sociology, 21,* 207-218.

Dawe, A. (1978). Theories of social action. In T. Bottomore & R. Nisbet (Eds.), *A history of sociological analysis* (pp. 362-417). New York: Basic Books.

Deetz, S. (1992a). *Democracy in an age of corporate colonization.* Albany: State University of New York Press.

Deetz, S. (1992b). Disciplinary power in the modern corporation, discursive practice and conflict suppression. In M. Alvesson & H. Willmott (Eds.), *Critical management studies* (pp. 106-142). London: Sage.

Deetz, S. (1994). Representative practices and the political analysis of corporations: Building a communication perspective in organization studies. In B. Kovacic (Ed.), *Organizational communication: New perspectives* (pp. 209-242). Albany: State University of New York Press.

Deetz, S. (1995). *Transforming communication, transforming business: Building responsive and responsible workplaces.* Cresskill, NJ: Hampton.

Deetz, S., & Mumby, D. K. (1990). Power, discourse, and the workplace: Reclaiming the critical tradition. In J. A. Anderson (Ed.), *Communication yearbook 13* (pp. 18-47). Newbury Park, CA: Sage.

Deleuze, G., & Guattari, F. (1983). *Anti-Oedipus: Capitalism and schizophrenia.* Minneapolis: University of Minnesota Press. (Original work published 1977)

DeSanctis, G., & Poole, M. S. (1994). Capturing the complexity in advanced technology use: Adaptive structuration theory. *Organization Science, 5,* 121-147.

Downs, C., Clampitt, P., & Pfeiffer, A. (1988). Communication and organizational outcomes. In G. Goldhaber & G. Barnett (Eds.), *Handbook of organizational communication* (pp. 171-212). Norwood, NJ: Ablex.

Drecksel, G. L. (1991). Leadership research: Some issues. In J. A. Anderson (Ed.), *Communication yearbook 14* (pp. 535-546). Newbury Park, CA: Sage.

Eagleton, T. (1983). *Literary theory: An introduction.* Minneapolis: University of Minnesota Press.

Eaves, M., & Leathers, D. (1991). Context as communication: McDonald's vs. Burger King. *Journal of Applied Communication Research, 19,* 263-289.

Ebers, M. (1985). Understanding organizations—The poetic mode. *Journal of Management, 7*(2), 51-62.

Ehrenhaus, P. (1993). Cultural narratives and the therapeutic motif: The political containment of Vietnam veterans. In D. Mumby (Ed.), *Narrative and social control* (pp. 77-96). Newbury Park, CA: Sage.

Eisenberg, E. M., & Goodall, H. L. (1997). *Organizational communication: Balancing creativity and constraint* (2nd ed.). New York: St. Martin's.

Eisenberg, E. M., & Riley, P. (1988). Organizational symbols and sense-making. In G. Goldhaber & G. Barnett (Eds.), *Handbook of organizational communication* (pp. 131-150). Norwood, NJ: Ablex.

Ellis, B. H., & Miller, K. (1993). The role of assertiveness, personal control, and participation in the prediction of nurse burnout. *Journal of Applied Communication Research, 21,* 327-335.

Elster, J. (1984). *Ulysses and the sirens.* Cambridge, UK: Cambridge University Press.

Euske, N. A., & Roberts, K. H. (1987). Evolving perspectives in organization theory: Communication implications. In F. M. Jablin, L. L. Putnam, K. H. Roberts, & L. W. Porter (Eds.), *Handbook of organizational communication: An interdisciplinary perspective* (pp. 41-69). Newbury Park, CA: Sage.

Everett, J. L. (1994). Communication and sociocultural evolution in organizations and organizational populations. *Communication Theory, 4,* 93-110.

Fairhurst, G. T. (1988). Male-female communication on the job: Literature review and commentary. In M. McLaughlin (Ed.), *Communication yearbook 11* (pp. 83-116). Newbury Park, CA: Sage.

Fairhurst, G. T. (1993). The leader-member exchange patterns of women leaders in industry. *Communication Monographs, 60,* 321-351.

Fairhurst, G. T., & Chandler, T. (1989). Social structure in leader-member interactions. *Communication Monographs, 56,* 215-239.

Fairhurst, G. T., Green, S., & Snavely, B. (1984a). Face support in controlling poor performance. *Human Communication Research, 11,* 272-295.

Fairhurst, G. T., Green, S., & Snavely, B. (1984b). Managerial control and discipline: Whips and chains. In R. N. Bostrom (Ed.), *Communication yearbook 8* (pp. 558-593). Beverly Hills, CA: Sage.

Fairhurst, G. T., Rogers, L. E., & Sarr, R. A. (1987). Manager-subordinate control patterns and judgments about the relationship. In M. McLaughlin (Ed.), *Communication yearbook 10* (pp. 395-415). Newbury Park, CA: Sage.

Falcione, R. L., Sussman, L., & Herden, R. P. (1987). Communication climate in organizations. In F. M. Jablin, L. L. Putnam, K. H. Roberts, & L. W. Porter (Eds.), *Handbook of organizational communication: An interdisciplinary perspective* (pp. 195-227). Newbury Park, CA: Sage.

Falcione, R. L., & Wilson, C. E. (1988). Socialization processes in organizations. In G. Goldhaber & G. Barnett (Eds.), *Handbook of organizational communication* (pp. 151-170). Norwood, NJ: Ablex.

Ferraris, C., Carveth, R., & Parrish-Sprowl, J. (1993). Interface precision benchworks: A case study in organizational identification. *Journal of Applied Communication Research, 21,* 336-357.

Feyerabend, P. K. (1993). *Against method* (3rd ed.). London: Verso. (Original work published 1975)

Fielding, N. (Ed.). (1988). *Actions and structure.* London: Sage.

Fink, E. L., & Chen, S. (1995). A Galileo analysis of organizational climate. *Human Communication Research, 21,* 484-521.

Franz, C., & Jin, K. G. (1995). The structure of group conflict in a collaborative work group during information systems development. *Journal of Applied Communication Research, 23,* 108-127.

Frost, P. J. (1987). Power, politics, and influence. In F. M. Jablin, L. L. Putnam, K. H. Roberts, & L. W. Porter (Eds.), *Handbook of organizational communica-*

*tion: An interdisciplinary perspective* (pp. 503-548). Newbury Park, CA: Sage.

Frye, N. (1957). *Anatomy of criticism*. Princeton, NJ: Princeton University Press.

Fulk, J., & Dutton, W. (1985). Videoconferencing as an organizational information system: Assessing the role of electronic meetings. *Systems, Objectives, Solutions, 4*, 105-118.

Fulk, J., & Mani, S. (1986). Distortion of communication in hierarchical relationships. In M. McLaughlin (Ed.), *Communication yearbook 9* (pp. 483-510). Beverly Hills, CA: Sage.

Fulk, J., Schmitz, J., & Steinfield, C. (1991). A social influence model of technology use. In J. Fulk & C. Steinfield (Eds.), *Organizations and communication technology* (pp. 117-140). Newbury Park, CA: Sage.

Gayle, B. M. (1991). Sex equity in workplace conflict management. *Journal of Applied Communication Research, 19*, 152-169.

Gergen, K. (1982). *Toward transformation in social knowledge*. New York: Springer-Verlag.

Gergen, K. (1992). Organization theory in the postmodern era. In M. Reed & M. Hughes (Eds.), *Rethinking organization: New directions in organization theory and analysis* (pp. 207-226). London: Sage.

Giddens, A. (1976). *New rules of sociological method*. New York: Basic Books.

Giddens, A. (1979). *Central problems in social theory*. Berkeley: University of California Press.

Giddens, A. (1984). *The constitution of society*. Berkeley: University of California Press.

Giddens, A. (1990). *The consequences of modernity*. Stanford, CA: Stanford University Press.

Gitlin, T. (1988, November 1). Hip-deep in postmodernism. *New York Times Book Review*, pp. 35-36.

Goldhaber, G. M., & Barnett, G. (1988a). Foreword. In G. Goldhaber & G. Barnett (Eds.), *Handbook of organizational communication* (pp. 1-4). Norwood, NJ: Ablex.

Goldhaber, G. M., & Barnett, G. (Eds.). (1988b). *Handbook of organizational communication*. Norwood, NJ: Ablex.

Goodall, H. L. (1990). Theatre of motives and the meaningful orders of persons and things. In J. A. Anderson (Ed.), *Communication yearbook 13* (pp. 69-94). Newbury Park, CA: Sage.

Goodall, H. L., Wilson, G., & Waagen, C. (1986). The performance appraisal interview. *Quarterly Journal of Speech, 72*, 74-87.

Gouldner, A. (1980). *The two Marxisms*. New York: Oxford University Press.

Granovetter, M. (1985). Economic action and social structure: The problem of embeddedness. *American Journal of Sociology, 91*, 481-510.

Greenbaum, H. H., Hellweg, S. A., & Falcione, R. L. (1988). Organizational communication evolution: An overview 1950-1981. In G. Goldhaber & G.

Barnett (Eds.), *Handbook of organizational communication* (pp. 275-318). Norwood, NJ: Ablex.

Gregg, N. (1993). Politics of identity/politics of location: Women workers organizing in a postmodern world. *Women's Studies in Communication, 16*, 1-33.

Habermas, J. (1979). *Communication and the evolution of society* (T. McCarthy, Trans.). Boston: Beacon.

Habermas, J. (1981). Modernity versus postmodernity. *New German Critique, 22*, 3-14.

Habermas, J. (1984). *The theory of communicative action* (Vol. 1). (T. McCarthy, Trans.). Boston: Beacon.

Habermas, J. (1986). The genealogical writing of history: On some aporias in Foucault's theory of power. *Canadian Journal of Political and Social Theory, 10*, 1-9.

Habermas, J. (1987). *The theory of communicative action* (Vol. 2). (T. McCarthy, Trans.). Boston: Beacon.

Habermas, J. (1991). A reply. In A. Honneth & H. Joas (Eds.), *Essays on Jürgen Habermas's* The Theory of Communicative Action (pp. 215-264). Cambridge, UK: Cambridge University Press.

Hammer, M. R., & Martin, J. N. (1992). The effects of cross-cultural training on American managers in a Japanese-American joint venture. *Journal of Applied Communication Research, 20*, 161-182.

Harris, C. C. (1980). *Fundamental concepts and the sociological enterprise*. London: Croom Helm.

Harrison, T. (1994). Communication and interdependence in democratic organizations. In S. A. Deetz (Ed.), *Communication yearbook 17* (pp. 247-274). Thousand Oaks, CA: Sage.

Held, D. (1980). *Introduction to critical theory*. Berkeley: University of California Press.

Helmer, J. (1993). Storytelling in the creation and maintenance of organizational tension and stratification. *Southern Communication Journal, 59*, 34-44.

Hess, J. A. (1993). Assimilating newcomers into the organization: A cultural perspective. *Journal of Applied Communication Research, 21*, 189-196.

Hirokawa, R. M., Mickey, J., & Miura, S. (1991). Effects of request legitimacy on the compliance-gaining tactics of male and female managers. *Communication Monographs, 58*, 421-436.

Hogan, J. M. (1989). Managing dissent in the Catholic Church. *Quarterly Journal of Speech, 75*, 400-415.

Holowitz, J., & Wilson, C. (1993). Structured interviewing in volunteer selection. *Journal of Applied Communication Research, 21*, 41-52.

Howard, L. A., & Geist, P. (1995). Ideological positioning in organizational change: The dialectic of control in a merging organization. *Communication Monographs, 62*, 110-131.

Huber, G. (1990). A theory of the effects of advanced information technologies on organizational design, intelligence, and decision making. In J. Fulk & C. Steinfield (Eds.), *Organizations and communication technology* (pp. 237-274). Newbury Park, CA: Sage.

Huber, G. P., & Daft, R. L. (1987). The information environments of organizations. In F. M. Jablin, L. L. Putnam, K. H. Roberts, & L. W. Porter (Eds.), *Handbook of organizational communication: An interdisciplinary perspective* (pp. 130-164). Newbury Park, CA: Sage.

Husband, R. (1985). Toward a grounded typology of organizational leadership behavior. *Quarterly Journal of Speech, 71,* 103-118.

Huspek, M. (1993). Dueling structures. *Communication Theory, 1,* 1-25.

Huspek, M., & Kendall, K. (1991). On withholding political voice: An analysis of the political vocabulary of a "nonpolitical" speech community. *Quarterly Journal of Speech, 77,* 1-19.

Jablin, F. M. (1979). Superior-subordinate communication. *Psychological Bulletin, 86,* 1201-1222.

Jablin, F. M. (1987a). Formal organization structure. In F. M. Jablin, L. L. Putnam, K. H. Roberts, & L. W. Porter (Eds.), *Handbook of organizational communication: An interdisciplinary perspective* (pp. 389-419). Newbury Park, CA: Sage.

Jablin, F. M. (1987b). Organizational entry, assimilation, and exit. In F. M. Jablin, L. L. Putnam, K. H. Roberts, & L. W. Porter (Eds.), *Handbook of organizational communication: An interdisciplinary perspective* (pp. 679-740). Newbury Park, CA: Sage.

Jablin, F. M., Putnam, L. L., Roberts, K. H., & Porter, L. W. (Eds.). (1987). *Handbook of organizational communication: An interdisciplinary perspective.* Newbury Park, CA: Sage.

Jablonski, C. (1988). Rhetoric, paradox and the movement for women's ordination in the Roman Catholic Church. *Quarterly Journal of Speech, 74,* 164-183.

Johnson, J. D. (1988). On the use of communication gradients. In G. Goldhaber & G. Barnett (Eds.), *Handbook of organizational communication* (pp. 361-384). Norwood, NJ: Ablex.

Keen, P. (1990). Telecommunications and organizational choice. In J. Fulk & C. Steinfield (Eds.), *Organizations and communication technology* (pp. 295-312). Newbury Park, CA: Sage.

Keough, C., & Lake, R. (1993). Values as structuring properties of contract negotiations. In C. Conrad (Ed.), *The ethical nexus* (pp. 171-192). Norwood, NJ: Ablex.

Krone, K. J., Jablin, F. M., & Putnam, L. L. (1987). Communication theory and organizational communication: Multiple perspectives. In F. M. Jablin, L. L. Putnam, K. H. Roberts, & L. W. Porter (Eds.), *Handbook of organizational communication: An interdisciplinary perspective* (pp. 18-40). Newbury Park, CA: Sage.

Knuf, J. (1993). "Ritual" in organizational culture theory. In S. A. Deetz (Ed.), *Communication yearbook 16* (pp. 61-103). Newbury Park, CA: Sage.

Kramer, M. (1993). Communication after job transfers: Social exchange processes. *Human Communication Research, 20,* 147-174.

Kunda, G. (1991). *Ritual and the management of corporate culture: A critical perspective.* Paper presented at the 8th International Conference on Organizational Symbolism, Copenhagen, Denmark.

Laird-Brenton, A. (1993). Demystifying the magic of language: A critical linguistic case analysis of legitimation of authority. *Journal of Applied Communication Research, 21,* 227-244.

Leipzig, J. S., & Moore, E. (1982). Organizational communication: A review and analysis of three current approaches to the field. *Journal of Business Communication, 19,* 77-92.

Levitt, B., & Nass, C. (1994). Organizational narratives and person/identity distinction. In S. A. Deetz (Ed.), *Communication yearbook 17* (pp. 236-246). Thousand Oaks, CA: Sage.

MacIntyre, A. (1981). *After virtue.* Notre Dame, IN: Notre Dame University Press.

Marshall, A., & Stohl, C. (1993). Participating as participation. *Communication Monographs, 60,* 137-157.

Marshall, J. (1993). Viewing organizational communication from a feminist perspective. In S. A. Deetz (Ed.), *Communication yearbook 16* (pp. 122-143). Newbury Park, CA: Sage.

McMillan, J., & Cheney, G. (1996). The student as consumer: The implications and limitations of a metaphor. *Communication Education, 45,* 1-15.

McPhee, R. (1985). Formal structure and organizational communication. In R. McPhee & P. Tompkins (Eds.), *Organizational communication: Traditional themes and new directions* (pp. 149-178). Beverly Hills, CA: Sage.

McPhee, R. D. (1993). Cultural-ideological modes of control: An examination of concept formation. In S. A. Deetz (Ed.), *Communication yearbook 16* (pp. 43-53). Newbury Park, CA: Sage.

McPhee, R. D., & Corman, S. R. (1995). An activity-based theory of communication networks in organizations, applied to the case of a local church. *Communication Monographs, 62,* 132-151.

McPhee, R., & Tompkins, P. (Eds.). (1985). *Organizational communication: Traditional themes and new directions.* Beverly Hills, CA: Sage.

Miller, K. I., & Monge, P. R. (1987). The development and test of a system of organizational participation and allocation. In M. McLaughlin (Ed.), *Communication yearbook 10* (pp. 431-455). Newbury Park, CA: Sage.

Miller, V. D., Johnstone, J. R., & Grau, J. (1994). Antecedents to willingness to participate in a planned organizational change. *Journal of Applied Communication Research, 22,* 59-80.

Monge, P. R., & Eisenberg, E. M. (1987). Emergent communication networks. In F. M. Jablin, L. L. Putnam, K. H. Roberts, & L. W. Porter (Eds.), *Hand-*

book of organizational communication: An interdisciplinary perspective (pp. 304-342). Newbury Park, CA: Sage.

Monge, P. R., & Miller, K. I. (1988). Participative processes in organizations. In G. Goldhaber & G. Barnett (Eds.), Handbook of organizational communication (pp. 213-230). Norwood, NJ: Ablex.

Monge, P. R., Cozzens, J., & Contractor, N. (1992). Communication and motivation predictors of the dynamics of innovation. Organization Science, 2, 1-25.

Morrill, C., & Thomas, C. K. (1992). Organizational conflict management as disputing process. Human Communication Research, 18, 400-428.

Mumby, D. (1987). The political function of narrative in organizations. Communication Monographs, 54, 113-127.

Mumby, D. (1988). Communication and power in organizations. Norwood, NJ: Ablex.

Mumby, D. (1989). Ideology and the social construction of meaning: A communication perspective. Communication Quarterly, 37, 18-25.

Mumby, D. (1993a). Critical organizational communication studies. Communication Monographs, 60, 18-25.

Mumby, D. (1993b). Feminism and the critique of organizational communication. In S. A. Deetz (Ed.), Communication yearbook 16 (pp. 155-166). Newbury Park, CA: Sage.

Mumby, D., & Putnam, L. (1992). The politics of emotion: A feminist reading of bounded rationality. Academy of Management Review, 17, 465-486.

O'Connell, S. E. (1988). Human communication in the high tech office. In G. Goldhaber & G. Barnett (Eds.), Handbook of organizational communication (pp. 473-482). Norwood, NJ: Ablex.

Olson, M. H. (1982). New information technology and organizational culture. MIS Quarterly, pp. 426-478.

O'Neill, J. (1995). The disciplinary society: From Weber to Foucault. British Journal of Sociology, 37, 42-60.

O'Reilly, C. A., Chatman, J. A., & Anderson, J. C. (1987). Message flow and decision making. In F. M. Jablin, L. L. Putnam, K. H. Roberts, & L. W. Porter (Eds.), Handbook of organizational communication: An interdisciplinary perspective (pp. 600-623). Newbury Park, CA: Sage.

Pacanowsky, M., & O'Donnell-Trujillo, N. (1983). Organizational communication as cultural performance. Communication Monographs, 50, 126-147.

Papa, M., Arwal, M. A., & Singhal, A. (1995). Dialectic of control and emancipation in organizing for change. Communication Theory, 5, 189-223.

Peterson, M. F., & Sorenson, R. L. (1991). Cognitive processes in leadership: Interpreting and handling events in an organizational context. In J. A. Anderson (Ed.), Communication yearbook 14 (pp. 501-534). Newbury Park, CA: Sage.

Plax, T., Beatty, M., & Feingold, P. (1991). Predicting verbal plan complexity from decision rule orienta-

tion among business students and corporate executives. Journal of Applied Communication Research, 19, 242-262.

Poole, M. S. (1985). Communication and organizational climates: Review, critique, and a new perspective. In R. McPhee & P. Tompkins (Eds.), Organizational communication: Traditional themes and new directions (pp. 79-108). Beverly Hills, CA: Sage.

Poole, M. S. (1994). A turn of the wheel: The case for a renewal of systems inquiry in organizational communication research. Paper presented at the annual meeting of the Speech Communication Association, Atlanta, GA.

Poole, M. S., & DeSanctis, G. (1990). Understanding the use of group decision support systems: The theory of adaptive structuration. In J. Fulk & C. Steinfield (Eds.), Organizations and communication technology (pp. 173-193). Newbury Park, CA: Sage.

Poole, M. S., & DeSanctis, G. (1992). Microlevel structuration in computer-supported group decision-making. Human Communication Research, 19, 5-49.

Poole, M. S., & Holmes, M. (1995). Decision development in computer-assisted group decision making. Human Communication Research, 22, 90-127.

Poole, M. S., & McPhee, R. D. (1983). A structurational analysis of organizational climate. In L. L. Putnam & M. E. Pacanowsky (Eds.), Communication and organizations: An interpretive approach (pp. 195-220). Beverly Hills, CA: Sage.

Poole, M. S., & McPhee, R. D. (1994). Methodology in interpersonal communication research. In M. Knapp & G. R. Miller (Eds.), Handbook of interpersonal communication (2nd ed., pp. 42-100). Thousand Oaks, CA: Sage.

Poole, M. S., Seibold, D. R., & McPhee, R. D. (1985). Group decision-making as a structurational process. Quarterly Journal of Speech, 71, 74-102.

Poole, M. S., & Van de Ven, A. H. (1989). Using paradox to build management and organization theories. Academy of Management Review, 14, 562-578.

Putnam, L., & Sorenson, R. (1982). Equivocal messages in organizations. Human Communication Research, 8, 114-132.

Putnam, L., & Stohl, C. (1990). Bona fide groups: A reconceptualization of groups in context. Communication Studies, 41, 248-265.

Putnam, L. L., & Poole, M. S. (1987). Conflict and negotiation. In F. M. Jablin, L. L. Putnam, K. H. Roberts, & L. W. Porter (Eds.), Handbook of organizational communication: An interdisciplinary perspective (pp. 549-599). Newbury Park, CA: Sage.

Ralston, S. (1993). Applicant communication satisfaction, intent to accept second interview offers, and recruiter communication style. Journal of Applied Communication Research, 21, 53-65.

Ralston, S. M., & Kirkwood, W. G. (1995). Overcoming managerial bias in employment interviewing. *Journal of Applied Communication Research, 23,* 75-92.

Reed, M. (1985). *Redirections in organizational analysis.* London: Tavistock.

Richmond, V. P., & Roach, K. D. (1992). Willingness to communicate and employee success in U.S. organizations. *Journal of Applied Communication Research, 20,* 95-115.

Riley, P. (1983). A structurationist account of political cultures. *Administrative Science Quarterly, 28,* 414-438.

Ritzer, G. (1997). *Postmodern social theory.* New York: McGraw-Hill.

Roberts, K., & O'Reilly, C. (1978). Organizations as communication structures: An empirical approach. *Human Communication Research, 4,* 283-293.

Rogers, E. M. (1988). Information technologies: How organizations are changing. In G. Goldhaber & G. Barnett (Eds.), *Handbook of organizational communication* (pp. 437-452). Norwood, NJ: Ablex.

Rosenau, P. M. (1992). *Postmodernism and the social sciences.* Princeton, NJ: Princeton University Press.

Salaman, G. (1986). *Working.* London: Tavistock.

Salvador, M., & Markham, A. (1995). The rhetoric of self-directive management and the operation of organizational power. *Communication Reports, 8,* 45-53.

Sambamurthy, V., & Poole, M. S. (1993). The effects of variations in capabilities of GDSS designs on management of cognitive conflict in groups. *Information Systems Research, 3,* 224-251.

Scott, C. R. (1996, May). *Identification with multiple targets in a geographically dispersed organization.* Paper presented at the annual meeting of the International Communication Association, Chicago.

Scott, J. C. (1993). *Domination and the arts of resistance: Hidden transcripts.* New Haven, CT: Yale University Press.

Seibold, D. R., & Contractor, N. (1993). Issues for a theory of high-speed management. In S. A. Deetz (Ed.), *Communication yearbook 16* (pp. 237-246). Newbury Park, CA: Sage.

Shils, E. (1968). The concept and function of ideology. In D. Sills (Ed.), *The international encyclopedia of the social sciences* (Vol. 7, pp. 66-76). New York: Crowell, Collier and Macmillan.

Shockley-Zalabak, P., & Morley, D. D. (1994). Creating a culture. *Human Communication Research, 20,* 334-355.

Sias, P., & Jablin, F. M. (1995). Differential superior-subordinate relations, perceptions of fairness, and coworker communication. *Human Communication Research, 22,* 5-38.

Simons, H. (1989). *Rhetoric in the human sciences.* London: Sage.

Simons, H. (1990). *The rhetorical turn, invention and persuasion in the conduct of inquiry.* Chicago: University of Chicago Press.

Smircich, L., & Calás, M. B. (1987). Organizational culture: A critical assessment. In F. M. Jablin, L. L. Putnam, K. H. Roberts, & L. W. Porter (Eds.), *Handbook of organizational communication: An interdisciplinary perspective* (pp. 228-263). Newbury Park, CA: Sage.

Smith, R. C., & Turner, P. K. (1995). A social constructionist reconfiguration of metaphor analysis: An application of "SCMA" to organizational socialization theorizing. *Communication Monographs, 62,* 152-181.

Stewart, L. P., Gudykunst, W. B., & Ting-Toomey, S. (1986). The effects of decision-making style on openness and satisfaction within Japanese organizations. *Communication Monographs, 53,* 236-251.

Stohl, C. (1986). Bridging the parallel organization: A study of quality circle effectiveness. In J. Burgoon (Ed.), *Communication yearbook 10* (pp. 473-496). Beverly Hills, CA: Sage.

Stohl, C. (1993). European managers' interpretations of participation: A semantic network analysis. *Human Communication Research, 20,* 97-117.

Stohl, C. (1995). *Organizational communication: Connectedness in action.* Thousand Oaks, CA: Sage.

Stohl, C., & Redding, W. C. (1987). Messages and message exchange processes. In F. M. Jablin, L. L. Putnam, K. H. Roberts, & L. W. Porter (Eds.), *Handbook of organizational communication: An interdisciplinary perspective* (pp. 451-502). Newbury Park, CA: Sage.

Strine, M. S. (1992). Understanding "how things work": Sexual harassment and academic culture. *Journal of Applied Communication Research, 20,* 391-400.

Sypher, B. D. (1991). A message-centered approach to leadership. In J. A. Anderson (Ed.), *Communication yearbook 14* (pp. 547-559). Newbury Park, CA: Sage.

Taylor, B. (1992). The politics of the nuclear text. *Quarterly Journal of Speech, 78,* 429-449.

Taylor, B. (1993). Register of the repressed. *Quarterly Journal of Speech, 79,* 267-285.

Taylor, B., & Conrad, C. (1992). Narratives of sexual harassment: Organizational dimensions. *Journal of Applied Communication Research, 20,* 401-418.

Thayer, L. (1988). Leadership/communication: A critical review and a modest proposal. In G. Goldhaber & G. Barnett (Eds.), *Handbook of organizational communication* (pp. 231-264). Norwood, NJ: Ablex.

Therborn, G. (1980). *The ideology of power and the power of ideology.* London: Verso.

Tompkins, P. K. (1987). Translating organizational theory: Symbolism over substance. In F. M. Jablin, L. L. Putnam, K. H. Roberts, & L. W. Porter (Eds.), *Handbook of organizational communication: An interdisciplinary perspective* (pp. 70-96). Newbury Park, CA: Sage.

Tompkins, P. K., & Cheney, G. (1983). Account analysis of organizations: Decision making and identification. In L. L. Putnam & M. E. Pacanowsky (Eds.), *Communication and organizations: An interpretive approach* (pp. 123-146). Beverly Hills, CA: Sage.

Tompkins, P. K., & Cheney, G. (1985). Communication and unobtrusive control in contemporary organizations. In R. McPhee & P. Tompkins (Eds.), *Organizational communication: Traditional themes and new directions* (pp. 179-210). Beverly Hills, CA: Sage.

Touraine, A. (1985). An introduction to the study of social movements. *Social Research, 52,* 763-771.

Tracy, K., & Baratz, S. (1993). Intellectual discussion in the academy as situated discourse. *Communication Monographs, 60,* 300-320.

Treadwell, D. F., & Harrison, T. (1994). Conceptualizing and assessing organizational image. *Communication Monographs, 61,* 63-85.

Trevino, L. K., Daft, R. L., & Lengel, R. H. (1990). Understanding managers' media choices: A symbolic interactionist perspective. In J. Fulk & C. Steinfield (Eds.), *Organizations and communication technology* (pp. 71-94). Newbury Park, CA: Sage.

Triandis, H. C., & Albert, R. D. (1987). Cross-cultural perspectives. In F. M. Jablin, L. L. Putnam, K. H. Roberts, & L. W. Porter (Eds.), *Handbook of organizational communication: An interdisciplinary perspective* (pp. 264-296). Newbury Park, CA: Sage.

Trice, H., & Beyer, J. (1993). *The cultures of work organizations.* Englewood Cliffs, NJ: Prentice Hall.

Tushman, M. L., & Romanelli, E. (1985). Organizational evolution: A metamorphosis model of convergence and reorientation. In B. Staw & L. Cummings (Eds.), *Research in organizational behavior* (Vol. 7, pp. 171-222). Greenwich, CT: JAI.

Turner, B. (1992). The symbolic understanding of organizations. In M. Reed & M. Hughes (Eds.), *Re-thinking organization: New directions in organization theory and analysis* (pp. 46-66). London: Sage.

Van de Ven, A. H., & Poole, M. S. (1988). Paradoxical requirements for a theory of organizational change. In R. Quinn & K. Cameron (Eds.), *Paradox and transformation: Toward a theory of change in organizations and management* (pp. 19-63). Cambridge, MA: Ballinger.

Waldron, V. (1991). Achieving communication goals in superior-subordinate relationships. *Communication Monographs, 58,* 289-306.

Weick, K. E. (1979). *The social psychology of organizing* (2nd ed.). Reading, MA: Addison-Wesley.

Wert-Gray, S., Center, C., Brashers, D., & Meyers, R. (1991). Research topics and methodological orientations in organizational communication: A decade in review. *Communication Studies, 42,* 141-154.

West, C., & Zimmerman, D. (1987). Doing gender. *Gender & Society, 1,* 125-151.

Wigand, R. T. (1988). Communication network analysis: History and overview. In G. H. Goldhaber & G. A. Barnett (Eds.), *Handbook of organizational communication* (pp. 319-360). Norwood, NJ: Ablex.

Witten, M. (1993). Narrative and the culture of obedience at the workplace. In D. Mumby (Ed.), *Narrative and social control: Critical perspectives* (pp. 97-118). Newbury Park, CA: Sage.

Wood, J. T. (1992). Telling our stories: Narratives as a basis for theorizing sexual harassment. *Journal of Applied Communication Research, 20,* 349-362.

Zmud, R. (1990). Opportunities for strategic information manipulation through new information technology. In J. Fulk & C. Steinfield (Eds.), *Organizations and communication technology* (pp. 95-116). Newbury Park, CA: Sage.

# 3

# Discourse Analysis in Organizations

## Issues and Concerns

LINDA L. PUTNAM
*Texas A&M University*

GAIL T. FAIRHURST
*University of Cincinnati*

Language analysis has moved into a prominent place in organizational studies. Once the domain of scholars of linguistics and sociology, language is more than just a specialized vernacular or a unique code system. Although language is vital for understanding organizational symbols, recent shifts in both organizational theory and discourse analysis suggest that language is more than elements of narrative structure and words that reflect themes, rules, and norms of behavior. Even though discourse analysis is clearly a type of methodology, language is more than an analytical tool used to gain insights about organizational constructs. Finally, although the study of language is an interdisciplinary pursuit in its own right, discourse patterns fuse with organiza-tional processes in ways that make language and organizations a unique domain—one that differs from the study of linguistics in general and discourse analysis in other social settings. To begin the process of building theory in this area, this chapter reviews the literature on language and organization and delineates specific challenges in this research domain.

The interdisciplinary roots of language analysis date back to rhetorical and literary studies, particularly ones that originated with the philosophical treatises of the ancient Greeks more than 2,000 years ago (van Dijk, 1985). The rhetorical and literary perspectives drew from poetics and examine figures of speech such as metaphors, metonymy, synecdoche, and irony (Brown, 1977). Other approaches in the rhetorical tradition focused on persuasion, argumentation, and reasoning (Toulmin, 1958). These studies centered on language's strategic functions of making claims, supporting positions, and developing relationships between audiences and speakers/writers. The entry of anthropology and sociology into the study of words and grammatical forms marked the beginning of applying modern linguistics to social and historical texts. In the 1960s, the French structuralists broadened linguistic analyses by focusing on the context of utterances, genres of discourse, and social situations. Drawing from these views, theorists of social construction and phenomenology examined subjective and intersubjective meanings that emanated from language use, and critical theorists highlighted the way discourse aids in suppressing voice through hegemony, unobtrusive control, and ideology.

The rise of poststructuralism, with its emphasis on the science of signs, cast language as a structural system of relationships in which meanings and signification are constantly deferred (Huyssen, 1986; Saussure, 1916/1974). Poststructuralists contend that words and texts have no fixed or stable meanings. Object, ideas, and symbols are constituted through signifiers or referents linked to other referents. They purport that webs of practices embodied in discourses become logics of surveillance, disciplinary practices, and histories of texts (Foucault, 1979; Townley, 1993). Discourse is also a salient component of deconstruction, in which researchers disassemble texts by examining the privileging and concealing of words and antinomies (Derrida, 1982). Another postmodern approach that centers on discourse is actor-network theory in which scripts reflexively constitute networks of texts that become centered and decentered (Akrich & Latour, 1992; Latour, 1988, 1996b). Clearly, the study of language and discourse in the process of organizing has reached its maturity; consequently, it needs synthesis and critique as an ontological base for the study of organizations.

## DEFINITIONS AND FRAMEWORK FOR THE CHAPTER

Discourse analysis, in this chapter, is defined as the study of words and signifiers, including the form or structure of these words, the use of language in context, and the meanings or interpretation of discursive practices (Fairhurst & Putnam, 1998). Language analyses encompass the study of verbal codes, utterances, conversations, interaction patterns, and signs. In this chapter, discourse is viewed as a way of knowing or a perspective for understanding organizational life. It is a lens or a point of entry for seeing, learning, and understanding ongoing events. As a lens, it provides a unique way to focus on the subtle aspects of organizing and to determine what is figure and ground in the framing of organizational events.

Even though language is intertwined with organizational symbols such as myths, rituals, and narratives, this review focuses directly on studies that make linguistic patterns the key to examining organizational life. Language is clearly central to the development of narrative text, but it is not identical to the structure of narratives as reflected in such elements as theme, plot, characterization, and scene. Hence, this chapter includes only those narrative studies of organizations that focus on the linguistics of storytelling. This essay includes studies on rhetorical analyses of organizations, particularly those that examine figures of speech such as troupes, irony, paradoxes, and dialogue.

Moreover, this chapter excludes essays that treat language and metaphors as metatheoretical perspectives for understanding the field (Boland & Greenberg, 1988; Morgan, 1980, 1997; Putnam, Phillips, & Chapman, 1996). Although these studies make valuable contributions, they represent a different body of literature, one that uses discourse to study the sociology of knowledge about organizational theory (Pinder & Bourgeois, 1982). In addition, this review mainly centers on studies that cross multiple organizational levels and units. Hence, investigations of doctor-patient interaction and clerk-customer exchanges that are primarily dyadic are not included in the purview of this chapter.

This essay undertakes a review and critique of the organizational discourse literature through unpacking the relationships among the constructs *language* and *organization.* Rather than presuming the existence of these constructs, this chapter seeks out the assumptions and their interconnections implicit in the use of these terms. This argument develops through a review, classification, and analysis of the organizational discourse literature.

To review and classify the literature, we employ a typology based on eight categories of language analysis: sociolinguistics, conversation analysis, cognitive linguistics, pragmatics, semiotics, literary and rhetorical language analysis, critical language studies, and postmodern language analysis. This classification scheme emanates from the literatures on discourse and organizations (Donnellon, 1986; Grant, Keenoy, & Oswick, 1998; Keenoy, Oswick, & Grant, 1997; Tulin, 1997) and represents a synthesis of the standard linguistic typologies (Haslett, 1987; van Dijk, 1985, 1997b). Even though these approaches differ in their emphases on discourse features, the categories are not "pure," nor are they mutually exclusive. Scholars often merge several approaches or borrow methodologies, foci, and constructs from different perspectives. What is critical in this chapter is an effort to reveal how language is defined and conceived in different studies, what features of discourse are privileged, and how discourse patterns relate to organizational processes and constructs.

These eight approaches draw from and highlight different features that become central in a particular discourse study. Discourse features refer to the characteristics or elements that comprise the language analysis. We contend that one or more features of language emerge as figure or become prominent in a study and the other elements remain in the background or are omitted from investigations. Eight interrelated features surface in this literature:

*Codes:* The features of naming, such as labels, jargon, vernacular, terminology, and signs

*Structure:* The patterns, order, syntax, sequence of words and phrases, and implicit/explicit rules for the use of discourse

*Function:* The purposes for language use and the links between discourse and organizational functions

*Language user:* The knowledge representations, expectations, scripts, frames, and cognition of users

*Meaning:* Interpretation, understandings, and reading of texts

*Text:* Sets of structured discourse patterns inscribed in organizations

*Context:* Organizational events, history, and parameters that shape interpretations of texts

*Intertextuality:* The interfaces between discourse, text, and institutional contexts

Although discourse analysts define these elements differently (e.g., shifting definitions of *texts* sometimes in the same studies), these elements frame the nature of studies and serve as a basis for analyzing language patterns. Determining which ones are privileged in a study and how these units are intertwined with organizational constructs and processes is the critical factor in organizational language analysis.

In addition, this review examines the way that discourse patterns relate to organizational processes and constructs. That is, researchers typically employ language as a tool for analyzing particular organizational constructs or processes. Hence, in many studies language analysis is a technique for conducting qualitative analysis. Researchers, then, are less interested in understanding discourse as a process of organizing and more concerned with particular constructs, for example, leadership, control/power, identity/image, conflict, or change. In other studies, language is treated as constitutive; therefore, organizational constructs grow out of the discourse, for example, identity or conflict. This chapter examines the language-organization relationship to see how discourse processes shape and are shaped by organizational constructs.

## DISCOURSE TYPOLOGIES IN ORGANIZATIONAL STUDIES

In the organizational arena, language analysis has focused on both written and oral discourse, including the talk of administrators (Gronn, 1983; Gummer, 1984), analysis of the production of corporate documents (Keller-Cohen, 1987), and the links between writing and talking at work (Baxter, 1993; Hawes, 1976; Kaufer & Carley, 1993). These studies have embraced both the rhetorical and literary traditions and the traditional linguistic roots for studying discourse.

Early research on the study of language in organizations grew out of two major strands of work: professional talk and organizational culture. About a decade before organizational researchers became interested in discourse, language researchers began to focus on talk in institutional settings. Drawing from the work in conversation analysis and sociolinguistics, researchers examined the patterns of talk that characterized doctor-patient interaction (Fisher & Todd, 1983; Korsch & Negrete, 1972; Mishler, 1984), legal settings (Conley & O'Barr, 1990; Levi & Walker, 1990), therapist-counselor interviews (Labov & Fanshel, 1977; Turner, 1972), and classroom interactions (Gumperz & Herasimchuk, 1975; Mehan, 1979; Sinclair & Coulthard, 1975; Stubbs, 1976). In general, these studies centered on the form and structure of everyday talk framed by roles, identity, or occupational constraints. Hence, the process of organizing per se was not a central feature of these studies.

Culture was another strand of research that championed the critical role of discourse in organizational studies (see Eisenberg & Riley,

Chapter 9, this volume). Defined as a unique sense of place that each organization offers (Pacanowsky & O'Donnell-Trujillo, 1983), studies of organizational culture examine the use of slogans, creeds, jokes, and stories as a lens for understanding organizational life. Often referred to as "organizational symbolism" (Dandridge, Mitroff, & Joyce, 1980), studies of language use in organizations became fused with myths, rituals, and cultural artifacts (Ouchi & Wilkins, 1985; Schein, 1985).

These pioneers of language analysis in organizations developed typologies rooted in linguistics and literary forms. For example, in the late 1970s, Pettigrew (1979) defined organizations "as language systems" and Pondy (1978) treated leadership as a "language game" in which linguistic formations were connected to actions. The dominant typologies that surfaced in the early organizational culture literature adhered to symbolic views of language, for example, vocabularies, themes, tropes (Johnson, 1977), or to linguistic views of discourse analysis, for example, ethnomethodology and speech acts (Hawes, 1976). Drawing from the linguistic perspective, Donnellon (1986) set forth a typology for examining language as a system of cognitions. She posited six approaches: linguistics, psycholinguistics, sociolinguistics, ethnography of speaking, ethnomethodology, and interaction analysis and advocated focusing on conversation analysis to investigate how language displayed and enacted organizational cognitions. Tulin (1997) echoed this commitment to conversation analysis, but she employed structuration theory as a way of moving conversation analysis beyond its ethnomethodological roots. For Tulin, conversation was an accomplishment, a process that engendered social order and constituted organizational phenomena.

Other approaches to discourse studies include linguistics, rhetoric, philosophy, literature, and cognitive science (O'Connor, 1994). These approaches illustrate how language functions as a reflexive social act that represents cultural production. More recently,

Keenoy et al. (1997) and Grant et al. (1998) highlight the critical and postmodern perspectives to the study of language. Through focusing on text and intertexuality, they trace the conceptual roots of organizational discourse to speech acts, ethnomethodology, and semiology, but note that these origins infuse contemporary studies that center on organizational stories, metaphors, language games, and texts. They introduce an important distinction between monologic and dialogic views of discourse analysis. A monologic view centers on an uncontested singular interpretation or preferred reading of a text while a dialogic focus examines the multiple voices that contribute to pluralistic, contested, and paradoxical meanings that evolve from the interpenetration of texts among groups over time. Pragmatic approaches to discourse analysis also make this distinction between monologic and dialogic readings of texts (Haslett, 1987).

This review of literature integrates and draws from these summaries to present a typology of eight categories of language analysis in organizations: sociolinguistics, conversation analysis, cognitive linguistics, pragmatics and discourse analysis, semiotics, literary and rhetorical analyses, critical language studies, and postmodern language analysis (Fairhurst & Putnam, 1998; Haslett, 1987; Putnam, 1990a, 1994). These eight differ in the features of discourse that are privileged and the way discourse relates to organizational processes and constructs. Some approaches differ radically in the definitions and assumptions that underlie language analysis in organizations.

## SOCIOLINGUISTICS

Sociolinguists treat language as an outgrowth of social categories. Researchers who embrace this perspective emphasize semantics or the lexicon that emanates from societal and structural differences, for example, so-cioeconomic class, education, or geographic location. Organizational studies on social class treat linguistic repertoires as housed within social systems. For example, Tompkins's (1962, 1965) study of communication within labor unions reveals semantic barriers and patterns of semantic information distance between hierarchical levels within the union. Tracing the roots of language to economic class, Tompkins also observes that union and corporate leaders share similar definitions of terminology while the rank and file differ from both groups in their perceptions of workplace vernacular. A study on language and the life-worlds of blue-collar and white-collar workers noted a similar pattern in that white-collar employees relied on bureaucratic language profiles while blue-collar workers draw from linguistic patterns rooted in technical production (Sands, 1981). To enhance their social and organizational positions, blue-collar women who have different ways of writing and talking pursue language education (Krol, 1991).

These class differences, however, become secondary to organizational variables in accounting for diversity in linguistic patterns. Basically, Tway (1975) reports no difference in lexical use between management and workers within the same department, but observes considerable variation across departments, especially when these units are geographically separated. Thus, departmental stratification and geographic separation account for distinct linguistic patterns among units.

Structural variables such as occupation, subculture groups, and hierarchical position also contribute to variations in linguistic repertoires. Specifically, scientists, especially biochemists, rely on technical and empirical talk in professional discourse but switch to contingency language in informal interactions about the field (Gilbert & Mulkay, 1984). These discourses produce contradictory positions when scientists engage in decision making about a pension fund (Cray, 1989).

For Barley (1983, 1986), differences between the vernacular of radiologists and technicians emanate from occupational training and organizational roles rather than from a universal scientific discourse. Occupations, then, functioned as speech communities that infuse organizations with specialized vocabularies (Coleman, 1985; Van Maanen & Barley, 1984). For example, bank tellers in a British financial institution emerge as a subculture through their routine avoidance of denominational words, such as *pound, note,* and *pence,* to shift attention away from the vast sums of money that flow through their hands (Taylor, 1987). In like manner, physicians employ highly specialized linguistic registers to produce medical reports. These registers incorporate abbreviations, use of technical terms, active verbs, length of utterances, and depersonalized pronouns (van Naerssen, 1985). Since doctors rarely receive formal training on how to write medical records, these patterns point to the existence of an occupationally based linguistic repertoire. Language also distinguishes occupational classification in the U.S. Navy with cadets using words like *spark, skivvy waver,* and *spook* to identify a radio operator, signal operator, and communication technician, respectively (Evered, 1983). Words, then, become markers for the class, occupation, and professional roles in organizations.

Linguistic repertoires also emerge from informal interactions among members of an organizational subculture. For instance, the nursing staff of a regional hospital uses a slang system to distinguish patients, referring to the more demanding ones as *crocks,* the members of stigmatized groups as *gomers,* and the physically unresponsive as *gorks* (Gordon, 1983). Although this language system seems dehumanizing and derogatory, it provides nurses with tension release that distances them from highly emotional situations. Drawing from the work of dialectical geographers and sociolinguists, Bastien (1992) examines different lexical systems in use within and between a parent company and an acquired company. In this study, individuals who either learn the language of the new com-

pany or hold onto their own lexical patterns are retained as employees in the new organization. Ironically, the groups that switch codes to adapt to both cultures either voluntarily resign or are downsized in the reorganization.

Finally, hierarchical position and organizational status are also structural features that differentiate lexical codes in organizations. Coleman (1985) links these different lexical systems to expertise and status in talking shop at work. Moreover, early organizational studies on the use of titles and forms of address reveal that this linguistic pattern is nonreciprocal and signifies status differences among employees (Brown & Ford, 1961; Slobin, Miller, & Porter, 1968, 1972). However, in organizations today, CEOs on down to the lower-ranked workers often exchange first names and refer to title and last name only in formal situations or in interactions with strangers (Morand, 1996). Morand hypothesizes that these changes evolve from an increase in lateral communication, organic forms of organizing, and informality in organizations over the past 30 years. Thus, in ambiguous or uncertain situations, name avoidance bridges power differences and enables subordinates to cope psychologically with the unfamiliar situations.

From a sociolinguistic perspective, language becomes a system or code in which organizational communities define their identities and relationships. Discourse indexes social structures; defines communication styles; and emanates from training, enculturation, and class systems that operate within and outside of the organization. In many ways, language as an artifact of organizations reflects occupation, department, and organizational role.

What is problematic in this approach is the treatment of organizational structures as social facts. Structures become fixtures or static forms rather than dynamic processes that emerge from organizational struggles. Meanings and interpretations of discourse are assumed rather than questioned; lexical codes surface as the central features of discourse.

Organizational constructs that this perspective privileges include structural units, roles, and levels. Issues of status and identity surface within the context variables of class, occupation, and position and emanate from organizational tasks and interaction settings (Drew & Heritage, 1992).

# CONVERSATION ANALYSIS

Unlike sociolinguistics, conversation analysis (CA) focuses on the structure of language rather than its code. Order, syntax, and sequence of interaction occur within a dynamic rather than a static context. Conversations are accomplishments, ones produced, renewed, and transformed locally through interactions (Drew & Heritage, 1992). The term *accomplishment,* derived from ethnomethodology, refers to implicit rules that guide the syntax and structure of successive talk turns. Although traditional CA examines the way institutions constrain interactions (Drew & Heritage, 1992), the enactment of talk in organizations differs from the accomplishment of conversations in everyday interaction.

Organizational studies that employ CA cluster into five areas: (1) the opening and closing of interactions (McLaughlin, 1984; Pomerantz & Fehr, 1997); (2) turn taking, including hesitations, interruptions, silences, and talkovers (Boden, 1994; Sacks, Schegloff, & Jefferson, 1974); (3) adjacency pairs, such as question/answer (Boden, 1994; Levinson, 1983); (4) the initiation and management of topics (McLaughlin, 1984); and (5) patterns for handling conversational problems, such as disclaimers, alignments, accounts, and repairs (Hewitt & Stokes, 1975; Stokes & Hewitt, 1976).

## *Openings and Closings*

Openings and closings of conversations played a critical role in shaping identities and managing impressions in institutional settings. For example, in a hospital setting, su-

pervisory physicians must oversee the performance of internists without undermining the student's competency or authority as the "physician in charge" (Pomerantz, Fehr, & Ende, 1997). Hence, supervising physicians employ spatial positioning, ambiguous references, and such words as *working with, working together,* to equalize the role of intern and physician. In a job interview setting, recruiters manage impressions of their companies through using a sequence of summaries, positive statements, and continuity of interactions to close conversations with applicants (Ragan, 1983).

## *Turn Taking*

Turn taking, the second area of conversational research in organizations, is aligned with power and control and the very concept of organizing. A turn refers to the utterances that mark a speaker's control of the floor. Coordinating conversations through turn taking focuses on the length of a turn, the rules for holding and allocating the floor, and the use of overlaps and interruptions to gain the floor (McLaughlin, 1984). Specifically, in market negotiations bargainers use hesitations, self-correction, and slow speech followed by increased volume and interruptions to gain control of the floor and signal agreement (Neu, 1988).

Other studies, particularly ones concerned with gender in organizations, focus on turn taking as manifestations of power (Tannen, 1994). In committee meetings, male supervisors talk longer and interrupt their colleagues more often than do female supervisors (James & Clarke, 1993; Woods, 1988; Zimmerman & West, 1975); their interruptions are aimed at clarifying issues, voicing agreements, and influencing the directions of conversations (Kennedy & Camden, 1983). However, in meetings in which both genders share the agenda, female committee members talk as long as their male counterparts do and joke, argue, and solicit responses more often than their male members do (Edelsky, 1981). Thus, opportunity to communicate and expectations mediate the use of talk turns and exert control in meetings. In a similar way, conversational sequences both tighten and loosen administrative reins in interactions between a school principal and his immediate subordinates (Gronn, 1983). Thus, turn taking in conversations functions both to empower and to control organizational meetings, depending on whether organizational members are involved in shaping agendas and meeting activities.

Leaving aside power issues, Boden (1994) emphasizes the organizing capacity of turn taking and turn-taking mechanisms such as adjacency pairs (e.g., question-answer, query-response). Because organizational action coheres as a sequence, the sequential pacing of talk is "deeply implicative of organizations themselves" (Boden, 1994, p. 206). She examines organizational agenda setting, report giving, decision making, and turn taking in interactional and sequential terms, thus highlighting what is organizing about discourse itself.

### Adjacency Pairs

The third area of CA in organizations, the use of adjacency pairs or message sequences, is also linked to power and control. The term *adjacency pair* refers to a message/response sequence that occurs in a predictable manner, for example, question/answer, request/acceptance, demand/response. In job interview and training sessions, power relationships surface through the use of question-answer sequences. For example, answers to a job interviewer's question signal the applicant's comprehension or misunderstanding of the prior utterance. To keep the process controlled, interviewers rarely restate questions or correct the applicant. Rather, the applicant's ability to understand the interviewer's questions becomes a criterion for evaluating interviewee competence (Button, 1993). In job training programs, the use of marked speech and cryp-

tic answers disadvantage ethnic minorities in comparison with native speakers (Gumperz, 1992).

The use of adjacency pairs also reveals the way conversational patterns influence the design and management of communication systems. In an emergency dispatch setting, the management of call processing—the way that calls develop and are concluded—and the policies of particular organizations are oriented to the accomplishments of a request/response sequence (Whalen & Zimmerman, 1987; Zimmerman, 1992). Moreover, in a teachers' negotiation, use of a question-answer sequence is more effective than a demand-response sequence in eliciting information and concessions (Donohue & Diez, 1985).

### Topic Shifts

Power and control also surface as dominant organizational features in the fourth area of CA: topic shifts. Topic shifts refer to changes in the themes or sequences of events from one utterance to the next. In one study, male physicians exert more control in decision making through introducing a higher frequency of topic shifts than women doctors do (Ainsworth-Vaughn, 1992). In a labor-management negotiation, bargainers, by using question-answer sequences, position their own side's proposals as salient in the discussion (Frances, 1986). Ironically, mediators of organizational disputes also use topic shifts to control the interactions of disputants, reduce emotional outbursts, and move disputants toward settlements (Frances, 1986; Greatbatch & Dingwall, 1994).

### Disclaimers and Alignments

Differences between powerful and powerless speech are particularly salient in studies of the fifth area of CA in organizations: disclaimers and alignments (Haslett, 1987). Disclaimers are feedback strategies that aid in preventing conversational breakdowns, while alignments, accounts, and explanations are corrections used to repair conversational problems. Disclaimers qualify the force of utterances to avoid negative judgments through the use of metatalk, hedges, tag questions, and qualifiers. For example, statements like "I didn't mean it that way," "I'm not an authority on this issue," "This is your opinion, isn't it?" and "We *usually* take this course of action" exemplify the use of disclaimers.

Using disclaimers as indexes of speech, Fairhurst and Chandler (1989) illustrate the way subordinates display both powerful and powerless language to exert influence over their supervisors and preserve deference. Unlike in-group subordinates, out-group members use disclaimers and a verbatim report style to maintain social distance. In other studies, use of disclaimers reduces expert power, softens criticism, and facilitates group discussion (Dubois & Crouch, 1975; Holmes, 1984; Preisler, 1986). But in computer-mediated groups, use of disclaimers and powerless speech reduces credibility and the persuasiveness of group member messages (Adkins & Brashers, 1995). These studies indicate that disclaimers maintain role and status boundaries, foster efforts to include or empower subordinates, and influence judgments of credibility and persuasiveness among colleagues (Baker, 1991). Use of disclaimers in organizations, then, indicates that this language pattern is not necessarily a form of powerless speech. Mediating variables such as gender, expectations, and status influences both the use of and reaction to disclaimers.

Patterns of powerful and powerless speech surface in studies of alignments in organizational conversations. Alignments refer to the way that speakers use conversational devices to buffer or anticipate disruptions and misunderstandings (Stokes & Hewlitt, 1976). Through formulations, metatalk, accounts, and side sequences, alignments clarify meanings, convey intentions, and repair conversations. In employment situations, interviewers control conversational pacing through the use of summaries, formulations, and metatalk while applicants employ powerless forms of speech, such as qualifiers, speech fillers, and accounts (Ragan, 1983; Ragan & Hopper, 1981). But rather than suggesting powerlessness, the giving of accounts in selection interviews hinges on the interviewer's questions, the vulnerability of the job, and the applicant's recognition of his or her role (Morris, 1988). In selection interviews, accounts are regarded legitimate when they express doubts or interpretations of what the interviewer "is really asking." Account giving in conversations, then, underscores the relationship between interaction and social structure. That is, even when low-status participants offer accounts to gain access to the floor, these moves reflexively reaffirm the asymmetry and power differences between doctors and patients (Fisher & Groce, 1990) and between senators and witnesses in the Watergate hearings (Molotch & Boden, 1985).

CA highlights the structure of language through focusing on the syntax and coherence of interactions in organizations. Unlike the sociolinguistic perspective, both language and organizations are accomplishments; that is, power and control emanate from the way organizational members produce conversations and organizational roles influence the way that conversations are interactively structured. This perspective shows how conversations contribute to the production of organizational roles, for example, superiors-subordinates, labor-management, and interviewers-applicants; however, it presumes that organizations as entities exist prior to conversations. The focus of traditional CA, then, is primarily dyadic, centering on skilled activities and goal accomplishment of organizational members.

Within its ethnomethodological roots, moving CA to the macrolevel of analysis incurs inferential leaps. It is difficult to determine, even at the microlevel of meaning, that interruptions, silences, and sequencing of conversations reflect power or produce patterns of organizational control. That is, the structure of conversation itself is not necessarily reflective of the purposes, situations, and contextual history of participants (Haslett, 1987). Hence, differences in conversational patterns among men and women may reflect a number of organizational processes that are not apparent in the dyadic or group-level measures of interaction, for example, organizational culture, organizational identity, and even socialization patterns. However, work that explicitly combines ethnomethodology and conversation analysis, such as that by Boden (1994), has begun to address these issues.

In CA, producing, maintaining, and repairing conversations accomplish communication. Traditional conversation analysts rarely move away from a level of meaning or contextual understanding that is not embodied in the discourse. In like manner, language surfaces as conversational forms and structures that signify communication, for example, patterns of power and control in organizations. Although this perspective has a number of weaknesses, CA joins with speech act studies to form the foundation for discourse studies in organizations.

## COGNITIVE LINGUISTICS

One spin-off of CA is cognitive linguistics, the study of discourse patterns that arise from mental processes, such as scripts, schemata, and frames (Schank & Abelson, 1977; Weick, 1995). Unlike CA, cognitive linguistics privileges the link between discourse forms and language users. Individuals as language users interpret or make sense of discourse through matching linguistic patterns with commonsense knowledge of events (Haslett, 1987). This knowledge stems from personal and vicarious experiences, prototypes for grammatical forms, expected sequences of events, and the framing of events.

In organizational studies, cognitive linguistics falls into the broad category of sensemaking, an interpretive perspective that focuses on assigning meaning to organizational activities and processes (Gioia, 1986; Weick, 1995).

Language contributes to sensemaking through identifying how cognitive texts are structured, how they are read, and how they break from routine conversational patterns (Louis & Sutton, 1991). The use of metaphors, speech acts, and sociolinguistics evokes particular schemata, ones rooted in cultural practices and organizational structures (Moch & Fields, 1985). Studies of cognitive linguistics also centers on message production and on the ways that the mind stores and retrieves linguistic texts (Lord & Kernan, 1987). Four areas of organizational research exemplify the cognitive linguistic perspective: scripts and schemata, cognitive mapping, semantic networks, and frames.

### Scripts and Schemata

Scripts refer to mental representations or stereotypical sets of conversational events, for example, making a complaint, ordering a meal at a restaurant, conducting a job interview (Gioia & Poole, 1984). In the organizational literature, scholars employ language analysis to analyze scripts in performance appraisals (Gioia, Donnellon, & Sims, 1989), superior-subordinate relationships (Gioia & Sims, 1986), task coordination (Saferstein, 1992), and negotiations (Carroll & Payne, 1991). Interviewer use of positive expressions, subordinate use of acknowledgments early in the deliberations, and interviewer use of denials with low performers evolve from scripts that distinguish between low- and high-performing subordinates (Gioia et al., 1989). Other studies demonstrate that superiors' attributions of performance shift after they interact with their subordinates (Gioia & Sims, 1986).

In a negotiation setting, linguistic patterns reveal that novices share a common bargaining script, one that consists of incompatible interests, sequential issue settlement, impasse, and competitive behaviors (O'Connor & Adams, 1999). Many of these elements are linked to departures from rationality, such as faulty perceptions, encoding errors, and misinterpretation of information in negotiation situations (Carroll & Payne, 1991; Thompson & DeHarpport, 1994).

Schemata differ from scripts in referring to standards or general rules for moment-to-moment coordination (Weick, 1979). Language reflects organizational schemata, ones formed through hierarchical role and occupational expertise. Through schemata and semantic indirectness, discourse sedates targets and facilitates compliance with influence attempts (Drake & Moberg, 1986). Then, in interactions among members of a TV production team, individuals develop a common schema that translates into the script for a television drama (Saferstein, 1992).

## Cognitive Mapping

Cognitive mapping differs from scripts and schemata through focusing on causal links among elements of organizing (Weick, 1979; Weick & Bougon, 1986). Language functions as nodes or codes in which meaning resides in the pattern among words rather than in any one concept. Linguistic phrases, then, constitute a coherent set of meanings in a cause map (Weick, 1979). Cause maps are collective structures in which shared explanations for events emerge from composites of individual mental models. For example, in Hall's (1984) study of the *Saturday Evening Post,* policy concepts fit into a tight-fitting cognitive map that reveals an imbalance in strategic thinking, leading to the organization's ultimate demise. In the Utrecht Jazz Orchestra, phrases linked to organizational actions intertwine in causal links to form an orderly social structure. This structure reflects different patterns of phrases arrayed on a continuum from left to right (Ford & Hegarty, 1984; Roos & Hall, 1980).

In addition to actions, underlying values form a key component of cognitive maps. For instance, Huff's (1988, 1990) analysis of goals, values, and chain relationships in superintendents' and school board members' speeches impinge on the context in which

strategic planning occurs. In negotiations, bargainers who treat utility as a subjective value reach more integrative agreements than dyads who regard it as an outgrowth of interpersonal relations (Simons, 1993).

## Semantic Networks

Semantic networks, as a third arena of cognitive linguistics, also focus on patterns of meanings among organizational members (see Monge & Contractor, Chapter 12, this volume). The concept of *semantic networks* refers to the network patterns derived from linkages among individuals who have similar interpretations for the same words (Danowski, 1982; Monge & Eisenberg, 1987). Studies of semantic networks reveal differences between adopters and users of voice mail systems (Rice & Danowski, 1993), in annual reports prepared for U.S. and Japanese stockholders (Jang & Barnett, 1994), and in shared meanings for the concept *worker participation* within and between managers in five European countries (Stohl, 1993). Semantic networks, then, focus on the mapping or linkage of individuals who have similar meanings for words and phrases.

## Framing

Framing, as the fourth area of cognitive linguistic studies, refers to worldviews, fields of vision, or perspectives for managing meaning (Fairhurst & Sarr, 1996; Putnam & Holmer, 1992). Theorists differ as to whether frames are primarily cognitive heuristics that shape human judgment (Neale & Bazerman, 1991) or whether they are processes developed through discourse and interaction patterns (Fairhurst & Sarr, 1996; Gray, 1997; Putnam & Holmer, 1992). Despite its origins, framing is both mental and social and linked to the labels members assign to situations. A frame encompasses figure-ground relationships, ties abstract words to concrete cues, and defines the parameters for what is included or excluded in an event.

Organizational studies on framing examine such constructs as leadership, new information technology, organizational memory, and conflict. Leaders frame organizational experiences through creating and communicating visions, confronting unanticipated events, and influencing others (Fairhurst, 1993a; Fairhurst & Sarr, 1996). The development of language tools through metaphor, jargon, contrast, spin, and catchphrases are ways that leaders enact and convey corporate visions. Fairhurst (1993a) highlights how managers use these linguistic devices to link actions to the new vision, to tie this vision to old norms, and to reduce ambiguity about change. Managers who use framing to personalize changes during this process are more effective than leaders who ignore framing when communicating this vision.

Executive frames also function as filters for shaping what is noticed, how it should be managed, and how events should be categorized (Starbuck & Milliken, 1988). Discourse about corporate strategy among middle managers frames the microdynamics of inclusion and exclusion within the corporate inner circle (Westley, 1990). The framing of technological innovations as either concrete or abstract is another arena in which mental models influence organizational experiences, particularly in the way employees first notice and label a new feature as novel or innovative (Orlikowski & Gash, 1994).

Research on cognitive linguistics also surfaces as collective remembering in organizations (Edwards & Middleton, 1986; Kaha, 1989; Middleton & Edwards, 1990). Specifically, conversations about the past reaffirm collective frames when members recall moments of socialization, precedents in decision making, and breaks from routines (Walsh & Ungson, 1991; Weick & Roberts, 1993). In effect, language is the way that organizational members coconstruct remembering and for-

getting (Shotter, 1990) and embody organizational memory (Yates, 1990). In the arena of conflict management, framing functions as a cognitive heuristic for decision making, as a representation of categories of experience, and as a means of redefining and transforming contract issues (Putnam & Holmer, 1992).

The cognitive approach privileges meaning rather than linguistic structures and codes. Meanings, however, are stored in cognitive systems of users; thus, language is a behavioral code to reveal cognitive interpretations (Donnellon, 1986) and to represent knowledge structures of a collective mind (Fairclough, 1989). Organizations, in this sense, resemble the human brain (Morgan, 1997). Studies of leadership, performance appraisals, and negotiation within this perspective privilege sensemaking as the fundamental approach to studying discourse and organization.

## PRAGMATICS

Pragmatics is a broad term that refers to the study of language in context; hence, it is often treated as a generic category for a variety of discourse perspectives. Unlike cognitive linguistics and conversation analysis, pragmatics incorporates both the linguistic form and the communicative context of discourse; however, it privileges contextual features and focuses on discourse as action and symbolic interaction in speech communities. Although early studies examine isolated utterances, contemporary research centers on extended sequences of talk and the role of language in social contexts (Blum-Kulka, 1997). As with cognitive linguistics, meaning is a central feature of pragmatics, but action, context, and relationships contribute to the generative nature of meaning. In this perspective, individuals construct social actions through working out discrepancies between what is said and what is meant. This review of the pragmatic perspective highlights three schools: speech acts, ethnography of speaking, and interaction analysis. These schools of pragmatic studies, however, differ in the assumptions they make about language, the role of structure, and the way meaning enters into the organizing process.

## Speech Acts

Speech act theory, drawn from the writings of Austin (1962) and Searle (1969), treats language as action. That is, by simply being uttered, words such as *promising, requesting, warning, asserting,* and *apologizing* perform actions through what is said. Speech acts, then, focus on functions and language texts rather than on code or linguistic structure. This approach assumes that a speaker's motives and intentions are embodied in what he or she says. Research on speech acts also addresses appropriate conventions of expression and ways to execute utterances effectively. The success of a speech act depends on the condition and rules necessary to execute actions embodied in the utterances. Searle (1979) sets forth five general types of speech acts, but only three of them, directives, politeness, and accounts, surface in the organizational literature.

*Directives.* Directives are speech acts that convey requests, invitations, instructions, orders, and/or commands. In the organizational arena, researchers study both the explicit and implicit use of directives. Comparing men and women in a volunteer task group, K. Jones (1992) finds no gender differences in the frequency, target, and types of directives in a group. Status variation and context intertwine to set the conditions for appropriate use of directives. Specifically, using expressions of solidarity in combination with speech acts overcomes the face-threatening potential of directive use. Similarly, in a formal contract negotiation, alignment of goals between teachers and administrators affect the appropriateness of directives (Donohue & Diez, 1985). Questions are more effective than imperative statements in eliciting information from the other side and in softening the blow of directives, particularly in the early stages of bargaining.

Another factor that affects the use of directives is expertise. In a study that compares different mediums of communication (e.g., e-mail, teleconferencing, face-to-face), Murray (1987) reports that project managers at IBM use promises to comply with requests or they reject them implicitly by invoking background knowledge and expertise. Moreover, novices lack detail in specifying their requests while experts overspecify their directives. Expertise also differentiates knowledge of radiologists and technologists, as evident in Barley's (1986) study of direction giving, countermands, and questions among new CT scanner users in an urban hospital.

As Murray's (1987) study illustrates, implicit use of directives functions as a form of politeness, particularly when subordinates communicate with superiors. Referred to as mitigators, implicit directives use words that soften the impact of requests and avoid triggering offense, such as *might, could, okay,* and *right.* In a study of Air Force crew members, Linde (1988) notes that the use of mitigators affects the interactional success of requests, which, in turn, influences safety and crew performance. Excessive use of indirect requests, particularly combined with topic change, however, may lead to ignoring requests and endangering the safety of the crew. Hence, excessive use of this type of directive may reduce compliance with a message.

*Politeness and facework.* Just as mitigators convey politeness, facework uses language to negotiate rights and obligations, to protect face, and to preserve autonomy. During bargaining, negotiators phrase demands ambiguously to defend face and to repair identity damaged through exchanging concessions. Politeness remarks simultaneously attack opponents through asserting a firm position and protect them through conceding on issues (Wilson, 1992). In a more relationally based negotiation, a cyclical pattern develops in which negotiators seek to restore a hostage taker's face while the hostage taker attacks the negotiator's face. Hostage situations are more likely to end in suicide if the perpetrator attacks his or her own face (Rogan & Hammer, 1994). However, status hierarchies may impinge on facework, as in a quality of work life program when managers engage in explicit face-threatening acts while employees respond with off-the-record and negative politeness strategies (O'Donnell, 1990). Thus, politeness remarks function as double-edged strategies for negotiating rights and preserving identity and autonomy.

*Accounts and justifications.* Accounts are linguistic patterns that function as explanations for unanticipated or untoward behavior (Scott & Lyman, 1968). As explanations, they address why something happened or why someone failed to do what was expected. Accounts encompass the use of excuses and justifications to address problematic actions. However, in using excuses the offending party admits that the behavior in question is wrong, but he or she denies responsibility for it; in using justifications a person admits personal responsibility for the untoward action but he or she denies the negative consequence of the action.

Analysis of accounts in organizations falls into the categories of superior-subordinate interaction, job interviews, conflict management, and decision making. In superior-subordinate interaction, managers give accounts in performance evaluations, budget request denials, announcements of layoffs, and justifications for unethical conduct (Bies & Sitkin, 1992). Research also focuses on the believability and effectiveness of subordinates' accounts when managers confront them about performance problems. In general, research suggests that use of accounts enhances subordinate perceptions of fairness in performance reviews and budget cuts (Bies & Shapiro, 1988; Bies, Shapiro, & Cummings, 1988; Greenberg, 1991), reduces a subordinate's feelings of anger (Baron, 1990), and enhances

adjustments and organizational commitment in layoff situations (Rousseau & Anton, 1988). Use of accounts in unethical situations reduces the negative effects of such actions as a boss taking credit for a subordinate's ideas (Bies & Shapiro, 1987), an employee disclosing information about errors to customers (Sitkin, Sutcliffe, & Reed, 1993), and a boss responding to charges of unethical company behavior (Garrett, Bradford, Meyers, & Becker, 1989). However, the prior history of the excuse-giver and the gender of the target influence the acceptability of accounts. That is, males and females evaluate excuses differently (Giacalone, 1988).

Employees also use social accounts to mitigate evaluations of poor performance. Even though these accounts reduce blame (Wood & Mitchell, 1981) and lead to more lenient disciplinary actions (Gioia & Sims, 1986), their plausibility depends on whether managers have experienced a similar situation, the employee has a good reputation, and the subordinate provides corroborating evidence (Morris & Coursey, 1989). Moreover, the use of apologies coupled with expressions of regret and promises to rectify the problem are more effective than the use of excuses (Braaten, Cody, & DeTienne, 1993).

Accounts enter into job interviews when applicants express doubts about their qualifications and when they interpret interviewers questions (Morris, 1988). Interviewers who provide excuses for rejecting job candidates receive higher ratings of fairness than do those who fail to give explanations (Bies & Moag, 1986; Bies & Shapiro, 1988). In other types of asymmetric interviews, such as a doctor-nurse interactions, subordinates give accounts through telling stories to display competence, to manage impressions, and to maintain institutional dominance (Fisher & Groce, 1990).

In addition to superior-subordinate interactions and job interviews, accounts aid in managing conflicts. Three types of accounts surface in conflict situations: provision of mitigating circumstances, exonerating explanations, and reframing (Sitkin & Bies, 1993).

Managers typically combine mitigating circumstances with control-oriented actions to handle confrontations. They typically avoid fault finding and seek explanations based on exonerating circumstances (Morris, Gaveras, Baker, & Coursey, 1990). In conflict situations, use of multiple explanations results in more effective outcomes than does providing only one account.

Accounts also function to buffer interactions against the potential for a conflict and to justify decisions (Bies, 1989; Schonbach, 1990). In commodity negotiations, accounts function as ways to identify and challenge relevant information and to secure agreements (Firth, 1994). They serve as premises for supporting and opposing proposals, for selecting targets of identification, and for developing decision premises (Geist & Chandler, 1984; Tompkins & Cheney, 1983). In effect, organizational accounts function proactively as strategies in conflict management and as creative ways to solve problems.

In addition to the study of accounts, speech acts serve as metaphors for understanding organizational change and business communication conventions. In this sense, organizational change emanates from discourses of initiating, understanding, performing, and closing— types of speech acts that invoke actions (Ford & Ford, 1995). Speech acts also provide a grammar for business failures through opting out, clashing, flouting, and violating rules (Ewald & Strine, 1983). These macrolevel approaches treat planned change and business failures as discursive practices composed of networks of speech acts rather than programs of strategic decisions.

Overall, the study of speech acts integrates language research with organizational action. In these studies, speech acts produce the process of organizing by simply being spoken. The shortcomings of this approach evolve from the speaker-listener relationship, the role of meaning in this perspective, and the link between discourse and action. Studies of speech acts often neglect the role of the listener in producing what is said; hence, meaning becomes removed from the dynamics of interaction. Similarly, the link between language and action in research on speech acts is too linear, sequential, literal, and direct to address complex relationships between communicating and organizing. Organization intentions are not neatly embodied in what is said, and the execution of utterances has political as well as contextual ramifications.

## Ethnography of Speaking

Ethnography of speaking differs from speech acts in its focus on the immediate interactive context and the local accomplishments of organizing. Ethnography combines research on discourse, speech acts, and conversations to provide a basis for understanding expectations and typifications of actors (Spencer, 1994). In this perspective, discourse is more than talk— it is a way of encompassing the everyday routines of organizational members. Discourse and social meanings intertwine with immediate context to constitute the process of organizing and the nature of speech communities. Researchers within this perspective rely on naturalistic observations, field notes, and transcriptions to analyze how discourse is reflexively linked to organizational context. Studies of ethnography of speaking cluster into five categories: speech communities, communication rules, conversational performances, storytelling as performances, and symbolic interaction.

*Speech communities.* In this cluster of studies, speech situations provide a multilevel taxonomy for studying the appropriateness of language use in particular settings (Hymes, 1972). Speech communities coalesce around shared language use and schemata for interpreting linguistic codes. Studies that fall into this category typically highlight the lexical and semantic fields, cultural functions of language, and ways that language enacts community. Rather than being treated in isolation, communities shape the rules for and enact the meanings of speech acts such as joking, requesting, and demanding.

Research on language and speech communities contrast newcomers with veterans (Fletcher, 1990, 1991; Sigman, 1986; Van Maanen, 1973, 1978), note differences between professional and lay audiences in educational decision making (Mehan, 1983), and identify in-group and out-group members in leadership situations (Fairhurst, 1993b; Fortado, 1998; Morrill, 1991). Research on speaking culturally in organizations highlights the distinctiveness and functions of speech codes in Teamsterville (Philipsen, 1975, 1992), the language of veterans versus rookies at the police academy (Van Maanen 1973, 1978), and the native views of cultures and subcultures among Silicon Valley employees (Gregory, 1983). In the blue-collar, multiethnic working class of Teamsterville, language varies in levels of abstraction across occupational communities (Philipsen, 1992). In like manner, aphorisms, tag questions, denials, and indexical pronouns are guides to the underworld of cops. They paradoxically signal inclusion while they reaffirm that outsiders are excluded (Fletcher, 1991).

The accomplishment of task coordination and decision making also differentiates language use among organizational subgroups. For example, the activities of client selection and decision making about services emanate from different understandings of the term *battered woman* that surfaces in a women's clinic (Loseke, 1989). Labeling also influences expectations and behaviors of staff members who adjust to work at the women's shelter and to new residents in a nursing home. Terminology such as *Dr. Johnson's syndrome* and *auditions* characterizes residents who either refuse to accept their new home or are shunned by other residents. Labels, in this sense, indicate how similar or how different a new employee is from other individuals in his or her immediate area (Sigman, 1986).

The development of written documents involves task coordination rooted in negotiations between speech communities. Writing and talking, then, become forms of social interaction in which contrasting expectations of the function and audience of texts differentiate discourse communities (Pogner, 1999), shape who uses and has access to different modes of discourse (Hawes, 1976), and privilege speech community preferences for "talking things through" versus "putting them in writing" (Baxter, 1993). Use of imperative statements in technical communication becomes instances of task negotiation in which knowledge engineers and domain experts interpret ambiguity in standards and present diverse views of organizational accountability (Irons, 1998).

In like manner, educators responsible for making decisions about student enrollments in a special education program differentiate between the language of lay and professional advisers. In particular, phrases such as "the child has problems" locates the child's difficulties in internal and private causes rather than in institutional conditions. The mystique of this technical vocabulary privileges the judgment of professionals in these decisions (Mehan, 1983). Additional studies reveal that the laws governing public education, the amount of money allotted to school districts, and political considerations such as "out of district placement" also influence the pragmatics of what is said in decision-making meetings (Mehan, 1987).

Language also identifies informal speech communities in organizations. In conflicts among executives of CEO corporations, discourse that characterizes chivalry, warfare, and sports serves as a code of honor to distinguish the more from the less honorable employees. The culture of honor provides stability and predictability in uncertain and ambiguous times (Morrill, 1991, 1995). Use of nicknames in six different organizations also creates a speech community in which subordinates pit themselves against authorities to humanize the organizational process (Fortado, 1998).

The role of humor in organizations demonstrates how talk unites subcultures, relieves tension, and orders the social world. Ironically, the use of humor in the workforce also segments subcultures, creates stress, and highlights incongruencies. Self-deprecating jokes told by organizational newcomers create a bond to unite new and returning employees and to facilitate the accomplishment of work tasks (Vinton, 1989), but humor divides through separating high-authority figures from low-status personnel, as Coser (1959, 1960) observes in hospital administration meetings. In like manner, use of hyperboles and analogies in a university-based outpatient clinic segments physicians from residents and residents from nurses (Yoels & Clair, 1995). Humor unifies school staff members through embracing organizational values, but it also segments them through accenting belittling behaviors (Meyer, 1997). Joking lessens social distance between managers and workers (Duncan, 1983; Duncan & Feisal, 1989), but it maintains group boundaries through types of jokes told and behaviors deemed acceptable (Linstead, 1985; Sykes, 1966).

While humor releases tension and defuses nervousness, it also creates stress through increasing ambiguity and challenging the status quo. For example, lower-ranking police officers poke fun at shift sergeants and test the limits of permissible behaviors (Pogrebin & Poole, 1988). Poking fun aids in processing new information, reducing uncertainty (Ullian, 1976), and relieving boredom of meaningless work (Roy, 1960). However, it also demands a playfulness with language that highlights the incongruency of the absurd, irrational, and unexpected while helping participants establish order and consistency at work (Boland & Hoffman, 1986). Research on language in organizations, then, demonstrates how humor unites and divides, releases tension and creates stress, and reveals incongruencies while enabling employees to reaffirm multiple perspectives and develop a congruent social order.

Research on leadership also demonstrates how language aids in developing speech communities, particularly through enabling leaders to promote visions for change and to define in-group and out-group relationships. Leaders employ discourse to mobilize mean-ing, to alter the prevailing wisdom, and to define what needs to be done. For example, in a case study of an insurance company president, Smircich and Morgan (1982) observe how the military phrase and imagery of "Operation June 30th" failed to incite action in getting employees to act with urgency and cooperation to reduce a backlog of claims.

Moreover, leaders and subordinates bond together in speech communities through using linguistic resources to constitute relational and group identities. Fairhurst (1993b) analyzes the work conversations of six leaders and 16 subordinates to identify discourse patterns that characterize high, medium, and low leader-member exchange (LMX). She reports that high LMX members are marked by the posing of broad questions, brainstorming, building common ground, and engaging in nonroutine problem solving, while low LMXs demonstrate more performance monitoring, face-threatening acts, and power games.

*Communication rules.* The study of rules that govern language use in particular settings extends the research on speech communities (Hymes, 1972). Communication rules are guidelines for appropriate actions; that is, rules are "followable, prescriptive, and contextual" (Haslett, 1987, p. 35) and account for the enactment of genres, roles, and rituals (Shimanoff, 1980). Through commonsense knowledge and past experiences, individuals share agreement on and an understanding of communication rules. Reactions to rule-governed behavior include compliance, noncompliance, ignorance, forgetfulness, and reflectiveness. In cases where misunderstandings occur and rules are violated, interactants may negotiate new rules for language use.

Organizational studies on communication rules examine how broadly defined rules emerge as narrowly defined procedures, for example, in the interactions within two narcotics enforcement units (Manning, 1977). Research also centers on rule invocation, simulation, and implementation in a health care group involved in potential layoffs (Sigman & Donnellon, 1989); on rules as a master contract (Harris & Cronen, 1979); and on insider-confirmed rules for exercising influence in two interfacing work groups (Schall, 1983). These studies affirm Manning's (1977) finding that participants invoke communication rules to influence interaction behaviors, bureaucratic procedures, and task activities in organizations.

*Conversational performances.* Within the broad rubric of ethnography of speaking, researchers also focus on the enactment of speech events rather than on the characteristics of speech communities or the rules for appropriate discourse in these settings. Hence, language not only symbolizes and manifests speech communities, it creates the performances of organizational life. Studies on conversational performances typically examine talk in the enactment of an event, a process, or an activity. Talk is the way conversation events are accomplished or the way discourse fuses with action to produce performances.

Just as leaders use language to manage meanings and negotiate in-group and out-group relationships, they also engage in conversational performances that are interactional, contextual, episodic, and improvisational (Pacanowsky & O'Donnell-Trujillo, 1983). Trujillo's (1983, 1985) study of Lou Polito, the owner of a car dealership, demonstrates how a leader invokes hierarchy, engages in playful episodes, accomplishes mutual recognition, and develops knowledge through conversational performances. Both Polito's selection of words and his sequences of discourse enact routines that illustrate how he leads. Leadership, in this sense, mobilizes resources and enacts organizing.

In a similar way, flight attendants engage in conversational performances. They perform highly patterned public announcements through engaging in increased loudness, use of pauses, elevation of pitch changes, and segmentation of phrases (Banks, 1994). These performances contribute to self-efficacy by controlling and regulating passenger safety while simultaneously attending to their com-

fort. These stylized performances also aid in managing tensions between contradictory goals and loss of self-identity in the presence of social fragmentation.

Other studies examine conversation performances in informal meetings and within cross-functional teams. Namely, informal problem-solving sessions, as unplanned activities, occur in high-tech manufacturing firms against the backdrop of frequent formal meetings (Mangrum & Wieder, 1997). The use of short turns, frequent shifts in turn talk, and immediate feedback keeps participants on track and integrates contributions more effectively than do conversations in formal meetings. Cross-functional teams employ conversational performances to balance integration and differentiation across units (Donnellon, 1994, 1996). Use of imperative verbs, linguistic markers, and repeated pronoun references allow members to negotiate the contradictions that emerge from conflicting goals between units, the need for control, and the drive to both assimilate and distance team members from their functional units.

Conversational performances also enact major events such as the decision to strike or the enactment of a merger/acquisition. In a simulation of an organization, Donnellon, Gray, and Bougon (1986) examine the sequential and multilevel interactions among department members who use language to legitimate a decision to strike. Their reliance on linguistic indirection, argumentative appeals, and changes in affect result in a climate of confusion, which, in turn, supports the decision to strike. In a similar manner, the language of takeover in a merger situation facilitates diffusion and legitimation through sustaining order despite disruption. Stages and patterns that depict a hostile takeover vary over time, as reflected in the public discourse of courtship, warfare, and chivalry (Hirsch, 1986). In both instances, language legitimates decisions and shapes organizational actions.

Studies of conversational performances center on the way discourse and action intertwine to accomplish organizing and to enact speech communities. This approach to discourse analysis centers on the patterns or regularities that define speech episodes of leading, managing tensions, negotiating contradictory goals, and accomplishing organizational events.

*Storytelling performances.* In a similar manner, storytelling in organizations involves linguistic performances as well as narrative scripts. Studies of organizational narratives typically highlight the characters, scene, plots, and themes of narratives; they rarely center on the linguistic features of telling a story. Storytelling as performance occurs naturally in conversations through turn-by-turn situations (Jefferson, 1978), the joint construction, and the enactment of narratives (Boje, 1991). The dynamics of storytelling examine the way narratives are introduced in ongoing interactions, how listeners react and alter stories, and how stories affect subsequent dialogues. When stories become eclipsed, terse, or reduced to clichés and labels, language enacts these changes through narrative patterns and structures (Gabriel, 1998).

Research suggests that narrative performances differentiate among organizational subgroups, signal turbulence and organizational change, and aid in diagnosing problems. In particular, executives, venders, and salespeople use different mechanics such as filling in the blanks, glossing, and digressions to tell stories about organizational change (Boje, 1991). In times of turbulence and organizational change, members share terse and highly abbreviated narratives. As storytelling increases, the decision to proceed often weaves together multiple and ongoing narratives to enact themes for why and how changes are occurring (O'Connor, 1997). In many cases, storytelling emanates from organizational situations, such as repairing a broken copier, and it involves constructing identities between the past and present, socializing novices, and addressing problems in ambiguous situations. In these performances, storytelling moves from second to first person, from general to concise, and from descriptive

to didactic purposes (Orr, 1990). Moreover, each retelling of stories must incorporate different contexts, audience members, and historical circumstances. For example, Holt (1989) examines linguistic devices that constrain narrative characters and restrict performance features of storytelling in organizations. Transcriptions from six different organizations demonstrate how storytellers are bound by rules and yet free to act and how their reinterpretations of events emanate from codefinitions of self and organizations.

*Symbolic interaction.* The fifth type of research in ethnography of speaking privileges context and meaning rather than lexical codes, communication rules, or speech communities. Drawing from the work of G. H. Mead (1934) and Hubert Blumer (1969), symbolic interaction is a metatheory that includes a variety of schools of thought, particularly ones aligned with constructivist views of social reality. This perspective purports that human beings act toward other people based on meanings that are derived from social interactions and rooted in language and symbols. Symbolic interaction is situated directly in the world of social experience in which meanings are the keys to rich descriptions of self, social settings, and organizational actions (Schwandt, 1994).

Organizational structures and practices emerge through ongoing interactions and negotiations. Following Strauss's (1978) work, all social order is negotiated; hence, organizing is not possible without negotiation. Negotiations are patterned through lines of communication that establish, renew, revise, and reconstitute structural changes in organizing (Eisenberg & Riley, 1988; Fine, 1984). Most negotiated order studies focus on social actions and treat discourse as a taken-for-granted feature of organizations. However, Mellinger (1994) examines medical directives in radio calls between paramedics and emergency room nurses at a hospital. In this situation, the use of *if-then* language, mitigators, suggestions, and directive-response sequences function as directives to shape organizational reality. Paramedics and nurses are more likely to use directives to negotiate organizational order, if new information is provided, if actions need hospital coordination, and if paramedics are unable to fulfill an original suggestion. In like manner, Donohue and Roberto (1993) employ negotiated order to study the interaction patterns of ten FBI hostage negotiations. Disputants in this setting make, accept, and reject orders implicitly through using verbal immediacy to define the limits of their relationship.

Overall, ethnography of speaking centers on the way language accomplishes organizing through defining speech communities, adhering to communication rules, enacting conversational performances, producing storytelling, and negotiating orders. Ethnography of speaking combines semantic patterns of speech communities with linguistic structures to examine the social meanings of organizing. Studies center on the distinctiveness and functions of professional codes, accomplishments of task coordination and decision making, informal processes of conflict management, leader-member relationships, and organizational change. Sensemaking arises from the way that language typifies speech communities as well as from the meanings that organizational actors coconstruct through the process of organizing.

## Interaction Analysis

Interaction analysis shifts the focus of pragmatics away from speech acts, codes, and communication rules to the functions and structures of talk. This approach uses standardized procedures for coding verbal behavior to examine categories and meanings embedded in structural patterns of talk (Poole, Folger, & Hewes, 1987). The literature in this area clusters into five different types of research: interaction process analysis, behaviorist studies, systems-interaction research, negotiation research, and adaptive structuration interpretive coding. Studies across the five types differ in their observational modes (real-time observation, time sampling, or coding from tapes and transcripts); unit of analyses (speaking turn, thought unit, speech act; act, interact, double interact; act-to-act or phase); study designs (simulation vs. naturally occurring conversation); length of interactions studied (20 minutes or more); nature of the coding scheme (a priori or derived from the data); type of coding required (univocal or multifunctional); type of analyses (distributional or sequential); and theoretical base (e.g., reinforcement theory, systems theory, negotiation, structuration).

*Interaction process analysis.* Among the earliest interactional studies are those based on Bales's (1950) interaction process analysis (IPA), a coding scheme for analyzing the task/instrumental and socioemotional/expressive functions of group communication. Of the few organizational studies using IPA, Sargent and Miller's (1971) investigation of autocratic and democratic leaders is perhaps the best known. They report that democratic leaders use more questions and encouragement to increase participation, while autocratic leaders aim to enhance productivity by giving more orders and answering more questions. The SYMLOG (an acronym for systematic, multiple-level observation of groups) scheme, also based on Bales's pioneering work, is used to assess group interaction along three dimensions: dominance-submissiveness, friendly-unfriendly, and task orientation-emotional expressiveness (Bales & Cohen, 1979; for a review, see Keyton & Wall, 1989). Although Bales and Cohen (1979) present an interaction scoring method for observers, most organizational studies use retrospective rating methods for coding social interaction (e.g., Boethius, 1987; Cegala, Wall, & Rippey, 1987; Farrell, Schmitt, & Heinemann, 1988; Jesuino, 1985; Schantz, 1986).

*Behaviorist studies.* A second type of interactional analysis draws from reinforcement theory and the behaviorist tradition (Skinner, 1957, 1974). Based on the principles of operant conditioning, Komaki and colleagues employ the Operant Supervisory Taxonomy and Index (OSTI) to study the impact of leader monitoring on improved work unit performance (Komaki, Zlotnick, & Jensen, 1986). A comprehensive review of this research program can be found in Komaki (1998). Among the findings, Komaki (1986) reports that effective managers in a medical insurance firm spend more time in performance monitoring than do marginally effective managers. In a sailboat regatta where supervisory effectiveness is gauged by series standings, Komaki, Desselles, and Bowman (1989) observe that a skipper's racing success correlates significantly with the use of performance monitors and consequences. Finally, Komaki and Citera (1990) note that monitoring stimulates employees to talk about their own performance consequences, which encourages continued monitoring.

Based on work in leader reinforcement and punishment theory (Sims, 1977), goal setting theory (Locke, 1968), and social learning theory (Bandura, 1986), Sims and colleagues also address the relationship between employee performance and leader verbal behavior in their research on cognitive scripts. The organizational verbal behavior (OVB) categorization system codes for evaluation of employee performance and leader goal setting, task information, and attributions (Gioia et al., 1989; Gioia & Sims, 1986; Sims & Manz, 1984). Although this research is reviewed earlier in this chapter, it is worth noting that low-performing employees elicit several pronounced leader verbal behaviors, including frequent task-oriented statements, punitive statements and comparisons, and attribution requests (e.g., "Why haven't you finished this job?") (Gioia & Sims, 1986).

*Systems-Interaction Research.* Systems-interaction analysis, the third major type of research, is rooted in the application of systems theory to social interaction (e.g., Bateson,

1972; Fisher, 1978; Watzlawick, Beavin, & Jackson, 1967). This approach assumes that communicative acts in a social system constrain the options for future communicative behaviors in ways that develop unique and recognizable structured sequences. Redundancy or predictability of recurring communication patterns defines the structure of a system, while the nature and complexity of these patterns determine the system's function. The empirical focus of this research examines statistical patterning of acts and interacts to reveal how relational control arises from competing and dominating moves as opposed to neutral or leveling actions.

For example, Fairhurst and her colleagues use a relational control coding scheme developed by Rogers and Farace (1975) to examine control patterns in routine work interaction. Fairhurst, Rogers, and Sarr (1987) observe that manager dominance is linked to lower employee performance ratings, less understanding of employees, and lower employee desire for decision making. Courtright, Fairhurst, and Rogers (1989) examine control patterns in organic and mechanistic systems. They support Burns and Stalker's (1961) theory and observe more question-answer combinations in the organic system and more manager dominance and competitive patterns in the mechanistic system. Fairhurst, Green, and Courtright (1994) investigate the impact of plant history (organic from start-up or conversion to organic from mechanistic) and plant manager style (participative or autocratic) on manager-employee communication in five manufacturing plants. Conceptualized as sources of organizational inertia, a mechanistic history and an autocratic plant manager produce fewer challenges to managers' assertions and more employee approval seeking. When these inertial forces are absent, employees challenge manager assertions, initiate discussions, and experience less manager control than in mechanistic systems.

Other relational control studies include Watson (1982) and Watson-Dugan (1989), who employ Ellis's (1979) relational control coding scheme to study performance feedback and goal setting. Glauser and Tullar (1985) examine relational communication patterns of satisfying and dissatisfying officer-citizen telephone interactions and note that officers who engage in fewer competitive control struggles elicit more satisfying conversations than do ones who exert more control. Tullar's (1989) study of relational control patterns in the employment interview reveals that successful applicants are submissive when the interviewer is dominant and are dominant when the interviewer is submissive.

*Negotiation research.* Interactional analysis of negotiation forms the fourth category of organizational studies. Much of this literature draws from a systems-interaction approach or what Putnam (1990b) calls a process perspective. A process perspective is neither a variable nor a method, but an approach aimed at understanding the stages or phases of negotiations, message patterns or sequences of bargaining tactics, and the enactment of rules and norms in this context.

Several studies examine the effects of message functions on bargaining outcomes (Chatman, Putnam, & Sondak, 1991). For example, Theye and Seiler (1979) use Bales's (1950) IPA to code strategies and tactics in teacher-school board negotiations. Donohue (1981a, 1981b) tests a coding scheme based on the rules that govern attack, defend, and aggression tactics for distributive tasks. He reports that successful negotiators make more offers and stick to them, present fewer concessions, and deny others' arguments more often than do unsuccessful negotiators. Putnam and Wilson (1989) investigate four levels of outcomes in integrative bargaining (bridging, sharpening, trade-offs, and win-lose). Among their findings, exploratory problem solving and workability arguments are linked to bridging outcomes, while voicing preferences for positions and evaluating propositions result in win-lose settlements. Drawing from this investigation, Putnam, Wilson, and Turner (1990) compare early- and late-phase variations in a teacher-school board negotiation. Teachers and board members differ in

their argumentation strategies at both early and late stages of the negotiations.

Weingart, Thompson, Bazerman, and Carroll (1990) examine negotiation behavior and individual-joint gains in a variable-sum buyer-seller negotiation task. They note that initial offers affect final outcomes differently across buyers and sellers, that negotiators reciprocate and balance both distributive and integrative tactics, and that information sharing has a positive effect on the efficiency of the arguments. Weingart, Bennett, and Brett (1993) report on two studies concerning the effect of motivation (cooperative, individualistic) and issue consideration (simultaneous, sequential) on negotiation process and outcome. Among the more notable findings, groups who exchange issues simultaneously share more information and have a greater understanding of the other sides' priorities than do those who discuss issues sequentially. Finally, Olekalns, Smith, and Walsh (1996) simulate an employment contract negotiation to test for cuing and response strategies across four types of distributive and integrative outcomes: stalemate, win-lose, suboptimum, and optimum.

While previous studies focus on the effects of communication on bargaining outcomes, other investigations center on the intervening effects of communication on outcomes. Using a modified version of Hopmann and Walcott's (1976) bargaining process analysis (BPAII), Putnam and Jones (1982) investigate the way frequency and sequence of bargaining talk mediates the effects of negotiated outcomes in a simulated grievance case study. In labor-management dyads that result in an agreement, an attack-defend cycle guards against conflict escalation. In impasse dyads, an act-react cycle, in which the parties match each other's offensive and defensive moves, produces an escalating pattern of one-upmanship.

Still other studies primarily describe bargaining tactics and language patterns rather than test for effects of communication on outcomes (e.g., Chatman et al., 1991; Donohue, Diez, & Hamilton, 1984). Bednar and Curington (1983), using the relational control coding scheme, examine the content and relationship aspects of negotiations in an oil company contract dispute. Holmes and Sykes (1993) and Holmes (1997) investigate phases in actual versus simulated hostage negotiations.

*Adaptive structuration theory.* The fifth type of interactional studies, adaptive structuration theory (AST), draws from structuration theory (Giddens, 1979, 1984; Poole, Seibold, & McPhee, 1985) and focuses on the mutual influence of technology and social processes on organizational change. DeSanctis and Poole (1994) call their analysis "interpretive coding" because, unlike most interaction analyses studies, they go beyond conventional meanings of message sequence and pattern to infer actor intentions (Poole & DeSanctis, 1992). Although some of their research is interpretive in character (DeSanctis, Poole, Dickson, & Jackson, 1993; Poole, DeSanctis, Kirsch, & Jackson, 1995), other studies employ a priori category schemes to focus on structural claims.

AST analysis centers on the way that groups incorporate a computerized decision support system (GDSS) into their processes (Watson, DeSanctis, & Poole, 1988). Interpretive coding uses AST to document the appropriation of structures as they arise from and occur within the discourse (e.g., direct use, relate to other structures, constrain the structure, or express judgments about the structure). This analysis, when combined with distinctions made between faithful and unfaithful appropriations and the attitudes that group members display toward the technology, demonstrates how AST coding extends beyond microlevel analyses to global (i.e., conversations, meetings, or documents as a whole) and institutional (e.g., longitudinal observation with the goal of identifying persistent patterns) levels. Two prominent studies include Poole and DeSanctis (1992) and DeSanctis and Poole (1994). Poole and DeSanctis (1992) report that consensus change and variations in the restrictiveness of the GDSS are related to differences in the structuration process.

DeSanctis and Poole (1994) illustrate how the same technology can be introduced to two difference groups, yet the effects of the technology differ according to each group's appropriation. Specifically, appropriations that are consistent with the intended use of the technology produce desirable decision processes and outcomes.

Other studies examine the impact of GDSSs on influence patterns in group interaction (Zigurs, Poole, & DeSanctis, 1988) and on conflict behavior (Poole, Holmes, & DeSanctis, 1991) in both laboratory and field contexts (e.g., DeSanctis, Poole, Lewis, & Desharnais, 1992). Finally, Contractor and Seibold (1993) use simulation data to show the AST deficiencies in explaining GDSSs appropriation over time. With the aim of advancing AST, they offer self-organizing systems theory as a solution to the problems with GDSS research.

Interaction analysis draws from studies of message functions and language structures to assess the frequency and types of verbal behaviors, the redundancy and predictability of talk in a communicative system, the sequences and stages of talk, and the links between structures of talk and interpretations of these patterns. As a form of pragmatics, interaction analysis is grounded in regularities and recurring patterns within a communication system. For the most part, with the exception of AST approaches, this research locates meaning in the unfolding process of the social system and treats language users as elements in the background of social systems. Communication, then, resides within the system of interaction patterns and meaning emanates from the functions and patterns of talk. Organizational constructs, such as leadership, managerial dominance, and strategies and tactics of negotiation, evolve from message patterns and communication systems rather than from semantics or conversational forms. Interaction analysis, as an approach for understanding linguistic systems, is criticized for its proliferation of category systems, its reliance on a priori categories, and the practice of specifying and categorizing meanings of utterances

(Firth, 1995). In effect, interaction analysis uses a static framework for analyzing a dynamic activity. In actuality, participants jointly constitute social meanings in ways that are more ephemeral, malleable, and negotiable than interaction analysis depicts.

Overall, pragmatics is a broad category of discourse, one that privileges the role of language in organizational context. Given the variation that exists among the three major clusters of discourse studies—speech acts, ethnography of speaking, and interaction analysis—pragmatics is not a uniform perspective, but rather an umbrella for studies that fit into subcategories of different relationships among discourse, meaning, action, and organizations. In research on speech acts, language is action that shapes organizing by being uttered. Both meaning and organizing are embodied in the utterances of what is said. In contrast, research on the ethnography of speaking centers on the way that language accomplishes organizing through developing speech communities, enacting performances, and negotiating orders. Accomplishments rather than utterances embody action and meaning as processes that actors coconstruct. Interaction analysis moves the study of language into systems of communication through focusing on the structure and regularities of message categories. Interaction systems depict such processes as leadership and negotiation by combining function and meaning into a priori forms. Thus, each of these schools privileges different features of discourse analysis and casts the link between language and organization differently.

## SEMIOTICS

Semiotics, unlike the pragmatic perspective, centers on the way that interpretations evolve from signs or code systems. By examining a sign as anything that represents something else, semiotics broadens the focus of linguistic studies to include not only discourse but also nonverbal codes, images, actions, and objects. Semiotics emphasizes how language signifies, how it is related to an association among codes, and how it becomes a system of symbols (Stewart, 1986). Two different schools of semiotics surface in the organizational literature and serve as precursors to the postmodern approaches. The first approach, drawn from structuralism (Saussure, 1916/1974), casts language as a system of differences rooted in surface and deep levels of structure. The second approach, semiosis, treats language as a signifying process in which symbols become referents for objects and ideas (Peirce, 1931).

### Structuralism

A structuralist perspective to the study of semiotics addresses the way deep structures give rise to surface forms. Deep structures underlie language system in which meaning develops through a system of logical opposites, narratives, or part-whole relationships. Even labels, metaphors, and platitudes function as symbol systems that signify deeper structures of organizational control (Czarniawska-Joerges & Joerges, 1988). Lexical variation and nonverbal behaviors of factory workers also function as semiotic code systems that reveal deep-level meanings of work and play (Tway, 1976). Semiotic analysis begins by identifying signs or signal units through searching for a set of codes, the rules that link these codes together, and the underlying values embedded in these codes (Fiol, 1989). In this analysis, semioticians uncover the hidden meanings or fundamental values that produce and organize sign systems through a set of constraints, rules, or choices. The deep structure, then, rests on central or universal principles that unify chains of signifiers. This unifying principle might be power/knowledge relationships, modes of production, or capitalist relations.

For example, Barley (1983) illustrates how a recurrent underlying value, the denial of death, permeates the culture of a funeral home and conveys the themes of naturalness and familiarity. By comparing the codes of a living sleeping person with those of a dead person, he illustrates how the signs that seem opposite are actually similar and how code rules at the deep level reinforce those at the surface level to form an interrelated semiotic system. With a similar focus on oppositional forms, Manning (1982a, 1982b, 1986, 1988) examines the underlying beliefs about crime in a study of emergency 911 or 999 telephone calls within two police departments. His analyses of caller times, sources, locations, and directions at the surface level reveal a system of codes in which action-inaction, complete-incomplete, and construction-reconstruction at the deep level produce loosely coupled webs of meanings for processing events. The occupational culture of police and the division of labor in the organization severely constrain interactions with callers and subvert representations of events.

Patterns of beliefs about the appropriate way to define internal and external relations characterize Fiol's (1989) semiotic narrative analysis of letters to shareholders in ten chemical companies, five of whom had engaged in joint ventures. Using the semiotic square to identify the underlying oppositions between strong-weak and internal-external, Fiol demonstrates how the belief systems of risky behaviors unify the semiotic codes of loss and gain in company images and justify the pursuit of joint ventures.

Structuralist approaches to semiotics lay the foundation for examining language as a system of codes, signs, and signifiers. However, this approach tends to reify structures, fixing form at surface and deep levels and treating meanings as unified and universal. By ignoring history and temporality, structuralists also fail to account for the production and reproduction of structures through language use.

## Semiosis

A second type of semiotic analysis, known as semiosis, centers on the signifying process.

Developed by Peirce (1931), semiosis focuses on the relationship among the sign, the object or referent, and the interpretant. The sign stands for something or somebody, while the referent refers to the object or form in the material world. The interpretant is the mental image of the interpreter created or stimulated by the sign. In this perspective, signs are transparent in that they mirror the nature of being itself.

This approach to semiotics underlies research on organizational identity, corporate image, and marketing communication (Nöth, 1988). Organizational identity, as noted in Cheney and Christensen (Chapter 7, this volume), is what the company comes to represent or its formal profile, while corporate image is the impression created by a set of signs or the company's reputation (Christensen, 1995). In a semiotic analysis, corporate identity functions as sign, corporate image becomes the interpretant, and the organization is the referent or object. However, these elements are complex, interchangeable, and even contradictory in the dynamics of the signifying process. Such complexities include the way organizations become self-reflexive through processing data from marketing studies and image analyses (see Cheney & Christensen, this volume) and the way that corporate identities surface as referents behind the use of logos, names, merchandise, and ads (Balmer, 1995). Semiotics, then, demonstrates how the interplay between organizational identity and corporate image is a dynamic negotiation between sign and interpretant and one rooted in representations that are sociohistorical rather than based on fit with reality (Christensen & Askegaard, in press). This view of organizational identity and corporate image evolves through the interplay of texts and the relationships that exist among multiple signs (Eco, 1976).

In both of these perspectives, signs and symbols stand for something else; thus, language is representation in that it refers, substitutes, or interprets something else. Whether through a system of codes rooted in surface and deep structures or a set of meanings developed through a signifying process, this perspective treats discourse as a system of symbols that represents a nonlinguistic world of objects. By privileging codes and interpretants, semiotics treats organizing as developing chains of signifiers that represent belief systems and characterize corporate identity and images.

## LITERARY AND RHETORICAL ANALYSES

Literary and rhetorical perspectives share an interest with semiotics in treating language as a signifying process. However, this approach centers on symbols rather than signs and highlights the meaning and contextual elements of language instead of the code and structural features. Rhetoric is often defined as using the available means of persuasion; hence, rhetorical approaches draw from classical methods of argumentation to examine corporate messages in crisis situations, organizational decision making, identification, and conflict management. Rhetorical and literary perspectives center on the text of discourse and the ways that meaning intertwines with function to shape messages and message responses.

Research on literary and rhetorical perspectives cluster into the following categories: rhetorical strategies in corporate advocacy, argument in organizational decision making and identification, and rhetorical and literary tropes. The last category includes literary approaches to organizations that conduct analyses on metaphors, metonymy, synecdoche, and irony.

### *Rhetorical Strategies in Corporate Advocacy*

Research on corporate advocacy focuses on the management of public messages in promoting company positions, acknowledging events, and responding to organizational crises. Since this literature is reviewed extensively in Cheney and Vibbert (1987), this section synthesizes current studies on organizational crisis communication. The way that organizations respond to crisis situations parallels work on conversational repairs by focusing on how companies make excuses, provide explanations and justifications, and offer apologies and recompense (Barton, 1993; Benoit & Brinson, 1994; Hearit, 1994; Lukaszewski & Gmeiner, 1993). Often classified as rhetorical apologia, communication during corporate crises draws from research on facework, impression management, and persuasion (Allen & Caillouet, 1994; Benoit, 1992; Pinsdorf, 1987).

Most practitioners of corporate advocacy recommend candor in providing accounts for organizational disasters (Dougherty, 1992); however, given the legal constraints that corporations face, candor is typically couched in equivocal messages aimed at instilling labels or names for the event, promoting collective sensemaking, and persuading diverse audiences (Tyler, 1997). Selection of rhetorical strategies hinges on the goals of the organization, the type of crises, the prevailing attributions about the situation, and the primary target audience (Coombs, 1995).

Although maintaining a positive organizational image remains the dominant aim of these messages, the desire to shift blame, express mortification, and implement corrective action also guides the selection of strategies (Benoit & Brinson, 1994; Campbell, Follender, & Shane, 1998). To distance companies from a crisis event, corporations often label the crisis as an accident, a transgression, a faux pas, or sabotage, depending on whether the public sees the event as emanating from internal or external forces and from intentional or unintentional motives (Coombs, 1995). In an effort to shift blame, the company might separate the actions of culpable members from the corporate body (Brinson & Benoit, 1999; Gephart, 1993). To express mortification and ingratiation, a company might offset negative attributions with positive impressions or make promises for corrective action.

Corporations who fail to achieve these goals often select inappropriate strategies for particular audiences. Targets of corporate messages include victims, organizational members, shareholders, customers, clients, and the general public. Messages that are aimed at the financial, scientific, and legal communities may alienate victims and the general public, as occurred in Union Carbide's response to the Bhopal accident (Ice, 1991). In like manner, legal issues, as surfaced in the Exxon Valdez oil spill and the Dalkon Shield case, may influence corporations to target their messages to stockholders rather than to victims (Tyler, 1997). In contrast, the use of mortification and corrective action strategies, as exemplified in the Tylenol incident, seems appropriate to the external nature of the incident and the general public as an audience. In some situations, paradoxical messages emerge in which a company denies responsibility for a crisis while simultaneously being accountable for its actions or it may apologize for the crisis while disavowing any ownership of it (Tyler, 1997). In effect, in crisis situations the general public wants to hear ownership and apologies rather than excuses and justifications. Failure to acknowledge events, take ownership of the situation, or address particular stakeholders may lead to public rejection.

Although influenced by the work on speech acts and conversational repairs, rhetorical studies in crisis situations broaden discourse analysis to embrace both the content and context of communication. Rhetorical strategies in these situations not only invoke social action, but they also reveal ways that "speaking the right words" influences definitions of social reality and patterns of sensemaking in times of crisis. Public communication embodies persuasive appeals shaped by contextual constraints and aimed at particular audiences. Hence, meaning is inter-twined with text and context, but messages are conceived in light of senders and receivers rather than through the way they are embedded in an interactive process.

### Argument in Organizational Decision Making and Identification

Another persuasive strategy commonly used in organizations is argument. Defined as reason-giving aimed at supporting a claim, argument is linked to rationality or a coherent set of agreed-on rules and procedures (Weick & Browning, 1986). However, argument is more than a set of procedures, it is a form of discourse aimed at enhancing understanding. Reasoning, then, is a process of drawing inferences and making connections among events, motives, and actions. As Anderson (1983) demonstrates in his analysis of the Cuban missile crisis, organizational members come to understand a situation through novel arguments embedded in objections to a course of action rather than through presenting a prevailing position. Although a variety of perspectives on argument exist, the literature on organizational argument clusters into two areas: (1) decision premises and identification and (2) argument as policy deliberation.

*Decision premises and organizational identification.* Organizations are texts composed of connections among arguments (Tompkins, Tompkins, & Cheney, 1989). A text in this sense is not a written document, but a body of discourse produced through organizational actions and interactions. Tompkins and Cheney (1985) draw from Simon's (1976) notion of decision premises to show how organizations exert decision-making control through inculcating major premises in key words and topics. Thus, using the term *innovation* may signal that "innovation is desirable" through a process of reasoning known as the *enthymeme.* An enthymeme is an incomplete syllogism or a form of logic in which the major premise is implied and the audience draws the logical conclusion from linking the stated to the implied premises. For example, by stating the minor premise, "This product will make you look youthful," the audience completes the conclusion, "This product is desirable" through reasoning from a premise widely held in American society, "Looking youthful is desirable" (Tompkins et al., 1989).

Research in this area examines the way organizations inculcate decision premises as forms of identification and unobtrusive control. Drawn from Burke's (1950/1969b) theory of identification, Tompkins and Cheney (1985) note that the process of identification is necessary to cope with mystery and estrangement inherent in division of labor. Organizations aim to overcome the separation, estrangement, and mystery of hierarchy through creating and extending terminology (e.g., the naming of events) and through stretching old meanings into new "terministic screens" (Meyer, 1996; Tompkins, Fisher, Infante, & Tompkins, 1975).

Studies of organizational identification examine different written and oral texts to uncover decision premises. Using account analysis as a method, Tompkins and Cheney (1983) investigate the decision premises of teaching assistants who depart from a standardized course design. Their study reveals that accounts of deviation fit normative premises, reveal targets of identification, and are linked to zones of ambiguity in teaching assistant requirements. In a study of corporate periodicals, Cheney (1983) illustrates the way identification and decision premises arise in appeals to common ground, use of common enemies, and reference to the transcendent "we." DiSanza and Bullis (1999) extend this work by analyzing member responses to rhetorical appeals published in Forest Service newsletters. Their study reveals that organizational members recognize and complete decision premises, especially ones communicated through common ground appeals and "we" strategies in CEO policy statements. Quality circle manuals also promote identification

through subtle messages embedded in the rationale, criteria, and procedures that inculcate managerial concerns (Stohl & Coombs, 1988).

Other studies on decision premises demonstrate how the U.S. Catholic bishops recast their identity as a national unit through the use of enthymemes in peace initiatives (Cheney, 1991) and how organizations such as the U.S. Forest Service alter decision premises through changes in training of professionals (Bullis & Tompkins, 1989). Overall, decision premises embodied in organizational texts and inculcated through rhetorical strategies promote identification and underscore the pervasiveness of organizations as arguments.

*Argument as policy deliberation.* Persuasion and rhetorical strategies also underlie the research on policy deliberation and conflict management. Argument plays a critical role in this process because effective decisions often emerge from the interactive clash of opposing viewpoints (Anderson, 1983). These decisions emanate from shifts in language that define new themes and reformulate decision strategies (Huff, 1983). Research in this area clusters into two categories: arguments in bargaining and value-laden arguments.

Different perspectives guide the research on argumentation in bargaining and negotiation. Drawing from both simulated and actual negotiations, researchers examine arguments as persuasive tactics (Putnam & Jones, 1982; Roloff, Tutzauer, & Dailey, 1989), as invention (Bacharach & Lawler, 1981), and as issue development (Putnam et al., 1990). As persuasive tactics, arguments function as strategic maneuvers aimed at changing the opponents' attitudes and fostering concession making. As invention, arguments provide the rationale and justification for making claims about legitimacy and independence (Bacharach & Lawler, 1981; Keough & Lake, 1993). In issue definition, arguments center on the attack and defense of proposals, reason-giving through evidence and claims, case making, and stock issues (Putnam & Geist, 1985; Putnam & Wilson, 1989; Putnam, Wilson, Waltman, &

Turner, 1986; Schmidt, 1986). Bargainers often specialize in argument types in different stages of negotiation. In the early stages, they rely on harm and workability arguments to prepare their cases, but in the later stages they employ inherency and disadvantage arguments to weigh the costs of concessions and to rationalize a settlement (Putnam et al., 1990).

A second area of research on argumentation is value-laden appeals. Reasonableness and "good arguments" are not simply tightly reasoned cases. Rather, conflicting arguments produce and reproduce organizational values (Conrad, 1993; Smithin, 1987). In a study of boycotts against organizations, Meyers and Garrett (1993) investigate argument themes emanating from the corporate values of profitability and social responsibility. Using structuration theory, they note how contradictions serve as sites for incompatible values, how opposing values define communication differently for protest and target groups, and how organizations use competing arguments to reproduce their current structures. Conflicting and incompatible values also surface in studies on environmental innovation, as demonstrated in comparing UK and German companies (Steward & Conway, 1998). Documents on innovation from the UK corporations employ a limited environmental vocabulary, rooted in accountability and a knowledge/customer network. In contrast, German companies ground their arguments in an ethics of conviction, which privileges a broad environmental vocabulary and a regulator/supplier type of network.

Other studies demonstrate how multiple value hierarchies pervade organizational life, as Keough and Lake (1993) observe in their investigation of teaching assistants' bargaining. These hierarchies create different logics of action that link to core values of efficiency and growth evident in corporate annual reports (Cheney & Frenette, 1993). Discourse, then, is reconstituted in light of shifting constraints, as Hamilton (1997) illustrates in his study of rational and emotional appeals in the pay system of the National Health Service

Trust. Arguments reveal a shift from a public service ethos to an enterprise-culture logic through supporting or refuting wage issues.

In each of these approaches, argument is more than causal attributions (Bettman & Weitz, 1983) in which researchers focus on the amount or stability of reasoning; rather, argument is a means of persuasion rooted in controversy about the merits of issues. The content of the argument, the type of case making, and the joint interaction of participants play a critical role in organizational policy deliberations. In some ways, organizations are argument fields in which persuasive appeals are interwoven with praxis. Thus, the concept of "argument field" treats interaction at the microlevel as shaping and being influenced by arguments made at the macrolevel (Keough, 1987). In this sense, research on argument in organizational studies moves from emphasis on function and text to a focus on the relationship between text and context.

## Rhetorical and Literary Tropes

Rhetoric is not just using language to persuade; it is also a means of human understanding and a process of constructing social reality (Watson, 1994). This perspective stands in opposition to the view that rhetoric is embellishment distinct from some other social reality (Bowles & Coates, 1993; Keenoy, 1990; Vaughn, 1994). In like manner, the use of literary tropes reveals both style and creation of text, but style is more than mere ornamentation. Literary tropes entail a variety of rhetorical forms, including alliteration, icons, euphemisms, and clichés. However, the four classic tropes, as presented by Burke (1945/1969a), Brown (1977), and Manning (1979), are metaphor, metonymy, synecdoche, and irony.

*Metaphor.* As the most basic of the master tropes, metaphor is a way of seeing things as if they were something else. By casting the unfamiliar in light of the known, metaphor bridges cognitive domains, legitimates actions, and guides behaviors (Lakoff & Johnson, 1980). Metaphor creates imagery that shifts figure-ground relationships by highlighting some features of language while suppressing others. As rich summaries of worldviews, metaphors subsume other metaphors, exist in clusters, and shift perspectives, often between surface and deep levels (Smith & Eisenberg, 1987; Smith & Turner, 1995).

Metaphor contributes to organizational analysis in three primary ways: creating and developing organizational theory, describing and understanding the discursive texture of organizations, and conducting organizational research (Cazal & Inns, 1998). Given the scope of literature in each of these areas, this review centers on metaphor analysis in two particular research domains: organizational change and conflict management (Grant & Oswick, 1996a). Other texts overview essays on metaphors as theory-building and methodological tools (see Alvesson, 1993; Brink, 1993; Grant & Oswick, 1996b; Morgan, 1980, 1997; Oswick & Grant, 1996b; Putnam et al., 1996; Tsoukas, 1991).

Through its generative quality, metaphor is an appealing approach for investigating organizational change, particularly in studies about information transfer in unfamiliar situations and in research on the organizational logic for change (Pondy, 1983; Sackmann, 1989). Metaphor facilitates new knowledge production (Morgan & Ramirez, 1984); introduces new perspectives and worldviews (Marshak, 1993, 1996); and contributes to transforming organizational processes and experiences through painting visions, arousing emotions, and inspiring commitment (Höpfl & Maddrell, 1996; Sackmann, 1989; Srivastva & Barrett, 1988; Vaughn, 1995). Although metaphors facilitate new knowledge and bridge the known with the unfamiliar (Barrett & Cooperrider, 1990), they also constrain learning and action through preserving ideologies (Tsoukas, 1993) and deepening organizational meanings and values (Broussine & Vince, 1996). Hence, within a symbol system, metaphor functions simultaneously to facilitate change and preserve stability.

Research on the role of root metaphors in conflict situations illustrates the way that metaphor functions at this dual level. For example, analysis of metaphors in the change management literature shows how downsizing becomes aligned with improving health and physical environment (e.g., "trim the fat," "bulging," "stormy seas of competition") as well as with violence and damaged bodies (e.g., "butchers," "frontal assault," "cutting muscle not just fat," "organizational anorexia") (Dunford & Palmer, 1996). Moreover, in a study of ownership of commodities, metaphors of the short-term logic of cost control run counter to images of long-term processes of human investment (Watson, 1994, 1995). Thus, the relationship between metaphors of change and the emergence of countermetaphors preserves continuity while promoting organizational changes. These contradictions often lead to conflict when efforts to alter root metaphors elicit overt struggles between competing ideologies (Dunn, 1990; Hirsch & Andrews, 1983; Smith & Eisenberg, 1987).

The way that metaphor reveals contradictions underscores the need to capture shifts in meaning and relationships among chains of images across organizational texts (Alvesson, 1993). Thus, metaphors do not represent inherent or stable meanings; rather, they function at the nexus of evolving symbols, text, and meaning. In this sense, organizations are living texts and metaphors are repertoires of meanings that point to the connections among terms in an evolving symbol system.

*Metonymy, synecdoche, and irony.* For the most part, the research on organizational metaphors overshadows organizational studies on metonymy, synecdoche, and irony. The broad concept of metaphor, however, subsumes and intertwines with the other three tropes (Manning, 1979; Oswick & Grant, 1996a). Whereas the term *metaphor* signifies diverse perspectives, the term *metonymy* refers to reduction. That is, metonymy is a figure of speech in which the whole stands for the parts, for example, the use of the word *heart* to stand for *emotions*. In particular, the term *culture* is often used as a metonymy for an organization's rites and rituals, myths, stories, and values. The whole of culture is represented through its different symbol systems. Through the process of reduction, an integrating term such as *culture* intertwines its parts into an associated pattern, one that is similar to using abbreviated phrases to refer to well-known jokes. In this sense, an organization, as an intangible unit, is likened to its visible and concrete parts (Burke, 1950/ 1969b).

Research on metonymy reveals how whole-part relationships develop alternative meanings and new patterns of association. In a study of police discourse, Manning (1979) illustrates how the concept of *drug use* becomes a crime through aligning this whole with parts of the criminal process, such as crime statistics, seizure data, and number of warrants. In Watson's (1995) study of a trade union talk, the National Health Service Trust employs metonymy to signify steps in a pendulum shift arbitration in which the parties agree to a no-strike policy. Drawing on a similar context, Putnam (1995) demonstrates how the terms *language* and *money* in a teachers' bargaining moves from referencing sections of the contract to signifying competing commodities that serve as a formula for a settlement.

Synecdoche reverses this process by using the part to signify the whole, for example, the term *crown* or *throne* to represent the king or queen. Synecdoche operates from the concept of representation. For example, some theorists use the terms *hierarchy* and *bureaucracy* to stand for organizations as reified entities. Manning (1979) points out how the concepts of *detective* and *case* in policing operate differently in drug investigations. Unlike regular policing, cases are not placed in central locations and delegated to drug investigators; rather, a case is a synecdoche that represents

storing information in an officer's head, developing key informant relationships, and processing files individually rather than as a unit.

Slogans, jargon, clichés, and credos also function as synecdoche to represent an organization's image. For instance, slogans about quality often function in a redundant and iconic way to proclaim standards of precision that, in turn, produce expectations for organizational action (Gorden & Nevins, 1987). However, a juxtaposition of jargon and themes from total quality management with those from high-commitment work systems reveals a critical gap in the concept of ownership, change, and organizational image of a manufacturing company (Fairhurst & Wendt, 1993).

Clichés also become persuasive by connecting taken-for-granted actions to corporate-wide mission statements, such as using the phrase "the bottom line" to represent big-budget firms and using the expression "work hard, play hard" to capture the glamour, long hours, and lucrative activity of modern accounting (Anderson-Gough, Grey, & Robson, 1998). In effect, the general and ubiquitous nature of clichés normalizes professional and organizational practices, functions as synecdoche to represent the corporation, and operates unobtrusively to exert managerial control.

When intended meanings in discourse contradict with conventional ones, irony becomes a way of producing unexpected outcomes (Brown, 1977; Westenholz, 1993). Irony parallels and closely relates to contradiction in its reliance on discourse to uncover tensions between what was said and what was meant. Ironies often lead to contradictions and paradoxes that contribute to theory building (Poole & Van de Ven, 1989) and to the conception of contradiction-centered organizations (Putnam, 1986; Trethewey, 1999). But as a rhetorical trope, irony arises from the context in which a speaker or researcher foregrounds a conventional meaning and then provides a twist or surprising reversal in interpretation (Weick & Browning, 1986). Contradictions arise in the text/subtext of a message and in the discursive practices of what an organization purports and what actually happens.

Irony opens new possibilities through uncovering perspectives on incongruity and exposing new meanings that challenge normative conventions and historical practices (Burke, 1950/1969b; Hatch & Ehrlich, 1993). As an example, Hatch's (1997) study of spontaneous humor reveals how managers coconstruct experiences about what is possible or impossible to change or what is valued and devalued in the organization. Managers interpret ironic remarks by invoking contextual knowledge; then, they reflexively construct their own identities as they reconstitute the organization.

Ironies also reveal contradictions, as noted in Manning's (1979) discovery of similarities between narcotic agents and drug users (e.g., meeting at strange hours, hanging out in bars, and dressing like criminals) and Filby and Willmott's (1988) finding that ironic humor produces trained incapacity through reifying self-image while exaggerating opposition to bureaucracy. Ironies facilitate engaging in paradoxical thinking to "deframe" meanings and establish new lines of communication (Westenholz, 1993). Employees who embrace the contradictions between solidarity and market orientation, internal and external, and ambiguous and unambiguous cut across frames of reference and argue for a new approach to organizational problems.

In summary, the rhetorical approach to discourse analysis in organizations centers on the interconnections among messages, functions, meanings, and contexts. Researchers intertwine these features in complex ways to examine rhetorical strategies that emanate from persuasion, argumentation, and literary tropes. Working with oral and written texts, researchers infer meanings through subtexts of discourse rooted in organizational circumstances and contexts. The immediacy of the rhetorical situation and the audience for a given message play a prominent role in interpreting meaning and constructing organizational reality. In many ways, literary and rhetorical studies of organizational texts provide the building blocks for discourse analysis in the critical and postmodern traditions.

## CRITICAL LANGUAGE STUDIES

Unlike previous sections that examine language through particular methods of discourse analysis, critical and postmodern traditions focus on discourse and society (van Dijk, 1993, 1997a). Hence, these perspectives borrow from modes of discourse analysis previously discussed to achieve particular goals and uncover ways that language constitutes and reconstitutes social arrangements. Specifically, as Mumby notes in Chapter 15 in this volume, discourse analysis in critical theory centers on power and control, particularly the way different groups compete to serve their own interests and to control symbolic and discursive resources. In this perspective, discourse produces, maintains, and/or resists systems of power and inequality through ideology and hegemony (Mumby & Clair, 1997). Ideology is a system of beliefs and interpretive frames that mediates discourse and social structures, and hegemony is the way that subtle and often hidden forms of consent constitute power relationships (Mumby, 1988).

With the aim of exposing these relationships and suggesting alternative arrangements, critical theory examines the way hegemony shapes and is shaped by language use, the way powerful groups control language systems, and the way deep structures reveal power and ideology. For instance, Riley (1983) examines the deeply layered structures that sustain organizational cultures through the power embedded in political imagery and verbal symbols. Since other chapters in this handbook review literature on critical theory (see Deetz, Chapter 1; Conrad & Haynes, Chapter 2; Mumby, Chapter 15), this chapter centers on language as a particular feature of this research perspective. Specifically, it concentrates on four major features: narrative talk; rituals and texts; everyday talk; and ironies, contradictions, and paradoxes.

## Narrative Talk

In this perspective, storytelling is not a neutral process; rather, stories function ideologically to represent the interests of dominant groups, instantiate values, reify structures, and reproduce power (Mumby, 1988). In Witten's (1993) view, narrative discourse is a mode of persuasion used to create and maintain a culture of obedience, to invent a credible history, and to exert covert control. For example, Mumby (1987) illustrates how reading narrative discourse through the lens of gender reproduces power relationships at IBM. In the classic story of Tom Watson, chair of the board, and the young female security officer who stopped Watson and asked him to put on his badge, use of the words such as *bride, ill-fitting uniform, white-shirted men,* and *trembling* reproduces power relationships through signifiers of class and gender. Even though the story argues for equality in following the rules, it reaffirms inequality through male and class dominance in the social order.

Similarly, in horse track racing, women grooms reproduce each other as marginalized members through telling stories about the "girls" who use their sexuality to gain success among the big trainers, while being alienated professionally from the legitimate grooms (Helmer, 1993). Through these oppositions, women participate in and provide consent for their exclusion from the structures of power and privilege. Finally, stories of sexual harassment, rooted in an ideology of denial and surprise, reveal the tensions between private and public arenas of organizational life (Strine, 1992; Taylor & Conrad, 1992; Wood, 1992). Victims of harassment often sequester their

stories by treating them as normal yet abnormal, inevitable yet immutable, and trivial but significant (Clair, 1993b). These oppositional tensions create doubt that often leads to responses of silence and inaction. Thus, through constructing, telling, and concealing stories, organizational members reproduce power relationships rooted in the institutional and societal structures.

## Rituals and Texts

*Rituals and rites.* Discourse plays a critical role in enacting organizational rituals and rites, such as interviews, planning meetings, award ceremonies, and company parties. As routine events, rituals are patterned and repeated social activities and rites are scripted public ceremonies. Rituals and rites often consist of normative ways of speaking through situating control in routine practices. Performance interviews, as a genre of discourse, demonstrate how discourse reconstitutes power relationships. In an interview between the sales director and Japanese American employees of a large hotel chain, the sales director's use of indexical expressions and nonstandard speech enacts the linguistic pattern of "markedness," which, in turn, isolates minorities from the organizational mainstream (Banks, 1987). Power is also constituted in team meetings through juxtaposing seriousness and humor to create a cultural drama that melds occupational and personal frames into group objectives. For example, balancing seriousness and humor in the training workshops of a high-tech company elicits an ideology of strong organizational commitment (Kunda, 1992). Moreover, simultaneous use of humor and seriousness often results in a climate of ambiguity in which anecdotes and nuances of such terms as *wallop, slap, stunner* conceal gender and class and treat domestic violence as a normal activity (Saferstein, 1994).

Symbolic struggles also surface in business planning when alternative discourses replace original organizational expressions. In a reengineering team, business planning controls capital allocations through introducing new vocabularies to displace existing labels, as with the case of the Canadian government (Oakes, Townley, & Cooper, 1998). Thus, use of linguistic patterns, humor, and labeling construct and reaffirm power relationships through enacting collaborative processes that reflect dominant ideologies.

Even social rites such as award ceremonies and company parties enact power relationships through organizational dramas. At an annual awards breakfast, public orations that feature such words as *we are one, body of the church,* and *salary adjustment* reconstitute elite power in an advertising agency through enacting a ritual that unifies while separating, praises while criticizing, and rewards seniority while extolling performance (Rosen, 1985). Similarly, speeches at an annual Christmas party function to obscure and thus secure the economic foundation of the ad agency (Rosen, 1988). Organizational rites, then, are not simply social activities; they enact relations of domination and control, often embedded in the deep-level contradictory meanings that evolve from discursive practices.

*Formal texts.* Rituals as normative ways of speaking interface with written documents to instantiate ideology and power relationships. Critical analyses of these texts, including organizational policy statements, advertisements, budgets, and program documents, demonstrate how microlevel linguistic practices reflect back on and draw from social and institutional structures (Dent, 1991; Munro, 1995). For example, Clair's (1993a) study of policy statements on sexual harassment illustrates how bureaucracy treats sexuality in the workplace as a commodity. Use of such phrases as "just say no," "keep a record," and "report it" in conjunction with such strategies as minimizing the act, ambiguity, and joking fosters confessional and exclusionary discourses that, in turn, reify power relationships.

The rhetoric of commodity also surfaces in job advertisements and program materials (Fairclough & Wodak, 1997). Fairclough (1993) observes how universities, in their quest to be entrepreneurial, shift from a traditional academic mission to a goal of marketing educational services. Use of action verbs, managerial language, and self-promotion in these materials reflects how organizations enact commodity values that shift from an ideology of obligation. Organizations also sediment certain ideologies and themes (e.g., cost cutting, secrecy) in official documents, ones in which management and workers appropriate in different ways (Bastien, McPhee, & Bolton, 1995; Knights & Willmott, 1987). In effect, formal texts are genres in which organizations reproduce power relationships through constituting ideologies discursively.

### Everyday Talk

Power relationships are also actively constructed through the work routines of everyday organizational life. These routines surface as members develop special vocabularies to depict organizational processes, to reflect political interests, and to resist managerial ideologies. That is, the labeling or naming of objects, people, and events exerts control over organizational processes. For instance, labeling the computer as *the smart machine, machine of the year,* and *the brain power* serves to legitimate information technology; defer decisions; blame machines; and root problems in professionalism, consumption, and technical power (Prasad, 1995).

In like manner, labeling or naming a discursive practice, such as sexual harassment, inscribes patterns of sensemaking that affect what people see, what gets silenced, and what is regarded as reasonable and acceptable (Wood, 1994). Even communication about such seemingly objective processes as pay scales are intertwined with language and power (Lang, 1986). In pay differentials, women and minorities are often isolated from the power relationships that control the definition and norms of equity (Clair & Thompson, 1996).

Language also becomes a source of power as speech communities vie to have their words and meanings accepted as legitimate. In particular, lumber workers' use of political vocabularies (e.g., "political hires," "shit talk," "gettin' down on workers") develops an ideology aimed at resisting the dominant group discourse but one that prohibits them from exerting organizational voice (Huspek & Kendall, 1991). Similar studies demonstrate how working-class males use humor to resist managerial control, conform to masculine norms, and influence fellow workers (Collinson, 1988, 1992). This form of resistance, however, rooted in an individualist ideology, proves to be ineffective in resisting managerial control.

## Ironies, Contradictions, and Paradoxes

Everyday interactions also conceal contradictions in power relationships that reside at deep-structure levels. These contradictions surface through the way routine practices disclose the opposite of their intentions. Examples of these contradictions appear in reward structures and goal systems, when organizations expect performance while rewarding seniority and develop rules and regulations that act against the achievement of group goals (Kerr, 1975).

Contradictions also arise because ideologies shift over time revealing power struggles in primary and secondary contradictions. Using Giddens's structuration theory, Howard and Geist (1995) illustrate how the primary contradictions of autonomy and dependence in a utility company merger lead to secondary tensions of change versus stability, empowerment versus powerlessness, and identification versus estrangement. Employees assume positions of invincibility, diplomacy, defection, and betrayal through recognizing or ignoring

these contractions and through accepting or rejecting the new ideology. In a similar way, cynicism and ironic slogans conceal tensions between self and organizational identity, as noted in the contradictions between embracing and distancing organizational roles, affirming and denying identities, and blurring work and nonwork activities (Kunda, 1992).

Contradictions also lead to paradoxes in which mutually exclusive alternatives reflect back on and constrain organizational actions (Putnam, 1986). Contradictions that emanate from organizational documents and training programs underlie the paradoxes of participation and diversity training. Ironically, the most effective participation programs offer workers the least amount of input in decisions. In unpacking this irony, Stohl (1995) uncovers contradictions in the design, control, and compatibility of workplace participation that lead to paradoxes in commitment and cooperation. By ordering workers to participate voluntarily, employees often avoid conflicts, participate by not participating, and exert concertive control over team members (Barker, 1993; Stohl, 1995).

In a similar way, programs aimed at recruiting and promoting women and minorities develop ironies that result in paradoxical practices. For example, to avoid discrimination, companies isolate women and minorities and train them in special programs, and to reduce inequality in personnel actions, they develop separate criteria for hiring and promoting women (Wood & Conrad, 1983). These practices rooted in societal discourses on affirmative action invoke feelings of confusion and helplessness that, ironically, reconstitute women and minorities as powerless. Feelings of powerlessness in a small design company also emanate from paradoxes, particularly ones in which the exercise of control contradicts the ideology of autonomy (Markham, 1996). Through fusing the language of teamwork and strategic ambiguity with explosive negative feedback, organizational members enact a culture in which self-direction functions as a constraint rather than a freedom.

Organizational ironies and contradictions, then, reveal tensions and uncover ruptures in deep-seated meanings. In effect, the contradictions that surface in organizational discourse point out how language mystifies power relationships and identifies the fault lines for resistance against domination and control.

Studies that adopt a critical theory approach to discourse root language in ideology and power relationships. Thus, critical language studies privilege the context, function, and meaning to show how discourse enacts, reveals, and conceals the exercise of control. Empirical investigations highlight words and phrases, structures and patterns, and contextual meanings that link language to hegemonic processes and dominant ideologies. The use of semantics as a process of naming shapes ideologies that emanate from deep-structure understandings rather than from surface analysis of speech communities, texts, and organizational functions. Contradictions and ironies not only reveal the way that power operates in organizational discourse, but they also unearth the fault lines in which resistance can emerge.

## POSTMODERN LANGUAGE ANALYSIS

Power and resistance are dominant themes in postmodern approaches to discourse analysis. But rather than being fixed within dominant coalitions, power is a contested concept, one instantiated in discourse through a dialectic of control. Power and resistance, then, develop from multiple and conflicting discourses linked to different knowledge regimes (Deetz, 1992, 1995). Hegemony is dialectical—subject to negotiation through competing meanings (Mumby & Stohl, 1991). For example, Murphy's (1998) study of flight attendants' "hidden transcripts" illustrates how discourse opens possibilities for resistance and change. Through the use of speech acts, euphemisms, and joking, flight attendants enact situations rooted in ambiguity that allow them to renegotiate their identities and modify localized practices. Thus, resistance arises from local rather than deep-seated meanings and power intertwines with knowledge to frame events within a historical and cultural context (Foucault, 1979; D. Jones, 1992).

Postmodern assumptions about power and local meanings have direct implications for discourse analysis. Specifically, postmodernism rejects grand narratives, challenges traditional notions of representation, and centers on the instability of meaning. Power and knowledge are produced, not in universal narratives, but in temporary language games and small stories located in space and time (Mauws & Phillips, 1995). Words and symbols do not represent or stand for a referent or idea, as the majority of linguistic approaches purport. Since no stable core or foundation exists on which to ground meaning, understanding emanates from inscribing value and creating signification within a particular process. Meanings, then, are often deferred from one linguistic symbol to another (Chia, 1996). In effect, postmodernism sets forth a crisis in representation. Since language functions as a system of difference, devoid of any stable and direct relationship with the natural world, texts are meaningful only as different people read and interpret them in multiple ways. Thus, texts slide into other texts as referents and meanings shift over time (Calás & Smircich, 1999).

Grounded in the work of Saussure (1916/ 1974), postmodernism privileges semiotics and rhetoric and treats language as a set of structured relations rather than a system of codes. However, these relations emanate from a system of difference, grounded in movement from presence to absence, metaphysics to irony, and text to intertextuality (Hassan, 1985). What is present in the text conceals what is absent or implied in this discourse. Difference makes the "the other term" visible through using presence and absence to show how language inscribes what it seeks to suppress and how it excludes the devalued other.

Postmodern approaches to language analysis privileges irony, metonymy, and rhetoric as discursive processes for reading and interpreting texts (Chia, 1996).

This review of discourse studies in the postmodern tradition clusters into three major categories: language as fragmentation and ambiguity, discourse as irony and paradox, and language as texts. The third category of language as texts subdivides into deconstructing texts, texts and conversations, and texts as dialogue.

### Fragmentation and Ambiguity

Fragmentation and ambiguity are key constructs in a postmodern perspective. Both concepts stem from the way meaning shifts within the discursive terrain. Ambiguity refers to the absence of a clear interpretation or the presence of multiple plausible interpretations (Eisenberg, 1984; Weick, 1979). Fragmentation results from multiple voices and interpretations that separate rather than coalesce into a consensus (Martin, 1992; Meyerson, 1991). Multiple discourses contribute to fragmentation through the way different dynamics surface in the process of organizing. In particular, different discourses simultaneously infuse reflexive cycles and continuous changes in a global agency such as the Institute of Cultural Affairs (Thatchenkery & Upadhyaya, 1996). They also contribute to fragmentation through the use of localized meanings and situated discourses, such as phrases like "the bottom line" and "profit and loss" that have particular meanings across different accounting practices (Miller & O'Leary, 1987).

Ambiguities also open space to embrace multiple discourses through the contradictions and antagonisms that exist among organizational members. For example, supporters of a regional symphony use the terms *professionals, activists, volunteers,* and *business resources* in diverse ways to reflect the tensions among and sustain a multivocal culture (Rudd, 1995). Through ambiguity, the symphony becomes a place that is simultaneously creative and uncreative, passionate and pas-

sionless, realistic and unrealistic. In like manner, introducing novel discourse in a total quality management process (e.g., *cross-functional teams* and *empowerment*) juxtaposed with resistance language such as "beat it to death" and "not submit until we wave the white flag" creates ambiguity that simultaneously preserves and changes an organization (Barrett, Thomas, & Hocevar, 1995).

Ambiguity and fragmentation also characterize the interplay between acceptance and rejection of organizational identities. Phillips and Hardy (1997) demonstrate how the term *refugee* constructs the self as a product of the discursive struggles among four different governmental organizations. These agencies constitute refugees in fragmented ways as *bogus applicants, disguised economic migrants, clients, constituencies* and/or *dependents,* depending on the prevailing local practices of refugee determination.

Through analysis of a Working Together program, Holmer-Nadesan (1996) illustrates how responses to contradictory discourses in a large university provide space for service workers to shift among identification, counteridentification, and disidentification. "Bitching" as a form of discourse also serves as an ambivalent communication practice that constitutes organizational identities as both maintaining secretarial stereotypes and destabilizing clerical identities (Sotirin & Gottfried, 1999). For Pringle (1988), secretarial moments of bitching, gossiping, and joking enact a form of sexual power play that contributes not only to resistance but also to the tensions between rationality and emotionality in the workplace. In general, ambiguity and fragmentation arise from multiple discourses and the interplay of contradictions. These discourses, in turn, open up space for resistance and for shifting organizational power relations.

### Irony and Paradox

Tensions between rationality and emotionality underlie postmodern views of irony and paradox. Unlike the rhetorical and critical perspectives, ironies and contradictions in this orientation stem from shifting meanings and fragmented practices rather than from deep-seated structures or rhetorical functions. In the postmodern perspective, irony aids in recognizing incongruity, holding incompatibilities together, and celebrating the contingencies of discourse. For instance, in her study of a women's social service organization, Trethewey (1999) demonstrates how an ironic stance both celebrates client resistance and "problematize[s] the distinctions between resistance and accommodation, between power and powerlessness, and between agency and subjection" (p. 161). Irony fosters contradictions that lead to paradoxes, such as promoting self-sufficiency by creating client dependency, empowering clients through controlling their behaviors, and developing trust through objectifying others (Trethewey, 1997).

Paradoxical discourse, as the simultaneous enactment of two mutually exclusive imperatives, surfaces in the postmodern perspective as chaotic, spontaneous, and nonrational. As with the rhetorical and critical perspectives, paradoxes are self-referential and often lead to vicious circles and double binds; hence, organizations typically want to eliminate, resolve, or transcend them (Smith & Berg, 1987). In the postmodern perspective, however, paradoxes, as illogical aspects of organizing, are empowering and beneficial. They provide counterintuitive insights, encourage nonrational thinking, and counterbalance organizations with Zen-like wisdom (Wendt, 1998).

In her analysis of organizational change, O'Connor (1995) illustrates how organizations learn from paradoxes. Applying narrative to an analysis of a high-tech manufacturing firm, O'Connor shows how involvement in organizational change entails coping with the paradoxes of absence/presence, inclusion/exclusion, retaining/losing jobs, and siding with/against champions of change. Organizations that embrace the *both-and* of these paradoxes engage in counterintuitive learning and feel empowered from the constant interplay of these contradictions. Overall, the study of irony and paradox in the postmodern perspective celebrates the contingencies of language through providing counterintuitive insights and promoting a self-referential process. Rather than creating paralysis, paradoxes open up discourse and embrace diversity.

## Language as Texts

In addition to ironies and paradox, the concept of text takes on different nuances in the postmodern perspective. Linguistic and rhetorical scholars often treat *text* as written documents, reifications of experience, or social facts that represent coherent meanings or thematic unity (Cheney & Tompkins, 1988; Kets de Vries & Miller, 1987). Critical theorists, in turn, view texts as institutionalized forces or networks of intertextual relations that sustain power. In the postmodern perspective, *text* becomes a metaphor for organizing, the constellation of discursive practices, and the array of multiple fragmented meanings. Texts are temporal, self-reflexive, and grounded in both local experiences and historical meanings (Strine, 1988; Thatchenkery, 1992). Postmodernists also privilege intertextuality, as the way a given text embodies other texts within it. Studies of texts in the postmodern perspective cluster into these categories: deconstructing texts, texts and conversations, and dialogue as texts.

*Deconstructing texts.* In the postmodern perspective, language is inherently unstable. Its illusion of stability derives from a system of binary opposites in which one term of a pair is privileged over the other. Deconstruction is a literary method in which researchers disassemble a text through revealing the concealed and marginalized terms and opening the text for alternative interpretations (Derrida, 1976). A number of scholars have deconstructed classic texts to introduce multiple readings of organizational theory (see Calás & Smircich, 1999, for these citations). This review, however, centers on the analyses of empirical and practical texts aimed at exposing dualisms and providing alternative readings.

Four articles deconstruct the discourses of popular and practitioner textbooks on leadership, workforce diversity, constituent corporate directors, and stakeholders. Through juxtaposing leadership with seduction, Calás and Smircich (1991) demonstrate how the rhetoric of leadership parallels a seductive game and how leadership embodies multiple rather than unitary meanings. Similarly, Litvin's (1997) deconstruction of workforce diversity shows how society prescribes essentialistic categories and ignores the way that ongoing interaction accomplishes the presence of difference. In her analysis of recent texts, Bradshaw (1996) shows how oppositional pairs in the corporate boardroom discourse reaffirms the status quo and excludes women board members. Finally, Calton and Kurland (1996) recast organizational stakeholders as connected knowers in webs of relationships through deconstructing the oppositional pairs linked to autonomy, impartial reasoning, competition, and environmental control.

Empirical studies that deconstruct organizational texts focus on tensions between public and private and presence and absence in organizational life. In her analysis of a CEO memo, Martin (1990) examines the text and subtext of this message to illustrate how a high-ranking executive's pregnancy suppresses gender conflict, reifies existing structures, and challenges traditional dichotomies. The dialectic of presence/absence also characterizes worker accounts of quality management teams (Mumby & Stohl, 1991). Obligations to substitute for an absent team member leads employees to blame each other rather than management for an inadequate workforce. Thus, physical absence becomes a way of enacting the tensions between presence and absence at both the team and system levels.

The tensions between public and private and insider and outsider surface in Boje's (1995) deconstruction of the modernist and postmodernist readings of the Disney Corporation. Through examining the dualities embedded in documents and interviews, Boje ob-serves how Disney struggles to maintain a grand narrative while marginalizing multiple voices and counterculture views. As a literary technique, deconstruction of organizational texts reveals the shadow-side of organizing and shows how power marginalizes certain discourses while privileging other voices.

*Texts as dialogue.* One way of fragmenting grand narratives into multiple local discourses is to privilege dialogue rather than monologue. Dialogue is a mode of communication that builds mutuality through the awareness of others, use of genuine or authentic discourse, and reliance on the unfolding interaction. Although viewed as a momentary accomplishment (Cissna & Anderson, 1998), the conditions for engaging in dialogue serve as the "praxis for mediating competing and contradictory discourses" (Hawes, 1999). Drawn from the work of Bakhtin (1981) and Buber (1923/1958), organizational studies of dialogue center on promoting learning through opening a "third space" for questioning, critiquing, reconfiguring interests, and affirming differences (Evered & Tannenbaum, 1992). Dialogue stresses balanced communication by providing parties with a chance to speak and be heard and to challenge the traditional positioning of authority (Eisenberg & Goodall, 1993).

Dialogue, then, is a genre of discourse that mediates the instabilities of difference through not only creating something new but also altering the identity of a system (Hawes, 1999). Thus, dialogue is closely linked to organizational learning (Isaacs, 1993, 1999) and the interplay of stability and change (Kristiansen & Bloch-Poulsen, 2000). Through developing a caring container, Kristiansen and Bloch-Poulsen illustrate how dialogic competencies and sequences of interaction enable managers and employees in a Danish industrial company to transcend a priori ways of relating, speak the unspoken across different organizational status positions, and become valid partners in producing new meanings. Similar approaches to understanding organizations surface in the work on appreciative inquiry (Barrett, 1995; Barrett & Cooperrider, 1990) and workplace relationships (Fletcher, 1999; McNamee, Gergen, & Associates, 1999). Although originating in modernism, dialogue as a postmodern discourse embraces fragmentation and ambiguity, privileges differences, and offers an alternative for parties to mediate contradictions and develop a third space.

*Text and conversations.* Playing off the tensions between text and conversation, Taylor and Cooren set forth a postmodern approach that embraces the duality between action and structure (Cooren, 1997, 1999, 2000; Cooren & Taylor, 1997, 1998; Groleau & Cooren, 1998; Taylor, 1995; Taylor & Cooren, 1997; Taylor, Cooren, Giroux, & Robichaud, 1996; Taylor & Van Every, 2000). They posit the discursive equivalent of the structure maxim—that structure is the medium and outcome of action. However, they substitute text for structure and treat text as the medium and outcome of conversation. Thus, the agency they ascribe to text, a non-human agent, fits the tenets of postmodern thinking and positions this approach within actor-network theory (Callon, 1986; Callon & Latour, 1981; Latour, 1993, 1994, 1996a), semiotics (Greimas, 1987), and activity theory (Engeström, 1987, 1990).

Taylor (1993) purports that language has inherent organizing properties similar to speech acts, sentence grammars, story grammars, argument structures, and lexicons. Cooren and Taylor (1997) also argue that the concept of interaction should be broadened to include the active role of non-human agents. This non-human agency is especially illustrated by the important role played by texts, machines, and architectural elements in organizational settings. These agents have struc-

turing properties that are typically neglected in traditional organizational analyses.

Although the work in this area is primarily theoretical, recent articles test these ideas with empirical data. For example, Cooren and Fairhurst (in press) examine story grammars in an organizational downsizing to demonstrate the way "restorying" through workforce restructuring alters management policy. Groleau and Cooren (1998), Cooren and Taylor (1998), and Robichaud (1998) apply this approach to the implementation of organizational technology, the development of a parliamentary commission in a national assembly, and the way a municipality organizes a public discussion. Finally, Cooren and Taylor (2000) use this approach to analyze the organization of a coalition during an environmental controversy. Drawing from linguistic traditions, the interplay of text and conversation seeks to understand how the inherent properties of language ascribe organizing as texts. In this sense, text is both the medium and outcome of conversation.

Postmodern approaches privilege structural relations, texts, and intertexuality of meaning; however, meaning is unstable and often shifts among multiple and contradictory discourses. Power arises through a duality of control enacted in language games and local narratives. The self-referential and contradictory nature of meaning surfaces in paradoxes and ambiguities. As the embodiment of discursive practices and fragmented meanings, texts become the metaphors for organizing.

One particular problem that arises in both the postmodern and critical perspectives is a tendency to overlay a particular linguistic form onto an organizational phenomenon, without a careful inductive analysis of the underlying processes that influence this choice (Dunford & Palmer, 1996). Hence, the research functions deductively to label a pattern without noting the linguistic elements and discursive practices that comprise this form. That is, linguistic forms should not become templates to impose on organizational processes.

Linguistic analyses rooted in deconstruction typically avoid this pitfall. Deconstruction introduces alternative readings of texts by dismantling binary opposites, and dialogue mediates the tensions among disparate interpretations. Through focusing on the inherent properties of language, text and conversations in the postmodern perspective surface as isomorphic with organizing.

## SUMMARY AND DISCUSSION

This chapter reviews the empirical literature on discourse and organizations in eight perspectives: sociolinguistics, conversation analysis, cognitive linguistics, pragmatics, semiotics, literary and rhetorical analysis, critical language studies, and postmodern language analysis. These approaches differ in definitions of language, salient linguistic features, and organizational processes. In the sociolinguistic perspective, language is a system of codes that indexes static organizational structures, occupational communities, and gender/class variables.

Conversation analysts focus on the syntax and coherence of talk, treating conversation as an accomplishment. Studies center on the opening and closings of talk in performance appraisals, turn taking and interruptions in organizational meetings, adjacency pairs in job interviews, topic shifts in decision making, and disclaimers in superior-subordinate interactions. Both sociolinguistics and conversation analysis treat organizations as institutional structures that exist prior to language use.

Cognitive linguistics shifts the focus of language to meanings that reside within language users; hence, organizing is a process of collective sensemaking triggered by discourse. Organizational studies focus on scripts and schemata, cognitive mapping, semantic networks, and frames. In the pragmatic perspective, discourse produces organizing through being uttered as a speech act, constituting speech communities, performing conversations, telling stories, negotiating orders, and enacting interaction sequences and patterns. Semiotics emphasizes sign systems and how language signifies through patterns of meaning in factory work, emergency call systems, and corporate images.

Literary and rhetorical perspectives highlight meaning, text, and context as the key features of language analysis. Studies in this area focus on rhetorical strategies in corporate advocacy, argument in decision making, and literary tropes in organizational change. Context plays a dominant role in critical language studies. Grounded in a concern about power and control, critical studies highlight narrative talk, rituals and texts, everyday talk, and contradictions in organizations. With an emphasis on text and intertexuality, postmodern language analysis treats discourse as a set of relations in which meaning shifts through fragmentation, ambiguity, and paradox. Studies on language as texts include deconstructions of popular and practitioner textbooks, dialogue as texts, and the links between text and conversations.

Whereas a decade ago there were relatively few studies on discourse processes in organizations, this review suggests that research is becoming prolific. Scholars from a wide range of backgrounds within the organizational sciences focus on an increasing number and variety of discursive forms that constitute organizational life. Analysis of this growing body of literature leads to several implications for future research.

First, analysis of the implicit relationship between language and communication supports a meaning-centered view of communication over a transmission model. Only interaction analysis and sociolinguistics depart from this general trend. The pendulum has also swung away from variable analytic models and the scientific method because they lose too many distinctive qualities of communication (Cronen, 1995). Correspondingly, scientific approaches to language analysis, which focus on the function, frequency, and regularity of organizational messages, appear less often than do interpretive methods, which focus on meaning, context, and structure. However, it is too soon to dismiss scientific methods because neither a focus on meaning nor frequency alone can answer the relevant questions about discourse and organizations.

Second, different approaches to language analysis share important conceptual distinctions that figure prominently in the debate about discourse and organization. In this debate, the relationships between discourse and organization emerge as reflective, constitutive, or equivalent (Cooren & Taylor, 1997; Smith, 1993). In the reflective relationship, language represents or reflects organizations as structures, occupational communities, levels of meanings, or systems of codes. In the constitutive relationship, discourse and organizations are active and dynamic and develop a relationship in which organizations produce language, language produces organizations, or the two coproduce each other. In the equivalency relationship, discourse and organizing are one in the same. That is, organizing is communicating through the intersection of conversation and text.

Fewer contemporary analyses of discourse and organization adopt a reflective relationship and a container view of organizations. This stance trivializes communication and language use, reifies the organization, and pays little attention to organizational change (Cooren & Taylor, 1997). Most perspectives included in this review embrace variations of social constructivism, which supports the production relationship of discourse and organization. These perspectives acknowledge the organizing potential of discourse while they maintain an assumption of organizational primacy (i.e., discourse and organization are inextricably bound but *separate* phenomena). By contrast, language analysis influenced by postmodernism is most compatible with an equivalency view, which casts organization and discourse as simultaneous achievements.

Fragmentation and decentering of the subject in postmodern perspectives parallels the way in which equivalency problematizes organization and discourse in each other's terms.

However, organizational discourse analysts in general are guilty of mixing their perspectives. Even within the same article, container-view descriptions, such as language as an *actualizing process* or discourse that *uncovers* or *reflects* the organization, are mixed with production-view descriptors, such as discourse that *accomplishes, defines,* or *produces* the organization. These references, in turn, are coupled with equivalency notions of discourse that are *simultaneously organizational.* As these perspectives become intertwined, either intentionally or inadvertently, the theoretical status of the discourse-organization relationship becomes unclear. In essence, organizational researchers need to be explicit in articulating their positions on the discourse-organization relationship.

Third, most of these perspectives struggle with the problem of context. These problems include (1) reifying context by treating the organization as static (e.g., sociolinguistics, ethnography of speaking), (2) focusing on conversational structures and failing to discern the broader organizational and societal issues (e.g., interaction analysis, conversation analysis), (3) analyzing excerpts of discourse out of context (e.g., discourse analysis, critical discourse analysis, postmodern analysis), and (4) failing to determine which aspects of organizational context contribute to particular language forms (e.g., ethnography of speaking).

Because context consists of any element that shapes the way people think and what they expect, its unwieldy nature creates a tendency to simplify levels of analysis and to treat context as a frame for social interaction rather than as an interactional achievement (Beach, 1995). But to fully understand the relationship between discourse and organization, language analysts need to complicate their views of context through "thick descriptions" of organizational processes that form a nexus of influences on discursive production.

Fourth, Mauws and Phillips (1999) recently note that the vast array of practices that constitute organizations not only requires identification, but also involves understanding patterns that emerge from these practices. This requirement raises a number of empirical questions about the relationship between discourse and organization, the sampling of discourse as a structured sets of texts, and differentiating between discursive and nondiscursive organizational practices.

Other empirical questions regarding the meaning of the term *organization* need to be raised. Like a Procrustean bed, different studies cast the organization in terms of its leadership; a set of team dynamics; a set of genres for communicating; or a response to an event, a controversy, or a change effort. Relatedly, examining the way individual linguistic forms contribute to a larger unit is not the same as examining how discourse and organization work in concert (i.e., the contingent basis on which they operate and take shape). The application of different linguistic perspectives complicates this issue (e.g., interaction analysis and ethnography). Finally, researchers need to investigate how linguistic patterns combine over time and how they contribute to larger and larger organizational units.

Boden's (1994) work is a case in point. Citing Giddens (1979, 1984) and drawing from Goffman's (1974) notion of the lamination of conversations, Boden argues that patterns take shape from multiple conversations on common topics and roles to knit together the organization as a whole. Even though she illustrates this process with a number of discursive forms (e.g., question-answer, turn taking, categorization devices), she never fully unpacks the lamination question. In essence, *how* do conversations layer to form patterns? Given that patterns form around common topics and roles, how do linguistic features combine to create an internal structure in this layering process, especially given the wide variety of linguistic patterns that contribute to this process? Moreover, how does one layered set of conversations connect to another set to construct larger organizational units? The lamination metaphor is a useful heuristic that most discourse analysts accept as a generating mechanism for structure, but the question of how the lamination process actually works remains unanswered.

Unfortunately, even if language analysts could resolve the lamination question, they must face a second dilemma; that is, discourse analysis primarily examines traces of conversation rather than conversations or texts per se. Even though texts have certain properties that conversations do not, including the capacity to transcend the local (Derrida, 1988), they are only partial. Inevitably, researches face a major sampling question because organizations produce an innumerable number and variety of texts from which to select. Conversations, briefings, meetings, e-mail messages, reports, and press releases are just a few of the discourses that organizations produce day after day, month after month, and year after year. How does a language analyst determine which texts to select? While some analysts argue that any text is part of the organization and thus worthy of study, ethnographic studies and event-related analyses often reveal that this assumption is risky. Not all texts have equal saliency in the process of organizing.

Finally, most of these studies, with the exception of semiotics and postmodernism, accept an artificial separation between discursive and nondiscursive practices, one that biases research toward discursive analyses. Even though conventional folk wisdom often demeans talk in favor of organizational action (Marshak, 1998), many language analysts continue to view talk and action as disjoint activities, even though they shift the emphasis to discourse. The problem is not their view of the relationship between talk and action; rather, it stems from their treatment of nondiscursive action as underrepresented in the analyses. More attention to context should address this concern.

However these issues get resolved, the study of discourse and organizations has come of age. Increasing numbers of organizational scholars recognize language and communication as fields of study that are intertwined, interdependent, and among the most promising in the search for knowledge about organizational life.

# REFERENCES

Adkins, M., & Brashers, D. E. (1995). The power of language in computer-mediated groups. *Management Communication Quarterly, 8,* 289-322.

Ainsworth-Vaughn, N. (1992). Topic transitions in physician-patient interviews: Power, gender, and discourse change. *Language in Society, 21,* 409-426.

Akrich, M., & Latour, B. (1992). A summary of a convenient vocabulary for the semiotics of human and nonhuman assemblies. In W. Bijker & J. Law (Eds.), *Shaping technology, building society: Studies in sociotechnical change* (pp. 259-264). Cambridge, MA: MIT Press.

Allen, M. W., & Caillouet, R. H. (1994). Legitimate endeavors: Impression management strategies used by an organization in crisis. *Communication Monographs, 61,* 44-62.

Alvesson, M. (1993). The play of metaphors. In J. Hassard & M. Parker (Eds.), *Postmodernism and organizations* (pp. 114-131). London: Sage.

Anderson, P. A. (1983). Decision making by objection and the Cuban missile crisis. *Administrative Science Quarterly, 28,* 201-222.

Anderson-Gough, F., Grey, C., & Robson, K. (1998). "Work hard, play hard": An analysis of organizational cliché in two accountancy practices. *Organization, 5,* 565-592.

Austin, J. L. (1962). *How to do things with words.* Cambridge, MA: Harvard University Press.

Bacharach, S. B., & Lawler, E. J. (1981). *Bargaining: Power, tactics, and outcomes.* San Francisco: Jossey-Bass.

Baker, M. A. (1991). Gender and verbal communication in professional settings. *Management Communication Quarterly, 5,* 36-63.

Bakhtin, M. (1981). *The dialogic imagination* (C. Emerson & M. Holquist, Trans.). Austin: University of Texas Press.

Bales, R. F. (1950). *Interaction process analysis.* Cambridge, MA: Addison-Wesley.

Bales, R. F., & Cohen, S. P. (1979). *SYMLOG: A system for the multiple level observation of groups.* New York: Free Press.

Balmer, J. M. T. (1995). Corporate branding and connoisseurship. *Journal of General Management, 21*(1), 24-46.

Bandura, A. (1986). *Social foundations of thought and action.* Englewood Cliffs, NJ: Prentice Hall.

Banks, S. P. (1987). Achieving "unmarkedness" in organizational discourse: A praxis perspective on ethnolinguistic identity. *Journal of Language and Social Psychology, 6,* 171-189.

Banks, S. P. (1994). Performing public announcements: The case of flight attendants' work discourse. *Text and Performance Quarterly, 14,* 253-267.

Barker, J. (1993). Tightening the iron cage: Concertive control in self-managing teams. *Administrative Science Quarterly, 38,* 408-437.

Barley, S. R. (1983). Semiotics and the study of occupational and organizational culture. *Administrative Science Quarterly, 28,* 393-413.

Barley, S. R. (1986). Technology as an occasion for structuring: Evidence from observation of CT scanners and the social order of radiology departments. *Administrative Science Quarterly, 31,* 78-108.

Baron, R. A. (1990). Countering the effects of destructive criticism: The relative efficacy of four interventions. *Journal of Applied Psychology, 75,* 235-245.

Barrett, F. J. (1995). Creating appreciative learning cultures. *Organizational Dynamics, 24*(2), 36-49.

Barrett, F. J., & Cooperrider, D. L. (1990). Generative metaphor intervention: A new behavioral approach for working with systems divided by conflict and caught in defensive perception. *Journal of Applied Behavioral Science, 26*(2), 219-239.

Barrett, F. J., Thomas, G. F., Hocevar, S. P. (1995). The central role of discourse in large-scale change: A social construction perspective. *Journal of Applied Behavioral Science, 31,* 352-372.

Barton, L. (1993). *Crisis in organizations: Managing and communicating in the heat of chaos.* Cincinnati, OH: South-Western, College Division.

Bastien, D. T. (1992). Change in organizational culture: The use of linguistic methods in corporate acquisition. *Management Communication Quarterly, 5,* 403-442.

Bastien, D. T., McPhee, R. D., & Bolton, K. A. (1995). A study and extended theory of the structuration of climate. *Communication Monographs, 62,* 87-109.

Bateson, G. (1972). *Steps to an ecology of the mind.* New York: Ballantine.

Baxter, L. (1993). "Talking things through" and "putting it in writing": Two codes of communication in an academic institution. *Journal of Applied Communication Research, 21,* 313-326.

Beach, W. A. (1995). Conversation analysis: "Okay" as a clue for understanding consequentiality. In S. J. Sigman (Ed.), *The consequentiality of communication* (pp. 121-162). Hillsdale, NJ: Lawrence Erlbaum.

Bednar, D. A., & Curington, W. P. (1983). Interaction analysis: A tool for understanding negotiations. *Industrial and Labor Relations Review, 36,* 389-401.

Benoit, W. L. (1992, November). *Union Carbide and the Bhopal tragedy.* Paper presented at the annual meeting of the Speech Communication Association, Chicago.

Benoit, W. L., & Brinson, S. L. (1994). AT&T: "Apologies are not enough." *Communication Quarterly, 42,* 75-88.

Bettman, J. R., & Weitz, B. A. (1983). Attributions in the board room: Causal reasoning in corporate annual reports. *Administrative Science Quarterly, 28,* 165-183.

Bies, R. J. (1989). Managing conflict before it happens: The role of accounts. In M. A. Rahim (Ed.), *Managing conflict: An interdisciplinary approach* (pp. 83-91). New York: Praeger.

Bies, R. J., & Moag, J. S. (1986). Interactional justice: Communication criteria of fairness. In R. J. Lewicki, B. H. Sheppard, & M. H. Bazerman (Eds.), *Research on negotiation in organizations* (pp. 43-55). Greenwich, CT: JAI.

Bies, R. J., & Shapiro, D. L. (1987). Interactional fairness judgments: The influence of causal accounts. *Social Justice Research, 1,* 199-218.

Bies, R. J., & Shapiro, D. L. (1988). Voice and justification: The influence on procedural fairness judgements. *Academy of Management Journal, 31,* 676-685.

Bies, R. J., Shapiro, D. L., & Cummings, L. L. (1988). Causal accounts and managing organizational conflict: Is it enough to say it's not my fault? *Communication Research, 15,* 381-399.

Bies, R. J., & Sitkin, S. B. (1992). Excuse-making in organizations: Explanation as legitimation. In M. L. McLaughlin, M. J. Cody, & S. Read (Eds.), *Explaining one's self to others: Reason giving in a social context* (pp. 183-198). Hillsdale, NJ: Lawrence Erlbaum.

Blum-Kulka, S. (1997). Discourse pragmatics. In T. A. van Dijk (Ed.), *Discourse as social interaction* (Vol. 2, pp. 38-63). London: Sage.

Blumer, H. (1969). *Symbolic interactionism: Perspective and method.* Englewood Cliffs, NJ: Prentice Hall.

Boden, D. (1994). *The business of talk: Organizations in action.* Cambridge, UK: Polity.

Boethius, S. B. (1987). The view from the middle: Perceiving patterns of interaction in middle management groups. *International Journal of Small Group Research, 3,* 1-15.

Boje, D. M. (1991). The storytelling organization: A study of story performance in an office-supply firm. *Administrative Science Quarterly, 36,* 106-126.

Boje, D. M. (1995). Stories of the storytelling organization: A postmodern analysis of Disney as "Tamara-land." *Academy of Management Journal, 38,* 997-1035.

Boland, R. J., Jr., & Greenberg, R. H. (1988). Metaphorical structuring of organizational ambiguity. In L. R. Pondy, R. J. Boland, & H. Thomas (Eds.), *Managing ambiguity and change* (pp. 17-36). New York: John Wiley.

Boland, R. J., Jr., & Hoffman, R. (1986). Humor in a machine shop: An interpretation of symbolic action. In P. Frost, V. Mitchell, & W. Nord (Eds.), *Organization reality: Reports from the firing line* (pp. 371-376). Glenview, IL: Scott, Foresman.

Bowles, M. L., & Coates, G. (1993). Image and substance: The management of performance as rhetoric or reality? *Personnel Review, 22*(2), 3-21.

Braaten, D. O., Cody, M. J., & DeTienne, K. B. (1993). Account episodes in organizations: Remedial work and impression management. *Management Communication Quarterly, 6,* 219-250.

Bradshaw, P. (1996). Women as constituent directors: Re-reading current texts using a feminist-postmodernist approach. In D. M. Boje, R. P. Gephart, & T. J. Thatchenkery (Eds.), *Postmodern management and organization theory* (pp. 95-124). London: Sage.

Brink, T. L. (1993). Metaphor as data in the study of organizations. *Journal of Management Inquiry, 2,* 366-371.

Brinson, S. L., & Benoit, W. L. (1999). The tarnished star: Restoring Texaco's damaged public image. *Management Communication Quarterly, 12,* 483-510.

Broussine, M., & Vince, R. (1996). Working with metaphor towards organizational change. In C. Oswick & D. Grant (Eds.), *Organization development: Metaphorical explorations* (pp. 557-572). London: Pitman.

Brown, R., & Ford, M. (1961). Address in American English. *Journal of Abnormal and Social Psychology, 62,* 375-385.

Brown, R. H. (1977). *A poetic for sociology.* Cambridge, UK: Cambridge University Press.

Buber, M. (1958). *I and thou* (2nd ed., R. G. Smith, Trans.). New York: Scribner. (Original work published 1923)

Bullis, C., & Tompkins, P. K. (1989). The forest ranger revisited: A study of control practices and identification. *Communication Monographs, 56,* 287-306.

Burke, K. (1969a). *A grammar of motives.* Berkeley: University of California Press. (Original work published 1945)

Burke, K. (1969b). *A rhetoric of motives.* Berkeley: University of California Press. (Original work published 1950)

Burns, T., & Stalker, G. M. (1961). *The management of innovation.* London: Tavistock.

Button, G. (Ed.). (1993). *Technology in working order: Studies of work, interaction, and technology.* London: Routledge.

Calás, M. B., & Smircich, L. (1991). Voicing seduction to silence leadership. *Organization Studies, 12*(4), 567-602.

Calás, M. B., & Smircich, L. (1999). Past postmodernism? Reflections and tentative directions. *Academy of Management Review, 24*(4), 649-671.

Callon, M. (1986). Some elements of sociology of translation: The domestication of the scallops and the fishermen of St-Brieuc Bay. In J. Law (Ed.), *Power, action, belief* (pp. 196-233). London: Routledge and Kegan Paul.

Callon, M., & Latour, B. (1981). Unscrewing the big Leviathan: How actors macro-structure reality and how sociologists help them to do so. In A. Cicourel & K. Knorr-Cetina (Eds.), *Advances in social theory and methodology: Towards an integration of micro- and macro-sociologies* (pp. 277-303). Boston: Routledge and Kegan Paul.

Calton, J. M., & Kurland, N. B. (1996). A theory of stakeholder enabling: Giving voice to an emerging postmodern praxis of organizational discourse. In D. M. Boje, R. P. Gephart, & T. J. Thatchenkery (Eds.), *Postmodern management and organization theory* (pp. 154-177). London: Sage.

Campbell, K. S., Follender, S. I., & Shane, G. (1998). Preferred strategies for responding to hostile questions in environmental public meetings. *Management Communication Quarterly, 11*, 401-421.

Carroll, J. S., & Payne, J. W. (1991). An information processing approach to two party negotiations. In M. H. Bazerman, R. J. Lewicki, & B. H. Sheppard (Eds.), *Research on negotiation in organizations* (pp. 3-34). Greenwich, CT: JAI.

Cazal, D., & Inns, D. (1998). Metaphor, language, and meaning. In D. Grant, T. Keenoy, & C. Oswick (Eds.), *Discourse and organization* (pp. 177-192). London: Sage.

Cegala, D., Wall, V. D., & Rippey, G. (1987). An investigation of interaction involvement and the dimensions of SYMLOG: Perceived communication behaviors of persons in task-oriented groups. *Central States Speech Journal, 38*, 81-93.

Chatman, J. A., Putnam, L. L., & Sondak, H. (1991). Integrating communication and negotiation research. In M. H. Bazerman, R. J. Lewicki, & B. H. Sheppard (Eds.), *Research on negotiation in organizations* (pp. 139-164). Greenwich, CT: JAI.

Cheney, G. (1983). The rhetoric of identification and the study of organizational communication. *Quarterly Journal of Speech, 69*, 143-158.

Cheney, G. (1991). *Rhetoric in an organizational society: Managing multiple identities.* Columbia: University of South Carolina Press.

Cheney, G., & Frenette, G. (1993). Persuasion and organization: Values, logics, and accounts in contemporary corporate public discourse. In C. Conrad (Ed.), *Ethical nexus* (pp. 49-73). Norwood, NJ: Ablex.

Cheney, G., & Tompkins, P. K. (1988). On the facts of the text as the basis of human communication research. In J. A. Anderson (Ed.), *Communication yearbook 11* (pp. 455-481). Newbury Park, CA: Sage.

Cheney, G., & Vibbert, S. L. (1987). Corporate discourse: Public relations and issue management. In F. M. Jablin, L. L. Putnam, K. H. Roberts, & L. W. Porter (Eds.), *Handbook of organizational communication: An interdisciplinary perspective* (pp. 165-194). Newbury Park, CA: Sage.

Chia, R. (1996). *Organizational analysis as deconstructive practice.* New York: Walter de Gruyter.

Christensen, L. T. (1995). Buffering organisational identity in the marketing culture. *Organization Studies, 16*, 651-672.

Christensen, L. T., & Askegaard, S. (in press). Corporate identity and corporate image revisited: A semiotic perspective. *European Journal of Marketing.*

Cissna, K. N., & Anderson, R. (1998). Theorizing about dialogic moments: The Buber-Rogers position and postmodern themes. *Communication Theory, 8*(1), 63-104.

Clair, R. P. (1993a). The bureaucratization, commodification, and privatization of sexual harassment through institutional discourse. *Management Communication Quarterly, 7*, 123-157.

Clair, R. P. (1993b). The use of framing devices to sequester organizational narratives: Hegemony and harassment. *Communication Monographs, 60*, 113-136.

Clair, R. P., & Thompson, K. (1996). Pay discrimination as a discursive and material practice: A case concerning extended housework. *Journal of Applied Communication Research, 24*, 1-20.

Coleman, H. (1985). Talking shop: An overview of language and work. *International Journal of Sociology of Language, 51*, 105-129.

Collinson, D. (1988). Engineering humor: Masculinity, joking and conflict in shop-floor relations. *Organization Studies, 9*, 181-199.

Collinson, D. (1992). *Managing the shopfloor: Subjectivity, masculinity and workplace culture.* New York: Walter de Gruyter.

Conley, J. M., & O'Barr, W. M. (1990). *Rules versus relationships: The ethnography of legal discourse.* Chicago: University of Chicago Press.

Conrad, C. (1993). The ethical nexus: Conceptual grounding. In C. Conrad (Ed.), *Ethical nexus* (pp. 7-22). Norwood, NJ: Ablex.

Contractor, N. S., & Seibold, D. R. (1993). Theoretical frameworks for the study of structuring processes in group decision support systems: Adaptive structuration theory and self-organizing systems theory. *Human Communication Research, 19*, 528-563.

Coombs, W. T. (1995). Choosing the right words: The development of guidelines for the selection of the "appropriate" crisis-response strategies. *Management Communication Quarterly, 8*, 447-476.

Cooren, F. (1997). Actes de langage et semio-narrativite: Une analyse semiotique des indirections. *Semiotica, 116,* 339-273.

Cooren, F. (1999). Applying socio-semiotics to organizational communication: A new approach. *Management Communication Quarterly 13,* 294-304.

Cooren, F. (2000). *The organizing property of communication.* Amsterdam and Philadelphia: John Benjamins.

Cooren, F., & Fairhurst, G. T. (in press). The leader as a practical narrator: Leadership as the art of translating. In D. Holman & R. Thorpe (Eds.), *The manager as a practical author.* London: Sage.

Cooren, F., & Taylor, J. R. (1997). Organization as an effect of mediation: Redefining the link between organization and communication. *Communication Theory, 7,* 219-260.

Cooren, F., & Taylor, J. R. (1998). The procedural and rhetorical modes of the organizing dimension of communication: Discursive analysis of a parliamentary commission. *Communication Review, 3*(1-2), 65-101.

Cooren, F., & Taylor, J. R. (2000). Association and dissociation in an ecological controversy: The great whale case. In N. W. Coppola & B. Karis (Eds.), *Technical communication, deliberative rhetoric, and environmental discourse: Connections and directions* (pp. 171-190). Stamford, CT: Ablex.

Coser, R. L. (1959). Some social functions of laughter. *Human Relations, 12,* 171-182.

Coser, R. L. (1960). Laughter among colleagues. *Psychiatry, 23,* 81-95.

Courtright, J. A., Fairhurst, G. T., & Rogers, L. E. (1989). Interaction patterns in organic and mechanistic systems. *Academy of Management Journal, 32,* 773-802.

Cray, D. (1989). The use of symbols in multicriteria decision making. *Lecture Notes in Economics and Mathematical Systems, 335,* 100-111.

Cronen, V. E. (1995). Coordinated management of meaning: The consequentiality of communication and the recapturing of experience. In S. J. Sigman (Ed.), *The consequentiality of communication* (pp. 17-66). Hillsdale, NJ: Lawrence Erlbaum.

Czarniawska-Joerges, B., & Joerges, B. (1988). How to control things with words: Organizational talk and control. *Management Communication Quarterly, 2,* 170-193.

Dandridge, T. C., Mitroff, I., & Joyce, W. F. (1980). Organizational symbolism: A topic to expand organizational analysis. *Academy of Management Review, 5,* 77-82.

Danowski, J. A. (1982). A network-based content analysis methodology for computer-mediated communication: An illustration with a computer bulletin board. In R. Bostrum (Ed.), *Communication yearbook 6* (pp. 904-925). New Brunswick, NJ: Transaction Books.

Deetz, S. (1992). *Democracy in an age of corporate colonization.* Albany: State University of New York Press.

Deetz, S. (1995). *Transforming communication, transforming business: Building responsive and responsible workplaces.* Cresskill, NJ: Hampton.

Dent, J. (1991). Accounting and organizational cultures: A field study of the emergence of a new organizational reality. *Accounting, Organizations and Society, 18,* 705-732.

Derrida, J. (1976). *Of grammatology.* Baltimore: Johns Hopkins University Press.

Derrida, J. (1982). *Margins of philosophy.* Chicago: University of Chicago Press.

Derrida, J. (1988). *Limited Inc.* Chicago: Northwestern University Press.

DeSanctis, G., & Poole, M. S. (1994). Capturing the complexity in advanced technology use: Adaptive structuration theory. *Organizational Dynamics, 5,* 121-147.

DeSanctis, G., Poole, M. S., Dickson, G. W., & Jackson, B. M. (1993). Interpretive analysis of team use of group technologies. *Journal of Organizational Computing, 3,* 1-29.

DeSanctis, G., Poole, M. S., Lewis, H., & Desharnais, G. (1992). Using computing in quality team meetings: Initial observations from the IRS-Minnesota Project. *Journal of Management Information Systems, 8,* 7-26.

DiSanza, J. R., & Bullis, C. (1999). "Everybody identifies with Smokey the Bear": Employee responses to newsletter identification inducements at the U.S. Forest Service. *Management Communication Quarterly, 12,* 347-399.

Donnellon, A. (1986). Language and communication in organizations: Bridging cognition and behavior. In H. P. Sims, Jr. & D. A. Gioia (Eds.), *The thinking organization: Dynamics of organizational social cognition* (pp. 136-164). San Francisco: Jossey-Bass.

Donnellon, A. (1994). Team work: Linguistic models of negotiating differences. In R. J. Lewicki, B. H. Sheppard, & R. Bies (Eds.), *Research on negotiation in organizations* (Vol. 4, pp. 71-123). Greenwich, CT: JAI.

Donnellon, A. (1996). *Team talk: The power of language in team dynamics.* Boston: Harvard Business School Press.

Donnellon, A., Gray, B., & Bougon, M. G. (1986). Communication, meaning, and organized action. *Administrative Science Quarterly, 31,* 43-55.

Donohue, W. A. (1981a). Analyzing negotiation tactics: Development of a negotiation interact system. *Human Communication Research, 7,* 273-287.

Donohue, W. A. (1981b). Development of a model of rule use in negotiation interaction. *Communication Monographs, 48,* 106-120.

Donohue, W. A., & Diez, M. E. (1985). Directive use in negotiation interaction. *Communication Monographs, 52,* 305-318.

Donohue, W. A., Diez, M. E., & Hamilton, M. (1984). Coding naturalistic negotiation interaction. *Human Communication Research, 10,* 403-425.

Donohue, W. A., & Roberto, A. J. (1993). Relational development as negotiated order in hostage negotiation. *Human Communication Research, 20,* 175-198.

Dougherty, D. (1992). *Crisis communications: What every executive needs to know.* New York: Walker.

Drake, B. H., & Moberg, D. J. (1986). Communicating influence attempts in dyads: Linguistic sedatives and palliatives. *Administrative Science Quarterly, 11,* 567-584.

Drew, P., & Heritage, J. (Eds.). (1992). *Talk at work.* Cambridge, UK: Cambridge University Press.

Dubois, B. L., & Crouch, I. (1975). The question of tag questions in women's speech. *Language in Society, 4,* 289-294.

Duncan, W. J. (1983). The superiority theory of humor at work: Joking relationships as indicators of formal and informal status patterns in small, task-oriented groups. *Small Group Behavior, 16,* 556-564.

Duncan, W. J., & Feisal, J. P. (1989). No laughing matter: Patterns of humor in the work place. *Organizational Dynamics, 17,* 18-30.

Dunford, R., & Palmer, I. (1996). Metaphors in popular management discourse: The case of corporate restructuring. In D. Grant & C. Oswick (Eds.), *Metaphor and organizations* (pp. 95-109). Thousand Oaks, CA: Sage.

Dunn, S. (1990). Root metaphor in the old and new industrial relations. *British Journal of Industrial Relations, 28,* 1-31.

Eco, U. (1976). *A theory of semiotics.* Bloomington: University of Indiana Press.

Edelsky, C. (1981). Who's got the floor? *Language in Society, 10,* 383-421.

Edwards, D., & Middleton, D. (1986). Joint remembering: Constructing an account of shared experience through conversational discourse. *Discourse Processes, 9,* 423-459.

Eisenberg, E. M. (1984). Ambiguity as strategy in organizational communication. *Communication Monographs, 51,* 227-242.

Eisenberg, E. M., & Goodall, H. L., Jr. (1993). *Organizational communication: Balancing creativity and constraint.* New York: St. Martin's.

Eisenberg, E. M., & Riley, P. (1988). Organizational symbols and sense-making. In G. M. Goldhaber & G. A. Barnett (Eds.), *Handbook of organizational communication* (pp. 131-150). Norwood, NJ: Ablex.

Ellis, D. G. (1979). Relational control in two group systems. *Communication Monographs, 46,* 156-166.

Engeström, Y. (1987). *Learning by expanding: An activity-theoretical approach to developmental research.* Helsinki: Orienta-Konsultit Oy.

Engeström, Y. (1990). *Learning, working and imagining.* Helsinki: Orienta-Konsultit Oy.

Evered, R. (1983). The language of organizations: The case of the Navy. In L. R. Pondy, P. J. Frost, G. Morgan, & T. C. Dandridge (Eds.), *Organizational symbolism* (pp. 125-143). Greenwich, CT: JAI.

Evered, R., & Tannenbaum, R. (1992). A dialog on dialog. *Journal of Management Inquiry, 1,* 43-55.

Ewald, H. R., & Strine, D. (1983). Speech act theory and business communication conventions. *Journal of Business Communication, 20*(3), 13-25.

Fairclough, N. (1989). *Language and power.* New York: Longman.

Fairclough, N. (1993). Critical discourse analysis and the marketization of public discourse: The universities. *Discourse & Society, 4,* 133-168.

Fairclough, N., & Wodak, R. (1997). Critical discourse analysis. In T. A. van Dijk (Ed.), *Discourse as social interaction* (pp. 258-284). London: Sage.

Fairhurst, G. T. (1993a). Echoes of the vision: When the rest of the organization talks total quality. *Management Communication Quarterly, 6,* 331-371.

Fairhurst, G. T. (1993b). The leader-member exchange patterns of women leaders in industry: A discourse analysis. *Communication Monographs, 60,* 321-351.

Fairhurst, G. T., & Chandler, T. A. (1989). Social structure in leader-member interaction. *Communication Monographs, 56,* 215-239.

Fairhurst, G. T., Green, S. G., & Courtright, J. A. (1994). Inertial forces and the implementation of a socio-technical systems approach: A communication study. *Organization Science, 6,* 168-185.

Fairhurst, G. T., & Putnam, L. L. (1998). Reflections on the organization-communication equivalency question: The contributions of James Taylor and his colleagues. *Communication Review, 31,* 1-19.

Fairhurst, G. T., Rogers, L. E., & Sarr, R. A. (1987). Manager-subordinate control patterns and judgments about the relationship. In M. McLaughlin (Ed.), *Communication yearbook 10* (pp. 395-415). Newbury Park, CA: Sage.

Fairhurst, G. T., & Sarr, R. A. (1996). *The art of framing: Managing the language of leadership.* San Francisco: Jossey-Bass.

Fairhurst, G. T., & Wendt, R. F. (1993). The gap in total quality: A commentary. *Management Communication Quarterly, 6,* 441-451.

Farrell, M. P., Schmidt, M. H., & Heinemann, G. D. (1988). Organizational environments of health care teams: Impact on team development and implications for consultation. *International Journal of Small Group Research, 4,* 31-54.

Filby, I., & Willmott, H. (1988). Ideologies and contradictions in a public relations department: The seduction and impotence of a living myth. *Organization Studies, 9,* 335-349.

Fine, G. (1984). Negotiated orders and organizational cultures. *Annual Review of Sociology, 10,* 239-262.

Fiol, C. M. (1989). A semiotic analysis of corporate language: Organizational boundaries and joint venturing. *Administrative Science Quarterly, 34,* 277-303.

Firth, A. (1994). "Accounts" in negotiation discourse: A single-case analysis. *Journal of Pragmatics, 23,* 199-226.

Firth, A. (Ed.). (1995). *The discourse of negotiation: Studies of language in the workplace.* Oxford, UK: Pergamon.

Fisher, B. A. (1978). *Perspective on human communication.* New York: Macmillan.

Fisher, S., & Groce, S. B. (1990). Accounting practices in medical interviews. *Language in Society, 19,* 225-250.

Fisher, S., & Todd, D. D. (Eds.). (1983). *The social organization of doctor-patient communication.* Washington, DC: Center for Applied Linguistics.

Fletcher, C. (1990). *What cops know.* New York: Villard.

Fletcher, C. (1991). The police war story and the narrative of inequality. *Discourse & Society, 2,* 297-331.

Fletcher, J. K. (1999). *Disappearing acts: Gender, power, and relational practice at work.* Cambridge, MA: MIT Press.

Ford, J. D., & Ford, L. W. (1995). The role of conversations in producing intentional change in organizations. *Academy of Management Review, 20,* 541-570.

Ford, J. D., & Hegarty, W. H. (1984). Decision makers' beliefs about the causes and effects of structure: An exploratory study. *Academy of Management Journal, 27,* 271-291.

Fortado, B. (1998). Interpreting nicknames: A micropolitical portal. *Journal of Management Studies, 35,* 13-34.

Foucault, M. (1977). *Discipline and punish: The birth of the prison* (A. S. Smith, Trans.). New York: Random House.

Frances, D. W. (1986). Some structure of negotiation talk. *Language in Society, 15,* 53-79.

Gabriel, Y. (1998). Same old story or changing stories? In D. Grant, T. Keenoy, & C. Oswick (Eds.), *Discourse and organizations* (pp. 84-103). London: Sage.

Garrett, D. E., Bradford, J. L., Meyers, R. A., & Becker, J. (1989). Issues management and organizational accounts: An analysis of corporate responses to accusations of unethical business practices. *Journal of Business Ethics, 8,* 507-520.

Geist, P., & Chandler, T. (1984). Account analysis of influence in group decision-making. *Communication Monographs, 51,* 67-78.

Gephart, R. P., Jr. (1993). The textual approach: Risk and blame in disaster sense making. *Academy of Management Journal, 36,* 1465-1514.

Giacalone, R. A. (1988). The effect of administrative accounts and gender on the perception of leadership. *Group and Organization Studies, 13,* 195-207.

Giddens, A. (1979). *Central problems in social theory.* Berkeley: University of California Press.

Giddens, A. (1984). *The constitution of society.* Berkeley: University of California Press.

Gilbert, G. N., & Mulkay, M. (1984). *Opening Pandora's box: An analysis of scientists' discourse.* Cambridge, UK: Cambridge University Press.

Gioia, D. A. (1986). The state of the art in organizational social cognition. In H. P. Sims, Jr. & D. A. Gioia (Eds.), *The thinking organization* (pp. 336-356). San Francisco: Jossey-Bass.

Gioia, D. A., Donnellon, A., & Sims, H. P., Jr. (1989). Communication and cognition in appraisal: A tale of two paradigms. *Organization Studies, 10,* 503-530.

Gioia, D. A., & Poole, P. P. (1984). Scripts in organizational behavior. *Academy of Management Review, 9,* 449-459.

Gioia, D. A., & Sims, H. P., Jr. (1986). Cognition-behavior connections: Attribution and verbal behavior in leader-subordinate interactions. *Organizational Behavior and Human Decision Processes, 37,* 197-229.

Glauser, M. J., & Tullar, W. L. (1985). Citizen satisfaction with police officer-citizen interaction: Implications for changing the role of police organizations. *Journal of Applied Psychology, 70,* 514-527.

Goffman, E. (1974). *Frame analysis.* New York: Harper-Colophon.

Gorden, W. I., & Nevins, R. J. (1987). The language and rhetoric of quality: Made in the U.S.A. *Journal of Applied Communication Research, 15,* 19-34.

Gordon, D. P. (1983). Hospital slang for patients: Crocks, gomers, gorks, and others. *Language in Society, 12,* 173-185.

Grant, D., Keenoy, T., & Oswick, C. (1998). Organizational discourse: Of diversity, dichotomy and multi-disciplinarity. In D. Grant, T. Keenoy, & C. Oswick (Eds.), *Discourse and organization* (pp. 1-13). London: Sage.

Grant, D., & Oswick, C. (1996a). Introduction: Getting the measure of metaphors. In D. Grant & C. Oswick (Eds.), *Metaphor and organizations* (pp. 1-20). Thousand Oaks, CA: Sage.

Grant, D., & Oswick, C. (Eds.). (1996b). *Metaphor and organizations.* Thousand Oaks, CA: Sage.

Gray, B. (1997). Framing and reframing of intractable environmental disputes. In R. Lewicki, B. Sheppard, & B. Bies (Eds.), *Research on negotiation in organizations* (pp. 95-112). Greenwich, CT: JAI.

Greatbatch, D., & Dingwall, R. (1994). The interactive construction of interventions by divorce mediators. In J. P. Folger & T. S. Jones (Eds.), *New directions in mediation* (pp. 84-109). Thousand Oaks, CA: Sage.

Greenberg, J. (1991). Using explanations to manage impressions of performance appraisal fairness. *Employee Responsibilities and Rights Journal, 4,* 51-60.

Gregory, K. L. (1983). Native-view paradigms: Multiple cultures and culture conflicts in organizations. *Administrative Science Quarterly, 28,* 359-376.

Greimas, A. (1987). *On meaning: Selected writings in semiotic theory* (P. J. Perron & F. J. Collins, Trans.). Minneapolis: University of Minnesota Press.

Groleau, C., & Cooren, F. (1998). A socio-semiotic approach to computerization: Bridging the gap between ethnographers and system analysts. *Communication Review, 3*(1-2), 125-164.

Gronn, P. C. (1983). Talk as the work: The accomplishment of school administration. *Administrative Science Quarterly, 28,* 1-21.

Gummer, B. (1984). All we ever do is talk: Administrative talk as advice, influence and control. *Administration in Social Work, 8,* 113-123.

Gumperz, J. (1992). Contextualization and understanding. In A. Duranti & C. Goodwin (Eds.), *Rethinking context: Language as an interactive phenomenon* (pp. 229-252). Cambridge, UK: Cambridge University Press.

Gumperz, J., & Herasimchuk, E. (1975). The conversational analysis of social meaning: A study of classroom interaction. In B. Blount & M. M. Sanches (Eds.), *Sociocultural dimensions of language use* (pp. 81-115). New York: Academic Press.

Hall, R. I. (1984). The natural logic of management policy making: Its implications for the survival of an organization. *Management Science, 30,* 905-927.

Hamilton, P. M. (1997). Rhetorical discourse of local pay. *Organization, 4,* 229-254.

Harris, L., & Cronen, V. E. (1979). A rules-based model for the analysis and evaluation of organizational communication. *Communication Quarterly, 27,* 12-18.

Haslett, B. J. (1987). *Communication: Strategic action in context.* Hillsdale, NJ: Lawrence Erlbaum.

Hassan, I. (1985). The culture of postmodernism. *Theory, Culture and Society, 2*(3), 119-132.

Hatch, M. J. (1997). Irony and the social construction of contradiction in the humor of a management team. *Organization Science, 8,* 275-288.

Hatch, M. J., & Ehrlich, S. B. (1993). Spontaneous humor as an indicator of paradox and ambiguity in organizations. *Organization Studies, 14,* 505-526.

Hawes, L. C. (1976). How writing is used in talk: A study of communicative logic-in-use. *Quarterly Journal of Speech, 62,* 350-360.

Hawes, L. C. (1999). The dialogics of conversation: Power, control, and vulnerability. *Communication Theory, 9,* 229-264.

Hearit, K. M. (1994). Apologies and public relations crises at Chrysler, Toshiba, and Volvo. *Public Relations Review, 20,* 113-125.

Helmer, J. (1993). Storytelling in the creation and maintenance of organizational tension and stratification. *Southern Communication Journal, 59,* 34-44.

Hewitt, J. P., & Stokes, R. (1975). Aligning actions. *American Sociological Review, 41,* 838-849.

Hirsch, P. M. (1986). From ambushes to golden parachutes: Corporate takeovers as an instance of cultural framing and institutional integration. *American Journal of Sociology, 91,* 800-837.

Hirsch, P. M., & Andrews, J. A. Y. (1983). Ambushes, shootouts, and knights of the roundtable: The language of corporate takeovers. In L. R. Pondy, P. J. Frost, G. Morgan, & T. C. Dandridge (Eds.), *Organizational symbolism* (pp. 145-155). Greenwich, CT: JAI.

Holmer-Nadesan, M. (1996). Organizational identity and space of action. *Organization Studies, 17,* 49-81.

Holmes, J. (1984). Hedging your bets and sitting on the fence. *Te Reo, 27,* 47-62.

Holmes, M. E. (1997). Optimal matching analysis of negotiation phase sequences in simulated and authentic hostage negotiations. *Communication Reports, 10,* 1-9.

Holmes, M. E., & Sykes, R. E. (1993). A test of the fit of Gulliver's phase model to hostage negotiations. *Communication Studies, 44,* 38-55.

Holt, G. R. (1989). Talk about acting and constraint in stories about organizations. *Western Journal of Speech Communications, 53,* 374-397.

Höpfl, H., & Maddrell, J. (1996). Can you resist a dream? Evangelical metaphors and the appropriation of emotion. In D. Grant & C. Oswick (Eds.), *Metaphor and organizations* (pp. 200-212). Thousand Oaks, CA: Sage.

Hopmann, P. T., & Walcott, C. (1976). The impact of international conflict and debate on bargaining in arms control negotiations: An experimental analysis. *International Interactions, 2,* 189-206.

Howard, L. A., & Geist, P. (1995). Ideological positioning in organizational change: The dialectic of control in a merging organization. *Communication Monographs, 62,* 110-131.

Huff, A. S. (1983). A rhetorical examination of strategic change. In L. R. Pondy, P. J. Frost, G. Morgan, & T. C. Dandridge (Eds.), *Organizational symbolism* (pp. 167-183). Greenwich, CT: JAI.

Huff, A. S. (1988). Politics and argument as a means of coping with ambiguity and change. In L. R. Pondy, R. J. Boland, & H. Thomas (Eds.), *Managing ambiguity and change* (pp. 79-90). New York: John Wiley.

Huff, A. S. (Ed.). (1990). *Mapping strategic thought.* Chichester, UK: Wiley.

Huspek, M., & Kendall, K. (1991). On withholding political voice: An analysis of the political vocabulary of a "nonpolitical" speech community. *Quarterly Journal of Speech, 77,* 1-19.

Huyssen, A. (1986). *After the great divide.* Bloomington: Indiana University Press.

Hymes, D. (1972). Models for the interaction of language in social life. In J. J. Gumperz & D. Hymes (Eds.), *Directions in sociolinguistics: The ethnography of communication* (pp. 35-71). New York: Holt, Rinehart & Winston.

Ice, R. (1991). Corporate publics and rhetorical strategies: The case of Union Carbide's Bhopal crisis. *Management Communication Quarterly, 4,* 341-362.

Irons, L. R. (1998). Organizational and technical communication: Terminological ambiguity in representing work. *Management Communication Quarterly, 12,* 42-71.

Isaacs, W. (1999). *Dialogue and the art of thinking together.* New York: Doubleday.

Isaacs, W. N. (1993). Taking flight: Dialogue, collective thinking, and organizational learning. *Organizational Dynamics, 22*(2), 24-39.

James, D., & Clarke, S. (1993). Women, men and interruptions: A critical review. In D. Tannen (Ed.), *Gender and conversational interaction* (pp. 231-280). Oxford, UK: Oxford University Press.

Jang, H., & Barnett, G. A. (1994). Cultural differences in organizational communication: A semantic network analysis. *Bulletin de Methodologie Sociologique, 44,* 31-59.

Jefferson, G. (1978). Sequential aspects of story-telling in conversation. In J. Schenkein (Ed.), *Studies in the organization of conversational interaction* (pp. 219-248). New York: Academic Press.

Jesuino, J. C. (1985). Assessment of leaders by SYMLOG. *International Journal of Small Group Research, 1,* 887-888.

Johnson, B. (1977). *Communication: The process of organizing.* Boston: Allyn & Bacon.

Jones, D. (1992). Postmodern perspectives on organisational communication. *Australian Journal of Communication, 19,* 30-37.

Jones, K. (1992). A question of context: Directive use at a Morris team meeting. *Language in Society, 21,* 427-445.

Kaha, C. W. (1989). Memory as conversation. *Communication, 11,* 115-122.

Kaufer, D. S., & Carley, K. M. (1993). *Communication at a distance: The influence of print on sociocultural organization and change.* Hillsdale, NJ: Lawrence Erlbaum.

Keenoy, T. (1990). Human resource management: Rhetoric, reality and contradiction. *International Journal of Human Resource Management, 1*(3), 363-384.

Keenoy, T., Oswick, C., & Grant, D. (1997). Organizational discourses: Text and context. *Organization, 4,* 147-157.

Keller-Cohen, D. (1987). Literate practices in a modern credit union. *Language in Society, 16,* 7-23.

Kennedy, C. W., & Camden, C. T. (1983). A new look at interruptions. *Western Journal of Speech Communications, 47,* 45-58.

Keough, C. M. (1987). The nature and function of argument in organizational bargaining research. *Southern Speech Communication Journal, 53,* 1-17.

Keough, C. M., & Lake, R. A. (1993). Values as structuring properties of contract negotiation. In C. Conrad

(Ed.), *Ethical nexus* (pp. 171-189). Norwood, NJ: Ablex.

Kerr, S. (1975). On the folly of rewarding A, while hoping for B. *Academy of Management Journal, 47,* 469-483.

Kets de Vries, M. F. R., & Miller, D. (1987). Interpreting organizational texts. *Journal of Management Studies, 24*(3), 233-247.

Keyton, J., & Wall, V. D. (1989). SYMLOG: Theory and method for measuring group and organizational communication. *Management Communication Quarterly, 2,* 544-567.

Knights, D., & Willmott, H. (1987). Organizational culture as management strategy: A critique and illustration from the financial service industry. *International Studies of Management and Organization, 17,* 40-63.

Komaki, J. L. (1986). Toward effective supervision: An operant analysis and comparison of managers at work. *Journal of Applied Psychology, 71,* 270-278.

Komaki, J. L. (1998). *Leadership from an operant perspective.* London: Routledge.

Komaki, J. L., & Citera, M. (1990). Beyond effective supervision: Identifying key interactions between superior and subordinate. *Leadership Quarterly, 1,* 91-106.

Komaki, J. L., Desselles, M. L., & Bowman, E. D. (1989). Definitely not a breeze: Extending an operant model of effective supervision to teams. *Journal of Applied Psychology, 74,* 522-529.

Komaki, J. L., Zlotnick, S., & Jensen, M. (1986). Development of an operant-based taxonomy and observational index of supervisory behavior. *Journal of Applied Psychology, 71,* 260-269.

Korsch, B. M., & Negrete, V. F. (1972). Doctor-patient communication. *Scientific American, 227,* 66-74.

Krol, T. F. (1991). Women talk about talk at work. *Discourse & Society, 2,* 461-476.

Kristiansen, M., & Bloch-Poulsen, J. (2000). The challenge of the unspoken in organizations: Caring container as a dialogic answer? *Southern Communication Journal, 65*(2-3), 176-190.

Kunda, G. (1992). *Engineering culture: Control and commitment in a high-tech corporation.* Philadelphia: Temple University Press.

Labov, W., & Fanshel, D. (1977). *Therapeutic discourse: Psychotherapy as conversation.* New York: Academic Press.

Lakoff, G., & Johnson, M. (1980). *Metaphors we live by.* Chicago: University of Chicago Press.

Lang, K. (1986). A language theory of discrimination. *Quarterly Journal of Economics, 51,* 363-382.

Latour, B. (1988). *The pasteurization of France.* Cambridge, MA: Harvard University Press.

Latour, B. (1993). *We have never been modern.* Cambridge, MA: Harvard University Press.

Latour, B. (1994). On technical mediation—Philosophy, sociology, and genealogy. *Common Knowledge, 3,* 29-64.

Latour, B. (1996a). *Aramis, or the love for technology.* Cambridge, MA: Harvard University Press.

Latour, B. (1996b). On interobjectivity. *Mind, Culture, and Activity, 3,* 228-245.

Levi, J., & Walker, A. G. (Eds.). (1990). *Language in the judicial process.* New York: Plenum.

Levinson, S. C. (1983). *Pragmatics.* Cambridge, UK: Cambridge University Press.

Linde, C. (1988). The quantitative study of communicative success: Politeness and accidents in aviation discourse. *Language in Society, 17,* 375-399.

Linstead, S. (1985). Jokers wild: The importance of humor and the maintenance of organizational culture. *Sociological Review, 33,* 741-767.

Litvin, D. R. (1997). The discourse of diversity: From biology to management. *Organization, 4,* 187-209.

Locke, E. A. (1968). Toward a theory of task motivation and incentives. *Organizational Behavior and Human Performance, 3,* 179-180.

Lord, R. G., & Kernan, M. C. (1987). Scripts as determinants of purposive behavior in organizations. *Academy of Management Review, 12,* 265-277.

Loseke, D. R. (1989). Creating clients: Social problems work in a shelter for battered women. In J. A. Holstein & G. Miller (Eds.), *Perspectives on social problems* (Vol. 1, pp. 173-193). Greenwich, CT: JAI.

Louis, M. R., & Sutton, R. I. (1991). Shifting cognitive gears: From habits of mind to active thinking. *Human Relations, 44,* 55-76.

Lukaszewski, J. E., & Gmeiner, J. (1993). The Exxon Valdez paradox. In J. A. Gottschalk (Ed.), *Crisis response: Inside stories on managing image under stress* (pp. 185-213). Detroit, MI: Visible Ink.

Mangrum, F. G., & Wieder, D. L. (1997, November). *Ad hoc gatherings for informal problem solving: Ordinary conversation with co-workers as labor for the company.* Paper presented at the annual conference of the National Communication Association, Chicago.

Manning, P. K. (1977). Rules in organizational context: Narcotics law enforcement in two settings. *Sociological Quarterly, 18,* 44-61.

Manning, P. K. (1979). Metaphors of the field: Varieties of organizational discourse. *Administrative Science Quarterly, 24,* 660-671.

Manning, P. K. (1982a). Organisational work: Enstructuration of the environment. *British Journal of Sociology, 2,* 118-139.

Manning, P. K. (1982b). Producing drama: Symbolic communication and the police. *Symbolic Interaction, 5,* 223-241.

Manning, P. K. (1986). Signwork. *Human Relations, 39,* 283-308.

Manning, P. K. (1988). *Symbolic communication: Signifying calls and the police response.* Cambridge, MA: MIT Press.

Markham, A. (1996). Designing discourse: A critical analysis of strategic ambiguity and workplace control. *Management Communication Quarterly, 9,* 389-421.

Marshak, R. J. (1993). Managing the metaphors of change. *Organizational Dynamics, 22,* 44-56.

Marshak, R. J. (1996). Metaphors, metaphoric fields and organizational change. In D. Grant & C. Oswick (Eds.), *Metaphor and organizations* (pp. 147-165). Thousand Oaks, CA: Sage.

Marshak, R. J. (1998). A discourse on discourse: Redeeming the meaning of talk. In D. Grant, T. Keenoy, & C. Oswick (Eds.), *Discourse and organization* (pp. 15-30). London: Sage.

Martin, J. (1990). Deconstructing organizational taboos: The suppression of gender conflicts in organizations. *Organization Science, 1,* 339-359.

Martin, J. (1992). *Cultures in organizations: Three perspectives.* New York: Oxford University Press.

Mauws, M. K., & Phillips, N. (1995). Understanding language games. *Organization Science, 6,* 322-334.

Mauws, M. K., & Phillips, N. (1999, May). *Beyond language games: Studying organizational change from a discourse analytic perspective.* Paper presented at the International Conference on Language in Organizational Change: What Makes a Difference, Ohio State University, Columbus.

McLaughlin, M. L. (1984). *How talk is organized.* Beverly Hills, CA: Sage.

Mead, G. (1934). *Mind, self, and society.* Chicago: University of Chicago Press.

Mehan, H. (1979). *Learning lessons: Social organization in the classroom.* Cambridge, MA: Harvard University Press.

Mehan, H. (1983). The role of language and the language of role in institutional decision making. *Language in Society, 12,* 187-211.

Mehan, H. (1987). Language and power in organizational process. *Discourse Processes, 10,* 291-301.

McNamee, S., Gergen, K. J., & Associates. (1999). *Relational responsibility: Resources for sustainable dialogue.* Thousand Oaks, CA: Sage.

Mellinger, W. M. (1994). Negotiated orders: The negotiation of directives in paramedic-nurse interaction. *Symbolic Interaction, 17,* 165-185.

Meyer, J. (1996). Seeking organizational unity: Building bridges in response to mystery. *Southern Communication Journal, 61,* 210-219.

Meyer, J. C. (1997). Humor in member narratives: Uniting and dividing at work. *Western Journal of Communication, 61,* 188-208.

Meyers, R. A., & Garrett, D. E. (1993). Contradictions, values, and organizational argument. In C. Conrad (Ed.), *Ethical nexus* (pp. 149-170). Norwood, NJ: Ablex.

Meyerson, D. E. (1991). Acknowledging and uncovering ambiguities in cultures. In P. J. Frost, L. F. Moore, M. R. Louis, C. C. Lundberg, & J. Martin (Eds.), *Reframing organizational culture* (pp. 254-270). Newbury Park, CA: Sage.

Middleton, D., & Edwards, D. (1990). Conversational remembering: A social psychological approach. In D. Middleton & D. Edwards (Eds.), *Collective remembering*. London: Sage.

Miller, P., & O'Leary, T. (1987). Accounting and the construction of the governable person. *Accounting, Organizations and Society, 12*, 235-265.

Mishler, E. (1984). *The discourse of medicine: Dialectics of medical interviews*. Norwood, NJ: Ablex.

Moch, M. K., & Fields, W. C. (1985). Developing a content analysis for interpreting language use in organizations. In S. B. Bacharach (Ed.), *Research in the sociology of organizations* (Vol. 4, pp. 81-126). Greenwich, CT: JAI.

Molotch, H. L., & Boden, D. (1985). Talking social structure: Discourse, domination, and the Watergate hearings. *American Sociological Review, 50*, 273-288.

Monge, P. R., & Eisenberg, E. M. (1987). Emergent communication networks. In F. M. Jablin, L. L. Putnam, K. H. Roberts, & L. W. Porter (Eds.), *Handbook of organizational communication: An interdisciplinary perspective* (pp. 304-342). Newbury Park, CA: Sage.

Morgan, G. (1980). Paradigms, metaphors, and puzzle solving in organization theory. *Administrative Science Quarterly, 24*, 605-622.

Morgan, G. (1997). *Images of organization* (2nd ed.). Thousand Oaks, CA: Sage.

Morgan, G., & Ramirez, R. (1984). Action learning: A holographic metaphor for guiding social change. *Human Relations, 37*, 1-28.

Morand, D. A. (1996). What's in a name? An exploration of the social dynamics of forms of address in organization. *Management Communication Quarterly, 9*, 422-451.

Morrill, C. (1991). Conflict management, honor and organizational change. *American Journal of Sociology, 97*, 585-621.

Morrill, C. (1995). *The executive way: Conflict management in corporations*. Chicago: University of Chicago Press.

Morris, G. H. (1988). Accounts in selection interviews. *Journal of Applied Communication Research, 15*, 82-98.

Morris, G. H., & Coursey, M. L. (1989). Negotiating the meaning of employees' conduct: How managers evaluate employees' accounts. *Southern Communication Journal, 54*, 185-205.

Morris, G. H., Gaveras, S. C., Baker, W. L., & Coursey, M. L. (1990). Aligning actions at work: How managers confront problems of employee performance. *Management Communication Quarterly, 3*, 303-333.

Mumby, D. K. (1987). The political function of narrative in organizations. *Communication Monographs, 54*, 113-127.

Mumby, D. K. (1988). *Communication and power in organizations: Discourse, ideology and domination*. Norwood, NJ: Ablex.

Mumby, D. K., & Clair, R. P. (1997). Organizational discourse. In T. A. van Dijk (Ed.), *Discourse as social interaction* (Vol. 2, pp. 181-205). London: Sage.

Mumby, D. K., & Stohl, C. (1991). Power and discourse in organizational studies: Absence and the dialectic of control. *Discourse & Society, 2*, 313-332.

Munro, R. (1995). Management by ambiguity: An archeology of the social in the absence of management accounting. *Critical Perspectives on Accounting, 6*, 433-482.

Murphy, A. G. (1998). Hidden transcripts of flight attendant resistance. *Management Communication Quarterly, 11*, 499-535.

Murray, D. E. (1987). Requests at work: Negotiating the conditions for conversation. *Management Communication Quarterly, 1*, 58-83.

Neale, M. A., & Bazerman, M. H. (1991). *Cognition and rationality in negotiation*. New York: Free Press.

Neu, J. (1988). Conversation structure: An explanation of bargaining behaviors in negotiations. *Management Communication Quarterly, 2*, 23-45.

Nöth, W. (1988). The language of commodities: Groundwork for a semiotics of consumer goods. *International Journal of Research in Marketing, 4*, 173-186.

Oakes, L. S., Townley, B., & Cooper, D. J. (1998). Business planning as pedagogy: Language and control in a changing institutional field. *Administrative Science Quarterly, 43*, 257-292.

O'Connor, E. S. (1994, August). *A modest proposal: The contribution of literacy theory and methods to organizational studies*. Paper presented at the Academy of Management meeting, Dallas, TX.

O'Connor, E. S. (1995). Paradoxes of participation: Textual analysis and organizational change. *Organization Studies, 16*, 769-803.

O'Connor, E. S. (1997). Telling decisions: The role of narrative in organizational decision making. In Z. Shapira (Ed.), *Organizational decision making* (pp. 304-323). New York: Cambridge University Press.

O'Connor, K. M., & Adams, A. A. (1999). What novices think about negotiation: A content analysis of scripts. *Negotiation Journal, 15*(2), 135-148.

O'Donnell, K. (1990). Difference and dominance: How labor and management talk conflict. In A. D. Grimshaw (Ed.), *Conflict talk* (pp. 210-240). Cambridge, UK: Cambridge University Press.

Olekalns, M., Smith, P. L., & Walsh, T. (1996). The process of negotiating: Strategies, timing, and outcomes. *Organizational Behavior and Human Decision Processes, 68*, 68-77.

Orlikowski, W. J., & Gash, D. C. (1994). Technological frames: Making sense of information technology in organizations. *ACM Transactions on Information Systems, 12,* 174-207.

Orr, J. E. (1990). Sharing knowledge, celebrating identity: Community memory in a service culture. In D. Middleton & D. Edwards (Eds.), *Collective remembering* (pp. 169-189). London: Sage.

Oswick, C., & Grant, D. (1996a). The organization of metaphors and the metaphors of organization: Where are we and where do we go from here? In D. Grant & C. Oswick (Eds.), *Metaphor and organizations* (pp. 213-226). Thousand Oaks, CA: Sage.

Oswick, C., & Grant, D. (Eds.). (1996b). *Organization development: Metaphorical explorations.* London: Pitman.

Ouchi, W. G., & Wilkins, A. L. (1985). Organizational culture. *Annual Review of Sociology, 11,* 457-483.

Pacanowsky, M. E., & O'Donnell-Trujillo, N. (1983). Organizational communication as cultural performance. *Communication Monographs, 50,* 126-147.

Peirce, C. S. (1931). *Collected papers.* Cambridge, MA: Harvard University Press.

Pettigrew, A. (1979). On studying organizational cultures. *Administrative Science Quarterly, 24,* 570-581.

Philipsen, G. (1975). Speaking "like a man" in Teamsterville: Cultural patterns of role-enactment in urban neighborhoods. *Quarterly Journal of Speech, 62,* 13-22.

Philipsen, G. (1992). *Speaking culturally: Explorations in social communication.* New York: State University of New York Press.

Phillips, N., & Hardy, C. (1997). Managing multiple identities: Discourse, legitimacy and resources in the UK refugee system. *Organization, 4,* 159-185.

Pinder, C. C., & Bourgeois, V. W. (1982). Controlling tropes in administrative science. *Administrative Science Quarterly, 27,* 641-652.

Pinsdorf, M. K. (1987). *Communicating when your company is under siege: Surviving public crisis.* Lexington, MA: D. C. Heath.

Pogner, K. (1999). Discourse community, culture and interaction: On writing by consulting engineers. In F. Bargiela-Chiappini & C. Nickerson (Eds.), *Writing business: Genres, media and discourse* (pp. 101-127). New York: Pearson Education Limited.

Pogrebin, M. R., & Poole, E. D. (1988). Humor in the briefing room: A study of the strategic uses of humor among police. *Journal of Contemporary Ethnography, 17,* 183-210.

Pomerantz, A., & Fehr, B. J. (1997). Conversation analysis: An approach to the study of social action as sense making practices. In T. A. van Dijk (Ed.), *Discourse as social interaction* (pp. 64-91). London: Sage.

Pomerantz, A., Fehr, B. J., & Ende, J. (1997). When supervising physicians see patients. *Human Communication Research, 23,* 589-615.

Pondy, L. R. (1978). Leadership is a language game. In M. W. McCall, Jr. & M. M. Lombardo (Eds.), *Leadership: Where else can we go?* (pp. 88-99). Durham, NC: Duke University Press.

Pondy, L. R. (1983). The role of metaphors and myths in organizations and in the facilitation of change. In L. R. Pondy, P. J. Frost, G. Morgan, & T. D. Dandridge (Eds.), *Organizational symbolism* (pp. 157-166). Greenwich, CT: JAI.

Poole, M. S., & DeSanctis, G. (1992). Microlevel structuration in computer-supported group decision-making. *Human Communication Research, 91,* 5-49.

Poole, M. S., DeSanctis, G., Kirsch, L., & Jackson, M. (1995). Group decision support systems as facilitators of quality team efforts. In L. R. Frey (Ed.), *Innovations in group facilitation techniques: Case studies of applications in naturalistic settings* (pp. 299-320). Creskill, NJ: Hampton.

Poole, M. S., Folger, J. P., & Hewes, D. (1987). Analyzing interpersonal interaction. In M. E. Roloff & G. R. Miller (Eds.), *Interpersonal processes: New directions in communication research* (pp. 220-256). Newbury Park, CA: Sage.

Poole, M. S., Holmes, M. E., & DeSanctis, G. (1991). Conflict management in a computer-supported meeting environment. *Management Science, 37,* 926-953.

Poole, M. S., Seibold, D. R., & McPhee, R. D. (1985). Group decision-making as a structurational process. *Quarterly Journal of Speech, 71,* 74-102.

Poole, M. S., & Van de Ven, A. H. (1989). Using paradox to build management and organization theories. *Academy of Management Review, 14,* 562-578.

Prasad, P. (1995). Working with the "smart" machine: Computerization and the discourse of anthropomorphism in organizations. *Studies in Cultures, Organizations and Societies, 1,* 253-265.

Preisler, B. (1986). *Linguistic sex roles in conversation.* Berlin: Mouton de Gruyter.

Pringle, R. (1988). *Secretaries talk: Sexuality, power, and work.* London: Verso.

Putnam, L. L. (1986). Contradictions and paradoxes in organizations. In L. Thayer (Ed.), *Organization–communication: Emerging perspectives I* (pp. 151-167). Norwood, NJ: Ablex.

Putnam, L. L. (1990a, August). *Language and meaning: Discourse approaches to the study of organizations.* Paper presented at the Academy of Management meeting, San Francisco.

Putnam, L. L. (1990b). Reframing integrative and distributive bargaining: A process perspective. In B. H. Sheppard, M. H. Bazerman, & R. J. Lewicki (Eds.), *Research on negotiation in organizations* (pp. 3-30). Greenwich, CT: JAI.

Putnam, L. L. (1994, August). *Language and meaning in organizations: A facilitator or a barrier?* Paper presented at the Academy of Management meeting, Dallas, TX.

Putnam, L. L. (1995). Formal negotiations: The productive side of organizational conflict. In A. M. Nicotera (Ed.), *Conflict and organizations: Communication processes* (pp. 183-200). Albany: State University of New York Press.

Putnam, L. L., & Geist, P. (1985). Argument in bargaining: An analysis of the reasoning process. *Southern Speech Communication Journal, 50,* 225-245.

Putnam, L. L., & Holmer, M. (1992). Framing, reframing, and issue development. In L. L. Putnam & M. E. Roloff (Eds.), *Communication and negotiation* (pp. 128-155). Newbury Park, CA: Sage.

Putnam, L. L., & Jones, T. S. (1982). Reciprocity in negotiations: An analysis of bargaining interaction. *Communication Monographs, 49,* 171-191.

Putnam, L. L., Phillips, N., & Chapman, P. (1996). Metaphors of communication and organization. In S. R. Clegg, C. Hardy, & W. R. Nord (Eds.), *Handbook of organization studies* (pp. 375-408). London: Sage.

Putnam, L. L., & Wilson, S. R. (1989). Argumentation and bargaining strategies as discriminators of integrative outcomes. In M. A. Rahim (Ed.), *Managing conflict: An interdisciplinary approach* (pp. 121-141). New York: Praeger.

Putnam, L. L., Wilson, S. R., & Turner, D. B. (1990). The evolution of policy arguments in teachers' negotiations. *Argumentation, 4,* 129-152.

Putnam, L. L., Wilson, S. R., Waltman, M. S., & Turner, D. (1986). The evolution of case arguments in teachers' bargaining. *Journal of the American Forensic Association, 23,* 63-81.

Ragan, S. L. (1983). A conversational analysis of alignment talk in job interviews. In R. Bostrum (Ed.), *Communication yearbook 7* (pp. 502-516). Beverly Hills, CA: Sage.

Ragan, S. L., & Hopper, R. (1981). Alignment talk in the job interview. *Journal of Applied Communication Research, 9,* 85-103.

Rice, R. E., & Danowski, J. A. (1993). Is it really just like a fancy answering machine? Comparing semantic networks of different types of voice mail users. *Journal of Business Communication, 30,* 369-397.

Riley, P. (1983). A structurationist account of political cultures. *Administrative Science Quarterly, 28,* 414-437.

Robichaud, D. (1998). Textualization and organizing: Illustrations from a public discussion process. *Communication Review, 3*(1-2), 103-124.

Rogan, R. G., & Hammer, M. R. (1994). Crisis negotiations: A preliminary investigation of facework in naturalistic conflict discourse. *Journal of Applied Communication Research, 22,* 216-231.

Rogers, L. E., & Farace, R. V. (1975). Relational communication analysis: New measurement procedures. *Human Communication Research, 1,* 222-239.

Roloff, M. E., Tutzauer, F. E., & Dailey, W. O. (1989). The role of argumentation in distributive and integrative bargaining contexts: Seeking relative advantage but at what cost? In M. A. Rahim (Ed.), *Managing conflict: An interdisciplinary approach* (pp. 109-119). New York: Praeger.

Roos, L. L., & Hall, R. I. (1980). Influence diagrams and organizational power. *Administrative Science Quarterly, 25,* 57-71.

Rosen, M. (1985). Breakfast at Spiro's: Dramaturgy and dominance. *Journal of Management, 11,* 31-48.

Rosen, M. (1988). You asked for it: Christmas at the bosses' expense. *Journal of Management Studies, 25,* 463-480.

Rousseau, D. M., & Anton, R. J. (1988). Fairness and implied contract obligations in job terminations: A policy-capturing study. *Human Performance, 1,* 273-289.

Roy, D. (1960). Banana time: Job satisfaction and informal interaction. *Human Organization, 18,* 156-168.

Rudd, G. (1995). The symbolic construction of organizational identities and community in a regional symphony. *Communication Studies, 46,* 201-221.

Sackmann, S. (1989). The role of metaphors in organization transformation. *Human Relations, 42,* 463-485.

Sacks, H., Schegloff, E. A., & Jefferson, G. (1974). A simplest systematics for the organization of turn-taking for conversation. *Language, 50,* 696-735.

Saferstein, B. (1992). Collective cognition and collaborative work: The effects of cognitive and communicative processes on the organization of television production. *Discourse & Society, 3,* 61-86.

Saferstein, B. (1994). Interaction and ideology at work: A case of constructing and constraining television violence. *Social Problems, 41,* 316-345.

Sands, R. (1981). Language and consciousness in industrial workers: Homeless minds? *International Journal of Sociology of Language, 32,* 55-64.

Sargent, J. F., & Miller, G. R. (1971). Some differences in certain communication behaviors of autocratic and democratic group leaders. *Journal of Communication, 21,* 233-252.

Saussure, F., de. (1974). *Course in general linguistics* (W. Baskin, Trans.). London: Fontana. (Original work published 1916)

Schall, M. S. (1983). A communication-rules approach to organizational culture. *Administrative Science Quarterly, 28,* 557-581.

Schank, R. C., & Abelson, R. P. (1977). *Scripts, plans, goals, and understanding.* Hillsdale, NJ: Lawrence Erlbaum.

Schantz, D. (1986). The use of SYMLOG as a diagnostic tool in drug-related problems on the job. *International Journal of Small Group Research, 2,* 219-224.

Schein, E. H. (1985). *Organizational culture and leadership*. San Francisco: Jossey-Bass.

Schmidt, D. P. (1986). Patterns of argument in business ethics. *Journal of Business Ethics, 5*, 501-509.

Schonbach, P. (1990). *Account episodes: The management of escalation of conflict*. Cambridge, UK: Cambridge University Press.

Schwandt, T. A. (1994). Constructivist, interpretivist approaches to human inquiry. In N. K. Denzin & Y. S. Lincoln (Eds.), *Handbook of qualitative research* (pp. 118-137). Thousand Oaks, CA: Sage.

Scott, M., & Lyman, S. (1968). Accounts. *American Sociological Review, 22*, 46-62.

Searle, J. R. (1969). *Speech acts: An essay in the philosophy of language*. London: Cambridge University Press.

Searle, J. R. (1979). *Expression and meaning: Studies in the theory of speech acts*. New York: Cambridge University Press.

Shimanoff, S. (1980). *Communication rules: Theory and research*. Beverly Hills, CA: Sage.

Shotter, J. (1990). The social construction of remembering and forgetting. In D. Middleton & D. Edwards (Eds.), *Collective remembering* (pp. 120-138). London: Sage.

Sigman, S. J. (1986). Adjustment to the nursing home as a social interaction accomplishment. *Journal of Applied Communication Research, 14*, 37-58.

Sigman, S. J., & Donnellon, A. (1989). Discourse rehearsal: Interaction simulating interaction. In D. Crookall & D. Saunders (Eds.), *Communication and simulation: From two fields to one theme* (pp. 69-81). London: Multilingual Matters.

Simon, H. A. (1976). *Administrative behavior* (3rd ed.). New York: Free Press.

Simons, T. (1993). Speech patterns and the concept of utility in cognitive maps: The case of integrative bargaining. *Academy of Management Journal, 36*, 139-156.

Sims, H. P., Jr. (1977). The leader as a manager of reinforcement contingencies: An empirical example and a model. In J. G. Hunt & L. L. Larson (Eds.), *Leadership: The cutting edge*. Carbondale: Southern Illinois University Press.

Sims, H. P., Jr., & Manz, C. C. (1984). Observing leader verbal behavior: Toward reciprocal determinism in leadership theory. *Journal of Applied Psychology, 69*, 222-232.

Sinclair, J. M., & Coulthard, M. (1975). *Towards an analysis of discourse: The English used by teachers and pupils*. Oxford, UK: Oxford University Press.

Sitkin, S., & Bies, R. J. (1993). Social accounts in conflict situations: Using explanations to manage conflict. *Human Relations, 46*, 349-370.

Sitkin, S. B., Sutcliffe, K. M., & Reed, L. (1993). Prescriptions for justice: Using social accounts to legitimate the exercise of professional control. *Social Justice Research, 6*, 87-111.

Skinner, B. F. (1957). *Verbal behavior*. Englewood Cliffs, NJ: Prentice Hall.

Skinner, B. F. (1974). *About behaviorism*. New York: Vintage.

Slobin, D., Miller, S., & Porter, L. (1968). Forms of address and social relations in a business organization. *Journal of Personality and Social Psychology, 8*, 289-293.

Slobin, D. I., Miller, S. H., & Porter, L. W. (1972). Forms of address and social relations in a business organization. In S. Moscovici (Ed.), *The psychosociology of language* (pp. 263-272). New York: Pergamon.

Smircich, L., & Morgan, G. (1982). Leadership: The management of meaning. *Journal of Applied Behavioral Studies, 18*, 257-273.

Smith, K. K., & Berg, D. N. (1987). *Paradoxes of group life*. San Francisco: Jossey-Bass.

Smith, R. C. (1993, May). *Images of organizational communication: Root metaphors of the organization-communication relation*. Paper presented at the annual conference of the International Communication Association, Washington, DC.

Smith, R. C., & Eisenberg, E. M. (1987). Conflict at Disneyland: A root-metaphor analysis. *Communication Monographs, 54*, 367-380.

Smith, R. C., & Turner, P. (1995). A social constructionist reconfiguration of metaphor analysis: An application of "SCMA" to organizational socialization theorizing. *Communication Monographs, 62*, 152-181.

Smithin, T. (1987). Argument in organizations. In C. L. Cooper & I. L. Mangham (Eds.), *Organizational analysis and development: A social construction of organizational behaviour* (pp. 61-80). Chichester, UK: Wiley.

Sotirin, P., & Gottfried, H. (1999). The ambivalent dynamics of secretarial "bitching": Control, resistance, and the construction of identity. *Organization, 6*, 57-80.

Spencer, J. W. (1994). Mutual relevance of ethnography and discourse. *Journal of Contemporary Ethnography, 23*, 267-279.

Srivastva, S., & Barrett, F. (1988). The transformation nature of metaphors in group development: A study in group theory. *Human Relations, 41*, 31-64.

Starbuck, W. H., & Milliken, F. J. (1988). Executives' perceptual filters: What they notice and how they make sense. In D. C. Hambrick (Ed.), *The executive effect: Concepts and methods for studying top managers* (pp. 35-65). Greenwich, CT: JAI.

Steward, F., & Conway, S. (1998). Situating discourse in environmental innovation networks. *Organization, 5*, 479-502.

Stewart, J. (1986). Speech and human being: A complement to semiotics. *Quarterly Journal of Speech, 72*, 55-73.

Stohl, C. (1993). European managers' interpretations of participation: A semantic network analysis. *Human Communication Research, 20,* 97-117.

Stohl, C. (1995). Paradoxes of participation. In R. Cesaria & P. Shockley-Zalabak (Eds.), *Organization means communication: Making the organizational communication concept relevant to practice* (pp. 199-215). Rome: Sipi Editore.

Stohl, C., & Coombs, W. T. (1988). Cooperation or co-optation: An analysis of quality circle training manuals. *Management Communication Quarterly, 2,* 63-89.

Stokes, R., & Hewitt, J. P. (1976). Disclaimers. *American Sociological Review, 40,* 1-11.

Strauss, A. (1978). *Negotiations: Varieties, contexts, processes, and social order.* San Francisco: Jossey-Bass.

Strine, M. S. (1988). Constructing "texts" and making inferences: Some reflections on textual reality in human communication research. In J. A. Anderson (Ed.), *Communication yearbook 11* (pp. 494-500). Newbury Park, CA: Sage.

Strine, M. S. (1992). Understanding "how things work": Sexual harassment and academic culture. *Journal of Applied Communication Research, 20,* 391-400.

Stubbs, M. (1976). *Language, schools and classrooms.* London: Methuen.

Sykes, A. J. M. (1966). Joking relationships in an industrial setting. *American Anthropologist, 68,* 188-193.

Tannen, D. (1994). *Talking from 9 to 5: Women and men in the workplace.* New York: Avon.

Taylor, B., & Conrad, C. R. (1992). Narratives of sexual harassment: Organizational dimensions. *Journal of Applied Communication Research, 20,* 401-418.

Taylor, J. R. (1993). *Rethinking the theory of organizational communication: How to read an organization.* Norwood, NJ: Ablex.

Taylor, J. R. (1995). Shifting from a heteronomous to an autonomous worldview of organizational communication: Communication theory on the cusp. *Communication Theory, 5,* 1-35.

Taylor, J. R., & Cooren, F. (1997). What makes communication "organizational"? How the many voices of a collectivity become the one voice of an organization. *Journal of Pragmatics, 27,* 409-438.

Taylor, J. R., Cooren, F., Giroux, N., & Robichaud, D. (1996). The communicational basis of organization: Between the conversation and the text. *Communication Theory, 6,* 1-39.

Taylor, J. R., & Van Every, E. (2000). *The emergent organization: Communication as its site and surface.* Mahwah, NJ: Lawrence Erlbaum.

Taylor, M. E. (1987). Functions of in-house language: Observations on data collected from some British financial institutions. *Language in Society, 16,* 1-7.

Thatchenkery, T. (1992). Organizations as "texts": Hermeneutics as a model for understanding organizational change. In W. A. Pasmore & R. W. Woodman (Eds.), *Research in organization development and change* (Vol. 6, pp. 197-233). Greenwich, CT: JAI.

Thatchenkery, T. J., & Upadhyaya, P. (1996). Organizations as a play of multiple and dynamic discourses: An example from a global social change organization. In D. M. Boje, R. P. Gephart, & T. J. Thatchenkery (Eds.), *Postmodern management and organization theory* (pp. 308-330). London: Sage.

Theye, L. D., & Seiler, W. J. (1979). Interaction analysis in collective bargaining: An alternative approach to the prediction of negotiated outcomes. In D. Nimmo (Ed.), *Communication yearbook 3* (pp. 375-392). New Brunswick, NJ: Transaction Books.

Thompson, L., & DeHarpport, T. (1994). Social judgment, feedback, and interpersonal learning in negotiation. *Organizational Behavior and Human Decision Processes, 58,* 327-345.

Tompkins, E. V. B., Tompkins, P. K., & Cheney, G. (1989). Organizations, texts, arguments, premises: Critical textualism and the study of organizational communication. *Journal of Management Systems, 1,* 35-48.

Tompkins, P. (1962). *An analysis of communication between headquarters and selected units of a national labor union.* Unpublished doctoral dissertation, Purdue University, West Lafayette, IN.

Tompkins, P. (1965). General semantics and "human relations." *Central States Speech Journal, 16,* 285-289.

Tompkins, P., Fisher, J., Infante, D., & Tompkins, E. (1975). Kenneth Burke and the inherent characteristics of formal organizations: A field study. *Speech Monographs, 42,* 135-142.

Tompkins, P. K., & Cheney, G. (1983). The uses of account analysis: A study of organization decision-making and identification. In L. L. Putnam & M. E. Pacanowsky (Eds.), *Communication and organizations: An interpretive approach* (pp. 123-146). Beverly Hills, CA: Sage.

Tompkins, P. K., & Cheney, G. (1985). Communication and unobtrusive control in contemporary organizations. In R. D. McPhee & P. K. Tompkins (Eds.), *Organizational communication: Traditional themes and new directions* (pp. 179-210). Beverly Hills, CA: Sage.

Toulmin, S. E. (1958). *The uses of argument.* Cambridge, UK: Cambridge University Press.

Townley, B. (1993). Foucault, power/knowledge, and its relevance for human resource management. *Academy of Management Review, 18,* 518-545.

Trethewey, A. (1997). Resistance, identity, and empowerment: A postmodern feminist analysis of clients in a human service organization. *Communication Monographs, 64,* 281-301.

Trethewey, A. (1999). Isn't it ironic: Using irony to explore the contradictions of organizational life. *Western Journal of Communication, 63,* 140-167.

Trujillo, N. (1983). "Performing" Mintzberg's roles: The nature of managerial communication. In L. L.

Putnam & M. E. Pacanowsky (Eds.), *Communication and organizations: An interpretive approach* (pp. 73-98). Beverly Hills, CA: Sage.

Trujillo, N. (1985). Organizational communication as cultural performance: Some managerial considerations. *Southern Speech Communication Journal, 50*, 201-224.

Tsoukas, H. (1991). The missing link: A transformational view of metaphors in organizational science. *Academy of Management Review, 16*, 566-585.

Tsoukas, H. (1993). Analogical reasoning and knowledge generation in organization theory. *Organization Studies, 14*, 323-346.

Tulin, M. F. (1997). Talking organization: Possibilities for conversation analysis in organizational behavior research. *Journal of Management Inquiry, 6*, 101-119.

Tullar, W. L. (1989). Relational control in the employment interview. *Journal of Applied Psychology, 74*, 971-977.

Turner, R. (1972). Some formal properties of therapy talk. In D. Sudnow (Ed.), *Studies in social interaction* (pp. 367-396). New York: Free Press.

Tway, P. (1975). Workplace isoglosses: Lexical variation and change in a factory setting. *Language in Society, 4*, 171-183.

Tway, P. (1976). Verbal and nonverbal communication of factory workers. *Semiotica, 16*, 29-44.

Tyler, L. (1997). Liability means never being able to say you're sorry: Corporate guilt, legal constraints, and defensiveness in corporate communication. *Management Communication Quarterly, 11*, 51-73.

Ullian, J. A. (1976). Joking at work. *Journal of Communication, 26*, 479-486.

van Dijk, T. A. (Ed.). (1985). *Handbook of discourse analysis*. New York: Academic Press.

van Dijk, T. A. (1993). Principles of critical discourse analysis. *Discourse & Society, 4*, 249-283.

van Dijk, T. A. (Ed.). (1997a). *Discourse as social interaction* (Vol. 1). London: Sage.

van Dijk, T. A. (1997b). The study of discourse. In T. A. van Dijk (Ed.), *Discourse as structure and process* (Vol. 1, pp. 1-34). London: Sage.

Van Maanen, J. (1973). Observations on the making of policemen. *Human Organization, 32*, 407-418.

Van Maanen, J. (1978). The asshole. In P. K. Manning & J. Van Maanen (Eds.), *Policing* (pp. 221-238). New York: Random House.

Van Maanen, J., & Barley, S. R. (1984). Occupational communities: Culture and control in organizations. In B. M. Staw & L. L. Cummings (Eds.), *Research in organizational behavior* (pp. 287-366). Greenwich, CT: JAI.

van Naerssen, M. M. (1985). Medical records: One variation of physicians' language. *International Journal of Sociology of Language, 51*, 43-73.

Vaughan, E. (1994). The trial between sense and sentiment: A reflection on the language of HRM. *Journal of General Management, 19*(3), 20-32.

Vaughn, M. A. (1995). Organization symbols: An analysis of their types and functions in a reborn organization. *Management Communication Quarterly, 9*, 219-250.

Vinton, K. L. (1989). Humor in the workplace: It is more than telling jokes. *Small Group Behavior, 20*, 151-166.

Walsh, J. P., & Ungson, G. R. (1991). Organizational memory. *Academy of Management Review, 16*, 57-91.

Watson, K. M. (1982). An analysis of communication patterns: A method for discriminating leader and subordinate roles. *Academy of Management Journal, 25*, 107-120.

Watson, R. T., DeSanctis, G., & Poole, M. S. (1988). Using a GDSS to facilitate group consensus: Some intended and unintended consequences. *MIS Quarterly, 12*, 463-478.

Watson, T. J. (1994). *In search of management: Culture, chaos and control in managerial work*. London: Routledge.

Watson, T. J. (1995). Rhetoric, discourse and argument in organizational sense making: A reflexive tale. *Organization Studies, 16*, 805-821.

Watson-Dugan, K. M. (1989). Ability and effort attributions: Do they affect how managers communicate performance feedback information? *Academy of Management Journal, 32*, 87-114.

Watzlawick, P., Beavin, J. H., & Jackson, D. D. (1967). *Pragmatics of human communication: A study of interactional patterns, pathologies, and paradoxes*. New York: Norton.

Weick, K. E. (1979). *The social psychology of organizing* (2nd ed.). Reading, MA: Addison-Wesley.

Weick, K. E. (1995). *Sensemaking in organizations*. Thousand Oaks, CA: Sage.

Weick, K. E., & Bougon, M. G. (1986). Organizations as cause maps. In H. P. Sims, Jr. & D. A. Gioia (Eds.), *Social cognition in organizations* (pp. 102-135). San Francisco: Jossey-Bass.

Weick, K. E., & Browning, L. D. (1986). Argument and narration in organizational communication. *Journal of Management, 12*, 243-260.

Weick, K. E., & Roberts, K. H. (1993). Collective mind in organizations: Heedful interrelating on flight decks. *Administrative Science Quarterly, 38*, 357-381.

Weingart, L. R., Bennett, R. J., & Brett, J. M. (1993). The impact of consideration of issues and motivational orientation on group negotiation process and outcome. *Journal of Applied Psychology, 78*, 504-517.

Weingart, L. R., Thompson, L. L., Bazerman, M. H., & Carroll, J. S. (1990). Tactical behavior and negotiation outcomes. *International Journal of Conflict Management, 1,* 7-31.

Wendt, R. F. (1998). The sound of one hand clapping: Counterintuitive lessons extracted from paradoxes and double binds in participative organizations. *Management Communication Quarterly, 11,* 323-371.

Westenholz, A. (1993). Paradoxical thinking and change in the frames of reference. *Organization Studies, 14,* 37-58.

Westley, F. R. (1990). Middle managers and strategy: Microdynamics of inclusion. *Strategic Management Journal, 11,* 337-351.

Whalen, M., & Zimmerman, D. H. (1987). Sequential and institutional contexts in calls for help. *Social Psychology Quarterly, 50,* 172-185.

Wilson, S. R. (1992). Face and facework in negotiation. In L. L. Putnam & M. E. Roloff (Eds.), *Communication and negotiation* (pp. 176-205). Newbury Park, CA: Sage.

Witten, M. (1993). Narrative and the culture of obedience at the workplace. In D. K. Mumby (Ed.), *Narrative and social control: Critical perspectives* (pp. 97-118). Newbury Park, CA: Sage.

Wood, J. T. (1992). Telling our stories: Narratives as a basis for theorizing sexual harassment. *Journal of Applied Communication Research, 20,* 349-362.

Wood, J. T. (1994). Saying it makes it so: The discursive construction of sexual harassment. In S. G. Bingham (Ed.), *Conceptualizing sexual harassment as discursive practice* (pp. 17-30). Westport, CT: Praeger.

Wood, J. T., & Conrad, C. (1983). Paradox in the experiences of professional women. *Western Journal of Communication, 47,* 305-322.

Wood, R. E., & Mitchell, T. R. (1981). Manager behavior in a social context: The impact of impression management on attributions and disciplinary action. *Organizational Behavior and Human Decision Processes, 28,* 356-378.

Woods, N. (1988). Talking shop: Sex and status as determinants of floor apportionment in a work setting. In J. Coates & D. Cameron (Eds.), *Women in their speech communities* (pp. 141-157). London: Longman.

Yates, J. (1990). For the record: The embodiment of organizational memory, 1850-1920. *Business and Economic History, 19,* 172-182.

Yoels, W. C., & Clair, J. M. (1995). Laughter in the clinic: Humor as social organization. *Symbolic Interaction, 18,* 39-58.

Zigurs, I., Poole, M. S., & DeSanctis, G. L. (1988). A study of influence in computer-mediated group decision making. *MIS Quarterly, 12,* 625-644.

Zimmerman, D. H. (1992). Achieving context: Openings in emergency calls. In G. Watson & R. Seiler (Eds.), *Text in context: Contributions in ethnomethodology* (pp. 35-71). Newbury Park, CA: Sage.

Zimmerman, D. H., & West, C. (1975). Sex roles, interruptions and silences in conversation. In B. Thorne & N. Henley (Eds.), *Language and sex: Differences and dominance* (pp. 105-129). Rowley, MA: Newbury House.

# 4

# Quantitative Research Methods

KATHERINE MILLER
*Texas A&M University*

During its history, the field of organizational communication has been marked by a variety of methodological traditions. Early lab experiments examining information flow were supplanted by survey research investigating perceptions of communication processes. In the 1970s, these methods were joined by sophisticated multivariate field and laboratory methodologies based largely on systems theory concepts. In the 1980s, the growing popularity of the culture metaphor and increasing dissatisfaction with scientific methods led many organizational communication scholars to embrace interpretive methods. And in the past ten years, more and more scholars are wedding those interpretive approaches with a critical theoretical stance.

As new methods have come onto the organizational communication scene, the old ones have not necessarily left quietly. Indeed, the "debates" and "conversations" in our literature (see, e.g., Hawes, Pacanowsky, & Faules, 1988; Putnam, Bantz, Deetz, Mumby, & Van Maanen, 1993) suggest that a variety of approaches still exist and that the proponents of these approaches are even willing to talk to each other and learn from each other. Thus, organizational communication scholarship today is marked by a healthy eclecticism in which a variety of research methods are accepted as legitimate.

In this chapter, I will consider quantitative approaches to organizational communication research by discussing their assumptive bases, typical practices, and emerging challenges. Before beginning this discussion, it is important to comment on the label used for the research methods considered in this chapter. The theoretical school that has spawned many of the methods discussed here has variously been referred to as functionalism (Burrell & Morgan, 1979; Putnam & Pacanowsky, 1983), postpositivism (Phillips, 1987), postempiricism (Manicas, 1987), normative (Deetz, 1994), and even naturalism (Bernstein, 1976). However, the research *methods* considered here share a value for understanding and explaining organizational communication process through some kind of quantification process (at widely varying levels of exactitude). Thus, because the concentration in this chapter is on *methodological* practices and challenges, the term *quantitative* will be used throughout.

## BACKGROUND AND ASSUMPTIVE BASE

Quantitative approaches to research methodology within organizational communication have their roots in a logical positivist philosophy of science (e.g., Hempel, 1966). Though space does not permit a full exploration of these origins (see Suppe, 1977), logical positivism was marked by operationalism (the belief that all theoretical terms can and must be reduced to observable phenomena) and by the belief that a totally unbiased account of the world can be achieved through the careful application of the scientific method.[1] Logical positivists held that the physical and social worlds exist independent of our appreciation of them (realist ontology) and that an understanding of that world is found in a search for causal relationships and universal laws (positivist epistemology).

Allegiance to the logical positivist school of thought began waning soon after World War II, as philosophers of science began to question some of its main tenets, especially operationalism. New notions of "how science works" and "how science *should* work" became prominent on the scene (see, e.g., Feyerabend, 1975; Kuhn, 1962; Lakatos, 1970; Popper, 1962). Today, the classical form of logical positivism has been thoroughly debunked and is widely regarded as dead. However, allegiance to the principles of realism and objectivity has not died with it. Indeed, these assumptions are still viewed as highly viable by many organizational communication researchers, though in slightly altered form. The description of postpositivism presented by Phillips (1987, 1990) closely parallels the assumptive base of many quantitative researchers in organizational communication today. Thus, his work will be drawn on extensively in the following two sections.

### Ontological Assumptions

Guba and Lincoln (1994) summarize the ontological position of postpositivists as "critical realism." Researchers in this tradition are realists in that they support "the view that entities exist independently of being perceived, or independently of our theories about them" (Phillips, 1987). However, this realism is tempered by the argument that humans cannot *fully* apprehend that reality and that the driving mechanisms in the social and physical world cannot be *fully* understood. As Smith (1990) states, "Realism is essential . . . because it poses 'at least in principle, a standard by which all human societies and their beliefs can be judged: they can all have beliefs about the world which turn out to be mistaken' (Trigg, 1985, p. 22)" (p. 171).

Phillips argues, however, that a realist ontology does not prohibit the advocacy of a "social construction of reality" (Berger & Luckmann, 1967). Rather, Phillips (1990) draws the distinction between *beliefs* about the reality and the objective reality (pp. 42-43). Making this distinction allows a quantitative researcher to appreciate (and investigate) multiple "realities" that are constructed by social collectives through communicative interaction. Quantitative researchers also argue that the social construction *process* is a regular one that can be studied through traditional social scientific methods. Wilson (1994) argues convincingly for this point regarding her own study of children's responses to the mass media:

> I believe that children's interpretations and responses are as richly individualistic as snowflakes. However, I also believe that there are common patterns that characterize a majority of young viewers and that those patterns are as predictable and explainable as the basic process by which all those unique snowflakes are formed from water. (p. 25)

Theorists advocating ontological positions clearly opposed to realism also see the usefulness of quantitative research methods in scholarship. For example, Deetz (1994), in arguing for an "emergent" ontology in communication studies, states that "in communication-based studies, quantitative analysis is a situated slice of the total research process arising out of and returning to constitutive processes" (p. 595). That is, quantitative researchers can contribute to the study of emergent processes by taking informative snapshots of those processes as they unfold.

### *Epistemological Assumptions*

Quantitative researchers' assumptions about the grounds of social knowledge are also largely based on tenets originally developed by positivists in the physical sciences (Burrell & Morgan, 1979). These assumptions include the interlinked notions that (1) knowledge can best be gained through a search for regularities and causal relationships among components of the social world, (2) regulari-

ties and causal relationships can best be discovered if there is a complete separation between the investigator and the subject of the investigation, and (3) this separation can be guaranteed through the use of the scientific method. The scientific method is necessary because "scientists, like all men and women, are opinionated, dogmatic, ideological. . . . That is the very reason for insisting on procedural objectivity; to get the whole business outside of ourselves" (Kerlinger, 1979, p. 264).

Like ontological assumptions, however, most quantitative researchers in organizational communication have tempered these epistemological bases to what Guba (1990) has termed "modified objectivist." Quantitative scholars generally hold to the first assumption listed above. That is, the search for knowledge remains centered on causal explanations for regularities observed in the physical and social world. However, postpositivists have largely rejected the second assumption above, concluding that "the hope for a formal method, capable of being isolated from actual human judgment about the content of science (that is, about the nature of the world), and from human values seems to have evaporated" (Putnam, 1981, p. 192). Because this assumption of value-free inquiry is rejected, postpositivists have similarly rejected blind obedience to the scientific method. Instead, objectivity is seen as a "regulatory ideal." In other words, a quantitative researcher will use methods that strive to be as unbiased as possible and will attempt to be aware of any values that might compromise neutrality. However, because the possible fallibilities of the scientific method are recognized, the researcher will also rely on the critical scrutiny of a community of scholars to safeguard objectivity and maximize the growth of social scientific knowledge. As Bernstein (1976) argues, "The theorist must always be willing to submit his [*sic*] hypothetical claims to public discussion and testing, and ought to abandon any claims which have been refuted according to the canons of scientific research" (p. 44).

## QUANTITATIVE METHODS: RESEARCH PRACTICES

In this section, I will consider several specific research methodologies widely used by quantitative organizational communication researchers: experimental methods, survey methods, and behavioral observation. For each methodology, I will briefly consider typical procedures for data collection and data analysis and cite exemplary studies from the organizational communication literature that have used the method being considered. The division of quantitative methods into these three categories is useful for the purpose of discussion, but it is also somewhat artificial. Experimental, survey, and behavioral observation techniques are not mutually exclusive, and a great many studies triangulate these techniques to gain a more complete and complex explanation of organizational communication phenomena (Albrecht & Ropp, 1982).

### Experimental Research

Experimental research can be distinguished from all other types of research in that it involves the manipulation or control of the independent variable (Campbell & Stanley, 1963). Further, a true experiment can be distinguished from a quasi-experiment in that a true experiment involves the random assignment of participants to treatment conditions. The goal of an experimental study is to maximize the ability of a researcher to draw conclusions about the causal relationship between the independent variable and dependent variable. By controlling the independent variable, the researcher takes the first step in making these causal claims. The ability to infer causality is further enhanced if the researcher can rule out alternative explanations through randomization and other design and procedural choices (see classic texts by Campbell & Stanley, 1963, and Cook & Campbell, 1979, for detailed discussion).

Experimental studies can be undertaken in a variety of research settings. Because a true experiment involves the random assignment of participants to treatment groups as well as tight control over research procedures, such studies typically take place in laboratory settings. Though laboratory settings involve some sacrifice in terms of organizational realism (though see Locke, 1986, for an alternative view), they are often used to ferret out the specific mechanisms involved in organizational communication processes. Control over the independent variable can also be exercised in field experiments conducted in actual organizations. Such studies are typically quasi-experiments and may involve the manipulation of the independent variable through the use of scenarios or through organizational programs or subgroups that provide a "naturally occurring" field experiment. Quasi-experimental designs can also be employed to investigate organizational programs in which effects are evaluated over extended periods of time.

The data gathered in an experimental study are typically analyzed with statistical techniques that allow for the comparison of groups on the dependent variable(s) of interest. The procedures most typically used are from the family of techniques based on analysis of variance (ANOVA) (for complete discussion, see Keppel, 1982; Keppel & Zedeck, 1989). Variants of the basic ANOVA model allow for the analysis of multiple dependent variables (multivariate analysis of variance —MANOVA; for review, see Bochner & Fitzpatrick, 1980) or the analysis of additional variables that serve as covariates (analysis of covariance—ANCOVA). Some methodologists have also advocated the use of structural equation modeling in experimental research (Bagozzi, 1980) to allow the researcher to explicitly assess the impact of the manipulation on participant perceptions of the independent variable and to examine causal ordering among multiple dependent variables.

In organizational communication, several recent studies have used experimental methods. Papa and Pood (1988) studied the effect of coorientational accuracy on conflict resolution tactics in a field experiment. These researchers created dyads with either high or low coorientational accuracy regarding the organization's plan to use participative management, then analyzed the dependent variables of conflict resolution tactics and discussion satisfaction. Ellis (1992) investigated the impact of source credibility and uncertainty in the organizational change process by creating messages with varying types of social information about an upcoming departmental reorganization and measuring subsequent attitudes about the planned change. Both of these experimental designs are interesting in that they use naturally occurring organizational events (e.g., a plan to use participative management and a departmental reorganization) as a springboard for the manipulation of theoretically driven independent variables. The use of experimental techniques was particularly appropriate in that each researcher was attempting to delineate specific causal connections (e.g., between coorientation and tactic selection or between uncertainty and message acceptance) that would advance an established theoretical body of literature.

## Survey and Interview Research

Researchers using survey and interview techniques within the quantitative tradition rely on the self-reports of research participants to make inferences about organizational communication processes (for more detail on survey research techniques, see Kerlinger, 1986; Warwick & Lininger, 1975). Researchers using these techniques generally base their work on the psychological perspective of organizational communication (Krone, Jablin, & Putnam, 1987), proposing that individual perceptions about communication processes have important theoretical and pragmatic implications. The self-reports of research participants are used to measure attitudes about communication events or relationships, to measure predispositions for particu-

lar communication behavior, or as a marker of other organizational communication behavior. Whether collecting data through written questionnaires, phone interviews, or face-to-face interviews, quantitative researchers typically use *structured* measurement instruments that include forced-choice items or structured open-ended questions.

In analyzing data from survey research, the investigator generally follows two sequential steps. First, the quality of the scales must be determined. Then, the theoretical relationships among the scales can be analyzed. At the simplest level, scale quality is assessed through face validity and a consideration of scale consistency such as Cronbach's alpha (Cronbach, 1951). In initial studies where scale development is the goal, exploratory factor analysis (EFA) might be used to uncover the dimensionality of the scales (Nunnally, 1978). However, many communication researchers have become disillusioned with this technique and have turned to confirmatory factor analysis (CFA) as a method for analyzing the quality of both newly developed and well-validated scales (for thorough discussions of CFA techniques, see Fink & Monge, 1985; Hunter & Gerbing, 1982; James, Mulaik, & Brett, 1982). The challenge of making choices regarding the assessment of measurement quality will be discussed later in this chapter.

After confirming the quality of the measurement instruments, the survey researcher then assesses the relationships among the constructs. At the simplest level, relationships are considered through techniques including correlation and multiple regression (for complete discussions, see Keppel & Zedeck, 1989; Pedhazur, 1982). However, because many organizational communication researchers are interested in more complex systems of relationships, in recent years scholars have turned to more sophisticated analytical techniques.[2] For example, many researchers now use path analytic techniques or structural equation modeling (for discussion, see Cappella, 1980; McPhee & Babrow, 1987) in their analysis of survey data in organizational communication. Again, choices among these more complex analytical techniques will be discussed later in this chapter.

Finally, if the self-report data collected are designed to be indicators of communicative activity in the organization, network analytic techniques are often employed. As Rice and Richards (1985) note, "The goal of network analysis is to obtain from low-level or raw relational data higher-level descriptions of the structure of the system" (p. 106). This higher-level description might be construed either in the form of "cohesion" (e.g., individuals are linked in the network if they talk to each other) or in the form of "structural equivalence" (e.g., individuals are linked in the network if they talk with a similar set of people) (Burt, 1978). These network constructs can then be used either as descriptions of organizational social systems or as antecedent or consequent conditions in higher-level explanations of organizational communication behavior (e.g., Eisenberg, Monge, & Miller, 1983; McPhee & Corman, 1995). For a more complete review of network analytic assumptions, techniques, and computer programs, see Wasserman and Faust (1994).

A wide range of recent organizational communication research has used survey research techniques (for a sampling of recent studies, see Barker & Tompkins, 1994; Fink & Chen, 1995; Kramer, 1993; Miller, Birkholt, Scott, & Stage, 1995; Treadwell & Harrison, 1994). I will briefly discuss three representative examples. Marshall and Stohl (1993) were interested in assessing the ways in which participation in communication networks and the empowerment derived from that participation led to valued organizational outcomes. Their survey design involved measures of network participation, perceived involvement, empowerment, and satisfaction. Performance appraisals were also obtained from members of the management team. Through correlational and regression techniques, Marshall and Stohl were able to explore the differential relationships among em-

powerment, involvement, satisfaction, and performance.

A more complex analytical strategy was employed by Fulk (1993) in survey research taking a social constructivist approach to the investigation of communication technology in organizations. Using a survey of electronic mail users and structural equation modeling techniques (Joreskög & Sörbom, 1989), Fulk determined that social influences on technology-related attitudes and behaviors were consistently stronger when individuals reported a high level of attraction to their work groups.

A third recent study (Stohl, 1993) is useful in demonstrating the ways in which quantitative research methods can be applied to explain the processes through which organizational actors *interpret* their working worlds. Phillips (1990) argues that the "socially constructed realities" of actors can be objectively investigated with appropriate quantitative research methods. One method for doing this that has gained considerable favor in organizational communication is semantic network analysis (Monge & Eisenberg, 1987). This method allows the researcher to analyze the self-reported interpretations of research participants to create a map of the degree to which meanings for key organizational processes are shared. Stohl (1993) recently used this method to investigate the ways in which managers from varying national cultures differ in their interpretation of the participation construct.

## Coding of Communication Behaviors and Archives

A third general research strategy used by quantitative organizational communication researchers involves the objective coding of communication behaviors or communication artifacts (see Bakeman & Gottman, 1986, for general discussion). Work in this genre is distinguished by its attempt to view the interaction or archives in an objective and reliable manner and by its search for systematic explanations of communication phenomena.

The first step for researchers in this tradition involves the collection of behavioral or archival data to be coded. The major concern at this point in the research is to assemble a data set that provides a valid representation of the communicative phenomenon under investigation. After the data set has been assembled, attention shifts to analysis. The first analytical step (often taken before or concomitantly with data collection) is the development of a coding scheme to be used in analyzing the data. Poole and McPhee (1995) discuss two routes for developing a coding system. First, an analytically complete coding system can be deduced through rules of formal logic (e.g., a logical choice tree). Second, and more typically, categories can be developed based on theoretical concerns and the text being studied. Poole and McPhee note a natural trade-off between these two techniques: "The second approach to designing classification systems is advantageous because it is more responsive to the particular nature of the discourse than the first, but it is correspondingly less 'clean' and its rules harder to apply consistently" (p. 62).

Application of the coding scheme typically involves having multiple independent coders both divide the data into the proper units to be coded and apply the coding scheme to those units. There are two assessments that can be made to support the validity of the classification system. The first of these, unitizing reliability (e.g., Guetzkow, 1950), involves the extent to which coders agree on the division of the text into analytical units. The second assessment to be made is classificatory reliability (e.g., Cohen, 1960; Holsti, 1969), and involves the extent to which coders agree on the classification of units into categories. For complete discussions of reliability assessment options and problems that often arise in the process of coding, see Folger, Hewes, and Poole (1984), Hewes (1985), and Zwick (1988).

After the data are coded, the researcher typically looks for patterns in the categorization. Because these data are usually coded at the nominal level, techniques such as ANOVA and regression are generally inappropriate as analytical choices. At the most basic level, then, coded interaction and archival data can be analyzed with nonparametric statistics such as chi-square. However, recent trends in organizational communication research point to the continuing importance of more advanced categorical data analysis techniques, particularly log-linear analysis (see, e.g., Bishop, Feinberg, & Holland, 1975) or, for the analysis of sequential categorical data, Markov modeling (see Hewes, 1975, 1979). Though these techniques are not without problems,[3] they allow for assessments of causality and the influence of time that are unavailable in more elementary procedures.

Several important examples of the use of behavioral observation and analysis are prominent in the organizational communication research literature. For example, Gail Fairhurst and her colleagues (see, e.g., Fairhurst, 1993; Fairhurst & Chandler, 1989; Fairhurst, Green, & Courtright, 1995; Fairhurst, Rogers, & Sarr, 1987) have used interaction analysis (along with discourse analysis) to investigate the relational control patterns used in supervisor-subordinate relationships. Research in decision making conducted by Scott Poole and his colleagues provides another example of behavioral coding in organizational communication research. In early work, Poole and Roth (1989) developed a typology of group decision paths and a procedure for coding types of interaction in decision-making groups. In subsequent work, these researchers have used the coding procedures to explore the nature of computer-mediated decision making, concentrating on conflict management (Poole, Holmes, & DeSanctis, 1991), microstructurational processes (Poole & DeSanctis, 1992), and the distinction between computer-mediated and face-to-face groups (Poole, Holmes, Watson, & DeSanctis, 1993). They have also extended the coding methodology in the development of a computer program for analyzing over-time decision sequences (Holmes & Poole, 1991).

## CRITERIA FOR JUDGING QUANTITATIVE RESEARCH

The ontological and epistemological foundations that undergird quantitative scholarship suggest a clear direction for judging the quality of research efforts. That is, high-quality quantitative research in the postpositivist tradition provides an accurate and relatively unbiased account of the social world, provides well-supported explanations of relationships within that social world, and contributes to the advance of our knowledge about the social world. This suggests that such research can be judged in two ways. First, a piece of research can be compared with standards for how "proper" quantitative research should be conducted. As Smith (1990) notes, "The notion of the properly done study is central to postempiricists and they hold it is possible to distinguish unbiased, open, honest, and precise research from that which is not" (p. 172). Second, a piece of research can be judged in the context of the larger body of scholarship to which it is contributing.

The technical merits of functional research are typically assessed with standards of validity and reliability established in a wide array of social scientific disciplines (see, e.g., Kerlinger, 1986).[4] The standards of internal validity, external validity, measurement reliability, and measurement validity are summarized in Table 4.1.

Although these standards are well accepted among scholars using quantitative research methods, they are not without controversy. For example, several debates have centered around issues of external validity in organizational research, both in terms of generalizability of research participants and generalizability of research settings. This debate will be considered later in this chapter as one of the "challenges" facing quantitative researchers.

If a study is determined to be valid and reliable in the ways outlined in Table 4.1, the quantitative researcher would conclude that it provides a defensible explanation for the phe-

nomenon under investigation. However, the technical quality of the study does not necessarily mean that it makes a meaningful contribution to our knowledge about organizational communication. As Wilson (1994) notes, "All of us have encountered empirical studies that are technically proficient and highly rigorous but which report findings that seem rather meaningless in light of current issues in communication" (p. 29).

Two general criteria can be offered regarding the contribution made by functionalist research. First, quantitative research should be grounded in established theory and research, or as Marshall (1990) states, the research should be tied to "the big picture" and be sensitive to "historical context" (pp. 194-195). Second, research in the postpositivist tradition should move beyond the extant literature and make an independent and significant contribution to that theoretical groundwork. The question of what constitutes a "significant" contribution is, of course, difficult to determine. Certainly, significance of contribution means more than deriving results that are statistically significant, and perhaps the significance of research can best be judged retrospectively. That is, if a piece of research stands the test of time by generating additional research questions, contributing to theoretical development, and motivating dialogue among scholars, it is truly significant scholarship.

## QUANTITATIVE METHODS: RESEARCH CHALLENGES

Despite the entrenchment of quantitative methods in our scholarship, there are still a number of areas in which researchers using these approaches are confronted with challenges that are either inherent in quantitative methodology or have sprung from the typical conduct of quantitative research. These challenges are associated with all phases of the research process, from the conceptualization of the research program and design, to the

**TABLE 4.1** Basic Criteria for Judging the Technical Merits of Quantitative Research

| Criterion | Description | Methodological Strategies |
|---|---|---|
| Internal validity | The extent to which the researcher is sure that no confounding variables have influenced the relationship between the independent and dependent variables. | Use of random assignment to treatment groups and other design strategies that minimize alternative explanations for study results. |
| External validity | The extent to which the researcher can generalize study results to other actors, behaviors, and contexts. | Use of random sampling, representative organizational field sites, and realistic organizational activities. |
| Measurement reliability | The extent to which a measure is repeatable (over time) and consistent (with regard to multiple indicators or multiple coders). | Assess reliability through alpha, repeated measures, or interrater reliability coefficient. Enhance reliability through careful item construction, pretesting, and thorough training of coders. |
| Measurement validity | The extent to which a measure assesses the concept it is designed to assess. Includes content (face), construct, and pragmatic validity. | Assess through review of item content, comparison to relevant outcome variables, relationships within nomothetic network, consideration of multitrait-multimethod matrix. |

collection of data, to statistical analysis, and to substantive interpretation. Although these portions of the research process are clearly interdependent, challenges associated with each of these areas will be considered separately in the remainder of this chapter.

## Challenges of Research Design

Organizational communication scholars face the daunting task of investigating and understanding processes that are becoming increasingly complex. Organizations are messy sites—characterized by multiple layers of activity and constant change over time. Thus, an important challenge for quantitative scholars is to design research that is capable of captur-

ing the complexities of organizational life. Two aspects of this challenge are discussed below: Dealing with multiple levels of analysis in quantitative research, and incorporating time into our research designs.

### Challenges Associated With Levels of Analysis

In some areas of communication scholarship, research interest is largely defined by the level of analysis. An example of such an area is small-group communication. Organizational communication, as well, could appear to the outsider to be a "single-level" phenomenon. However, systems theorists in communication have long recognized that multiple levels must be considered in an investigation of organizational phenomena (see, e.g., Farace,

Monge, & Russell, 1977). A look at our journals confirms this notion, as research investigations in organizational communication include the psychological processes of individuals, dyadic and group interaction, organizational culture and climate, and interorganizational transactions. Klein, Dansereau, and Hall (1994) suggest that levels issues should be considered in terms of (1) theory development, (2) data collection, and (3) data analysis.

Klein et al. (1994) first argue that an organizational theorist should carefully consider levels assumptions being made in theory. For example, a theory could specify the homogeneity of a group, the independence of individuals within a group, or a distinct patterning of individuals within a group. These distinctions are far from straightforward. For example, a debate has raged in the management literature regarding the status of the "climate" construct (see, e.g., Glick, 1988; James, Joyce, & Slocum, 1988). Is climate an individual-level variable that can be aggregated to the organizational level? Or is climate a property of the organization or subgroup apart from individual perceptions of climate? Further, many theories include attention to two or more levels. For example, leader-member exchange theory (see Graen & Scandura, 1987) includes constructs and effects on the individual, dyadic, and work group levels.

Once the level of theory is carefully considered and delineated, decisions about data collection and analysis must be addressed. Klein et al. (1994) argue that the researcher can either choose to collect data in a way that *conforms* to the level of the theory or to collect data in a way that will allow the researcher to *test* assumptions about the level of theory. For example, a theory of group decision making may propose that the *process* of decision making is substantively different from the process of individual decision making. The researcher could choose to either explore the process of group decision making further by collecting extensive data from groups or could test the assumptive base of the

theory by contrasting data collected from individuals and groups. Klein et al. argue that "the ideal approach, however, is to employ multiple and varied measures of the constructs of a theory. When diverse measures of a construct demonstrate the variability predicted for the construct, researchers' confidence in the level of the construct is enhanced" (p. 211). As Klein et al. (1994) point out, similar dilemmas face the researcher in the analysis of data, and the picture becomes particularly complicated when the theory includes multiple levels:

> The development and testing of multiple-level theories magnifies these concerns. The strength of multiple-level theories is their complexity; they do not oversimplify organizational realities (Burstein, 1980). Specifying the level of each construct within a multiple-level theory aids theorists and researchers in managing such complexity. So, too, do efforts to align the assumptions of variability underlying the independent and dependent constructs. (p. 225)

A more specific proposal regarding the level-of-analysis challenge has recently been proposed by House, Rousseau, and Thomas-Hunt (1995). These scholars suggest that organizational research has traditionally been bifurcated into "micro" and "macro" camps and that fuller understanding of organizational phenomena will come only when we also look at the "meso" level. Mesotheory and research are defined as

> the simultaneous study of at least two levels of analysis wherein (a) one or more levels concern individual or group behavioral processes . . . , (b) one or more levels concern organizational processes . . . , and (c) the processes by which the levels of analysis are related are articulated in the form of bridging, or linking, propositions. (House et al., 1995, p. 73)

House et al. continue by proposing and discussing three ways in which micro- and macroprocesses can interact: isomorphisms (constituent components of a phenomenon are similar across levels of analysis), discontinuities (components manifest themselves differently at different levels of analysis), and interlevel relationships (bridging propositions are proposed to specify the process by which components at various levels of analysis affect each other). House et al.'s specific suggestions for dealing with interlevel relationships could be very useful for organizational communication scholars who routinely struggle with multiple-level research issues.

Consider, for example, the work of communication scholars investigating organizational groups. Though early scholars recognized the impact of individual members on small-group interaction, recent investigations have advocated adding another layer to our models of group functioning. Stohl began making this extension in organizational communication over ten years ago by considering quality circles as group structures "parallel" to the larger organizational structure (Stohl, 1986). More recently, Putnam and Stohl (1990) have advocated the study of "bona fide groups" in which organizational groups are characterized in terms of their stable yet permeable boundaries and their interdependence with the larger organizational context (see also Stohl, 1995). Lammers and Krikorian (1997) have demonstrated the complexity of research stemming from a bona fide group perspective in their study of hospital surgical teams. Lammers and Krikorian did not use the vocabulary of House et al. (1995) in their discussion of surgical teams, but their efforts to examine and operationalize some of the concepts proposed in Putnam and Stohl's original development of the bona fide group concept demonstrate some of the complex decisions that must be confronted in multilevel organizational communication research. For example, Lammers and Krikorian consider the complexity of using network analytic concepts such as connectedness across multiple levels of analysis. Though they note that connectedness scores could be computed at varying levels of analysis (e.g., perhaps

connectedness is an isomorphism), they further argue (Lammers & Krikorian, 1997, p. 23) that "it may be that the logics of connectedness vary across level" (e.g., perhaps connectedness is a discontinuity). Lammers and Krikorian's related discussions of tight and loose coupling, resource dependency, and internal and external authority systems demonstrate the challenging nature of cross-level organizational research.

### Challenges Associated With Over-Time Processes

In addition to considering the complexity of multileveled organizational processes, communication researchers using quantitative methods must also deal with appropriate ways for incorporating the concept of process into their theorizing and research. The call for more attention to process in organizational communication has been most fully developed by Peter Monge and his colleagues (Monge, 1982, 1990; Monge, Farace, Eisenberg, White, & Miller, 1984) and has been echoed by scholars throughout disciplines of organization study. For example, two recent issues of *Organization Science* were devoted to issues of longitudinal design and analysis (see Huber & Van de Ven, 1995).

Scholars advocating longitudinal approaches argue that most of our theories of organizational communication are either explicitly or implicitly processual, but that our research methods have lagged behind these theories by considering cross-sectional data analyzed with regression or analysis of variance. To provide but one example, theories of organizational socialization are inherently processual. Yet it is the rare study (e.g., Kramer, 1993) that includes multiple data collection periods, let alone the observation and analytic procedures that would allow for a full mapping and understanding of the assimilation process. Thus, Monge and his colleagues urge organizational communication researchers to move beyond the strictures of cross-sectional research designs and analytical tools to consider methods that will allow a more complete assessment of organizational communication processes.

Monge's (1990) suggestions for moving ahead with processual research closely parallel Klein et al.'s suggestions regarding the issue of levels in research. Specifically, Monge recommends a careful conceptualization of the process notions inherent in our theories by considering each construct in terms of its continuity, magnitude of change, rate of change, trend, periodicity, and duration. After the processual qualities of theoretical constructs are carefully delineated, the researcher can follow up with appropriate longitudinal data collection procedures and appropriate analytical tools (e.g., Markov modeling, event history analysis, multivariate time series analysis).[5] However, Monge (1982) argues that progress with processual theorizing can be accomplished only by considering the correspondence among the nature of the theory, the nature of the data, and the analytical tools used. For explications of specific strategies useful in the design, conduct, and analysis of longitudinal research, the interested reader is referred to Van de Ven and Poole (1990), Glick, Huber, Miller, Doty, and Sutcliffe (1990), and Pettigrew (1990).

Consider, for example, the complications faced by scholars investigating the process of innovation adoption in organizations (e.g., Monge, Cozzens, & Contractor, 1992; Van de Ven & Poole, 1990). The study of innovation requires processual theories and methods because, as Van de Ven and Poole (1990) note, "although many studies have examined the antecedents to or consequences of innovation, very few have directly examined how and why innovations emerge, develop, grow, or terminate over time" (p. 313; see also Tornatsky et al., 1983). Van de Ven and Poole describe the procedures used to study the development of innovation in the Minnesota Innovation Research Program. Their multilayered and longitudinal approach involved the classification of innovation incidents, the coding of those incidents, the transformation of incidents into a "bit-map event sequence," the analysis of sequence data with appropriate statistical techniques, and the identification of patterns among various sequences. This highly complex process yields important insights about the innovation process that would be unavailable through static techniques, but it also poses numerous land mines for the researcher. Each step of the process poses new and complex dilemmas regarding reliability, validity, appropriate statistical choice, and meaningful interpretation.

## Challenges of Data Collection

The preceding section considered some of the challenges of designing research that considers the complexity of time and level in organizational research. Part of dealing with that complexity involved *collecting* data at multiple points in time and from multiple levels of these organization. But there are other challenges associated with data collection that must be considered by the quantitative researcher. Two of these challenges are considered in this section: challenges associated with the use of self-report data and challenges of gathering data that are representative of the people and processes under theoretical consideration.

### Challenges Associated With Self-Report Data

Although the trend in communication research has been shifting toward an emphasis on interactional data, a great deal of organizational communication research remains grounded in the self-reports of research participants. This is not necessarily bad. When psychological variables or perceptions of communication processes constitute the phenomenon of interest, self-reports are the most appropriate means for collecting data. However, if the researcher is using the self-report as an indicator of actual communication behavior, there can be a great deal of slippage between the self-report and interaction. Further, there are other inherent challenges of using self-report data that must be considered by the quantitative researcher.

The first challenge associated with self-report data is the assessment of whether the self-report is a valid representation of the construct being considered. For example, there has been substantial debate regarding what is actually measured when researchers collect self-reports about conflict management style (see Knapp, Putnam, & Davis, 1988). Are these self-reports indicative of actual behavior, planned behavior, recalled behavior, or preferred behavior? Or are the self-reports totally unrelated to communicative interaction? This issue has been most thoroughly investigated with regard to communication network participation. A series of studies in the early 1980s (Bernard, Killworth, Kronnenfeld, & Sailer, 1984; Bernard, Killworth, & Sailer, 1982) demonstrated that perceptions of network participation are not valid indicators of observable communication behavior. Since then, communication scholars have been grappling with this issue (see Corman, 1990; Corman & Scott, 1994; Monge & Contractor, 1988; Monge & Eisenberg, 1987) by looking for better measurement techniques, assessing the importance of perceived communication apart from actual behavior, and considering theoretical models that could provide a vehicle for explaining and modeling these gaps between perception and behavior. The important development here is that self-reports are no longer seen as perfectly reliable stand-ins for behavioral assessment, and researchers are dealing with this lack of isomorphism both theoretically and methodologically.

Other challenges also come with the territory when using self-report data. One of these is the problem of social desirability (see Crowne & Marlowe, 1964). How can we know that respondents are giving us true reports of their perceptions and not simply telling us "what we want to hear" (or, just as dan-

gerous, what management wants to hear)? Social desirability problems can be particularly vexing when assessing communicative behavior in which the goal is to assess *use* of the behavior rather than *appropriateness* of behavior. Social desirability problems have been argued to be present in measures of compliance-gaining techniques (Burleson et al., 1988; though see responses by Boster, 1988; Hunter, 1988; Seibold, 1988) and conflict management techniques (Wilson & Waltman, 1988). Within the confines of survey research, the problem of social desirability can probably best be curtailed by emphasizing the researcher's independent role, by assuring confidentiality or anonymity, and by convincing participants that their honesty and straightforwardness is truly valued. Wilson and Waltman (1988) also recommend eschewing "checklist" measures in favor of open-ended responses to hypothetical situations.

Finally, self-report data may lead to erroneous conclusions about the relationship between variables. When two or more constructs are measured using self-reports, those constructs might appear to be related simply because of the measurement techniques used (common method variance). For example, Wagner and Gooding (1987) conducted a meta-analysis of the participative decision-making literature and concluded that studies using self-reports of both participation and outcome variables yielded consistently stronger relationships than those in which alternative methods were used. Avoiding this problem requires a shifting from self-report to behavioral measures, or the careful development of self-report measures through multitrait/multimethod techniques (Althauser, 1974; Campbell & Fiske, 1959).

## Challenges of Sample Representativeness

When considering organizational communication processes, quantitative scholars typically want to generalize the research to people, settings, and processes beyond the confines of the research project. This concern with external validity has most traditionally considered the generalizability of research participants and research settings. The debate regarding research participants typically considers the appropriateness of using college students in research investigating organizational processes. This issue is far from settled (see, e.g., Gordon, Slade, & Schmitt, 1986, 1987; Greenberg, 1987), but there does seem to be agreement on several issues. First, as Greenberg (1987) states, "student and nonstudent samples may be equally useful sources of information about the processes underlying organizational phenomena" (p. 158). However, this is the case only when care is taken to support the student sample as similar to the population being generalized to on relevant theoretical variables and when the student-based study is part of a larger research program justifying generalization to the organizational population of interest (see Gordon et al., 1986, 1987, for arguments; Walther, 1995, for organizational communication example). A similar debate has raged about the use of the laboratory setting in studies of organizational phenomena. This debate was thoroughly investigated in a volume edited by Edwin Locke (1986) in which meta-analytic techniques were used to compare laboratory and field-based investigation of critical organizational phenomena. The conclusion of these investigations was that "the data do not support the belief that lab studies produce different results than field studies" (Campbell, 1986, p. 276). This is not to suggest, though, that either setting is appropriate for any research question. Instead, choice of research participants and research site must be guided by the substantive issues of interest.

Drawing a generalizable sample of *people* is only part of the challenge for today's organizational communication researcher, however. With increasing reliance on text-based research, scholars must also consider the representativeness of the discourse or text under consideration. This debate has been most thoroughly explored in the area of discourse and interaction analysis in a consideration of what is to "count as evidence" in the study of texts and conversations. For example, Cappella (1990) vehemently argued against what he called "the method of proof by example" (p. 237) arguing that this method capitalizes on random occurrences in the text and is susceptible to selection bias. Jacobs (1990) disagrees, arguing that these biases are unlikely to occur, especially if there is "a community of analysts who actively set out to falsify the analysis of any particular study" (p. 247). No closure has been reached on this debate, but Fitch (1994) defends a middle road in which the researcher attempts to balance richness with precision. She argues for the criterion that "claims should be based on an adequate selection of the total corpus of data. In other words, claims should be saturated in data" (p. 36).

## Analytical Challenges

In the previous sections on research design and data collection, it is clear that a challenge continually faced by quantitative researchers is dealing with the interdependence of the various phases of the research effort. Nowhere are the connections made more clear than in the process of analyzing quantitative data. Our care in designing research that captures the complexity of organizational communication processes will be of little use if we cannot analyze those data in a way that usefully informs us about those conceptual processes. Monge (1982) raised this issue over 15 years ago, arguing that although scholars in the systems theory tradition were proposing complex abstract insights about organizational communication behavior, those insights were of little use if they were not investigated through commensurably complex analytical tools. In this section, I will consider four specific quantitative analysis techniques that can be used to enhance the "match" between our theorizing and analysis at various phases of the research process. It should be noted, of course, that complex analytical tools are not always appropriate in organizational communication research. When asking simple questions, scholars should avoid the tendency to "kill gnats with a cannon" and use simple techniques capable of answering research questions in a straightforward and elegant manner. However, when required by complex theorizing, the following analytical strategies are useful components of the organizational communication researcher's arsenal.

First, as noted earlier, quantitative researchers are usually trying to contribute to an accumulation of knowledge about organizational communication processes, and thus try to build research attempts on past literature. Surprisingly, though, quantitative researchers rarely perform quantitative methods in the research review process. Instead, scholars typically rely on a narrative literature review, occasionally "counting" the number of significant and nonsignificant findings, in reaching conclusions about extant knowledge on a topic. However, a more comprehensive literature review strategy is available in the form of meta-analysis (Glass, McGaw, & Smith, 1981; Hunter, Schmidt, & Jackson, 1982). With meta-analytic techniques, a scholar is able to quantitatively cumulate findings over a variety of research projects, accounting for research artifacts such as sample size, measurement techniques, research context, and era of publication. Though meta- analyses are not without their problems (e.g., the "file drawer problem," incommensurability of measures and methods across studies, and problems of quantification from incomplete results), they provide an important avenue for organizing and summarizing the results of past research in an area (see, e.g., Miller & Monge, 1986).

A second area in which our analytical techniques should more appropriately mirror our theoretical sophistication is in the assessment of measurement instruments. We often have highly developed ideas about the constructs under investigation in our research, and we typically work hard to develop instruments designed to tap those constructs. However, we

usually assess the quality of those instruments using overly simplistic methods such as test-retest reliability or coefficient alpha or using inherently underidentified methods such as exploratory factor analysis (EFA; see Fink & Monge, 1985). These techniques do not allow a thorough consideration of the strengths and flaws of our measurements, for they do not require the researcher to put theoretical assumptions about measurement to a specific test. A stronger alternative in many research situations is CFA. CFA requires the researcher to specify an a priori factor structure, then *confirm* that factor structure by statistically comparing the correlations created by the specified factor structure and the observed correlations. Model confirmation can involve either microanalytical tests of internal consistency and parallelism (see Hunter & Gerbing, 1982) or macroanalytic tests of goodness of fit (see Fink & Monge, 1985). CFA techniques are superior to EFA and simple tests of reliability both in terms of statistical rigor and theoretical grounding. As with most statistical procedures, the GIGO ("garbage in, garbage out") principle guides CFA operations. The strength of the final model confirmed through CFA is largely dependent on the quality of theorizing and on the quality of individual items created in the measurement development process.

Third, in investigating the relationship among variables, we often squander opportunities to gain insight about organizational communication processes because our analytical techniques do not match the complexity of our theorizing. For example, we might dichotomize or trichotomize an independent variable and analyze with ANOVA or MANOVA, rather than take advantage of the full range of our independent variable with regression techniques. Or if we use regression techniques, we might choose to investigate simple bivariate relationships or relationships with single dependent variables through the use of correlation and multiple regression. However, our theoretical frameworks, more often than not, propose more complex processes in which constructs are embedded in systems of relationships. Thus, a useful analytical alternative for investigating *relationships* among variables is structural equation modeling (Marcoulides & Schumacker, 1996; Schumacker & Lomax, 1996), sometimes known as path modeling or causal modeling. These techniques are generally based on the same mathematical model as regression and correlation but allow the investigation of systems with multiple causes and effects and complex feedback loops (see Monge, 1982). With some estimation procedures (e.g., full information maximum likelihood), the researcher is also able to assess the fit of the model to the data with tests of overidentifying restrictions.[6]

McPhee and Babrow (1987) argue convincingly that causal modeling is often underutilized in communication research. In their discussion of the "disuse" of causal modeling, they suggest a wide range of research situations in which causal modeling techniques are desirable (e.g., unreliable measurement, partial correlational analyses, extended systems of propositions). But McPhee and Babrow (1987) also point to a number of ways in which causal modeling is *mis*used in communication research in terms of theoretical standards, methodological standards, and presentational standards. Several issues seem particularly important to organizational communication researchers. First, causal modeling, like CFA, is a *confirmatory* technique and should be used only to test theoretically derived systems of relationships. Second, the power of the estimation procedures in causal modeling packages should be respected, especially when the researcher is attempting to simultaneously estimate measurement and causal models. Indeed, McPhee and Babrow (1987) recommend that "where there is substantial ambiguity about the causal structure of the measurement model" (p. 361) a least-squares technique should be used initially, followed by the maximum likelihood techniques of LISREL or a similar program.

A fourth area in which more sophisticated analytical strategies could be used to enhance

organizational communication research is in the actual theory development process. Theory development has often been construed as an "armchair" activity, in which insight is derived from past literature and extant theoretical frameworks. Theoretical insights created in the armchair are then taken to the field for testing. However, advances in computer technology can be used to make the theory *development* process a more exacting and exciting process. Specifically, through the use of computer simulations, various theoretical propositions can be "put to the test" with various starting values and taken to their logical conclusions. In this way, the theorist can explore the implications of a variety of theoretical assumptions and refine theory before taking the costly step of moving to the field for empirical testing. These procedures have been proposed as a means through which systems concepts can be rejuvenated in organizational communication theorizing (Poole, 1996) and have been demonstrated in recent work by Contractor and Seibold (1993). These researchers were looking for a theoretical system that would explain appropriation patterns for group decision support systems (GDSSs). Through the use of a computer simulation, Contractor and Seibold (1993) demonstrated that self-organizing systems theory has the potential to provide a dynamic and precise explanation of GDSS appropriation.

## Interpretive Challenges

The quantitative researcher's job does not end with the computation of statistics and the assessment of significance. Indeed, it has often been noted that statistical significance should be evaluated separately from practical significance and that the import of results must be evaluated with reference to the larger corpus of knowledge about organizational communication processes. In the final section of this chapter, I will consider several challenges facing quantitative researchers as they attempt to make sense of their research findings.

### The Art of Quantitative Interpretation

Qualitative research in organizational communication and throughout the social sciences has often been labeled "interpretive" (e.g., Putnam & Pacanowsky, 1983). Though the argument is rarely made explicitly, the implication of this labeling is that quantitative research does not involve the process of interpretation. This implicit argument has been taken to task in a recent article by Herbert M. Kritzler (1996) on interpretation in quantitative research. Kritzler makes a compelling case for the centrality of interpretation in quantitative research endeavors. Indeed, he argues:

> As one moves from previously existing texts of the type central to the humanities, through the textual materials of qualitative social science, to the quantitative data many of us use, the role of interpretation—which I broadly define as *the process of ascertaining the meaning(s) and implication(s) of a set of materials*—actually increases. . . . In quantitative social science, the analyst constructs both a first order text (in assembling the data) and a second order text (in the form of statistical results). With each additional step in the process, the role of interpretation increases, as do the technical elements that must be considered as part of the interpretive process. Thus, rather than being more divorced from the human process of interpretation, quantitative social science probably involves more levels of interpretation than does qualitative social science. (Kritzler, 1996, pp. 2-3, emphasis in original)

Kritzler goes on to detail the nature of interpretation in quantitative research. He first considers the multiple *levels* at which quantitative researchers must interpret results. At the first level, the results of statistical tools used in analysis must be understood. For example, how is one to interpret a significant canonical correlation? What does it mean to have a large "critical $N$" in a structural equation model? At the second level of interpretation, statistical results are used to identify anomalies and problems in the analysis. Is there restriction in range that must be considered? Have unreliable measurement instruments attenuated observed correlations? Has a small sample limited power to an untenable extent? These issues of interpretation are more complex than first-level interpretation and require an experienced analyst to fully appreciate. Finally, at the third level of interpretation, statistical patterns must be connected to broader theoretical concerns. Kritzler believes this level of analysis is "the most complex and the least understood" (p. 9) and suggests that third-level interpretation is accomplished both through reference to the context in which data were collected and theory was generated and to common "tropes" of quantitative analysis. He concludes by arguing that, as in qualitative analysis, the efficacy of an analyst's interpretation depends largely on the interaction between the researcher and the data. Even quantitative data "will speak only when they are properly questioned" (Bloch, 1953, p. 64).

Consider, for example, work in the area of participative decision making. There is little doubt from years of research that participation *can* have positive effects on employee satisfaction and productivity. Yet the questions of *how* and *why* with regard to participation in organizations are still up for some debate. Miller and Monge (1986) argued that theorists and researchers have variously advocated cognitive and affective channels through which participation could affect productivity and satisfaction. More recently, Barker and his colleagues (e.g., Barker, 1993; Barker & Tompkins, 1994) have proposed that concertive control processes are critical explanatory factors for understanding participative group effects. Clearly, these explanatory mechanisms cannot be sorted out without careful attention at all stages of the research process. The appropriate constructs must be measured (in ways commensurate with conceptualization), data must be collected at research sites and in a manner that will allow observation of critical processes, and data must be analyzed with tools that facilitate the assessment of various underlying causal structures.

## Articulation With Qualitative Methods

In this chapter, I have reviewed quantitative approaches to organizational communication research. Obviously, these approaches are often seen as radically different from qualitative methods (see Taylor & Trujillo, Chapter 5, this volume). Quantitative approaches to research, based in the largely realist and objective assumptions of postpositivism, provide systematic means for generating and accumulating generalizable explanations about organizational communication processes. Research in this tradition is judged on the extent to which it meets classical standards of reliability and validity and contributes meaningfully to an accumulation of knowledge about organizational communication processes. Qualitative approaches to organizational communication research, in contrast, are based on a subjective or emergent (see Deetz, 1994) ontology and epistemology and view the research enterprise as one in which meaning and understanding are constructed through the interaction of knower and known.

Are these two general approaches to organizational communication research diametrically opposed and locked in a battle for supremacy in the field of organizational communication? Or can these approaches exist independently as alternative—but equally viable—approaches? Or is there a way that these approaches can be seen as interdependent parts of the greater research endeavor?

The contrasting ontological and epistemological assumptions of these two schools of thought would suggest that there are some points at which quantitative and qualitative researchers will *necessarily* diverge (though see Lee, 1991). That is, if a qualitative researcher denies the possibility of generalization and causal relationships, many quantitative practices must be rejected (e.g., significance testing, random sampling, experimental control). Similarly, if a quantitative researcher believes that it is desirable to achieve a detached and scientific explanation of organizational life, an ethnographic case study involving the active participation of the researcher will not be accepted as valid research. Further, it is unlikely that some "solutions" that have been proposed for this dilemma will be satisfactory to either camp. For example, the notion of using qualitative methods to "develop" research questions and quantitative methods to "test" those research questions (or vice versa) is probably distasteful to members of both schools of thought.

A more fruitful direction might be the one proposed by Gioia and his colleagues (Gioia & Pitre, 1990; Weaver & Gioia, 1994) in arguing for a multiparadigmatic approach to theory building. Gioia and Pitre (1990) examine the "transition zones" between various paradigms and suggest strategies for bridging these zones. Weaver and Gioia (1994) further the argument for the commensurability of paradigms, positing that various paradigms of inquiry serve to "selectively bracket" social phenomena. They maintain that structuration theory (Giddens, 1976, 1979, 1984) provides means for understanding this selective bracketing and a point of connection between assumptions of interpretivists and postpositivists. Weaver and Gioia (1994) explain:

> Structuration provides a basis for seeing how organizational scholars can invoke different assumptions, pursue different goals, ask different research questions, and use different approaches, but nonetheless be engaged in inquiry with commonalities despite such diversities. . . . Structuration theory shows just how the selective bracketing of social phenomena can occur. (pp. 577-578)

Weaver and Gioia (1994) then go on to argue that structuration theory's central construct of the "dualism" can serve to break down oppositional dichotomies and illuminate "positions, processes or entities whose various aspects may be temporarily bracketed" (p. 578). For example, in proposing the "duality of structure," Giddens (1976) argues that social structures "are both constituted 'by' human agency, and yet at the same time are the very 'medium' of this constitution" (p. 121). Thus, the structuration process, by considering both the *process* of social structure constitution and the *effects* those constitutions have on practices, provides a fertile ground for both postpositivist and interpretive theorists and for both quantitative and qualitative researchers. Qualitative methods are necessary for gaining a local understanding of how the interaction of organizational members creates rules and structures. Quantitative research methods can be used to investigate the more stable ways in which those reified structures constrain and enable organizational behavior and communication.

Interestingly, scholars within the field of organizational communication are poised to take a leading role in this theoretical bridging of the qualitative and quantitative camps. Organizational communication scholars have been vocal proponents of structuration theory for many years. For example, this framework has been used to enhance our understanding of the political nature of organizational cultures (Riley, 1983), formal organizational communication structures (McPhee, 1985), group decision making (Poole, Seibold, & McPhee, 1986), and communication network participation (Corman & Scott, 1994).

Two recent research programs are particularly illustrative of the power of this theoretical paradigm for understanding communication phenomena through both quantitative and qualitative lenses. Joanne Yates and Wanda Orlikowski (e.g., Orlikowski & Yates, 1994; Yates & Orlikowski, 1992) draw on structuration theory in examining the ways in which "communication genres" are enacted in organizations or organizational communities. In a second line of research, Gerardine DiSanctis and Marshall Scott Poole have advocated the use of adaptive structuration theory for understanding the complexity of communication technologies such as group decision support systems (see DeSanctis & Poole, 1994, for a recent and comprehensive discussion). These scholars advocate a multilevel and multimethod research approach that holds great promise for explaining the ways in which "technology and social structures mutually shape one another over time" (DeSanctis & Poole, 1994, p. 125). DeSanctis and Poole's (1994) discussion of the analytical research strategies necessary for a consideration of the appropriation process is notable in its inclusion of both quantitative and qualitative techniques (see pp. 138-139).

In conclusion, though quantitative and qualitative researchers advance very different research agendas and goals, structuration theory provides one possible framework that can allow both schools to work together in enhancing our knowledge of the creation, sustenance, and constraining effects of organizational communication processes. Because of these metatheoretical possibilities, and the tradition of healthy dialogue within the field of organizational communication, it seems likely that both quantitative and qualitative research programs will continue to thrive in our research.

## NOTES

1. Watt and van den Berg (1995), in a recent explication of quantitative research methods for communication, note the following requirements that differentiate scientific methods from "naive science" (pp. 12-14): selection of abstract concepts to represent observable phenomena, defining concepts both conceptually and operationally, linking concepts through propositions, testing theories with observable evidence, controlling alternative explanations through study design, making definitions and procedures public for scrutiny by the scientific community, using unbiased evidence in making truth claims, and objective reconciliation of theory and observation.

2. Several multivariate techniques used by organizational communication researchers are discussed in this chapter. Others that cannot be discussed due to space limitations include multivariate multiple regression, canonical correlation, and discriminant analysis. For a discussion of the use of these, and other, multivariate techniques in human communication research, see Monge and Cappella (1980).

3. McPhee and Corman (1995) note problems with this family of techniques including the complexity and difficulty of interpretation and reliance on statistical tests that are overly sensitive to sample size.

4. Technical merits of the study can also be considered with regard to the appropriate choice and execution of statistical techniques. Because these issues vary substantially depending on the analytical choices made in a study, they will not be discussed in detail here. The interested reader is referred to relevant sources on specific statistical procedures referenced in the course of this chapter.

5. More complete information on analytical techniques and choices can be found in the following sources. For event history analysis, see Allison (1984). For Markov analysis, see Bartholomew (1976). For time series analysis, see Box and Jenkins (1976). For an overview of sequence methods, see Abbott (1990).

6. A variety of goodness-of-fit tests are available in statistical software packages such as LISREL (Jöreskog & Sörbom, 1989). Because these goodness-of-fit indexes (based on chi-square) are sensitive to sample size, Hoetler (1983) has suggested the use of the "critical $N$" statistic to account for sample size. The use of the chi-square to degrees of freedom ratio (Bentler & Bonett, 1980) for this correction is not recommended, however.

# REFERENCES

Abbott, A. (1990). A primer on sequence methods. *Organization Science, 1*, 375-392.

Albrecht, T. L., & Ropp, V. A. (1982). The study of network structuring in organizations through the use of method triangulation. *Western Journal of Speech Communication, 46*, 162-178.

Allison, P. D. (1984). *Event history analysis.* Beverly Hills, CA: Sage.

Althauser, R. P. (1974). Inferring validity from the multitrait-multimethod matrix: Another assessment. In H. L. Costner (Ed.), *Sociological methodology 1974* (pp. 106-127). San Francisco: Jossey-Bass.

Bagozzi, R. M. (1980). *Causal models in marketing.* New York: John Wiley.

Bakeman, R., & Gottman, J. M. (1986). *Observing interaction.* Cambridge, UK: Cambridge University Press.

Barker, J. R. (1993). Tightening the iron cage: Concertive control in self-managing teams. *Administrative Science Quarterly, 38*, 408-437.

Barker, J. R., & Tompkins, P. K. (1994). Identification in the self-managing organization: Characteristics of target and tenure. *Human Communication Research, 21*, 223-240.

Bartholomew, D. J. (1976). *Stochastic models for social processes.* New York: John Wiley.

Bentler, P. M., & Bonett, D. G. (1980). Significance tests and goodness of fit in the analysis of covariance structures. *Psychological Bulletin, 88*, 588-606.

Berger, P., & Luckmann, T. (1967). *The social construction of reality.* London: Penguin.

Bernard, H. R., Killworth, P. D., Kronnenfeld, D., & Sailer, L. (1984). On the validity of retrospective data: The problem of informant accuracy. *Annual Review of Anthropology, 13*, 495-517.

Bernard, H. R., Killworth, P. D., & Sailer, L. (1982). Informant accuracy in social network data V: An experimental attempt to predict actual communication from recalled data. *Social Science Research, 11*, 30-66.

Bernstein, R. (1976). *The restructuring of social and political theory.* Philadelphia: University of Pennsylvania Press.

Bishop, Y. M. M., Feinberg, S. E., & Holland, P. W. (1975). *Discrete multivariate analysis: Theory and practice.* Cambridge, MA: MIT Press.

Bloch, M. (1953). *The historian's craft.* New York: Knopf.

Bochner, A. P., & Fitzpatrick, M. A. (1980). Multivariate analysis of variance: Techniques, models, and applications in communication research. In P. R. Monge & J. N. Cappella (Eds.), *Multivariate techniques in human communication research* (pp. 143-174). New York: Academic Press.

Boster, F. J. (1988). Comments on the utility of compliance-gaining message selection tasks. *Human Communication Research, 15*, 169-177.

Box, G. E. P., & Jenkins, G. M. (1976). *Time series analysis: Forecasting and control.* Oakland, CA: Holden-Day.

Burleson, B. R., Wilson, S. R., Waltman, M. S., Goering, E. M., Ely, T. K., & Whaley, B. B. (1988). Item desirability effects in compliance-gaining research: Seven studies documenting artifacts in the strategy selection procedure. *Human Communication Research, 14*, 429-486.

Burrell, G., & Morgan, G. (1979). *Sociological paradigms and organisational analysis.* London: Heinemann.

Burstein, L. (1980). The analysis of multilevel data in educational research and evaluation. In D. C. Berliner (Ed.), *Review of research in education* (Vol. 8, pp. 153-233). Washington, DC: American Educational Research Association.

Burt, R. S. (1978). Cohesion versus structural equivalence as a basis for network subgroups. *Sociological Methods and Research, 7,* 189-212.

Campbell, D. T., & Fiske, D. W. (1959). Convergent and discriminant validation by the multitrait-multimethod matrix. *Psychological Bulletin, 56,* 81-105.

Campbell, D. T., & Stanley, J. C. (1963). *Experimental and quasi-experimental designs for research.* Chicago: Rand-McNally.

Campbell, J. P. (1986). Labs, fields, and straw issues. In E. A. Locke (Ed.), *Generalizing from laboratory to field settings* (pp. 269-279). Lexington, MA: Lexington Books.

Cappella, J. N. (1980). Structural equation modeling: An introduction. In P. R. Monge & J. N. Cappella (Eds.), *Multivariate techniques in human communication research* (pp. 57-110). New York: Academic Press.

Cappella, J. N. (1990). The method of proof by example in interaction analysis. *Communication Monographs, 57,* 236-242.

Cohen, J. (1960). A coefficient of agreement for nominal scales. *Educational and Psychological Measurement, 20,* 37-46.

Contractor, N. S., & Seibold, D. R. (1993). Theoretical frameworks for the study of structuring processes in group decision support systems: Adaptive structuration theory and self-organizing systems theory. *Human Communication Research, 19,* 528-563.

Cook, T. D., & Campbell, D. T. (1979). *Quasi-experimentation: Design and analysis issues for field settings.* Chicago: Rand-McNally.

Corman, S. R. (1990). A model of perceived communication in collective networks. *Human Communication Research, 16,* 582-602.

Corman, S. R., & Scott, C. R. (1994). Perceived networks, activity foci, and observable communication in social collectives. *Communication Theory, 4,* 171-190.

Cronbach, L. (1951). Coefficient alpha and the internal structure of tests. *Psychometrika, 16,* 297-334.

Crowne, D. P., & Marlowe, D. (1964). *The approval motive: Studies in evaluative dependence.* New York: John Wiley.

Deetz, S. A. (1994). Future of the discipline: The challenges, the research, and the social contribution. In S. A. Deetz (Ed.), *Communication yearbook 17* (pp. 565-600). Thousand Oaks, CA: Sage.

DeSanctis, G., & Poole, M. S. (1994). Capturing the complexity in advanced technology use: Adaptive structuration theory. *Organization Science, 5,* 121-147.

Eisenberg, E. M., Monge, P. R., & Miller, K. I. (1983). Involvement in communication networks as a predictor of organizational commitment. *Human Communication Research, 10,* 179-201.

Ellis, B. H. (1992). The effects of uncertainty and source credibility on attitudes about organizational change. *Management Communication Quarterly, 6,* 34-57.

Fairhurst, G. T. (1993). The leader-member exchange patterns of women leaders in industry: A discourse analysis. *Communication Monographs, 60,* 321-351.

Fairhurst, G. T., & Chandler, T. A. (1989). Social structure in leader-member interaction. *Communication Monographs, 56,* 215-239.

Fairhurst, G. T., Green, S., & Courtright, J. (1995). Inertial forces and the implementation of a socio-technical systems approach: A communication study. *Organization Science, 6,* 168-185.

Fairhurst, G. T., Rogers, L. E., & Sarr, R. A. (1987). Manager-subordinate control patterns and judgments about the relationship. In M. McLaughlin (Ed.), *Communication yearbook 10* (pp. 395-415). Newbury Park, CA: Sage.

Farace, R. V., Monge, P. R., & Russell, H. M. (1977). *Communicating and organizing.* Reading, MA: Addison-Wesley.

Feyerabend, P. (1975). *Against method.* London: New Left Books.

Fink, E. M., & Chen, S.-S. (1995). A Galileo analysis of organizational climate. *Human Communication Research, 21,* 494-521.

Fink, E. M., & Monge, P. R. (1985). An exploration of confirmatory factor analysis. In B. Dervin & M. J. Voigt (Eds.), *Progress in communication sciences* (Vol. 5, pp. 167-197). Norwood, NJ: Ablex.

Fitch, K. L. (1994). Criteria for evidence in qualitative research. *Western Journal of Communication, 58,* 32-38.

Folger, J. P., Hewes, D., & Poole, M. S. (1984). Coding social interaction. In B. Dervin & M. J. Voigt (Eds.), *Progress in communication sciences* (Vol. 4, pp. 115-161). New York: Ablex.

Fulk, J. (1993). Social construction of communication technology. *Academy of Management Journal, 36,* 921-950.

Giddens, A. (1976). *New rules for sociological method.* New York: Basic Books.

Giddens, A. (1979). *Central problems in social theory.* Berkeley: University of California Press.

Giddens, A. (1984). *The constitution of society: Outline of the theory of structure.* Berkeley: University of California Press.

Gioia, D. A., & Pitre, E. (1990). Multiparadigm perspectives on theory building. *Academy of Management Review, 15,* 584-602.

Glass, G. V., McGaw, B., & Smith, M. L. (1981). *Meta-analysis in social research.* Beverly Hills, CA: Sage.

Glick, W. H. (1988). Response: Organizations are not central tendencies: Shadowboxing in the dark, round 2. *Academy of Management Review, 13,* 133-137.

Glick, W. H., Huber, G. P., Miller, C. C., Doty, D. H., & Sutcliffe, K. M. (1990). Studying changes in organizational design and effectiveness: Retrospective event histories and periodic assessments. *Organization Science, 1,* 293-312.

Gordon, M. E., Slade, L. A., & Schmitt, N. (1986). The "science of the sophomore" revisited: From conjecture to empiricism. *Academy of Management Review, 11,* 191-207.

Gordon, M. E., Slade, L. A., & Schmitt, N. (1987). Students as guinea pigs: Porcine predictors and particularistic phenomena. *Academy of Management Review, 12,* 160-163.

Graen, G. B., & Scandura, T. A. (1987). Toward a psychology of dyadic organizing. In B. Staw & L. L. Cummings (Eds.), *Research in organizational behavior* (Vol. 9, pp. 175-208). Greenwich, CT: JAI.

Greenberg, J. (1987). The college sophomore as guinea pig: Setting the record straight. *Academy of Management Review, 12,* 157-159.

Guba, E. G. (1990). The alternative paradigm dialog. In E. G. Guba (Ed.), *The paradigm dialog* (pp. 17-27). Newbury Park, CA: Sage.

Guba, E. G., & Lincoln, Y. S. (1994). Competing paradigms in qualitative research. In N. K. Denzin & Y. S. Lincoln (Eds.), *Handbook of qualitative research* (pp. 105-117). Thousand Oaks, CA: Sage.

Guetzkow, H. (1950). Unitizing and categorizing problems in coding qualitative data. *Journal of Clinical Psychology, 6,* 47-57.

Hawes, L., Pacanowsky, M., & Faules, D. (1988). Approaches to the study of organizational communication: A conversation among three schools of thought. In G. M. Goldhaber & G. A. Barnett (Eds.), *Handbook of organizational communication* (pp. 41-53). Norwood, NJ: Ablex.

Hempel, C. (1966). *Philosophy of natural science.* Englewood Cliffs, NJ: Prentice Hall.

Hewes, D. E. (1975). Finite stochastic modeling of communication processes. *Human Communication Research, 1,* 217-283.

Hewes, D. E. (1979). The sequential analysis of social interaction. *Quarterly Journal of Speech, 65,* 56-73.

Hewes, D. E. (1985). Systematic biases in coded social interaction data. *Human Communication Research, 11,* 554-574.

Hoetler, J. H. (1983). The analysis of covariance structures: Goodness-of-fit indices. *Sociological Methods and Research, 11,* 325-344.

Holmes, M., & Poole, M. S. (1991). The longitudinal analysis of interaction. In B. Montgomery & S. Duck (Eds.), *Studying interpersonal interaction* (pp. 286-302). New York: Guilford.

Holsti, O. R. (1969). *Content analysis for the social sciences and humanities.* Reading, MA: Addison-Wesley.

House, R., Rousseau, D. M., & Thomas-Hunt, M. (1995). The meso paradigm: A framework for the integration of micro and macro organizational behavior. *Research in Organizational Behavior, 17,* 71-114.

Huber, G. P., & Van de Ven, A. H. (Eds.). (1995). *Longitudinal field research methods: Studying processes of organizational change.* Thousand Oaks, CA: Sage.

Hunter, J. E. (1988). Failure of the social desirability response set hypothesis. *Human Communication Research, 15,* 162-168.

Hunter, J. E., & Gerbing, D. W. (1982). Unidimensional measurement, second order factor analysis, and causal models. *Research in Organizational Behavior, 4,* 267-320.

Hunter, J. E., Schmidt, F. L., & Jackson, G. B. (1982). *Meta-analysis: Cumulating research findings across studies.* Beverly Hills, CA: Sage.

Jacobs, S. (1990). On the especially nice fit between qualitative analysis and the known properties of conversation. *Communication Monographs, 57,* 243-249.

James, L. R., Joyce, W. F., & Slocum, J. W. (1988). Comment: Organizations do not cognize. *Academy of Management Review, 13,* 129-132.

James, L. R., Mulaik, S. A., & Brett, J. M. (1982). *Causal analysis: Assumptions, models, and data.* Beverly Hills, CA: Sage.

Jöreskog, K. G., & Sörbom, D. (1989). *LISREL 7 user's reference guide.* Mooresville, IN: Scientific Software.

Keppel, G. (1982). *Design and analysis: A researchers handbook.* Englewood Cliffs, NJ: Prentice Hall.

Keppel, G., & Zedeck, S. (1989). *Data analysis for research designs.* New York: Freeman.

Kerlinger, F. N. (1979). *Behavioral research: A conceptual approach.* New York: Holt, Rinehart & Winston.

Kerlinger, F. N. (1986). *Foundations of behavioral research.* New York: Holt, Rinehart & Winston.

Klein, K. J., Dansereau, F., & Hall, R. J. (1994). Levels issues in theory development, data collection, and analysis. *Academy of Management Review, 19,* 195-229.

Knapp, M. L., Putnam, L. L., & Davis, L. J. (1988). Measuring interpersonal conflict in organizations: Where do we go from here? *Management Communication Quarterly, 1,* 414-429.

Kramer, M. W. (1993). Communication after job transfers: Social exchange processes in learning new roles. *Human Communication Research, 20,* 147-174.

Kritzler, H. M. (1996). The data puzzle: The nature of interpretation in quantitative research. *American Journal of Political Science, 40,* 1-32.

Krone, K. J., Jablin, F. M., & Putnam, L. L. (1987). Communication theory and organizational communication: Multiple perspectives. In F. M. Jablin, L. L. Putnam, K. H. Roberts, & L. W. Porter (Eds.), *Handbook of organizational communication: An interdisciplinary perspective* (pp. 18-40). Newbury Park, CA: Sage.

Kuhn, T. S. (1962). *The structure of scientific revolutions.* Chicago: University of Chicago Press.

Lakatos, I. (1970). Falsification and the methodology of scientific research programmes. In I. Lakatos & A. Musgrave (Eds.), *Criticism and the growth of knowledge* (pp. 91-196). Cambridge, UK: Cambridge University Press.

Lammers, J. C., & Krikorian, D. (1997). Theoretical extension and operationalization of the bona fide group construct with an application to surgical teams. *Journal of Applied Communication Research, 25,* 17-38.

Lee, A. S. (1991). Integrating positivist and interpretive approaches to organizational research. *Organization Science, 2,* 342-365.

Locke, E. A. (Ed.). (1986). *Generalizing from laboratory to field settings.* Lexington, MA: Lexington Books.

Manicas, P. (1987). *A history and philosophy of the social sciences.* Oxford, UK: Basil Blackwell.

Marcoulides, G. A., & Schumacker, R. E. (1996). *Advanced structural equation modeling: Issues and techniques.* Mahwah, NJ: Lawrence Erlbaum.

Marshall, A. A., & Stohl, C. (1993). Participating as participation: A network approach. *Communication Monographs, 60,* 137-157.

Marshall, C. (1990). Goodness criteria: Are they objective or judgment calls? In E. G. Guba (Ed.), *The paradigm dialog* (pp. 188-197). Newbury Park, CA: Sage.

McPhee, R. D. (1985). Formal structure and organizational communication. In R. D. McPhee & P. K. Tompkins (Eds.), *Organizational communication: Traditional themes and new directions* (pp. 149-177). Beverly Hills, CA: Sage.

McPhee, R. D., & Babrow, A. (1987). Causal modeling in communication research: Use, disuse, and misuse. *Communication Monographs, 54,* 344-366.

McPhee, R. D., & Corman, S. R. (1995). An activity-based theory of communication networks in organizations, applied to the case of a local church. *Communication Monographs, 62,* 132-151.

Miller, K., Birkholt, M., Scott, C., & Stage, C. (1995). Empathy and burnout in human service work: An extension of a communication model. *Communication Research, 22,* 123-147.

Miller, K. I., & Monge, P. R. (1986). Participation, satisfaction, and productivity: A meta-analytic review. *Academy of Management Journal, 29,* 727-753.

Monge, P. R. (1982). Systems theory and research in the study of organizational communication: The correspondence problem. *Human Communication Research, 8,* 245-261.

Monge, P. R. (1990). Theoretical and analytical issues in studying organizational processes. *Organization Science, 1,* 406-430.

Monge, P. R., & Cappella, J. N. (Eds.). (1980). *Multivariate techniques in human communication research.* New York: Academic Press.

Monge, P. R., & Contractor, N. S. (1988). Communication networks: Measurement techniques. In C. H. Tardy (Ed.), *A handbook for the study of human communication: Methods and instruments for observing, measuring, and assessing communication processes* (pp. 107-138). Norwood, NJ: Ablex.

Monge, P. R., Cozzens, M. D., & Contractor, N. S. (1992). Communication and motivational predictors of the dynamics of organization innovation. *Organization Science, 3,* 250-274.

Monge, P. R., & Eisenberg, E. M. (1987). Emergent communication networks. In F. M. Jablin, L. L. Putnam, K. H. Roberts, & L. W. Porter (Eds.), *Handbook of organizational communication: An interdisciplinary perspective* (pp. 304-342). Newbury Park, CA: Sage.

Monge, P. R., Farace, R. V., Eisenberg, E. M., White, L., & Miller, K. I. (1984). The process of studying process in organizational communication. *Journal of Communication, 34,* 22-43.

Nunnally, J. (1978). *Psychometric theory.* New York: McGraw-Hill.

Orlikowski, W. J., & Yates, J. (1994). Genre repertoire: The structuring of communicative practices in organizations. *Administrative Science Quarterly, 39,* 541-574.

Papa, M. J., & Pood, E. A. (1988). Coorientational accuracy and organizational conflict: An examination of tactic selection and discussion satisfaction. *Communication Research, 15,* 3-28.

Pedhazur, E. J. (1982). *Multiple regression in behavioral research.* New York: Holt, Rinehart & Winston.

Pettigrew, A. M. (1990). Longitudinal field research on change: Theory and practice. *Organization Science, 1,* 267-292.

Phillips, D. C. (1987). *Philosophy, science, and social inquiry.* Oxford, UK: Pergamon.

Phillips, D. C. (1990). Postpositivistic science: Myths and realities. In E. G. Guba (Ed.), *The paradigm dialog* (pp. 31-45). Newbury Park, CA: Sage.

Poole, M. S. (1996, February). *Another turn of the wheel: A return to systems theory in organizational communication.* Paper presented at the Conference on Organizational Communication and Change, Austin, TX.

Poole, M. S., & DeSanctis, G. (1992). Microstructural processes in computer-supported group decision-making. *Human Communication Research, 19,* 5-49.

Poole, M. S., Holmes, M., & DeSanctis, G. (1991). Conflict management in a computer-supported meeting environment. *Management Science, 37,* 926-953.

Poole, M. S., Holmes, M., Watson, R., & DeSanctis, G. (1993). Group decision support systems and group communication: A comparison of decision making in computer-supported and nonsupported groups. *Communication Research, 20,* 176-213.

Poole, M. S., & McPhee, R. D. (1995). Methodology in interpersonal communication research. In M. L. Knapp & G. R. Miller (Eds.), *Handbook of interper-*

*sonal communication* (2nd ed., pp. 42-100). Thousand Oaks, CA: Sage.

Poole, M. S., & Roth, J. (1989). Decision development in small groups IV: A typology of group decision paths. *Human Communication Research, 15,* 323-356.

Poole, M. S., Seibold, D. R., & McPhee, R. D. (1986). A structurational approach to theory-building in group decision-making research. In R. Y. Hirokawa & M. S. Poole (Eds.), *Communication and group decision-making* (pp. 237-264). Beverly Hills, CA: Sage.

Popper, K. (1962). *Conjectures and refutations.* New York: Harper.

Putnam, H. (1981). *Reason, truth, and history.* Cambridge, UK: Cambridge University Press.

Putnam, L. L., Bantz, C., Deetz, S., Mumby, D., & Van Maanen, J. (1993). Ethnography versus critical theory: Debating organizational research. *Journal of Management Inquiry, 2,* 221-235.

Putnam, L. L., & Pacanowsky, M. E. (Eds.). (1983). *Communication and organizations: An interpretive approach.* Beverly Hills, CA: Sage.

Putnam, L. L., & Stohl, C. (1990). Bona fide groups: A reconceptualization of groups in context. *Communication Studies, 41,* 248-265.

Rice, R. E., & Richards, W. D. (1985). An overview of network analysis methods and programs. In B. Dervin & M. J. Voigt (Eds.), *Progress in communication sciences* (Vol. 6, pp. 105-165). Norwood, NJ: Ablex.

Riley, P. (1983). A structurationist account of political cultures. *Administrative Science Quarterly, 28,* 414-437.

Schumacker, R. E., & Lomax, R. G. (1996). *A beginner's guide to structural equation modeling.* Mahwah, NJ: Lawrence Erlbaum.

Seibold, D. R. (1988). A response to "Item desirability in compliance-gaining research." *Human Communication Research, 15,* 152-161.

Smith, J. K. (1990). Goodness criteria: Alternative research paradigms and the problem of criteria. In E. G. Guba (Ed.), *The paradigm dialog* (pp. 167-187). Newbury Park, CA: Sage.

Stohl, C. (1986). Bridging the parallel organization: A study of quality circle effectiveness. In M. McLaughlin (Ed.), *Communication yearbook 10* (pp. 473-496). Beverly Hills, CA: Sage.

Stohl, C. (1993). European managers' interpretations of participation: A semantic network analysis. *Human Communication Research, 20,* 97-117.

Stohl, C. (1995). *Organizational communication: Connectedness in action.* Thousand Oaks, CA: Sage.

Suppe, F. (Ed.). (1977). *The structure of scientific theories* (2nd ed.). Urbana: University of Illinois Press.

Tornatsky, L. G., Eveland, J. D., Boylan, M. G., Hetzner, W. A., Johnson, E. C., Roltman, D., & Schneider, J. (1983). *The process of technological innovation: Reviewing the literature.* Washington, DC: National Science Foundation.

Treadwell, D. F., & Harrison, T. M. (1994). Conceptualizing and assessing organizational image: Model images, commitment, and communication. *Communication Monographs, 61,* 63-85.

Trigg, R. (1985). *Understanding social science.* Oxford, UK: Basil Blackwell.

Van de Ven, A. H., & Poole, M. S. (1990). Methods for studying innovation development in the Minnesota Innovation Research Program. *Organization Science 1,* 313-335.

Wagner, J. A., III, & Gooding, R. Z. (1987). Effects of societal trends on participative research. *Administrative Science Quarterly, 32,* 241-262.

Walther, J. B. (1995). Relational aspects of computer-mediated communication: Experimental observations over time. *Organization Science, 6,* 186-203.

Warwick, D., & Lininger, C. (1975). *The sample survey: Theory and practice.* New York: McGraw-Hill.

Wasserman, S., & Faust, K. (1994). *Social network analysis: Methods and applications.* Cambridge, UK: Cambridge University Press.

Watt, J. H., & van den Berg, S. A. (1995). *Research methods for communication science.* Boston: Allyn & Bacon.

Weaver, G. R., & Gioia, D. A. (1994). Paradigms lost: Incommensurability vs. structurationist inquiry. *Organization Studies, 15,* 565-590.

Wilson, B. J. (1994). A challenge to communication empiricists: Let's be more forthcoming about what we do. *Western Journal of Communication, 58,* 25-31.

Wilson, S. R., & Waltman, M. S. (1988). Assessing the Putnam-Wilson Organizational Communication Conflict Instrument (OCCI). *Management Communication Quarterly, 1,* 367-388.

Yates, J., & Orlikowski, W. J. (1992). Genres of organizational communication: A structurational approach to studying communication and media. *Academy of Management Review, 17,* 299-326.

Zwick, R. (1988). Another look at interrater agreement. *Psychological Bulletin, 103,* 274-378.

# 5

# Qualitative Research Methods

BRYAN C. TAYLOR
*University of Colorado at Boulder*

NICK TRUJILLO
*California State University, Sacramento*

In the past two decades, a growing number of researchers have used qualitative methods to study various aspects of organizational communication. Researchers have turned to qualitative methods for a variety of reasons, including the recognition of the limitations of positivist epistemology and quantitative methods, as well as the acceptance of multiple approaches to the study of organizations. The increased use of qualitative methods in organizational communication also has reflected (or, more often, has followed) the trend set by scholars in anthropology, sociology, management, and other disciplines (see Denzin & Lincoln, 1994, for a review).

We welcome—indeed, we celebrate—the widespread use of qualitative methods by contemporary organizational communication scholars. In this chapter, we consider some of the issues and challenges that continue to confront researchers using these methods. Spe-

cifically, we begin the chapter with a discussion of some trends in the evolution of qualitative research in organizational communication. We then focus the majority of the chapter on key methodological issues and challenges confronting qualitative researchers. We conclude with a discussion of future trends in qualitative research.

## THE EVOLUTION OF QUALITATIVE RESEARCH IN ORGANIZATIONAL COMMUNICATION

### *Defining Qualitative Research*

We believe it is futile to propose any single, comprehensive definition of qualitative research. Like the term *postmodernism, qualita-*

*tive research* defies complete resolution. For some, the term connotes a general paradigm, involving epistemological and theoretical assumptions. For others, the term denotes a specific methodology with guiding implications for data collection and analysis. Consider, for example, the following multiple-choice question:

Qualitative research . . .

(a) is "a field of inquiry in its own right" that "privileges no single methodology over any other" (Denzin & Lincoln, 1994, pp. 1, 3);

(b) is "drawn to a broad, interpretive, postmodern, feminist and critical sensibility" as well as to "more narrowly defined positivist, postpositivistic, humanistic, and naturalistic conceptions of human experience" (Nelson, Treichler, & Grossberg, 1992, p. 4);

(c) "emphasizes inductive, interpretive methods applied to the everyday world which is seen as subjective and socially created" (Anderson, 1987, p. 384);

(d) "examines the qualities . . . of communication phenomena" whereby "data tend to be continuous rather than discrete, and the emphasis is on description and explanation more than on measurement and prediction" (Fitch, 1994a, p. 32); or

(e) "encompasses a variety of methods variously referred to as interpretive, naturalistic, phenomenological, or ethnographic" (Kreps, Herndon, & Arneson, 1993, p. 1).

The correct answer is, of course, "all of the above." A trick question perhaps, but qualitative research is a tricky area to define with much precision, because it is so large and amorphous, and because it is growing and changing even as you read this chapter. As Van Maanen (1995) noted, "New journals, new theories, new problems, new topics, and new critiques of older works multiply with each passing year" (p. 27). In fact, a truly comprehensive survey of qualitative research in organizational communication would likely result in a handbook at least the size of this volume (see Denzin & Lincoln, 1994) because it would include reviews of conversation analysis (see Drew & Heritage,

1992), ethnomethodology (see Heritage, 1984), grounded theory (see Browning, 1978), ethnography (see Schwartzman, 1993), rhetorical criticism (see McMillan, 1987), semiotics (see Barley, 1983), critical theory (see Deetz, 1992), feminism (see Buzzanell, 1994; Marshall, 1993), postmodernism (see Alvesson & Deetz, 1996), and others. We take heart in our current task from Van Maanen's (1995) observation that no single scholar can keep up with the developments in all of these subfields and that some filtering is inevitable: "It seems the best we can do these days is to selectively pursue and cultivate an ever diminishing proportion of the relevant literature that comes our way and assume an attitude of benign neglect towards the rest" (p. 27).

Although we do not have the space to fully review these various areas, we do not fully neglect them either. However, because we were commissioned to discuss the *methodological* issues and challenges facing scholars who conduct qualitative research, we proceed with the following agenda. Specifically, we discuss two issues that have been long-standing concerns of qualitative researchers—the relationship between qualitative and quantitative methods, and the criteria used to evaluate qualitative research—and two issues that have been raised recently in light of the popularity of critical approaches—the role of critical theory in qualitative research, and the poetics and politics of representation. Before we address these issues, though, we briefly review the evolution of qualitative research in organizational communication.

## Trends in the Evolution of Qualitative Research in Sociology and Anthropology

In the introduction to their own massive handbook, Denzin and Lincoln (1994) described what they called five "moments" in the evolution of qualitative research in sociology and anthropology, two disciplines that have a rich history of qualitative research. We briefly review their discussion here because the trends they discuss have influenced other disciplines as well, including organizational communication. Although they discussed five discrete moments or phases, their model does not report deterministic sequences of exhaustive or mutually exclusive stages. Rather, these phases overlap with one another, and researchers continue to conduct scholarship reflecting trends from each period.

Denzin and Lincoln described the first moment, which occurred roughly from the early 1900s until World War II, as a "traditional period," one characterized by researchers "who wrote 'objective,' colonizing accounts of field experiences that were reflective of the positivist scientific paradigm" (p. 7). They billed Malinowski (1916/1948) as the pioneer of the period and cited the classic anthropological ethnographies of Radcliffe-Brown, Margaret Mead, and Gregory Bateson and the classic sociological ethnographies of Robert Park and the "Chicago school" as defining exemplars. They had Rosaldo (1989) eulogize the phase, debunking the now-transparent objectivism, imperialism, monumentalism, and timelessness of this research.

The second moment they described was the "modernist phase," a period that extended through the post-World War II years into the 1970s. Qualitative researchers of this period attempted to "formalize qualitative methods" through "postpositivist discourse" in a conscious effort to demonstrate reliability and validity (p. 8). It was the "golden age of rigorous qualitative analysis" (p. 8), an age when sociologists such as Howard Becker (Becker, Geer, Hughes, & Strauss, 1961) and Glaser and Strauss (1967) produced important work and when theories of ethnomethodology, phenomenology, feminism, and critical theory started to receive attention.

Denzin and Lincoln described the third phase as "the moment of blurred genres," a period from the early 1970s through the mid-1980s, when qualitative researchers embraced the use of multiple perspectives. They cast anthropologist Clifford Geertz (1973), with his call for "thick description," as the hero of this phase. They also suggested that the "naturalistic, postpositivistic, and constructionist paradigms gained power in this

period" (p. 9) as new journals such as *Urban Life* (now *Journal of Contemporary Ethnography*), *Qualitative Sociology,* and *Symbolic Interaction* came onto the scene.

Denzin and Lincoln noted that the fourth phase was triggered by a "profound rupture" in the mid-1980s that resulted in two related "crises." First, a "crisis of legitimation" problematized and politicized issues such as reliability, validity, truth, and meaning that had been viewed as "settled" in earlier phases. This crisis has led qualitative researchers to further embrace critical theory, feminism, ethnic studies, poststructuralism, and postmodernism in an effort to de- and reconstruct the very nature of scholarship. Second, a "crisis in representation" was articulated in the writings of Marcus and Fischer (1986), Clifford and Marcus (1986), and others who "made research and writing more reflexive, and called into question the issues of gender, class, and race" (p. 10) as influences on the research process. This crisis of representation problematized the very nature of authorship and led qualitative researchers to confront the autobiographical and political dimensions of all scholarship.

Denzin and Lincoln described the fifth moment of qualitative research as one of "coping with the present" (p. 576). They suggested that we are coping with the crises of legitimation and representation from the fourth moment; with the ongoing challenges of critical theory, feminism, ethnic studies, and postmodernism to the status quo; with the introduction of new research technologies; and with the juxtaposition of the sacred and the scientific as influences on research.

### Trends in the Evolution of Qualitative Research in Organizational Communication

Several of the trends described by Denzin and Lincoln (1994) also characterize trends in the evolution of qualitative research in organizational communication. However, as an area of study distinct from sociology and anthropology, organizational communication has its own unique history (see Redding, 1985) and its own unique trends in the use of qualitative research. Here we briefly review some of the trends in the evolution of qualitative research in organizational communication. Again, these trends do not reflect any sort of deterministic sequence, but are suggestive of the historical development of qualitative research in our discipline.

Unlike sociology and anthropology, the field of organizational communication never really experienced a "traditional period" of *qualitative* research. However, Tompkins and Redding (1988) noted that the period from 1900 to 1940—what they called the "era of preparation" (p. 7)—included several areas of study such as "business speech," "industrial journalism," "proto-human relations," and even Dale Carnegie courses, which shared a "speech" tradition and reflected a rhetorical—and, thus, a more or less qualitative—approach (see also Redding, 1985). In addition, certain seminal management books of this early period that influenced subsequent research in organizational communication were based on extensive case studies, such as Barnard's (1938) *Functions of the Executive,* Roethlisberger and Dickson's (1939) *Management and the Worker,* and Simon's (1945) *Administrative Behavior.*

"Modernist" trends in organizational communication began in the 1940s and dominated research well into the early 1970s as researchers struggled to define "organizational communication" as a distinct and legitimate field. Tompkins and Redding (1988) referred to the early modernist period as one of "identification and consolidation," noting that researchers tried to deal with "the identity problem" of our emerging field (p. 15). In fact, Redding (1985) nominated *1959* as "The Year of Crystallization," when "industrial communication" had become recognized as a distinct field of study, and *1967* as "The Year of Official Acceptance," when the landmark Conference on Organizational Communication occurred in Huntsville, Alabama where researchers offered state-of-the-art reviews of the *empirical research* in organizational communication.

Although most of the methodologies that characterize "modernist" research in organizational communication were—and still are—quantitative ones applied by proponents of mechanistic, psychological, and systems approaches, some scholars also developed more qualitatively oriented approaches. Early in this period, communication scholars—like scholars in other fields—grappled with the implications of the famous "Hawthorne Studies" and subsequent debates about "human relations" approaches to management. Numerous case studies of communication in organizations dominated the early years of this period—especially in the form of doctoral dissertations at universities such as Northwestern, Ohio State, and Purdue (see Redding, 1985, for a review). Case study approaches, however, became post-World War II casualties when scholars in communication and other disciplines advocated large-scale experiments and surveys to satisfy institutional goals of prediction and control. Later in this period, scholars such as Ernest Bormann (1972; Bormann, Pratt, & Putnam, 1978), Phil Tompkins (Tompkins, Fisher, Infante, & Tompkins, 1975), and others (e.g., Chesbro, Cragan, & McCullough, 1973; Cowell, 1972; Sharf, 1978) drew on the unique rhetorical roots of our discipline and applied rhetorical criticism to the study of organizational communication, setting the stage for subsequent rhetorical analyses of organizational communication and corporate discourse (see Cheney, 1991; Cheney & Vibbert, 1987; McMillan, 1987; Putnam, Van Hoeven, & Bullis, 1991; Tompkins, 1978). Finally, other researchers suggested that ethnomethodology (Garfinkel, 1967) could be a useful qualitative method for studying the interactional reproduction of social order, leading to the development of conversation analysis, which has since become a thriving area of study in communication and which has been used to study organizational discourse (see Banks, 1994; Beach, 1994, 1995; Drew & Heritage, 1992; Geist & Hardesty, 1990).

Like other disciplines, organizational communication also experienced a period characterized by the blurring of genres as described in Denzin and Lincoln's "third moment." This trend in our field was incited during the 1970s and 1980s by the "new" idea that the expressive and symbolic dimensions of organizations warranted their study as cultures (see Eisenberg & Riley, Chapter 9, this volume). Even though sociologists had treated organizations as cultures for decades in their ethnographic studies of urban settings, scholars (and popular writers and consultants) in management, followed closely by those in organizational communication, fervently embraced the cultural model. Our field initiated in 1981 what became the annual Conference on Interpretive Approaches to the Study of Organizational Communication in Alta, Utah.[1] Following that first conference, and the subsequent publications resulting from the conference (Pacanowsky & Putnam, 1982; Putnam & Pacanowsky, 1983), there was a groundswell of conferences, curriculum offerings, journal articles, and books on organizational culture and symbolism. Organizational communication scholars such as Pacanowsky and O'Donnell-Trujillo (1982, 1983), Riley (1983), Eisenberg (1984), Goodall (1989), and others followed the lead of management scholars such as Van Maanen (1979), Burrell and Morgan (1979), Deal and Kennedy (1982), Smircich (1983), and others, paving the way for a bountiful decade of research. In fact, Allen, Gotcher, and Seibert (1993) noted that "organizational culture and symbolism" was the third most frequent topic in organizational communication from 1980 to 1991, resulting in 99 of the 889 journal articles they surveyed, outdistanced only by "interpersonal relations in organizations" (233) and "communication skills and strategies" (120). Perhaps most important, scholars in organizational communication started to use "new" qualitative methods of field research (such as ethnography) that forced us to spend more time in organizations; these qualitative methods continue to be used by researchers today (see Brown, 1985; Carbaugh, 1988; Goodall, 1991; Muto, 1993; Neumann & Eason, 1990; Smith & Eisenberg, 1987; Trujillo, 1992).

The "crises of legitimation and representation" that defined Denzin and Lincoln's fourth phase of qualitative research have also stimulated much discussion and debate in organizational communication. Although scholars first identified these crises during the counter-cultural ferment of the 1960s, debates surrounding these crises reached fruition during the late 1980s and 1990s as scholars offered widespread critiques of rationality, consumer-capitalism, militarism, racism, imperialism, and sexism that have implicated the academy in structures of oppression (see Trice & Beyer, 1993, pp. 23-32). For example, scholars in organizational communication have experienced *crises of legitimation* as we alternately embrace and react against critical theories in the organizational communication literature. These theories address how power and control dominate virtually every aspect of organizational communication and of research about its phenomena. Communication scholars such as Deetz (1982), Conrad (1983), Tompkins and Cheney (1983), Mumby (1987), and others followed the lead of management scholars such as Clegg (1975), Giddens (1979), Burawoy (1979), and others in paving the way for various programs of critical research that have thrived in the 1990s (see Deetz, Chapter 1, and Mumby, Chapter 15, this volume).

In addition, organizational communication scholars have experienced *crises of representation* in our struggles to articulate and evaluate the choices available for writing qualitative reports, choices that now include fictional and autobiographical forms as well as traditional social science formulas (see Brown & McMillan, 1991; Goodall, 1989, 1991; Jones, 1996; Pacanowsky, 1983, 1988; Phillips, 1995). Further, some researchers are arguing for the legitimacy of *performing* one's qualitative research (see Conquergood, 1989, 1991; Jackson, 1993; Maguire & Mohtar, 1994; Paget, 1990).

And, so, we in organizational communication, just like scholars in other disciplines, have arrived at the present moment of "coping," as we try to address the challenges of critical theory, feminism, ethnic studies, and postmodernism in the context of modernist and naturalistic traditions of qualitative research in organizational communication. As Lindlof (1995) commented on qualitative communication research in general:

> There is a growing sense that disciplinewide agreement about the goals and epistemology of a communication science may not be achievable. Communication research now accommodates many different styles of inquiry, living side by side. Some accept this situation reluctantly, some welcome it, and some resist it. (p. 7)

Lindlof explained that this theoretical and methodological pluralism characteristic of our discipline (and of most other disciplines) has been fostered by long-standing and ongoing debates among proponents of various perspectives (see "Ferment in the Field," 1983; Hawes, Pacanowsky, & Faules, 1988; Putnam, Bantz, Deetz, Mumby, & Van Maanen, 1993). As Faules (in Hawes et al., 1988) noted, pluralism "recognizes that all of the positions . . . have strengths and weaknesses" (p. 45). Indeed, we believe that it is naive and narrow-minded to assume that one particular theoretical or methodological perspective can completely reveal the complexities of organizational communication. Thus, we welcome the adoption of different perspectives and styles of inquiry, and we find much comfort in the range of theoretical and methodological choices available to organizational communication scholars. However, we also recognize that the selection of any particular theoretical and methodological perspective is always a political one that must be defended at virtually every step in the research process and that will be contested by advocates of alternative perspectives. Accordingly, we find the present to be an exciting and disturbing time to be a qualitative researcher, filled with paradox and politics, and with clarity and confusion, as we express our own sense—and try to push the boundaries—of what constitutes qualitative research in organizational communication.

# KEY ISSUES AND CHALLENGES FACING QUALITATIVE RESEARCHERS

Several issues and challenges have confronted researchers as their applications of qualitative methods have evolved over the past several years. In this section, we discuss some of these issues and challenges that face us as we continue to conduct this research. In particular, we examine the relationship between qualitative and quantitative research, the role of critique in qualitative studies, the poetics and politics of representation, and criteria for evaluating qualitative studies.

## The Relationship Between Quantitative and Qualitative Methods

There are many possible relationships between qualitative and quantitative approaches, depending, of course, on who is defining the relationship. Some scholars have argued that the two approaches can work very well together and have advocated the use of triangulation—the use of qualitative and quantitative methods in the same study (e.g., Albrecht & Ropp, 1982; Faules, 1982; Flick, 1992). Others have suggested that the two approaches are based ultimately on incompatible, even contradictory, epistemological underpinnings such that they should never be used together (e.g., Anderson, 1987; Bostrom & Donohew, 1992).

We believe it is relatively pointless to debate the merits of each approach in a qualitative-versus-quantitative type of debate. We agree with Miles and Huberman (1994) that "the quantitative-qualitative argument is essentially unproductive" and that there is "no reason to tie the distinction to epistemological preferences" (p. 41). Like Miles and Huberman, we believe that "the question is not whether the two sorts of data and associated methods can be linked during study design, but whether it should be done, how it will be done, and for what purposes" (p. 41).

Miles and Huberman (1994) suggested that each approach can help the other approach during the design, data collection, and data analysis stages of research. They argued that a quantitative approach can help a qualitative study during *design* "by finding a representative sample and locating deviant cases"; during *data collection* "by supplying background data, getting overlooked information, and helping avoid 'elite bias' "; and during *data analysis* "by showing the generality of specific observations . . . and verifying or casting new light on qualitative findings" (p. 41). On the other hand, a qualitative approach can help a quantitative study during *design* "by aiding with conceptual development and instrumentation"; during *data collection* "by making access and data collection easier"; and during *data analysis* "by validating, interpreting, clarifying, and illustrating quantitative findings" (p. 41).

In general, we support the use of multiple methods, quantitative and/or qualitative, in organizational communication research. However, we do not believe that triangulation can be used to "validate" data or findings in a directly positivistic sense. We believe that different methods tap into different dimensions of organizational communication and that no one method has more privileged access to organizational "reality" than any other. As Deetz (1982) argued with respect to interview methods in the context of observational methods, "Asking organizational members what they mean generates more talk, not privileged insight" (p. 135). Thus, we agree with Denzin and Lincoln (1994), who argued that "triangulation is not a tool or a strategy of validation, but an alternative to validation" such that "the combination of multiple methods . . . in a single study is best understood, then, as a strategy that adds rigor, breadth, and depth to any investigation" (p. 2; see also Flick, 1992). Similarly, Richardson (1994) suggested "crystallization" as an analytic stance

that deconstructs the traditional idea of validity as capturing a single, comprehensive truth: "The central image for 'validity' for postmodern texts is not the triangle—a rigid, fixed, two-dimensional object. Rather, the central image is the crystal, which combines symmetry and substance with an infinite variety of shapes, substances, transmutations, multidimensionalities, and angles of approach" (p. 522).

Several organizational communication scholars have used multiple methods in various ways in their research. Virtually all ethnographers use interview and participant-observation methods to collect data in organizations, and some use document analysis, content analysis, and other methods (see Bantz, 1993; Carbaugh, 1988; Goodall, 1991; Neumann, 1992; Scheibel, 1992). Other organizational communication scholars have used a variety of methods in their research as well. For example, Burrell, Buzzanell, and McMillan (1992) used questionnaire and open-ended interviews to collect data, and metaphor-analysis and content-analysis to analyze data, in their study of images of conflict among women in government. Similarly, Finet (1993) used questionnaire and open-ended interviews in her study of boundary-spanning and conflict in a New York agency. Waldron and Krone (1991) used open-ended interviews and an a priori coding system to collect data, and content analysis and log-linear analysis to analyze data in their study of the experience and expression of emotion in a corrections organization. Clair (1993a) conducted interviews and analyzed organizational documents in her critical analysis of sexual harassment in Big Ten universities. Putnam (1994) used survey and ethnographic data in her analysis of conflict in two teacher-school board negotiations. Watkins and Caillouet (1994) used participant observation and content analysis in their examination of impression management strategies used by members of a recycling facility experiencing crisis.

In sum, we believe that debates regarding which approach is "better" have become tiresome. After all, the worth of any theory or method is demonstrated not in debate, however clever, but in its utility for various communities of scholars and practitioners. We believe there are many possible relationships between qualitative and quantitative approaches to organizational communication, and we encourage researchers to demonstrate the value of these relationships in actual studies.

## The Role of Critical Theory in Qualitative Research

The various crises of legitimation and representation discussed above have led scholars to examine the political nature of organizational reality and organizational research. These crises have encouraged many to adopt "critical" approaches that encourage researchers to *critique* (i.e., judge, evaluate) the organizations they study. In this section, we examine issues and challenges related to critique in qualitative research, as suggested by those who adopt the (often-overlapping) discourses of critical theory, feminism, and postmodernism. We emphasize that while we treat these discourses discretely, they often overlap in specific research projects (see, e.g., Holmer-Nadesan, 1996).

### Critical Theory

Critical theory has become a popular perspective for organizational communication research in the 1990s. The term *critical theory* designates a tradition of social inquiry derived from Hegelian and Marxist philosophies, as well as more contemporary, neo-Marxist and Frankfurt schools of thought (see Mumby's chapter for a review). Applied to the study of organizational communication, critical theory is generally concerned with revealing, interrupting, and transforming the oppressive dimensions of corporate capitalism. These dimensions include hegemonic "deep-structures" and identities (such as "technical ratio-

nality" and "individualism") that are reproduced through language and interaction (such as in performance reviews). These elements function to maximize the profit and power of elites, alienate workers from authentic experience of their desires, inhibit their achievement of human potential and solidarity, and distort the democratic expression of diverse interests in organizational routines (such as decision making). Critical theory is explicitly political, and it has as its ultimate goal the "emancipation" of organizational members—the development of new lines of thought and practice that may enable undistorted dialogue and resolve unjust power asymmetries. In this view, organizational reality is inherently *contested* as different groups conduct their institutionalized struggles through various means (such as lockouts and sabotage), with the most important being *discursive* attempts to control the meanings and consequences of "work." Browner and Kubarski (1991), for example, argued that the managerial rhetoric of "professionalism" works to secure the loyalty and productivity of even low-paid clerical employees.

With respect to research "methodology," critical theorists typically engage in some form of "deconstruction." Proponents of this approach diverge from the classical interpretive goal of describing presences to argue the significance of absences—of possibilities for meaning that are systematically prevented from materializing in the repetitions and compulsions of organized interaction. Critical theorists hold that it is not the practice of research per se (such as the gathering of empirical data) that distinguishes different paradigms of organizational research so much as the nature of the assumptions and values used in developing research problems, and especially in interpreting data (Melody & Mansell, 1983). Indeed, although early critical studies in organizational communication tended to be meta-analyses[2] of other studies (e.g., Mumby, 1987), recent critical theorists have used participant-observation, interviewing, and other qualitative methods for data collection (see

Barker & Cheney, 1994; Cheney, 1995; Clair, 1993b; Deetz, 1994). What clearly distinguishes critical theorists from others who use qualitative methods is how they approach the data that they—or someone else—produce. For critical theorists, the goals of "data analysis" are, by definition, "to expose and critique the process by which a particular organizational ideology produces and reproduces the corresponding structure of power within the organization" and to provide "social actors themselves with the means by which to both critique and change the extant meaning structures of an organization" (Mumby, 1988, pp. 146, 147).

This condition that researchers *must* analyze the power relations in organizations—and provide a means for changing them—has led to inevitable debates between critical theorists and other researchers. Not surprisingly, critical theorists have vigorously indicted positivistic researchers—quantitative or qualitative—because positivists often claim objectivity, neglect the historical and cultural contexts of organizational processes, and unreflectively promote management priorities (such as effectiveness and efficiency). Indeed, critical researchers wish to expose how organizational research is subsequently implicated in perpetuating repressive systems of labor discipline.

However, critical theorists have also indicted interpretive researchers on a number of counts (see Fiske, 1991; Putnam et al., 1993; Thomas, 1993). Critical theorists have argued that ethnographers often display a political naiveté and narrow insularity in their depictions of order in organizational culture (due perhaps to a historical bias in anthropology toward studying tribal, "integrationist" cultures). From this critical view, interpretivism is not a politically neutral stance, but is one that potentially serves dominant managerial rationality (seeking, e.g., to design and impose a "strong" culture). Critical researchers argue that superficial accounts of apparently shared meanings can miss the hegemonic organization of "false consciousness" that often

underlies expressions of consensus. Qualitative research can also encourage passive spectatorship by its audiences toward the "interesting" features of organizational culture, cultivating an aesthetic experience that does not disturb or radicalize its consumers. Such accounts create premature closure on the fracturing absurdity, cruelty, and paradox that pervade the experiences of organizational members. Finally, critical researchers argue that ethnographers often do not problematize the means by which power is produced in organizations and in the qualitative research process itself. The ways that research goals are developed, and that researchers and subjects interact in the field, often confirm that the power to manage and the power to represent the Other are complementary. As Mumby stated, "The failure of ethnography lies in its refusal to assume an evaluative position" (in Putnam et al., 1993, p. 225). Thus, qualitative research may perpetuate oppression if for no other reason than that it fails to conceptualize and oppose it (one controversy here involves the "correct" theory of organizational ideology; see Beyer, Dunbar, & Meyer, 1988; Fitch, 1994b; Lannamann, 1994; Neumann, 1994). In this view, the research imperatives of "expose" and "awaken" replace those of "describe" and "interpret" (Hawes, 1983), and irony—an orientation that acknowledges how ambiguity and contradiction suffuse the production of knowledge among organizational members and researchers—replaces realism.

These claims have generated strong reactions from ethnographers, including those who counter that critical theorists hold a distorted view of their practices and that critical theory is a flawed and inappropriate foundation for qualitative research. Hammersley (1992, chap. 6), for example, argued that critical theorists have failed to demonstrate that the ideal of emancipation is itself either undistorted or inevitable, and is therefore any different from the "irrational" ideologies that it opposes. He also suggested that a "brute" Marxist position oversimplifies how power operates in organizational practice (because oppression is overdetermined by extraorga-nizational forces, because power inevitably begets resistance, and because organizational members may simultaneously be powerful victimizers and powerless victims). An addi-tional flashpoint involves the criteria by which ethnographers may claim examples of false consciousness and ideological distortion. Re-searchers in the "ethnography of communica-tion" tradition (see Carbaugh, 1991) hold that claims regarding struggle and ideological in-fluence must be supported by explicit treat-ment of those features in the discourse of or-ganizational members. Ethnographers in this tradition also disdain the Marxist-political in-vestment by critical theorists in the subjects and outcome of their research; as Carbaugh (1989-1990) put it: "One does not necessarily have to evaluate a system in order to describe and theorize about it" (p. 264; see also Alvesson & Deetz, 1996; Philipsen, 1989-1990; Van Maanen, in Putnam et al., 1993, p. 229). For its opponents, critical theory com-pels a biased imposition of ideological values onto the research process and thus violates the goals of discovery and description essential to interpretive research. The elements of *intel-lectualism* (favoring abstract concepts and elaborate processes), *essentialism* (presuming the desire for autonomy in all workers), *nega-tivism* (continually attacking management ac-tivity without providing workable solutions), and *elitism* (invalidating employees' sense-making as false) in critical theory have inhib-ited its acceptance among communication scholars, even those influenced by democratic and progressive ideologies.

Despite this tension, there have been recent signs of rapprochement between ethnog-raphers and critical theorists. Ethnographers are increasingly drawing on critical-theoreti-cal conceptualizations of power and discipline in their studies of communication (see, e.g., Communication Studies, 1997; Conquergood, 1989, 1991; Goodall, 1991; Scheibel, 1994; Taylor, 1990, 1993; Trujillo, 1993; West, 1993). Alternately, some critical theorists are drawing on ethnographic methods to produce careful, detailed, and empathic descriptions of everyday organizational phenomena (Alves-son & Willmott, 1992; Barker & Cheney, 1994; Deetz, 1994; Forester, 1992; Willis, 1977). These descriptions assist critical theo-rists in exploring the contradictions between intersubjective understandings and objective social conditions, in detailing the discursive (re)production of organizational subjectiv-ities, and in developing appropriate programs for action and change. These trends indicate that the tensions between critical theory and ethnography will continue to be productive —if not resolvable—ones for the study of or-ganizational communication.

In summary, critical theorists have chal-lenged organizational communication schol-ars to use research methods that enable us to uncover the ways in which organizational members use and are used by power. This crit-ical challenge works best not as a litmus test for the quality and depth of a given study, but as a reminder that power is a prevalent and naturalized phenomena that we should con-sider in organizational research. In addition, critical theorists have challenged us to actu-ally emancipate those who are oppressed by organizations. This is a far greater challenge, and it requires very different forms of research than currently used (such as the participatory research suggested but not practiced by Mumby, 1994), and very different forms of public-a(c)tion than the traditional textual me-dia of journal articles or books (such as politi-cal activism; see Andersen, 1993).

## Feminism

Like critical theory, feminism has become a popular perspective. And, like critical the-ory, "feminism" is not one particular theory, but a highly charged field of competing narra-tives about gender and sexual identities. These narratives include *liberal feminism,* which is primarily concerned with the inclusion of women in the rights and benefits traditionally afforded to men; *ideological/Marxist femi-nism,* which links female oppression to the system of social organization under capitalism; *radical feminism,* which celebrates women as fundamentally different from and better than their male oppressors, and emphasizes sexual separatism; *standpoint feminism,* which argues that women's marginalized position as Other in culture provides a resource of difference useful in critiquing and transforming misogynist institutions; and *poststructuralist and postmodern feminism,* which analyzes discourse to understand how gender identities are constructed and deployed as political processes. This last perspective diverges from other feminisms in not presuming, a priori, inherent differences between the sexes (see Bullis, 1993; Buzzanell, 1994; Donovan, 1985; Fine, 1993; Marshall, 1993; Ollenburger & Moore, 1992; Tong, 1989).

Despite their differences, feminist researchers share a commitment to critiquing gender bias in organizations and in organizational theory and research. Feminists have established that patriarchal and misogynistic elements of organizational structure and culture guide members to systematically devalue, marginalize, and annihilate women (e.g., in excluding them from important networks of informal communication). Women's "different" needs (e.g., maternity leave), which expose the organizational normalization of masculine values, are often ignored or dismissed by authorities. Beyond the "normal" demands of work, women are often subjected to ubiquitous forms of domination ranging from mundane degradation to sexual harassment to violent assault (see Clair, 1993a, 1993b; Loy & Stewart, 1984; Taylor & Conrad, 1992; Wood, 1992a, 1992b).

Feminist scholars have also challenged an implicit, "androcentric" gender bias in organizational theory and research. They argue that in their uncritical depictions of impersonal and hierarchical control systems, of technical and professional expertise, and of aggressive competition among amoral "individuals" concerned with victory and profit, many organizational researchers have naturalized ele-

ments of male sexuality as the essence of organizations. In addition, feminists argue that organizational researchers have adopted binary thinking that oversimplifies and reifies gender differences. From a (particularly poststructuralist) feminist perspective, researchers should not simply document the perceptions and behaviors of organizational members varied by biological sex (such as "male" and "female" styles of leadership), but they also should investigate the practices by which organizations conceptualize gender, and then deploy its meanings in ways that alternately oppress and please members (Gutek, 1985; Hearn, Sheppard, Tancred-Sheriff, & Burrell, 1989). In this view, gender is not simply an individual variable (a noun), but is an epistemological and political construct that guides the processes of both organization and research (a verb; see Rakow, 1986). Organizational scholars have been complicit, feminists argue, in sustaining the very structures that oppress women and in blinding their constituents to alternative forms of thought and practice (Calás & Smircich, 1991; Martin, 1990; Mumby & Putnam, 1992).[3]

While feminists continue to critique the gender bias of organizations and theory, they also make several challenges with respect to methodology. Feminists have criticized several elements of the "traditional" (primarily quantitative) research format, including its elitist selection of research topics (of those advancing the interests of men); its ritualized reproduction (in exclusively required quantitative methods courses in graduate curriculums); its biased research designs (those primarily sampling male subjects); its hierarchical exploitation of subjects; its illusion of objectivity; its improper interpretation and overgeneralization of findings (of those derived from male samples to mixed-sex populations); and finally, its inadequate use of data (e.g., in maintaining sexist policies).

This suspicion of quantitative methods does not mean, however, that there is a simple or direct mapping between feminist interests and *qualitative* methods. Qualitative methods are neither a necessary nor sufficient condition for the production of feminist research; feminist goals may be situationally met through the unique contributions of experimental and survey research, or through crystallizations of quantitative and qualitative methods (see Jayaratne & Stewart, 1991). We agree instead with arguments that "truly" feminist research (a highly contested term) is established in the content of research questions posed, in the selection of subjects, in the relations established between and among researchers and subjects, in the assumptions guiding the interpretation of data, and in the political uses to which research findings are put. With these elements in mind, we turn to five issues in feminist methodology that intersect with qualitative methods and organizational communication research.

First, we can identify a concern with *diversity*. Reinharz (1992), for example, has argued that "feminist research strives to recognize diversity" (p. 252) and that "diversity has become a new criterion for feminist research excellence" (p. 253). This concern is based on the belief that gender interacts with related constructs of race and class and sexual preference in the overlapping cultural contexts of postcolonialism, late capitalism, and patriarchy. As a result, the oppression of women through sexism is not independent from their oppression through racism and classism. Thus, feminists challenge organizational researchers to study women (and men) across a wide range of demographic categories and contexts. Feminists are struggling in this process to overcome a bias against representing working-class women of color in the production of social theory (Ollenburger & Moore, 1992). Sadly, the literature in organizational communication has offered very little diversity in terms of studies of women in organizations. With a few notable exceptions (see Eastland, 1993; Ligtenberg, 1994; Lont, 1990), most of the women studied by organizational communication scholars have been white, heterosexual, middle class, and corporate-managerial. We agree with Reinharz that

we need to embrace a form of *scholarly* "affirmative action to alter research projects" (p. 253). Obvious candidates for research, thus, involve "alternative" organizational forms that are explicitly lesbian and feminist in their characteristic structures, cultures, norms for emotional expression, patterns of development, and modes of conflict (see Ferree & Martin, 1995; Weston & Rofel, 1984).

Second, we can identify a concern with *involvement* among researchers and subjects. Reinharz (1992) has suggested that the relationship between these two groups inherently "leaves the realm of research and enters the personal lives of the individuals involved" (p. 263). The traditional authority of the researcher to unilaterally define problems, to determine methods of inquiry, and to interpret findings is rejected by feminists to emphasize the relational, collaborative, and nonhierarchical development of research goals and procedures. These qualities ideally permeate relationships among research team members, and between researchers and subjects. Research should also directly meet the needs of women and reflect a valuing of women as authorities on their own experience (Bristow & Esper, 1984; Duffy, 1985; Gergen, 1988). As Foss and Foss (1994) pointed out, feminist scholars "continually remind themselves and participants that the research product is a joint construction of the participants' experiences and interpretations and researchers' presentational expertise," and they concluded that feminist scholarship "produces not only knowledge—information about others' lives —but understanding—a capacity for insight, empathy, and attentive caring—that emerges from interaction with participants" (p. 41). Thus, researchers should not just develop "rapport" with these participants; they should develop meaningful relationships that transcend the research project and play an important part in the lives of those participants. Not surprisingly, few studies in organizational communication have reached this ideal. One exception is Kauffman's (1992) study of women artists, in which she argues that ethnographic interviews are not simply a means to *produce* data (in the form of a transcript text) reflecting theoretical concerns. They are, instead, *in and of themselves data* of collaborative performances of evolving, politically inflected relationships between interviewers and interviewees. Such data, she argued, should not be stripped to be aggregated, or to typify abstract concepts.

Third, we can identify a feminist concern with *accountable investment* by researchers. Feminist qualitative researchers are decidedly *not* objective (Mies, 1981)—a state that is viewed as neither possible nor desirable. Alternately, feminist researchers are explicitly accountable about their investment in their work (e.g., as a function of their class positions, sexual orientations, and personal histories), and about its consequences for those studied. Reinharz (1992) expressed this image of holistic research when she stated that feminism encourages "the involvement of the researcher as a person" (p. 258). This process, however, is neither straightforward nor easy. Marshall (1993), for example, reported that some feminist researchers face a dilemma involved in "exposing" through publication the "secrets" of vulnerable, subordinate women (which may subsequently be used by male authorities against their interests). Foss and Foss (1994) suggested that feminist researchers should "constantly monitor their own perspectives in regard to the personal experiences they gather" (p. 41).

Fourth, we can identify a feminist concern with *achieving social change* through qualitative research. Like other critical theories, emancipation and liberation are fundamental goals of feminist research. As Foss and Foss (1994) put it: "Feminist research is conducted for the purpose of improving women's lives. It is done to empower women—to assist them in developing strategies to make sense of and make choices about the world in which they live" (p. 42). With respect to organizations, feminists seek to "call out" and "disentangle" elements of gender and sexuality that are commonly distorted and suppressed in organi-

zational communication, such as empathy, intuition, cooperation, and dialogue (Ferguson, 1984). In this view, these elements need to be reintegrated as ethical principles to guide managers and researchers in revising androcentric assumptions about the "typical" traits and performances of organizational members. Clair (1993a), for example, suggested that "emancipatory discourse"—"discourse that promotes dialogue rather than closure" (p. 148)—can help in this endeavor, but feminists challenge us in organizational communication to do far more to accomplish change. Like critical theorists, feminists who study organizational politics must ultimately engage in meaningful political action of their own (see Harding, 1986; West, 1993). After all, if we only change the nature of what is published in our journals without changing the lives of the people we study, the goals of critical theory and feminism will never be reached.

Finally, we can identify a feminist concern with the *gendered nature of the qualitative research experience* (Bell, 1993; Golde, 1986). Given that organizations are often sexist cultures, female researchers are confronted with fieldwork challenges that their male counterparts are not (or, more precisely, generic challenges that are inflected by the researcher's gender). These challenges include the real and perceived need for sponsors, patrons, and general "protection" in negotiating hostile cultures (both resistant subjects and "protectors" may, in different ways, inhibit the research process); pressures to conform to sexual stereotypes and even to have sexual relations during data gathering (a gendered manifestation of the dilemmas of mutual obligation and reciprocity between fieldworkers and subjects); and the ongoing negotiation of suspicion from patriarchal interests toward the doubled Otherness of "woman" and "researcher." These challenges suggest the need for reflective pedagogy in the training of ethnographers, and for ongoing discussions of gendered "tactics" in fieldwork.

In summary, feminist organizational theory has challenged organizational communication scholars to use research methods for particular ends, including the creation of preservationistic accounts of situated experience; the satisfaction of real needs of organizational women (both those "in" and also "invisible" to the organization, such as organizational wives; see Kanter, 1977); the revision of assumptions and practices in organizational research so that gender "differences" are reflexively considered at every stage of the research process; and finally, the reform of organizational authority and theory in the interests of sexual justice.

## Postmodernism

Postmodernism is another critical perspective that gained prominence in the organizational literature in the 1990s. Postmodernism has been described as everything from a social mood and historical period to a theoretical perspective (see Alvesson, 1995; Featherstone, 1991; Thompson, 1993). As applied to the study of organizations, Alvesson and Deetz (1996) described postmodernism as a "philosophically based research perspective" providing several topics and agendas for scholarship, including *the centrality of discourse* (defined as the use of language in interaction, as well as linguistically constituted systems of thought); *the fragmentation of self* (the existence of multiple, decentered, linguistically constituted and often competing forms of consciousness as identity "subject positions"); *the critique of the philosophy of presence* (in favor of the linguistic construction of reality); *the loss of master narratives* (the rejection of unified and authoritative images of the world in favor of local, situated narratives of experience); *the power/ knowledge connection* (the construction and reproduction of power through authoritative knowledge claims); *hyperreality* (reality experienced as intensive, pervasive mediation and simulation of material phenomena); and *resistance* (the attempt to open up the indeterminacy that modern science closes in its quest

for certainty and progress). These concerns are addressed to communication in both "modern" industrial-corporate organizations (which embody hierarchical differentiation, control, performativity, and rationality) and in emerging, postindustrial organizational forms (which embody fragmentation, turbulence, ambiguity, and creative play). (See Deetz's chapter for a more detailed discussion of these issues.)

With respect to *methodology*, proponents of postmodernism have offered a wide, vague, and contradictory range of options. Some suggest that postmodernism is best achieved through meta-analyses of organizational texts, including published research on organizations, while others argue that postmodernism energizes field research methods, especially ethnography.

Reading postmodernism in the context of critical theory, Alvesson and Deetz (1996) suggested that organizational researchers who draw on postmodernism typically use one of three methods: deconstruction, resistance readings, and/or genealogy (p. 36). *Deconstruction* describes the process of uncovering the tensions, contradictions, absences, and paradoxes in texts. Meaning is held to be not *in* the form of the text, but in the relationships among its signs; between those signs and their social, political, and economic uses; between the text and all other texts from which it draws its form and content (i.e., its *intertextuality*); and between the text and its readers. Calás and Smircich (1991), for example, provide a dizzying deconstruction of conventional discourse about organizational leadership to demonstrate its suppressed homosocial dimension in which masculine values dominate as a strategy for "seducing" masculine-identified organizational subjects. As Kilduff (1993) concluded, "Deconstruction is used not to abolish truth, science, logic, and philosophy, but to question how these concepts are present in texts and how they are employed to systematically exclude certain categories of thought and communication" (p. 15; see also Martin, 1992, pp. 135-141).

Although postmodernist deconstruction tends to focus on how organizations fragment, confound, and control members, Goodall (1992) has also used deconstruction to illustrate how organizations can empower people by examining one particular organizational artifact: the Nordstrom's employee handbook. He showed that by producing a brief (one-page) and strategically ambiguous "handbook" containing a single rule ("use your good judgment in all situations") followed by the statement "there will be no more additional rules," Nordstrom employees are encouraged to accept responsibility and to value creativity and initiative. As he concluded: "From a postmodern vantage, organizational communication is dedicated to sharing power, accepting responsibility, recognizing interdependence, and embodying—through appropriate displays of attitude and style—the 'unique sense of place' as a consumable commodity within fluid, ambiguous contexts of everyday business life" (p. 29).

*Resistance readings* similarly deconstruct textual meaning, but they do so by problematizing the role of the organizational analyst as a privileged observer who possesses the expertise to construct an authoritative metanarrative of organizational reality. Such readings are typically meta-analyses that reread organizational research accounts not as direct reflections of the organizations themselves, but of the logics and procedures by which researchers represent those organizations. Examples include Gusterson's (1993) and Taylor's (1996) reflections on "dialogic" representation of conflicting voices in nuclear weapons organizations.

Finally, Foucault's *genealogy* emphasizes how apparently divergent discourses of knowledge are embedded within a modern "episteme" (the dominant ways of knowing and speaking that characterize a particular historical period). For Foucault, these discourses lead to a network of practices that—despite their assertions—do not so much reflect truth as accomplish discipline. Working from this perspective, researchers

employ a historical focus to describe how particular methods for understanding and managing organizational members achieve authority, and thus, bear particular consequences for those members. Frequently, this perspective focuses on how the body is a symbolic "site" through which discourses create "technologies of the self" that attempt to maintain labor's productivity and efficiency. Barker and Cheney's (1994) analysis of how ostensibly progressive team-based management forms that have succeeded Taylorism, Fordism, and human relations lead to increasingly coercive control is one example of this strategy. Another is Jacques's (1996) study of the circular and fragmented "evolution" of American management's images of workers as, alternately, spiritual pilgrims, federal citizens, labor professionals, and bureaucratic cases.

Some scholars worry that empirical research will suffer with the postmodern emphasis on conducting meta-analyses of organizational documents and of organizational research texts. Dorst (1989) suggested that one implication of the postmodern breakdown between the researcher and the subject is that "field techniques for gathering information, participant observation and informant interview, will be conceptually demoted" (p. 208). Similarly, Vidich and Lyman (1994) hinted that the postmodern research enterprise "may become one devoted to reading texts and writing critiques" and that "the 'field' may be located in one's library or one's study" (p. 42).

However, other researchers, especially ethnographers, have exhibited excitement about integrating postmodern ideas into their field research. Trujillo (1993), for example, examined the hyperreality and commodification of experience at Dealey Plaza on the 25th anniversary of the assassination of John F. Kennedy. Gottschalk (1995) examined Las Vegas—a perennial favorite of postmodern ethnographers—as a (dis-)organized mediascape. Vidich and Lyman (1994) proposed that we may take "the onset of the postmodern condition as the very occasion for presenting a new kind of ethnography," one that reflects "an ethnographic attitude of engagement with a world that is ontologically absurd but always meaningful to those who live in it" (p. 42). Increasingly, ethnographers adopting this perspective turn to—if not corporate organizations in the traditional sense—what Foucault discussed as the increasing organization of the world (Burrell, 1988): the pervasive commercialization and rationalization of both public life and private experience. Linstead (1993) put the challenge this way:

> Postmodern ethnography interrogates traditional practice, asking of every representation "is this fact?" and refusing to come to any final conclusions. . . . It throws into question its own authority as an account, and whether it introduces the device of co-authorship or multiple voices or not, it nevertheless points to the possibility of an infinitude of interpretations and accounts. (p. 66)

As West (1993) concluded, "The future of ethnography lies in the ability of researchers to understand how Others articulate their sensemaking of their lives, while at the same time having the perspicacity to reveal the relations of power in which these Others' sensemaking is articulated" (p. 214).

In summary, critical theory, feminism, and postmodernism challenge organizational communication researchers to confront issues of power at every step in the research process. They challenge us to critique how power relations influence the lives of organizational women and men, and the ways that we design, conduct, and report our research. We now consider this latter issue of reporting research results.

## The Poetics and Politics of Representation

As noted earlier, researchers across disciplines have experienced a crisis of representation. This dis-ease with realistic forms of research reporting was initially articulated by sociologists and anthropologists (Brown, 1977; Clifford & Marcus, 1986; Geertz, 1988; Marcus & Fischer, 1986; Myerhoff & Ruby, 1982) and has been further developed by those embracing postmodernism. "The postmodern critique has engendered something of a crisis," wrote Vidich and Lyman (1994), one in which "a new self-and-other consciousness has come to the fore, and the imperatives of reflexivity have shifted attention onto the literary, political, and historical features" of research (p. 41).

As suggested by these and other scholars, there are related political and poetic dimensions to this crisis in representation. The political dimension suggests that power is now understood to influence the very research processes of gathering and analyzing data as well as writing about our findings. For example, Rosaldo (1989) pointed out that "the dominant idea of a detached observer using neutral language to explain 'raw' data has been displaced by an alternate project that attempts to understand human conduct as it unfolds through time and in relation to its meaning for the actors" (p. 37). Accordingly, researchers are now advised to articulate not only how relations of power influence the members of the organizations we study but also how they influence the research process itself. Indeed, researchers are now disclosing the role we ourselves play in constructing images of the subjects we study. As Denzin (1994) put it: "Representation . . . is always self-presentation" because "the Other's presence is directly connected to the writers' self-presence in the text" (p. 503).

The self-awareness generated during this crisis of representation has led to a new concern for the poetics of scholarship, a movement that can be found in calls for new perspectives for conducting research and for new forms of presenting our scholarship. Many qualitative researchers—including those in organizational communication—have turned to "performance-centered research." One benefit of this perspective is that it orients researchers to situated, improvisational, and collaborative enactments of cultural scripts (see Lindlof, 1995, pp. 13-18). It is also productive for critical and postmodern researchers, however, because it "privileges particular, participatory, dynamic, intimate, precarious, embodied experience grounded in historical process, contingency, and ideology," and because it focuses on the "preeminently rhetorical nature" of communicative processes such as "ceremony, celebration, festival, parade, pageant, feast, and so forth" (Conquergood, 1991, pp. 187, 188; see also Banks, 1994; Bell & Forbes, 1994; Goodall, 1991; Knight, 1990; Presnell, 1994; Rogers, 1994; Trujillo & Dionisopoulos, 1987). Reflecting this postmodern stance, several studies in special issues of *Text and Performance Quarterly* (Hawes, 1994) and the *Journal of Contemporary Ethnography* (Ellis & Bochner, 1996) depict organizational performers and researchers as fluid subjectivities that are coconstructed through evolving, collaborative enactments of cultural identities such as gender, class, race, and profession. Organizational performance emerges in these articles as the locus of productive tensions between cultural disciplining of the subject and the disorganizing impulses of individual and group desires. Some of these studies problematize their own narrative form to promote reflexivity about the process by which knowledge claims are produced. In this way, the researchers are not documentarians but are implicated as coperformers. Both the process and the product of their research, in this view, become "performances" that evoke the situated performances of organizational members.

Researchers have turned to new forms of representation as well, especially with respect to *writing*. In his primer on ethnographic writing, Van Maanen (1988) identified two forms of writing in particular that some contemporary researchers have adopted. After he described conventional social science reports (or "realist" tales[4]) Van Maanen discussed "confessional" and "impressionist" tales, two related forms of writing that are not mutually exclusive or exhaustive, but are illustrative of the forms that qualitative researchers can use in their representation of claims and data.

According to Van Maanen, *confessional tales* are distinguished by their "highly personalized styles and their self-absorbed mandates" (p. 73), and they exhibit *personalized author(ity)*, whereby "the details that matter . . . are those that constitute the field experience of the author" (p. 76) and a focus on the *fieldworker's point of view,* revealing tensions as the author struggles "back and forth between an insider's passionate perspective and an outsider's dispassionate one" (p. 77). Richardson (1994) referred to confessional writing as "the narrative of the self," and she concluded that by "writing these frankly subjective narratives, [researchers] are somewhat relieved of the problems of speaking for the 'Other,' because they are the Other in their texts" (p. 521).

We believe that confessional writing is important because our writing does not "capture" the essential truth of the organizations we study. Rather, it reveals how we as writing actors are materially and symbolically involved with those organizations through a process of reflecting on and describing our relationships with them. Unfortunately, while there have been many calls for confessional writing, there remain very few exemplars, especially in organizational communication.

One of the most provocative examples can be found in the work of Bob Krizek (1992) in his ethnography of the closing of Chicago's Comiskey Park in 1990. In the course of the article, Krizek framed the emotions of the "mourners" who narrated their memories of the ballpark with his own emotions, as he recalled going to the same ballpark to watch baseball games as a child with his father, who had died the year before the park closed. Here is how Krizek told his tale:

> Research was secondary in my mind . . . as I instinctively negotiated the ramps and stairways to those sacred seats [where we used to sit]. . . . I paused, took a few deep breaths, and then

held one as I sank into the chair closest to the aisle. For one brief moment the confidence of adulthood drifted away, replaced by the feelings of a lost five- or six-year-old boy, and I began to cry.

This may have been the first time I truly missed my dad or genuinely mourned his passing. . . . Like a frightened child, I rocked up and back in my chair and reached for his hand. The pain was immense and I reached our to hold my father's hand. I believe I succeeded. (pp. 34-35, 41)

Krizek (p. 50) concluded the article by putting the study in the context of his life (and perhaps vice versa): "This project was both painful and cleansing for me. The relationship with my father that I 'never quite understood' has become a bit clearer. I only wish that the five- or six-year-old boy still within me had a place to visit with him. Goodbye Comiskey; goodbye Dad" (see also Trujillo & Krizek, 1994).

Other examples of confessional writing in organizational communication can be found in Crawford's (1996) "personal ethnography," Eastland's (1993) discussion of liminality in her study of a 12-step recovery program, Pacanowsky's (1988) "fictional" story about the angst that a professor experiences at academic conventions, Benson's (1981) account of politics on the campaign trail, Goodall's (1989, 1991) books on his identity as "consulting detective," team ethnographers' personal reflections on their experiences at a "postmodern bar" (Communication Studies, 1997), Taylor's (1997) examination of the dialectical relationship between "personal" and "professional" interests in the production of nuclear weapons, and the special issue on sexual harassment in the *Journal of Applied Communication Research,* edited by Wood (1992a). Examples from other disciplines include Ronai's personal accounts of fieldwork as a topless dancer (1992) and of child sexual abuse (1995), Zola's (1983) compelling portrait of living with a disability, and Ellis's (1993) "story of a sudden death."

*Impressionist writing* can be as provocative as confessional writing, for it focuses on the drama of conducting a qualitative study. Van Maanen (1988) argued that impressionist writing exhibits *textual identity,* such that "dramatic recall" is used to recreate the experience of fieldwork; *fragmented knowledge,* revealed in a "novelistic" form whereby the tale "unfolds event by event" (p. 104); *characterization,* whereby various figures are developed as unique individuals with "such poses as befuddlement, mixed emotions, moral anguish, heightened sensitivity, compassion, enchantment, skepticism," and other emotions (p. 104); and *dramatic control,* whereby the writer produces an evocative *story,* with a plot line that has "interest (does it attract?), coherence (does it hang together?), and fidelity (does it seem true?)" (p. 105).

Not surprisingly, there are few exemplars of impressionistic writing in the organizational communication literature. One example can be found in Goodall's (1991) book *Living in the Rock 'n Roll Mystery,* which may be read as a postmodern update of classical studies of organizational and community life. Here, he describes his feelings about people in the Deep South of Birmingham, Alabama:

I fear the mere possibility of human connections between me and them based on the joke of a life that rushes us all too quickly to nowhere, regardless of our birth, looks, language, or money, and that requires us all to pay taxes along the way, taxes that are taken from wages that are never enough, wages that take time away from a life that is never enough, when what waits for us is the great trapdoor at the bottom end of the twentieth century that should mark our common generational tombstones thusly:

This citizen was born, reared, and
   educated,
Got a job in order to consume,
Consumed like hell,
Was famous, locally, for it
Realized that no matter how much was
   consumed it was
Never Enough,
Then retired,
Then died. (p. 180)

Other examples in organizational communication include Pacanowsky's (1983) fictional story of a police officer, based on his fieldwork at a police station; Brown and McMillan's (1991) "synthetic" narrative of socialization in a nursing home; and Jones's (1996) "kaleidoscopic" tale of women musicians at a folk music club. Examples from other disciplines include Richardson's (1992) long poem based on her interviews with unmarried mothers, Freeman's (1992) feminist interpretation of her "perfect Valentine," Hayano's (1982) portrait of poker players, and a special issue of the *Journal of Contemporary Ethnography,* edited by Ellis and Bochner (1996).

There are several strengths of confessional, impressionist, and other unconventional forms of writing. First, they vividly and sensitively use lyricism, nonlinearity, and pastiche (combinations of different textual fragments) to subvert the positivist premises of detachment, monologic authority, and noncontingent Truth. This writing demonstrates the "politics of form" that qualitative researchers can use to disrupt patriarchal and other realist theories. They also demonstrate how, as opposed to the belief that researchers choose methods ("the fallacy of the present choice"; Frost, Moore, Louis, Lundberg, & Martin, 1991, p. 331), *qualitative methods seem to choose researchers.* We refer here to the sense of fulfillment experienced by many researchers as they discover in qualitative methods a resonant "permission" that enables them to work through in their research the contradictions and ambiguities created in their personal histories and professional socializations (Martin, 1989; Weil, 1989).

Second, unconventional forms of writing are—despite sneering from some traditionalists about "rigor" (discussed below)—more challenging to write well, and they are almost always more interesting to read. Indeed, when we receive our quarterly issues of the *Journal of Contemporary Ethnography,* we read them with the same interest and passion that we experience when reading our monthly issues of the *New Yorker* or *Atlantic Monthly.* We have the fond hope that someday in the 21st cen-

tury, audiences will read our communication journals with the same impassioned responses.[5] Such a hope, however, will come to fruition only if authors and editors are willing to risk their own professional identities to push the traditional boundaries of academic scholarship.

There are, however, some potential pitfalls and challenges associated with these forms of writing. One potential danger is that we may narcissistically emphasize ourselves over the very people we interact with in the field. As Fitch (1994a) pointed out, "The extended attention and heavy emphasis directed toward the researcher's place and state of mind sometimes degenerate into a kind of self-indulgence that [is] unproductive at best" (p. 35). We believe that the best research narratives focus on the organizational others while, at the same time, revealing how we as researchers are transformed during the process of studying the organization. In addition, the use of unconventional writing formats does not guarantee by fiat that a qualitative report is a quality report. As Van Maanen noted in his review of the first draft of this chapter, it is inappropriate if "novel work [is] simply assumed to be worthy poetics," adding that "there are lousy poems too and an ethnography cast as a short story is not necessarily a good short story." We treat the issues raised by these challenges in our subsequent discussion of evaluative criteria for qualitative research.

Perhaps the greatest challenge associated with unconventional forms of writing is that they are far more difficult to publish than conventional forms. Confessional and impressionist writing is subject to the highly arbitrary and selective tastes of editors and reviewers, and it is also subject to the ideological apparatus of academic publishing. Our own personal experience with manuscript submissions to journals suggests that criteria among editors and reviewers for "innovative" writing are often wildly divergent, idiosyncratic, poorly articulated, and occasionally approach ineffability.[6] In fact, responding to the question "What is 'good' postmodern ethnography?" one journal editor (D. Loseke, personal communication with Bryan Taylor,

April 9, 1996) stated: "I think of it like I think of 'pornography': I can't define it but I know it when I see it." We now briefly examine some of the issues involved in the politics of poetic representation.

## The Politics of Poetics

Clearly, there are more calls for creative writing in organizational communication than there are exemplars. We believe this void is by no means surprising or accidental; rather, it is quite predictable given the politics of academia. We socialize our graduate students to use conventional forms of writing, and we employ publishing practices that encourage conventional forms of writing. West (1993) pointed out that "ethnography is enmeshed within the ideological practices of the academy" that "establish standards that are in direct opposition to the concerns of ethnographers" (p. 216). Some of these practices include truncating manuscripts to fit journal slots preformatted for shorter, quantitative reports; demanding that ethnographies conform to traditional, linear protocols of social science reporting formats; and devaluing narratives of personal experience as "subjective." These practices are in turn related to other traditional academic conventions, such as funding priorities for "traditional" research topics and methods; institutionally required rituals such as the literature review (and increasingly, the meta-analysis of statistical findings in a particular research area) that "box" researchers within a sedimented encoding of deductive and often sexist theorizing and that constrain (as a narrative performed for professional authorities) the questions they may legitimately ask about topics (see Aldag & Stearns, 1988); and requirements for academic retention and promotion (such as high numbers of rapidly produced, "well-placed" journal articles) that encourage reproduction of the status quo in "established" lines of research. These conventions often discourage researchers from using time- and labor-intensive ethnographic methods (particularly as these qualities aggravate

women's competing responsibilities involving childbearing and -rearing; see Moore, 1991; Podsakoff & Dalton, 1987). West concluded that changing the current situation will require qualitative researchers in communication to engage in actions that include publishing outside our field, "becoming editors of existing communication journals, creating new journals with new formats, and becoming more active in the political battles for power in our discipline and its organizations" (p. 218).[7]

Of course, writing is but one form of representation. And given the challenges of feminism and postmodernism, it may not be the most powerful form. As Conquergood (1991) challenged:

> It is one thing to talk about performance as a model for cultural process . . . as long as that performance-sensitive talk eventually gets "written down." . . . The hegemony of inscribed texts is never challenged by fieldwork because, after all is said and done, the final word is on paper. . . . It is interesting to note that even the most radical deconstructions still take place on the page. (p. 190)

Conquergood offered as one alternative *performance* itself, a form of representation advocated by Victor Turner (1986) and treated by Conquergood (1991) "as a complement, alternative, supplement, and critique of inscribed texts" (p. 191). Conquergood is one of the few scholars in communication to pursue this form of representation (see Conquergood, Friesema, Hunter, & Mansbridge, 1990; see also Welker & Goodall, 1997), and he has coproduced at least two documentaries based on his fieldwork: "Between Two Worlds: The Hmong Shaman in America" (1985) and "The Heart Broken in Half" (1990). Similarly, Mara Adelman and Peter Shultz (1994) produced a video, titled "The Pilgrim Must Embark: Living in Community," about community among people living with the AIDS virus.

Another intriguing use of performance has been adopted by Bonnie Johnson, Eric

Dishman, and their colleagues at Interval Research Corporation in Palo Alto, California (Burns, Dishman, Johnson, & Verplank, 1995). These researchers have been conducting "informances" (informative performances) for corporate clients and design engineers that draw upon ethnographic observations of computer users, conversation analytic methods to interpret field data, scenario-based interactive design techniques such as storytelling and storyboarding, and performances that they call "bodystorming" and "repping" (reenacting everyday people's performances). These informances are designed by these researchers to help engineers understand how technologies are actually used and imagine potential future uses, and to present new designs and prototypes within grounded and imagined future contexts.

In summary, the crisis of representation has radically challenged our assumptions about what constitutes the appropriate conduct and representation of our research. In our view, this crisis has provided opportunities to adopt alternative forms of writing and other strategies of representation that were unavailable to previous generations of organizational communication scholars. However, it must be remembered that these opportunities are available only in a highly politicized academic environment. We need to take more chances with our research, but in doing so, we run the risk of not finishing our dissertations on time, of having our article submissions rejected, and of being denied tenure and promotion, all because our research does not meet traditional requirements for "quality" scholarship. We now turn our attention to the issues involved in defining criteria for assessing the quality of qualitative research.

## Criteria for Evaluating Qualitative Research

Scholars across disciplines have a wide variety of ideas regarding the appropriate criteria for evaluating qualitative research. In this section, we briefly review some of the criteria proposed by various scholars, especially those for "validity" in qualitative research, and we discuss the politics of assessing qualitative research in organizational communication.

Until recently, the standards used to assess qualitative research were primarily defined through a positivistic framework. When judged by positivist standards, qualitative studies of organizational communication usually have been found wanting. Indeed, they have been dismissed using such stereotypes as "soft," "imprecise," "unverifiable," "unreliable," and "nongeneralizable" (Aldag & Stearns, 1988; Lindlof, 1995). Often, these judgments have been unreflective, asserting positivist epistemology as the sole, correct, and seemingly inevitable approach to studying organizational phenomena. They have assumed the necessity of exact "correspondence" between a singular, objective reality, its quantitative measurement, and the representation of measurement activities and outcomes in the research text. In positivism, validity is guaranteed through the rigorous adoption of protocols that control against "bias" and that lead inexorably to either falsification or confirmation of hypotheses. In this way, positivists have presumed to develop universal and lawlike explanations of causal relationships between organizational variables to enable their prediction and control. Deployed against qualitative research, such reasoning has led critics such as Staw (1985) to complain that "beyond the hand-waving and travelogue that characterize most articles devoted to symbolism, we are still waiting for the real contributions to organizational science" (pp. 117-180). Such comments imply that qualitative research may be interesting but that it is ultimately unfit for the "higher" purposes of organization studies. Other positivists concede a preliminary and heuristic role for qualitative research in discovering organizational variables that can then be studied through more rigorous experimental and survey methodologies.

Qualitative researchers and their supporters have been equally vigorous in defending the integrity of their work, and they have done so through a variety of strategies. These strategies reflect the eclectic and contested nature of "qualitative research" as an interdisciplinary enterprise that spans a variety of methodological positions. As a result, multiple sets of criteria have emerged for the evaluation of qualitative research. These criteria are applied differently by different "interpretive communities" (e.g., by ethnographers, rhetorical critics, organizational consultants) to particular research texts. Although some standards seem consistent across these audiences (e.g., the description of meanings and practices among organizational members), disagreement exists among and between audiences about which evaluative criteria should be applied, and how they should be applied. This disagreement confirms a controversial but important tenet of qualitative research: Validity is attributed by audiences through the researcher's rhetorical evocation and satisfaction of normative standards in the research text itself. Ultimately, the value and significance of qualitative research are the province of *readers* (such as journal editors and manuscript reviewers) applying standards that are themselves contested, fluid, and rapidly evolving (Strine & Pacanowsky, 1985). As a result, we cannot claim here to represent a definitive consensus on standards of validity in qualitative research. We can, however, identify the seams and overlaps of an ongoing debate on the topic.

In general, we find arguments in this debate reflecting a continuum of epistemological positions ranging from "quasi-positivism" to "intepretivism" to "critical postmodernism." It is important to note that these positions are less pure types than heuristic punctuations of epistemological differences. There is as much debate within as between these positions, and any particular research text may reflect the influence of more than one position.

At the *quasi-positivist* end of the continuum, researchers value the programmatic execution of predetermined research protocols (e.g., involving the initial definition and rationalization of research questions), the confirmation of reliability through multiple observers, the generalization of "representative" textual and case study findings to larger populations, and the relevance of findings for prior, deductively tested theory (see, for examples in rhetorical and discourse analysis, Tompkins, 1994; Waitzkin, 1993). Here, qualitative methods achieve legitimacy as valued adjuncts to survey, experimental and variable analytic methods by achieving greater precision and detail in the analysis of actual micropractices in organizations. These benefits form trade-offs, however, against decreased researcher control over the organizational variables studied, and decreased ability to effectively generalize from the setting(s) studied to larger populations.

Recently, some theorists and methodologists (Eisenhardt, 1989; Hammersley, 1992; Tsoukas, 1989) have attempted to recuperate qualitative research within the larger (and more direct) opportunities for validity presented by idiographic, case study research. Such research, the authors note, is not restricted only to qualitative methods, and may involve the collection of quantitative data to offset the vivid but misleading impressions occasionally created by "soft" and "sensational" qualitative data. These authors draw on Yin's (1984) distinction between "sampling" and "replication" logics to explore how, through careful planning and execution, case studies can successfully generate and test theories. They do so by adding to—if not statistical generalizations about the distribution of variables within the population—*theoretical* understanding of the *operations* of those variables within that population. This process requires researchers to establish in advance the larger, aggregate population within which they wish the case to be understood as an exemplar. After deciding which target aggregate is desired, researchers can use official, published data to maximize the similarity between the characteristics of the aggregate and of the case. They can collaborate with other researchers to combine case studies as a series of quasi-experiments that generate, confirm, and disconfirm hypotheses. Cases that confirm emergent hypotheses enhance confidence in their validity, while cases that disconfirm them often provide an opportunity to refine and extend theory (Eisenhardt, 1989, p. 544).

Voices positioned at the *interpretivist* point in this continuum of criteria celebrate the inductive and meaning-centered focus of ethnographic research (see Anderson, 1987; Bantz, 1983; Bryman, 1988; Conrad, 1985; Fitch, 1994a; Kirk & Miller, 1986; Rosen, 1991; Silverman, 1993). External validity (i.e., generalizability) is construed as irrelevant, since any specific organization is viewed as a unique site of meanings and practices, whose complexity is to be explored and evoked by the researcher (Hansen & Kahnweiler, 1993). Description, interpretation, narrative skill, and empathic understanding take precedence; analytic claims may relate indirectly to existing concepts, but must be "relevant"—a somewhat generous and ambiguous criteria.

To elaborate, this interpretivist position on qualitative research holds that although organizational reality may admit a variety of interpretations, not all of them are equal. A valid, useful, and significant account is generally held to be one that

1. *Provides evidence of an involved and committed study* (i.e., it specifies the length of time spent by the researcher in the field, the number of organizational members studied, the frequency and quality of contact with informants, the groups that have been "theoretically sampled," etc.).

2. *Uses emic and inductive analysis* to preserve the naturally occurring features and discourse of the organizational scene and to depict both consensual and contested meanings among organizational members (i.e., it provides historical and cultural context necessary to understand the significance of events for both organizational members and professional audiences).

3. *Provides sufficient types and amounts of evidence to warrant the analytic claims being made* (i.e., it "saturates" claims with support and achieves relevance and richness by grounding them in the ongoing concerns of professional audiences regarding the topic, method, and theory).

4. *Provides evidence of a continuous and reflexive movement between explanations and data* (i.e., it indicates that initial, interpretive categories have been revised through expanding contact with the organizational scene, and may include "confessional" discourse about elements in the nonlinear process of ethnographic discovery, including false starts, backtracking, good and bad luck, serendipity, epiphanies, effects of the researcher on the researched—and vice versa— regrets, obstacles to access and inclusion posed by funding bodies and gatekeepers, and unfinished business).

5. *Shows rhetorical skill in language use* (i.e., it creates a clear, vivid, plausible, provocative, and compelling story of organizational life—also known as *verisimilitude*—that enables the reader to imaginatively enter the organizational life-world at issue and to reflect on the adequacy of its potential explanations).

6. *Uses representative data drawn from a corpus that is publicly available for review* (e.g., from transcripts of public speeches to copies of fieldnotes that are edited for confidentiality).

7. *Employs triangulation of multiple researchers, data sources, and/or methods, in addition to member checks, debriefings, and/or negative-case analysis* (which serve to enhance the accuracy and consistency of observations).

Collectively, these criteria establish the general conditions for credible qualitative accounts of organizational communication. Such accounts, however, may be indirectly related to theory. Theory here is held in tension as a resource establishing the significance of the ethnographic argument, and as a powerful "hammer" that may potentially shatter its emic character. In this view, the goal of interpretivist research is to contribute to the disciplinary enterprise of theory without succumbing to positivist tendencies toward totalization and reductionism. To achieve this goal, researchers suspend the introduction of theory into analysis until they have developed a holistic understanding of the scene. The separate discourses of organizational members and of theory are then brought into contact by researchers in a tentative, reflective manner. Heuristic connections that preserve the integrity of the documented scene are strengthened in the research report through the use of exemplars: condensed scenes of interaction that demonstrate relevant patterns and themes of interaction. Because the relationship between theory and ethnographic argument is a site of tension between inductive and deductive processes, it can also be a source of ambiguity in ethnographic pedagogy.

Finally, at the other end of the continuum is qualitative research from critical perspectives. A quality critical study is one that (1) discusses the relevant historical and cultural struggles between class, gender, and ethnic groups under study; (2) analyzes multiple forms and practices of power, ranging from outright coercion and the active constraint of minority voices to the normalization of premises that inhibit the very imagination of alternatives (see Lukes, 1974); (3) analyzes the various "tactics" of the powerless as they alternately accommodate, appropriate, resist, and transform the "strategies" of the powerful (see De Certeau, 1984); and (4) reflects on the extent to which research potentially or actually leads to changes in oppressive power relations and the emancipation of the powerless (see Lincoln, 1990, for a discussion of "catalytic" and "tactical" authenticity). In many ways, this fourth criterion of emancipation is the most important to critical studies. Mumby (in Putnam et al., 1993), for example, argued that validity from a critical perspective should not be "tied to conditions of verifiability or verisimilitude," but to "social transformation" whereby members "engage in self-reflection

and hence re-evaluate their conditions of existence" (p. 225). Similarly, West (1993) argued that ethnography is meaningful only in "its ability as a potential counter-hegemonic force" (p. 218). It is important to note that this ideal is contingent on the successful collaboration between researchers and subjects in developing and applying criteria for defining and resolving "distortions." This is a process, Deetz (1982, p. 147) conceded, that requires patience and faith.

With respect to criteria for *postmodern* qualitative research, we should note Lather's (1993) provocative discussion of "validity after poststructrualism" in which she explores the "antifoundational possibilities outside the limits of the normative framings of validity in the human sciences" (p. 677). In developing a reflexive "validity of transgression," she identifies the following four types: (1) an *ironic validity* that proliferates possible explanations to foreground the insufficiency of language for capturing and exhausting truth; (2) a *neopragmatic validity* that preserves contradictions within and between discourses to inhibit their resolution through imposition of master narratives; (3) a *rhizomatic validity* that simultaneously asserts and undermines interpretations by deferring the authority of claims to a network of competing, interanimating explanations; and (4) a *situated validity* that privileges partial, disruptive, and excessive feminine discourse to clarify patriarchal framing of knowledge fields.

These evaluative positions of quasi-positivism, interpretivism, and critical postmodernism reflect a range of standards by which qualitative researchers legitimate their studies of organizational communication. It is important to remember that these "technologies of validation" are not equally desired by all qualitative research audiences; indeed, each will have its preferred standards. Interpretivist-oriented readers, for example, may reject the quasi-positivistic demand for researchers to predetermine the aggregate contexts of their sites as an obstacle to achieving inductive understanding. In this view, such a practice might influence researchers to "see" organizational phenomena as exemplars of larger trends, rather than as local, practical accomplishments. Alternately, quasi-positivists may see this criterion as necessary to standardize and focus succeeding generations of qualitative research. Ultimately, these disagreements indicate how qualitative researchers *socially construct* validity in their discourse, within particular sets of codes and contracts with readers. The validity of qualitative methods hinges, then, not on their accuracy per se, but on their utility for the various evolving projects of organizational communication study (such as teaching, theory building, consulting, and research). At present, it appears that the participants in those projects—either through tolerance or failure to reflect on their root assumptions (Stewart, 1994)—are willing to live with ambiguity and diversity in evaluative criteria. The process by which disciplines develop and apply evaluative criteria for organizational research, of course, merits its own study (Jacques, 1992).

## FUTURE ISSUES AND CHALLENGES FOR QUALITATIVE RESEARCHERS

Several issues and challenges will confront qualitative researchers in organizational communication in the new millennium, two of which we will consider here. First, we are excited about the challenges and possibilities for organizational communication research created by the emerging phenomena of *virtuality* and *cyberspace* (see Davidow & Malone, 1992; King & Cushman, 1995; Markham, 1998; Pruitt & Barrett, 1991; Reid, 1995). These terms index large-scale economic, technological, and cultural forces currently transforming post-Fordist organizational reality that must be studied by communication scholars. For example, researchers will need to become more sensitive to how computer networks and virtual workspaces destabilize the presumably formal structures of organizations by facilitating the bypassing of hierarchies and the development of fine, complex gradations of fluid memberships (staff, consultant, "temp," etc.) available to employees through these technologies. In addition, the increasing use of computer-mediated communication and virtual reality systems among members affords researchers new opportunities to study the remapping of communicative codes and conventions from face-to-face onto mediated cultural realms. Researchers who engage in text-based qualitative research will need to understand how multimedia and hypertext technologies complicate and destabilize the very notion of the organizational "text." Finally, researchers should investigate how virtual systems recode working bodies into organizational cyborgs, holograms, and tokens of desire (see Stone, 1991).

Second, we are intrigued by the challenges and opportunities created by the topic of organizational *spirituality* (see Goodall, 1996; Reason, 1993). We believe that spirituality offers powerful narratives of purpose that alternately complement and subvert "official" organizational culture and control practices. As a medium of communion with a "higher power," spirituality potentially relativizes organizational authority and forms a competing source of identification for organizational members. Of course, the relationship between spirituality and organization is not only oppositional, because spirituality also provides a reassuring and nurturing narrative that compensates for the transient, fragmented experience of organizational life. In addition, members of "minority" groups present alternative spiritualities (besides traditional Western European Judeo-Christianity) that circulate in organizational cultures and structures, with important consequences for the legitimation of power.[8] Organizational communication researchers, as a result, can study spirituality as a form of community and experience that alternately flows with, in opposition to, and parallel to existing organizational structures.

In the final analysis, we in organizational communication must find ways to make more meaningful changes in our organizations and our communication. If we are truly honest with ourselves, we must admit that, for the most part, we have not really made a difference in the lives of the men and women we have studied. Certainly, we will continue to publish our research in academic books and journals, but we must energize those publications with better and more provocative writing so they are read by more than the students and instructors in our classes (who often do so involuntarily). We should also continue to engage in cross-disciplinary research with scholars from other fields. We should develop more meaningful relationships with the men and women we study in organizations. And we should engage in activist research and political action to make organizations safe and humane places for the work of communication, and the communication of work.

## NOTES

1. I (Trujillo) was a Ph.D. student at Utah in 1981, and I felt truly blessed to be a participant at the first Alta conference and what seemed to be a defining moment in the field. Although I had read many organizational ethnographies as an undergraduate sociology major in the 1970s, I experienced a powerful excitement as I realized that scholars in organizational communication were crying for alternatives to the functionalist tradition. Several graduate students from the University of Texas also attended the conference, and I believe, no doubt naively, that we added an enthusiasm to the gathering that can only come from young, happy, and ripening grad students. In fact, after the conference, grad students from Utah and Texas declared our universities to be "sister schools," and we even had T-shirts printed with our new logo: an armadillo skiing down a mountain slope.

I (Taylor) was a member of the graduate cohort that succeeded Trujillo at Utah between 1984 and 1990. While I did not attend an Alta conference until 1989, I was drawn inexorably to the phenomena (if not the traditional research practices) of organizational communication due to my interest in critical theory and interpretive methods. I consider myself to be a highly interested "poacher" whose interests in discourse, power, and institutions intersect with the evolving projects of organizational communication research. It is significant in the writing of this chapter that Trujillo is primarily an ethnographer who has made use of critical theory, while I am primarily a cultural critic who has made use of organizational ethnography.

2. We use the term *meta-analysis* in two ways in this chapter. In most cases—such as the use of the term here—we are referring to reflexive intellectual work that investigates the premises and processes of published research. Only once do we use the term in its specialized meaning as a research technology for resolving statistical variance in the cumulative findings of a particular research area. When we use the term in this latter sense, we refer explicitly to its objectivist function.

3. We would like to offer a personal caveat at this point. Although some of our scholarship has been conducted from an avowedly feminist perspective (see Taylor, 1993; Taylor & Conrad, 1992; Trujillo, 1991, 1995), one of us (Trujillo) considers himself to be a "feminist," while the other (Taylor) is more comfortable with the label "pro-feminist," believing that biology is to some extent both boundary and destiny. However, I (Trujillo) have tired of continuing to debate those who argue—often in convention hotel hallways—that men cannot be feminists. Recently, I was pressured to drop out of an online discussion group after a debate raged on for several weeks about whether or not men should be "allowed" to participate, since the group involved women telling very personal stories. Even though most in the group agreed that the men who were part of the group were sensitive to the issues discussed by the women (and that it was virtually impossible to tell whether someone was really a man or a woman from their e-mail address anyway), the consensus was that men would be allowed to read messages but could not post any replies. When I quit the group in protest and called myself a "feminist," I received several replies, some of which chastised me for using that label, since I "could not possibly know what it was like to experience life as a woman."

I (Taylor) offer a similar exchange in which a feminist scholar in our field disclosed her reluctance to read one of my articles (1993) because "you're, well . . . you know . . . " Generally, I concede my limits in embracing all feminisms equally, and I try to keep the conversation going as a means of personal and professional growth. We both agree that our field should support all men and women who take the difficult and self-implicating journey to promote feminist research in organizational communication.

4. According to Van Maanen (1988), *realist tales* are characterized by four conventions: (1) *experiential author(ity)*, "the almost complete absence of the author from most segments of the finished text" (p. 46) focusing solely on the members of the culture who were studied; (2) a *documentary style* of writing "focused on minute, sometimes precious, but thoroughly mundane details of everyday life among the people studied" (p. 48); (3) a focus on the *native's point of view* using "accounts and explanations by members of the culture of the events in their lives" (p. 49); and (4) *interpretive omnipotence* whereby the researcher implies or directly asserts that his or her interpretations are the plausible ones with few questions about "whether they got it right, or whether there might be yet another, equally useful way to study,

characterize, display, read, or otherwise understand the accumulated field materials" (p. 51).

5. In his review of the first draft of this chapter, John Van Maanen shared a story with us that was told to him by the former editors of the *Journal of Contemporary Ethnography.* The story described how typesetters and copyeditors at Sage (the press that publishes *JCE*) fight for their assignments to *JCE* issues, because the articles are far more interesting and fun to edit than articles from most other scholarly journals.

6. For example, one of the authors (Trujillo) submitted a team-written postmodern ethnography for the special issue on ethnography in *Communication Studies* edited by Anderson and Holmes (1995). Anderson returned our manuscript *unreviewed* because, as he wrote, it was "too avant-garde." We subsequently submitted the same manuscript to the *Journal of Contemporary Ethnography;* it received a "revise and resubmit" review and was subsequently accepted for publication (see Communication Studies, 1997).

7. The formation in 1998 of an Ethnography Division within the National Communication Association is a significant development in this regard. We also experienced the politics of poetics firsthand in writing this chapter. When we decided to write the chapter together, we were in constant contact with each other through e-mail. As we developed our ideas (and our relationship), we challenged each other to think of ways to represent some of the issues and challenges of the chapter in the *writing* (the form) of the chapter. We came up with the idea of writing the chapter as an e-mail conversation, revealing our own personal perspectives on the issues while reflexively positioning ourselves in the chapter. However, when we ran this idea past Jablin and Putnam, the editors of this handbook, they instructed us not to write it as a dialogue but to write it in a more traditional didactic style to conform to the other chapters in the book. We are not condemning this decision per se, since we respect the editors and their editorial judgment (and we did, after all, want our chapter to be included in their handbook), but we noted the irony nonetheless.

8. One author (Taylor) knows a woman who has been both the subject and object of *pagan hexes* in conflicts with her fellow employees, actions that certainly exceed the boundaries of traditional disciplinary procedures.

# REFERENCES

Albrecht, T. L., & Ropp, V. A. (1982). The study of network structuring in organizations through the use of method triangulation. *Western Journal of Speech Communication, 46,* 162-178.

Aldag, R. J., & Stearns, T. M. (1988). Issues in research methodology. *Journal of Management, 14,* 253-276.

Allen, M. W., Gotcher, J. M., & Seibert, J. H. (1993). A decade of organizational communication research: Journal articles 1980-1991. In S. A. Deetz (Ed.), *Communication yearbook 16* (pp. 252-330). Newbury Park, CA: Sage.

Alvesson, M. (1995). The meaning and meaninglessness of postmodernism: Some ironic remarks. *Organization Studies, 15,* 1047-1075.

Alvesson, M., & Deetz, S. (1996). Critical theory and postmodernism approaches to organizational studies. In S. R. Clegg, C. Hardy, & W. R. Nord (Eds.), *Handbook of organization studies* (pp. 191-217). London: Sage.

Alvesson, M., & Willmott, H. (1992). *Critical management studies.* London: Sage.

Andersen, P. A. (1993). Beyond criticism: The activist turn in ideological debate. *Western Journal of Communication, 57,* 247-256.

Anderson, J. (1987). *Communication research: Issues and methods.* New York: McGraw-Hill.

Anderson, J. (Ed.), & Holmes, M. E. (Assoc. Ed.). (1995). Ethnography [Special issue]. *Communication Studies, 46.*

Banks, S. P. (1994). Performing flight announcements: The case of flight attendants' work discourse. *Text and Performance Quarterly, 14,* 253-267.

Bantz, C. R. (1983). Naturalistic research traditions. In L. L. Putnam & M. E. Pacanowsky (Eds.), *Communication and organizations: An interpretive approach* (pp. 55-72). Beverly Hills, CA: Sage.

Bantz, C. R. (1993). *Understanding organizations: Interpreting organizational communication cultures.* Columbia: University of South Carolina Press.

Barker, J. R., & Cheney, G. (1994). The concept and the practices of discipline in contemporary organizational life. *Communication Monographs, 61,* 19-43.

Barley, S. R. (1983). Semiotics and the study of occupational and organizational cultures. *Administrative Science Quarterly, 28,* 393-413.

Barnard, C. I. (1938). *The functions of the executive.* Cambridge, MA: Harvard University Press.

Beach, W. A. (1994). Orienting to the phenomenon. In F. L. Casmir (Ed.), *Building communication theories: A socio-cultural approach* (pp. 133-163). Hillsdale, NJ: Lawrence Erlbaum.

Beach, W. A. (1995). Preserving and constraining options: "Okays" and "official" priorities in medical interviews. In G. H. Morris & R. Cheneil (Eds.), *Talk of the clinic* (pp. 259-289). Hillsdale, NJ: Lawrence Erlbaum.

Becker, H. S., Geer, B., Hughes, E. C., & Strauss, A. L. (1961). *Boys in white: Student culture in medical school.* Chicago: University of Chicago Press.

Bell, D. (1993). Introduction 1: The context. In D. Bell, P. Caplan, & W. J. Karim (Eds.), *Gendered fields: Women, men and ethnography* (pp. 1-17). New York: Routledge.

Bell, E., & Forbes, L. C. (1994). Office folklore in the academic paperwork empire: The interstitial space of gendered (con)texts. *Text and Performance Quarterly, 14,* 181-196.

Benson, T. W. (1981). Another shooting in Cowtown. *Quarterly Journal of Speech, 67,* 347-406.

Beyer, J. M., Dunbar, R. L., & Meyer, A. D. (1988). *Academy of Management Review, 13,* 483-489.

Bormann, E. G. (1972). Fantasy and rhetorical vision: The rhetorical criticism of social reality. *Quarterly Journal of Speech, 58,* 396-407.

Bormann, E. G., Pratt, J., & Putnam, L. (1978). Power, authority, and sex: Male response to female leadership. *Communication Monographs, 45,* 119-155.

Bostrom, R., & Donohew, L. (1992). The case for empiricism: Clarifying fundamental issues in communication theory. *Communication Monographs, 59,* 109-129.

Brown, M. H. (1985). That reminds me of a story: Speech action in organizational socialization. *Western Journal of Speech Communication, 49,* 27-42.

Brown, M. H., & McMillan, J. (1991). Culture as text: The development of an organizational narrative. *Southern Communication Journal, 57,* 49-60.

Brown, R. H. (1977). *A poetic for sociology.* Cambridge, UK: Cambridge University Press.

Browner, C. H., & Kubarski, K. (1991). The paradoxical control of American clerks. *Organization Studies, 12,* 233-250.

Bristow, A. R., & Esper, J. A. (1984). A feminist research ethos. *Humanity and Society, 8,* 489-496.

Browning, L. D. (1978). A grounded organizational communication theory derived from qualitative data. *Communication Monographs, 45,* 93-109.

Bryman, A. (1988). Introduction: Inside accounts and social research in organizations. In A. Bryman (Ed.), *Doing research in organizations* (pp. 1-20). New York: Routledge.

Bullis, C. (1993). Organizational socialization research: Enabling, constraining, and shifting perspectives. *Communication Monographs, 60,* 10-17.

Burawoy, M. (1979). *Manufacturing consent: Changes in the labor process under monopoly capitalism.* Chicago: University of Chicago Press.

Burns, C., Dishman, E., Johnson, B., & Verplank, B. (1995, August 8). *"Informance": Min(d)ing future contexts for scenario-based interaction design.* Performance, Palo Alto, CA.

Burrell, G. (1988). Modernism, postmodernism and organizational analysis 2: The contribution of Michel Foucault. *Organization Studies, 9,* 221-275.

Burrell, G., & Morgan, G. (1979). *Sociological paradigms and organizational analysis.* London: Heinemann.

Burrell, N. A., Buzzanell, P. M., & McMillan, J. J. (1992). Feminine tensions in conflict situations as revealed by metaphoric analyses. *Management Communication Quarterly, 6,* 115-149.

Buzzanell, P. M. (1994). Gaining a voice: Feminist organizational communication theorizing. *Management Communication Quarterly, 7,* 339-383.

Calás, M. B., & Smircich, L. (1991). Voicing seduction to silence leadership. *Organization Studies, 12,* 567-601.

Carbaugh, D. (1988). Cultural terms and tensions in the speech at a television station. *Western Journal of Speech Communication, 52,* 216-237.

Carbaugh, D. (1989-1990). The critical voice in ethnography of communication research. *Research on Language and Social Interaction, 23,* 261-282.

Carbaugh, D. (1991). Communication and cultural interpretation. *Quarterly Journal of Speech, 77,* 336-342.

Cheney, G. (1991). *Rhetoric in an organizational society: Managing multiple identities.* Columbia: University of South Carolina Press.

Cheney, G. (1995). Democracy in the workplace: Theory and practice from the perspective of communication. *Journal of Applied Communication Research, 23,* 167-200.

Cheney, G., & Vibbert, S. L. (1987). Corporate discourse: Public relations and issue management. In F. M. Jablin, L. L. Putnam, K. H. Roberts, & L. W. Porter (Eds.), *Handbook of organizational communication: An interdisciplinary perspective* (pp. 165-194). Newbury Park, CA: Sage.

Chesbro, J. W., Cragan, J. F., & McCullough, P. (1973). The small group techniques of the radical revolutionary: A synthetic study of consciousness raising. *Speech Monographs, 40,* 136-146.

Clair, R. P. (1993a). The bureaucratization, commodification, and privatization of sexual harassment through institutional discourse: A study of the "Big Ten" universities. *Management Communication Quarterly, 7,* 123-157.

Clair, R. P. (1993b). The use of framing devices to sequester organizational narratives: Hegemony and harassment. *Communication Monographs, 60,* 113-136.

Clegg, S. R. (1975). *The theory of power and organization.* London: Routledge and Kegan Paul.

Clifford, J., & Marcus, G. E. (Eds.). (1986). *Writing culture: The poetics and politics of ethnography.* Berkeley: University of California Press.

Communication Studies 298 [California State University, Sacramento]. (1997). Fragments of self at the postmodern bar. *Journal of Contemporary Ethnography, 26,* 251-292.

Conquergood, D. (1989). Poetics, play, process, and power: The performative turn in anthropology. *Text and Performance Quarterly, 9,* 82-88.

Conquergood, D. (1991). Rethinking ethnography: Towards a critical cultural politics. *Communication Monographs, 58,* 179-187.

Conquergood, D., Friesema, P., Hunter, A., & Mansbridge, J. (1990). *Dispersed ethnicity and community integration: Newcomers and established residents in the Albany Park area of Chicago.* Evanston: Northwestern University, Center for Urban Affairs and Policy Research.

Conrad, C. (1983). Organizational power: Faces and symbolic forms. In L. L. Putnam & M. E. Pacanowsky (Eds.), *Communication and organizations: An interpretive approach* (pp. 173-194). Beverly Hills, CA: Sage.

Conrad, C. (1985). Chrysanthemums and swords: A reading of contemporary organizational communication theory and research. *Southern Speech Communication Journal, 50,* 189-200.

Cowell, C. (1972). Group process as metaphor. *Journal of Communication, 22,* 113-123.

Crawford, L. (1996). Personal ethnography. *Communication Monographs, 63,* 158-170.

Davidow, W. H., & Malone, M. S. (1992). *The virtual corporation: Structuring and revitalizing the corporation for the 21st century.* New York: Harper Collins.

Deal, T. E., & Kennedy, A. A. (1982). *Corporate cultures: The rites and rituals of corporate life.* Reading, MA: Addison-Wesley.

De Certeau, M. (1984). *The practice of everyday life.* Berkeley: University of California Press.

Deetz, S. (1982). Critical interpretive research in organizational communication. *Western Journal of Speech Communication, 46,* 131-149.

Deetz, S. (1992). *Democracy in the age of corporate colonization.* Albany: State University of New York Press.

Deetz, S. (1994). The micro-politics of identity formation in the workplace: The case of a knowledge intensive firm. *Human Studies, 17,* 23-44.

Denzin, N. K. (1994). The art and politics of interpretation. In N. K. Denzin & Y. S. Lincoln (Eds.), *Handbook of qualitative research* (pp. 500-515). Thousand Oaks, CA: Sage.

Denzin, N. K., & Lincoln, Y. S. (1994). Introduction: Entering the field of qualitative research. In N. K. Denzin & Y. S. Lincoln (Eds.), *Handbook of qualitative research* (pp. 1-17). Thousand Oaks, CA: Sage.

Donovan, J. (1985). *Feminist theory: The intellectual traditions of American feminism.* New York: Unger.

Dorst, J. (1989). *The written suburb: An American site, an ethnographic dilemma.* Philadelphia: University of Philadelphia Press.

Drew, P., & Heritage, J. (Eds.). (1992). *Talk at work: Interaction in institutional settings.* Cambridge, UK: Cambridge University Press.

Duffy, M. E. (1985). A critique of research: A feminist perspective. *Health Care for Women International, 6,* 341-352.

Eastland, L. S. (1993). The dialectical nature of ethnography: Liminality, reflexivity, and understanding. In S. L. Herndon & G. L. Kreps (Eds.), *Qualitative research: Applications in organizational communication* (pp. 121-138). Cresskill, NJ: Hampton.

Eisenberg, E. M. (1984). Ambiguity as strategy in organizational communication. *Communication Monographs, 51,* 227-242.

Eisenhardt, K. E. (1989). Building theories from case study research. *Academy of Management Review, 14,* 532-550.

Ellis, C. (1993). Telling a story of a sudden death. *Sociological Quarterly, 34,* 711-730.

Ellis, C., & Bochner, A. (Eds.). (1996). Taking ethnography into the twenty-first century [Special issue]. *Journal of Contemporary Ethnography, 25.*

Featherstone, M. (1991). *Consumer culture and postmodernism.* London: Sage.

Faules, D. (1982). The use of multi-methods in the organizational setting. *Western Journal of Speech Communication, 46,* 150-161.

Ferguson, K. E. (1984). *The feminist case against bureaucracy.* Philadelphia: Temple University Press.

Ferment in the field. (1983). *Journal of Communication, 33.*

Ferree, M. M., & Martin, P. Y. (1995). *Feminist organizations: Harvest of the new women's movement.* Philadelphia: Temple University Press.

Fine, M. G. (1993). New voices in organizational communication: A feminist commentary and critique. In S. P. Bowen & N. Wyatt (Eds.), *Transforming visions: Feminist critiques in communication studies* (pp. 125-166). Cresskill, NJ: Hampton.

Finet, D. (1993). Effects of boundary spanning communication on the sociopolitical delegitimation of an organization. *Management Communication Quarterly, 7,* 36-66.

Fiske, J. (1991). Writing ethnographies: Contributions to a dialogue. *Quarterly Journal of Speech, 77,* 330-335.

Fitch, K. L. (1994a). Criteria for evidence in qualitative research. *Western Journal of Communication, 58,* 32-38.

Fitch, K. L. (1994b). Culture, ideology and interpersonal communication research. In S. A. Deetz (Ed.), *Communication yearbook 17* (pp. 104-135). Thousand Oaks, CA: Sage.

Flick, U. (1992). Triangulation revisited: Strategy of validation or alternative? *Journal for the Theory of Social Behavior, 22,* 175-198.

Forester, J. (1992). Critical ethnography: On fieldwork in a Habermasian way. In M. Alvesson & H. Willmott (Eds.), *Critical management studies* (pp. 46-65). Newbury Park, CA: Sage.

Foss, K. A., & Foss, S. K. (1994). Personal experience as evidence in feminist scholarship. *Western Journal of Communication, 58,* 39-43.

Freeman, J. (1992). The perfect Valentine. *Journal of Contemporary Ethnography, 20*, 478-483.

Frost, P. J., Moore, L. F., Louis, M. R., Lundberg, C. C., & Martin, J. (1991). Contexts and choices in organizational research. In P. J. Frost, L. F. Moore, M. R. Louis, C. C. Lundberg, & J. Martin (Eds.), *Reframing organizational culture* (pp. 327-334). Newbury Park, CA: Sage.

Garfinkel, H. (1967). *Studies in ethnomethdology.* Englewood Cliffs, NJ: Prentice Hall.

Geertz, C. (1973). *The interpretation of cultures.* New York: Basic Books.

Geertz, C. (1988). *Works and lives: The anthropologist as author.* Stanford, CA: Stanford University Press.

Geist, P., & Hardesty, M. (1990). Ideological positioning in professionals' narratives of quality medical care. In N. K. Denzin (Ed.), *Studies in symbolic interaction* (Vol. 11, pp. 257-284). Greenwich, CT: JAI.

Gergen, M. M. (1988). Toward a feminist metatheory and methodology in the social sciences. In M. M. Gergen (Ed.), *Feminist thought and the structure of knowledge* (pp. 87-104). New York: New York University Press.

Giddens, A. (1979). *Central problems in social theory.* London: Macmillan.

Glaser, B. G., & Strauss, A. L. (1967). *The discovery of grounded theory: Strategies for qualitative research.* Chicago: Aldine.

Golde, P. (1986). *Women in the field: Anthropological experiences* (2nd ed.). Berkeley: University of California Press.

Goodall, H. L. (1989). *Casing a promised land: The autobiography of an organizational detective as cultural ethnographer.* Carbondale: Southern Illinois University Press.

Goodall, H. L. (1991), *Living in the rock 'n roll mystery: Reading context, self, and others as clues.* Carbondale: Southern Illinois University Press.

Goodall, H. L. (1992). Empowerment, culture, and postmodern organizing: Deconstructing the Nordstrom Employee Handbook. *Journal of Organizational Change Management, 5*, 25-30.

Goodall, H. L. (1996). *Divine signs: Connecting spirit to community.* Carbondale: Southern Illinois University Press.

Gottschalk, D. (1995). Ethnographic fragments in postmodern spaces. *Journal of Contemporary Ethnography, 24*, 195-228.

Gusterson, H. (1993). Exploding anthropology's canon in the world of the bomb. *Journal of Contemporary Ethnography, 22*, 59-79.

Gutek, B. A. (1985). *Sex in the workplace.* San Francisco: Jossey-Bass.

Hammersley, M. (1992). *What's wrong with ethnography? Methodological explorations.* London: Routledge.

Hansen, C. D., & Kahnweiler, W. M. (1993). Storytelling: An instrument for understanding the dynamics of corporate relationships. *Human Relations, 46,* 1391-1409.

Harding, S. (1986). *The science question in feminism.* Ithaca, NY: Cornell University Press.

Hawes, L. C. (1983). Epilogue. In L. L. Putnam & M. E. Pacanowsky (Eds.), *Communication and organizations: An interpretive approach* (pp. 257-259). Beverly Hills, CA: Sage.

Hawes, L. C. (Ed.). (1994). Performance, organization and culture [Special issue]. *Text and Performance Quarterly, 14.*

Hawes, L., Pacanowsky, M., & Faules, D. (1988). Approaches to the study of organizations: A conversation among three schools of thought. In G. M. Goldhaber & G. A. Barnett (Eds.), *Handbook of organizational communication* (pp. 41-54). Norwood, NJ: Ablex.

Hayano, D. M. (1982). *Poker faces.* Berkeley: University of California Press.

Hearn, J., Sheppard, D. L., Tancred-Sheriff, P., & Burrell, G. (Eds.). (1989). *The sexuality of organization.* London: Sage.

Heritage, J. (1984). *Garfinkel and ethnomethodology.* Cambridge, UK: Polity.

Holmer-Nadesan, M. (1996). Organizational identity and space of action. *Organization Studies, 7*, 49-81.

Jackson, S. (1993). Ethnography and the audition: Performance as ideological critique. *Text and Performance Quarterly, 13*, 21-43.

Jacques, R. (1992). Critique and theory building: Producing knowledge "from the kitchen." *Academy of Management Review, 17*, 582-606.

Jacques, R. (1996). *Manufacturing the employee: Management knowledge from the 19th to the 21st centuries.* Thousand Oaks, CA: Sage.

Jayaratne, T. E., & Stewart, A. J. (1991). Quantitative and qualitative methods in the social sciences. In M. M. Fonow & J. A. Cook (Eds.), *Beyond methodology: Feminist scholarship as lived research* (pp. 85-106). Bloomington: Indiana University Press.

Jones, S. H. (1996). *Kaleidoscope notes: An ethnography.* Master's thesis, California State University, Sacramento.

Kanter, R. M. (1977). *Men and women of the corporation.* New York: Basic Books.

Kauffman, B. J. (1992). Feminist facts: Interview strategies and political subjects in ethnography. *Communication Theory, 2*, 187-206.

Kilduff, M. (1993). Deconstructing organizations. *Academy of Management Review, 18*, 13-31.

King, S. S., & Cushman, D. P. (1995). The high-speed management of organizational communication: Cushman, King and associates. In D. P. Cushman & B. Kovacic (Eds.), *Watershed research traditions in human communication theory* (pp. 177-210). Albany: State University of New York Press.

Kirk, J., & Miller, M. L. (1986). *Reliability and validity in qualitative research.* Beverly Hills, CA: Sage.

Knight, J. P. (1990). Literature as equipment for killing: Performance as rhetoric in military training camps. *Text and Performance Quarterly, 10,* 157-168.

Kreps, G. L., Herndon, S. L., & Arneson, P. (1993). Introduction: The power of qualitative research to address organizational issues. In S. L. Herndon & G. L. Kreps (Eds.), *Qualitative research: Applications in organizational communication* (pp. 1-18). Cresskill, NJ: Hampton.

Krizek, B. (1992). Remembrances and expectations: The investment of identity in the changing of Comiskey. *Elysian Fields Quarterly, 11,* 30-51.

Lannamann, J. W. (1994). The problem with disempowering ideology. In S. A. Deetz (Ed.), *Communication yearbook 17* (pp. 136-147). Thousand Oaks, CA: Sage.

Lather, P. (1993). Fertile obsession: Validity after poststructuralism. *Sociological Quarterly, 35,* 673-693.

Ligtenberg, A. K. (1994). *A woman's place is in the organization: An analysis of women's metaphors and stories of organizational life.* Master's thesis, California State University, Sacramento.

Lincoln, Y. S. (1990). The making of a constructive: A remembrance of transformations past. In E. G. Guba (Ed.), *The paradigm dialog* (pp. 67-87). Newbury Park, CA: Sage.

Lindlof, T. R. (1995). *Qualitative communication research methods.* Thousand Oaks, CA: Sage.

Linstead, S. (1993). Deconstruction in the study of organizations. In J. Hassard & M. Parker (Eds.), *Postmodernism and organizations* (pp. 49-70). Newbury Park, CA: Sage.

Lont, C. M. (1990). Persistence of subcultural organizations: An analysis surrounding the process of subcultural change. *Communication Quarterly, 38,* 1-12.

Loy, P. H., & Stewart, L. P. (1984). The extent and effects of the sexual harassment of working women. *Sociological Focus, 17,* 31-43.

Lukes, S. (1974). *Power: A radical view.* London: Macmillan.

Maguire, M., & Mohtar, L. F. (1994). Performance and the celebration of a subaltern counterpublic. *Text and Performance Quarterly, 14,* 238-252.

Malinowski, B. (1948). *Magic, science, and religion, and other essays.* New York: Natural History Press. (Original work published 1916)

Marcus, G., & Fischer, M. (1986). *Anthropology as cultural critique: An experimental moment in the human sciences.* Chicago: University of Chicago Press.

Markham, A. (1998). *Life online: Researching real experiene in virtual space.* Walnut Creek, CA: Alta Mira Press.

Marshall, J. (1993). Viewing organizational communication from a feminist perspective: A critique and some offerings. In S. A. Deetz (Ed.), *Communication yearbook 16* (pp. 122-143). Newbury Park, CA: Sage.

Martin, P. Y. (1989). The moral politics of organizations: Reflections of an unlikely feminist. *Journal of Applied Behavioral Science, 25,* 451-470.

Martin, J. (1990). Re-reading Weber: A feminist analysis. In E. Freeman (Ed.), *Ruffin series in business ethics.* Oxford, UK: Oxford University Press.

Martin, J. (1992). *Cultures in organizations: Three perspectives.* New York: Oxford University Press.

McMillan, J. J. (1987). In search of the organizational persona: A rationale for studying organizations rhetorically. In L. Thayer (Ed.), *Organization–communication: Emerging perspectives II* (pp. 21-45). Norwood, NJ: Ablex.

Melody, W. H., & Mansell, R. E. (1983). The debate over critical vs. administrative research: Circularity or challenge? *Journal of Communication, 33,* 103-116.

Mies, M. (1981). Towards a methodology for feminist research. In G. Bowles & R. Duelli-Klein (Eds.), *Theories of women's studies* (Vol. 2, pp. 25-46). Berkeley: University of California, Women's Studies Department.

Miles, M. B., & Huberman, A. M. (1994). *Qualitative data analysis* (2nd ed.). Thousand Oaks, CA: Sage.

Moore, L. F. (1991). Inside Aunt Virginia's kitchen. In P. J. Frost, L. F. Moore, M. R. Louis, C. Lundberg, & J. Martin (Eds.), *Reframing organizational culture* (pp. 366-372). Newbury Park, CA: Sage.

Mumby, D. K. (1987). The political function of narrative in organizations. *Communication Monographs, 54,* 113-127.

Mumby, D. K. (1988). *Communication and power in organizations: Discourse, ideology, and domination.* Norwood, NJ: Ablex.

Mumby, D. K. (1994). Critical organizational communication studies: The next 10 years. *Communication Monographs, 60,* 18-25.

Mumby, D., & Putnam, L. L. (1992). The politics of emotion: A feminist reading of bounded rationality. *Academy of Management Review, 17,* 465-486.

Muto, J. (1993). "Who's that in my bed?" The strange bedfellows made by the politics of applied qualitative organizational research. In S. L. Herndon & G. L. Kreps (Eds.), *Qualitative research: Applications in organizational communication* (pp. 19-28). Cresskill, NJ: Hampton.

Myerhoff, B., & Ruby, J. (1982). Introduction. In J. Ruby (Ed.), *A crack in the mirror: Reflexive perspectives in anthropology.* Philadelphia: University of Pennsylvania Press.

Nelson, C., Treichler, P. A., & Grossberg, L. (1992). Cultural studies. In L. Grossberg, C. Nelson, & P. A. Treichler (Eds.), *Cultural studies* (pp. 1-6). New York: Routledge.

Neumann, M. (1992). The trail through experience: Finding self in the recollection of travel. In C. Ellis & M. G. Flaherty (Eds.), *Investigating subjectivity:*

*Research on lived experience* (pp. 176-204). Newbury Park, CA: Sage.

Neumann, M. (1994). The contested spaces of cultural dialogue. In S. A. Deetz (Ed.), *Communication yearbook 17* (pp. 148-158). Thousand Oaks, CA: Sage.

Neumann, M., & Eason, D. (1990). Casino world: Bringing it all back home. *Cultural Studies, 4,* 45-60.

Ollenburger, J. C., & Moore, H. A. (1992). *A sociology of women: The intersection of patriarchy, capitalism and colonization.* Englewood Cliffs, NJ: Prentice Hall.

Pacanowsky, M. E. (1983). A small-town cop: Communication in, out, and about a crisis. In L. L. Putnam & M. E. Pacanowsky (Eds.), *Communication and organizations: An interpretive approach* (pp. 261-282). Beverly Hills, CA: Sage.

Pacanowsky, M. E. (1988). Slouching towards Chicago. *Quarterly Journal of Speech, 74,* 453-467.

Pacanowsky, M. E., & O'Donnell-Trujillo, N. (1982). Communication and organizational cultures. *Western Journal of Speech Communication, 46,* 115-130.

Pacanowsky, M. E., & O'Donnell-Trujillo, N. (1983). Organizational communication as cultural performance. *Communication Monographs, 50,* 126-147.

Pacanowsky, M. E., & Putnam, L. L. (1982). Introduction. *Western Journal of Speech Communication, 46,* 114.

Paget, M. (1990). Performing the text. *Journal of Contemporary Ethnography, 19,* 136-155.

Philipsen, G. (1989-1990). Some initial thoughts on the perils of "critique" in the ethnographic study of communicative practices. *Research on Language and Social Interaction, 23,* 251-260.

Phillips, N. (1995). Telling organizational tales: On the role of narrative fiction in the study of organizations. *Organization Studies, 16,* 625-649.

Podsakoff, P. M., & Dalton, D. R. (1987). Research methodology in organizational studies. *Journal of Management, 13,* 419-441.

Presnell, M. (1994). Postmodern ethnography: From representing the other to co-producing a text. In K. Carter & M. Presnell (Eds.), *Interpretive approaches to interpersonal communication* (pp. 11-43). Albany: State University of New York Press.

Pruitt, S., & Barrett, T. (1991). Corporate virtual workspace. In M. Benedikt (Ed.), *Cyberspace: First steps* (pp. 383-409). Cambridge, MA: MIT Press.

Putnam, L. L. (1994). Productive conflict: Negotiation as implicit coordination. *International Journal of Conflict Management, 5,* 284-298.

Putnam, L. L., Bantz, C., Deetz, S., Mumby, D., & Van Maanen, J. (1993). Ethnography versus critical theory: Debating organizational research. *Journal of Management Inquiry, 2,* 221-235.

Putnam, L. L., & Pacanowsky, M. E. (Eds.). (1983). *Communication and organizations: An interpretive approach.* Beverly Hills, CA: Sage.

Putnam, L. L., Van Hoeven, S. A., & Bullis, C. A. (1991). The role of rituals and fantasy themes in teachers' bargaining. *Western Journal of Communication, 55,* 85-103.

Rakow, L. F. (1986). Rethinking gender research in communication. *Journal of Communication, 36,* 11-26.

Reason, P. (1993). Sacred experience and sacred science. *Journal of Management Inquiry, 2,* 10-27.

Redding, W. C. (1985). Stumbling toward identity: The emergence of organizational communication as a field of study. In R. D. McPhee & P. K. Tompkins (Eds.), *Organizational communication: Traditional themes and new directions* (pp. 15-54). Beverly Hills, CA: Sage.

Reid, E. (1995). Virtual worlds: Culture and imagination. In S. Jones (Ed.), *Cyberspace: Computer-mediated communication and community* (pp. 164-183). Thousand Oaks, CA: Sage.

Reinharz, S. (1992). *Feminist methods in social research.* New York: Oxford University Press.

Richardson, L. (1992). The consequences of poetic representation: Writing the other, rewriting the self. In C. Ellis & M. G. Flaherty (Eds.), *Investigating subjectivity: Research on lived experience* (pp. 125-140). Newbury Park, CA: Sage.

Richardson, L. (1994). Writing: A method of inquiry. In N. K. Denzin & Y. S. Lincoln (Eds.), *Handbook of qualitative research* (pp. 516-529). Thousand Oaks, CA: Sage.

Riley, P. (1983). A structurationist account of political culture. *Administrative Science Quarterly, 28,* 414-437.

Roethlisberger, F. J., & Dickson, W. (1939). *Management and the worker.* New York: John Wiley.

Rogers, R. A. (1994). Rhythm and the performance of organization. *Text and Performance Quarterly, 14,* 222-237.

Ronai, C. R. (1992). The reflexive self through narrative: A night in the life of an erotic dancer/researcher. In C. Ellis & M. G. Flaherty (Eds.), *Investigating subjectivity: Research on lived experience* (pp. 102-124). Newbury Park, CA: Sage.

Ronai, C. R. (1995). Multiple reflections of child sex abuse: An argument for a layered account. *Journal of Contemporary Ethnography, 18,* 271-298.

Rosaldo, R. (1989). *Culture and truth: The remaking of social analysis.* Boston: Beacon.

Rosen, M. (1991). Coming to terms with the field: Understanding and doing organizational ethnography. *Journal of Management Studies, 28,* 1-24.

Scheibel, D. (1992). Faking identity in Clubland: The communicative performance of "fake ID." *Text and Performance Quarterly, 12,* 160-175.

Scheibel, D. (1994). Graffiti and "film school" culture: Displaying alienation. *Communication Monographs, 61,* 1-18.

Schwartzman, H. B. (1993). *Ethnography in organizations.* Newbury Park, CA: Sage.

Sharf, B. F. (1978). A rhetorical analysis of leadership emergence in small groups. *Communication Monographs, 45,* 156-172.

Silverman, D. (1993). *Interpreting qualitative data: Methods for analyzing talk, text and interaction.* London: Sage.

Simon, H. A. (1945). *Administrative behavior.* New York: Free Press.

Smircich, L. (1983). Concepts of culture and organizational analysis. *Administrative Science Quarterly, 28,* 339-358.

Smith, R. C., & Eisenberg, E. M. (1987). Conflict at Disneyland: A root-metaphor analysis. *Communication Monographs, 54,* 367-379.

Staw, B. M. (1985). Spinning on symbolism: A brief note on the future of symbolism in organizational research. *Journal of Management, 11,* 117-118.

Stewart, J. (1994). An interpretive approach to validity in interpersonal communication research. In K. Carter & M. Presnell (Eds.), *Interpretive approaches to validity in interpersonal communication research* (pp. 45-81). Albany: State University of New York Press.

Stone, A. R. (1991). Will the real body please stand up? Boundary stories about virtual cultures. In M. Benedikt (Ed.), *Cyberspace: First steps* (pp. 81-118). Cambridge, MA: MIT Press.

Strine, M. S., & Pacanowsky, M. (1985). How to read interpretive accounts of organizational life: Narrative bases of textual authority. *Southern Speech Communication Journal, 50,* 283-297.

Taylor, B. (1990). *Reminiscences of Los Alamos:* Narrative, critical theory, and the organizational subject. *Western Journal of Speech Communication, 54,* 395-419.

Taylor, B. (1993). Register of the repressed: Women's voice and body in the nuclear weapons organization. *Quarterly Journal of Speech, 79,* 267-285.

Taylor, B. (1996). Make bomb, save world: Reflections on dialogic nuclear ethnography. *Journal of Contemporary Ethnography, 25,* 120-143.

Taylor, B. (1997). Home zero: Images of home and field in nuclear-cultural studies. *Western Journal of Communication, 61,* 209-234,

Taylor, B., & Conrad, C. (1992). Narratives of sexual harassment: Organizational dimensions. *Journal of Applied Communication Research, 20,* 401-418.

Thomas, J. (1993). *Doing critical ethnography.* Newbury Park, CA: Sage.

Thompson, P. (1993). Post-modernism: Fatal distraction. In J. Hassard & M. Parker (Eds.), *Postmodernism and organizations* (pp. 183-203). London: Sage.

Tompkins, P. K. (1978). Organizational metamorphosis in space research and development. *Communication Monographs, 45,* 110-118.

Tompkins, P. K. (1994). Principles of rigor for assessing evidence in "qualitative" communication research. *Western Journal of Communication, 58,* 44-50.

Tompkins, P. K., & Cheney, G. (1983). Account analysis of organizations: Decision making and identification. In L. L. Putnam & M. E. Pacanowsky (Eds.), *Communication and organizations: An interpretive approach* (pp. 123-146). Beverly Hills, CA: Sage.

Tompkins, P. K., Fisher, J. Y., Infante, D. A., & Tompkins, E. L. (1975). Kenneth Burke and the inherent characteristics of formal organizations: A field study. *Speech Monographs, 42,* 135-142.

Tompkins, P. K., & Redding, W. C. (1988). Organizational communication: Past and present tenses. In G. M. Goldhaber & G. A. Barnett (Eds.), *Handbook of organizational communication* (pp. 5-33). Norwood, NJ: Ablex.

Tong, T. (1989). *Feminist thought: A comprehensive introduction.* Boulder, CO: Westview.

Trice, H. M., & Beyer, J. M. (1993). *The cultures of work organizations.* Englewood Cliffs, NJ: Prentice Hall.

Trujillo, N. (1991). Hegemonic masculinity on the mound: Media representations of Nolan Ryan and American sports culture. *Critical Studies in Mass Communication, 8,* 290-308.

Trujillo, N. (1992). Interpreting (the work and the talk of) baseball: Perspectives on ballpark culture. *Western Journal of Communication, 56,* 350-371.

Trujillo, N. (1993). Interpreting November 22: A critical ethnography of an assassination site. *Quarterly Journal of Speech, 79,* 447-466.

Trujillo, N. (1995). Machines, missiles, and men: Images of the male body on ABC's "Monday Night Football." *Sociology of Sport Journal, 12,* 403-423.

Trujillo, N., & Dionisopoulos, G. (1987). Cop talk, police stories, and the social construction of organizational drama. *Central States Speech Journal, 38,* 196-209.

Trujillo, N., & Krizek, B. (1994). Emotionality in the stands and in the field: Expressing self through baseball. *Journal of Sport and Social Issues, 18,* 303-325.

Tsoukas, H. (1989). The validity of idiographic research explanations. *Academy of Management Review, 14,* 551-561.

Turner, V. (1986). *The anthropology of performance.* New York: PAJ.

Van Maanen, J. (1979). The fact of fiction in organizational ethnography. *Administrative Science Quarterly, 24,* 539-550.

Van Maanen, J. (1988). *Tales of the field: On writing ethnography.* Chicago: University of Chicago Press.

Van Maanen, J. (1995). An end to innocence: The ethnography of ethnography. In J. Van Maanen (Ed.), *Representation in ethnography* (pp. 1-35). Thousand Oaks, CA: Sage.

Vidich, A. J., & Lyman, S. M. (1994). Qualitative methods: Their history in sociology and anthropology. In N. K. Denzin & Y. S. Lincoln (Eds.), *Handbook of* qualitative research (pp. 23-59). Thousand Oaks, CA: Sage.

Waitzkin, H. (1993). Interpretive analysis of spoken discourse: Dealing with the limitations of quantitative and qualitative methods. *Southern Communication Journal, 58,* 128-146.

Waldron, V. R., & Krone, K. J. (1991). The experience and expression of emotion in the workplace: A study of a corrections organization. *Management Communication Quarterly, 4,* 287-309.

Watkins, M., & Caillouet, R. H. (1994). Legitimation endeavors: Impression management strategies used by an organization in crisis. *Communication Monographs, 61,* 44-62.

Weil, M. (1989). Research on vulnerable populations. *Journal of Applied Behavioral Science, 25,* 419-437.

Welker, L. L., & Goodall, H. L. (1997). Representation, interpretation, and performance: Opening the text of Casing a Promised Land. *Text and Performance Quarterly, 17,* 109-122.

West, J. T. (1993). Ethnography and ideology: The politics of cultural representation. *Western Journal of Communication, 57,* 209-220.

Weston, K. M., & Rofel, L. B. (1984). Sexuality, class and conflict in a lesbian workplace. *Signs, 9,* 623-646.

Willis, P. (1977). *Learning to labour: How working class kids get working class jobs.* Franborough, UK: Saxon House.

Wood, J. T. (Ed.). (1992a). "Telling our stories": Sexual harassment in the communication discipline [Special issue]. *Journal of Applied Communication Research, 20.*

Wood, J. T. (1992b). "Telling our stories": Narratives as a basis for theorizing sexual harassment. *Journal of Applied Communication Research, 20,* 349-362.

Yin, R. (1984). *Case study research: Design and methods.* Beverly Hills, CA: Sage.

Zola, I. K. (1983). *Missing pieces: A chronicle of living with a disability.* Philadelphia: Temple University Press.

# PART II

# Context: Internal and External Environments

# 6

# Organizational Environments and Organizational Information Processing

KATHLEEN M. SUTCLIFFE
*University of Michigan*

Organizations survive by making sense of and giving sense to their environments. Organizations acquire, interpret, and control flows of environmental information in order not to be blindsided by threats, unprepared for opportunities, or ineffective in managing interdependencies with resource controllers and other important stakeholders. It is this essential role of information and its effective use that makes communication fundamental to the study of organizational behavior. Because coping with environments can be both reac-

tive, as organizations respond to pressing problems and issues, and proactive, as organizations create opportunities previously unforeseen, any information-oriented treatment of organization-environment relations must account for outward as well as inward information flows. This chapter does both.

This chapter is focused on organizational environments and organizational information processing and is concerned with cross-boundary information flows oriented toward minimizing threats and maximizing opportu-

AUTHOR'S NOTE: I am grateful to Dennis Gioia, James Grunig, Fred Jablin, Sim Sitkin, and Karl Weick for helpful comments on a previous version and to Daniel Koger for help in sharpening many ideas in this chapter.

nities. The environment and information processing are dominant concepts in organization studies because processing information about the external environment is a key organizational and managerial activity. It is critical for adaptation and long-term survival (Galbraith, 1973; Weick, 1979). In fact, some scholars argue that information-gathering and information-processing roles—such as the kind of information managers have to work with, and the handling of information prior to decisions—are more crucial to the success of the firm than strategic decision making itself (Pfeffer & Salancik, 1978; Starbuck & Milliken, 1988; Weick, 1974). Consequently, at the heart of this chapter is the assumption that environmental information flows—the gathering and interpretation of environmental information—are crucial inputs to many organizational decisions and as such represent important processes to scholars of organizational communication. Yet information flows from organizations to their environments are as critical for organizational success as flows of information from environments to organizations.

It has long been accepted that organizations enhance their effectiveness and long-term legitimacy by proactively using communication to manage environmental interdependencies and shape their identities (Pfeffer & Salancik, 1978), yet interest in this area is gaining renewed momentum and is of increasing importance to scholars and others interested in organizational legitimacy (Elsbach, 1994; Elsbach & Sutton, 1992; Suchman, 1995), issues management and risk communication (Chess, Saville, Tamuz, & Greenberg, 1992; Chess, Tamuz, Saville, & Greenberg, 1992; Heath, 1988, 1994; Elsbach & Kramer, 1996; Heath & Nelson, 1986; Marcus & Goodman, 1991), and public relations (Cheney & Dionisopoulos, 1989; Cheney & Vibbert, 1987; Grunig, 1992), and to strategic management practitioners as well (Lev, 1992). Therefore, a second key assumption is that outflows of information related to strategy formulation, implementation, and

consequent outcomes serve as inputs to change the environment (Pfeffer & Salancik, 1978; Weick, 1979); a changed environment may have important implications for organizational legitimacy, performance, and future organizational behaviors.

This chapter departs from other treatments of organizational environments and information processing such as the chapter coauthored by Huber and Daft in the first edition of this handbook in two fundamental ways. First, it considers both the processing of incoming environmental information and the outward flow of information across organizational boundaries. Previous research in the management and organizational communication literatures examining how organizations manage environmental information has often been focused either on the processing of incoming environmental information or on the processing of outgoing information to the environment. This chapter not only reviews and updates the traditional literature on environments and information processing, but it also draws together several disparate research streams to develop a framework to better understand how organizations make sense of their environments and how organizations direct or control the flow of information back to the environment, presumably to affect organizational outcomes and identities.

Second, the chapter is directed by concerns for how organizations process and manage something they call an environment to enhance organizational effectiveness. By focusing on environmental sensing and interpretation systems and how organizations strategically use environmental information to enhance organizational effectiveness, this chapter takes a more macro-oriented approach to managerial and organizational communication processes, which is in stark contrast to many previous treatments of these issues. For example, prior work has considered the more micro-information processes related to the transmission and distribution of information internally (see Huber, 1982, 1991), and the use of information in decision making includ-

ing the derivation of alternative courses of action, their evaluation, and the implementation
of alternatives (see Huber, 1991; Huber &
McDaniel, 1986; O'Reilly, 1983; and a special issue of *Strategic Management Journal,*
1993, 14[S2]).

My discussion in this chapter unfolds as
follows. The first section is devoted to a historical overview of key perspectives on organizational environments and organizational
information processing and more fully elaborates important issues overlooked or underdeveloped in previous work. In the second section, I discuss the processes by which
environmental information is noticed and interpreted. The third section is focused on a
discussion of information flows across organizational boundaries intended to preempt anticipated problems or hedge against unanticipated ones. The fourth section develops a
framework to link incoming and outgoing
flows of environmental information. The final
section is devoted to a discussion of implications and future research directions.

## ORGANIZATIONAL
## ENVIRONMENTS AND
## ORGANIZATIONAL
## INFORMATION PROCESSING:
## A HISTORICAL OVERVIEW

Concern with the concept of organizational
environment has drawn serious academic attention for over 40 years, dating roughly
from about 1956 to the present. Still, to date,
only a few key perspectives describing environments are reflected in the literature. The
assumptions underlying these key perspectives differ dramatically and are important
not only because they influence our understanding of organization-environment relations, but also because they affect a discussion of communication-related implications.
Several key perspectives on the environment
are reviewed in the next section followed by a
more general discussion of organizational information-processing theory.

### Key Perspectives on the Environment

#### Objectivist Perspective

Most generally, the environment has been
portrayed as a source of resources or as a
source of information. The resource dependence perspective as developed by some scholars (e.g., Aldrich, 1979; Aldrich & Pfeffer,
1976; Pfeffer & Salancik, 1978) treats the environment as consisting of scarce resources
for which organizations compete. Organizational outcomes are a function of both the
level of resources (including the importance
of a resource to the organization and the number of sources from which the resource is
available) and the extent to which these resources are made available to organizations
(i.e., the number, variety, and relative power
of organizations competing for the resource).
The resource dependence perspective suggests that organizations attempt to avoid becoming dependent on other organizations and
seek to make other organizations dependent
on them (Aldrich, 1979). Scholars adopting
the resource dependence approach pay little
attention to the processes by which organizations either obtain information about the environment or communicate information about
the environment; however, they pay close attention to characteristics or dimensions of
task environments.

The range of dimensions or characteristics
describing task environments is large. In the
organizational theory literature, organizational environments have been characterized
as a set of components (e.g., economic, regulatory, technical, social), stakeholders (e.g.,
customers, competitors, suppliers), or as a set
of attributes (e.g., instability, munificence,
complexity) (Aldrich, 1979; Bourgeois, 1980;
Dess & Beard, 1984). Industrial economists
(e.g., Caves, 1980; Khandwalla, 1981), on the
other hand, have characterized environments
more broadly in terms of industry characteristics such as concentration of market power,
entry barriers, changes in demand, or changes
in product characteristics (Yasai-Ardekani,
1986). Organization theorists generally agree

that three dimensions—stability, munificence, and complexity—are key environmental dimensions affecting organizations (Dess & Beard, 1984). These three dimensions reflect the nature and distribution of resources in environments thereby reflecting the extent of dependence and typically have been assessed using archival industry data such as industry sales, net assets, or capital expenditures.

The characterization of the environment as components, stakeholders, or attributes is often referred to as the "objective environment." The notion of an objective environment presumes that organizations are embedded within external independent environments that "constitute some thing or some set of forces to be adapted to, coaligned with, controlled, or controlled by" (Smircich & Stubbart, 1985, p. 725). As Smircich and Stubbart (1985) and others (e.g., Weick, 1979) highlight, conceptualizing environments as objective, concrete, external, or tangible implies that attributes, events, and processes are hard, measurable, and determinant. The goal of strategic management in an objective environment is to initiate strategic actions that will meet the real constraints and demands that exist "out there" (Smircich & Stubbart, 1985, p. 726).

### Perceptual and Interpretivist Perspectives

In contrast to the characterization of environments as stocks of resources, environments also have been portrayed as a source of data that serves as the raw material from which organizational members fabricate information and subsequent organizational responses (Dill, 1962; Tushman & Nadler, 1978; Weick, 1979). Scholars adopting this perspective—sometimes known as the information-processing perspective—are concerned with the conditions under which information is noticed and how it is communicated and interpreted. In fact, viewing the environment as flows of data and information highlights the importance of perceptions and interpretations. It is generally agreed that variations in environmental data as filtered through members' perceptions and interpretive schemes are a major factor explaining organizational change (Weick, 1979).

Scholars adopting the information view traditionally have considered environmental uncertainty and the equivocality of information available to decision makers as critical variables affecting organizational actions and outcomes (Aldrich, 1979; Weick, 1979). Environmental complexity, and unpredictability in terms of the frequency and direction of change, supposedly generates uncertainties for organizations and their members, which complicates rational decision-making processes and ultimately affects organizational outcomes. A way of linking the information view of environments with the resource view is to focus on perceived uncertainty and how executives perceive their environment. Scholars adopting the resource perspective generally agree that decision makers' perceptions of uncertainty and other external constraints or demands play a part in determining an organization's response to the situation of dependence (Pfeffer & Salancik, 1978).

The perceptual perspective on environments is similar to the objectivist perspective in that it also assumes that there is a real, material, external environment out there to be perceived (Smircich & Stubbart, 1985). Thus, in essence, there is little difference between the conception of objective and perceived environments. The difference between perceived and objective environments lies in the extent to which decision makers are (or can be) accurate assessors of the supposed "real" environment.

Much of the previous research examining the adaptation of organizations to their environments has implicitly assumed that decision makers accurately perceive environmental changes and demands and subsequently develop adaptive strategies based on their accurate perceptions. Yet empirical evidence supporting the idea that executives are veridical assessors of their environments is scant, and recent research has advanced several important theories that help to account for the lack of significant associations between objective (archival) and perceived environments (see Boyd, Dess, & Rasheed, 1993; Sutcliffe, 1994; and Sutcliffe & Huber, 1998, for analyses of probable causes).

## Enactment Perspective

The enactment perspective to environments poses an alternative to the concreteness implied in the previous conceptualizations. The enactment or social construction perspective suggests that the environment is not an objective given; it is not even perceived. Rather, it is made or enacted (Weick, 1979). The central premise of the enactment perspective is that organizations create the environments that subsequently impinge on them (Abolafia & Kilduff, 1988). Enacted environments are socially created rather than concrete or material in that the environment is the joint product of the actions of purposeful actors and accompanying efforts to make sense out of these actions (Abolafia & Kilduff, 1988). Enactment transpires through communication processes in that entities involved in interactive relationships read each other's behavior and make attributions to make sense of the situation.

Enacted environments are not synonymous with perceived environments although perception is involved: "An enactment model implies that an environment of which strategists can make sense has been put there by strategists' patterns of action—not by a process of perceiving the environment, but by a process of making the environment" (Smircich & Stubbart, 1985, p. 727). Enactment occurs through the processes of attention and action (Weick, 1988). From an enactment perspective, the world is an ambiguous field of experience devoid of threats and opportunities. Decision makers pay attention to certain aspects of their environments as a consequence of attentional processes. Once data or information in the environment become stimuli and

penetrate an organization's cognitive system, decision makers give meaning to the information so that it makes sense and subsequently act on their interpretations. The resulting actions and outcomes are informational inputs for other entities in the environment, who ascribe meaning to the acts and subsequently react. As Weick (1988) highlights:

An *enacted environment* is the residuum of changes produced by enactment. The word "residuum" is preferred to the word "residue" because residuum emphasizes that what is left after a process cannot be ignored or left out of account because it has potential significance (*Webster's Dictionary of Synonyms*, 1951, p. 694). The product of enactment is not an accident, an afterthought, or a byproduct. Instead it is an orderly, material, social construction that is subject to multiple interpretations. Enacted environments contain real objects such as reactors, pipes, and valves. The existence of these objects is not questioned, but their significance, meaning, and content is. These objects are inconsequential until they are acted upon and then incorporated retrospectively into events, situations, and explanations. (p. 307)

## Information Environments

As noted earlier, traditional views of the environment highlight that organizations exist within environments that are independently given—no matter whether objective or perceived. If environments are seen as external and concrete, then it is natural for researchers and managers to be concerned with the extent to which managers accurately discern their environments. In a concrete world, "a premium is placed on the ability to measure, predict, and influence the environment to ensure successful adaptation to the contingencies it presents" (Smircich, 1983, p. 227). An implication of this line of thinking is that environmental information is a thing "out there" to be discovered and is independent from the meanings ascribed by organizational members.

In the first edition of this handbook, Huber and Daft (1987, p. 130) developed the concept of the information environment. The information environment constitutes the "raw material of organizational communication and actions" and as such is the sensable environment. Huber and Daft (1987) argued that the information environment mediates between the objective environment and the environment that is sensed by organizational members. One way to think about the components of the information environment is as follows: (a) occurrences, anything happening or changing in the environment; (b) acts, specific behaviors (including specific communication behaviors) stemming from resource allocation actions and decisions of other entities in an organization's environment; and (c) messages, events resulting from the decisions of other environmental actors that have specific, predetermined targets (Vertzberger, 1984, pp. 12-13). In other words, the information environment can be viewed as the interactive communication behaviors between organizations and the entities in their environment, the cognitions and meanings that executives develop from this communication or other messages, or the cognitions or meanings that executives develop from directly perceiving and interpreting other environmental information (i.e., occurrences or acts) (Grunig, 1997).

The information perspective is similar to the traditional perspectives recounted earlier in that it supports the notion of environments as independent, external, and tangible. Yet the notion of an information environment may be potentially misleading from a communication standpoint because it implies that information is a thing "out there" to be discovered and fails to take into account that information in the environment is not inherently meaningful or predefined (Heath, 1994, p. 41). Information is a variable in the communication process; it becomes meaningful only as a consequence of the evaluative schema that are used to process and assess it. Organizational members, through the sharing of information, and

through interpretive and enactment processes, socially construct information filters through which information is selected and interpreted and subsequently enacted through communication (Heath, 1994). Shared information and its accompanying interpretations are what communication is about. In other words, communication results when what one entity does and says is meaningful to another (Heath, 1994). Because the goals and actions of organizational subgroups are not monolithic and are likely to vary, organizational subgroups are likely to come into contact with different aspects of an organization's environment, are likely to differentially focus their attention and therefore notice only certain aspects of their organization's environment, and are likely to have unique zones of meaning (Heath, 1994) through which they filter information. Thus, it may be more accurate to think of information "environments" rather than a single environment.

Before concluding the discussion of the key perspectives of the environment, it is important to highlight the issue of boundaries. In contrast to the enactment perspective that favors a socially created symbolic world and abandons the idea of concrete material organizations/environments, the objective, perceived, and interpreted environmental perspectives presume real, material environments whose boundaries are clearly distinct from the concrete material organizations located within them. What is inside and outside the firm is clearly differentiated in more traditional perspectives because of legal factors (i.e., ownership issues) or as a consequence of other factors such as varied senses of identity, culture, or strategic priorities. Although some theorists acknowledge that boundaries are not fixed (Aldrich, 1979), more often than not, traditional perspectives have assumed that organization-environment boundaries are relatively static and well defined. Recent foci on process and value-chain management and viewing organizations and their environments as "boundaryless" strengthen the view that the boundaries between organizations and their environments are fluid, dynamic, and constantly evolving.

To summarize, few researchers would say that environments are totally objective, but even fewer would say that environments are totally constructed (Weick, 1983). Still, nothing has really emerged to replace these extreme views in spite of over 40 years of work. One way to accommodate the differences between perspectives is to postulate, as Weick (1983, p. 18) suggests, that grains of preexisting reality are at the core of decision makers' representations. Small, objective details are enlarged into constructions by interdependent actions. Sales fall, sales skyrocket, new competitors enter tight markets. Representations do not materialize out of thin air; things do exist.

## *Organizational Information Processing*

Organizational information processing is often treated as an organizing concept for understanding a broad and interrelated range of phenomena of significance in organizational decision making, strategy formulation, and strategy implementation. In essence, organizational information-processing theory attempts to explain organizational behaviors by examining information flows occurring in and around organizations (Knight & McDaniel, 1979), and traditional approaches to information processing have been grounded primarily in the objectivist or perceptual perspectives. An organization's information-processing system is thought to include

- The exposure to information, readiness to attend to various environmental elements, and the development of strategies and sensory systems for searching the environment (Dill, 1962, p. 97)
- Communication and storage of information (Galbraith, 1973; Thompson, 1967; Tush-

man & Nadler, 1978) and mechanisms for transmitting information

- Development of interpretations systems that influence the transformation of data into information (Daft & Weick, 1984)
- Routines for translating information into action or for using information in decision making, strategy formulation, and strategy implementation

Early research drawing on the organizational information-processing perspective focused on the idea that uncertainty arises from certain characteristics in the environment, and to cope with this uncertainty, effective organizations match their information-processing capabilities (i.e., their designs) to the information-processing demands of the environment (i.e., level of uncertainty) (Galbraith, 1973; Huber, 1982; Thompson, 1967; Tushman & Nadler, 1978). Also known as the logistical perspective of information processing, this perspective focused on the capacity of organizational structures and processes to enhance or impede the transfer and transformation of data or information and subsequent decision-making capabilities (Huber, 1982). Empirical studies reflecting this perspective have focused on the effects of structural variables on communication networks, channels, and amount of communication. Specifically, studies drawing on the logistical perspective have examined the intraorganizational and more microlevel aspects of information processing and found, for example:

- Effective decision-making units differentially structure themselves depending on perceived environmental uncertainty (Duncan, 1973).
- For high-performing units, the greater the task interdependence, the greater the frequency of communication (Tushman, 1979).
- The credibility of the information source rather than expertise determines the extent

to which information is believed and used in decision making (O'Reilly & Roberts, 1974).

To summarize, the logistical view has examined how information processing and communication are enhanced or impeded by organizational design characteristics. An implicit assumption underlying the logistical view is that information is something that flows or is conveyed from one entity to another. The logistical view fails to take into account the idea that information has no inherent meaning and that it is given meaning through interpretive processes (Heath, 1994).

In contrast to the logistical perspective, much of the more recent work on organizational information processing, grounded in the interpretive and enactment perspectives, has focused more heavily on cognition and construction, viewing organizations as sensemaking and learning systems (Daft & Weick, 1984; Dutton & Jackson, 1987; Milliken, 1990; Starbuck & Milliken, 1988; Thomas, Clark, & Gioia, 1993). Information processing is reflected in the individual or collective abilities of organizational members to scan and interpret environmental information in order to increase knowledge of action-outcome links between the organization and its environment (Corner, Kinicki, & Keats, 1994; Daft & Weick, 1984, p. 286), presumably to enhance organizational performance (Thomas et al., 1993). Empirical studies reflecting these perspectives have explored, for example, the effects of antecedent and contextual factors on decision makers' interpretations of strategic information (Milliken, 1990; Thomas, Shankster, & Mathieu, 1994), the role that managerial characteristics play in issue identification and interpretation processes (Walsh, 1988), and how heuristics and framing may affect managers' strategic decision-making processes (Bateman & Zeithaml, 1989; Schwenk, 1984). The focus of the interpretive view is primarily on how information processing, and in particular, the interpretation of information, is influenced by factors unique to

the context such as organizational structures, organizational processes (i.e., communication processes), and the psychological and social-psychological characteris- tics of organizational members.

While some scholars suggest that the logistical and interpretive information-processing perspectives noted above are contradictory, in fact, they are complementary—especially from an organizational communication perspective. Organizational information processing includes both the transfer of information and the inference of meaning, and as such can be thought of as a communication process (O'Reilly & Pondy, 1979). In analyzing organizational information processing of organizational environments and evaluating its outcomes, it is natural to be concerned with the factors that affect how organizations and their members single out information in the environment or how messages penetrate an organizational system; the factors that affect how environmental information is interpreted; and how organizational responses, in particular communication responses, subsequently reshape the environment.

Concern with how environmental information is noticed, the individual and organizational factors that influence the interpretation of environmental information and the development of a representation of the environment and how it changes over time, and how organizations and their members use information and communication subsequently to reshape the environment are considered more fully below.

## HOW ENVIRONMENTS BECOME KNOWN

In the following sections, I review research grounded primarily in the perceptual, interpretive, and enactment perspectives related to how organizations and their members come to know and cope with their environments through the processes of attention, interpretation, and action. Noticing environmental data or information is one key step in coping with environments. However, noticing information is not the only process that is important. Information is not inherently meaningful. As Ford and Baucus (1987, p. 367) note, facts don't speak for themselves—data are generally interpreted before they are useful for strategy formulation. This means that even though two organizations may notice the same things, their interpretations may differ and subsequent responses may differ as a result. Disentangling the process of noticing environmental stimuli from the process of interpreting environmental stimuli is useful for better understanding organizational adaptation and responsiveness and for isolating the communication dynamics related to each of the processes (Daft & Weick, 1984; Kiesler & Sproull, 1982; Starbuck & Milliken, 1988).

Many scholars have used the term *scanning* to refer to the observation of stimuli; other scholars argue that *noticing* is a more accurate term since scanning implies proactivity, or a more stimulus-specific search. In this chapter, I use the term noticing to refer to an awareness of environmental stimuli. The process of noticing stimuli can be both formal and informal, as well as voluntary and involuntary. Interpreting refers to the process of making sense of what is noticed.

## Noticing Environmental Information

Noticing may be dominated by strategy or tactics. Strategic information processing generally is concerned with the fundamental position of an organization with its environment and higher-level organizational goals, is focused on nonroutine—perhaps discontinuous—problems and situations, is broad in scope, has a longer time horizon, and generally involves the top managers of an organization (Knight & McDaniel, 1979). In contrast, tactical information processing deals with more routine day-to-day problems and situa-

tions, generally operating and administrative issues, and often involves the middle and lower levels of an organization. Notwithstanding these distinctions, tactics can be thought of as strategy in that once they are implemented, they generate strategy. Nonetheless, this chapter is focused on the processing of environmental information of importance to the whole organization more generally. Consequently, in the following section I highlight the clusters of influences that are likely to enhance or impede the detection of important environmental information by an organization's top decision makers.

With few exceptions (see Bourgeois, 1985), the limited research examining the determinants of executives' environmental perceptions has been focused on the perceptions of a single manager (or CEO). However, there is reason to focus on the perception of a team of executives rather than on single individuals. First, few decisions affecting the entire organization and its relationship with its environment are made unilaterally by any single person. The chief executive often shares tasks, and to some extent, power with other members of the top management team (Hambrick & Mason, 1984). Further, while a number of organizational members may be involved in boundary-spanning roles collecting environmental data and channeling the data into the organization, the information generally converges at the organization's top level (Daft & Weick, 1984) and it is the collective that affects organizational decisions and subsequent responses (Hinz, Tindale, & Vollrath, 1997; Klimoski & Mohammed, 1994; Walsh, Henderson, & Deighton, 1988).

Second, as Zucker (1983) argues, attitudes and behaviors in formal organizations are highly institutionalized or governed by "common understandings about what is appropriate and, fundamentally, meaningful behavior" (p. 5). Organizational settings have been characterized as strong situations that exert powerful influences on individual perceptions, attitudes, and behaviors (Mischel, 1977). Consequently, it is assumed that the environmental characteristics noticed by a team of top managers amount to something more than what individual team members' notice. This stems from the assumption that, through social interchange, decision makers create collectively shared or consensual reality (Daft & Weick, 1984; Klimoski & Mohammed, 1994). Therefore, although individual processes serve to filter and distort decision makers' perceptions of what is going on, and what should be done about it, individual perceptions are likely to be influenced significantly by social information processes.

Before proceeding with a discussion of noticing, two comments are in order. First, as is often the case with complex phenomena, previous research has tended to focus on selected relationships between variables hypothesized to affect the detection of environmental information rather than on developing an integrated conceptual framework. Nonetheless, in recent years, managerial variables such as top management group structure and beliefs and other social characteristics, as well as organizational variables such as characteristics of the organization's information system, structure, and strategy, are frequently cited as the key determinants that affect the detection and selection of information. In essence, these factors moderate the degree to which data, information, and messages in the environment penetrate an organization's cognitive system and are transmitted, analyzed, or otherwise taken into account in strategic decisions and actions. The list of antecedents of effective environmental information noticing is not meant to be exhaustive.

A second limitation of the current literature on noticing processes, and perhaps an even more important one, is that researchers who study noticing/scanning often treat information and communication as one and the same. In fact, in much of the work related to noticing or scanning, information transfer can be substituted for communication. This is unfortunate and unnecessarily restrictive because communication is a big part of noticing or

sensing aspects of the environment. Thus, my discussion in the next section reflects the current state of the art, and not an effort to treat information and communication synonymously.

## Top Management Group Characteristics

Past research suggests that environmental perceptions may be influenced by individuals' psychological characteristics such as tolerance for ambiguity or cognitive complexity (Downey, Hellriegel, & Slocum, 1977; Downey & Slocum, 1975; Gifford, Bobbitt, & Slocum, 1979). Still, empirical findings are inconsistent (Boyd et al., 1993), and no strong conclusions have been drawn about the influence of these factors. More recently, researchers have focused on demographic characteristics related to the composition of the top management group, hypothesizing that these factors more strongly influence the information processing of the team as a whole and how organizations and their members attend and select among data, information, and messages in the information environment (Hambrick, 1994; Hambrick & Mason, 1984).

Studies examining demographic factors have largely focused on the diversity of a team's work history and length of team tenure. For example, the work of Dearborn and Simon (1958) suggests that individuals with similar functional backgrounds will have similar perceptions. Each member of the top management team develops a way of seeing the world based on his or her past or current experience in a particular functional area. If this holds true, a more functionally diverse top management team not only will notice different environmental events but also will notice different features of the same events. "If people look for different things, when their observations are pooled they collectively see more than any one of them alone would see" (Weick, 1987, p. 116). Still, it also may be true that too much diversity may hinder team interactions or in other ways hamper managers' abilities to communicate effectively (Glick, Miller, & Huber, 1993; O'Reilly, Caldwell, & Barnett, 1989), which will constrain the group's information-processing capabilities as a whole. Although this reasoning makes sense, Hambrick (1994) argues that top management groups will quickly develop norms of interaction that facilitate frequent and fluid communication. In one of the few empirical studies to shed light on this issue, Sutcliffe (1994) found a negative association between work history diversity and the accurate detection of information related to the level of resources available in an organization's environment. Her results suggest that team interactions or other communication processes are repressed in more highly diverse teams and this hinders the sharing of certain types of information among team members.

The length of team tenure may also affect the environmental information that is sensed. The amount of time the members of a group have been together is related strongly to the degree of interaction and communication among group members (O'Reilly et al., 1989) and is critical to the development of shared attitudes and perspectives. Although longevity may lead to a similarity of perspectives and, perhaps, diminished communication because members think they know what everyone else is thinking (Katz, 1982), shorter-tenured teams may not know what to look for. Shorter-tenured teams may lack well-defined organizational frameworks or cognitive schemas, which hinders the recognition of salient information.

Hambrick and D'Aveni (1992) provide empirical support for the idea that longer-tenured teams are better at detecting important environmental information. In a comparative study of bankrupt and surviving firms, they found that the average team tenure in bankrupt firms was significantly shorter than the average team tenure in matched survivors. In addition, the average tenure of bankrupt teams declined monotonically over the five-year period prior to bankruptcy. They concluded that shorter-tenured teams fall victim to flawed perceptions, deficient information processing, and subsequent strategic errors based on bad detection systems (Hambrick & D'Aveni, 1992, p. 1447). More direct evidence about the importance of enduring teams is provided by Sutcliffe (1994), who found a positive association between team tenure and the extent to which teams accurately detected the level of resources in their environment. She concluded that longer-tenured teams have more effective team communication patterns and/or more effective external communication networks, which gives them better access to information about resources than shorter-tenured teams.

In addition to team background characteristics, executives' capacities to notice information may also be shaped by other factors such as managerial discretion (Hambrick & Finkelstein, 1987), managerial values (Beyer, 1981; Hambrick & Brandon, 1988), managerial ideologies (Meyer, 1982), and beliefs about efficacy (Wood & Bandura, 1989). Managerial discretion—the latitude for action—may act as a perceptual lens by influencing both the range and the intensity of stimuli to which managers attend. Management teams who have a greater latitude of action will be attentive to a wider range of environmental information and may be more likely to pick up weak variations in environmental stimuli as a consequence of wider attention processes. If managers think they can take lots of action, "they can afford to pay attention to a wider variety of inputs because, whatever they see, they will have some way to cope with it" (Weick, 1988, p. 311). Meyer (1982) found that hospital administrators with a high degree of perceived discretion more carefully attended to the environment and attended to a wider range of environmental sectors than administrators with a low degree of perceived discretion. Managerial and organizational values and ideologies and collective efficacy also may be important filters that affect the screening and selection of stimuli.

## Organizational Characteristics

Factors related to an organization's processes, structure, and design will also affect the detection of important environmental information. In the following section, I examine organizational information acquisition processes including organizational scanning routines, performance-monitoring routines, and top executives' scanning routines as well as factors related to an organization's structure, strategy, and resources.

Organizational scanning refers to the acquisition of information about the environment by lower-level and middle-level boundary spanners or subunits dedicated to the task of intelligence gathering and the subsequent communication of this information to relevant parties. Organizational scanning systems vary in intensity, formalization, and complexity (Fahey & King, 1977; Huber, 1991). Organizations may be highly vigilant in their scanning, may routinely scan, may probe for specific information in response to actual or suspected problems or opportunities or whenever the need arises, or simply may be on the alert for "nonroutine" (but relevant) information (Huber, 1991, p. 97). Intensive scanning routines are generally considered to lead to a more "wide-ranging sensing of the environment" (Huber, 1991, p. 97). Fundamental to these perspectives is the idea that more frequent scanning (i.e., a greater amount) enhances the recognition of environmental changes, threats, or opportunities—an idea empirically validated by Sutcliffe (1994).

Organizational scanning provides information about the overall business environment critical for planning, strategy formulation, and decision making. In contrast to scanning, performance monitoring provides more specific information about an organization's specific business situation and its effectiveness in fulfilling goals and the requirements of stakeholders (Eisenhardt, 1989; Huber, 1991). Information about current competitors, existing technologies, and product markets in which a firm operates is useful for making operational and tactical decisions; is important for uncovering or discovering idiosyncratic threats,

problems, or trends; and leads to a more timely and accurate detection of problems and opportunities (Eisenhardt, 1989). Decision makers in firms where performance is monitored continually sense the environment more quickly and accurately because they have frequent, mandatory, intense, face-to-face operations meetings (not limited to discussions of internal operations) and frequently receive written reports detailing performance targets (Eisenhardt, 1989). This enables decision makers to initiate corrective actions before substantial problems materialize (Eisenhardt, 1989). In addition to its effect on sensing processes, performance monitoring may also lead to higher performance indirectly through its effect on trust. It is possible that frequent interactions enable executive teams to develop social routines and patterns of trust that permit quick and reliable responses when situations get tough.

Executives also acquire information directly through their own efforts. The frequency or intensity of managerial scanning indirectly reflects the amount of information top management team members obtain about the environment (Hambrick, 1982). For example, studies by Kefalas and Schoderbek (1973) and Daft, Sormunen, and Parks (1988) suggest that top managers gain experience in selecting stimuli to attend to by scanning more, and as a consequence, are more adept at building an accurate picture of the environment. Consequently, when managers' observations are pooled they collectively formulate a better representation of their environment. Related to scanning is the idea that the choice of communication media will affect the extent to which executives get a deeper—and perhaps more accurate—picture of their environment. For example, studies by Daft and his colleagues (Daft, Bettenhausen, & Tyler, 1993; Daft & Lengel, 1984) have shown that richer media not only may allow for the resolution of ambiguity and the enhancement of understanding but also may induce deeper processing of environmental information.

An organization's design and structural characteristics such as the organization's internal pattern of tasks, roles, and administrative mechanisms also will affect the detection and selection of information. Organizational structures not only affect decisions about what information to collect but also the transmission, analysis, and interpretation of environmental information.

Formalization and complexity, for example, affect the detection and selection of environmental information by circumscribing patterns of attention and information collection as well as constraining opportunities for interaction and communication between boundary spanners and upper managers. High levels of differentiation and formalization may contribute to a widening reality gap if top executives become increasingly detached from those more closely connected with the environment (Aldrich & Auster, 1986, pp. 169-170). Centralization may affect executives' noticing capacities more directly. Orton and Weick (1990) and Weick (1976) have argued that loosely coupled systems more accurately register their environments than tightly coupled systems. To the extent that decentralization implies diversity in the goals and preferences of decision makers, decentralized executive teams may form a more complete picture of an environment because they tend to focus their attention on more, and more varied, indicators. Consequently, when managers pool their observations, they collectively formulate a better picture of the current environmental trends, threats, and opportunities than managers in more centralized organizations—an idea recently validated by Sutcliffe (1994).

In addition to organization structure, an organization's strategic orientation, degree of inertia (Boyd et al., 1993), and the presence of slack (Hambrick, 1994; Tushman & Romanelli, 1985) also may be influential in affecting what information is noticed. A firm's strategic orientation is associated with differing assumptions regarding the external environment (Daft & Weick, 1984), and this may directly affect executives' attentional processes. The strong pursuit of a dominant single strategy may lead executives to overlook important environmental features (Hambrick & Snow, 1977) because it delimits the focus of their attentions. This highlights that notic-

ing is a limiting process in that the noticing of one thing eliminates the simultaneous noticing of something else (Pfeffer & Salancik, 1978; Weick, 1979). For example, firms pursuing cost leadership strategies are likely to be concerned with efficiency and other issues related to streamlining internal processes, and this may prove to be problematic for survival. A recent study of failing firms and matched survivors showed that managers in failing firms appear to pay less attention to certain aspects of their environment than do managers in the survivors (D'Aveni & MacMillan, 1990). Executives in firms surviving external crises differed significantly from executives in failing firms in that they (1) paid more attention to the external rather than internal environment, and (2) paid increasing attention to the output side of their environment by focusing on customers and other general economic factors affecting demand. In addition to the effects of strategic orientation on noticing processes, organizational inertia may also affect attention and the selection of information because inertia often leads organizational members to focus internally as search and decision-making processes atrophy (Boyd et al., 1993). Finally, slack may affect the extent to which executives notice environmental information because it often promotes a complacency or a decreased vigilance in searching out information about environmental changes (Tushman & Romanelli, 1985).

## *Interpreting Environmental Information*

In the previous section, I reviewed the major factors that affect the sensing or noticing of environmental data and information and various communication-related implications. I now turn to a discussion of the factors that affect sensemaking or the interpretation of data and information. Once organizations and their members become aware of environmental information, further processing occurs as executives make sense of it and formulate an interpretation that provides the basis for decisions and actions. The interpretation process has a number of distinct aspects including "comprehending, understanding, explaining, attributing, extrapolating, and predicting" (Starbuck & Milliken, 1988, p. 51). Communication is integral to this process as meanings are shaped through advocacy, persuasion, and other power and influence processes.

Fundamental to the interpretation process is the categorization of data or information, which involves placing stimuli into frameworks (or schemata) to make sense of the stimuli (Starbuck & Milliken, 1988). While numerous categories are possible, the literature in strategic management highlights "opportunity" and "threat" as two salient general categories used by decision makers when interpreting information in regard to environmental changes, events, trends, or developments (Dutton & Jackson, 1987; Fredrickson, 1985; Jackson & Dutton, 1988). These general labels capture top executives' beliefs about the potential effects of environmental events and trends on the organization more broadly, and may even determine those effects because the extent to which top decision makers interpret environmental conditions as opportunities or threats predisposes them to respond in predictable ways (Dutton & Jackson, 1987).

Prior studies of interpretation processes often have focused on the characteristics of environmental issues and events (magnitude, urgency, etc.) and how issue characteristics affect the likelihood that executives will label environmental events as "threats" or "opportunities" (Dutton, Walton, & Abrahamson, 1989; Jackson & Dutton, 1988). Less attention has been paid to examining how managerial and contextual characteristics affect decision makers' interpretations, although recent research suggests there are several potential sources of influence (see Dutton, 1993a; Gioia & Thomas, 1996; Thomas et al., 1994). Three particularly important factors that are likely to affect executives' interpretations include managerial ideologies and beliefs (Dutton, 1993b; Meyer, 1982; Starbuck & Milliken, 1988), an organization's recent performance history (Milliken & Lant, 1991), and the changing nature of the context (Dutton, 1993a).

Interpretations are conditioned by decision makers' repertoire of shared beliefs, values, and ideologies—by habits, beliefs about what is, and beliefs about what ought to be (Starbuck & Milliken, 1988). Shared beliefs and assumptions about possible future events, alternative courses of action, and consequences attached to these alternatives (i.e., the extent that managers perceive they have the latitude to take action) have been found to be important influences on managerial interpretations (Child, 1972; Daft & Weick, 1984; Hambrick & Finkelstein, 1987).

Opportunities are more likely to be constructed in organizations where multiple courses of action are envisioned and favored (Dutton, 1993b), or where decision makers perceive they have more control. Managers with a higher degree of discretion are likely to envision many courses of action and to perceive that they have a higher degree of control, which means they will be more likely than their counterparts with a low degree of discretion to frame environmental variations or discontinuities as opportunities.

An organization's recent performance history is another potentially important factor that influences how executives make sense of their environment (McCabe & Dutton, 1993; Milliken, 1990; Milliken & Lant, 1991). The degree to which decision makers believe their organization is performing more or less successfully activates powerful psychological processes that influence the extent to which managers view their environment as more or less threatening and subsequently influences top decision makers' thinking about strategic change (Milliken & Lant, 1991). Milliken (1990), for example, found that managers in high-performing organizations were less likely to interpret a particular environmental change as threatening than managers in low-performing organizations. This suggests that managers are more likely to interpret environmental contingencies as opportunities and less as threats when they believe their organization is performing well.

Differences in contextual conditions also create different motivating conditions for decision makers to construct their environments in particular ways (Dutton et al., 1989). Change is often seen as threatening (Staw, Sandelands, & Dutton, 1981), which suggests that decision makers in contexts that are unstable and changing may be more likely to interpret these events and conditions as threatening than decision makers in more stable contexts. Similarly, decision makers in contexts where resources are constrained are more likely to interpret environmental contingencies as threatening than are decision makers in more munificent contexts.

### Action as a Mechanism to Enhance the Plausibility of Interpretations

This chapter is guided by the assumption that information processing is purposeful behavior by which individuals, groups, or organizations become aware of, handle, make sense of, resolve, or control data and information about the environment. One outcome of environmental information processing is a representation of the environment—a schema reflecting important trends, threats, and opportunities that decision makers use as the basis for strategic action. However, because of bounded rationality, individuals and organizations are limited as information processors, which suggests that a certain level of misperception is inevitable in every information-processing system. This may not be a problem when competition is low, when resources are plentiful, or when organizations are loosely coupled to other organizations in their environment. However, it may be a problem in very competitive markets, when organizations are tightly coupled to other organizations in their environments, or in industries where resources are constrained or limited. Thus, as Vertzberger (1990) and Weick (1995, pp. 56-57) argue, better information process-

ing may not so much be characterized by an ability to choose between accurate images and misperceptions, but rather the ability to enhance plausibility and choose between different potential misperceptions.

Recent empirical research has shown that executives in failing and surviving firms differ in the speed with which they update mental models (Barr, Stimpert, & Huff, 1992; Hambrick & D'Aveni, 1992). One promising explanation to account for the performance differences relates to the idea that surviving firms engage less in more formalized scanning, strategic planning, and competitor analysis, and more in trial-and-error action, which may enhance plausibility because it facilitates both learning and dramatic changes in mental models of a firm's environment (Lyles & Mitroff, 1980; Weick, 1990a).

Formal systems for learning about competitive environments bog down in detail, are slow to operate, and often represent the environment as it was, not as it is. In these systems, opportunities for interaction and communication are often circumscribed. Consequently, executives in organizations relying on more formalized strategic planning or information systems are less likely to be aware of current environmental information than their counterparts in organizations without such systems. Action taking may be a better mechanism for generating data and for instantiating opportunities for dialogue, bargaining, negotiation, and persuasion that are essential for developing a good sense of what is going on. Further, action and cognition are mutually reinforcing, and communication is critical to this process. Actions allow for the assessment of causal beliefs that subsequently lead to new actions undertaken to test the newly asserted relationships. Over time, as supporting evidence mounts, more significant changes in beliefs and actions evolve (Barr et al., 1992; Weick, 1990a).

Some researchers have gone so far as to suggest that accurate environmental maps may be less important than any map that brings some order to the world and prompts action (Weick, 1990a). Action is important in organizations because it facilitates learning (Sitkin, Sutcliffe, & Weick, 1998). The pursuit of action generates new information and increases opportunities for communication that helps executives modify erroneous understandings and allows them to update previously held inaccurate perceptions (Sutcliffe, 1997). Consequently, executives in more action-oriented organizations are likely to develop better representations of a current environment and to more quickly update existing environmental models than their counterparts in organizations that are less action oriented. Second, more action-oriented organizations are likely to be more adaptable to future, changing environments than less action-oriented organizations. As noted earlier, however, how executives make sense of environmental data may be a critical factor in influencing action. For example, upbeat interpretations of the environment—sometimes called positive illusions—may enable managers to overcome inertial tendencies by propelling them to pursue goals that might look unattainable in environments assessed in utter objectivity. If current environments aren't seen accurately but executives remain non-threatened, managers may undertake potentially difficult courses of action with enthusiasm, effort, and self-confidence necessary to bring about success.

To summarize, environments become known through the processes of noticing and interpreting, and communication dynamics are critical to each. Taken together, the results of the research presented earlier suggest that the observation or detection of environmental stimuli is enhanced or impeded by executives' interaction patterns (both intraorganizational and interorganizational); their communication capabilities including their abilities (and willingness) to share, surface, and attend to unique information; their abilities to resolve conflicts; the media used in communication; and intense scanning and performance-monitoring routines that provide opportunities for interaction and communication. Communica-

tion is equally important in the interpretation process. Communication is critical to the construction of information filters through which information is interpreted and is an integral part of enacting those interpretations.

## OUTWARD INFORMATION FLOWS: AN OVERVIEW

To this point, I have focused on incoming information flows, and more specifically, on the processing of environmental information oriented primarily at adapting or reacting to environmental demands, contingencies, or constraints. However, as noted earlier, organizations proactively and strategically manage the flow of information outward to the environment to preempt anticipated problems or hedge against unanticipated ones (Grunig, 1984; Vertzberger, 1990), to manage the real or potential consequences of risks and crises (Heath, 1988; Heath & Nelson, 1986), to alter dependencies by affecting the relationship of the organization relative to other entities in its environment (Pfeffer & Salancik, 1978), and to enhance legitimacy and create value for the firm (Elsbach, 1994; Lev, 1992; Suchman, 1995). Understanding the flow of information outward from an organization to its environment is the focus of the following section.

Organizational communication scholars have paid attention to information flows from organizations to their environments—particularly in the areas of mass communication, issues management, and risk communication. Notwithstanding this attention, however, to a large extent, scholarship in mainstream organizational communication has focused on intraorganizational information processing and interpersonal communication among organizational members. Much of the work examining how organizations manage the flow of information to their environments has been done by scholars in the public relations domain. However, the contributions of public relations scholars have not yet been deeply incorporated into mainstream organizational communication and organizational theory literatures.

Information flows from organizations to their environments have received fragmented attention in the organizational theory literature. Two major theoretical perspectives in organizational theory have made reference to how organizations use information to manage their environments and improve legitimacy: impression management theories and institutional theories. Drawing on impression management theories, recent work in organizational theory has focused on the use of justifications to improve an organization's image to enhance performance (Bettman & Weitz, 1983; Salancik & Meindl, 1984; Staw, McKechnie, & Puffer, 1983), and on identifying the form and content of effective organizational accounts (Elsbach, 1994; Marcus & Goodman, 1991). Institutional theorists have focused on how organizations attempt to project legitimacy by highlighting the adoption of widely used and accepted practices (DiMaggio & Powell, 1983; Elsbach & Sutton, 1992; Feldman & March, 1981). Although organizational scholars assume that "managing strategically" means to accomplish the organization's mission coincident with managing environmental relationships, there has been little effort by organizational theorists to consolidate research examining differences in how and why organizations choose to manage the flow of information to the environment, the information tactics used, or the factors and mechanisms that affect external communication behaviors.

Corporate communication, public relations, and information/communication management have been used interchangeably in the organizational communication, public relations, and organization theory literatures (and are used here) to mean the management of information or communication between an organization and its environment, or more specifically, between an organization and its publics or stakeholders (Cheney & Dionisopoulos, 1989; Grunig & Hunt, 1984, p. 6).

According to Grunig and Hunt (1984, p. 6), communication management (i.e., strategic public relations) includes a myriad of activities (i.e., planning, execution, evaluation) aimed at enhancing an organization's communication with the external and internal groups that affect its ability to meet its goals. The presumed goal of strategic public relations is to increase a firm's autonomy and limit or circumscribe its dependence.

In the following sections, to further our understanding of how organizations manage flows of information to their environments, I draw heavily on research and theory in public relations, issues management, and crisis communication and examine (1) typologies of organizational information management behaviors, (2) determinants of information management behaviors and the mechanisms that influence outward information flows, and (3) the effectiveness of particular communication strategies.

### Classifying External Information Behaviors

Typologies of communication behaviors are grounded in Thayer's (1968) concepts of synchronic and diachronic communication. "The purpose of synchronic communication is to 'synchronize' the behavior of a public with that of the organization so that the organization can continue to behave in the way it wants without interference. The purpose of diachronic communication is to negotiate a state of affairs that benefits both the organization and the public" (Grunig & Grunig, 1992, p. 287). Grunig and Hunt (1984) expanded these ideas and developed a typology of public relations behaviors useful not only for categorizing the types of communication behaviors exhibited in organizations but also for thinking about how organizations manage communicative relationships with their environments. The four types—*press agentry/ publicity, public information, two-way asymmetric,* and *two-way symmetric*—are described more fully below.

The press agentry model describes communication behaviors aimed at seeking favorable publicity or media attention in almost any way possible, especially in the mass media. Organizations practicing the public information model, on the other hand, disseminate relatively objective information—mostly accurate and positive rather than negative—through mass media, and other controlled media such as newsletters, brochures, and direct mail (Grunig, 1990). Both the press agentry and public information models are considered one-way communication models because they try to manipulate stakeholders for the benefit of the organization through hype or by disseminating exclusively favorable information without conducting research or planning.[1] The two-way asymmetrical model describes organizations that conduct research to identify the types of messages that are likely to produce the support of important stakeholders without having to change the behavior of the organization. Finally, the two-way symmetrical model describes organizations that use dialogue, bargaining, negotiation, and conflict management strategies to improve understanding and build relationships between an organization and its stakeholders.

Research examining these four behavioral types has shown that few organizations practice two-way symmetrical communication even though it is hypothesized to enhance firm performance (Grunig & Grunig, 1992). More typical is one-way (or even two-way) asymmetrical communication in which organizations refuse to accept responsibility for negative controversies, withhold information in hopes of diminishing alarm, or put a positive spin on events to frame situations in a more favorable light (e.g., Elsbach, 1994; Marcus & Goodman, 1991).

### Determining External Information Behaviors

Early theories predicting communication management practices were contingency based and examined how the types of communication behaviors exhibited by organizations vary as a consequence of organization type, the nature of the environment, and organization structure. Grunig and Hunt (1984), for example, argued that communication behaviors would vary depending on an organization's fundamental mission and goals (e.g., the type of organization). They proposed that sports, theater, or consumer product organizations would be most likely to employ the press agent model; government agencies and nonprofit organizations such as universities would be most likely to use the public information model; competitive firms would practice the two-way asymmetrical model; and regulated businesses would practice the two-way symmetrical model. Findings from a number of studies appear to support this line of thinking (Grunig & Grunig, 1992) with much of the variation attributed to an organization's history and the institutionalization of routines. For example, Grunig and Grunig (1992, p. 307) explain that public information may be most common in government because of the institutionalized confinements placed on its practice there.

Another stream of research examining determinants of organizational communication practices is grounded in assumptions related to resource dependence, autonomy, and the idea that organizations naturally want to dominate their environments and reduce their dependence by managing interdependencies with entities in the environment that restrict their autonomy (Pfeffer & Salancik, 1978). Central to these studies is the idea that environmental constraints or dependence influence external communication behaviors. For example, Grunig (1976) and Schneider (1985) hypothesized that symmetrical communication will be more likely in organic organizations facing constraining, uncertain environments. They argued that organizations facing environmental constraints and uncertainty will be prompted to establish symmetrical information flows to achieve stable, predictable, and dependable relations with other actors in the environment. Thus, as the complexity and uncertainty of the environment increase, the complexity of communication practices increases because effective coping requires organizations to seek information from their environments and also to disseminate information to the environment to forecast or forestall uncertainty and achieve a more reliable pattern of resource exchanges. While intuitively appealing, the hypotheses were not supported (Grunig, 1976; Schneider, 1985). Other studies in public relations have failed to support these ideas as well (Grunig & Grunig, 1989).

Recently, researchers have abandoned their focus on contingency explanations and have adopted a power-control perspective to explain externally directed communication behaviors (Grunig, 1990). Results from a five-year study of public relations by Grunig and his colleagues (see Grunig, 1992) suggest that external communication practices are affected by

- Organizational power (i.e., the worldview held by the dominant coalition and whether the dominant coalition includes a senior public relations executive)

- Organizational culture (an organizational culture that is flexible and favors shared responsibility for problem solving, and a dominant coalition whose beliefs and values are consistent with information sharing)

- The expertise and knowledge of the top public relations executive (a relatively powerful and valued senior public relations executive that can advise organizations about ways to implement two-way symmetrical communication; Dozier, 1992)

In addition to the influence of political and normative pressures arising internally, communication behaviors may also be affected by normative external forces. In fact, the institutional environment may impose pressures on organizations to justify activities or outputs (DiMaggio & Powell, 1983; Elsbach, 1994; Meyer & Rowan, 1977), and

these legitimacy pressures may affect outward information flows and organizational information management strategies more generally. The flow of information for purposes of increasing legitimacy can originate when an organization is motivated to demonstrate or improve its reputation, image, prestige, or congruence with prevailing norms in its institutional environment. Thus, it is important to consider the more symbolic aspects of information management and the idea that corporate communication may help to shape identity and legitimize an organization and its actions (Feldman & March, 1981; Sitkin, Sutcliffe, & Barrios-Choplin, 1992).

Public relations theory advances the prescription that organizations engaging in two-way symmetrical communication will be more effective than organizations practicing asymmetrical communication. This line of thinking is based on the idea that organizations can enhance their autonomy and legitimacy by proactively managing their interdependencies through interactive communication with the publics that provide the greatest threats and opportunities for the organization. Two-way communication including bargaining, negotiating, and strategies to reduce conflict help to bring about "symbiotic changes in the ideas, attitudes, and behaviors of both the organization and its publics" (Grunig, 1992, p. 29). Yet it is not surprising to find that effective organizations often mix the two-way models (Grunig & Grunig, 1992).

Organizations have multiple and conflicting goals and multiple and conflicting stakeholders interested in and affected by a constantly shifting mix of issues or problems. To deal with the stream of goals, stakeholders, and issues, organizations must balance the necessity of persuading stakeholders or publics with the necessity of negotiating with them. Thus, organizations mixing the two-way asymmetrical and symmetrical models, in fact, may be "strategically" managing the flow of outward information in that "it is in the strategic interest of organizations to change their behavior when they provoke opposition from the environment as well as to try to change the behavior of environmental stakeholders" (Grunig & Repper, 1992, p. 123).

Strategically managing communication with the environment is inextricably tied to environmental information processing and, more specifically, to the processes of noticing and interpreting environmental information concerning stakeholders, publics, and issues. Researchers in public relations and issues management emphasize that organization-environment relationships can best be understood by thinking of the environment in terms of organizations, stakeholders, publics, and issues (Grunig, 1992) in dynamic competition. Stakeholders, individuals, groups, or other organizations that can affect or are affected by organizational decisions, actions, policies, or practices become publics when they recognize organizational decisions or actions, outcomes, or related consequences as a problem and organize to do something about the issue(s) recognized (Grunig & Repper, 1992). While these relations are portrayed as simple and linear in theory, in reality, organization-stakeholder relations are more complex, dynamic, and ambiguous since different focal organizations are competing with one another for the attention and support of the same stakeholders. Communication, in particular, persuasion and advocacy, is critical for influencing interpretations that will predominate.

One potential concern with defining the environment as a network of important stakeholders and active publics concerned with problems is that it implies that communication management behaviors are primarily reactive, aimed at minimizing the potential threats of active publics. Yet organizations do more than respond to their environments in a cybernetic way. Rather than merely adapting to them, organizations proactively attempt to shape their environments through communication. That is, through communication, many organizations try to impose their preferred definition of situations and issues on their environments. The processes of how information penetrates an organization's cognitive system and how it is interpreted are underdeveloped and sometimes taken for granted in much of the public relations literature (see Heath, 1994, for an exception). Yet, as noted throughout this chapter, understanding the dynamics and antecedents that pertain to how key organizational decision makers attend to and make sense of environmental elements, how interpretations affect subsequent organizational actions (including communication acts), and how environmental entities subsequently make sense of organizational actions and communication is at the heart of environmental information processing.

Although issues don't come automatically labeled as threats or opportunities, the way an issue is labeled (i.e., interpreted) may predictably affect organizational communication behaviors. Evidence by Chess, Tamuz, et al. (1992) suggests that two-way communication is often initiated when organizational members perceive that stakeholders or issues pose a moderate degree of threat or uncontrollability (rather than high or low degree of threat). This implies two things. First, if stakeholders are perceived as entirely quiescent, distant, or disinterested there is no motivation for symmetrical communication. Second, if stakeholder scrutiny or hostility is perceived to be too great, an organization may choose to ignore the threat and wall itself off to protect itself (Chess, Tamuz, et al., 1992). This reconfirms the importance interpretations play in affecting organizational actions—in this case communication actions. Research examining strategic decision makers' interpretations about their environments, publics, or issues may provide important insights about these issues.

## External Information Flows, Legitimacy, and Organizational Performance

So far, I have described typical information management behaviors and discussed the factors and mechanisms that relevant theory suggests may influence outward information flows more generally. In this section, I examine information tactics more specifically, and how they differentially affect organizational legitimacy and performance. In an increasingly turbulent world, outward communication is particularly relevant before, during, or after scandals, accidents, crises, or other situations that threaten an organization's legitimacy. I use specific examples from risk communication, organizational theory, and strategic management to illustrate the outward communication strategies organizations use in preparation for or in response to legitimacy threats and how these tactics are related to organizational outcomes (for examples, see Heath, 1988, 1994; Heath & Nelson, 1986; Rowland & Rademacher, 1990; Small, 1991; for a more extensive discussion of specific communication tactics). The examples cited are meant to be illustrative, and I have not been exhaustive in citing relevant work. Thus, the examples are not wholly representative of each of the literatures sampled.

Chess, Tamuz, et al. (1992) and Chess, Saville, et al.'s (1992) in-depth case study of Sybron Chemicals provides insights not only into how firms can respond to volatile publics but also into the internal mechanisms, structures, and processes that influence both the type of and effectiveness of external communication. As Chess and her colleagues note, research into external communication is particularly relevant and timely given that, in the past ten years, technological failures have eroded public confidence in organizations' capabilities to reduce the likelihood of such crises. After several small crises (see Chess, Saville, et al., 1992, p. 432), Sybron Chemicals Inc. determined that its survival depended on improving relations with the community and subsequently developed effective, ongoing, two-way symmetrical communication practices aimed at managing risk. The results of the Chess, Saville, et al. study suggest that five internal factors affect the propensity to establish effective risk communication practices. First, risk communication is inextrica-

bly linked with risk management and other goals to improve health and safety. Second, symmetrical communication is more likely when a firm perceives important stakeholders as threatening the company's profitability. Third, diffusion of communication responsibilities among multiple organizational members at varying hierarchical levels is likely to increase two-way symmetrical communication with stakeholders; however, the success of such practices depends on the effectiveness of internal communication.[2] Fourth, risk communication requires the sensing and amplification of bad news, which often depend on a high degree of trust and openness among organizational members at all levels in the hierarchy. Finally, effective two-way communication is more likely when there are mechanisms to institutionalize organizational learning.

The case of Sybron Chemicals (Chess, Saville, et al., 1992; Chess, Tamuz, et al., 1992) and Small's (1991) analysis of Exxon's handling of the Valdez oil spill highlight that two-way communication aimed at preempting anticipated problems and managing the real or potential consequences of risks and crises can enhance firm legitimacy and performance in the long run. Still, it is more often the case that organizations fail to communicate with stakeholders until after a scandal or crisis occurs. Recent studies by Marcus and Goodman (1991) and Elsbach (1994) demonstrate, more specifically, how organizations construct communication intended to deflect public criticism following a crisis and how these different communication efforts influence performance.

Marcus and Goodman (1991) examined public managerial announcements after scandals, accidents, and public safety violations to determine investor reactions to two types of statements: accommodative statements in which management admits to the problem, accepts responsibility, and is ready to take remedial actions, and defensive statements in which management denies problem existence, confirms the firm's ability to generate revenue, and suggests the rapid resumption of normal operations (Marcus & Goodman, 1991, p. 286). They found that following accidents investors reacted more positively to defensive statements rather than to accommodative statements and that following scandals investors reacted more positively to accommodative statements rather than to defensive statements. Thus, in the short term, defensive accounts were more effective in protecting an organization's legitimacy; however, as the authors note, it was not possible to determine the longer-term effects of such a defensive posture. Nonetheless, Marcus and Goodman's study holds a very important implication. If defensiveness is the predominant response after serious accidents or crises, paradoxically, two-way communication will be curtailed at the precise time it is most needed because diminished interactions between an organization and its environment may constrain opportunities to ferret out unique solutions and remedies for resolving or rectifying the calamity.

Marcus and Goodman's (1991) findings are contrary to results reported by Elsbach (1994). In a more finely grained study exploring the construction and effectiveness of organizational accounts, Elsbach found that accommodative accounts containing references to widely institutionalized characteristics (e.g., legitimate hierarchies and roles, legitimate rules and procedures, legitimate goals or outcomes) are the most effective in protecting organizational legitimacy following moderately negative controversies. Both studies provide insights (albeit contradictory) into the types of accounts that are most effective in enhancing or regaining organizational legitimacy and performance following untoward events. More work needs to be done in this area to link organizational accounts, external communication practices, and organizational outcomes more generally.

In summarizing the discussion on outward information flows, several conclusions can be drawn. First, in theory, organizations reactively, proactively, and interactively communicate with their environments to preempt or hedge against problems, to alter dependencies, to enhance legitimacy, and to create value for the firm; in practice, there are many variations in the ways organizations communicate with entities in their environments. Second, current research suggests external communication practices are determined at least in part by power, culture, the roles played by senior public relations executives, and institutional requirements. Third, linking current research describing organizational communication strategies with research examining organizational sensing and interpretative mechanisms can provide useful insights into questions related to what determines outward communication, what affects the form and content of organizational communication, and how communication is linked with organizational performance.

## TOWARD AN INTEGRATIVE FRAMEWORK: AN ENVIRONMENTAL SENSEMAKING AND SENSEGIVING MODEL

In this chapter, I have conceptually separated environmental information coming into an organization from information going out to the environment for ease in discussing the two processes. This is not to imply, however, that the processes are independent. In fact, the processes are inextricably linked. Organizations survive by making sense of environmental information, and in the process of making sense of their environment and to gain legitimacy organizations attempt to influence the opinions and interpretations of stakeholders and other environmental entities by communicating and asserting "themselves into the community around them" (Heath, 1994, p. 27). The process continues as stakeholders confirm or disconfirm an organization's proposed vision and attempt to influence its realized form. Borrowing from the work of Gioia and Chittipeddi (1991), the concepts of "sensemaking" and "sensegiving" provide a useful framework for better understanding the link between the two processes. The framework is discussed more fully below.

Once environmental data, information, or messages are selected, somehow penetrate, or flow into an organization's cognitive system, they are interpreted and given meaning and are often used as the basis on which organizational actions are built. Therefore, interpretations related to the information to which organizational members attend is a critical component of processing information about the external environment. The sensemaking label highlights this meaning construction by organizational participants and that environmental data and information are often ambiguous and do not come neatly packaged. In the process of developing a meaningful framework for understanding the nature of the environment, organizational members construct and reconstruct their interpretations (Gioia & Chittipeddi, 1991), and this is the essence of sensemaking.

The sensegiving label highlights the process by which organizations and their members communicate with entities in their environment. The sensegiving process is focused on influencing the "sensemaking and meaning construction of others toward a preferred redefinition of organizational reality" (Gioia & Chittipeddi, 1991, p. 442). By what they do and what they say, organizations attempt to attract attention, gain acceptance, and assert opinions. Because information is not inherently meaningful, organizations use symbols and symbolic action to give sense to their environments: to communicate their (i.e., the organization's) preferred interpretative scheme, and also to negotiate, build harmony, and resolve conflict.

Although I describe sensemaking and sensegiving in an orderly and linear way, these processes are nonlinear, reciprocal, iterative, and dynamic. Executives single out particular information in the environment as a consequence of a number of factors; develop a cognitive representation of contingencies; label or interpret perceived pressing demands, threats, or opportunities; refine their conception of the organization in relation to its environment; and subsequently create a guiding vision for the organization (sensemaking). Following this interpretive work, organizations communicate this vision to stakeholders and other constituencies (sensegiving). Stakeholders and constituencies engage in sensemaking processes as they try to figure out the meaning of the organization's communication and in the process revise their understanding of the organization and their relationship to it (sensemaking). Following this interpretive process, these entities engage in sensegiving efforts as they provide feedback and confirm or disconfirm the organization's vision. In this way, sensemaking and sensegiving cycles correspond to periods dominated by *understanding* and *influencing*. "Sensemaking phases are those that deal primarily with understanding processes and the sensegiving phases are those that concern attempts to influence the way that another party understands or makes sense" (Gioia & Chittipeddi, 1991, p. 443).

Organizational sensemaking and sensegiving processes are not random. Weick and Daft's (1983) description of organizational interpretation modes provides a platform for understanding how differences in interpretation modes systematically affect information gathering and interpreting behaviors and subsequent communication acts aimed toward affecting other actors in their environment. Differences in interpretation systems affect how active organizations are in collecting environmental information, the information to which they attend, the labels organizations apply to the information they collect, and the predominant type of organizational communication practices (i.e., asymmetrical vs. symmetrical). In addition, interpretation modes affect the general communication stance an organization takes in giving sense to its environment by affecting how strongly an organization tries to influence stakeholder perceptions toward itself (i.e., the assertiveness of organizational communication).

Daft and Weick (1984; Weick & Daft, 1983) argue that interpretation systems vary along two dimensions—the extent to which management believes the environment to be objectively given or analyzable, and the degree to which organizations actively penetrate their environments to gather information. Combined, these distinctions form the basis of a framework of four interpretive modes— enacting, discovering, undirected viewing, and conditioned viewing—that differentially affect organizational sensemaking and sensegiving behaviors.

Enacting organizations construct their own environments because they believe the environment to be unanalyzable. They experiment, test, stimulate, and ignore precedent. Enacting organizations are likely to be the most assertive in attempting to influence or shape stakeholder attitudes. In this way, enacting organizations are likely to "give the most sense to" their environments than the other types. Consequently, enacting organizations may be predisposed to two-way asymmetrical communication behaviors (Grunig, 1984). The discovering mode also represents an active organization, but discovering organizations assume the external environment is concrete. Discovering organizations actively gather attitudinal data from stakeholders, and these data are interpreted as perceived environmental requirements. The externally directed communication of discovering organizations is likely to be adaptive and responsive to stakeholder demands and less assertive in manipulating stakeholder attitudes toward themselves. Because discovering organizations are likely to engage in a dynamic process of negotiating with important environmental entities, they may be predisposed to two-way symmetrical communication (Grunig, 1984). Organizations characterized by undirected viewing are nonintrusive and assume the environment to be unanalyzable. An undirected-viewing organization will be assertive in shaping stakeholder opinions when the opportunity arises. Undirected-viewing organizations may be predisposed to engage in one-way public information behaviors (Grunig, 1984) and will use informal opportunities such as telephone contacts about questions or complaints or annual shareholder meetings to learn about stakeholder opinions and to shape and influence those opinions (Weick & Daft, 1983). Finally, the conditioned-viewing mode represents less active organizations that assume an the environment to be analyzable. Conditioned-viewing organizations rely on formal data collection, planning, and forecasting and develop traditional interpretations about "constraints" in the environment. Communication by these organizations is likely to be reactive and may reflect a more defensive stance than the other types. Thus, organizations in the conditioned-viewing mode may be predisposed to one-way press agentry type behaviors (Grunig, 1984).

Organizations attempt to do more than respond to their environments in a reactive or adaptive way. Organizations try to shape their environments as well as adapt to them. Sensemaking and sensegiving processes are inextricably and reciprocally tied as sensemaking guides sensegiving and sensegiving guides sensemaking. The sensemaking and sensegiving framework provides an integrative perspective for understanding the processing of environmental information in that it links incoming with outgoing informational processes. The sensemaking and sensegiving framework also highlights the dynamism involved in environmental information processing. Finally, a focus on sensemaking and sensegiving moves us away from thinking about information processing from an "information flows" perspective. Thinking about inward and outward information flows may be potentially misleading. Flow is the process of transmitting information, yet information is not inherently meaningful. Meanings are not transferred; individuals and organizations determine the meaning of information (i.e., communication acts) based on evaluative schemas in use. Consequently, sensemaking and sensegiving better reflect that meanings are constituted and reconstituted through the dynamic, reciprocal, and iterative processing of environmental information.

## IMPLICATIONS FOR RESEARCH

The purpose of this chapter was to explore organizational environments and organizational information processing with the intention of highlighting issues that have been underdeveloped, disregarded, or otherwise overlooked in previous examinations of these topics. In this chapter, I have focused on sensing and interpreting processes related to incoming information flows and have also examined the flow of information outward from organizations to their environments. Environmental information processing embodies exchanges of information and inferences of meaning at the heart of communication theory and consequently is important for scholars interested in organizational communication. This chapter points to a number of areas to extend and enhance current research in organizational and communication theory.

### Implications for Extending Current Research

One avenue of future research concerns the construct of environment. As noted in the discussion of the environment, despite over 40 years of work and widespread dissatisfaction with both extreme views (i.e., objective vs. enactment), little has emerged to replace them. This would seem a rich area for research. Are current models meaningful to strategic managers and other organizational members who analyze their organization's environment? Are they meaningful to researchers trying to understand communication issues related to how organizational members make sense of and give sense to their environments? For example, characterizing the envi-

ronment in terms of its attributes such as volatility, munificence, and complexity may be too abstract for managers and for researchers as well. Although these conceptualizations may make environmental analysis more tractable in theory, it may be of little use in practice. Consequently, researchers must continue with their efforts to redefine and refine the concept of "environment," both in terms of perceptions and in terms of objectively measured attributes and how subjectivity and objectivity are blended (Weick, 1983). Richer methods and longitudinal designs are needed (see Fahey & Narayanan, 1989). For example, studies linking the cognitive maps of the dominant coalition over time with descriptive data on the environmental context coupled with descriptions of internal and external communication processes may provide fruitful insights into how managers operationally think of their environments; how environmental maps are developed, changed, and updated over time; and the consequences of shifts in perceived boundaries.

A related question is whether the construct of "environment" is still useful in a post-industrial world (Huber, 1984). Given the increasing plurality of organizations and environments; their overlapping, shifting, and permeable boundaries; and multiple and conflicting goals, stakeholders, and publics interested in and affected by a constantly shifting mix of issues or problems, it may be more useful, as public relations scholars suggest (Grunig, 1997), to think of environments as networks or hierarchies of stakeholders, publics, and issues. Conceptualizing environments in network terms may be important for understanding external communication behaviors and for understanding the reciprocal influence of organizations on environments and environments on organizations. For example, by focusing on what information means to different units or entities within and among networks as well as how information flows and is distributed within and among networks, future studies may shed light on the extent to which the interpretive systems used by members in interlocking networks are compatible, complementary, or contradictory (Heath, 1994). Insights into these "zones of meaning" (Heath, 1994) will enable researchers to better understand and predict interlocking interactions between organizations and their environments. Studies in this area may also provide insights about the accuracy of decision makers' views of their environment and how accuracy is achieved because executives in organizations in tightly coupled systems, by necessity, may develop more accurate views of the environment than their counterparts in loosely coupled systems.

More needs to be said about accuracy. Even if a more tractable model of assessing the environment is found (i.e., stakeholders, publics, issues), the issue of accuracy is still salient. The question of how well organizations and their members are able to sense important trends or elements still remains. Although some researchers argue that perceptual accuracy is not necessary (Starbuck & Milliken, 1988), the quality of certain types of important organizational decisions or actions may be determined in large part by the degree to which perceptions of environmental information adequately or accurately represent reality. Planes crash (i.e., Tenerife) because airline crews misinterpret environmental information (Weick, 1990b). Wars get started because one side misinterprets the actions of the other (Vertzberger, 1984). Intel gets in trouble when it misreads the extent to which people care about flawed Pentium chips and subsequently adopts a cavalier communication stance. External communication based on flawed perceptions may negatively affect a firm's legitimacy.

An assumption underlying this chapter is that information processing is purposeful behavior by which individuals, groups, or organizations become aware of, handle, manage, resolve, or control data and information about the environment. The outcome of information processing is manifest in a representation of the environmental landscape. The quality of the information-processing process can be evaluated against its product by determining the accuracy of perception, or in other words, the extent of misperception produced (i.e., the discrepancy between the real world and perceptual world). This view is admittedly embedded in rational, strategic choice assumptions. However, because of bounded rationality, individuals and organizations are limited as information processors, which suggests, as noted earlier, that a certain level of misperception is inevitable in every information-processing system. Thus, better information processing may not so much be characterized by an ability to choose between accurate images and misperceptions, but rather the ability to enhance plausibility and choose between different potential misperceptions.

Although it is often true that the dynamism and complexity of environments preclude totally accurate perceptions, accuracy matters sometimes about some things. From a communication management perspective, the distinction between global accuracy and circumscribed accuracy may be important (Swann, 1984; Weick, 1995). Global accuracy is concerned with the perception of widely generalizable beliefs. Circumscribed accuracy is a more limiting concept and is focused on specific predictions in a limited number of contexts for short periods (Swann, 1984; Weick, 1995). Not all information in the environment is likely to be relevant for organizational success, and research suggests that attention to particular kinds of information may be crucial for survival (D'Aveni & MacMillan, 1990). One important implication is that some things must be sensed and communicated more accurately than others. Even though little is known about this or the communication processes that affect these attention and selection processes, it may be useful to investigate the communication dynamics related to how organizational members single out and give meaning to particular components of the information environment. Research in this area may be especially important for understanding the dynamic features of competitive interactions.

Two areas of future research may be relevant. First, studies examining symmetrical information flows within organizations (i.e., with internal stakeholders) may shed light on how communication affects attention and selection. For example, research by Smith, Grimm, Gannon, and Chen (1991) shows that firms respond faster to their competitors' tactical actions than to strategic actions. Two conclusions can be drawn from this study: (1) tactical actions in some way are more salient than strategic actions and therefore get detected more quickly and more frequently, and (2) it is much more difficult to interpret the information contained in strategic actions than tactical actions. Symmetrical information systems in which employees are provided mechanisms for dialogue with each other, with supervisors, and with top managers may help employees more deeply understand their organization's goals, plans, and relationships with key actors in the environment. This not only will enhance coordination among subsystems but also will enhance the achievement of strategic objectives because lower-level employees may be better primed to recognize important environmental signals and this ultimately will affect the quality of sensing and sensemaking processes. Second, symmetrical information will help organizational members to make sense of their situation, may facilitate commitment to work and to the organization, and may enhance rather than constrain organizational members' sensemaking abilities (Gioia & Chittipeddi, 1991).

In addition to research on symmetrical information within organizations, research related to organizational interpretation systems is also needed. Interpretation modes are not random, and differences in how organizations interpret environmental information is likely to play a critical role in responsiveness to the environment (Daft & Weick, 1984; Gioia & Thomas, 1996). One rich source of ideas for organizational communication scholars relates to systematically validating organizational interpretation modes, their determinants, and their consequences. Interpretation modes may determine an organization's responsiveness to its environment by affecting what gets sensed, how information is interpreted, and how an organization responds (including the type of communication behaviors such as asymmetrical vs. symmetrical and also the form and content of particular messages). Although these ideas are powerful, there is little empirical work in this area.

Additional research focused on the information environment may also be useful for understanding why important information is rejected, considered irrelevant, or unimportant or why unimportant information (i.e., noise) is considered meaningful, relevant, and important (Vertzberger, 1984). Organizational communication studies in the areas of deception, secrecy, silence, or the nonexistence of information may also provide useful insights about the information environment and information-processing quality.

Another avenue for extending current research builds on the idea that even though misperceptions of environmental information are inevitable as environmental complexity and turbulence increase, it is important to understand how such distortions occur particularly because distortions or misperceptions are likely to affect external communication practices. Although a number of perceptual errors or incongruencies may occur, there are two major mismatches. Executives may notice more of an environmental attribute when there is less or none, or may fail to notice an environmental attribute that is present in the environment. It is likely that seeing more when there is less will have a different effect on an organization's responsiveness and performance than seeing less when there is more. For example, seeing more when there is less may result in reduced efficiency or profitability as firms waste resources on unnecessary scanning or information-monitoring activities thereby hindering firm performance (Boyd et al., 1993). However, seeing less when there is more—failing to detect changes or conditions—may have a far greater potential for bringing about negative consequences for an organization. If the environment is changing and a firm fails to notice changes and initiate appropriate adaptive responses, the firm's survival may be threatened. This suggests that the performance consequences of failing to detect environmental changes will be more serious than the performance consequences of perceiving conditions that are not there.

## Promising Avenues for Future Research

Past work provides a foundation on which the study of organizational information processing and environmental information flows can build. However, there are several promising new avenues of research opportunity that have been largely neglected in past work.

First, as the trend of global competition becomes increasingly dominant, scholars are particularly interested in the transferability of theories developed in Western economies to other countries. There is some evidence to suggest that models describing environmental information-processing activities in developed countries fail to adequately explain and predict the information-processing activities in developing countries (Kiggundu, Jorgensen, & Hafsi, 1983; Sawyerr, 1993). For example, Sawyerr (1993) found that Nigerian executives differed in important ways from their American counterparts in their scanning behaviors (e.g., types of sources used) and in terms of the attributes of the environment they identified as most important in affecting the organization's behavior. There is also research suggesting major differences in environmental intelligence systems between the United States and other countries (Ghoshal & Kim, 1986) and also in interpretation systems (Triandis & Albert, 1987). An examination of differences and similarities in information-processing behaviors across nations coupled with studies focusing on intercultural communication related both to sensemaking and to sensegiving processes seem important avenues for future research. If

we assume that environmental information sensing and processing are major sources of competitive advantage among firms that are increasingly similar in terms of their technological and managerial competencies, these research avenues could provide many interesting insights into these issues.

To this point, I have focused primarily on extending research primarily in the sensemaking area related to the processing of incoming environmental information. However, there is more work to be done in examining how and why organizations differ in managing flows of information to their environments and in examining the processes that affect symmetrical communication between organizations and their environments. Three areas related to the outward flow of information are in need of attention.

First, more attention needs to be paid to incorporating the extensive body of work in the public relations domain examining organizational communication management behaviors into mainstream communication and organization theories. In particular, integrating ideas from organizational communication theory and ideas related to interpretation and its role in influencing communication behaviors with public relations theory could genuinely enhance our understanding of these issues.

Second, although research examining the development and consequences of communication norms across organizational boundaries is growing, more work needs to be done in assessing the antecedents of such communication practices (e.g., Chess, Saville, et al., 1992; Chess, Tamuz, et al., 1992; Elsbach, 1994; Marcus & Goodman, 1991). This seems particularly relevant with the increasing predominance of network organizations and increasing emphasis on quality and continuous learning. Organizations often develop standardized communication routines that match the expectations or requirements imposed by various environmental contingencies (Feldman & March, 1981; Sitkin et al., 1992). The adoption of particular methods acceptable to key external groups may contribute to a firm's legitimacy and may be essential for continued survival and success (Meyer & Rowan, 1977). Over time, information flows, interactions, or communication patterns may become routinized within an industry or organizational field such that no alternative methods are considered, even when alternatives may be more efficient and effective (Sitkin et al., 1992). Research drawing on the institutional theory perspective may provide important insights.

Finally, with increasing attention being paid to the issues of opportunism and trust between organizations, research investigating the development of collaborative versus competitive interorganizational relations also may provide useful insights about flows of information across organizational boundaries. While competitive opportunism by environmental actors has been largely taken for granted in much of the strategic management and organizational theory literature, it may be useful to question these assumptions regarding the behavior of economic actors. Perhaps trusting behavior between economic actors can be identified and may lead to better outcomes in an interdependent world. Research integrating ideas from the literatures on competitive strategies, conflict, collaboration, and risk communication may provide a rich mixture from which to formulate a more comprehensive framework to explain corporate communication behaviors.

## CONCLUSION

Organizations are information-obtaining and information-processing systems. Yet to think of organizations solely as thinking entities that make cybernetic adjustments to environments based on objective data regarding goal achievement can be misleading. It fails to acknowledge the inherent complexities in sensing and interpreting environmental information. Further, an information-processing perspective alone fails to highlight that organizations are more than adaptive systems. Organizations proactively attempt to shape their

environments by influencing the opinions and interpretations of stakeholders and other important environmental entities. This chapter has broadened the conception of organizational information processing by articulating the idea that organizations not only make sense of their environments but also give sense to their environments.

## NOTES

1. Early public relations theories were dominated by the presupposition that the purpose of public relations was to manipulate the behavior of publics for the benefit of the organization (Grunig, 1992) and assumed that one-way communication is manipulative or asymmetric and that two-way communication is informative or symmetric. Yet, as Grunig (1984) highlights, "many organizations, such as universities or government agencies, provide one-way communication that is truthful and informative and benefits publics as much as or more than it benefits the organization. Other organizations use two-way communication to manipulate rather than adapt to publics. Their public relations practitioners do research—seek information—to determine what publics like and dislike about the organizations and then give information to those publics that describes the organization as having attributes the public favors and ignores attributes the public does not favor" (p. 8).

2. The effectiveness of decentralized communication responsibilities depends, in part, on the effectiveness of an organization's internal communication. As Small (1991) highlights in his study of Exxon's response to the Valdez oil spill, decentralized communication responsibilities can be problematic if an organization's internal communication is weak. If there is good two-way internal communication among all levels in the hierarchy, there is likely to be enhanced coordination among subsystems and a deeper understanding of the organization's goals, plans, and relationships with key actors in the environment. However, Small also points out that decentralized communication structures may be ineffective during crises or other untoward events.

## REFERENCES

Abolafia, M. Y., & Kilduff, M. (1988). Enacting market crisis: The social construction of a speculative bubble. *Administrative Science Quarterly, 33,* 177-193.

Aldrich, H. (1979). *Organizations and environments.* Englewood Cliffs, NJ: Prentice Hall.

Aldrich, H., & Auster, E. R. (1986). Even dwarfs started small. In B. M. Staw & L. L. Cummings (Eds.), *Research in organizational behavior* (Vol. 8, pp. 165-198). Greenwich, CT: JAI.

Aldrich, H., & Pfeffer, J. (1976). Environments of organizations. *Annual Review of Sociology, 2,* 79-105.

Barr, P., Stimpert, J., & Huff, A. (1992). Cognitive change, strategic action, and organizational renewal. *Strategic Management Journal, 13,* 15-36.

Bateman, T. S., & Zeithaml, C. P. (1989). The psychological context of strategic decisions: A model and convergent experimental findings. *Strategic Management Journal, 9,* 71-78.

Bettman, J., & Weitz, B. (1983). Attributions in the board room: Causal reasoning in corporate annual reports. *Administrative Science Quarterly, 28,* 165-183.

Beyer, J. M. (1981). Ideologies, values, and decision making in organizations. In P. Nystrom & W. Starbuck (Eds.), *Handbook of organizational design* (pp. 166-202). New York: Oxford University Press.

Bourgeois, L. J. (1980). Strategy and environment: A conceptual integration. *Academy of Management Review, 5,* 25-29.

Bourgeois, L. J. (1985). Strategic goals, perceived uncertainty, and economic performance in volatile environments. *Academy of Management Journal, 28,* 548-573.

Boyd, B. K., Dess, G. G., & Rasheed, A. M. (1993). Divergence between archival and perceptual measures of the environment: Causes and consequences. *Academy of Management Review, 18,* 204-226.

Caves, R. E. (1980). Industrial organization, corporate strategy, and structure. *Journal of Economic Literature, 28,* 64-92.

Cheney, G., & Dionisopoulos, G. N. (1989). Public relations? No, relations with publics: A rhetorical-organizational approach to contemporary corporate communications. In C. H. Botan & V. Hazleton, Jr. (Eds.), *Public relations theory* (pp. 135-157). Hillsdale, NJ: Lawrence Erlbaum.

Cheney, G., & Vibbert, S. L. (1987). Corporate discourse: Public relations and issue management. In F. M. Jablin, L. L. Putnam, K. H. Roberts, & L. W. Porter (Eds.), *Handbook of organizational communication: An interdisciplinary perspective* (pp. 165-194). Newbury Park, CA: Sage.

Chess, C., Saville, A., Tamuz, M., & Greenberg, M. (1992). The organizational links between risk communication and risk management: The case of Sybron Chemicals Inc. *Risk Analysis, 12,* 431-438.

Chess, C., Tamuz, M., Saville, A., & Greenberg, M. (1992). Reducing uncertainty and increasing credibility: The case of Sybron Chemicals Inc. *Industrial Crisis Quarterly, 6,* 55-70.

Child, J. (1972). Organizational structure, environment, and performance: The role of strategic choice. *Sociology, 6,* 2-22.

Corner, P. D., Kinicki, A. J., & Keats, B. W. (1994). Integrating organizational and individual information processing perspectives on choice. *Organization Science, 5,* 294-308.

Daft, R. L., Bettenhausen, K. R., & Tyler, B. B. (1993). Implications of top managers' communication choices for strategic decisions. In G. P. Huber & W. H. Glick (Eds.), *Organizational change and redesign: Ideas and insights for improving performance* (pp. 112-146). New York: Oxford University Press.

Daft, R. L., & Lengel, R. H. (1984). Information richness: A new approach to managerial behavior and organization design. In B. M. Staw & L. L. Cummings (Eds.), *Research in organizational behavior* (Vol. 6, pp. 193-233). Greenwich, CT: JAI.

Daft, R. L., Sormunen, J., & Parks, D. (1988). Chief executive scanning, environmental characteristics, and company performance: An empirical study. *Strategic Management Journal, 9,* 123-139.

Daft, R. L. & Weick, K. E. (1984). Toward a model of organizations as interpretation systems. *Academy of Management Review, 9,* 284-295.

D'Aveni, R. A., & MacMillan, I. C. (1990). Crisis and the content of managerial communications: A study of the focus of attention of top managers in surviving and failing firms. *Administrative Science Quarterly, 35,* 634-657.

Dearborn, D. C., & Simon, H. A. (1958). Selective perception: A note on the departmental identification of executives. *Sociometry, 21,* 140-144.

Dess, G. G., & Beard, D. W. (1984). Dimensions of organizational task environments. *Administrative Science Quarterly, 29,* 52-73.

Dill, W. R. (1962). The impact of environment on organizational development. In S. Malick & E. H. Van Ness (Eds.), *Concepts and issues in administrative behavior* (pp. 94-109). Englewood Cliffs, NJ: Prentice Hall.

DiMaggio, P. J., & Powell, W. W. (1983). The iron cage revisited: Institutional isomorphism and collective rationality in organizational fields. *American Sociological Review, 48,* 147-160.

Downey, H. K., Hellriegel, D., & Slocum, J. W. (1977). Individual characteristics as sources of perceived uncertainty variability. *Human Relations, 30,* 161-174.

Downey, H. K., & Slocum, J. W. (1975). Uncertainty: Measures, research, and sources of variation. *Academy of Management Journal, 18,* 562-578.

Dozier, D. M. (1992). The organizational roles of communication and public relations practitioners. In J. E. Grunig (Ed.), *Excellence in public relations and communication management* (pp. 327-356). Hillsdale, NJ: Lawrence Erlbaum.

Duncan, R. B. (1973). Multiple decision-making structures in adapting to environmental uncertainty: The impact on organizational effectiveness. *Human Relations, 26,* 273-291.

Dutton, J. E. (1993a). Interpretations on automatic: A different view of strategic issue diagnosis. *Journal of Management Studies, 30,* 339-357.

Dutton, J. E. (1993b). The making of organizational opportunities. In L. L. Cummings & B. M. Staw (Eds.), *Research in organizational behavior* (Vol. 15, pp. 195-226). Greenwich, CT: JAI.

Dutton, J. E., & Jackson, S. E. (1987). Categorizing strategic issues: Links to organizational action. *Academy of Management Review, 12,* 76-90.

Dutton, J. W., Walton, E. J., & Abrahamson, E. (1989). Important dimensions of strategic issues: Separating the wheat from the chaff. *Journal of Management Studies, 26,* 379-396.

Eisenhardt, K. M. (1989). Making fast strategic decisions in high-velocity environments. *Academy of Management Journal, 32,* 543-576.

Elsbach, K. D. (1994). Managing organizational legitimacy in the California cattle industry: The construction and effectiveness of verbal accounts. *Administrative Science Quarterly, 39,* 57-88.

Elsbach, K. D., & Kramer, R. M. (1996). Members' responses to organizational identity threats: Encountering and countering *Business Week* rankings. *Administrative Science Quarterly, 41,* 442-476.

Elsbach, K. D., & Sutton, R. I. (1992). Acquiring organizational legitimacy through illegitimate actions: A marriage of institutional and impression management theories. *Academy of Management Journal, 35,* 699-738.

Fahey, L., & King, W. R. (1977). Environmental scanning for corporate planning. *Business Horizons, 20*(4), 61-71.

Fahey, L., & Narayanan, V. K. (1989). Linking changes in revealed causal maps and environmental change: An empirical study. *Journal of Management Studies, 26,* 361-378.

Feldman, M. S., & March, J. G. (1981). Information in organizations as signal and symbol. *Administrative Science Quarterly, 26,* 171-186.

Ford, J. D., & Baucus, D. A. (1987). Organizational adaptation to performance downturns: An interpretation-based perspective. *Academy of Management Review, 12,* 366-380.

Fredrickson, J. W. (1985). Effects of decision motive and organizational performance level on strategic decision processes. *Academy of Management Journal, 28,* 821-843.

Galbraith, J. R. (1973). *Designing complex organizations.* Reading, MA: Addison-Wesley.

Ghoshal, S., & Kim, S. K. (1986). Building effective intelligence systems for competitive advantage. *Sloan Management Review, 28,* 49-58.

Gifford, W. E., Bobbitt, H. R., & Slocum, J. W. (1979). Message characteristics and perceptions of uncertainty by organizational decision makers. *Academy of Management Journal, 22,* 458-481.

Gioia, D. A., & Chittipeddi, K. (1991). Sensemaking and sensegiving in strategic change initiation. *Strategic Management Journal, 12,* 433-448.

Gioia, D. A., & Thomas, J. B. (1996). Identity, image, and issue interpretation: Sensemaking during strategic change in academia. *Administrative Science Quarterly, 41,* 370-403.

Glick, W. H., Miller, C. C., & Huber, G. P. (1993). Upper-echelon diversity in organizations: Demographic, structural, and cognitive influences on organizational performance. In G. P. Huber & W. H. Glick (Eds.), *Organizational change and redesign: Ideas and insights for improving performance* (pp. 176-214). New York: Oxford University Press.

Grunig, J. E. (1976). Organizations and public relations: Testing a communication theory. *Journalism Monographs, 46* (Serial No. 46).

Grunig, J. E. (1984, Winter). Organizations, environments, and models of public relations. *Public Relations Research and Education, 1,* 6-29.

Grunig, J. E. (1990). Theory and practice of interactive media relations. *Public Relations Quarterly, 35*(3), 18-23.

Grunig, J. E. (Ed.). (1992). *Excellence in public relations and communication management.* Hillsdale, NJ: Lawrence Erlbaum.

Grunig, J. E. (1997). Public relations management in government and business. In J. L. Garnett (Ed.), *Handbook of administrative communication.* New York: Marcel Dekker.

Grunig, J. E., & Grunig, L. A. (1989). Toward a theory of the public relations behavior of organizations: Review of a program of research. In J. E. Grunig & L. A. Grunig (Eds.), *Public relations research annual* (Vol. 1, pp. 27-63). Hillsdale, NJ: Lawrence Erlbaum.

Grunig, J. E., & Grunig, L. A. (1992). Models of public relations and communication. In J. E. Grunig (Ed.), *Excellence in public relations and communication management* (pp. 285-325). Hillsdale, NJ: Lawrence Erlbaum.

Grunig, J. E., & Hunt, T. (1984). *Managing public relations.* New York: Holt, Rinehart & Winston.

Grunig, J. E., & Repper, F. C. (1992). Strategic management, publics, and issues. In J. E. Grunig (Ed.), *Excellence in public relations and communication management* (pp. 117-157). Hillsdale, NJ: Lawrence Erlbaum.

Hambrick, D. C. (1982). Environmental scanning and organizational strategy. *Strategic Management Journal, 3,* 159-174.

Hambrick, D. C. (1994). Top management groups: A conceptual integration and reconsideration of the "team" label. In B. M. Staw & L. L. Cummings (Eds.), *Research in organizational behavior* (Vol. 16, pp. 171-214). Greenwich, CT: JAI.

Hambrick, D. C., & Brandon, G. L. (1988). Executive values. In D. Hambrick (Ed.), *The executive effect:*

*Concepts and methods for studying top managers* (pp. 3-34). Greenwich, CT: JAI.

Hambrick, D. C., & D'Aveni, R. A. (1992). Top team deterioration as part of the downward spiral of large corporate bankruptcies. *Management Science, 38,* 1445-1466.

Hambrick, D. C., & Finkelstein, S. (1987). Managerial discretion: A bridge between polar views of organizational outcomes. In B. M. Staw & L. L. Cummings (Eds.), *Research in organizational behavior* (Vol. 9, pp. 369-406). Greenwich, CT: JAI.

Hambrick, D. C., & Mason, P. A. (1984). Upper echelons: The organization as a reflection of its top managers. *Academy of Management Review, 9,* 193-206.

Hambrick, D. C., & Snow, C. C. (1977). A contextual model of strategic decision making in organizations. *Academy of Management Proceedings,* pp. 109-112.

Heath, R. L. (1988). *Strategic issues management.* San Francisco: Jossey-Bass.

Heath, R. L. (1994). *The management of corporate communication.* Hillsdale, NJ: Lawrence Erlbaum.

Heath, R. L., & Nelson, R. A. (1986). *Issues management.* Beverly Hills, CA: Sage.

Hinz, V. B., Tindale, R. S., & Vollrath, D. A. (1997). The emerging conceptualization of groups as information processors. *Psychological Bulletin, 121,* 43-64.

Huber, G. P. (1982). Organizational information systems: Determinants of their performance and behavior. *Management Science, 28,* 138-155.

Huber, G. P. (1984). The nature and design of post-industrial organizations. *Management Science, 30,* 928-951.

Huber, G. P. (1991). Organizational learning: The contributing processes and literatures. *Organization Science, 2,* 88-115.

Huber, G. P., & Daft, R. L. (1987). The information environments of organizations. In F. M. Jablin, L. L. Putnam, K. H. Roberts, & L. W. Porter (Eds.), *Handbook of organizational communication: An interdisciplinary perspective* (pp. 130-164). Newbury Park, CA: Sage.

Huber, G. P., & McDaniel, R. R. (1986). The decision-making paradigm of organizational design. *Management Science, 32,* 572-589.

Jackson, S. E., & Dutton, J. E. (1988). Discerning threats and opportunities. *Administrative Science Quarterly, 33,* 370-388.

Katz, R. (1982). Project communication and performance: An investigation into the effects of group longevity. *Administrative Science Quarterly, 27,* 81-104.

Kefalas, A., & Schoderbek, P. P. (1973). Scanning the business environment—Some empirical results. *Decision Science, 4,* 63-74.

Khandwalla, P. N. (1981). Properties of competing organizations. In P. Nystrom & W. Starbuck (Eds.), *Handbook of organizational design* (pp. 409-432). New York: Oxford University Press.

Kiesler, S., & Sproull, L. (1982). Managerial responses to changing environments: Perspectives on problem sensing from social cognition. *Administrative Science Quarterly, 27,* 548-570.

Kiggundu, M. N., Jorgensen, J. J., & Hafsi, T. (1983). Administrative theory and practice in developing countries: A synthesis. *Administrative Science Quarterly, 28,* 66-84.

Klimoski, R., & Mohammed, S. (1994). Team mental model: Construct or metaphor? *Journal of Management, 20,* 403-437.

Knight, K. E., & McDaniel, R. R. (1979). *Organizations: An information systems perspective.* Belmont, CA: Wadsworth.

Lev, B. (1992). Information disclosure strategy. *California Management Review, 34,* 9-32.

Lyles, M. A., & Mitroff, I. I. (1980). Organizational problem formulation: An empirical study. *Administrative Science Quarterly, 25,* 102-119.

Marcus, A., & Goodman, R. (1991). Victims and shareholders: The dilemmas of presenting corporate policy during a crisis. *Academy of Management Journal, 34,* 281-305.

McCabe, D. L., & Dutton, J. E. (1993). Making sense of the environment: The role of perceived effectiveness. *Human Relations, 46,* 623-643.

Meyer, A. D. (1982). Adapting to environmental jolts. *Administrative Science Quarterly, 27,* 515-537.

Meyer, J. W., & Rowan, B. (1977). Institutionalized organizations: Formal structure as myth and ceremony. *American Journal of Sociology, 83,* 340-363.

Milliken, F. J. (1990). Perceiving and interpreting environmental change: An examination of college administrators' interpretation of changing demographics. *Academy of Management Journal, 33,* 42-63.

Milliken, F. J., & Lant, T. K. (1991). The effect of an organization's recent performance history on strategic persistence and change: The role of managerial interpretations. *Advances in Strategic Management, 7,* 129-156.

Mischel, W. (1977). The interaction of person and situation. In D. Magnusson & N. S. Endler (Eds.), *Personality at the crossroads: Current issues in interactional psychology* (pp. 333-352). Hillsdale, NJ: Lawrence Erlbaum.

O'Reilly, C. A. (1983). The use of information in organizational decision making: A model and some propositions. In B. M. Staw & L. L. Cummings (Eds.), *Research in organizational behavior* (Vol. 5, pp. 103-139). Greenwich, CT: JAI.

O'Reilly, C. A., Caldwell, D. F., & Barnett, W. P. (1989). Work group demography, social integration, and turnover. *Administrative Science Quarterly, 34,* 21-37.

O'Reilly, C. A., & Pondy, L. R. (1979). Organizational communication. In S. Kerr (Ed.), *Organizational behavior* (pp. 119-150). Columbus, OH: Grid.

O'Reilly, C. A., & Roberts, K. (1974). Information filtration in organizations: Three experiments. *Organizational Behavior and Human Performance, 11,* 253-265.

Orton, D., & Weick, K. E. (1990). Loosely coupled systems: A reconceptualization. *Academy of Management Review, 15,* 203-223.

Pfeffer, J., & Salancik, G. R. (1978). *The external control of organizations: A resource dependence perspective.* New York: Harper & Row.

Rowland, R. C., & Rademacher, T. (1990). The passive style of rhetorical crisis management: A case study of the superfund controversy. *Communication Studies, 41,* 327-342.

Salancik, G., & Meindl, J. (1984). Corporate attributions as strategic illusions of control. *Administrative Science Quarterly, 29,* 238-254.

Sawyerr, O. O. (1993). Environmental uncertainty and environmental scanning activities of Nigerian manufacturing executives: A comparative analysis. *Strategic Management Journal, 14,* 287-299.

Schneider, L. A. (1985). *Organizational structure, environmental niches, and public relations: The Hage-Hull typology of organizations as predictor of communication behavior.* Unpublished doctoral dissertation, University of Maryland, College Park.

Schwenk, C. R. (1984). Cognitive simplification processes in strategic decision making. *Strategic Management Journal, 5,* 111-128.

Sitkin, S. B., Sutcliffe, K. M., & Barrios-Choplin, J. R. (1992). A dual-capacity model of communication media choice in organizations. *Human Communication Research, 18,* 563-598.

Sitkin, S. B., Sutcliffe, K. M., & Weick, K. E. (1998). Organizational learning. In R. Dorf (Ed.), *The technology management handbook* (pp. 70-76). Boca Raton, FL: CRC.

Small, W. J. (1991). Exxon Valdez: How to spend billions and still get a black eye. *Public Relations Review, 17*(1), 9-25.

Smircich, L. (1983). Implications for management theory. In L. L. Putnam & M. E. Pacanowsky (Eds.), *Communication and organizations: An interpretive approach* (pp. 221-242). Beverly Hills, CA: Sage.

Smircich, L., & Stubbart, C. (1985). Strategic management in an enacted world. *Academy of Management Review, 10,* 724-736.

Smith, K. G., Grimm, C. M., Gannon, M. J., & Chen, M. (1991). Organizational information processing, competitive responses, and performance in the U.S. domestic airline industry. *Academy of Management Journal, 34,* 60-85.

Starbuck, W. H., & Milliken, F. J. (1988). Executive's perceptual filters: What they notice and how they make sense. In D. Hambrick (Ed.), *The executive effect: Concepts and methods for studying top managers* (pp. 35-66). Greenwich, CT: JAI.

Staw, B., McKechnie, P., & Puffer, S. (1983). The justification of organizational performance. *Administrative Science Quarterly, 28,* 582-600.

Staw, B. M., Sandelands, L. E., & Dutton, J. E. (1981). Threat-rigidity effects in organizational behavior: A multilevel analysis. *Administrative Science Quarterly, 26,* 501-524.

Suchman, M. C. (1995). Managing legitimacy: Strategic and institutional approaches. *Academy of Management Review, 20,* 571-610.

Sutcliffe, K. M. (1994). What executives notice: Accurate perceptions in top management teams. *Academy of Management Journal, 37,* 1360-1369.

Sutcliffe, K. M. (1997). The nuances of learning. In J. Walsh & A. Huff (Eds.), *Advances in strategic management* (Vol. 14, pp. 331-336). Greenwich, CT: JAI.

Sutcliffe, K. M., & Huber, G. (1998). Firm and industry as determinants of executive perceptions of the environment. *Strategic Management Journal, 19,* 793-807.

Swann, W. B., Jr. (1984). Quest for accuracy in person perception: A matter of pragmatics. *Psychological Review, 91,* 457-477.

Thayer, L. (1968). *Communication and communication systems.* Homewood, IL: Irwin.

Thomas, J. B., Clark, S. M., & Gioia, D. A. (1993). Strategic sensemaking and organizational performance: Linkages among scanning, interpretation, action, and outcomes. *Academy of Management Journal, 36,* 239-270.

Thomas, J. B., Shankster, L. J., & Mathieu, J. E. (1994). Antecedents to organizational issue interpretation: The roles of single-level, cross-level, and content cues. *Academy of Management Journal, 37,* 1252-1284.

Thompson, J. (1967). *Organizations in action.* New York: McGraw-Hill.

Triandis, H. C., & Albert, R. D. (1987). Cross-cultural perspectives. In F. M. Jablin, L. L. Putnam, K. H. Roberts, & L. W. Porter (Eds.), *Handbook of organizational communication: An interdisciplinary perspective* (pp. 264-295). Newbury Park, CA: Sage.

Tushman, M. (1979). Work characteristics and subunit communication structure: A contingency analysis. *Administrative Science Quarterly, 24,* 82-98.

Tushman, M., & Nadler, D. A. (1978). An information processing approach to organizational design. *Academy of Management Review, 3,* 82-98.

Tushman, M. L., & Romanelli, E. (1985). Organizational evolution: A metamorphosis model of convergence and reorientation. In L. L. Cummings & B. M. Staw (Eds). *Research in organizational behavior* (Vol. 7, pp. 171-232). Greenwich, CT: JAI.

Vertzberger, Y. Y. (1984). *Misperceptions in foreign policymaking: The Sino-Indian conflict 1959-1962.* Boulder, CO: Westview.

Vertzberger, Y. Y. (1990). *The world in their minds.* Stanford, CA: Stanford University Press.

Walsh, J. P. (1988). Selectivity and selective perception: An investigation of managers' belief structures and information processing. *Academy of Management Journal, 31*, 873-896.

Walsh, J. P., Henderson, C. M., & Deighton, J. (1988). Negotiated belief structures and decision performance: An empirical investigation. *Organizational Behavior and Human Decision Processes, 42*, 194-216.

*Webster's dictionary of synonyms.* (1951). Springfield, MA: G & C Merriam.

Weick, K. E. (1974). Review of the book *The nature of managerial work. Administrative Science Quarterly, 18*, 111-118.

Weick, K. E. (1976). Educational organizations as loosely-coupled systems. *Administrative Science Quarterly, 21*, 1-19.

Weick, K. E. (1979). *The social psychology of organizing* (2nd ed.). Reading, MA: Addison-Wesley.

Weick, K. E. (1983). Organizational communication: Toward a research agenda. In L. L. Putnam & M. E. Pacanowsky (Eds.), *Communication and organizations: An interpretive approach* (pp. 13-29). Beverly Hills, CA: Sage.

Weick, K. E. (1987). Organizational culture as a source of high reliability. *California Management Review, 29*, 112-127.

Weick, K. E. (1988). Enacted sensemaking in crisis situations. *Journal of Management Studies, 25*, 305-317.

Weick, K. E. (1990a). Cartographic myths in organizations. In A. S. Huff (Ed.), *Mapping strategic thought* (pp. 1-10). New York: John Wiley.

Weick, K. E. (1990b). The vulnerable system: An analysis of the Tenerife air disaster. *Journal of Management, 16*, 571-593.

Weick, K. E. (1995). *Sensemaking in organizations.* Thousand Oaks, CA: Sage.

Weick, K. E., & Daft, R. L. (1983). Effectiveness of interpretation systems. In K. S. Cameron & D. A. Whetten (Eds.), *Organizational effectiveness: A comparison of multiple models* (pp. 71-93). New York: Academic Press.

Wood, R., & Bandura, A. (1989). Social cognitive theory in organizational management. *Academy of Management Review, 14*, 361-384.

Yasai-Ardekani, M. (1986). Structural adaptations to environments. *Academy of Management Review, 11*, 9-21.

Zucker, L. G. (1983). Organizations as institutions. In S. Bacharach (Ed.), *Research in the sociology of organizations* (Vol. 2, pp. 1-47). Greenwich, CT: JAI.

# 7

# Organizational Identity

*Linkages Between Internal and External Communication*

GEORGE CHENEY
*University of Montana*

LARS THØGER CHRISTENSEN
*Copenhagen Business School*

*As a man adjusts himself to a certain environment he becomes a different individual; but in becoming a different individual he has affected the community in which he lives. It may be a slight effect, but in so far as he has adjusted himself, the adjustments have changed the type of environments to which he can respond and the world is accordingly a different world.*

—George Herbert Mead (1934, p. 215)

With few exceptions, the externally directed communications of organizations have been defined by organizational communication scholars as activities outside the province of their concerns. Because the study of organizational communication traditionally has been focused on acts of communication between senders and receivers within the "container" of the organization—that is, within clearly defined organizational borders—most communication aimed at *external* audiences, and markets in particular, has been

AUTHORS' NOTE: We wish to thank Craig Carroll, James E. Grunig, Robert L. Heath, Fredric M. Jablin, Linda L. Putnam, Juliet Roper, Phillip K. Tompkins, Sarah Tracy, and Ted Zorn for their helpful comments on earlier drafts of this chapter.

regarded as alien to the field. Such a division is neither fruitful nor justifiable any longer. The notion of organizational boundaries is becoming increasingly problematic (although, it seems, an inescapable point of reference), and "internal" and "external" communications no longer constitute separate fields in practice (Ashforth & Mael, 1996; Berg, 1986; Christensen, 1994a; see also Alvesson, 1990; Berg & Gagliardi, 1985; Cheney, 1991). Further, from an epistemological perspective, organizational communication researchers are beginning to recognize the implications and limitations of their own metaphors, seeking to reconfigure notions such as "open" versus "closed" systems, the organization-environment interface, and the idea of the organization itself (cf. Putnam, Phillips, & Chapman, 1996; Smith, 1993; Taylor, 1993).

To secure and maintain a legitimate and recognizable place in material and symbolic markets, many organizations of today pursue a variety of complex communication activities. Such activities are not neatly circumscribed and often involve both internal and external functions in ways that blur their presumed boundaries. Nowhere is this clearer than in the fields and practices of public relations and issue management where internal groups now comprise part of the general audience that the organization wishes to address and where externally directed messages, accordingly, become an integral part of the organization's operating discourse. Many organizations have begun to realize the difficulties of convincing an external audience about their deeds (e.g., their protection of the environment or defense of human rights) if the *internal* audience does not accept the message—and vice versa. Although the stated goals of public relations and issue management traditionally have had a strong external orientation—for example, building relational bonds with publics, facilitating effective policy making, developing favorable images in the media, managing strategic stakeholders, and making the organization more responsible to society—practitioners are becoming aware

that the pursuit of these goals directly affects the organization itself and its own members. Public relations and issue management, therefore, should be regarded in close connection with other forms of organizational communication.

Within such a perspective, the most interesting question may not be what distinguishes the various kinds of communication practices from one another (although we do recognize that such differences are relevant in some contexts), but rather how these endeavors are integrated for the organization to communicate at least somewhat consistently to its many different audiences. Without such consistency, the organization of today will have difficulties sustaining and confirming a coherent sense of "self" necessary to maintain credibility and legitimacy in and outside the organization. As a consequence, a growing proportion of professional communication activities becomes integrated around the same overall concern: *identity* (see, e.g., Christensen & Cheney, 1994; Czarniawska-Joerges, 1994; Hatch & Schultz, 1997). While the problem of identity is not the only concern of large organizations and often not an explicitly stated objective, we observe the surprising extent to which the question of what the organization "is" or "stands for" or "wants to be" cuts across and unifies many different goals and concerns. In the corporate world of today, identity-related concerns have, in other words, become organizational preoccupations, even when organizations are ostensibly talking about other matters.

The preoccupation with *identity as an issue* indicates at least two difficulties facing contemporary organizations and their communication: (1) a persistent problem for organizations in drawing lines between themselves and the outside world—a problem that requires a thorough rethinking of our long-held notions of institutions as discrete units (such as a university's being "contained" by a campus or a multinational firm's having a "base" or a "headquarters"); and (2) the growing problem of *being heard* in a communication environment saturated with corporate messages. Of course, both of these trends are intensified by the rise of new computer and communications technologies. In the contemporary activities of public relations, issue management, marketing, advertising, and the like—what we might, for purposes of terminological economy here call "external organizational communication"—the ongoing rhetorical struggle for organizations of most kinds is to establish a clearly distinctive identity and at the same time connect with more general concerns so as to be maximally persuasive and effective. Because organizational messages are often organized around more than one purpose and aimed at more than one audience, we need to think of internal and external organizational communication as being closely intertwined, recognizing that along with attempts to speak "for" an organization using a unitary voice there will almost inevitably be the expression (or suppression) of multiple voices, identities, cultures, images, and interests (see Cheney, 1991, 1999; cf. Bakhtin, 1991).

## PURPOSE AND OUTLINE OF THE CHAPTER

In this essay, we discuss and illustrate the ways in which organizations attempt to manage both identifiable issues and their own identities, arguing that those efforts have become so interwoven as to make their analytical separation unproductive if not impossible except in a discussion that is largely divorced from the reality of contemporary corporate communications. To accomplish our purposes, the essay unfolds through a number of subthemes each discussed in relation to the overall question of managing issues and identities.

First, it is crucial to recognize central features of the communication environment if we are going to understand well how contemporary organizations are behaving today through their dazzling array of highly visible communication practices. One purpose of this essay,

then, is to establish a clear connection between the (post)modern symbolic environment of today and the integration of so-called external (e.g., public relations, marketing, and issues management) and internal (e.g., employee relations, statements of mission and policy, and organizational development) forms of organizational communications. Following this line of thought, we will consider how the contests over identity are related to such things as a growing fuzziness of organizational boundaries and the self-referential and sometimes nearly autonomous nature of public corporate symbols.

A second purpose of this essay is to bring together trends in corporate communications in seemingly disparate areas and in areas typically seen as foreign to the rubric of organizational communication (as a subdiscipline) — for example, corporate issue management, marketing, issue advertising—by revealing and analyzing their underlying and common concerns. None of this is to say that these various domains of communication activity are identical or that the differences between them are insignificant, but rather that their common features can be productively examined from the perspectives of communication and rhetoric, especially through assessments of the powerful and puzzling ways in which persuasion takes place in the organizational world of today.

A third purpose of our essay is to extend Cheney and Vibbert's (1987) commentary on the fields of public relations and issue management (in the previous handbook). Their analysis included both a historical section and an analysis of contemporary public relations practice. Among other things, their interpretive historical survey showed how conceptions of the organization as rhetor (or persuader) vis-à-vis its audiences have shifted over a century's time from a "reactive" and sometimes accommodative stance toward external threats toward more aggressive attempts to shape the *grounds* for discussing social and political issues of the day. That is, while public relations began with attempts by the railroads and oil companies to fend off harsh criticisms in the late 1800s, today the activity is far more broadly conceived. Cheney and Vibbert's analysis of contemporary practices and related research was organized around three dimensions, arguing that the public relations activity of large organizations today is (1) *rhetorical* in its attempt to establish the general premises for later and more specific claims, (2) *identity related* in that each organization must work to establish its unique "self" while connecting its concerns to those of the "cultural crowd," and (3) *political* in that many large organizations today are trying to exert political influence while usually avoiding being labeled as political actors. Together these features imply, as Cheney and Vibbert noted, that strict divisions between "internal" and "external" aspects of the corporate discourse become problematic. This observation is even more relevant today than it was a few years ago: The communication environment has intensified in a number of significant ways (see, e.g., Baudrillard, 1981, 1988), and with that intensification comes the need to integrate more fully the communicative efforts directed to the various publics of the organization (see, e.g., Cheney & Frenette, 1993). In our discussion, we will comment on these trends while extending Cheney and Vibbert's analysis and interpreting an even wider range of organizational communication activities (including some aspects of marketing, advertising, and strategic management).

Our discussion is based on descriptions and interpretations of current trends as they are represented in the scholarly literature. Moreover, we will draw on current and illustrative examples from print media, television, and the Internet. The overall purpose is to stimulate the discussion in and outside the broad field of organizational communication by offering a nontraditional and communication-centered perspective on the numerous and diverse ways in which large organizations relate to and "see" themselves as relating to their environments today and in the future.

The remainder of this essay is therefore divided into five sections: (1) an introduction to the area of external organizational communication, including a brief overview of the field of corporate issue management; (2) a characterization of the communication environment within which contemporary organizations operate and to which they contribute; (3) a discussion of the fuzziness of organizational boundaries and its implications for organizational identity and communication; (4) a reconceptualization of issue management through a discussion of self-reference and paradox in communication management; and (5) a conclusion, including a discussion of the wider context of this essay presented as surprises, paradoxes, and ethical concerns to which future research needs to be directed.

## CORPORATE ISSUE MANAGEMENT IN THE CONTEXT OF EXTERNAL ORGANIZATIONAL COMMUNICATION

Because scholars of organizational communication traditionally have regarded external communication as being outside their purview, there is only a vague idea of the nature of such activities within the field. And most often this idea confirms the self-image of organizational communication as a contained activity, confined within formal organizational boundaries. Today, this image makes little sense and actually tends to obscure important theoretical and practical questions (cf. Smith, 1993). If we define organizational communication in general terms as a set of processes through which organizations create, negotiate, and manage meanings (including those related to their own constitution), *external* organizational communication can be thought of as a subset of those processes specifically concerned with meaning construction by way of an "external" environment (Taylor, Flanagin, Cheney, & Seibold, in press). However, since this understanding implies assumptions about boundaries that our discussion later in the essay will work against, we will talk about external organizational communication as communication directed to and from audiences considered in everyday terms to be nonmembers of the organization.

## Convergence in External Organizational Communication

To conceive of internal and external communication as interrelated dimensions of organizational sensemaking means to move our focus beyond the "container" metaphor and to embrace communication activities traditionally relegated to academics and professionals in communication functions such as advertising, marketing, and public relations.

Each of these domains of activity, professions, and disciplines has its own history, tone, mythology, and reasons for announcing its importance in society. Advertising, born in the mid-19th century, used to concern itself primarily with the direct "selling" of a product or a service (Dyer, 1990). Public relations arose in the late 19th century as a defense-based means of responding to public attacks on an organization (Cheney & Vibbert, 1987). And marketing, developed as a response to the growing number of consumer movements after World War II, established itself strongly in the 1960s as a strategic perspective for anticipating, detecting, and responding to desires, needs, or preferences of target audiences of consumers (Kotler, 1991).

Today, each of these areas has a far less certain and specific orientation than previously. Advertising, for example, has expanded its focus to include "social advertising" on important sociopolitical causes, such as the preservation of tropical rain forests or the cancellation of the Third World debt. Public relations now embraces within its reach highly proactive activities such as "issues

management" and "identity management." And as we shall discuss below, the marketing perspective has gradually become a prevailing norm in the reordering of many organizations as customer driven or consumer driven (see the *Journal of Market-Focused Management*). This is to say that the genres have become blurred and may, as a consequence, have more in common than has usually been acknowledged within the self-promoting discourse of each field. As each area or profession has sought to extend its influence and reassert its specific importance, sometimes in a rather imperialistic way, this blurring of disciplinary boundaries becomes even more evident. Among the major external communications functions, marketing has probably been the most expansive in recent years.

## The Expansion of the Marketing Orientation

Since the consumer unrests of the 1960s made business aware of the potential power of the market, marketing has established itself as a dominant principle of organizing in institutions of many different types. Traditionally speaking, marketing has comprised organizational activities designed to detect, assess, and respond to consumers' needs, wants, and desires. In more general terms, marketing can be thought of as a managerial *orientation* concerned primarily with the *satisfaction* of target audiences. The mythos of the marketing field sees the discipline as being an important advancement over earlier mass-production and sales-oriented perspectives chiefly because marketing *respects and engages* the consumer and his or her preferences (e.g., Keith, 1960; Kotler, 1991); marketing thus asserts itself as participatory, responsive, and above all democratic.

Regarding publics as consumers or customers, the marketing orientation has gradually made its way into all sectors of society such that many organizations, public as well as private, now openly describe themselves as "customer driven" (see, e.g., Gay & Salaman, 1992). And even where such descriptions seem somewhat inappropriate (e.g., in health care), we still find marketing present as a managerial ethos committing the organization to monitor its environments to keep abreast of changes in the market.

The expansive tendencies of marketing have often been criticized by leading public relations thinkers eager to distinguish their discipline from that of marketing (e.g., Grunig & Grunig, 1991). Among the differences typically emphasized to justify such a distinction are orientations with respect to target groups and operational goals. Whereas marketing traditionally concentrates on building and maintaining mutually satisfactory relationships with *customers,* public relations often sees itself dealing with a much broader range of *publics* to attain not only satisfaction but "accord and positive behavior among social groupings" (Broom, Lauzen, & Tucker, 1991; see also Grunig, 1993).

While acknowledging the significance of such differences, we would point out that marketing and public relations today have more in common than is commonly believed. Since Kotler and Levy (1969) introduced their "broadened concept of marketing," the marketing discipline has widened its scope considerably to include activities traditionally thought of as belonging in the realm of public relations. In line with traditional public relation concerns, scholars and practitioners in marketing have gradually begun to realize the importance of creating and maintaining a hospitable environment by fostering goodwill among all relevant stakeholders. As a consequence, a growing number of marketers are broadening their notion of the "customer" to include families, friends, and sometimes even society. Moreover, marketing principles are no longer restricted to the realm of private business but are applied to an increasing extent in social change efforts, such as birth rate limitation programs, antismoking campaigns, and heart disease prevention programs (e.g.,

Fine, 1981; Fox & Kotler, 1980; Kotler & Andreasen, 1987; Kotler & Roberto, 1989; Lazer & Kelly, 1973; Zaltman, Kotler, & Kaufman, 1972).

Obviously, these tendencies are not without practical problems. Since marketers take their point of departure as the wish to satisfy the needs and wants of (more or less broadly defined) customers, they may typically, as Fennell (1987, p. 293) claims, "seek to participate in behavior that is underway" rather than work to change behavioral patterns as they find them. Although marketing as a principle has a democratic impulse (Bouchet, 1991; Laufer & Paradeise, 1990)—in seeking out public opinion and suitable responses—it may not be the most appropriate model for dealing with more complex social and political issues or for soliciting deeper forms of citizen participation (a problem we shall return to later in the essay).

Nevertheless, the ubiquity of the marketing orientation and its reflection in the discourse and practice of management (Christensen, 1995a; Gay & Salaman, 1992) deserve careful analysis in today's society where we commonly speak of the marketing of hospitals, churches, schools, and individuals and their careers (see, e.g., Coupland, 1996; Fairclough, 1993; McMillan & Cheney, 1996). In other words, although the specific influences from marketing are often odd or problematic we want to emphasize that marketing—as a way of seeing and responding to environmental changes and developments—has become deeply rooted in the institutions of contemporary society. In fact, so taken for granted is this orientation that in the United States the term *American consumers* has now largely replaced *American people* and *American citizens* in public discourse. The same is true in public discourse with reference to China and other nations (Cheney, 1999, in press).

Further, and even more interesting from the perspective of this essay, marketing and public relations often operate from similar perspectives concerning organizations, boundaries, and environments. Because both disciplines have historical reasons for seeing their audiences as external forces able to make potent and often expensive claims on a business corporation, they share an image of the organization as an open and externally influenced system. Moreover, confronted with challenging and sometimes hostile environments, both disciplines have realized the value of organizational flexibility and the importance of being responsive to changes in opinions and preferences of target audiences. Interestingly, the value of flexibility is often so pronounced that organizational identity—in terms of stability or essence—is ignored or downplayed as a central management issue (see Christensen, 1995a; Kaldor, 1971). Following these values and implicit prescriptions, public relations and marketing have come to conceive of their communication with the external world as an ongoing dialogue. Although PR and marketing have grown out of rather asymmetrical perspectives on the communication between organizations and their publics, they both emphasize today that communication is, or at least should be, a two-way process through which the voices of all relevant parties are heard (see, e.g., Cheney & Dionisopoulos, 1989; DeLozier, 1976; Grunig, 1992; Leitch & Neilson, in press; Nickels, 1976; Pearson, 1989; Shimp, 1990; Stidsen & Schutte, 1972). Consequently, most organizations influenced by public relations or marketing experts find themselves engaged in frequent and extensive scanning and information-gathering activities. The differences and similarities between marketing and public relations are summarized generally in Table 7.1.

Public relations and marketing conceive of their audiences with different global labels—as "publics" and as "consumers"—but the fields' notions of how the organization should conceive of its own role vis-à-vis these audiences have interesting points in common. While management practices often contradict these shared perspectives and ideals, these ideas are extremely relevant in terms of how

organizations of today see themselves handling their relations with their environments.

## Corporate Issue Management

We now turn our attention to the areas of study and practice commonly known today as "issue management" or "corporate advocacy." Issue management has become visible since the late 1970s, largely as a broader and more systematic analysis of how organizations engage the larger society through strategic communication. Although growing out of public relations, especially in its more proactive form, issue management also bears a resemblance to some contemporary marketing practices and concepts. Further, issue management (as an area of study) has come to employ a range of rhetorical principles while also drawing on the social-scientific study of persuasion. Issue management thus provides an important forum for exploring many of the ideas and concerns of this essay.

Corporate issue management grew out of a rising managerial concern with the intensified critique since the 1960s of industrial products (e.g., Nader & Green, 1973; Nader, Green, & Seligman, 1976), seductive advertising (e.g., Packard, 1969), and lack of environmental concern. Adding to this the attacks on the oil and other industries in the United States during the early to mid-1970s and the low ebb for U.S. public opinion of big business (Chase, 1984), it is hardly surprising that organizations of many types, but especially those in the embattled industries of oil, chemicals, and tobacco, began to address simultaneously in public discourse their own identities and the sociopolitical issues of the day (see the overview in Cheney & Vibbert, 1987, for a more detailed account).

Initially, corporate issue management was thought of as a "fire fighting" function centered primarily around bottom-line concerns (e.g., Ewing, 1987; Wartick & Rude, 1986). Issue management, thus, has often been de-

---

**TABLE 7.1**  Differences and Similarities Between Marketing and Public Relations

|  | *Marketing* | *Public Relations* |
|---|---|---|
| **Traditional differences** | | |
| Target group | Markets/customers/consumers | Politics/stakeholders |
| Principal goal | Attracting and satisfying customers through the exchange of goods and values | Establishing and maintaining positive and beneficial relations between various groups |
| **Shared perspectives** | | |
| General image of organization | An open and externally influenced system | |
| Communication ideal | Communication as an ongoing dialogue with the external world | |
| Prescription for management | Organizational flexibility and responsiveness vis-à-vis external wishes and demands | |

---

scribed as an "early warning system" that makes it possible for organizations to minimize surprises (e.g., Wartick & Rude, 1986) and to manage more effectively in a turbulent environment (see also Arrington & Sawaya, 1984). Since the early 1980s, issue management and the related terms *crisis management, issue diagnosis,* and (corporate) *advocacy advertising* have come to refer to a range of more intensive activities on the part of the modern organization to shape and manage its environment more directly (e.g., Chase, 1984). As Hainsworth and Meng (1988) found in their survey of 25 large U.S. corporations, issue management is now seen by managers as "an action-oriented management function" that helps the organization identify potential issues relevant for its business and to organize activities to influence the development of those issues "in an effort to mitigate their consequences for the organization" (p. 28). Thus, while the development of corporate issue management as a discipline had a defensive impetus, its primary focus has gradually become the question of how to maintain and expand corporate control. In the words of

Chase (1984), "History can be created, not just survived" (p. 7).

At the same time, we witness a growing interest in more *symmetrical* relations, meaning some form of real dialogue between organizations and their publics (Grunig, 1992, in press); however, issue management has typically been *asymmetrical* in terms of how the organization actually deals with its constituencies or publics. Asymmetrical tendencies are often downplayed or denied today by references to corporations' involvement and responsibility in public policy processes, but the idea that "issue management is about power [over]," as Ewing (1987, p. 1) puts it, is still quite prevalent. In this one-way view of the communication process, communication itself is seen largely as the transmission of information and the shaping of audiences' attitudes, beliefs, and perhaps actions.

## Issue Management as Communication

In line with Ewing's (1987) observation —though recognizing that the exercises of power and persuasion involved are more complex and subtle (see, e.g., Cheney & Frenette, 1993)—we would like to offer a definition of issue management that highlights its rhetorical dimension. Implicit in this definition is the view that communication not only mediates the space between human beings and "reality out there" but also helps to create the reality to which we respond. In this perspective, the world becomes real to us in large part through the symbolic and rhetorical constructions that we, as social actors, employ. For example, consider the point at which the mainstream media decide to recognize a "social movement" by calling it just that. While this is not to suggest that our words or labels bring the whole world into being—like a reduction (or extension) of the argument into mere "nominalism" would imply—it helps us to remember the creative, evocative, even "magical" potency of language in use and thus be aware of the powerfully creative *and* restrictive dimensions to the terms and images by which we describe our world (cf. Burke, 1966; Douglas, 1986).

In prevailing thought, an *issue* is often thought of as an unresolved or contestable matter "ready for decision" (Chase, 1984, p. 38). Understood this way, issues represent a more advanced stage in terms of awareness than simply trends or problems. According to Crable and Vibbert (1985, p. 5), issues are created "when one or more human agents [attach] significance to a situation or perceived problem" and, we should add, decide to *articulate* this attention publicly (see also Heath, 1988). In fact, this articulation may significantly affect the way an issue is understood to the general public. Such is precisely why debates over "what to call" important events and groups—even those yet to be noticed—can have such a broad persuasive impact. Rhetorical disputes over the meaning of such hallowed terms as *democracy, freedom, efficiency,* and *progress* often take on such importance in the United States and in other industrialized nations, although any measure of control over meaning must be seen as un-

certain, tentative, and often only localized. And such terms often function *simultaneously* as repositories of many meanings and as clichés almost devoid of meaning (cf. Cheney, 1999; McGee, 1980; White, 1984).

In rhetorical terms, *issue management* means that the organization attempts to both "read" the premises and attitudes of its audience and work to shape them, often *in advance* of any specific crisis or well-defined debate (Heath, 1980). Understood this way, then, the *issue* becomes a universe of discourse designed, managed, and ultimately, shaped by organizational rhetors and strategists in an attempt to shape the attitudes the audience hold toward the organization or its concerns. From this perspective, the audience or public becomes something that is "pursued" with the goals of understanding, persuasion, and control (cf. Bryant's, 1953, conception of the function of rhetoric as the adjustment of ideas to people and people to ideas; see also Crable and Vibbert's, 1986, reformulation of that famous definition in terms of organizations and their environments; see in addition Kuhn's, 1997, treatment of issue management as a genre of communication).

Clearly, the rhetorical perspective suggested here conceives of communication in much broader terms than is usually the case in prevailing theories of issue management (cf. Sproull, 1988, 1990). Rather than distinguishing between the strategic and the communication-related aspects of the issue management process (e.g., Grunig, in press; see also Chase, 1984), we see communication as a meta-concept that refers broadly to constructions and deconstructions of meaning at many different levels, including not only explicit communication campaigns but also the strategic planning process, the process of monitoring and analyzing issues, and corporate efforts to comply with changing norms and standards of social responsibility (cf. Heath & Cousino, 1990). In all such situations, corporate actors deal significantly with symbols and interpretations. To see communication merely as an identifiable campaign *tool* that supplements whatever an organization *does* (its behavior) is to fail to grasp the significance of interpretation in a wide range of organizational processes. Further, such a perspective ignores the possibility that corporate rhetorical persuasion has become more complex and subtle in the communication environment of today in which an excess of messages is the order of the day. (On the other hand, of course, we must resist the temptation to say that "everything is communication.")

Only recently have scholars in the communication discipline identified the fundamental rhetorical and communication-related aspects of corporate issue management practices. And only recently have organizational communication studies (and we perceive a similar trend in the transdisciplinary study of organizations) begun to reclaim the broad sociological and political interests that shaped the early works on organizations by Marx, Weber, Durkheim, and Simmel. Such research efforts are necessary and potentially significant for at least two reasons:

1. By continuing to refer unreflectively to a division of "internal" versus "external" organizational communication, we fail to recognize dramatically new communication practices. These practices include, for example, the intended influences on multiple audiences with a single organizational message and, conversely, adaptations made for different audiences. Also, observe the ways in which the "container" metaphor for organization has become so problematic even as it is still desired as a pragmatic and comforting point of reference (Cheney, 1992).

2. Note the ways organizational communication must be situated within the context of larger social and cultural trends, for example, in terms of the "marketing culture" and its relentless but problematic pursuit of consumers' opinions (Christensen, 1995a; Laufer & Paradeise, 1990).

In the following section, we will present and highlight a number of sociohistorical trends relevant for our understanding of external organizational communication and its specific conditions in contemporary society.

## SETTING THE SCENE: IDENTITY AND COMMUNICATION IN THE CORPORATE SOCIETY

A shipwrecked woman stranded on a remote island puts a message in a bottle. As she sets out to throw the bottle into the sea, she realizes that she cannot see the water. It is covered with messages in bottles. In a nutshell, this is the problem confronting corporate communications of today. At the beginning of the 21st century, any communicator is confronted with the fact that professional communications have taken on a previously unseen scope and intensity pervading almost all aspects of human life. "The space is so saturated," as Baudrillard (1988, pp. 24ff.) puts it, "the pressure of all which wants to be heard so strong that [we] are no longer capable of knowing what [we] want" or, perhaps more important, who we are. The "explosion" of communication that we are witnessing, in other words, goes hand in hand with the question of identity. "Standing out" with a distinct and recognizable identity in this cluttered environment is at once absolutely necessary and almost impossible. As an organizing problem, the issue of identity, however, has deeper sociohistorical roots.

### The Issue of Identity

The social order instituted by modernity implied a weakening of the bonds of local community and authority through which people traditionally defined their roles and positions in society (e.g., Nisbet, 1970). With the image of traditional society as a body (corpus) that provides its members with stable identities, Mongin (1982) describes modernity as a process of "decorporation" that dissolves ancient relations of community and authority. Without these relations, the modern individual is left without "markers of certainty" (Lefort,

1988) to guide the search for meaning and identity. Although modernity has established new and quite resilient points of guidance (e.g., individuality, the nation-state, the market, rationality, and bureaucracy), its foundations are open to questioning and are thus basically fragile (Bouchet, 1991; see also Weigert, Teitge, & Teitge, 1986). As a result, the question of identity has become a standing and often pressing issue for individuals and institutions in many different contexts (see Giddens, 1991; Lasch, 1978, 1984). The "extraordinary availability of identities" (Weigert et al., 1986) also signals a lack of and quest for meaning.

Today, individuals and organizations are in hot pursuit of solid, favorable identities even as such identities become harder to capture and sustain. This is especially the case in situations when issues turn into crises. For Royal Dutch Shell—today the largest corporation in Europe—identity has often been a salient issue. Well known for its controversial business interests in apartheid South Africa, the Shell name has for many years been associated, in the views of its critics, with cynicism and unethical business activities. To many observers, this negative image was confirmed by its 1995 decision, approved by the British government, to dump the oil platform Brent Spar into the North Sea. Following the announcement of the decision, the Shell corporation faced a previously unseen rash of negative reactions from organizations, consumers, and politicians, especially in northern Europe. While Greenpeace occupied Brent Spar to force Shell to scrap the platform on land, consumers and business corporations started a boycott of Shell that finally made the organization give up its dumping plans (see, e.g. Wätzold, 1996).

From the perspective of this essay, it is interesting to note that this case—behind the negotiations and strategic choices of the different actors—was *about* identity: that of Shell (that had struggled for several years with a bad image), of Greenpeace (that gradually had lost legitimacy and feared falling into oblivion), and of the involved politicians always eager to trade politically on the whims of the

public. In this game, the environmental issue (how to retire an oil platform most safely) was often pushed aside to the benefit of identities and power positions of influential actors. Obviously, Shell lost this battle, but that does not necessarily imply that the consumer, or the environment, *won*. In 1996, Brent Spar was "parked" in a fjord in Norway waiting to be scrapped on land: a solution far more harmful to the environment, according to many environmental experts, than a dumping at sea. Although later findings seem to support Shell's initial position on the issue, the organization has realized that negative connotations are still related to the name of Shell. And as the recent media attention to its activities in Nigeria and Turkey indicates, identity has indeed become a standing and very complex issue for the organization.

But even in less critical and problematic situations, the question of identity is quite evident. If we accept the idea that organizational communication is essentially a process through which meaning is created, negotiated, and managed, we should expect to find identity at issue in most organizing processes, especially in those explicitly concerned with addressing external audiences.

## The Communication Environment of Today

In the corporate landscape of today, the issue of identity is closely tied up with the ways organizations organize their "world" in terms of communication. To begin with, the key communication elements of source, message, and receiver are all much more complicated and less easily distinguished than in prior periods. As many organizations have come to realize, the principal management problem in today's marketplace of goods and ideas is not so much to provide commodities and services or to take stands on the salient issues of the day, but to do these things with a certain distinctiveness that allows the organization to create and legitimize itself, its particular "profile," and its advantageous position. This quest for visibility has made disciplines such as public relations, issue management, marketing, and advertising chief architects of organizational identity. To help organizations stand out and "break through the clutter," practitioners within these fields are continuously operating on the edge of established strategies and perspectives, hoping to discover the idea that will provide the organization with a momentary relief from the pressures of intensified communication. Interestingly, however, such measures are creating a situation in which established communication is continuously challenged and the *conditions* for communication are in constant change (Christensen, 1995b). Many organizations today engage in ongoing efforts to (re)shape their images, ever seeking the support of both internal and external audiences (see, e.g., Allen & Caillouet, 1994; Alvesson, 1990; Treadwell & Harrison, 1994), even though there may be in any given case little real harmony among various constituencies and the images they hold of the organization.

This problem is clearly present in advertising for consumer goods, but it is observable in the marketing of services and issues as well. As an example of the former, the strategies chosen by various computer companies in their attempts to emulate IBM comes to mind. Trading, for example, on IBM's well-known slogan "Think," another computer company, ICL, chose to suggest "Think ICL" (Olins, 1989). By *leaning on,* or exploiting, more well-known images or positions, such messages hope to "*capture* the mystery of other organizations" (Gallagher, 1990, emphasis added) while emphasizing small, but in a way still, significant differences. For less well-known companies or products, such "positioning" strategies are often necessary to gain visibility in a crowded marketplace.

Similar principles are activated when organizations take stands on prominent social and political issues. Benetton Corporation, for example, is well known for displaying tragedies and human disasters in its ads and this way attracting attention to pressing social and political issues. One recent example is its 2000 ad campaign, which features death row inmates. However, because Benetton's ads are not explicitly taking stands on these issues—the situations are merely *exhibited*—more directly expressed positions on these issues are open for other corporations to take up. Following the launch of one of Benetton's widely disputed ads showing a man dying of AIDS surrounded by his family, Esprit, another clothing company, tried to exploit the situation by stating that it was in fact donating money to *fight* AIDS. Similar strategies have been employed by other clothing companies. Although these companies will have difficulties challenging Benetton's number-one position in terms of media attention and public interest, their positioning attempts have definitely had an impact on Benetton and its communications. In later ads showing an undressed Luciano Benetton saying, "Give me back my clothes," the corporation asks the public to donate their used clothes to Caritas, a relief organization supported by Benetton. As this example demonstrates, corporate identities are often intertwined with the issues that organizations seek to address. Further, the case indicates that the *way* issues are managed is strongly affected by the dynamics of the communication environment.

In this complex and volatile environment, crowded with symbols referencing each other, any discourse on issues tends to develop its own logic relatively independent of its referent. The symbolism surrounding an organization's identity *can,* in other words, become something of a world of its own, even though it may often rely on other symbols to express what the organization is or is not. This is precisely why many contemporary consulting firms can speak of "giving organizations identities" or "creating identity packages." Further, because positions within this environment are defined in terms of other positions, the identity aimed at by the corporate actor is potentially reduced to what Perniola (1980) and Baudrillard (1981) call a "simulacrum," that is, an "autonomized" image without reference to anything but other images.[1]

Organizations that wish to express their stances on social issues need to take these dynamics of the communication environment into serious consideration. While striving to make the position of the organization clear, the issue manager of today has to realize that the impact of symbols employed to define a situation or bolster an image is fragile and often more dependent on the significance of other corporate symbols than on the specific issue in question.

At a more global level, issue managers need to realize that communication is not an unproblematic solution to crises or queries over identity. In terms of the plethora of corporate messages and their often peculiar character, the communication environment of today is radically different in substantive respects from that of, say, 40 to 50 years ago. On the one hand, *more* communication appears as a necessary solution to the constant challenges to corporate identity and legitimacy. The fact of more communication requires more communication, from the standpoint of any organization that seeks to be heard. On the other hand, we have to realize that communication itself, even in its widest sense, is an integral part of the problem it sets out to handle. A deeper understanding of the still emergent communication environment requires that the growing access to "information" and the mountain of messages are viewed not only in terms of the meanings or effects of *specific* or isolable messages but in terms of effects of the expansion of the communication universe *as a whole*. What is, on the one hand, the intensity of modern communication seems, on the other hand, to be the dissolution of communication itself, at least as understood in any deep or understanding-oriented way (cf. Baudrillard, 1983; Dervin, 1994).

## THE FUZZINESS OF ORGANIZATIONAL BOUNDARIES

At the same time that organizations have become preoccupied, even obsessed, with the communication of their identities, the problem of defining organizational boundaries has become more acute than ever. As a consequence, organizations find it increasingly difficult to maintain clear distinctions between their internal and external communication.

To be sure, the problem of defining organizational boundaries was recognized in the scholarly literature two decades ago (see, e.g., Starbuck, 1976; Weick, 1979), but its present manifestations are directly related to the marketing ethos. With its ideal of organizational flexibility and responsiveness vis-à-vis external demands, the marketing ethos and its related management practices not only defy established images of the organization but also question traditional notions of the organization-environment interface (Christensen, 1996). Because such notions are central for our understanding of how issues are perceived and managed, we will sketch out below some relevant trends that today challenge the traditional reliance on the "container" metaphor for understanding organizational life. We do not have the space to examine in detail all relevant trends, but we will mention a few powerful indicators of what we mean.

### Organizing Beyond the Organizational Boundary

It is well known that *service organizations* have often had difficulties in maintaining a clearly defined "sense of self," in large part because their clients or service recipients straddle the boundary of the organization (see, e.g., Adams, 1976). Long-term service recipients, in particular, are difficult to define as being fully "outside" the organization (see, e.g., Cheney, Block, & Gordon, 1986; Starbuck, 1976). Students, regular clients of advertising agencies, users of various therapies, and clients of image and identity consultants often find themselves in this category. Seemingly pedantic exercises such as determining whether an individual or group is "inside" or "outside" the organization (as depicted, e.g., with Venn diagrams) thus have tremendous practical implications.

This is especially the case today where the marketing orientation is being copied and implemented by organizations in all sectors. In many institutions of higher education in North America, Europe, and Australasia, the student is increasingly being talked about as a "consumer" or "customer," meaning not only that the organization is seeking to adapt to its primary audience (the service recipients) but also that the activities of many universities take on more and more of a self-promotional quality (see Fairclough, 1993; McMillan & Cheney, 1996), where the objective is often adding commodifiable "value" to the self and by extension to the institution (Gay, 1996). In such arrangements, students can become shapers of services to a greater degree than they have been in the past, largely through immediate responses to courses and instructors and through the registering of their desires with quick changes in curricula and student services. Such forms of "participation" or "engagement" tend to be rather shallow, however, requiring only limited exchanges of "information" and ignoring possibilities for intersubjective understanding.

Today, the spread of the marketing attitude seems to reach its apotheosis in some production arrangements where integration and flexibility have become central managerial criteria (see Christensen, 1996). In auto manufacturing, for example, the customer can be almost incorporated into the design process by way of new computer technology. As Achrol (1991) reports, some Japanese automobile companies have developed a system "by which the customer designs his or her car (from available options) in the dealer showroom on a computer linked directly to the factory production line" (p. 79). Such production arrangements are not necessarily dependent on advanced technology, although the expansion of e-commerce does facilitate this kind of consumer involvement. With relatively simple measures, the production of bicycles, for example, has in many cases become adapted considerably to individual preferences. Management practices like these seriously challenge the organization's ability to distinguish between inside and outside and, accordingly, its sense of "self." Because the specific operationalizations of the marketing ethos—as "consumer influence," "custom-made products," and so forth—are blurring the boundaries between the organization and its environment, identity is a standing issue for organizations influenced by this organizing ideal.

In principle, this is true as well for "network forms of organization," such as long-term strategic alliances and flexible manufacturing networks. These can be found in industries as diverse as construction, publishing, and film. Such organizational creatures are, as Powell (1990) observes, difficult to classify: Neither markets nor firms, they exhibit greater predictability than the former but greater flexibility than the latter (see also Arndt, 1979; Webster, 1992). Simultaneously, electronic and computerized communication systems now permit some organizations to exist without any spatially located headquarters. As a consequence, many employees now find themselves with "virtual offices" (e.g., James, 1993). As one example: In mountainous and long Norway, the health care system is experimenting with methods of electronic diagnosis where data collected from a patient in one place are received and "read" simultaneously by physicians in other locations. Such arrangements can serve to challenge traditional notions of where and what the organization *is*, especially because some service providers (in this example, physicians assistants or nurses) may rarely or never experience copresence with the doctors with whom they must coordinate efforts. These, and other, hard-to-classify organizational types, offer still more challenges to the idea of the organization as, in Richardson's (1972) apt description, "islands of planned coordination in a sea of market relations" (see Chapter 12, this volume)

Under all the circumstances mentioned here, the identity of the organization becomes more problematic and more precious (Scott & Carroll, 1999). This observation, however, is not restricted to these examples but applies as well to the management of *issues*. As contemporary organizations face a growing demand to listen to relevant publics before they carry out their operations, systematic efforts to *integrate* these publics somehow into deliberations when taking stands on salient issues gradually becomes a more common phenomenon. While this kind of integration may sometimes be more superficial than profound, organizations that implement such efforts no doubt find it increasingly difficult to distinguish clearly between themselves and their environment. This problem has important implications for contemporary corporate communications. Thus, it is hardly surprising that many organizations are consolidating their internal and external communications in a single office or function.

### Communicating Across Boundaries

To uphold a sense of "self" while being flexible or existing as part of a larger network, organizations of today seek to integrate internal and external dimensions of their activities with the overall purpose of communicating one identity, although they may indeed pursue variations on a central theme. And while changes in an organization's identity over time are necessary for the organization to be adaptable, they are also risky in potentially undermining employee or consumer identification with the organization (see, e.g., Carroll, 1995). People become accustomed to an organization's "look." Thus, changes in the Betty Crocker persona of General Mills are made incrementally and carefully in response to cultural shifts and the public's image of the "appropriate" woman for the label (now a composite, computer-generated figure). We find much corporate communication today organized around identity as the overarching

concern. In the following, we shall illustrate how this concern tends to blur the differences between external and internal messages.

In advertising, the content of messages often reflects the fact that contemporary organizations feel the need to remind not only consumers but also their own employees that they are still part of the corporate landscape, that their actions are legitimate, and their business ventures sound. Besides its functions as a traditional external medium, advertising may have an important *self*-enhancing dimension. When the German corporation Bayer expresses its concern for the environment in large expensive ads, it simultaneously addresses the consumer *and* tells its employees and investors that they are part of a "competent and responsible" corporation. An advertisement from BP America has a similar dual focus. Showing a dirty worker with a pipe wrench in his hand, the ad says: "It takes energy to make energy. From our riggers and roughnecks. From our planners, our traders, our service station attendants. From 38,000 BP America employees in all. Their energy has made BP America the largest producer of American oil, producing 800,000 barrels of oil a day. To make the most of our country's energy resources, we're making the most of our human ones." By linking the issue of energy resources to the question of work and employment, BP America hopes to establish in the minds of its many audiences an image of an industrious caretaker concerned at once with its employees and the environment. Speaking even more broadly, eight oil producers (BP, Norol, Shell, Chevron, Statoil, Texaco, Q8, and Total) have issued a joint ad that almost presents their product as the life-blood of society and a Promethean gift to humanity (cf. Crable & Vibbert, 1983). Composed of a number of simple images—icons of an oil refinery, an oil tanker, and an airplane—connected by pipelines, the ad says, trading on Walt Disney's famous TV show, "To all of you from all of us."

In these and similar cases, the messages are communicating both externally and internally, hoping to influence both consumers and stakeholders and to confirm the sending organization's own merits or good intentions. This way, market-related communication seeks to link internal and external audiences around the same concern, identity. And as van Riel (1995) points out, a strong corporate identity can raise employee motivation while inspiring confidence among an organization's external target groups.

Other kinds of corporate communications may serve a similar function. Corporate identity programs (Olins, 1989), design and architecture (Berg & Kreiner, 1990), art collections (Joy, 1993), and autobiographies (Ramanantsoa & Battaglia, 1991) are all examples of communications that cut across traditional organizational boundaries and seek to unify different audiences. As Ramanantsoa and Battaglia (1991) note, organizational autobiographies, memoirs, and self-portraits are becoming increasingly important for firms that actively want to manage their identity: "At first invisible and silent, later object of a discourse and battle-field, companies have now become the subject of their own discourse in an effort to win coherent identities, legitimacy, and institutionalization" (p. 2). Autobiographies are, in other words, playing several important roles for contemporary organizations. Externally, the autobiography may supplement more traditional public relations or marketing functions. Internally, it enacts a mirror structure that makes it possible for the members of the organization to perceive themselves as part of a whole, autonomous, and anthropomorphic entity with a strong and original (yet not too eccentric) personality. This is clearly the case with Procter & Gamble's own story as it is told in *The House That Ivory Built: 50 Years of Successful Marketing* (1989). Here an effort to claim a specific and very "personal" identity internally is combined with the wish to market itself externally as a legitimate corporate actor.

Whether or not such communications convince the audience about their *specific* content is, of course, an empirical question. In fact,

formal, established, and public symbols of an organization—as seen in the logo, mission statement, and so on—may well have little connection in a particular case with how individual organizational members image their organization. A full treatment of the range of influences inside the organization is certainly beyond the scope of this essay. But we emphasize that, despite the apparent "autonomy" of many of the public symbols that come to (re)present the organization, there is much that transpires between organizational members (both powerful decision makers and others) to determine the course of an organization's rhetorical enterprise. So in no way do we wish to presume a monolithic organization that speaks univocally to the world (cf. Bakhtin, 1981; Cheney, 1992; Christensen, 1997; Motion & Leitch, 2000), nor are we suggesting that corporate symbols have a complete life of their own. Still, given our intention here to bring activities such as marketing, public relations, and some kinds of advertising within the purview of organizational communication, we are necessarily stressing the creation, positioning, and transformation of those symbols that come to represent the organization to a variety of stakeholders.

When externally directed communication becomes an integral part of an organization's operating discourse, the self-enhancing dimension of communication may turn out to be more important than the substantive messages themselves. In such cases, organizations are not merely engaging in communication, in the sense of sending or receiving messages, but also *auto*-communicating, that is, communicating with themselves. Auto-communication, according to Lotman (1977, 1991), is a process of organizing through which a communicator evokes and enhances its own values or codes (see also Broms & Gahmberg, 1983). As many anthropologists (e.g., Geertz, 1973) and sociologists (e.g., Parsons, 1949) have noted, all societies communicate with themselves in a self-reinforcing manner about their most salient values or concerns (see also Lotman, 1977, 1991). In this process, the role of the external audience becomes more complex than is usually acknowledged: besides acting as receiver of the corporate message, the external audience represents an ideal reference point in terms of which the sender evaluates itself. In this "looking-glass" (Cooley, 1983), the communicator (person or group) recognizes itself, chiefly in terms of how it wants to be seen by others.

In contemporary organizations, auto-communication is stimulated by the quest for identity and a growing need among organizational members for identification and belongingness (see, e.g., Cheney, 1983a, 1983b, 1991; Cheney & Tompkins, 1987; Scott, Corman, & Cheney, 1998; Tompkins & Cheney, 1983, 1985). Rapid change in the job market makes organizational loyalty problematic, yet it is still desired by individuals and organizations. Within many organizations of varying types, members are searching for a connection with something larger than the self. This is particularly observable in value-based organizations such as religious and voluntary associations, but it applies as well to a range of organizations in all sectors. Under growing economic pressure and internal drives toward centralization, the Mondragón Cooperative Corporation, one of the largest systems of worker-owned co-ops in the world, is working to fortify its fundamental values, such as social solidarity and democracy, while reconfiguring itself as a "customer-driven" multinational corporation. However, it is clear that for this organization of 42,000 worker-owner-members, located in the Basque Country in Spain, many presumably externally driven programs and messages are serving also to maintain a need to identify with one's place of work. However, that strategy is meeting receptivity in some quarters and resistance from others, as internal constituencies struggle over the true "essence" or the defining goals and values of the corporation. Some worker-member-owners are identifying strongly with the cooperatives' new competitive posture toward the European Union and the global market (e.g., "We must grow or die"), while others

are maintaining greater allegiance to what they see as the "soul" or "heart" of the cooperatives: individual unit (or co-op) autonomy, employee participation in policy making, relative equality of members, and regional grounding of cooperative groups (or sectors). As the first author has discovered through his interviews in the worker-cooperative complex, a great deal of self-persuasion (about "who we are") is going on, fueled both by individual need and by perceived economic and social necessity. Interesting, too, is the fact that the organization is consciously moving into public relations and marketing activities at the same time that it is trying to expand its market base, maintain and increase jobs, implement self-directed work teams, and foster renewed member commitment to the larger cooperative enterprise (Cheney, 1999).

As these different examples indicate, organizations often communicate with themselves when they address audiences outside the "container" of the organization. Our discussion of the linkages between internal and external organizational communication, however, would be incomplete if it did not simultaneously acknowledge the significant ways in which *internal* communication activities and campaigns can be used for external purposes. Indeed, the organizational world of today is rich with such examples, with some being more apparent than others. In the following paragraphs, we will mention briefly a number of internal-external relationships ranging from unintentional effects of internal communication on external environments to deliberate and planned efforts to communicate externally by way of the organization's own employees (see Christensen, 1997).

Today, many organizations have come to realize that so-called internal matters—their organization of production, their use of resources, their handling of waste, and their treatment of employees—potentially communicate a strong message to the external world. For example, when the largest bank in Denmark, Danske Bank, announced internally that it would henceforth depend more on younger employees than on older ones in terms of its personnel policies, this message was caught by the media and turned into a public case of corporate cynicism, a case that severely damaged the bank's image.

Realizing that affairs *inside* the organization have shaping implications for *outside* communications, a growing number of organizations have begun to think of their employees as customers who, in accordance with the marketing orientation, also need to be satisfied. The concern for employees is not only reflected in public celebrations of internal achievements such as those found in annual reports, in the well-known "employee of the month" plaques (as displayed prominently for visitors of the organization to see), and in public awards ceremonies (e.g., for the most "family-friendly" governmental or third-sector agency, as is now popular in many communities in the United States and elsewhere) but also in efforts to respond to the needs and wants of employees beyond their worklife. While some organizations build fitness and child care centers for employees and families, others offer education and psychological support to spouses and offspring. Because such efforts are often described enthusiastically by the media, they have the potential of becoming part the organization's public relations campaign. But, of course, they can undermine PR efforts if the organization is seen as not living up to its very public standards.

It is not unusual that an organization makes a policy of building its business by building relationships with clients and other constituencies and is explicit in its commentary about this. For example, at Arthur Andersen, a group of accounting and consulting firms, employees are regularly urged to get involved in community organizations as a central part of their business. By doing so, the representatives of the companies can achieve several things at once: tout the accomplishments of the firm, make part of the external environment of the organization part of the organization (by "bring the community in"), and expand their client base.

Among the more direct efforts to communicate externally by way of internal voices we find attempts to use organizational members or employees as advocates or "ambassadors" to outside constituencies. General Motors, for example, consciously developed this strategy in the early 1980s when it integrated internal employee communications and external advertising and public relations. More specifically, the corporation relied on employees—who would receive both internally distributed memos and televised commercials—to spread the word about GM's new emphasis on safety as a foremost concern (Paonessa, 1982). In the case of an enormous organization like this one, employees can, in other words, be seen as a large "PR force" in themselves. Similarly, Gulf States Utilities (an electric and gas utility of Louisiana and Texas that was bought out by Entergy in the mid-1990s) invested a great deal of time and financial resources in communicating with employees in the early 1980s about a controversial nuclear power plant project in the clear hope that they, in turn, would talk with wider audiences about the company's record of safety, efficiency, and good management. In the view of top management, the corporation had over 3,500 potential employee-ambassadors (T. Zorn, personal communication, March 1997).

Clearly, the primary concern behind such efforts is the desire for control, not only of employees but also of the organization's identity, that is, how the organization is commonly represented. And since many organizations have come to believe that the points of contact between its members and the outside world communicate much stronger than well-crafted advertisements, the interest in understanding and managing these points of contact has increased remarkably. In line with Jan Carlzon's (former CEO of Scandinavian Airlines System) notion that every contact with a potential customer represents a "moment of truth" (i.e., a point when the customer decides to continue or discontinue further business with the organization) (Carlzon, 1987), many organizations have begun to think of their employees as fragments of their overall market communication strategy (see also Olins, 1989). Although there is a big difference between the sports organization that tries to foster a sense of internal cohesion and enthusiasm (and hopes that these feelings will be contagious to outsiders and potential supporters of a team) and the organization that develops extensive rules for how its employees can conduct their lives away from work, the same concern is at issue: the organization's identity.

Of course, many efforts at communicating an organization's preferred self-image, such as enhanced "efficiency," are today contradicted by employees' reports to outside "others" of, for example, wasted resources, cases of lavish spending, or cuts in staff that do not include reduced layers of upper administration. This seems to be precisely one of the problems faced by many institutions of higher education in the United States and elsewhere. Added to this is the complication of the public visibility of a campus. If a university complains of drastically limited funding and yet proudly displays new elegant buildings, the public will be understandably skeptical.

While acknowledging such limitations to organizational control of the external communication process, we need to be aware of the many ways in which presumably internal organizational communications emerge as or come to be part of an organization's external communication. Along with the cases of auto-communication mentioned earlier, these examples demonstrate that a clear distinction between internal and external organizational communication is impossible to uphold. Moreover, since the question of identity is so prominent—cutting across different messages often in attempts to link different audiences—we should expect this question to be present in most organizing processes that relate the organization to its surroundings, to shape the organization's outlook, and to affect its way of handling upcoming issues. In the following section, we shall discuss how this self-centeredness may prevent the organiza-

tion from being as open and responsive toward its surroundings as the disciplines of public relations, marketing, and issue management envision and prescribe.

## RETHINKING CORPORATE ISSUE MANAGEMENT: IDENTITY, SELF-REFERENCE, AND PARADOX

In contrast to traditional perspectives within issue management, public relations, and marketing, we offer in the next section of this essay a more detailed consideration of the possibility that internal perceptions (identities, expectations, and strategies) strongly affect what problems are "seen," what potential solutions are envisioned, and how the problems are ultimately addressed. The discussion will proceed from a rather straightforward example of how organizational identity affects the diagnosis of issues to notions of self-reference in organizational information management and then to the more complex question of how the organizational approach to the environment may define and shape the issue in question.

### Identity as Point of Reference

In their interesting study of the Port Authority of New York and New Jersey, Dutton and Dukerich (1991) illustrate very well how identity is a salient issue closely related to the ways organizations define, diagnose, and respond to problems in their surroundings. Dutton and her colleagues in other studies (e.g., Dutton, 1993; Dutton & Duncan, 1987) defined the diagnosis of strategic issues as an "individual-level, cognitive process through which decision makers form interpretations about organizational events, developments, and trends" (Dutton, 1993, p. 339). However, their interpretation of the Port Authority case necessarily moved them to a larger, social level of analysis. Among other things, Dutton and Dukerich found that "the organization's identity served as an important reference point that members used for assessing the importance of the issue at hand" (p. 543). Specifically, their study showed how much the organization's response to the growing homelessness problem in the 1980s and the organization's internal communication activities at the time were tied up with how organizational members *deliberately imagined* that their organization was being seen by outsiders. Further, Dutton and Dukerich even found that organization members' treatments of homelessness to some degree reflected how they perceived outsiders to be judging their *individual* characters.

While the case analysis of the Port Authority is quite revealing of the extent to which, even over time, an organization's response to an issue may be framed by perceptions of a collective identity, it fails to specify clearly the role of the external audience in shaping and in part constituting the organization's identity. Defining organizational identity in line with Albert and Whetten (1985), Dutton and Dukerich interpreted it as "what organizational members believe to be its central, enduring, and distinctive character" (p. 520). This definition focuses attention on what the organization's members think about their organization and does not address explicitly how the organization *is represented* either in its presumably univocal "corporate voice" or by outsiders (cf. Cheney & Tompkins, 1987). Although Dutton and Dukerich (1991) recognize the importance of outsiders in the construction of an organization's image, their definitions lead them to focus exclusively on the "inside" of the organization. Thus, the "mirror image" in terms of which the Port Authority, according to Dutton and Dukerich, judged and evaluated the issue of homelessness is simply seen as a passive reflection of the perception of the organization's members, not as a product related to social norms and values. In the

self-referential perspective that we will introduce below the "external" audience, by contrast, assumes a more central role. Besides being an ideal reference point in terms of which the organization continuously evaluates its own actions (e.g., through opinion polls and market analyses), the "external" audience becomes a social construct, shaped by prevalent managerial discourses and proactive organizations and constantly appealed to in the rhetoric of corporate actors (cf. Black's, 1970, notion of "the second persona").

## Information in the Context of Organizational Self-Reference

At the same time that organizations are preoccupied with the issue of identity, they display an almost compulsive concern about their publics: consumers, politicians, interest groups, and so on. This concern—fueled by increased environmental uncertainty and shaped by marketing-inspired management norms—implies that most organizations of today are involved in extensive information-gathering programs and in constant attempts to predict and manage their future (see also Sutcliffe, Chapter 6, this volume). For that reason, contemporary organizations appear more open and sensitive toward their environments than ever before. Ironically, this openness often coexists with organizing practices that tend to close the organization in on itself.

The continuous collection and analysis of information are regarded by both public relations and marketing experts as indispensable for organizations operating in turbulent environments; however, the attitude toward information is not unified or consistent. As Thompson and Wildavsky (1986, p. 275) argue, people and organizations often *do not want* more information (see also Fornell & Westbrook, 1984; Weick & Ashford, Chapter 18, this volume), and when they do, they tend to handle it automatically and rather reductively within established frames of knowledge (see also Manning, 1986, 1988). More specifically, Manning (1986) argues that organizations inevitably translate external data into "idiosyncratic semiotic worlds" that reduce the complexity of the environment to more or less predetermined codes. This way, internal aspects of organizational communication merge in with the dialogue that organizations carry on with their environments.

Often the culture of an organization constitutes a "terministic screen" through which the organization views and evaluates its environment (Burke, 1966; Heath, 1990). This is clearly the case for the successful and well-known toy producer LEGO. For three generations, the culture of the LEGO Corporation has been characterized by a remarkable stability—a stability reflected in explicit corporate values such as tradition, reliability, managed and steady growth, long-term planning, economic independence, and central coordination (Thygesen Poulsen, 1993). To bolster this stability, LEGO has defined itself as being outside more volatile "May-fly markets." Moreover, its product program is standardized to fit a global consumer. Rather than adapting to local differences, the LEGO Corporation is taking the position that LEGO is a product for "everybody" and that it should be available, in more or less the same form, all over the world. To back up this perspective, LEGO is involved in research into the themes of "play" and "creativity" in different cultures and is continuously conducting its own surveys and focus groups to test the universality of its own products. Still, most of these measures are organized to detect and confirm *similarities* across cultures (as found in the second author's field research). While LEGO managers *do* recognize differences between markets, their interests are primarily vested in the issue of "sameness." Information that challenges this position and points in the direction of more *adaptive* strategies in terms of segmentation and communication has often been encountered, both via external and internal sources, but has usually been rejected on the basis of LEGO's standardized global philosophy.

The interesting point here is the way organizations, such as the LEGO Corporation, establish systems of communication that tend to enhance organizational self-perceptions by grounding their own worldview and strategies in external opinions and demands. As initial assumptions are backed up by market research and strategic long-term planning, the relation with the environment tends to form a tightly closed circuit in which the organization confirms the basic elements of its own culture. Obviously, this practice can be quite detrimental to an organization. In his discussion of the asbestos industry and its earlier attempt to present its product as vital to society, Heath (1990) shows how management can be trapped by its own rhetoric and thus become insensitive to certain kinds of information. And clearly, this tendency may be one of the reasons why the LEGO Corporation was less successful for some years—a development that finally made the corporation move into new areas, such as computer technology.

Another important aspect of organizational information handling is related to the fact, explained so well by Feldman and March (1981), that often *the gathering process itself is more important than the actual information collected.* The sheer accumulation of information, in other words, is done by many organizations not so much because they use *all* those bits of data but because the gathering process and the heap assembled make organizations feel comfortable and appear rational to the outside world (see also Meyer & Rowan, 1977; Pfeffer, 1981; Pondy, Frost, Morgan, & Dandridge, 1983; Weick, 1979). Here too, the ritual *is* the message. Interestingly, formalized systems designed to help organizations perceive, analyze, and respond better to strategic issues (SIM systems) may serve similar functions. According to Dutton and Ottensmeyer (1987), "The simple presence of a formal SIM system may convey a sense of organizational potency or potential mastery over [the] environment" that helps preserve an illusion of organizational control (p. 361). In such cases, the rationalistic ritual of information pursuit becomes not only necessary but also sacred.

Through the use of systematic analyses and opinion polls, contemporary organizations demonstrate their adherence to a culture shaped by the marketing ethos. Likewise, by constantly putting out reports, organizations are able to assert their rational participation in the public discourse of the day (e.g., Feldman, 1989). However, as the following quotation suggests, the quest for information has further implications:

> The image given by the opinion poll is the image of opinion. It reflects to the perception of the politician a symmetrical image of the political activity that shapes it. As a consumer seduced by the images of products in the economic world, the man whose opinion is polled is also a consumer of images in the political sphere, which he regurgitates in the form of answers to survey questions. (Laufer & Paradeise, 1990, pp. 87-88)

In line with Baudrillard's writings on the masses (e.g., 1983), Laufer and Paradeise's essay on our "marketing democracy" points out that the relentless pursuit of "public opinion" enshrined in politics, public relations, advertising, and front-page surveys—and we could easily substitute "the organization" for "the politician" in the above passage—has created a world of discourse with its own internal dynamics. The talk about opinion polls that measure everything from political preferences to fashion consciousness engages everyone today in the sense that all are now able to participate in that discursive world. Having been polled on nearly every conceivable issue or preference, "the masses," according to Laufer and Paradeise, know they should be ready to express opinions on cue. Further, since the polling institution, according to Baudrillard (1983), has become a simulation process characterized by mutual seduction, the idea of uncovering or controlling a true or deep "public opinion" becomes

rather elusive (see Christensen & Cheney, in press). By "communicating" systematically with selected audiences, organizations promote the elusive ideal of "public opinion" while presuming to identify and respond to it. In this process, the message or text gives way to a metatext that communicates to the corporate culture of today its most basic myths about democracy, communication, and identity.

As a consequence, the "dialogue" between organizations and their environments takes on ironic, new meanings. In line with developments within self-referential systems (e.g., Luhmann, 1990; see also Maturana & Varela, 1980), it can be argued that organizations communicate with their "environment" not only to exchange information but also, and quite significantly, to maintain themselves and confirm their identities. As Maturana and Varela (1980) contend, identity is the primary issue of all living systems, an issue handled through self-referential communication, that is, communication through which the system specifies its own environment and the information necessary to maintain itself. As we have indicated above, organizations often seem to collect and handle information in such a self-referential manner. Of course, in a social system this tendency toward self-referential closure is modified by the need for external legitimacy and accreditation (e.g., Berg & Gagliardi, 1985; see also Meyer & Rowan, 1977). But this does not ensure the kind of openness prescribed by prevailing theories within public relations, marketing, and issue management. Since the preoccupation with *external* data often reflects an adherence to a certain management *discourse* rather than a sincere interest in information, organizations may still function as self-referentially closed even within an apparently open communication structure (cf. Luhmann, 1990).

Much organizational communication thus can be described as self-referential communication or auto-communication. And organizations often imitate one another in their attempts to be "cutting edge." As the management of corporate communications becomes more strategic—that is, proactive, integrative, and oriented toward long-term goals—this tendency is accentuated further.

## The Paradox of Proactivity

In the corporate world of today, issue management reaches far beyond the practice of collecting and responding to information. As Cheney and Vibbert (1987) explain with respect to transformations in public relations activity and research since the mid-1970s, this practice has become more aggressive, more forward looking, more proactive (see also Chase, 1984; Hainsworth & Meng, 1988; Heath, 1988).

In everyday managerial usage, *proactivity* has come to refer to a more or less unspecified set of nondefensive or nonreactive practices through which organizations handle their relations with the external world. Instead of waiting for threats and opportunities to become manifest imperatives, the proactive organization attempts to influence and shape external developments in ways considered favorable in terms of its own aspirations. Organizations are clearly displaying proactive behavior when they seek to avoid being "caught by surprise" by demands or pressures from the environment: for example, new rules of trade within the European Union, increasing regulation of industrial waste, rising quality standards, or changing demands by labor unions. While this idea of *non*reactivity certainly grasps an important aspect of the activities of contemporary organizations, the wide-ranging implications of proactive management actually necessitate a deeper understanding of the phenomenon.

Ironically, the proactive stance can be seen as a creative *re*action to the increasing turbulence and the related reduction of predictability experienced in the market since the late 1950s (see Heath & Cousino, 1990). Within the fields of marketing and strategic management, these developments gave birth to a more prescriptive theory-building effort simultaneously concerned with the consumer or the

public and the possibilities of extending managerial control through strategy and long-term planning. Together these considerations constitute what we have described above as the "marketing ethos." With its ambiguous norm of seeking to serve market needs and wants *before* these are expressed and objectified, the marketing orientation *is* largely proactive. As one marketing manager told the second author in a personal interview, the best strategy is "being at the forefront of the development we expect."

Being proactive means being involved in the definition and construction (albeit not necessarily control) of reality. Proactivity, thus, is implicated by Weick's (1979) notion of enactment whereby an organization's actions to a significant extent define the environments to which it is able to attend (e.g., governmental economic statistics, consultants' forecasts, the norms of competitors). By projecting internal concerns, intentions, and strategies onto its surroundings, the organization creates or simulates its own "environment" and, this way, sets the stage for its own future acts and sensemaking. But, because organizations are not always realizing just how narrowly they circumscribe their environments, this process can often be rather unintentional. In other cases, the process is largely intended through strong, controlling efforts to define the situation in self-serving and self-referential terms.

The relation between enactment and proactivity, thus, needs to be specified further. In contrast to Daft and Weick's (1984) often-cited model of organizations as interpretation systems, we need to emphasize that also apparently passive or reactive behaviors fall within the frame of enactment (cf. Weick, 1979). Interestingly, routine and largely reactive actions, such as explaining corporate performance to stockholders in annual reports, show the power of *defining* the situation. The "competitive edge" of the organization can be credited when the organization is successful, yet "fierce competition" from others can be blamed for sagging profits during the next year (Conrad, 1993). Whether the organization takes on the role of the accidental viewer, the passive detective, the active discoverer, or the experimenting doer (Daft & Weick, 1984), its ways of relating to its surroundings will always influence the definition of the situation in question. That is to say, diverse sorts of organizational "intentions" can lead to similar results. The differences among these different "enactment postures," however, are not trivial. Through *proactive* programs, the enactment dimension of organizational behavior becomes explicit and intensified to the extent of making the very enactment of the "environment" *itself* the primary goal of the management process. And clearly, organizations *have* become very self-conscious about their stances vis-à-vis the larger environment and about the "world" they are helping to bring into being. For example, as Bostdorff and Vibbert (1994) explain, large corporations and other organizations now routinely try to promote certain values (e.g., particular interpretations of "freedom") that they can then use to ground future persuasive campaigns.

What is at stake in this strategic approach is the desire for control. And often much of this activity is designed to get citizens as well as consumers to identify with some level of the organization. Whether the strategy involved can be characterized as "catalytic" or "dynamic"—that is, more or less offensive and assertive (Crable & Vibbert, 1985; cf. Jones & Chase, 1979)—its aim is to determine not only strategic outcomes but also the very *conditions* for business, including those of communication and competition themselves. Although the proactive approach claims to take its point of departure in the market or the larger environment, its preoccupation with *internal* aspirations and considerations makes proactivity in fact a rather self-centered enterprise. As Crable and Vibbert (1985) point out, an organization that wants to influence the development of issues needs continuously to "assess what it is, what it wants to be, and how the environment could be altered to the advantage of the organization" (p. 10).

This is not to suggest that various publics (e.g., activist groups, stockholders, govern-

ments, competitors, and communities) are insignificant in the process of shaping issues and images of major corporations. Such groups often make powerful claims on the corporate actor—claims that sometimes force organizations to reconsider fundamentally their activities (e.g., Heath, 1988). However, this is most often the case when organizations respond reactively to changes in their larger environments. The more proactively such changes are managed, the more the direct role of the public is circumscribed by the organization through determining, for example, which voices from the outside deserve a hearing or how different opinions should be prioritized. Further, as Sutcliffe (this volume) points out, simply knowing *what* issues publics or stakeholders are concerned with does not help us understand *how* these issues are perceived, defined, and managed by the organization. Although many issues originate and unfold in environments regarded as external to the organization, the process of managing such issues strategically brings the organization and its specific outlook into the process (see also Kaldor, 1971; Smircich & Stubbart, 1985).

## Issue Management as Proactive Communication

Through the pursuit of understanding and managing within a complex and turbulent environment of issues, organizations often establish the symbolic systems to which they are able to respond (Weick, 1979). This is especially the case when organizations are managed proactively.

Vibbert and Bostdorff (1993) offer an excellent example of corporate proactivity, spanning the private and public sectors, in their analysis of the behavior of the U.S. insurance industry during the so-called lawsuit crisis of the mid-1980s. In that instance, the Insurance Information Institute (III), an industrywide lobbying organization, employed a series of visible ads to explain rising insurance costs largely in terms of a litigation-crazy society and the corporate need for protective insurance. As the authors observe, there had been only a vague sense expressed in public discourse about something like a lawsuit "crisis." Yet the III apparently succeeded in locating the problem within the institution of the legal system, thereby defining a complex situation in polarizing terms, and clearly placing blame outside its own institutional borders.

It may be argued, of course, that the organizational rhetor in the case analyzed by Vibbert and Bostdorff (1993) not only defined the problem but also *identified* the problem in the first place, a strategy that could not have worked, rhetorically speaking, had the organization not "tapped into" some sort of suspicion or resentment already held by a significant segment of the citizenry. Whether this was exactly the case or not, Vibbert and Bostdorff's (1993) study clearly points out the way in which "crises" often emerge through being declared, defined, and interpreted by proactive corporate actors. This, of course, can be seen in a variety of discursive domains: political, economic, and social (see also Bostdorff's, 1994, treatment of the rhetorical shaping of various crises by U.S. presidents). To succeed in proclaiming a situation as urgent and especially to identify blameworthy parties is to mobilize opinion and responses. Conversely, if the reaction of an organizational rhetor comes to be viewed as insufficient or as minimizing a generally acknowledged crisis, then organizational credibility is threatened. This was indeed the case for the Exxon Corporation, following the Valdez oil spill in Alaska in 1989, as the corporation tried to define the disaster as an individual rather than a policy-related problem, focusing blame on the ship's captain and diverting attention away from potential regulations for strengthening ships' hulls (cf. Benson, 1988, on the Tylenol case; Ice, 1991, on the Bhopal disaster; and Benoit, 1995, on the image-restoration strategies of Sears).

What Vibbert and Bostdorff's (1993) analysis fails to describe is the relationship between issues and identities and the growing interrelatedness of internal and external organizational communication. In the self-referential perspective laid out in this chapter, the rhetorical efforts of the III would be described not only in terms of its presumed effects on an external audience but also as an auto-communicative ritual that helps constitute the rhetor itself and its identity in an emergent environment. The self-referential view, however, would include another important dimension. While a proactive management of issues may allow organizations (large, powerful organizations in particular) to define rhetorically their own discursive domain, it makes it possible for such organizations to determine the appropriate responses to the issues in question. And clearly, the III did have its own solution ready: raising insurance premiums. When organizational responses come, as some issue management scholars recommend (e.g., Chase, 1984), *before* the opinions by key audiences are crystallized, the organization has a tendency to close itself off from the larger, extraorganizational environment and communicate mainly within its own symbolic universe.

In proactive management, organizational responses may, in other words, often precede environmental stimuli. Still, the notion of a "response" suggests that even the proactive organization is in *dialogue* with its stakeholders. This assumption, however, needs to be modified. When organizations operate within a discursive universe enacted, in large part, through proactive strategies, they are significantly talking to themselves. The fact that many issues are not controlled, or controllable, by the organization (e.g., Hainsworth & Meng, 1988) does not undermine the logic of this particular argument: that organizations, when responding to their own enactments of an issue, are often communicating basically with themselves about their own expectations and concerns. Self-referential communication should thus be seen as a compelling tendency of issue management. This is clearly the case in the following example, which illustrates all the central dimensions discussed above: proactivity, auto-communication, and accordingly, identity.

The medical corporation Novo Nordisk (based in Denmark but with offices, manufacturing facilities, and associated companies in numerous countries) has become well known for its proactive stance on the "green" issue. In the early 1990s, the corporation issued a 40-page report on this issue, including a detailed evaluation of its own contributions to pollution. To disarm possible criticism, Novo Nordisk furthermore chose to let a well-known environmentalist evaluate publicly the report and the corrective measures taken. Managers within Novo Nordisk explained the report with reference to the growing environmental consciousness among investors and customers since the 1980s. While this influence is highly significant in the corporate world of today, the step taken by Novo Nordisk was proactive and not a reaction to *specific* environmental demands. The proactive strategy of Novo Nordisk has several interesting dimensions that will be discussed below.

As long as relatively few organizations are issuing comprehensive evaluations of themselves, those that *do* appear more responsible, internally as well as externally. And indeed, Novo Nordisk is now being cited widely as a *responsible organization* concerned about its employees, the local community, and the environment in general: an image that instills a sense of pride and belongingness among its employees and attracts new qualified personnel. The fact that this image or reputation most often is reproduced by people who have *not* read the report tells us a great deal about the communication environment of today. When the social space is saturated with corporate communication asserting social righteousness, only the indirect or more unusual messages are able to stand out and attract attention. And the report issued by Novo Nordisk is indeed communication. Although the report does reflect real changes in the *behavior* of the organization, including a number of internal measures taken to reduce pollution, it is first of all an elaborate piece of communication: a metatext that tells, by its very existence, the general public including Novo Nordisk's own members that this organization is willing to let action follow words.

And the report *did* commit Novo Nordisk to a number of specific goals. With its "eco-productivity index"—a notion that divides the amount of sold goods with the amount of raw materials, energy, water, and packing used in the production process—the report prescribed quite specifically how pollution was to be reduced: as an ongoing increase in the eco-productivity index. This self-imposed prescription is not easy to fulfill and puts a heavy burden on all departments of the organization. Interestingly, the proactive introduction of this index allows Novo Nordisk to define itself the measures necessary to reduce its pollution. This has tremendous advantages for the organization. Instead of responding *reactively* to environmental issues as they "pop up" in its surroundings, Novo Nordisk defines and shapes proactively the issues that it addresses: a strategy that allows it to operate in a more familiar universe defined, in large part, by its own actions.

Such measures cannot stand alone but require careful follow-up advocacy (see, e.g., Arrington & Sawaya, 1984) in many different fora: in the local community, the European Union, international environmental organizations, and the media. In the present case, the first steps to make environmental reporting compulsory in the chemical industry have already been taken by an industrial association of which Novo Nordisk is a prominent member. Further, Novo Nordisk carefully cultivates its relations with different publics by hosting regular meetings with neighbors, journalists, investors, insurance companies, employees, environmental groups, and politicians. In line with Grunig's (1992, in press) notion of "symmetrical public relations," these efforts seem to demonstrate a sincere interest on the part of Novo Nordisk in establishing a two-way dialogue with affected and relevant publics. Without rejecting this interpretation, it should be added that these relations also serve the very important function of making sure that the change measures imposed proactively by Novo Nordisk on itself in fact become the *future standards* of social responsibility. Since the organization's relations with these mentioned groups are very close—several powerful environmental groups publicly express their admiration of Novo Nordisk—there is a great likelihood that

Novo Nordisk will be successful in its efforts to shape future discussions on and standards of social responsibility.

In such cases, it is tempting to suggest that the relations are symbiotic and that the communication involved tends to establish a relatively closed universe of mutual understanding, not easily accessible to other publics. At least, this is an interesting possibility that any critical perspective on public relations needs to consider seriously. When operating effectively within this network, the organization is able to communicate with itself and, this way, confirm its up-to-date outlook and its identity as a responsible organization ready to take substantial measures to protect the environment.

Similar communication systems are being developed these days by many different kinds of organizations. German-based Bayer Corporation, for example, has established a communication center, BayKomm, that "actively seeks frank and open dialogue with the public about problems and questions relating to the chemical industry" (brochure from Bayer AG, Leverkusen, Germany). In its promotional material, Bayer describes BayKomm as "an important interface between the company and society." In BayKomm, the brochure continues, "Bayer tries to place dialogue with the public on a broad footing. BayKomm is designed as a bridge between Bayer and the outside world, between the chemical industry and society." For most of the public, however, the "communication" with Bayer is restricted to guided tours of the impressive BayKomm center. The professional dialogues and discussion rounds that BayKomm initiates are usually organized around selected *strategic* publics. Also, the topics discussed in these communication fora are not open questions of general interest but topics delimited to issues of strategic relevance to Bayer, such as recycling and gene technology. While such issues are often important to the general public as well, their shaping by Bayer in this particular setting implies that the dialogue may not be as open and symmetrical as it first appears.

Communication scholars who study organizations and their interactions with the environment, thus, should be aware of the possible limitations to the ideals of dialogue and responsiveness advocated so strongly today within public relations, marketing, and issue management. Such awareness is crucial, especially when we note that the restrictions on dialogue and responsiveness are not always intentional on the part of the organization. While many organizations today clearly hope to control their environment better by being proactive and at the forefront of new trends, the tendencies for proactive organizations to develop closed circuits of auto-communication may well be unintended consequences.

## CONCLUSION: PUBLIC DISCOURSE, ETHICS, AND DEMOCRACY

As this essay has argued, in an unstable symbolic world issue management becomes closely tied up with the question of organizational identity. Following our description of today's communication environment, we commented on the preoccupation with "identities" in the public discourse of contemporary organizations. Specifically, we observed how identity and image have become perhaps the central issue (or set of issues) for many organizations today as they "talk" about themselves in a variety of media and communication arenas.

A central and overarching theme of this essay concerns the blurring of domains of organizational communication. We have illustrated how so-called external communication activities of contemporary organizations must be seen as closely connected to those presumably inside the container of the organization. Moreover, we have presented theoretical, historical, and practical reasons for establishing such a linkage both more strongly and more clearly in the scholarship of organizational communication. Finally, we have demonstrated how this complex communication situation is structuring the way organizations of today perceive and manage issues *as* identities, and identities as issues. In the remaining part of this chapter, we will summarize major points of the essay in the form of paradoxes, indicate a number of ethical concerns, and finally, point out some implications for research and practice.

## Summary

To illustrate the complexity of managing issues in today's corporate world, it is useful to think of the communication involved as being based on a set of interrelated paradoxes. Besides summarizing and synthesizing the major points in the essay, it is our hope that these paradoxes will point the reader beyond the present text and stimulate further thinking within the field.

1. Because internal and external aspects of organizing are closely intertwined, communication that seems to be directed toward others may actually be auto-communicative, that is, directed primarily toward the self.
2. As a consequence of the "explosion" of information and communication that we are witnessing—an explosion that, ironically, seems to imply an *implosion* among receivers (see Baudrillard, 1983)—any corporate identity becomes a fragile construction whose uniqueness is entirely dependent on *other* identities and whose persistence over time requires even more communication.
3. Because proactive management, as we have indicated, has a *reactive* basis in the consumer unrest of the 1960s and beyond, the environments enacted through proactive corporate measures are rhetorically described as something "out there" to which the organization needs to adapt. However, within the self-referential perspective laid out in this essay, it can be argued that what is adapted (to) is in fact "the public," operating largely in a discursive universe defined by large corporate actors.
4. The kind of openness displayed by contemporary marketing-oriented organizations in their relentless pursuit of "the will of the market" may, in other words, represent a certain kind of organizational closedness. Indeed, as Luhmann (1990) has explained so well, identity—for an individual or for a group—rests on the tension between *openness* and *closedness* (cf. Morin, 1986). Too open a system has no identity at all, no possibility for being distinguished from the larger universe. Too closed a system, in contrast, has no possibility for adaptation, and in its extreme form, ceases to have any self-reference when it has no reference to the larger world. To the extent that these terms are still meaningful descriptors of organizational communication practices, openness and closedness should be seen in dialectical interdependence.

## Ethical Concerns

Our discussion of organizational communication, of course, has much wider social and political implications than even these paradoxes indicate, especially when we consider transformations in public and private discourse in recent decades (see, e.g., Habermas, 1981; Sennett, 1978). Although such developments are highly relevant to organizational communication scholarship, we do not have the space in this chapter to elaborate on all of the implications of these transformations. Instead, we will focus attention on a number of ethical concerns related to the major points in this essay. In doing so, we wish to distance ourselves from both a purely instrumental view of corporate communications and a perspective based in a hopeless form of postmodernism that implicitly argues that "there's nothing to be done."

Ethical-moral issues arise on multiple levels with respect to "external" organizational messages; these include (1) the posited character or integrity of the source of the message, (2) the defensibility of a particular message, (3) the legitimacy of a pattern or campaign of messages, (4) the practical impact of a message or the cumulative effect of a series of messages, (5) the openness of the structure of communication between an organization and its publics/audiences, (6) the articulation/representation of genuine public interests, and (7) the question of shared responsibility. Below we will comment briefly on each of these ethical arenas and their implications for practice.

1. *Integrity of the source of the message.* Our Western legal systems have enormous difficulties in dealing with the morality of corporate persons, largely because of the emphasis on definable and provable *intention*. At the same time, however, we do tend to ascribe intention, personality, and character to organizations, judging organizations by their actions. When the organization offers a *stated* purpose, we can hold the organization to its own word (see, e.g., Crable & Vibbert, 1983). To sidestep the thorny question of organizational intentionality yet hold organizations responsible, one option is to focus on the established awareness of harms. As Gibson (1994) observes, under certain conditions we may consider an organization as having a *culture* that suggests a disposition toward harmful actions. Thus, we may try to make a plausible case that an organization's culture encourages misrepresentations, intentional omissions of fact, and lies. But even in this case, the question of how to engage productively an organization's communication system remains how to penetrate and perhaps alter the organizational culture.

2. *The defensibility of a particular message.* This becomes a relevant domain of ethical evaluation for a variety of reasons, including questions about truth, the representation of interests, and the effect to which a message can be labeled propaganda (in its aggressive one-sidedness). The revelation of underlying interests is especially important in an age when, for example, many wholly private lobbying groups disguise their basic orientations with names such as "*Council* on Energy Awareness" and "Insurance Information *In-*

*stitute.*" Moreover, as we have argued, the closed nature of many communication systems means that "business as usual" is likely to prevail and that organizations in many cases will be unlikely to see beyond limited interests and concerns associated with their own survival and identity. Often, vigorous efforts are necessary to uncover "who" or "what" is behind a particular message. Organizations, like individuals, should be required to declare their interests and reveal the sources of messages.

3. *The legitimacy of a pattern or campaign of messages.* To look at a wider persuasive campaign by or for organizations requires the analysis of patterns in verbal and visual messages. From an ethical perspective, this affords the opportunity to examine such features as consistency, adaptation to multiple audiences, and openness in response to challenges from outsiders. In terms of communication and rhetorical studies, the central question about adaptation becomes: At what point does adjustment to different audiences become misrepresentation of what the organization "really *is*"? (see, e.g., Cheney & Dionisopoulos, 1989). Of course, this question requires at least passing consideration of the ontological-epistemological problem of the "essence" of the organization (Cooren, 2000). Conversely, as we have suggested with our analysis of auto-communication, one must ask: When does an organization's communication system become so closed that it is merely talking to itself? This question can be at least partially addressed through an assessment of an organization's relations with its various publics, with special attention to real opportunities for input into the organization's policy-making apparatus.

4. *The practical impact of a message or set of messages.* The analyst of ethical aspects of external organizational communication may also choose to emphasize the intended or un-

intended effects of messages. Obviously, there can often be a clash between the stated or actual intention and the actual consequences of a message or campaign, as when advertising for a particular product or service functions to "cultivate" an unrelated attitude or practice (cf. Gerbner, Gross, Morgan, & Signorielli, 1980). Importantly, the cumulative effect of a series of organizational messages perceived by some public to be untruthful or inauthentic can be a wide and deep breach of trust (just as occurs with reports of corporate and governmental scandals). Further, the interrelations of internal and external communication can become apparent. In a study by Finet (1994), an organization's attempt to limit the influence of one of its outspoken members who publicly criticized it were circumscribed by the organization's own public image. The critic who focuses on the practical consequences of messages, of course, does not have to consider intentionality at all if he or she chooses to evaluate organizational actions solely on the basis of their pragmatic effects. But the critic does need to explain and defend reasonably objective standards for judgment in the case of a "text"-centered or message-centered evaluation: that is, explaining clearly how inferences about the "nature" of the organization are being made from its messages. Even more difficult to evaluate than specific claims in corporate communication is the more general idea of organizational or corporate sincerity. Tracy (1995), for example, offers a probing meta-analysis of the marketing of social responsibility as a corporate strategy, drawing on cases such as the London-based Body Shop and Vermont's Ben and Jerry's Ice Cream. She urges consumers and critics to do their best to assess both intent (e.g., through looking at the scope of a social-responsibility program vis-à-vis its announced claims) and impact (i.e., considering what actual benefits accrue to society as a result of the program).

5. *The structure of communication between an organization and its publics.* In addition to a focus on messages (or in contrast to it),

the ethics analyst can focus attention on the *relationship* between an organization and its various publics or audiences, including employees, consumers/clients, competitors, governmental agencies, and the wider citizenry. This is precisely what Grunig (e.g., 1992) advocates by presenting a two-way symmetrical model of public relations. While recognizing that communication systems may often be dominated by the organization, Grunig promotes the idea of genuine dialogue between organizations and other actors in their environment. Grunig's model goes a long way toward addressing the alienated position of the individual or group that desires to have a real forum for addressing a "corporate audience" (cf. Coleman, 1974). Also, the model encourages organizational persuaders to engage their audiences in meaningful ways.

Of course, encouraging practices along these lines is often enormously difficult, not only in terms of political and resource-related obstacles but also because of the maddening nature of the communication environment itself. Moreover, the critic of corporate communications should be aware of the possibility indicated in this essay that so-called symmetrical communication fora established by responsive organizations to further a dialogue with relevant publics may turn out to be relatively closed universes of thought organized around the interests, expectations, and enactments of the organizations themselves (Cheney & Christensen, in press). This way, organizations may still be able to "auto-communicate" within a two-way symmetrical framework. In spite of these complex problems, it seems difficult in a Western democratic society to imagine better solutions to the management of issues than an ongoing two-way dialogue between organizations and their stakeholders—a dialogue in which questions of interests and representation are constantly negotiated.

6. *The articulation/representation of genuine public interests.* The question of authentic or genuine public interest is an extremely complex one that could take the analyst of

ethics into the domains of political representation, power, critical theories (see, e.g., Lukes, 1974), and perhaps, beyond. Clearly, when an organization professes to represent broad, public or societal interests, its claims merit careful scrutiny. However, in a time when public-private partnerships and quasi-governmental institutions in some countries and communities have become almost the rule rather than the exception, simply trying to say who or what is representing the broad public becomes very trying.

This is not to say that we are left with no place to stand in critiquing blatantly self-serving communication campaigns—such as continuing efforts by U.S. tobacco companies to proclaim a *freedom* to smoke in response to warnings about passive consumption—but to say that *locating* public and private interests along with their presumed constituencies is often not an easy task. Since organizations cannot respond equally to all public interests, they will often choose to establish closer relations to those stakeholders with the most power, influence, and/or media attention (Kingo, 1996), hoping perhaps that such groups do represent the interests of the general public. And in some situations, this may indeed be the case. Following our preceding discussion, however, the analyst interested in ethical and democratic issues should pay attention to the possibility that the communication systems that are being developed these days—though avowedly to satisfy the general public's demand for insight and participation—are too closed around organizations and their *active* and resource-rich publics and stakeholders, each monitoring the other and themselves. This pattern suggests the model of "corporatism" (cf. Held, 1996). What appear, to some observers, as symmetrical systems of communication may, in other words, turn out to be "corporatist" systems organized around specific issues with only limited access to the nonorganized (see also Christensen & Jones, 1996; Livesey, 1999). Such a pattern of communication by and among well-established and resource-rich entities can exacerbate the problem of dominance of the "free speech" arena by corporate and other large or-

ganization interests (Bailey, 1996). Again, although these challenges confront the question of the meaning of democracy in the context of organizational communication and urge scholars and practitioners to be sensitive to the possible limitations and problems of organized dialogues (cf. Pearson, 1989; Sutcliffe, this volume), they do not disqualify the two-way symmetrical model as an important communication ideal or beacon in today's society.

7. *Shared responsibility.* The question of public interests, however, has another important dimension. On the one hand, the consumer or citizen may not see himself or herself as sharing responsibility for the creation and development of the product, the service, or the ethical standard—for example, an automobile, an education, or a rule for dumping waste—even if he or she has been involved in the decision-making process. The fact that marketing has facilitated the consumption of ideas and social issues does not necessarily imply, as some social marketers seem to suggest (e.g., Fine, 1981), an increased attention to or participation in important societal questions. Since the consumption of ideas has become a trend, the opposite may sometimes be the case. Indeed, this problem represents the most serious drawback of the marketing ethos (cf. Hirschman, 1983). On the other hand, while marketing-oriented organizations have considerably improved their ability to respond to the wishes of specific audiences, their notion of *how* such wishes are related to the general well-being of society is still rather vague. Response-*ability*, in other words, does not necessarily entail responsibility. In contemporary, market-oriented society where corporations demonstrate social responsibility by being open and responsive to claims made by organized publics, the central question is still how such maneuvers correspond with the pursuit of "the overall good." This is especially true because some corporations are up front about using values merely for marketing advantage (see McDonald & Gandz, 1992).

In the writings of scholars who promote the idea of a symmetrical dialogue between organizations and their publics, one senses the implicit assumption that organizations are behaving in a socially responsible manner as long as they adapt to the will of the general public. Can we be sure, however, that active, vocal, or affected publics represent the "whole" and that *their* articulation of an issue reflects the necessary wider concerns (Davis & Blomstrom, 1971)? Clearly, such questions are of utmost importance in a society in which the "pulse" of the opinion has become a central indicator of economic and political vitality. Redefined from citizen to consumer, the modern man or woman is now being pursued by organizational rhetors, managers, and decision makers with all available means. His or her wants, or rather voice, have become the currency most prized and convertible in this phase of modernity. With this development in mind, it is not surprising that Laufer and Paradeise (1990) speak ironically and poignantly of "marketing democracy."

Together, these concerns represent important bases for ethically informed criticism of the communication that organizations carry on between themselves and their environment. The larger question of identifying a perspective from which to examine the (un)ethical nature of organizational communication remains. This question is vexing, especially in light of the popular view of ethics in business from an economic-utility standpoint (Cheney, in press). That is, arguments for ethical practice are most compelling in many sectors when it can be established clearly that ethical behavior will improve performance on the bottom line (see the results of a survey of U.S. business speeches by Finet & Bal, 1995). In other words, a view of worklife as essentially amoral persists in modern industrial society. To talk about the value of behaving ethically *in itself* is frequently not persuasive. A measurable, economic end product becomes the warrant for making a case for "good business." And "just business" becomes a shorthand justification for all sorts of questionable corporate practices.

Nevertheless, Thomas Donaldson (e.g., 1989) offers an informed, philosophically and practically sensitive model for large organizations, including multinational corporations. Among other principles, Donaldson advances the notion of a "micro-social contract," based on the idea that any organization enters into a social contract with the society or societies within which it operates. The parameters for the contract become "negotiated" through consideration of basic human rights (e.g., freedom from coercion), including the rights of organizations. While most of Donaldson's case examples do not feature issues of communication, we can make the case for application of his model to the parts of organizations that are most heavily engaged in the production of symbols (i.e., public relations, advertising, marketing, employee communications, and human resource management). Further, Donaldson's model can be usefully seen in conjunction with Deetz's (1995) multiple-stakeholder approach, with the latter offering as ideals genuine dialogue through overcoming unnecessary constraints in organizational communication patterns. Still, any apparently straightforward application of a model of ethical organizational practice to organizational communication systems becomes complicated by the aspects of the postmodern communication environment we have featured in this essay. As organizations become more conscious of their roles as cocreators of the "external" reality to which they claim to adjust, the organizational adjustments *themselves* become important loci of inquiry. Because many such adjustments change the environment to which organizations can respond, refined and penetrating ethical critiques of organizational communications and organizational understandings of the world become all the more urgent.

## Implications for Theory and Practice

In closing, the concepts and principles discussed in this essay present enormous practical and ethical challenges for analysts and practitioners in the broad and diverse field of organizational communication. We do not mean to suggest, however, that "there's *no* way through" the ambiguities, paradoxes, and circularities characterizing communication practices today. Below we will sketch out some possible implications based on the major points of the essay.

First, it is important to realize that there is great practical value in being *aware* of the features of an expanding yet constraining universe of communication. Awareness of the set of issues described here does not liberate the organizational message maker or critic from that universe, but it does give him or her certain places to stand, however contingent or local they may be, in making sense of what's going on and in saying something meaningful and perhaps helpful about it. Within the communication context we depict, coping becomes a reasonably high-minded goal. This does not imply that there cease to be opportunities for real betterment in the organization's relations with individuals and with the larger society. Clearly, the modernist confidence in advancing the human condition must be tempered and modified by postmodern understandings of the limits of all of our rational pursuits but that does not negate our noblest goals (such as vibrant democracy) as points of reference that are occasionally approachable and that keep us from allowing society to become worse than it would be without such images of progress. We simply must remember that our very own creations, symbols, can play games with us, such that today's vision of democracy through marketing can become tomorrow's antidemocratic or pseudo-democratic institution.

Second, and more specifically, there are a number of important implications related to the observation that internal and external aspects of organizational communication are interrelated. If traditional, internal communication is relevant to external audiences—and this may often be the case in a world that expects organizations to be socially and environmentally responsible—scholars and practitio-

ners need to understand much organizational communication as market-related communication, that is, as communication with the potential of shaping opinions and actions among consumers and other publics. If externally directed messages have the strongest impact on the organization and its members—and, as our discussion and examples suggest, this is often the case—we may need to think of marketing communications and public relations as an integral part of the organizational discourse. Whereas the former observation logically implies that organizational communications and relations should be evaluated not only as internal phenomena but also in terms of their impact on external audiences (an idea implicit in some approaches to public relations; see, e.g., Grunig, 1992, in press), the consequences of the latter observation are, as we shall indicate below, more complex.

As we have already pointed out, marketing, strategy, and issue management justify themselves primarily through their claimed sensitivity to symbols, trends, and developments in markets and other public arenas. To acknowledge fully their *internal* significance, these disciplines need to develop and widen their sensitivity to cover also an understanding of the organization and its own central symbols and values. This kind of sensitivity makes it possible to integrate external communications with such internal concerns as, for example, the need to mobilize human resources (Berg, 1986). Clearly, such integrative efforts are necessary for all kinds of organizations that wish to operate consistently with their goals. Moreover, since organizational symbols and values to a great extent determine what environments organizations are able to "see," this latter kind of sensitivity or *self-reflectivity* may sometimes be more important than collecting information about external trends. To know the environment better, organizations should, in other words, try to know themselves (cf. Weick & Ashford, this volume). This point is probably the most important practical implication of the self-referential perspective laid out in this chapter. Scholars and practitioners within the field of what traditionally is thought of as external communication need to learn to communicate consciously with themselves and their organizations about their most central meanings. These meanings include internal images and perceptions of what the organization "is," key symbols of pride and motivation, basic assumptions about relevant publics and environments, established procedures and routines involved in opinion polls and market analyses, tacit norms for interpreting data, briefing procedures and information exchange between departments, and more generally, perceptions of external information throughout the organization (see Christensen, 1994b). Being self-reflective and sensitive to such dimensions thus means trying to be aware of one's own auto-communicative predispositions. Only through such exercise can organizations hope to counter the self-referential tendencies described in this essay.

Third and finally, we are aware that our description of current communication and management practices can have negative consequences in the sense that some organizations, for strategic reasons, may choose to develop communication systems of a more closed and self-referential nature. Organizations, for example, that wish to *appear* open and responsive may find inspiration in our discussion of proactive organizing practices and the possibility of "integrating" stakeholders through the use of focused strategic dialogues. Although such *as-if dialogues* are not a new phenomenon confined to the corporate world but are part of our experience with politics, their present forms do present a real danger to our ideals of participation and democracy. Still, such worries should not keep us from describing, discussing, and critiquing significant tendencies in the corporate world—whether they conform to our ideals or not.

The tendencies discussed in this chapter indicate a great potential for changing the scope and outlook of a number of disciplines such as organizational theory, communication, marketing, management strategy, and issue management. Clearly, the greatest challenge for the organizational communication researcher

is to develop new and meaningful concepts able to reflect the real complexity of contemporary organizational communication, that is, concepts that are not confined within traditional dichotomies between "open" and "closed," "internal" and "external," "formal" and "informal," and so forth. Thus, we need to ask more probing questions about the relationships between various audiences and publics with organizations that would presume to speak to them. For example: How much openness is there in corporate communications that are seemingly directed outward? How much democracy is there even in debates and discussions that appear to include divergent parties and stakeholders? And how much concern is there on the part of people for corporate identities and other messages that organizations spend so much time, energy, and money on (Cheney & Christensen, in press; Christensen & Cheney, in press)? At the same time, of course, each researcher must make decisions about "where to stand" with respect to these phenomena. What practical-epistemological position to take, whether or not to seek social change, and what sort of ethical principles to develop represent perhaps the most crucial decisions.

## NOTE

1. We would like to circumnavigate the *"This* is postmodernity?" discussion by arguing simply that the point is not to label contemporary society but rather to understand it better. While we recognize the fact that trends brought together under the rubric of postmodernism have influenced a whole range of academic disciplines from literature to physics and that debates continue to rage over what each discipline "looks like" from a postmodernist perspective, the point of this essay is not to take sides in this debate.

## REFERENCES

Achrol, R. S. (1991, October). Evolution of the marketing organization: New forms for turbulent environments. *Journal of Marketing, 55,* 77-93.

Adams, J. S. (1976). The structure and dynamics of behavior in organizational boundary roles. In M. D.

Dunnette (Ed.), *Handbook of industrial and organizational psychology* (pp. 1175-1199). Chicago: Rand McNally.

Albert, S., & Whetten, D. A. (1985). Organizational identity. In B. M. Staw & L. L. Cummings (Eds.), *Research in organizational behavior* (Vol. 7, pp. 263-295). Greenwich, CT: JAI.

Allen, M. W., & Caillouet, R. H. (1994). Legitimation endeavours: Impression management strategies used by an organization in crisis. *Communication Monographs, 41*, 44-62.

Alvesson, M. (1990). Organization: From substance to image? *Organization Studies, 11*(3), 373-394.

Arndt, J. (1979). Toward a concept of domesticated markets. *Journal of Marketing, 43*, 69-75.

Arrington, C. B., & Sawaya, R. N. (1984). Managing public affairs: Issues management in an uncertain environment. *California Management Review, 26*(4), 148-160.

Ashforth, B. E., & Mael, F. A. (1996). Organizational identity and strategy as a context for the individual. *Advances in Strategic Management, 13*, 19-64.

Bailey, W. (1996). Corporate/commercial speech and the marketplace first amendment: Whose right was it anyway? *Southern Communication Journal, 61*, 122-138.

Bakhtin, M. (1981). *The dialogic imagination: Four essays* (C. Emerson & M. Holquist, Trans., M. Holquist, Ed.). Austin: University of Texas Press.

Baudrillard, J. (1981). *Simulacres et simulation.* Paris: Galilée.

Baudrillard, J. (1983). *In the shadow of the silent majorities.* New York City: Semiotext(e).

Baudrillard, J. (1988). *The ecstasy of communication.* New York: Semiotext(e).

Benoit, W. L. (1995). Sears' repair of its auto service image: Image restoration discourse in the corporate sector. *Communication Studies, 46*, 89-105.

Benson, J. A. (1988). Crisis revisited: An analysis of strategies used by Tylenol in the second tampering episode. *Central States Speech Journal, 39*, 28-36.

Berg, P. O. (1986). Symbolic management of human resources. *Human Resource Management, 25*, 557-579.

Berg, P. O., & Gagliardi, P. (1985). *Corporate images: A symbolic perspective of the organization-environment interface.* Paper presented at the SCOS Corporate Images conference, Antibes, France.

Berg, P. O., & Kreiner, K. (1990). Corporate architecture: Turning physical settings into symbolic resources. In P. Gagliardi (Ed.), *Symbols and artifacts: Views of the corporate landscape* (pp. 41-67). Berlin: Walter de Gruyter.

Black, E. (1970). The second persona. *Quarterly Journal of Speech, 56*, 109-119.

Bostdorff, D. M. (1994). *The presidency and rhetoric of foreign crisis.* Colombia: University of South Carolina Press.

Bostdorff, D. M., & Vibbert, S. L. (1994). Values advocacy: Enhancing organizational images, deflecting public criticism, and grounding future arguments. *Public Relations Review, 20*, 141-158.

Bouchet, D. (1991). Advertising as a specific form of communication. In H. H. Larsen, D. G. Mick, & C. Alsted (Eds.), *Marketing and semiotics* (pp. 31-51). Copenhagen, Denmark: Handelshøjskolens Forlag.

Broms, H., & Gahmberg, H. (1983). Communication to self in organizations and cultures. *Administrative Science Quarterly, 28*, 482-495.

Broom, G. M., Lauzen, M. M., & Tucker, K. (1991). Public relations and marketing: Dividing the conceptual domain and operational turf. *Public Relations Review, 17*(3), 219-225.

Bryant, D. (1953). Rhetoric: Its functions and its scope. *Quarterly Journal of Speech, 39*, 401-424.

Burke, K. (1966). *Language as symbolic action.* Berkeley: University of California Press.

Carlzon, J. (1987). *Moments of truth.* Cambridge, MA: Ballinger.

Carroll, C. (1995). Rearticulating organizational identity: Exploring corporate images and employee identification. *Management Learning, 26*, 467-486.

Chase, W. H. (1984). *Issue management: Origins of the future.* Stamford, CT: Issue Action.

Cheney, G. (1983a). On the various and changing meanings of organizational membership: A field study of organizational identification. *Communication Monographs, 50*, 343-363.

Cheney, G. (1983b). The rhetoric of identification and the study of organizational communication. *Quarterly Journal of Speech, 69*, 143-158.

Cheney, G. (1991). *Rhetoric in an organizational society: Managing multiple identities.* Columbia: University of South Carolina Press.

Cheney, G. (1992). The corporate person (re)presents itself. In E. L. Toth & R. L. Heath (Eds.), *Rhetorical and critical approaches to public relations* (pp. 165-184). Hillsdale, NJ: Lawrence Erlbaum.

Cheney, G. (1999). *Values at work: Employee participation meets market pressure at Mondragón.* Ithaca, NY: Cornell University Press.

Cheney, G. (in press). Arguing about the place of values and ethics in market-oriented discourses of today. In S. Goldzwig & P. Sullivan (Eds.), *New approaches to rhetoric for the 21st century.* East Lansing: Michigan State University Press.

Cheney, G., Block, B. L., & Gordon, B. S. (1986). Perceptions of innovativeness and communication about innovations: A study of three types of service organizations. *Communication Quarterly, 34*, 213-230.

Cheney, G., & Christensen, L. T. (in press). Public relations as contested terrain: A critical response. In R. L. Heath & G. Vazquez (Eds.), *Handbook of public relations.* Thousand Oaks, CA: Sage.

Cheney, G., & Dionisopoulos, G. (1989). Public relations? No, relations with publics: A rhetorical-organizational approach to contemporary corporate communications. In C. H. Botan & V. Hazleton, Jr. (Eds.), *Public relations theory* (pp. 135-158). Hillsdale, NJ: Lawrence Erlbaum.

Cheney, G., & Frenette, G. (1993). Persuasion and organization: Values, logics and accounts in contemporary corporate public discourse. In C. Conrad (Ed.), *The ethical nexus* (pp. 49-74). Norwood, NJ: Ablex.

Cheney, G., & Tompkins, P. K. (1987). Coming to terms with organizational identification and commitment. *Central States Speech Journal, 38,* 1-15.

Cheney, G., & Vibbert, S. L. (1987). Corporate discourse: Public relations and issue management. In F. M. Jablin, L. L. Putnam, K. H. Roberts, & L. H. Porter (Eds.), *Handbook of organizational communication: An interdisciplinary perspective* (pp. 165-194). Newbury Park, CA: Sage.

Christensen, L. T. (1994a). *Markedskommunikation som organiseringsmåde. En kulturteoretisk analyse.* Copenhagen, Denmark: Akademisk Forlag.

Christensen, L. T. (1994b, November). Talking to ourselves: Management through auto-communication. *MTC Kontakten* (Jubilæumstidsskrift), pp. 32-37.

Christensen, L. T. (1995a). Buffering organizational identity in the marketing culture. *Organization Studies, 16*(4), 651-672.

Christensen, L. T. (1995b). Fra kosmetisk markedsføring til integreret strategi. Reflektioner over den "grønne" kommunikation. In J. P. Ulhøi (Ed.), *Virksomhedens miljøhåndbog* (No. 5, pp. 1-10). Copenhagen, Denmark: Børsens Forlag.

Christensen, L. T. (1996, February). *Communicating flexibility: A critical investigation of the discourse of organizational change.* Paper presented at the Organizational Communication and Change: Challenges in the Next Century conference, Austin, Texas.

Christensen, L. T. (1997, May). Marketing as auto-communication. *Consumption, Markets & Culture, 3,* 197-227.

Christensen, L. T., & Cheney, G. (1994). Articulating identity in an organizational age. In S. A. Deetz (Ed.), *Communication yearbook 17* (pp. 222-235). Thousand Oaks, CA: Sage.

Christensen, L. T., & Cheney, G. (in press). Self-absorption and self-seduction in the corporate identity game. In M. Schultz, M. J. Hatch, & M. H. Larsen (Eds.), *The expressive corporation.* Oxford, UK: Oxford University Press.

Christensen, L. T., & Jones, R. (1996). En symmestrisk dialog om miljøspørgsmålet? En kritisk analyse af nye dialogformer mellem virksomheder og forbrugere. In J. P. Ulhøi & H. Madsen (Eds.), *Miljøledelse—Tanker, erfaringer og visioner* (pp. 151-167). Copenhagen, Denmark: Børsens Forlag.

Coleman, J. S. (1974). *Power and the structure of society.* New York: Norton.

Conrad, C. (Ed.). (1993). *The ethical nexus.* Norwood, NJ: Ablex.

Cooley, C. H. (1983). *Human nature and the social order.* New Brunswick, NJ: Transaction Books.

Cooren, F. (2000). *The organizing property of communication.* Amsterdam, the Netherlands: John Benjamins.

Coupland, J. (1996). Dating advertisements: Discourse of the commodified self. *Discourse & Society, 7,* 187-208.

Crable, R. E., & Vibbert, S. L. (1983). Mobil's epideictic advocacy: "Observations" of Prometheus-bound. *Communication Monographs, 50,* 380-394.

Crable, R. E., & Vibbert, S. L. (1985). Managing issues and influencing public policy. *Public Relations Review, 11,* 3-16.

Crable, R. E., & Vibbert, S. L. (1986). *Public relations as communication management.* Edina, MN: Bellweather.

Czarniawska-Joerges, B. (1994). Narratives of individual and organizational identities. In S. A. Deetz (Ed.), *Communication yearbook 17* (pp. 193-221). Thousand Oaks, CA: Sage.

Daft, R. L., & Weick, K. E. (1984). Toward a model of organizations as interpretation systems. *Academy of Management Review, 9,* 284-295.

Davis, K., & Blomstrom, R. L. (1971). *Business, society, and environment: Social power and social response* (2nd ed.). New York: McGraw-Hill.

Deetz, S. (1995). *Transforming communication, transforming business: Building responsive and responsible workplaces.* Cresskill, NJ: Hampton.

DeLozier, M. W. (1976). *The marketing communication process.* New York: McGraw-Hill.

Dervin, B. (1994). Information ↔ democracy. *Journal of the American Society of Information Science, 45,* 369-385.

Donaldson, T. (1989). *The ethics of international business.* New York: Oxford University Press.

Douglas, M. (1986). *How institutions think.* Syracuse, NY: Syracuse University Press.

Dutton, J. E. (1993). Interpretations on automatic: A different view of strategic issue diagnosis. *Journal of Management Studies, 30,* 339-357.

Dutton, J. E., & Dukerich, J. M. (1991). Keeping an eye on the mirror: Image and identity in organizational adaptation. *Academy of Management Journal, 34,* 517-554.

Dutton, J. E., & Duncan, R. (1987). The creation of momentum for change through the process of strategic issue diagnosis. *Strategic Management Journal, 8,* 279-295.

Dutton, J. E., & Ottensmeyer, E. (1987). Strategic issue management systems: Forms, functions, and contexts. *Academy of Management Review, 12,* 2, 355-365.

Dyer, G. (1990). *Advertising as communication.* London: Routledge.

Ewing, R. P. (1987). *Managing the new bottom-line: Issues management for senior executives.* Homewood, IL: Dow Jones-Irwin.

Fairclough, N. (1993). Critical discourse analysis and the marketization of public discourse: The universities. *Discourse & Society, 4*, 133-168.

Feldman, M. (1989). *Order without design: Information production and policy making.* Stanford, CA: Stanford University Press.

Feldman, M. S., & March, J. G. (1981). Information in organizations as signal and symbol. *Administrative Science Quarterly, 26*, 171-186.

Fennell, G. (1987). A radical agenda for marketing science: Represent the marketing concept! In A. F. Firat, N. Dholakia, & R. P. Bagozzi (Eds.), *Philosophical and radical thought in marketing* (pp. 289-306). Lexington, MA: D. C. Heath.

Fine, S. H. (1981). *The marketing of ideas and social issues.* New York: Praeger.

Finet, D. (1994). Sociopolitical consequences of organizational expression. *Journal of Communication, 44,* 114-131.

Finet, D., & Bal, V. (1995, May). *The rhetoric of ethics and economics in organizational discourse.* Paper presented at the annual meeting of the International Communication Association, Albuquerque, NM.

Fornell, C., & Westbrook, R. A. (1984). The vicious cycle of consumer complaints. *Journal of Marketing, 48,* 68-78.

Fox, K., & Kotler, P. (1980). The marketing of social causes: The first 10 years. *Journal of Marketing, 44,* 24-33.

Gallagher, V. J. (1990, November). *Symbolic action, culture, permanence and change: A critical addition to organizational studies.* Paper presented at the Speech Communication Association convention, Chicago.

Gay, P. du. (1996). *Consumption and identity at work.* London: Sage.

Gay, P. du, & Salaman, G. (1992). The cult[ure] of the customer. *Journal of Management Studies, 29*(5), 615-633.

Geertz, C. (1973). *The interpretation of cultures.* New York: Basic Books.

Gerbner, G., Gross, L., Morgan, M., & Signorielli, N. (1980). The "mainstreaming" of America: Violence profile No. 10. *Journal of Communication, 30,* 10-29.

Gibson, K. (1994). Fictitious persons and real responsibilities. *Journal of Business Ethics, 13,* 1-7.

Giddens, A. (1991). *Modernity and self-identity.* Palo Alto, CA: Stanford University Press.

Grunig, J. E. (1992). *Excellence in public relations and communication management.* Hillsdale, NJ: Lawrence Erlbaum.

Grunig, J. E. (1993, September). Forholdet mellem public relations og marketing. *Mediekultur, 20,* 6-14.

Grunig, J. E. (in press). Public relations management in government and business. In J. L. Garnett (Ed.), *Handbook of administrative communication.* New York: Marcel Dekker.

Grunig, J. E., & Grunig, L. A. (1991). Conceptual differences in public relations and marketing: The case of health-care organizations. *Public Relations Review, 17*(3), 257-278.

Habermas, J. (1981). Modernity versus postmodernity. *New German Critique, 22,* 3-22.

Hainsworth, B., & Meng, M. (1988). How corporations define issue management. *Public Relations Review, 14*(4), 18-30.

Hatch, M. J., & Schultz, M. (1997). Relations between organizational culture, identity and image. *European Journal of Marketing, 31,* 356-365.

Heath, R. L. (1980). Corporate advocacy: An application of speech communication perspectives and skills—and more. *Communication Education, 29,* 370-377.

Heath, R. L. (Ed.). (1988). *Strategic issues management: How organizations influence and respond to public interests and policies.* San Francisco: Jossey-Bass.

Heath, R. L. (1990). Effects of internal rhetoric on management response to external issues: How corporate culture failed the asbestos industry. *Journal of Applied Communication Research, 18,* 153-167.

Heath, R. L., & Cousino, K. R. (1990). Issues management: End of first decade progress report. *Public Relations Review, 16*(1), 5-18.

Held, D. (1996). *Models of democracy* (2nd ed.). Stanford, CA: Stanford University Press.

Hirschman, E. C. (1983). Aesthetics, ideologies and the limits of the marketing concept. *Journal of Marketing, 47,* 45-55.

Ice, R. (1991). Corporate publics and rhetorical strategies: The case of Union Carbide's Bhopal crisis. *Management Communication Quarterly, 4,* 341-362.

James, B. (1993, November 8). If only work could be virtual, too. *International Herald Tribune,* p. 1.

Joy, A. (1993). The modern Medicis: Corporations as consumers of art. *Research in Consumer Behavior, 6,* 29-54.

Jones, B. L., & Chase, W. H. (1979). Managing public policy issues. *Public Relations Review, 2,* 3-23.

Kaldor, A. G. (1971). Imbricative marketing. *Journal of Marketing, 35,* 19-25.

Keith, R. J. (1960). The marketing revolution. *Journal of Marketing, 24,* 35-38.

Kingo, L. (1996, March). *Stakeholder interaction—A future challenge.* Keynote paper presented at the 3rd Conference of the Nordic Business Environmental Management Network, Aarhus, Denmark.

Kotler, P. (1991). *Marketing management: Analysis, planning, implementation, and control* (7th ed.). Englewood Cliffs, NJ: Prentice Hall.

Kotler, P., & Andreasen, A. R. (1987). *Strategic marketing for non-profit organizations* (Vol. 1). Englewood Cliffs, NJ: Prentice Hall.

Kotler, P., & Levy, S. J. (1969). Broadening the concept of marketing. *Journal of Marketing, 33,* 10-15.

Kotler, P., & Roberto, E. L. (1989). *Social marketing: Strategies for changing public behavior.* New York: Free Press.

Kuhn, T. (1997). The discourse of issues management: A genre of organizational communication. *Communication Quarterly, 45,* 188-210.

Lasch, C. (1978). *The culture of narcissism.* New York: Norton.

Lasch, C. (1984). *The minimal self: Psychic survival in troubled times.* London: Picador.

Laufer, R., & Paradeise, C. (1990). *Marketing democracy: Public opinion and media formation in democratic societies.* New Brunswick, NJ: Transaction.

Lazer, W., & Kelly, E. J. (Eds.). (1973). *Social marketing: Perspectives and viewpoints.* Homewood, IL: Irwin.

Lefort, C. (1988). *Democracy and political theory.* Cambridge, UK: Polity.

Leitch, S., & Neilson, D. (in press). Public relations and a theory of publics. In R. L. Heath & G. Vazquez (Eds.), *Handbook of public relations.* Thousand Oaks, CA: Sage.

Livesey, S. (1999). McDonald's and the Environmental Defense Fund: A case study of a green alliance. *Journal of Business Communication, 36,* 5-39.

Lotman, J. M. (1977). Two models of communication. In D. P. Lucid (Ed.), *Soviet semiotics: An anthology* (pp. 99-101). London: Johns Hopkins.

Lotman, J. M. (1991). *Universe of the mind: A semiotic theory of culture.* London: I. B. Tauris.

Luhmann, N. (1990). *Essays on self-reference.* New York: Colombia University Press.

Lukes, S. (1974). *Power: A radical view.* New York: Macmillan.

Manning, P. K. (1986). Signwork. *Human Relations, 39*(4), 283-308.

Manning, P. K. (1988). *Symbolic communication: Signifying calls and the police response.* Cambridge, MA: MIT Press.

Maturana, H. R., & Varela, F. J. (1980). *Autopoiesis and cognition: The realization of the living.* Dordrecht, Holland: D. Reidel.

McDonald, P., & Gandz, J. (1992). Getting value from shared values. *Organizational Dynamics, 20*(3), 64-77.

McGee, M. C. (1980). The "ideograph": A link between rhetoric and ideology. *Quarterly Journal of Speech, 66,* 1-16.

McMillan, J., & Cheney, G. (1996). The student as consumer: Implications and limitations of a metaphor. *Communication Education, 45,* 1-15.

Mead, G. H. (1934). *Mind, self, & society* (Vol. 1). Chicago: University of Chicago Press.

Meyer, J. W., & Rowan, B. (1977). Institutionalized organizations: Formal structure as myth and ceremony. *American Journal of Sociology, 83,* 340-363.

Mongin, O. (1982, February). La democratie a corps perdu. *Esprit, 2,* 206-212.

Morin, E. (1986). *La méthode 3: La connaissance de la connaissance. Livre premier: Antropo logie de la connaissance.* Paris: Seuil.

Motion, J., & Leitch, S. (2000, March). *The technologies of corporate identity.* Working paper, University of Auckland and University of Waikato, Hamilton, New Zealand.

Nader, R., & Green, M. J. (1973). *Corporate power in America: Ralph Nader's conference on corporate accountability.* New York: Grossman.

Nader, R., Green, M. J., & Seligman, J. (1976). *Taming the giant corporation.* New York: Norton.

Nickels, W. G. (1976). *Marketing communication and promotion.* Columbus, OH: Grid.

Nisbet, R. (1970). *The sociological tradition.* London: Heinemann.

Olins, W. (1989). *Corporate identity: Making business strategy visible through design.* New York: Thames & Hudson.

Packard, V. (1969). *The hidden persuaders* (21st printing). New York: McKay.

Paonessa, K. A. (1982). *Corporate advocacy in General Motors Corporation.* Unpublished master's thesis, Purdue University, IN.

Parsons, T. (1949). *The structure of social action.* New York: Free Press.

Pearson, R. (1989). Business ethics as communication ethics: Public relations practice and the idea of dialogue. In C. H. Botan & V. Hazleton, Jr. (Eds.), *Public relations theory* (pp. 111-131). Hillsdale, NJ: Lawrence Erlbaum.

Perniola, M. (1980). *La societá dei simulacri.* Bologna, Italy: Capelli.

Pfeffer, J. (1981). Management as symbolic action: The creation and maintenance of organizational paradigms. In L. L. Cummings & B. M. Staw (Eds.), *Research in organizational behavior* (Vol. 3, pp. 1-52). Greenwich, CT: JAI.

Pondy, L. R., Frost, P. J., Morgan, G., & Dandridge, T. C. (Eds.). (1983). *Organizational symbolism.* Greenwich, CT: JAI.

Powell, W. M. (1990). Neither market nor hierarchy: Network forms of organization. In B. M. Staw & L. L. Cummings (Eds.), *Research in organizational behavior* (Vol. 12, pp. 295-336). Greenwich, CT: JAI Press.

Procter & Gamble. (1989). *The house that Ivory built: 150 years of successful marketing.* Lincolnwood, IL: NTC Business Books.

Putnam, L. L., Phillips, N., & Chapman, P. (1996). Metaphors of communication and organization. In S. R. Clegg, C. Hardy, & W. R. Nord (Eds.), *Handbook of organization studies* (pp. 375-408). London: Sage.

Ramanantsoa, B., & Battaglia, V. (1991, June). *The autobiography of the firm: A means of deconstruction of the traditional images.* Paper presented at the eighth International SCOS Conference, Copenhagen, Denmark.

Richardson, G. B. (1972). The organization of industry. *Economic Journal, 82,* 883-896.

Scott, C. R., & Carroll, C. E. (1999, November). *If not now, then when? Exploring situated identifications among members of a dispersed organization.* Paper presented at the annual conference of the National Communication Association, Chicago.

Scott, C. R., Corman, S. A., & Cheney, G. (1998). The development of a structurational theory of identification in the organization. *Communication Theory, 8,* 298-336.

Sennett, R. (1978). *The fall of public man: On the social psychology of capitalism.* New York: Vintage.

Shimp, T. A. (1990). *Promotion management and marketing communications* (2nd ed.). Chicago: Dryden.

Smircich, L., & Stubbart, C. (1985). Strategic management in an enacted world. *Academy of Management Review, 10,* 724-736.

Smith, R. (1993, May). *Images of organizational communication: Root-metaphors of the organization-communication relation.* Paper presented at the annual meeting of the International Communication Association, Washington, DC.

Sproull, J. M. (1988). The new managerial rhetoric and the old criticism. *Quarterly Journal of Speech, 74,* 468-486.

Sproull, J. M. (1990). Organizational rhetoric and the rational-democratic society. *Journal of Applied Communication Research, 74,* 192-240.

Starbuck, W. H. (1976). Organizations and their environments. In M. D. Dunnette (Ed.), *Handbook of industrial and organizational psychology* (pp. 1069-1123) Chicago: Rand McNally.

Stidsen, B., & Schutte, T. F. (1972). Marketing as a communication system: The marketing concept revisited. *Journal of Marketing, 36,* 22-27.

Taylor, J. R. (1993). *Rethinking the theory of organizational communication: How to read an organization.* Norwood, NJ: Ablex.

Taylor, J. R., Flanagin, A. J., Cheney, G., & Seibold, D. R. (in press). Organizational communication research: Key moments, central concerns, and future challenges. In W. B. Gudykunst (Ed.), *Communication yearbook 24.* Thousand Oaks, CA: Sage.

Thompson, M., & Wildavsky, A. (1986). A cultural theory of information bias in organizations. *Journal of Management Studies, 23*(3), 273-286.

Thygesen Poulsen, P. (1993). *LEGO—En virksomhed og dens sjæl.* Albertslund, Denmark: Schultz.

Tompkins, P. K., & Cheney, G. (1983). Account analysis of organizations: Decision making and identification. In L. L. Putnam & M. E. Pacanowsky (Eds.), *Communication and organizations: An interpretive approach* (pp. 123-147). Beverly Hills, CA: Sage.

Tompkins, P. K., & Cheney, G. (1985). Communication and unobtrusive control in contemporary organizations. In R. D. McPhee & P. K. Tompkins (Eds.), *Organizational communication: Traditional themes and new directions* (pp. 179-210). Beverly Hills, CA: Sage.

Tracy, S. (1995). *Can public relations about social responsibility be socially responsible?* Unpublished paper, University of Colorado at Boulder.

Treadwell, D. F., & Harrison, T. M. (1994). Conceptualizing and assessing organizational image: Model images, commitment, and communication. *Communication Monographs, 61,* 63-85.

van Riel, C. B. M. (1995). *Principles of corporate communication.* London: Prentice Hall.

Vibbert, S. L., & Bostdorff, D. M. (1993). Issue management in the "lawsuit crisis." In C. Conrad (Ed.), *The ethical nexus* (pp. 103-120). Norwood, NJ: Ablex.

Wartick, S. L., & Rude, R. E. (1986). Issues management: Corporate fad or corporate function. *California Management Review, 29*(1), 124-140.

Wätzold, F. (1996). When environmentalists have power: A case study of the Brent Spar. In J. P. Ulhøi & H. Madsen (Eds.), *Industry and the environment: Practical applications of environmental management approaches in business.* Aarhus, Denmark: Aarhus Business School.

Webster, F. E., Jr. (1992). The changing role of marketing in the corporation. *Journal of Marketing, 56,* 1-17.

Weick, K. E. (1979). *The social psychology of organizing* (2nd ed.). Reading, MA: Addison-Wesley.

Weigert, A. J., Teitge, J. S., & Teitge, D. W. (1986). *Society and identity: Toward a sociological psychology.* Cambridge, UK: Cambridge University Press.

White, J. B. (1984). *When words lose their meaning: Constitutions and reconstitutions of language, character, and community.* Chicago: University of Chicago Press.

Zaltman, G., Kotler, P., & Kaufman, I. (Eds.). (1972). *Creating social change.* New York: Holt, Rinehart & Winston.

# 8

# Sociopolitical Environments and Issues

◆ DAYNA FINET
◆ *Writer, Austin, Texas*

Historically, the field of organizational communication has prioritized analysis of *intra*organizational interaction. This focus involves a potentially infinite number of interesting and important questions. But it should not imply that organizational communication transcending organizational boundaries is less important. Rather, an organizational analyst might view the embeddedness of organizations in complex and dynamic sociopolitical environments, and the reciprocal influences of each upon the other, as good reason for concentrating even more directly on organizational communication within sociopolitical environments.

A note at the end of this chapter provides citations to a number of recent studies that

have explored relationships between organizations and sociopolitical environments.[1] Both the volume and scope of this research demonstrate the vitality of this topic. Most of this current work uses one, or a combination, of three dominant theoretical approaches: (a) population ecology (Aldrich, 1979; Hannan & Carroll, 1992; Hannan & Freeman, 1977), (b) resource dependency theory (Pfeffer & Salancik, 1978), and (c) institutional theory (DiMaggio & Powell, 1983; Meyer & Rowan, 1977; Meyer & Scott, 1983; Powell & DiMaggio, 1991; Scott, 1987; Zucker, 1988). In the previous version of this handbook, Euske and Roberts (1987) outlined the relevance of these three approaches in terms of organizational communication. Their effort represents a helpful step in the development of a communicative approach to the topic of interaction between organizations and environments. Yet like many other examples in the organizational communication literature, the Euske and Roberts chapter is unfortunately limited by the authors' strategy of pinning post hoc "communication implications" onto existing theories that never intended to make communication their primary concern. In this chapter, I attempt to build on the foundation provided by Euske and Roberts. I introduce a new model of sociopolitically oriented organizational communication where the organizational discourses of institutional rhetoric and everyday talk play essential roles.

The chapter is organized into two main parts. The first section elaborates the discourse-centered model of organizations and their relations with their sociopolitical environments. This model extends Karl Weick's (1979) notion of the "enacted" environment and Taylor's (1995) articulation of organizational communication as "conversation." The second part of the chapter applies this model, using as illustration current research on the sociopolitical topics of sexual harassment, and family-work conflict.

## THE DISCURSIVE MODEL OF ORGANIZATIONS AND SOCIOPOLITICAL ENVIRONMENTS

Early work on organizational environments emphasized market and technological environments (Burns & Stalker, 1961; Emery & Trist, 1965; Lawrence & Lorsch, 1967; Thompson, 1967). Later, this literature concentrated on sociopolitical environments (Aldrich, 1979; Hannan & Carroll, 1992; Hannan & Freeman, 1977; Meyer & Rowan, 1977; Meyer & Scott, 1983; Pfeffer & Salancik, 1978; Powell & DiMaggio, 1991; Scott, 1987; Zucker, 1988). Whichever its

orientation, all this literature is important for the reason that it acknowledges the significance of organizations' across-boundary interaction. Following Euske and Roberts's example, it thus makes sense to use this existing work as the initial foundation for a discursively grounded approach to the analysis of organizations and their relations with sociopolitical environments. Most basically, this discourse-centered model departs from the existing body of organization/environment research over an issue that has long preoccupied investigators. Much of the existing research in the field has assumed that organizations and environments are conceptually and empirically distinct. As a result, much of this work has involved the problem of "boundary specification," which distinguishes the organization from the environment with which it interacts. Its different strategy for handling this question represents the most elemental way in which a discourse-centered perspective prioritizes communication in the analysis of organizations' sociopolitical relations.

As Sutcliffe discusses in Chapter 6 in this handbook, discussion of the boundary specification question has centered on a debate over the comparatively objective or subjective character of organizational environments (Boyd, Dess, & Rasheed, 1993). This distinction has been variously labeled as, for example, a divergence between nominalist (objective) and realist (subjective) environments (Laumann, Marsden, & Prensky, 1983) or between archival (objective) and perceptual (subjective) ones (Boyd et al., 1993). The literature has tended to treat objective and subjective approaches to boundary specification as competing strategies, and the difference between them is easy to comprehend. Objectivists propose to establish empirical criteria for inclusion in the organization; whatever (or whoever) does not meet such criteria for organizational membership by definition then belongs to the organization's environment. Subjectivists are guided by organization members' perceptions of relevant external entities as the appropriate strategy for defining the organizational environment.

The problem of boundary specification is not insignificant, and both objective and subjective solutions have analytical utility if appropriately applied. But from the perspective of the discursive model developed in this chapter, this handling of the boundary specification question has encouraged two undesirable tendencies. First, it has led researchers to exaggerate the fixedness of organizational boundaries. Second, limiting boundary specification to objective and subjective techniques has caused researchers also to overlook the role of social practice, specifically as discourse, in organization-environment relations. At least two authors have created alternative conceptualizations of organization-environment relations that address these problems of boundary specification. Weick's (1979) notion of the "enacted" environment and Taylor's (1995) articulation of organizational "conversation" each lends conceptual support to a discourse-centered perspective on organizational relations within sociopolitical environments.

Weick's concept of the enacted environment addresses the problem of overly concretizing the organization-environment boundary as well as the problem of overlooking discursive social practices in the dynamics of organization and environment relations. In Weick's description, the concept of the enacted environment represents organizational boundaries as neither distinct nor static, but instead, as fundamentally permeable and fluid. According to Weick (1979), "boundaries between organizations and environment are never quite as clear-cut or stable as many organizational theorists think. These boundaries shift, disappear, and are arbitrarily drawn" (p. 132). Further, Weick's conceptualization of the enacted environment emphasizes the active (if not always self-reflective) role of patterned social practices as organizations and their members comprehend their external environments. According to Weick, enactment is naturally bound up with ecological change. On the one hand, organization members notice environmental occurrences and bracket these for collective attention. On the other hand, collective actions produce ecological change, which lead to other changes, and so on. Thus, in Weick's (1979) terms, "meaningful environments are the outputs of organizing, not inputs to it" (p. 131).

In his elaboration of organizational communication as conversation, Taylor likewise addresses both the issue of boundary precision and the role of social interaction in organization and environment relations. He rejects the notion of the organization-environment boundary as unambiguous, assumedly fixed. While not denying a distinctiveness of organization and environment, Taylor (1995) describes this boundary relationship as "self-generated [by the organization]: a membrane created from within by the process of self-reproduction. . . . Such boundary-establishing membranes, since they are constructed out of material common to all, do not totally isolate the organism from the world outside" (p. 8). Further, Taylor elaborates even more explicitly than does Weick the basic importance of discursive practices in organizations' communication within their social environments. Manifesting through organizational discourse the autopoietic quality of self-organizing, "an organization is not a physical structure . . . joined by material channels of communication, but a construction made out of conversation" (Taylor, 1995, p. 22) that simultaneously reflects and reproduces the social reality lived in the interactions of organization members. "Conversations are reflexive and self-organizing: they are produced by communication but are in turn the frame, or envelope, of the communication that generated them, in the absence of which communication would be impossible" (Taylor, 1995, p. 1).

In their ontological innovations, Weick and Taylor accomplish two common outcomes. First, they reduce the conceptual priority of the taken-for-granted separation of organization and environment and identify discursive practice as the principal feature in relationships between organizations and their larger environmental contexts. Second, they encourage an approach to organization-environment relations rooted in discursive process and practice, which the sociopolitically relevant example of "diversity" illustrates.

In analyzing diversity, traditional approaches to organization-environment relations would view the sociopolitical environment as the origin of normative change. Normative evolution would emerge in the form of specific demands regarding diversity, imposed on specific organizations from outside their boundaries. To cope, organizations would need to appropriately respond to these external expectations.

By contrast, Weick's and Taylor's work suggests that changing norms regarding gender and race actually reflect an ongoing cultural discussion occurring simultaneously within organizations and in their larger sociopolitical environments. These overlapping across-boundary conversations sometimes complement and sometimes conflict with, but always reciprocally influence, each other.

Traditional literature on organization-environment relations would also view the implications of diversity, for relations between organizations and sociopolitical environments, as either material or perceptual. A materialist conceptualization might focus on the numbers of women or minority group members in particular organizational roles, for example. A perceptual frame might examine the extent to which organizational decision makers feel threatened by gender- or race-relevant regulation.

Weick and Taylor concentrate instead on the means by which organizational discourse creates, sustains, or disestablishes particular sociopolitical understandings. This discourse might adopt infinite form. It could emerge as rhetorical labeling, apparent in such terms as *affirmative action, reverse discrimination,* and indeed, the term *diversity* itself. It could appear in patterns of organizational interaction that segregate organization members into subgroups along lines of gender or race. Or this diversity-oriented discourse could show up in the form of specific recruitment and training practices that use interaction to help overcome the often vast perceptual and experiential gaps between members of these subgroups.

What Weick and Taylor do not yet accomplish is the more detailed articulation of discourse processes in organizational relations with sociopolitical environments. Remaining sections of this chapter attempt this, conceptualizing organizations' sociopolitically relevant interaction at the intersecting organizational discourses of "institutional rhetoric" and "everyday talk."

## Conceptual Assumptions

Prior to a detailed presentation of the discursive model of organizational communication within sociopolitical environments, several preliminary conceptual assumptions warrant elaboration.

First, the relevant issues for understanding organizational communication within sociopolitical environments involves much more than just the ways in which social change affects (primarily internal) organizational communication "variables." Rather, the discursive practices of and within organizations also influence the larger sociopolitical context (Deetz, 1992), including the direction of social change. This means that organizations do not simply respond communicatively to societal changes that have occurred independent of these organizations' own discursive practices. Rather, organizational discourse contributes largely to the direction and nature of this societal transformation.

Second, to understand organizational discourse in the sociopolitical environment requires consideration of a multitude of diverse perspectives and voices both within and outside the organization. Certainly, organization members and those outside the organization's formal structure hold some common understandings based on their participation within a shared larger culture. Yet these people's experiences and meanings also vary by social location and personal history. The field of organizational communication has barely begun to explore such diversity of human experience. Such analysis is essential, though, to understand organizational discourse within a vastly complex and not necessarily coherent sociopolitical world.

Third, the analysis of sociopolitical issues and their importance for organizational discourse must emphasize politics. Social outcomes, good or bad, are not equally shared, and the preferences of some social interests, both within and outside organizations, are realized while the preferences of others are not. Thus, there will exist sometimes fierce conflict in the face of social change, and organizational discourse will both reflect and contribute to it. Because many of these issues are deeply affecting, they can involve exceptionally high-stakes conflict. To lose can cost dearly, often in the most essential human terms. Not surprisingly, then, politics are integral to the discussion of organizational discourse and sociopolitical environments.

The model presented in Figure 8.1 conceptualizes organizational interaction with sociopolitical environments as basically composed of the ongoing organizational discourses of institutional rhetoric and everyday talk. Organizational communication in the sociopolitical context includes both the externally directed corporate expression of relatively formal collective entities—"institutional rhetoric"—and the more diffuse but just as pervasive ongoing communication of the partially included individual members who people such collectives—"everyday talk." Adequate conceptualization of sociopolitically relevant organizational discourse must include both institutional rhetoric and everyday talk. Analysis of only one of these forms of discourse would significantly distort the representation of organizations' interaction in the sociopolitical context.

The corporate expression of interest advocacy inherent in practices of institutional rhetoric is relatively easy to recognize as sociopolitically relevant organizational discourse. However, the everyday interaction of individuals with multiple organizational affiliations also represents a significant means by which

sociopolitically relevant communication across organizational boundaries is accomplished. Weick's (1979) concept of "partial inclusion" suggests why the discourse of individuals must also represent a primary aspect of the model of organizations' sociopolitical interaction. The idea of partial inclusion refers to the multiple, overlapping collective memberships of individuals. One person may simultaneously hold membership in the collective contexts of work organization, church, political organization, and family, for example. In effect, these individuals produce linkages across organizational boundaries in their everyday talk with different individuals from different organizational contexts. To concentrate analysis only on the institutional voice of formal organizations and neglect the everyday interaction of the individuals who make up organizations would consequently leave out a crucial element of any model of organizations and sociopolitical environments.

## Institutional Rhetoric

Sociopolitically relevant organizational discourse in the form of institutional rhetoric involves collective expression intended to influence the larger social normative climate, with outcomes beneficial to the collective. Cheney's (1991) analysis of the rhetorical practices of the Roman Catholic Church in the United States exemplifies this form of discourse. Organizations engage in institutional rhetoric regarding social issues because these issues affect them, sometimes quite deeply. Institutional rhetoric promotes alternative interpretations of the meaning and significance of such changes, especially the degree to which they represent social problems and what policies and actions represent appropriate solutions. The primary role of institutional rhetoric in the discursive model of organizations' sociopolitical relations thus emphasizes the ways in which organizations strategically advocate their own perspectives, attempting to influence wider social meanings.

As a form of organizational discourse, institutional rhetoric demonstrates each of the

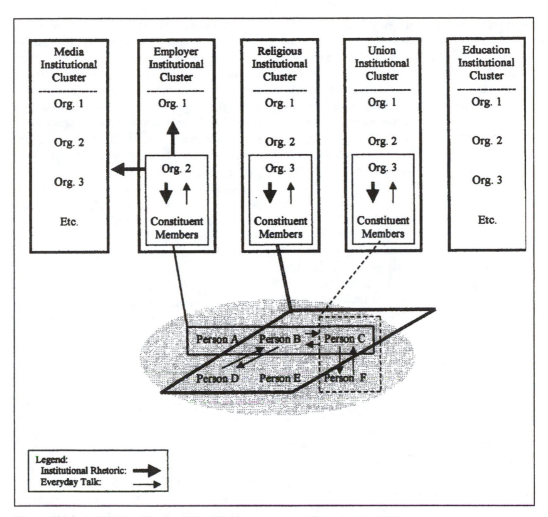

**Figure 8.1.** A Model of Sociopolitical Environments and Organizational Discourse

basic conceptual assumptions that underlies the discursive model of organizations' sociopolitical relations. Organizations that use institutional rhetoric to advocate their perspectives on sociopolitical issues may feel, and indeed, be deeply affected by, sociopolitical change. But they also influence, with varying degrees of conscious intent, the direction of this change. Certainly, the discursive practices of organizations from varied institutional contexts also reflect a multiplicity of social perspectives about which few common generalizations apply. And finally, the interaction among these various organizational viewpoints is clearly marked by often fierce competition for the sometimes zero-sum resource of societal legitimacy.

Discursive practices of institutional rhetoric are represented by the wide arrows in Figure 8.1. The model incorporates five exemplary institutional clusters—employing organizations, trade unions, media (journalism and popular culture), and educational institutions (primary, secondary, and higher education) and a cluster representing religious organizations—within which any number of specifically identifiable, relatively formal organizations might operate. Other institutional clusters are also possible (e.g., public interest groups, charitable organizations, policy institutions, branches of government).

Because the point of institutional rhetoric in the sociopolitical context is the strategic advocacy of organizational interests, the thick, solid lines represent rhetorical linkages established by the discursive engagement of organizations with other entities within the overall sociopolitical context to promote what are taken as these organizations' sociopolitical interests. Content of these rhetorical relations is infinitely variable, as is the variety of media used to convey its arguments. Depending on the target of its institutional rhetoric, the organization advocating its position on a given topic might employ a wide range of media, for example, employee handbooks, advocacy advertising, or lobbying communication.

To trace all possible linkages within the model would be confusing and, perhaps, incomprehensible, so the representation in Figure 8.1 illustrates as an example some of the discursive links that might be established by the institutional rhetoric of employing organizations. Organization members represent a common audience for sociopolitically relevant institutional rhetoric. In the example of an employing organization expressing its collective interest on a specific sociopolitically relevant topic, employees are (obviously) the organization members that the arguments of institutional rhetoric are designed to reach. Organizations also direct the discourse of institutional rhetoric to other organizations within the same or different institutional clusters to advocate their sociopolitical interests. Thus, the example in Figure 8.1 also includes a plausible, hypothetical institutionally rhetorical linkage from an employer to other organizations in its own cluster as well as the institutional cluster of media.

### Everyday Talk

Obviously very different from organizational discourse in the form of institutional rhetoric, organizational discourse as talk focuses on the everyday conversations shared among organization members and between organization members and important other people, such as family members. These discussions affect the subjective and intersubjective understandings characteristic of individuals and the collective. The scholarly literature in the field of organizational communication contains plentiful examples of interpretive theory and research (Putnam & Pacanowsky, 1983) that explore this type of organizational discourse. People talk about sociopolitical issues because often these affect life on an important personal level every single day. As organizational discourse, this talk helps individuals to both define themselves and negotiate relations with others. Thus, the discursive model of organizations and sociopolitical environments emphasizes the ways in which organization members use such talk creatively, to sort out and deal with the complexities of meaning and implications for human action of sociopolitical change.

Like the discourse of institutional rhetoric, organizational discourse as talk illustrates each of the main conceptual aspects of organizational discourse in the sociopolitical context. Social changes can transform the kinds of topics people discuss in organizations, the kinds of people they interact with, the meanings they hold. Yet individuals also influence the emergence of these meanings through their own discursive involvement with other individuals. No single voice monopolizes the everyday talk surrounding issues of sociopolitical transformation. Rather, this conversation represents the various perspectives of a great number of parties variously interested in these changes. Finally, the conversation often becomes an argument as the voices, in their everyday talk, dispute over competing interpretations of the meaning and significance of sociopolitical change.

Though analytically distinct, the sociopolitically relevant discursive practices of everyday organizational talk are, in actuality, embedded within the larger context of institutional rhetoric. Thus, organizational discourse in the form of everyday talk appears along with the discursive practices of institutional rhetoric represented in Figure 8.1. Here the model employs thin arrows to symbolically represent individuals linked through talk to other people, in one or more organizations, in one or more of the institutional clusters contained in the model. The cluster of individuals (Persons A, B, C, etc. contained within the oval shape) below the institutional clusters represent the individuals who collectively comprise separate organizations within those clusters.

Organizational discourse as everyday talk functions primarily as individuals use this discourse to interpret and make sense of consequential sociopolitical change. Thus, in addition to the wide arrows that represent the context of institutional rhetoric within which individuals are embedded, thin solid arrows appearing in Figure 8.1 represent the interpersonal everyday talk that enables individual organization members to interpret the personal and collective meanings of transformation in the larger sociopolitical environment. The content of this talk, like the content of institutional rhetoric, is infinitely variable. The content of individuals' everyday talk about a given sociopolitical issue might involve, for instance, the simple expression of pleasure or frustration or perhaps instrumental talk, useful for problem solving and decision making. Specific patterns of within-and-across-organization conversational linkage, for any given person in any given temporal context, also can assume an infinite variety of forms. One employee's everyday talk about any number of sociopolitical topics might reflect, for example, that person's embeddedness in a social network based on church membership. In turn, the sociopolitically related everyday talk of another employee may occur within a context of that person's active involvement with other people in a civic or political group.

For purposes of clarity, Figure 8.1 illustrates one possible pattern of linkages based on the relations of everyday talk for a person with overlapping organizational identities as employee, trade union member, and church member. In this example, the individual with multiple organizational affiliations discursively spans the boundaries of these identifiably different organizational contexts, through the social practices of ordinary interpersonal interaction.

# ORGANIZATIONAL DISCOURSE IN THE CONTEMPORARY SOCIOPOLITICAL ENVIRONMENT

A concern with topics of sociopolitical relevance has become increasingly apparent in recent organizational research, and a discourse-centered conceptualization of organization-environment relations in the sociopolitical context could productively inform much of this work. This section of the chapter applies the discursive model to two of these topics: sexual harassment and family-work conflict.

The number of specific topics that might be selected from the contemporary literature on sociopolitical issues and environments is large and wide ranging, and it would be impossible within the scope of a single chapter to provide an exhaustive survey of all the existing organizational research with sociopolitical relevance. The recent literature on the two topics examined here demonstrates especially clearly researchers' growing recognition of the mutuality of influence and effect between organizations, on the one hand, and the complex and often turbulent transformations taking place in the larger society, on the other. In other words, research on these topics demonstrates researchers' recognition that our society is in transition and organizations must deal with this while, at the same time, these organizations influence the directions such transitions take. But more important to its role exemplifying the discursive approach to organizations' sociopolitical relations, research on the topics of sexual harassment and family-work conflict (directly and indirectly) reflects both types of organizational discourse represented in the discursive model. Thus, these two issues have a special capacity to illustrate well how organizations' interaction within sociopolitical contexts can be more fruitfully understood from a perspective that makes organizational discourse analytically central.

## Sexual Harassment

Scholars have recognized the important consequences of sexual harassment at least since Catherine MacKinnon's (1979) influential analysis of the legal and public policy debates centered around this issue. But concern over sexual harassment has grown dramatically since the early 1990s when, during his confirmation hearings, attorney Anita Hill accused Supreme Court nominee Clarence Thomas of sexual harassment (Morrison, 1992; Ragan, 1996; Siegel, 1996). The body of research literature on the topic has now become substantial (Axelrod, 1993; Berryman-Fink, 1993; Braun, 1993; Brown, 1993; Clair, 1993a, 1993b, 1994; Clair, McGoun, & Spirek, 1993; Foegen, 1992; Galvin, 1993; Gutek, Cohen, & Konrad, 1990; Kreps, 1993; Strine, 1992; Taylor & Conrad, 1992; Terpstra & Baker, 1988, 1992; Wells & Kracher, 1993; Witteman, 1993). More specifically, organizational communication researchers have shown more interest in this topic than in most other sociopolitical issues, so the discursive model of organizations' sociopolitical communication processes readily applies to the topic of sexual harassment.

## Research on Sexual Harassment: Evidence of Institutional Rhetoric

Organizational discourse as institutional rhetoric involves the strategic collective advocacy of what organizations take to represent their sociopolitical interests. Organizations direct their institutional rhetoric at other organizations, within the same or different institutional clusters, and also toward their own individual members. Examples of institutional rhetoric in the context of sexual harassment include policy statements on harassment contained in company handbooks and training programs, press and popular cultural narratives from people who have experienced harassment, and legal definitions of harassment as articulated in court decisions.

Some existing research on the topic of harassment has specifically investigated organizational communication phenomena, which this chapter would label as institutional rhetoric. This work can be organized into three primary categories: (a) studies that describe organizations' efforts to use institutional rhetoric for positioning themselves, normatively, on the topic of sexual harassment; (b) work that has concerned the institutional rhetoric of media organizations on the topic of sexual harassment; and (c) research that has incorporated institutional rhetoric as an explanatory variable predictive of harassment-relevant organizational outcomes.

The first cluster of research on the topic of sexual harassment has focused on the rhetoric of organizational responses to societal concerns about harassment. These discursive efforts represent institutional rhetoric as they serve to strategically position organizational actors within the context of normative opinion on this controversial topic. Clair's (1993a) study provides an example of research within this cluster (see also Gutek, 1996). Her research examined official communication on the topic of harassment among the Big 10 universities. As institutional rhetoric, this discourse was intended to publicly situate the universities sympathetically within the context of a serious social problem. Ironically, Clair found this institutional rhetoric instead functioned to commodify, bureaucratize, and privatize the practice of harassment within the organizations.

Institutional rhetoric may also strategically situate employers with regard to their employees through policy statements and training programs that concentrate on the topic of harassment (Berryman-Fink, 1993; Blakely, Blakely, & Moorman, 1998; Galvin, 1993; Hulin, Fitzgerald, & Drasgow, 1996). Berryman-Fink describes organization-sponsored workshops and training programs in terms that the discursive model would call institutional rhetoric: collective statements of the normative positions that (a) harassment is not good, and (b) organizations bear some responsibility for reducing it. Berryman-Fink's research suggests that organizations can meet their obligations to discourage the undesirable practice of sexual harassment by promoting androgynous, "gender-flexible" communication among organization members. From a somewhat different perspective, Galvin's (1993) work explores the responsibility of academic organizations to clarify harassing statements and behavior for their faculties. Her research describes the discourse of institutional rhetoric in the sense that individual faculty members are not permitted to individually negotiate what statements and behaviors are considered to reflect sexual harassment. Rather, the institution determines which of these practices constitute harassment and then communicates these definitions to faculty members.

In the discursive model described in this chapter, media organizations represent a significant source of institutional rhetoric on practically any given sociopolitical topic, including sexual harassment. Institutional rhetoric functioning in this sense not only strategically positions media organizations in terms of their stance on a sociopolitical topic such as harassment but also contributes to the larger societal context of conversation and interpretation regarding such questions. Accordingly, a second group of studies has examined the harassment-related messages of mass media organizations. These messages represent institutional rhetoric in two ways. First, they strategically locate media organizations' own normative positions on the topic of harassment. Second, these messages also help to influence shifting interpretations of harassment within the larger normative culture. As an example of research along these lines, Axelrod (1993) studied representations of organizational sexuality in film, focusing on the ways in which institutional rhetoric embedded in films can influence broader societal norms about harassment. Axelrod concluded that film treatments that present harassment as amusing, or as an acceptable means for women to achieve organizational influence, in effect persuade the audiences to adopt these normative positions too. Braun's (1993) case study of an advertising agency's costly response to charges of sexism in its campaigns also provides an example of research that has examined the institutional rhetoric of mass media discourse about sexual harassment. In this study, institutional rhetoric took one form in the offensive content of campaigns developed for agency clients, which seemed to advocate greater tolerance of harassing behaviors. Institutional rhetoric also appeared in the agency's defensive and hostile response to complaints about these campaigns. Scornfully counterattacking its critics rather than listening and thoughtfully responding to them, the agency communicated its normative position on harassment in a misguided use of institutional rhetoric that angered agency critics and cost the agency both clients and income.

A third group of studies has implicitly identified institutional rhetoric as an explanation for the outcomes of harassment-related decision-making processes. For example, Wells and Kracher (1993) consider organizations' moral duty to define *hostile environment* not from an organizational point of view, but from the perspective of its (usually female) targets. These authors argue that if organizations can adopt in their own institutional rhetoric the voice of the women who most frequently experience sexual harassment, they can thereby better accomplish the overriding moral purpose of meeting the needs of those who have been harassed. Terpstra and Baker's (1988, 1992) research also demonstrates how institutional rhetoric may influence decision making in the context of sexual harassment. These studies examined the grounds associated with legal decisions favorable to harassment claimants. In this instance, institutional rhetoric is represented by the courts' articulation of criteria for determining that sexual harassment has occurred. Terpstra and Baker identified some of these criteria, including the severity of the harassing behavior, the presence of witnesses and documents, the notification of employers by harassment targets, and the remedial actions taken by companies in response to internal complaints. Outcomes affected by these criteria are tangible and significant. They include the determination itself that harassment has occurred, as well as decisions regarding the compensation awarded to its targets and the punishment dealt to its perpetrators.

## Research on Sexual Harassment: Evidence of Everyday Talk

As the discursive model suggests, sociopolitical organizational discourse in the form of everyday talk is analytically distinct, but actually embedded within a context of institutional rhetoric. Everyday talk does not focus on the advocacy of strategic collective interests. Instead, people use everyday talk in a much more personal way, creatively employing this form of discourse to help sort out and deal with the everyday human complexities that sociopolitical controversy and change imply. Everyday talk occurs among the members of a single organization, and also involves personal relationships that cross organizational boundaries. The private, personal stories of harassment told to friends, family members, therapists, lawyers, support groups, and other potential helpers provide an example of sociopolitical discourse as everyday talk. A very different type of everyday talk about sexual harassment occurred during the Hill-Thomas hearings, when innumerable intraorganizational conversations sparked by the proceedings helped organization members to make sense of this controversial subject.

Research on the topic of sexual harassment has frequently focused on organizational discourse as everyday talk. This literature is represented by two clusters: (a) a group of studies that has examined everyday talk about sexual harassment as it has occurred in the form of personal harassment narratives, and (b) research that has focused on everyday talk in the form of ordinary interpersonal interaction among organization members.

Research analyzing personal narratives of harassment represents one cluster of studies examining everyday talk on the subject of sex-

ual harassment. These narratives represent everyday talk in the sense that they are personal forms of expression, used both to recount and make sense of experiences that might represent sexual harassment. These narratives reflect everyday talk both influenced by the larger discursive context of institutional rhetoric about sexual harassment and also potentially capable of influencing it.

Among the number of studies that have examined sexual harassment from the perspective of personal narrative, Strine (1992) analyzed a series of personal harassment stories from a critical poststructuralist perspective. In this case, the everyday talk contained in her informants' narratives allowed Strine to detect means by which the individual, organizational, and social meanings of harassment are discursively constructed through everyday talk in organizations. In effect, everyday organizational talk privileges harassers' views of the severity and significance of their behavior and preserves a dominant patriarchal organizational order. Taylor and Conrad (1992) analyzed the same collection of harassment narratives. Like Strine, they identified the essentially political ways in which everyday talk about harassment respectively privileges and marginalizes organization members on gender grounds. Taylor and Conrad maintain that everyday talk about harassment systematically favors the interpretations given by perpetrators, usually men, and thereby reinforces existing patterns of male domination in the organizational setting. Brown (1993) used a somewhat different approach to explore the consequences of everyday talk, as personal narrative, for the construction of organizational meanings on the subject of sexual harassment. Based on actual interviews, Brown's "creative narrative" depicted a fictional conversation among female conference attendees. By relating their personal experiences with sexual harassment, these women were able to make sense of such incidents and discover creative means for dealing with them. Finally, Clair's (1993b) research also analyzed personal narrative to explore the role of women's everyday talk that reinforces more pervasive organizational understandings concerning harassment. Participants in Clair's research recounted incidents of harassment. These narrative accounts occasionally showed evidence of resistance by the women. More commonly, though, the narratives reflected the women's use of rhetorical framing devices to make sense of harassment in ways primarily unchallenging to dominant organizational ideology.

A second group of studies has examined interpersonal communication, which, as taken-for-granted, commonplace interaction among members of organizations, represents the discourse of everyday talk. For example, Clair et al. (1993) developed a typology of women's interpersonal responses to harassment. Forms of response in this typology range from the most passive, such as avoidance, to such aggressive responses as direct confrontation. As varieties of interpersonal interaction, these communicated responses to harassment represent the discursive domain of everyday talk. Witteman (1993) analyzed interactional characteristics common to the phenomena of sexual harassment and organizational romance, respectively, as well as the features of interaction that distinguish them. In this sense, Witteman's research explores interpersonal interaction as everyday discourse. Witteman considers such everyday talk as complimentary comments and looks to represent communication behaviors common to both sexual harassment and organizational romance. Analyses showed that nonreciprocated self-disclosure illustrates everyday talk more likely to be interpreted as harassment than as normal relational discourse. Similarly, Solomon and Williams (1997) have distinguished the communication characteristics of harassment as opposed to flirtation behavior. Gutek et al.'s (1990) research also features everyday talk as it influences collective meanings relevant to the topic of sexual harassment. These researchers found that greater sexualization of the workplace produced a higher level of harassing behavior. Significantly for the pur-

poses of this chapter, the researchers employed a discursive measure of workplace sexualization, operationalized as the degree of ongoing everyday communication between women and men. More simply put, the greater the level of everyday between-sex talk, the greater the incidence of workplace sexual harassment. Finally, Foegen (1992) also concentrated on interpersonal communication as a reflection of everyday organizational talk about sexual harassment. In Foegen's research, everyday talk emerged in the form of organizational discussions specifically on the topic of sexual harassment. These discussions eventually resulted in greater discomfort and interpersonal conflict in subsequent interactions among organization members.

## Interpenetration of Institutional Rhetoric and Everyday Talk

Organizational discourse at the levels of institutional rhetoric and everyday talk each has unique significance. Yet, and more important, these discourses interact with and mutually influence each other. For the sociopolitical example of sexual harassment, such discursive interpenetration might work in the following ways.

Though always subject to contestation and negotiation, the social practices of institutional rhetoric generate a societal context of meaning around sociopolitical questions such as sexual harassment (e.g., Mumby & Clair, 1997). This context represents the rhetorical voices of diverse collective interests with differing views on these issues. For example, positions advocated by institutional rhetoric might center on the very definition of harassment and whether it includes such behaviors as complimenting coworkers' appearance. In this example, social discourse, as institutional rhetoric, establishes what behaviors and communicative practices constitute harassment, whether these definitions represent widely consensual understandings, aggressively contested ones, or something in between. Thus, institutional rhetoric may contribute to the normative understanding that all commentary on the appearance of coworkers is inappropriate and, therefore, represents harassment.

Another example of the institutional rhetoric of sexual harassment might focus on responsibility for it. Assignment of responsibility might label perpetrators as wrongdoers, or on the other hand, just victims of confusion over changing social standards. In this sense, institutional rhetoric contributes to normative understandings about who should get the blame when harassment occurs. Thus, the discourse of institutional rhetoric might help to create a climate of sociopolitical meaning in which behaviors that offend other people are excused. In such a climate, people whose joking focuses on sexual topics or who use diminutive terms in communication with coworkers evade sanction because they "meant no harm."

Within the context of meaning generated through institutional rhetoric, individuals use everyday discourse to comprehend and interpret sociopolitical questions such as sexual harassment. These individuals generate meanings that may be complicit with or oppose certain positions expressed through institutional rhetoric. Two examples illustrate how discursive practices of everyday talk might play out within the contexts of institutional rhetoric about what constitutes harassment and whose responsibility it is.

In the first example, institutional rhetoric establishes a social context for defining what types of behaviors constitute harassment. Embedded in this normative context, discourse as everyday talk reflects and responds to these definitions. Thus, within a discursively influenced normative climate that classifies comments on personal appearance as inappropriate or offensive, a group of female coworkers discussing the supervisor's compliments may interpret these not as innocent pleasantries but instead as sexual harassment.

In the second example, institutional rhetoric establishes sociopolitical expectations regarding the question of responsibility for sexual harassment. Again, sociopolitically relevant organizational discourse in the form of everyday talk takes place within this context of normative meaning. Thus, when an organization's normative atmosphere dictates that responsibility for harassment is based not on the content of a message but on its (harmful) intent, older male employees may interpret their own communication as politeness rather than harassment. These men might accordingly continue to address young female employees using diminutive labels such as "honey" or "missy" or "sweetie." In turn, the women might employ everyday talk to express their objections to these terms.

Clair's (1994) study represents a rare example of research that has explored the intersecting discourses of institutional rhetoric and everyday talk. In this research, the target of a well-publicized harassment incident simulates the discourse of everyday talk in the form of interviews with the researcher, during which the research respondent interprets newspaper accounts—defined by the discursive model as institutional rhetoric—of the incident.

### Family-Work Conflict

Ongoing redefinition of American families has come to represent a topic of increasing societal concern. Accordingly, the interest of organizational researchers in the subject of family-work conflict has also grown (Adams, 1993; Bandow, 1991; Covin & Brush, 1993; Crosby, 1991; Falkenberg & Monachello, 1990; Frone, Russell, & Cooper, 1992; Goodstein, 1994; Karambayya & Reilly, 1992; Lilly, Pitt-Catsouphes, & Googins, 1997; Lobel, 1991; Lobel & St. Clair, 1992; Mele, 1989; Miller, Stead, & Pereira, 1991; Pitt-Catsouphes & Googins, 1999; Schneer & Reitman, 1993; Williams & Alliger, 1994). Communication research specifically has not shown as much interest in this topic as in the question of sexual harassment. Nevertheless, the existing research on family-work conflict indirectly reflects concern with discursive variables and processes.

## Research on Family-Work Conflict: Evidence of Institutional Rhetoric

Institutional rhetoric reflects the perspective of organizations, advocating their interests within the larger sociopolitical environment. One example of institutional rhetoric on the topic of family-work conflict might involve the promotion by organizations of their family-oriented benefits. Organizations' public arguments addressing legislation relevant to workers with families represent another illustration of the institutional rhetoric of family and work.

The literature on family-work conflict demonstrates extensive evidence of a concern with organizational features that resemble institutional rhetoric. This literature has included research concentrating on three primary themes: (a) specific arguments for and against progressive family and work policies, as these have been articulated through institutional rhetoric; (b) the identification of institutional rhetoric as a primary explanatory variable predicting organizations' responsiveness to their employees' family-related needs and expectations; and (c) the consequences, for individuals and families, of the emergent "mommy-track" and "daddy-track" phenomena, widely recognized contemporary terms largely constructed through the discursive processes of institutional rhetoric.

The public articulation of organizations' support of and opposition to progressive family and work policies reflects an important expression of institutional rhetoric that scholars have explored. Several investigators have examined the arguments used in the institutional rhetoric of the advocates of these progressive programs. In one such essay, Adams (1993) articulates common arguments made by organizations that employ institutional rhetoric strategically to position themselves as advocates for families. One such argument suggests that the morale benefits of these policies outweigh their costs. Another makes the point that supporting families is crucial to the long-term well-being of the whole society, business organizations included. Similarly, Mele (1989) analyzed the normative argument, expressed through institutional rhetoric, that organizations bear an ethical obligation to support the marital and parental responsibilities of their employees.

Scholars have also explored the logic evident in the institutional rhetoric of organizations that oppose progressive family-and-work policies. Adams (1993) identifies several of these arguments, which suggest that progressive family policies violate employee privacy, create perceptions of unfairness among employees (e.g., Young, 1999), unreasonably raise employee expectations, and pose excessive costs of regulatory compliance and liability. Bandow (1991) also examined the logic of opposition to progressive family policies as this has been articulated through institutional rhetoric. One such discursive theme maintains that more generous family benefits promote an economically detrimental ethic of entitlement among employees. Bandow also describes the rhetorically expressed logic that progressive family policies actually discriminate against married women and women with families, who earn less due to their family commitments.

Institutional rhetoric explains the responsiveness of organizations to their employees' family-related needs in a second category of research on the institutional rhetoric of family-work conflict. Consistent with this framework, Goodstein (1994) found that individual organizations respond strategically to external institutional pressures for their greater involvement in work and family issues (Witkowski, 1999), as these are communicated through institutional rhetoric. Organizations that experience more outside pressure to accommodate workers' family obligations do so. Organizations not facing such rhetorically expressed external expectations do little to assist with their employees' family obligations.

Institutional rhetoric has contributed to the discursive construction of meaning through its creation of such terms as the *mommy track* and its more contemporary parallel, the *daddy track*. These terms refer to the career patterns of women and men, respectively, who voluntarily choose to give their families priority over their work. Institutional rhetoric in this case has been articulated most obviously by media organizations, which have speculated on the practical consequences of these terms for the employees described by them. Findings from research have produced inconsistent conclusions about these effects. On the one hand, Lobel and St. Clair (1992) found that mommy-track and daddy-track workers with significant family commitments jeopardize their own compensation and opportunities for advancement. On the other hand, Schneer and Reitman (1993) discovered no apparent negative consequences for these workers, finding the earnings of men and women from "nontraditional" mommy-track and daddy-track families similar to those of their counterparts in "traditional" ones.

### Research on Family-Work Conflict: Evidence of Everyday Talk

In addition to institutional rhetoric, the discursive model includes sociopolitically relevant organizational discourse in the form of everyday talk. Researchers of family-work conflict have not yet investigated questions that might be translated directly into the terminology of the discursive model. But these researchers have explored topics that indirectly suggest a potentially important explanatory role for sociopolitically relevant organizational discourse in the form of everyday talk. This literature includes three clusters: (a) studies that have described differing perceptions regarding family-work conflict among members of various organizational classes, which might reflect their different patterns of everyday talk; (b) research that has examined the significance of family-work conflict for patterns of everyday interaction among family members; and (c) research that has explored the constructive uses of everyday talk as people

adapt creatively to the tensions sometimes produced when family and work demands collide.

A first group of studies has investigated differing perceptions regarding the nature and extent of family-work tension among various organizational subgroups. This research has not concentrated directly on discourse, or indeed, on any type of communication at all. Yet although these studies simply group respondents according to demographic or organizational role, the discursive model would suggest that these different categories actually imply diverse discursive experience, which could explain different views of family-work conflict. In other words, the overall everyday discursive pattern for workers with responsibility for children will naturally include some people and topics that childless workers would not ordinarily discuss. In turn, these variant discursive patterns could result in differing interpretations of the significance of family-work conflict. For example, Covin and Brush (1993) found significant differences between students and human resource professionals in their perceptions of issues such as support for child care, parental responsibility, work commitment, and the impact of children on achievement motivation. Covin and Brush did not directly examine the communication patterns of their respondents. Nevertheless, the discursive model would propose that the typically dissimilar everyday discursive experience of these two groups merits investigation as a factor influencing their diverse perceptions of family-work conflict. Falkenberg and Monachello (1990) proposed the presence of subgroups among dual-earner households, based on such factors as the spouses' individual reasons for working, the responsibilities assumed by spouses in the home, and the spouses' sex, which significantly affect the nature of problems experienced by families. The discursive model suggests that membership in these subgroups implies different patterns of everyday talk. These diverse discursive patterns in turn affect the variety of family and work problems that Falkenberg and Monachello observed. A final study (Miller et al., 1991) within this cluster of research explored different perceptions of top managers and employees, respectively, concerning employees' dependent care obligations. These researchers found two significant perceptual divergences between members of these two organizational subgroups. First, while employees considered family obligations to affect job performance, top managers did not. Second, while employees considered employers to have some responsibility to assist their employees in their family care obligations, top managers did not. Again, the discursive model would explore these differences in terms of the varied discursive experiences of everyday talk that underlie them.

A discourse-based strategy would also reinterpret a second group of recent studies that has focused on consequences of family-work conflict outside the workplace. The discourse-based model incorporates everyday talk across organizational boundaries. Accordingly, research in this group suggests that everyday talk at home, as well as everyday talk at work, plays an important role in the social dynamics of family-work conflict. One study within this cluster of research (Karambayya & Reilly, 1992) discovered that women's role repertoire has expanded disproportionately compared with men's as a result of family-work conflicts. Further, the study found that women restructure their time more often than men do to meet family commitments. In discursive terms, these findings suggest that family-work conflict may have created a more expansive pattern of women's everyday talk in comparison to men's because women's lives appear still to demand greater social role flexibility than do men's. In contrast, Williams and Alliger (1994) found the discursive consequences of family-work conflict similar for women and men. However, their research reports pervasive feelings of tension and negative "mood spillover" between family and work, and vice versa, regardless of sex. A discursive perspective would logically extend the examination of these feelings by concentrating on the ways in which women's and men's everyday talk both reflects and contributes to it. Everyday talk about family-work conflict also affected both men and women in Frone et al.'s (1992) study.

Both male and female respondents reported greater intrusion of work-related demands into family life than of family-related obligations into work. The discursive implications of such findings might indicate that the nature of everyday talk at home will be more disrupted when work-related expectations increase. By comparison, patterns of everyday talk at work might be predictably less affected by family demands.

A final development in research on families and work has relevance in the context of the discursive perspective. This work has begun to explore the constructive outcomes people experience as they use everyday talk to help themselves adapt to the tensions of competition between these two contexts. Crosby (1991), a primary exemplar of research within this group, suggests that people who juggle work and family responsibilities may experience stress and difficulty but also the immense satisfaction of a more complex and satisfying, competent personal identity. Investigation of the creative uses of everyday talk both to accomplish and reveal personally productive outcomes represents a relevant application of the discursive model. Another study, by Karambayya and Reilly (1992), surveyed both partners in a set of dual-earner couples. Despite pressures of role expansion and work restructuring, couples with greater family involvement reported higher marital satisfaction and lower stress. In discursive terms, these findings may imply the positive potential of a more complex discursive environment that includes everyday talk in both work and family contexts. Finally, Lobel (1991) focused on individuals' relative investment in work and family roles. Lobel maintained that the typical assumption of negative role conflict obscures the more significant capacity of individuals to enact a self-identity in which work and family roles both represent important elements. Like those of other researchers reviewed in this section, Lobel's perspective also has discursive implications. In this instance, everyday talk reflects not an inevitable tension between work and family. Rather, everyday talk serves as the constructive means by which individuals find personal and social meaning as they discursively negotiate their family and work involvement.

### Interpenetration of Institutional Rhetoric and Everyday Talk

Organizational discourse on the issue of family-work conflict demonstrates the discursive interpenetration of institutional rhetoric and everyday talk. Some examples illustrate how these processes of mutual influence might occur.

As for other sociopolitical issues, institutional rhetoric on the topic of family-work conflict serves to construct a societal context of meaning, composed of a variety of often competing rhetorical positions. For example, in the case of family-work conflict, the positions advocated by institutional rhetoric might focus on fairness in the development of solutions to the tension of competing family and work obligations. One such rhetorical view of fairness might suggest that organizations should more generously accommodate their employees' family commitments to compensate them for the societally significant responsibilities of childrearing and caretaking of the elderly. Yet, while such a normative inclination might prevail at any given time, the discourse of institutional rhetoric will also articulate competing logics of fairness as well. Such an alternative norm for fairness might argue, for example, that individuals who choose commitments to both work and family should take personal responsibility for the resulting extra strain on personal resources. In an alternative normative view, fairness might demand equality of treatment among employees regardless of differences in their personal lives.

The institutional rhetoric of family-work conflict might center on another normative question, the welfare of children. One position on this issue might argue that young children are permanently damaged when their mothers work outside the home. A competing view might emphasize the cognitive, emotional, and social benefits of a quality day care experience. Again, the discursive model predicts that one of these positions, expressed as insti-

tutional rhetoric, may dominate sociopolitical understanding at some times. At others, there may exist little consensus, and perhaps great social division, over which argument is "right."

Everyday discourse concerning the question of family-work conflict occurs within this larger societal context of meaning constructed largely through institutional rhetoric. In other words, institutional rhetoric establishes the positions in the larger sociopolitical discussion that various interests hold. Individuals variously attend to the arguments advanced through these rhetorical expressions, discuss them, interpret their significance, and act and speak in ways that either sustain or contradict certain positions articulated by this institutional rhetoric.

Examples suggest possible ways in which the discourse of everyday talk interacts with institutional rhetoric on the topic of family-work conflict, specifically the rhetoric that addresses questions of fairness and the welfare of children. In the first example, institutional rhetoric sets up the normative context for defining fairness relative to the sociopolitical issue of family-work conflict. In this example, a hypothetically dominant, rhetorically articulated normative perspective suggests that fairness is best served when employers make allowances for their employees' family obligations. Within this normative environment occur the discursive processes of everyday talk. Such everyday talk might challenge rather than accept norm-based accommodation of employees' family commitments. Thus, a group of single, childless employees may complain of the unfairness inherent when employees with families enjoy what others see as special, non-merit-based consideration. In the second example, institutional rhetoric about family-work conflict focused on the welfare of children. This discourse might argue that good day care programs actively benefit children. Within this rhetorically generated discursive field, individuals' everyday talk communicates a parallel concern with the well-being of children. Thus, parents who can visit their children at an on-site corporate day care facility enjoy a still rare (but increasingly common) form of everyday talk in their interaction with their children during the workday. More confident of their children's well-being through this proximity, the parents may also find everyday talk with their coworkers more satisfying and productive.

## SUMMARY

This chapter dealt with a topic relatively novel in organizational communication analysis, focusing on the interactions of organizations in the context of their sociopolitical environments. The thinking presented here was inspired by Weick's notion of the "enacted environment" and Taylor's conceptualization of organizational "conversation" within an environmental context. Based on these ideas, the chapter proposed a model of organizational communication with sociopolitical environments in terms of the intersecting organizational discourses of institutional rhetoric and everyday talk. The chapter illustrated this model using the contemporary sociopolitical issues of sexual harassment and family-work conflict.

A concern with sociopolitical questions equally involves both the consequences of sociopolitical transformation for organizations and the implications of organizational practices for the larger culture. Such a focus is far from established within the field of organizational communication. But its continued development offers many exciting possibilities for organizational communication analysts compelled by the purpose of better understanding the larger societal significance of organizational discourse.

## NOTE

1. In recent years, researchers have shown demonstrable enthusiasm for the three primary theoretical approaches to organization-environment relations, including studies based on *population ecology* (Barnett, 1990; Boeker, 1991, 1997; Castrogiovanni, 1991; Gimeno, Folta, Cooper, & Woo, 1997; Greve, 1999; Swaminathan & Delacroix, 1991; Tucker, Singh, & Meinhard, 1990;

Wholey & Sanchez, 1991), *resource dependence* (Baker, 1990; Boeker & Goodstein, 1991; Davis, 1991; Galaskiewicz & Wasserman, 1989; Goodstein & Boeker, 1991; Kraatz, 1998; Lang & Lockhart, 1990; Mizruchi, 1989, 1992; Mizruchi & Galaskiewicz, 1993; Mizruchi & Stearns, 1988; Oliver, 1991; Perrucci & Lewis, 1989; Singh & Harianto, 1989; Wade, O'Reilly, & Chandratat, 1990); and *institutional* (Abrahamson & Fairchild, 1999; Abrahamson & Rosenkopf, 1993; Baum & Oliver, 1991; D'Annuo, Sutton, & Price, 1991; DiMaggio, 1988; DiMaggio & Powell, 1983; Elsbach & Sutton, 1992; Finet, 1993, 1994a, 1994b; Gioia, Schultz, & Corley, 2000; Judge & Zeithaml, 1992; Leblebici, Salancik, & Copay, 1991; Mezias, 1990; Oliver, 1991; Tucker et al., 1990) perspectives.

## REFERENCES

Abrahamson, E., & Fairchild, G. (1999). Management fashion: Lifecycles, triggers, and collective learning processes. *Administrative Science Quarterly, 44,* 708-740.

Abrahamson, E., & Rosenkopf, L. (1993). Institutional and competitive bandwagons: Using mathematical modeling as a tool to explore innovation diffusion. *Academy of Management Review, 18,* 487-517.

Adams, J. (1993). Juggling job and family. *Vital Speeches of the Day, 60,* 125-128.

Aldrich, H. (1979). *Organizations and environments.* Englewood Cliffs, NJ: Prentice Hall.

Axelrod, J. (1993). Sexual harassment in the movies and its effect on the audience. In G. Kreps (Ed.), *Sexual harassment: Communication implications* (pp. 107-117). Cresskill, NJ: Hampton.

Baker, W. (1990). Market networks and corporate behavior. *American Journal of Sociology, 96,* 589-625.

Bandow, D. (1991). Should Congress play with family leave? *Business and Society Review, 77,* 41-45.

Barnett, W. (1990). The organizational ecology of a technological system. *Administrative Science Quarterly, 35,* 31-60.

Baum, J., & Oliver, C. (1991). Institutional linkages and organizational mortality. *Administrative Science Quarterly, 36,* 187-218.

Berryman-Fink, C. (1993). Preventing sexual harassment through male-female communication training. In G. Kreps (Ed.), *Sexual harassment: Communication implications* (pp. 267-280). Cresskill, NJ: Hampton.

Blakely, G. L., Blakely, E. H., & Moorman, R. H. (1998). The effects of training on perceptions of sexual harassment allegations. *Journal of Applied Social Psychology, 8*(1), 71-83.

Boeker, W. (1991). Organizational strategy: An ecological perspective. *Academy of Management Journal, 34,* 613-635.

Boeker, W. (1997). Strategic change: The influence of managerial characteristics and organizational growth. *Academy of Management Journal, 40,* 152-170.

Boeker, W., & Goodstein, J. (1991). Organizational performance and adaptation: Effects of environment and performance on changes in board composition. *Academy of Management Journal, 34,* 805-826.

Boyd, B., Dess, G., & Rasheed, A. (1993). Divergence between archival and perceptual measures of the environment: Causes and consequences. *Academy of Management Review, 18,* 204-226.

Braun, M. (1993). Fallongate: The ad agency, the feminist, and the $10 million case of sexual harassment. In G. Kreps (Ed.), *Sexual harassment: Communication implications* (pp. 90-106). Cresskill, NJ: Hampton.

Brown, M. H. (1993). Sex and the workplace: "Watch your behind or they'll watch it for you." In G. Kreps (Ed.), *Sexual harassment: Communication implications* (pp. 118-130). Cresskill, NJ: Hampton.

Burns, T., & Stalker, G. (1961). *The management of innovation.* London: Tavistock.

Castrogiovanni, G. (1991). Environmental munificence: A theoretical assessment. *Academy of Management Review, 16,* 542-565.

Cheney, G. (1991). *Rhetoric in an organizational society: Managing multiple identities.* Columbia: University of South Carolina Press.

Clair, R. (1993a). The bureaucratization, commodification, and privatization of sexual harassment through institutional discourses: A study of the Big 10 universities. *Management Communication Quarterly, 7,* 123-157.

Clair, R. (1993b). The use of framing devices to sequester organizational narratives: Hegemony and harassment. *Communication Monographs, 60,* 113-136.

Clair, R. (1994). Resistance and oppression as a self-contained opposite: An organizational communication analysis of one man's story of sexual harassment. *Western Journal of Communication, 58,* 235-262.

Clair, R., McGoun, M., & Spirek, M. (1993). Sexual harassment responses of working women: An assessment of current communication-oriented typologies and perceived effectiveness and response. In G. Kreps (Ed.), *Sexual harassment: Communication implications* (pp. 209-233). Cresskill, NJ: Hampton.

Covin, T., & Brush, C. (1993). A comparison of student and human resource professional attitudes toward work and family issues. *Group & Organization Management, 18,* 29-49.

Crosby, F. (1991). *Juggling: The unexpected advantages of balancing career and home for women and their families.* New York: Free Press.

D'Aunno, T., Sutton, R., & Price, R. (1991). Isomorphism and external support in conflicting institutional environments: A study of drug abuse treatment units. *Academy of Management Journal, 34,* 636-661.

Davis, G. (1991). Agents without principles? The spread of the poison pill through the intercorporate network. *Administrative Science Quarterly, 36,* 583-613.

Deetz, S. (1992). *Democracy in an age of corporate colonization.* Albany: State University of New York Press.

DiMaggio, P. (1988). Interest and agency in institutional theory. In L. Zucker (Ed.), *Institutional patterns and organizations: Culture and environment* (pp. 3-21). Cambridge, MA: Ballinger.

DiMaggio, P., & Powell, W. (1983). The iron cage revisited: Institutional isomorphism and collective rationality in organizational fields. *American Sociological Review, 48,* 147-160.

Elsbach, K., & Sutton, R. (1992). Acquiring organizational legitimacy through illegitimate actions: A marriage of institutional and impression management theories. *Academy of Management Journal, 35,* 699-738.

Emery, F., & Trist, E. (1965). The causal texture of organizational environments. *Human Relations, 18,* 21-32.

Euske, N. A., & Roberts, K. H. (1987). Evolving perspectives in organization theory: Communication implications. In F. M. Jablin, L. L. Putnam, K. H. Roberts, & L. W. Porter (Eds.), *Handbook of organizational communication: An interdisciplinary perspective* (pp. 41-69). Newbury Park, CA: Sage.

Falkenberg, L., & Monachello, M. (1990). Dual-career and dual-income families: Do they have different needs? *Journal of Business Ethics, 9,* 339-351.

Finet, D. (1993). Effects of boundary spanning communication on the sociopolitical delegitimation of an organization. *Management Communication Quarterly, 7,* 36-66.

Finet, D. (1994a). Interest advocacy and the transformation in organizational communication. In B. Kovacic (Ed.), *New approaches to organizational communication* (pp. 169-190). Albany: State University of New York Press.

Finet, D. (1994b). Sociopolitical consequences of organizational expression. *Journal of Communication, 44*(4), 114-131.

Foegen, J. (1992). The double jeopardy of sexual harassment. *Business and Society Review, 82,* 31-35.

Frone, M., Russell, M., & Cooper, M. (1992). Prevalence of work-family conflict: Are work and family boundaries asymmetrically permeable? *Journal of Organizational Behavior, 13,* 723-729.

Galaskiewicz, J., & Wasserman, S. (1989). Mimetic processes within an interorganizational field: An empirical test. *Administrative Science Quarterly, 34,* 454-479.

Galvin, K. (1993). Preventing the problem: Preparing faculty members for the issues of sexual harassment. In G. Kreps (Ed.), *Sexual harassment: Communica-*

*tion implications* (pp. 257-266). Cresskill, NJ: Hampton.

Gimeno, J., Folta, T., Cooper, A., & Woo, C. (1997). Survival of the fittest? Entrepreneurial human capital and the persistence of underperforming firms. *Administrative Science Quarterly, 42,* 750-783.

Gioia, D. A., Schultz, M., & Corley, K. G. (2000). Organizational identity, image, and adaptive instability. *Academy of Management Review, 25,* 63-81.

Goodstein, J. (1994). Institutional pressures and strategic responsiveness: Employer involvement in work-family issues. *Academy of Management Journal, 37,* 350-382.

Goodstein, J., & Boeker, W. (1991). Turbulence at the top: A new perspective on governance structure changes and strategic change. *Academy of Management Journal, 34,* 306-330.

Greve, H. R. (1999). The effect of core change on performance inertia and regression toward the mean. *Administrative Science Quarterly, 44,* 590-614.

Gutek, B. (1996). Sexual harassment at work: When an organization fails to respond. In M. Stockdale (Ed.), *Sexual harassment in the workplace: Perspectives, frontiers, and response strategies* (pp. 272-290). Thousand Oaks, CA: Sage.

Gutek, B., Cohen, A., & Konrad, A. (1990). Predicting social-sexual behavior at work: A contact hypothesis. *Academy of Management Journal, 33,* 560-577.

Hannan, M., & Carroll, G. (1992). *Dynamics of organizational populations: Density. legitimation and competition.* New York: Oxford University Press.

Hannan, M., & Freeman, J. (1977). The population ecology of organizations. *American Journal of Sociology, 82,* 929-964.

Hulin, C. L., Fitzgerald, L. F., & Drasgow, F. (1996). Organizational influences on sexual harassment. In M. Stockdale (Ed.), *Sexual harassment in the workplace: Perspectives, frontiers, and response strategies* (pp. 127-150). Thousand Oaks, CA: Sage.

Judge, W., & Zeithaml, C. (1992). Institutional and strategic choice perspectives on board involvement in the strategic decision process. *Academy of Management Journal, 35,* 766-794.

Karambayya, R., & Reilly, A. (1992). Dual earner couples: Attitudes and actions in restructuring work for family. *Journal of Organizational Behavior, 13,* 585-601.

Kraatz, M. S. (1998). Learning by association? Interorganizational networks and adaptation to environmental change. *Academy of Management Journal, 41,* 621-643.

Kreps, G. (Ed.). (1993). *Sexual harassment: Communication implications.* Cresskill, NJ: Hampton.

Lang, J., & Lockhart, D. (1990). Increased environmental uncertainty and changes in board linkage patterns. *Academy of Management Journal, 33,* 106-128.

Laumann, E., Marsden, P., & Prensky, D. (1983). The boundary specification problem in network analysis. In R. Burt & M. Minor (Eds.), *Applied network analysis: A methodological introduction* (pp. 18-34). Beverly Hills, CA: Sage.

Lawrence, P., & Lorsch, J. (1967). Differentiation and integration in complex organizations. *Administrative Science Quarterly, 12,* 1-47.

Leblebici, H., Salancik, G., & Copay, A. (1991). Institutional change and the transformation of interorganizational fields: An organizational history of the U.S. radio broadcasting industry. *Administrative Science Quarterly, 36,* 333-363.

Lilly, T. A., Pitt-Catsouphes, M., & Googins, B. (1997). *Work-family research: An annotated bibliography.* Westport, CT: Greenwood.

Lobel, S. (1991). Allocation of investment in work and family roles: Alternative theories and implications for research. *Academy of Management Review, 16,* 507-521.

Lobel, S., & St. Clair, L. (1992). Effect of family responsibilities, gender, and career identity salience on performance outcomes. *Academy of Management Journal, 35,* 1057-1069.

MacKinnon, C. (1979). *Sexual harassment of working women: A case of sex discrimination.* New Haven, CT: Yale University Press.

Mele, D. (1989). Organization of work in the company and family rights of employees. *Journal of Business Ethics, 8,* 647-655.

Meyer, J., & Rowan, B. (1977). Institutionalized organizations: Formal structure as myth and ceremony. *American Journal of Sociology, 83,* 340-363.

Meyer, J., & Scott, W. (1983). *Organizational environments: Ritual and rationality.* Beverly Hills, CA: Sage.

Mezias, S. (1990). An institutional model of organizational practice: Financial reporting at the *Fortune* 500. *Administrative Science Quarterly, 35,* 431-457.

Miller, J., Stead, B., & Pereira, A. (1991). Dependent care and the workplace: An analysis of management and employee perceptions. *Journal of Business Ethics, 10,* 863-869.

Mizruchi, M. (1989). Similarity of political behavior among large American corporations. *American Journal of Sociology, 95,* 401-424.

Mizruchi, M. (1992). *The structure of corporate political action: Interfirm relations and their consequences.* Cambridge, MA: Harvard University Press.

Mizruchi, M., & Galaskiewicz, J. (1993). Networks of interorganizational relations. *Sociological Methods & Research, 22,* 46-70.

Mizruchi, M., & Stearns, L. (1988). A longitudinal study of the formation of interlocking directorates. *Administrative Science Quarterly, 33,* 194-210.

Morrison, T. (1992). *Race-ing justice, en-gendering power: Essays on Anita Hill, Clarence Thomas, and the construction of social reality.* New York: Pantheon.

Mumby, D. K., & Clair, R. P. (1997). Organizational discourse. In T. A. van Dijk (Ed.), *Discourse as social interaction* (pp. 181-206). London: Sage.

Oliver, C. (1991). Strategic responses to institutional processes. *Academy of Management Review, 16,* 145-179.

Perrucci, R., & Lewis, B. (1989). Interorganizational relations and community influence structure: A replication and extension. *Sociological Quarterly, 30,* 205-223.

Pfeffer, J., & Salancik, G. (1978). *The external control of organizations: A resource dependence perspective.* New York: Harper & Row.

Pitt-Catsouphes, M., & Googins, B. K. (1999). Preface. *Annals of the American Academy of Political and Social Science, 562,* 8-15.

Powell, W., & DiMaggio, P. (1991). *The new institutionalism in organizational analysis.* Chicago: University of Chicago Press.

Putnam, L. L., & Pacanowsky, M. E. (Eds.). (1983). *Communication and organizations: An interpretive approach.* Beverly Hills, CA: Sage.

Ragan, S. (1996). *The lynching of language: Gender, politics, and power in the Hill-Thomas hearings.* Urbana: University of Illinois Press.

Schneer, J., & Reitman, F. (1993). Effects of alternate family structures on managerial career paths. *Academy of Management Journal, 36,* 830-843.

Scott, R. (1987). The adolescence of institutional theory. *Administrative Science Quarterly, 32,* 413-511.

Siegel, P. (1996). *Outsiders looking in: A communication perspective on the Hill/Thomas hearings.* Cresskill, NJ: Hampton.

Singh, H., & Harianto, F. (1989). Management-board relationships, takeover risk, and the adoption of golden parachutes. *Academy of Management Journal, 32,* 7-24.

Solomon, D. H., & Williams, M. L. M. (1997). Perceptions of social-sexual communication at work: The effects of message, situation, and observer characteristics on judgments of sexual harassment. *Journal of Applied Communication Research, 25,* 196-216.

Strine, M. (1992). Understanding "how things work": Sexual harassment and academic culture. *Journal of Applied Communication Research, 20,* 391-400.

Swaminathan, A., & Delacroix, J. (1991). Differentiation within an organizational population: Additional evidence from the wine industry. *Academy of Management Journal, 34,* 679-692.

Taylor, B., & Conrad, C. (1992). Narratives of sexual harassment: Organizational dimensions. *Journal of Applied Communication Research, 20,* 401-418.

Taylor, J. (1995). Shifting from a heteronomous to an autonomous worldview of organizational communication: Communication theory on the cusp. *Communication Theory, 5,* 1-35.

Terpstra, D., & Baker, D. (1988). Outcomes of sexual harassment charges. *Academy of Management Journal, 31,* 185-194.

Terpstra, D., & Baker, D. (1992). Outcomes of federal court decision on sexual harassment. *Academy of Management Journal, 35,* 181-190.

Thompson, J. (1967). *Organizations in action.* New York: McGraw-Hill.

Tucker, D., Singh, J., & Meinhard, A. (1990). Organizational form, population dynamics, and institutional change: The founding patterns of voluntary organizations. *Academy of Management Journal, 33,* 151-178.

Wade, J., O'Reilly, C., & Chandratat, I. (1990). Golden parachutes: CEOs and the exercise of social influence. *Administrative Science Quarterly, 35,* 587-603.

Weick, K. E. (1979). *The social psychology of organizing* (2nd ed.). Reading, MA: Addison-Wesley.

Wells, D., & Kracher, B. (1993). Justice, sexual harassment, and the reasonable victim standard. *Journal of Business Ethics, 12,* 423-431.

Wholey, D., & Sanchez, S. (1991). The effects of regulatory tools on organizational populations. *Academy of Management Review, 16,* 743-767.

Williams, K., & Alliger, G. (1994). Role stressors, mood spillover, and perceptions of work-family conflict in employed parents. *Academy of Management Journal, 37,* 837-868.

Witkowski, K. (1999). Becoming family-friendly: Work-family program innovation among the largest U.S. corporations. *Research in the Sociology of Work, 7,* 203-232.

Witteman, H. (1993). The interface between sexual harassment and organizational romance. In G. Kreps (Ed.), *Sexual harassment: Communication implications* (pp. 27-62). Cresskill, NJ: Hampton.

Young, M. (1999). Work-family backlash: Begging the question, what's fair? *Annals of the American Academy of Political and Social Science, 562,* 32-46.

Zucker, L. (Ed.). (1988). *Institutional patterns and organizations: Culture and environment.* Cambridge, MA: Ballinger.

# 9

# Organizational Culture

ERIC M. EISENBERG
*University of South Florida*

PATRICIA RILEY
*University of Southern California*

In the latter part of the 20th century, numerous scholars of organizational communication became entranced with the idea that understanding companies, churches, universities, government agencies, student clubs, or indeed any form of institution or organization could be enhanced through a cultural analysis or critique. The speed with which "organizational culture" emerged as a significant lens for communication scholars and other academics to examine or otherwise engage with organizations and institutions was astounding. The now ubiquitous nature of organizational culture as an academic concept likely began with its metaphorical success—it produced compelling narratives and insights that resonated with researchers who had previously lived in a world bounded by instruments, scales, networks, and central tendencies. The rather startling shift in organizational communication discourse and practice into this new arena of ethnographies, performances, tales, and texts will be examined in this chapter.

What may be most intriguing about the organizational culture concept, however, was the rapidity with which it became part of the folk taxa of everyday life. As the topic spread through the business press and everyday con-

AUTHORS' NOTE: We would like to thank Linda Putnam, Fred Jablin, Joanne Martin, and Nick Trujillo for their helpful comments on earlier drafts of this chapter.

versations, organizational discourse was soon peppered with such statements as "The culture here won't allow us to . . . " or "Our culture is very intense—we work hard and play harder." In our highly mediated and reflexive society, researchers and scholars often play a major role in the production and reproduction of ideas and practices that dramatically and recursively change the landscape of our existence (obvious examples would be communication campaigns designed to change dietary, smoking, or exercise patterns). Organizational culture was one of those interesting topics that quickly generated changes in both the community of scholars and the communities being studied. This chapter is thus an examination of organizational culture as well as the communication scholars who have been, and likely will continue to be, a part of one of the more visceral and enticing areas of organization studies.

This chapter differs from other reviews of organizational culture by setting forth a distinctively communicative view of the concept. It begins with a short "history" of organizational culture as a metaphor and its background in organizational communication. Next, we describe the basic assumptions that guide this communicative view of culture, and finally we review the significant contributions to the organizational culture literature. A subsequent section on future research is not only a list of what needs to be done but also a call for research that can continue to inform, illuminate, and excite organizational scholars.

## CONTEXTUALIZING THE ORGANIZATIONAL CULTURE METAPHOR

It is critical to begin this story with the premise that the culture metaphor itself displays our biases: a concern about relations to others, a need to understand the contexts of communication, and a desire to identify fairly stable or at least recognizable categories of institutional and organizational habits and practices. Put differently, the organizational culture concept, as it is typically invoked, is itself a kind of cultural artifact that speaks loudly about our need for closure and our discomfort with ambiguity. There is little consensus on a definition of culture because the concept is so rich—welcoming newcomers, alternative angles, and varied connotations. Like many other *grande idées* of our time (e.g., leadership, economics, communication), the beauty of the culture metaphor lies more in its heuristic value than in any determinant authority.

Any attempt to create a "history" of a metaphor is problematic—especially a concise one. Clearly, not all perspectives can be covered, or even known, and ultimately the positions and ideas that are included take on privileged status. While the issues surrounding the emergence of organizational culture are certainly more complicated than portrayed here, newcomers to this area of study might find a generally linear, broad-strokes description of the culture conversation beneficial.

The origin of the term *organizational culture* is unknown, but the notion that factories, schools, and other institutions have cultures has existed for at least a half century (e.g., Jaques, 1951). In the 1960s, it was not unusual to describe culture as the best way to get a handle on organizational development. Bennis (1969) explained that organizational culture was of the utmost importance because "the only viable way to change organizations is to change their 'culture,' that is, to change the systems within which people work and live" (p. v). By the next decade, the term *culture* had become increasingly commonplace in the organizational development literature as both work groups and organizations were viewed as having cultures (e.g., Katz & Kahn, 1978). For example, French and Bell (1973) defined organizational development as "a long range effort to improve an organization's problem-solving and renewal processes, particularly through a more effective and collaborative management of organization culture

—with special emphasis on the culture of formal work teams" (p. 15).

Other organization theorists soon began using the concept, if not always using the term: For example, Pondy and Mitroff (1979) argued that a cultural metaphor should replace the systems metaphor in organization theory; Weick's influential book *The Social Psychology of Organizing* (1979) attempted to bridge the gap between systems theory and sensemaking by identifying systems of interpretation (i.e., cause maps); and Pettigrew (1979) used symbols, ritual, ideology, language, and myth to take a detailed look at the creation and transformation of an organization's culture. New methodologies were appropriated, such as Whyte's (1943) formulation of "participant observation," along with ample borrowing of the ethnographic approach from anthropology (see Clifford, 1983; Clifford & Marcus, 1986; Van Maanen, 1988).

For scholars in organizational communication, the interest shown by anthropologists, sociologists, and management theorists was fortuitous but only a small part of the story. At least three other trends emerged. First, communication theorists with a background in rhetoric and symbolic interaction examined organizational issues through a variety of interpretive and symbolic analyses and mentored students and colleagues who were taking similar approaches (e.g., Ernest Bormann, Phil Tompkins). Second, the particular appropriation to systems theory that was being elucidated in organizational communication studies had relocated communication as the central process in organizations and equated communicating with organizing (e.g., Farace, Monge, & Russell, 1977; Johnson, 1977). Third, the focus on interpretive approaches led organizational communication scholars to theories and research in anthropology (e.g., Geertz, Turner), sociology (e.g., Goffman, Whyte), and increasingly to European scholars (e.g., Foucault, Giddens, Habermas, Lyotard) who fueled hermeneutic, critical, and later postmodern organizational studies.

This "interpretive turn" in organizational communication studies, however, was seen by many as either returning to or simply building on the rich intellectual roots of rhetorical theory and criticism, which has long been concerned with issues of meaning, identification, and persuasion in social and institutional contexts (e.g., Tompkins, 1987).

Unlike scholars in other areas of organization studies that did not initially grasp the power of the metaphor, communication researchers displayed an instinctive appreciation for organizations as social entities that were constituted in interaction. From the early 1980s forward, communication processes were recast as the way organizations were constructed, maintained, and transformed. Thus, communication's constitutive role in creating organizational culture was identified and elucidated.

Additionally, a pivotal role was played by conferences on interpretive approaches to organizational communication (cf. Putnam & Pacanowsky, 1983) where the contributions of communication scholars to the academic literature on organizational culture were refined and made available to those outside the communication discipline. For researchers in a discipline that had come to recognize, although in some cases reluctantly, both humanistic and scientific scholarship, this was not a very radical or oppositional mode of scholarship. The communicative study of "organizational cultures" was instead an intriguing amalgam of ideas that drew together people who were already studying organizational symbols, narratives, metaphors, identity, and politics.

Few academic concepts have received the public recognition that has been accorded to organizational culture. In the early 1980s, the organizational culture concept exploded in the media through stories in *Business Week* and *Fortune* magazines, as well as in the enormously popular business books *In Search of Excellence* (Peters & Waterman, 1982) and *Corporate Cultures* (Deal & Kennedy, 1982). Then in 1983, *Administrative Science Quar-*

*terly* (Jelinek, Smircich, & Hirsch, 1983) published a special issue devoted to academic studies of organizational culture, and *Organizational Dynamics* created its own special issue, which was also accessible to practitioners. With genuine excitement and a lot of hype, organizational culture became both a part of the language of the business world and a flourishing stream of academic research.

There is no single story that accounts for the rapid growth in popularity of cultural perspectives across related but distinct organizational literatures. One crucial factor was critiques of the value and status of science, rationality, and technology, along with other dominant institutions of society. As a result, there was a movement to give voice to those who were marginalized under the current system (e.g., women, minorities, subordinates, inhabitants of the so-called third world countries). Alvesson (1993b) purported that a constellation of issues was responsible for the emergence of the culture approach in organizational studies. His list included a disaffection with the methods and results of traditional organizational research; an increased emphasis on the lived experience of organizational members and an awareness of global societal issues; a call for alternatives to authoritarian leadership; the productivity problems of Western societies, and in particular the United States (as compared to Japanese management); the emergence of new organizational forms in which behaviors are controlled more through identification and loyalty than through direct supervision; and the marketing of the culture concept by consulting firms such as McKinsey, which sponsored popular business books in the early 1980s.

For some or all of these reasons, the culture concept encouraged a group of otherwise conservative researchers to explore aspects of organizational life under a new theoretical umbrella that legitimated alternative research methodologies. For others, it helped craft a larger community of scholars with whom they could share research and ideas. A number of theorists, particularly management scholars,

however, soon declared that organizational culture was a "dead" academic endeavor because it had been so quickly and uncritically appropriated by functionalist researchers and practitioners (Smircich & Calás, 1987). Although problems of managerial bias can be identified in the administrative literature, we were not persuaded that the organizational metaphor was significantly corrupted. First, the use of the term by change agents such as organizational development specialists and other practitioners was clearly not new, merely inflated by academic and media attention. Second, these instrumental approaches served different audiences, and they could not silence interpretive, critical, or postmodern voices in the arena of organizational culture scholarship unless one of two key situations arose: (1) the topic became "tainted" in the eyes of current or prospective non-managerially oriented researchers, who then left the research arena; or (2) it became difficult to publish stimulating, nonutilitarian work of high quality (Riley, 1993). We have not uncovered significant evidence of either scenario, and especially not in organizational communication literature. Instead we found a variety of fascinating research projects in the literature to review and discuss. The diversity of perspectives was illuminating and welcomed. In this chapter, we have attempted to examine each alternative theme or paradigm of culture research from the standpoint of its own goals and practices.

## A COMMUNICATIVE PERSPECTIVE ON ORGANIZATIONAL CULTURE

As previously mentioned, a communicative view of organizational culture sees communication as constitutive of culture. The process that we wish to label organizational culture consists solely of patterns of human action and its recursive behaviors (including talk and its symbolic residues) and meaning.

Our view of organizational culture is mediated by five assumptions that guide the typology we have developed for this review (for other typologies, see Bantz, 1993; Goodall, 1989, 1991; Pacanowsky & O'Donnell-Trujillo, 1983; Putnam, Phillips, & Chapman, 1996).

First, a communication perspective does not limit its interest to overt constructions with "extra meaning" such as central metaphors or key stories. It acknowledges the symbolic character of ordinary language and the ways in which cultural meanings are coconstructed in everyday conversation, textual evidence of patterns, and also the entire nonverbal, semiotic field, from the structure of parking lots (Goodall, 1989) to the structure of work processes (Alvesson, 1993a; Barley, 1983). Further, these fields are not simply observed but can also be cast in a physical, sensual way (Conquergood, 1991; Stoller, 1989).

Second, this vantage point offers a commentary on the tension between cognitive and behavioral approaches to human action, through a focus on communicative praxis. Of all human activities, human communication is the one in which interpretation and action most clearly coexist. Even though some explanations of human behavior may give weight to the constraining aspects of social and organizational structures, while others emphasize what is possible through individual agency, communication can be seen as an "interactive prism" through which all potentially enabling and constraining forces must pass (Mohan, 1993; Wentworth, 1980). Conceptualized this way, each instance of communication is a kind of crucible for culture, with the historical weight of language and past practices on the one hand, and the potential for innovation and novelty on the other. As power circulates within and between organizations, points of domination and of leverage for change coexist in the interactive moment.

Third, this approach takes into account broader patterns of communication in society and examines how they appear and interact at the organizational nexus. For example, studies of ethnicity, family systems, and media images of work may relate to an expanded notion of organizational culture, inasmuch as they act as constraints on behavior and serve as identity resources for members.

Fourth, a communication orientation takes full advantage of the various new options available for positioning the researcher. For example, Jackson's (1989) "radical empiricism" breaks down the perceived barriers between the researcher "self" and the organizational "other." Research on organizational culture can be either a tale told at a distance or something more impressionistic and confessional (Van Maanen, 1988).

Fifth, and perhaps most controversial, a communication perspective acknowledges the legitimacy of all motives for the study of culture, including the practical interests of organizational members seeking to enhance their effectiveness. An increased opportunity for dialogue about organizational culture, identity, and the change process (common topics in and around many companies and institutions) can potentially inform and empower organizational members. Workers (or managers) who are concerned about culture often acknowledge the interests and voices of multiple stakeholders and have used this information to reshape existing organizations and to launch new companies that seek alternatives to hierarchy and traditional, top-down models of organization. For example, a culturally "empowering" organization such as W. L. Gore (Pacanowsky, 1988) was described as a positive workplace that continuously improved itself in many arenas. And Cheney's (1995) article on a workers' cooperative in Spain (Mondragón) uncovered the organizational members' concern for effectiveness as the dialectic between an internal culture of workplace democracy and the exigencies of the global economic environment required an ongoing balancing act to maintain the cooperative's viability. This perspective does not, of course, condone attempts to engineer employee emotions or other manipulative uses of cultural knowledge that disadvantage workers.

# THEMES IN STUDYING
# ORGANIZATIONAL CULTURE

In the first version of this handbook, Smircich and Calás (1987) arrayed the organizational culture literature along three dimensions: paradigms, interests, and themes. The five cultural "themes" ranged from those that treat culture as a variable, something an organization has (e.g., comparative management and corporate culture), to those that treat culture as a root metaphor, something an organization is (organizational cognition, organizational symbolism, and unconscious processes). This category scheme is well known, often cited, and critiqued, but because it failed to capture a communicative perspective we developed an alternative schema for this chapter.

This chapter reviews the role of communication in the culture literature through the following thematic framework: culture as symbolism and performance, culture as text, culture as critique, culture as identity, culture as cognition, and culture as climate and effectiveness. This thematic display identified research that was rooted in a communicative process (symbolism and performance, text, critique, identity, and cognition) and in communicative goals (effectiveness and climate).

## Culture as Symbolism and Performance

It may at first appear that an "organizational symbolism" approach would be of greatest interest to—and perhaps even isomorphic with—an organizational communication perspective. But underneath this label was a host of divergent definitions and approaches—some in which communication played a central role, and others where communication was secondary, if not removed from the study.

The early studies of organizational symbolism, often characterized as the "management of meaning" perspective (e.g., Pfeffer, 1981), treated symbols similarly to the analysis of literary devices in basic English classes—as special expressions, artifacts, or events that occurred in organizations and were imbued with "extra" meaning. From this perspective, ordinary conversation and the arrangement of furniture would not constitute "symbolic action," but the dramatic choice of a metaphor in a speech to stockholders would. Taken this way, symbolic action was rare and significant, and such events were to be contrasted with the less "meaningful" substance of daily life.

To the communication scholar, this is a highly limited view of the symbolic, one that treats communication as a variable and places it "inside" of organizations. It ignored the symbolic nature of language and the semiotic significance of nonverbal communication. Some writers (e.g., Tompkins, 1987) rejected the distinction between "symbolism" and "substance" and assert that any substance that has meaning in organizations must also be symbolic. Partly in response to these critiques, an expanded view of organizational symbolism was developed by management theorists (cf. Frost, Moore, Louis, Lundberg, & Martin, 1991). The organizational symbolism perspective that they championed reflected a broad range of definitions and approaches to organizational culture, including "specialists" (Martin, 1992) who focus on vocabulary (e.g., Boland & Hoffman, 1983), narratives and stories (Brown, 1990a, 1990b; Mumby, 1988), ritual (Knuf, 1993), and hallway talk (Gronn, 1983) and "generalists" who attempt to develop a comprehensive view of all types of communication in creating, maintaining, and transforming organizational reality (e.g., Barley, 1990; Bormann, 1983; Van Maanen, 1991; Weick, 1991).

Several examples of such specialist work in organizational communication focused on the processual nature of culture. For instance, an early example in the communication literature was Conrad's (1983) work on power, which, borrowing from Giddens and Clegg, examined metaphors, myths, and rituals for their deep structuring patterns and implications in organizational conflict. Similarly, Smith and Eisenberg's (1987) examination of Disneyland used a root metaphor analysis to examine why this particularly "strong" culture was incapable of managing conflict and the tension between the practices the corporation engaged in during an economic downturn. What was unique about this particular incarnation of a "family" metaphor was its utopian nature—this conflict-free, paternalistic culture did not know how to engage in conflict and thus experienced traumatic results. A study by Putnam, Van Hoeven, and Bullis (1991) focused on the role of rituals and fantasy themes in teachers' bargaining. Their study located rites and ceremonies as mediators between public presentations of vision and the narratives generated in small-group interaction—an interesting cultural "mechanism." Another example was Trujillo's (1992) interpretation of the talk of baseball park culture for the reader to see both the interplay between talk and work and to the multivocal nature of the baseball environment.

Bantz (1993) attempted a comprehensive, generalist approach to the study of organizational culture. In his book, Bantz developed an integrated communication-based technique called organizational communication culture (OCC), which analyzed messages and their interpretations. Although the OCC method sometimes collapsed complex issues to provide an integrated approach, the technique demystified discourse on organizational culture and cleared the way for more field studies and less abstract debate. The OCC provided a fundamentally structurationist view of communication, in which all interactions are treated as inherently resource or constraint in pursuit of the maintenance or transformation of organizational reality.

Bantz was not alone in his application of structurationist approaches to the study of organizational culture. In an investigation of two professional firms' cultural politics, Riley's (1983) analysis of legitimation, domination, and signification processes uncovered

several subgroups with cultural norms different from those articulated by the public spokespersons of the larger organizations and that were amazingly distinct from each other. These "subcultures" often borrowed rules from their relationships with client organizations and enacted them in ways that protected their interests by symbolizing alternative power structures. In a study of a television station, Carbaugh (1988) focused on Giddens's notion of discursive consciousness and interpreted codes of communication as a way of analyzing cultural systems of communication. He delineated three types of symbols: symbols as persons, symbols of speaking, and epitomizing symbols. He argued that a cultural analysis is not about symbols or a set of symbols, but a system of symbols that when taken together with all their tensions, complexity, and contradictions enlightens our understanding of the situated use of work speech.

Witmer (1997) used a structurationist approach to culture to analyze an unusual Alcoholics Anonymous organization—1,000 to 1,200 attended weekly—and its strong, charismatic founder (a self-described "low-bottom drunk"). She found that powerful rituals bound participants together in the discourses of recovery and spirituality and that organizational practices were clearly codified and well articulated. The power imbalance between the founder and other organizational members generated a personal dependency on him and embedded the participants' personal identities within the discursive structuring of the group.

Although it is not an avowedly "cultural" study, Howard and Geist (1995) used structuration to help identify ideological positioning as one sensemaking mechanism used by organizational members as they work their way through the turbulent change of a merger. They found that the discourse of invincibility created the impression that some members were "bulletproof" and free from the detrimental effects of the merger; the discourse of diplomacy allowed other members to preserve a role for themselves in the merged organization. The last positioning device, betrayal, distanced organizational members from the dehumanized environment of the merger and prevented them from becoming another "cog in the machine" (p. 129).

In the management and organization studies literature, early symbolic analysis research was critiqued for its singular focus on "pure" symbols (e.g., stories, jokes, rituals) as well as for being disconnected from the organization and the work (ignoring tasks, jobs, and core work processes) (e.g., Alvesson, 1993b). Barley (1983) was one of the first to make this case, illustrating a semiotic approach to the significance of seemingly mundane actions, such as how the placement of furniture and standard operating procedures for jobs revealed deeper levels of interpretation that constituted work culture.

Kunda (1992) attended to these critiques and captured the high art of symbolic analysis in his book *Engineering Culture*. Written after a one-year stay in a high-technology organization, the study set out to learn about the way an organization attempts to create and maintain a strong culture specifically because the management executives believe that normative control is a better ideology than bureaucratic control. Kunda also focused on the performance of ritual as a framing device where members acting as agents of the corporate interest attempted to establish shared definitions through the use of slogans and metaphors (e.g., "We are like a football team," p. 154). Challenges to these ritual frames, which Kunda called mini-dramas, served to suppress dissent at Tech and distance those who disagreed with the corporate ideology. Kunda noted that "Tech management takes the implications of its own rhetoric seriously and invests considerable energy in attempting to embed the rules, prescriptions, and admonitions of the culture in the fabric of everyday life in the company" (p. 218). He concluded that "Tech's engineered culture appears to be a pervasive, comprehensive, and demanding system of normative control based on the use of symbolic power" (p. 219). His research

pointed to the paradoxes associated with complex and ambiguous circumstances and the self-reflexivity of organizational members —"Members evaluate each other on their ability to express both embracement and distancing and to know when to stop" (p. 158).

Kunda, however, was not the first to examine cultures as performance. Communication scholars Pacanowsky and O'Donnell-Trujillo (1983) earlier argued that organizational communication researchers should look at "performances" in their quest to understand cultural processes. They noted that "it is easy enough to answer that cultural structures come into being through processes of communication. The problem with this assertion is not that it is wrong (because it is not), but that it is not helpful" (p. 129). In their attempt to isolate a locus of interpretation, Pacanowsky and O'Donnell-Trujillo described two connotations of performance that should form the basis of research: First is Goffman's (1959) notion of theatricality, and the second is Turner's (1980) sense of "accomplishing" or "bringing to completion" of order in social life. They then described five cultural performances in organizations that have been examined in the literature: ritual, passion, sociality, politics, and acculturation. One vivid example of this sense of performance as theatricality was captured in Trujillo and Dionisopoulos's (1987) investigation of police talk and organization, where the performative nature of work was displayed and critiqued. In this study, police talk and actions were examined to focus attention on membership, difference, and discursive practices that established normative understanding of policing through their cultural enactments of masculinity.

A related perspective was offered by Conquergood (1991), who stated that the modes of "discussion" in cultures were "not always and exclusively verbal: Issues and attitudes are expressed and contested in dance, music, gesture, food, ritual, artifact, symbol, action, as well as words" (p. 189). Conquergood suggested that fieldwork itself was a collaborative performance and that consideration should be given to the "rhetorical problematics of performance as an alternative form of 'publishing' research" (p. 190).

Recent scholarship in organizational communication responded to these requests. For example, Rogers's (1994) study on the narrative of "rhythm" and the performance of organization was an investigation/argument that viewed rhythm as an organization's enactment of order—the "culture's means of identifying, differentiation, and relating objects, sensations, events, and processes in the world" (p. 223). Of particular interest was the link between a Foucauldian sense of discipline and the rhythm of production (e.g., the mass distribution of uniform, commodified music and factory or assembly line rhythm). In a related vein, Knight (1990) described military "Jody" performances (e.g., "I got a wife and she is keen, Traded her for my M-16") as a co-opted communication form that dehumanized women and exemplified "literature as equipment for killing" (p. 166).

As these studies indicate, culture as performance moved far beyond early notions of significant "symbols" and artifacts and began to embrace a multivocal, eclectic, contradictory, and celebratory sense of organizational culture.

## Culture as Text

A growing number of scholars situate themselves within a textual approach to organizational culture. Within this larger rubric, three rather distinct but loosely related approaches were uncovered. One approach focused on actual written texts in organizations such as newsletters, mission statements, and other documents written by organizational members. Another perspective expanded the textual metaphor to include the examination of spoken discourse. These studies analyzed the symbols, language, and practices produced in organizations as texts using literary theories and tools. Finally, a third enterprise conceived of the writing of organizational cul-

ture narratives (sometimes by scholars and sometimes the product of organizational members) as texts. Each of these perspectives is covered in turn.

The first of the three approaches—treatment of written organizational texts—was influenced by Ricoeur's (1971) notion of the "hermeneutics of suspicion," which helped shape the interpretive turn in literary theory and the humanities. For many organizational communication scholars, particularly those interested in rhetorical analysis, Ricoeur's specific focus on those signs that were "fixed by writing" (p. 529) renewed scholarly interest in organizational documents, interviews, and other textual manifestations of organizational life. One of the more interesting examples of written texts was Scheibel's (1994) reading of film school culture where he discovered that alienation was a key feature of the culture. Scheibel built his analysis around an important aspect of film school culture: its graffiti. He argued that cinema students romanticized their late nights of lonely editing by creating analogies between their isolation and the imagined experiences of great film directors. The students enacted their alienation through some plaintive and much humorous writing on the walls of the editing booths—for example, "those who can, direct; those who can't, edit" (p. 7) and "my film has turned against me" (p. 10).

The second perspective, which views spoken language as texts, has produced a number of interesting studies. Communication scholars Tompkins, Tompkins, and Cheney (1989) used "text" as a metaphor to analyze what we do and say in organizational life. In this sense, to see organizations as texts was to focus on the language and arguments of the organization (Tompkins & Cheney, 1988). The text metaphor legitimated the use of hermeneutic methods to unravel the symbolic document of a structured life-world by focusing on the modes of its production and interpretation.

A wonderful example of this approach is found in Taylor's (1990) analysis of personal narratives from the Manhattan Project (the production of the first atomic bomb at the Los Alamos Laboratory). This study was an example of a critical reading that aimed to reconstruct the organizational milieu. His reading suggested an organizational structure that authorized a "rational" subject for the first nuclear weapons organization. This rational culture allowed members to create a technical identity for themselves and for their work that sustained the hegemonic imperatives of nationalism and technological innovation.

Although it is not about a specific culture, Mumby and Putnam's (1992) rereading of the concept of bounded rationality has a similar flavor in that it is a critical reading of the discursive practices and the gendered identities that are a result of generic (read: masculine) organizational culture. Van Maanen and Kunda (1989) gave examples of these practices in their description of organizational cultures that act to emotionally control their members. Mumby and Putnam's reinterpretation of organizational practices as bounded emotionality had significant implications for researchers who are so used to their own vocabulary that they are unable "to recognize the cultural, historical, and political situatedness" of their analysis (p. 481).

The third and most common approach to texts focuses primarily on the written accounts of organizational culture. Following Geertz, many scholars have viewed organizational culture narratives as texts or as a kind of writing. In one of the better examples, Van Maanen (1988) categorized organizational ethnography into three basic types of "tales": realist, confessional, and impressionist, plus a cursory description of literary, formal, critical, and jointly told tales. Realist tales such as Whyte's (1943) *Street Corner Society,* a participant-observation of an Italian gang in the American Northeast, were easily recognized as traditional "objective" cultural descriptions from a somewhat detached observer (see Riley, 1991, for an alternative reading of "Cornerville" that used a narrative paradigm). Both latter types of ethnography—confessional and impressionist—implicate the re-

searcher and his or her biases and interactions as critical to the type of account that gets constructed. Impressionist tales, for example, are often tied to the chronological experiences of the ethnographer in the field, with the culture being inextricably bound to his or her particular encounters with it. Confessional tales are further distanced from traditional descriptive ethnography, in that they largely focus on the subjective experience of the researcher in the field. Confessional tales are closely paralleled by a movement in the social sciences toward autobiographical approaches to scholarship. For those who are familiar with Hunter Thompson and gonzo journalism, there was a close connection—in reading this work we learn more about the author than we do about the setting. Van Maanen's (1988) own studies of police work include examples of all three types of tales.

Martin (1992; see also Martin & Myerson, 1988) offered an alternative taxonomy of organizational culture research that, at a meta-level, treated organizational culture research as texts. She divided culture texts into three categories: integration, differentiation, and fragmentation. The integration text sought to define culture as everything that people in an organization "share" and was often closely associated with the themes of comparative management and corporate culture (although others investigating cognition and symbolism adopted this approach). The differentiation perspective, on the other hand, explicitly acknowledged the existence of different values, practices, and subcultures in organizations and highlighted the political struggles that were constantly a factor in achieving a negotiated order. This perspective is thus a close cousin of critical analysis, with its emphasis on power, conflict, and negotiation. Finally, the fragmentation perspective contended that so-called organizational cultures were characterized by ambiguity and that individuals and organizations had fluctuating boundaries and identities. These studies were most concerned with showing the practical and personal struggles involved in coping with wide-scale confusion and ambiguity. Consensus was seen as short-lived and issue specific (e.g., Kreiner & Schultz, 1993). This work captured the essence of postmodernism as applied to organizational cultures, in which "decentered" individuals constantly reconstructed their identities.

Martin's three-perspective system, when taken as a metatheory, implied that any culture, at any point in time, had some aspects congruent with all three perspectives. Further, if any of these points of view were excluded, then the potential power of cultural analysis was diminished (Martin, 1992). This is not dissimilar to Mumby and Putnam's (1992) request for scholars to draw on both the emotional and rational domains of experience. Such requests ask theorists to abandon efforts at constructing "final" organizational vocabularies but to, instead, maintain an ironic stance (Rorty, 1989).

An example of Martin's three-perspective system of cultural analysis is found in Eisenberg, Murphy, and Andrews (1998). This study of a university's search for a provost in a state that has a "sunshine law" (the search process is open to the public) uses narratives of integration, differentiation, and fragmentation as different "faces" from which to present the event and understand the multivocal nature of culture. In their analysis of the "nexus" of these three views—where a variety of cultural influences come together within a "[permeable and arbitrary] boundary" (p. 17)—they found that the varying perspectives appeared to be chosen for rhetorical reasons. Similar to a stucturationist study, Eisenberg et al. claimed that these perspectives could be drawn on as "resources that organizational actors use to communicate with multiple audiences" (p. 18).

In their postmodern questioning of the initial and common urge among culture researchers to seek integration and synthesis, Smircich and Calás (1987) have pushed scholars to think differently about their common-sense notions of culture. They posited that each "text" was an alternative "fiction" (in the sense of *fictive,* or something "made") and that the truth or falsity of a written account of culture was a meaningless question—what was salient were the rhetorical, political, and practical consequences of selecting one interpretation over another. They urged scholars to speak "culturally" in a multitude of voices and to transform the "organizational culture literature" into a "cultured organizational literature" (p. 257) in which all claims of knowledge about culture were open to investigation, and none would gain the status of permanent or totalizing truth.

Brown and McMillan (1991) also argued that unlike the move to focus on workplace documents or practices "as symbolic," postmodern scholars needed to redefine the terms *text* and *work* to distance "the work of an author from the 'work' of the receivers that might take the form of a response, and experience, a critique" (p. 50). Brown and McMillan reminded us of the authorial nature of all analytical descriptions. Whether it is the voice of the researcher or the voices of organizational members that is ultimately written down and "heard," Rabinow and Sullivan (1979) remarked that culture is "always multivocal and overdetermined, and both the observer and the observed are always enmeshed in it. . . . There is no privileged position, no absolute perspective, no final recounting" (p. 6).

## Culture as Critique

Critical cultural studies and the associated area of postmodern resistance characterized much communication research on culture in the 1980s and 1990s. We will first cover critical scholarship and then discuss the postmodern strains in organizational culture research. Early critical cultural studies of organizations (e.g., Deetz & Kersten, 1983) primarily emphasized power (see Mumby, Chapter 15, this volume). Many scholars in communication consider the cultural manifestations of concepts such as "resistance to domination" evident in "hidden transcripts" and in the discourse and practices of corporate colonization (Deetz, 1992). Drawing on the work of Habermas, Foucault, and other critical and postmodern theorists, Deetz (1992) recounted the growing spread of corporate control in a global society. His approach to both the structural and linguistic manifestations of organizations has allowed communication researchers (and others) to focus on the intersection of societal and local organizational practices at both philosophical and pragmatic levels. The enormous amount of time most everyone spends in organizations, as well as the powerful inscription of organizational routines in our everyday lives (e.g., standardized work hours, day care centers, insurance-driven medical care), forces us to look at cultural praxis in a more enduring way (Deetz, 1992). Deetz and Kersten (1983) noted, "In such cases of domination, communication is systematically distorted" (p. 165).

Critical approaches emphasize that any representation of culture always comes from a particular perspective, with particular interests, and encourages researchers to be more reflexive about what these interests and biases might be (Jermier, 1991). Central to this approach in the organizational context has been a shift away from notions of productivity and organizational effectiveness to a concern for employees' quality of life (Aktouf, 1992). Strains of this "culture as critique" theme have been articulated within some of the previously reviewed literature. Much of the structurationist culture literature—with its attention focused on dominant patterns of control—provides clear examples. Heavily grounded in Foucault's concern with power in organizations, Ferguson's (1984) classic feminist "case against bureaucracy" critiqued the whole of organization science literature as embedded in an overly rational, paternalistic, dominating conception of organizing. Scholarship such as Brown and McMillan's (1991) that problematizes author/authority is another example.

An excellent case study of culture as critique was included in Barker and Cheney's (1994) examination of the ways that discipline "works" discursively in organizations. In a company they call Tech USA, one of the authors observed the organization's conversion to self-managing teams (following the lead of Peters & Waterman, 1982). They found that the teams began to identify with and apply these values to each other's activities (e.g., Mumby & Stohl, 1991). Tech USA's management had "crafted a vision statement that articulated a set of core values, which all employees were to use to guide their daily actions" (Barker & Cheney, 1994, p. 33). In this organization, the teams created sets of disciplinary discourses that acted as a cultural system of control. In one example, an employee complained that "the whole team is watching what I do" (p. 35). Barker and Cheney posit an interesting paradox: As organizations work to become more ethical, achieve higher values, and allow members greater autonomy, the organization becomes more "concertive" in its influence and individual control is diminished.

In a more postmodern vein, Goodall (1989, 1991) approached ethnography with the ideas of the "plural present" and of "mystery" (borrowed from Kenneth Burke). Acknowledging the plural present means that in any organization, in any culture, there are always multiple voices telling multiple versions of what is "really" going on. This is not, however, necessarily a problem. Cultures, according to Goodall, are not problems to be solved, but mysteries to be experienced again and again, each time with new insight but without any final resolution other than the continual rediscovery of self (Rorty, 1989).

Conquergood's (1991) notion of postmodern cultural study, and specifically ethnography, required a radical rethinking in light of the "double fall of scientism and imperialism" (p. 179). As the image of an objective, detached observer who used neutral language to describe or represent a unitary culture has increasingly come under fire (e.g., Jackson, 1989; Marcus & Fischer, 1986; Van Maanen, 1988), various types of cultural analysis have emerged. These newer conceptions all situate the researcher deep in the cultural context, complete with personal biases and practical agendas. Conquergood asked that we consider a number of issues, but key among them are the return of the body and rhetorical reflexivity.

Return of the body referred to the importance of active, physical immersion in the organization whose culture one wishes to describe. Cultural study from this perspective was an embodied practice, and while there were costs to be paid for getting "close," there were also significant benefits. Bodily immersion opened the ethnographer to senses other than the visual (cf. Stoller, 1989) and to explicit consideration of issues such as investigating the connections between sexuality and power and specifically sexual harassment. For instance, Clair (1993) provided a feminist critique of harassment in a way that is easily aligned with organizational culture. In Clair's view, what was most interesting were the personal narratives of harassment and how they acted as frames for either challenging or reproducing the dominant ideology. That certain organizational cultures encouraged different ways of speaking and acting with regard to this subject was clear (e.g., Rogers, 1994).

By invoking rhetorical reflexivity, Conquergood (1991) suggested that cultural study is increasingly seen reflexively—meaning that there can be no final, authoritative account of a culture (Geertz, 1988). Instead, ethnographies invariably reflect the writer/researchers' biases and ways of life as much as they do those under study—the construction of a culture that is "strange" or "foreign" only serves to underscore the supposed "normalness" of the writer's home perspective. What flows from this insight is a recognition of the need to understand the kinds of "descriptions" of culture that are seen as "appropriate for publication," and the sorts of knowledge that are seen as legitimate within the institutional structures of academia and society.

As if she were responding directly to Conquergood, Martin's (1992) final chapter critiqued the "imperialism" of her own metatheory, her assertions that studies might fall into one category or another, and in the presumption of "truth" that the taxonomy makes. Similarly, she questioned her ability to present the voices of the employees she interviewed as part of her studies and admitted that as author she edited conversations and selected quotes to make her chosen arguments as best as she could. Finally, she speculated about ways of making the whole enterprise more open-ended and dialogic.

There are, obviously, ways in which "culture" and "postmodernism" have always coexisted uneasily since culture has traditionally been the study of common meanings, integration, community, and values (the language of unification), and postmodernism is about difference, suspicion, fragmentation, and the rejection of epistemology (the language of polysemy). And postmodernism is not without its critics, for several fairly obvious reasons. First, the language used is often accessible only to the initiated or the very patient, often replete with jargon, words in quotes, and phrases in a variety of languages. Second, some believe the focus on deconstructing texts, rather than on taking action to improve the lives of organizational members, makes postmodernism seem like "an elitist language game played by intellectual initiates while Rome (or Los Angeles) burns—a diversion or excuse for action paralysis and social nihilism" (see Martin & Frost, 1996, for a detailed discussion). But postmodernism is now a cultural phenomenon of its own, pressing researchers to rethink their values, methods, and goals.

In their review of such concerns, Linstead and Grafton-Small (1992) argued that we need to approach culture as a discursive complex and appreciate the importance of the other and the seductive process of forming culture and image. They stressed the detailed articulation and analysis of everyday practices as a means of exploring the marginal creativity of culture consumers, particularly with respect to their socioeconomic and historical contexts. It is in the articulation of everyday communication practices that so much work remains to be done.

## Culture as Identity

The concept of identity is a particularly important theme in the organizational culture literature, in part because of the postmodern "condition" of academic thought goaded by the rapidly changing face of our human geography. Many of the early conceptions of identity focused on national or ethnic identity, often under the rubric of comparative management, and delved into the ways organizations from different nations embodied characteristics or practices inherent in their cultural background. More recently, scholars have problematized the concept of identity in postmodern society. To explore the organizational culture research on identity, we have divided the review into subthemes: comparative management and self-identity.

### Comparative Management

The comparative management perspective treats culture as though it was imported into organizations through the national, regional, and ethnic affiliations of employees (see Stohl, Chapter 10 in this volume, for greater detail). This approach stresses the significance of nationality over the power of any individual organization to influence member behavior (Hofstede, 1991). Most studies of this kind treat culture as an external variable and employ a traditional, functionalist approach. Perhaps the best-known, and one of the most exhaustive, studies of cross-national differences in cultural orientation was conducted by Hofstede (1983). He studied matched populations of IBM employees across 64 countries. In general, differences in national value systems were found along four (and later, five) largely independent dimensions but Hofstede agreed that they said little that is specific about IBM's culture.

Similarly, Erez and Earley (1993) saw culture as a set of mental programs that con-

trolled behavior, and they argued that these mental sets varied from country to country. Their logic was that different national cultures produced people with different mental sets, who in turn both expected different behaviors of others and behaved differently themselves. In another well-known study, Shweder and LeVine (1984) contrasted Western egocentric cultures with Eastern sociocentric cultures and found them to have very different mental maps and behavioral expectations.

The simplistic nature of such research is called into question by research in organizational communication. Banks and Riley (1993) employed a structurationist lens to investigate the disembedding of rules and systems from other organizations or institutions in a Japanese subsidiary located in the United States. They found evidence of national identity and practices but also found disruptive contradictions, language confusion, and culturally based power systems that were interpreted differently by members of the various subcultures. In these days of permeable boundaries, joint ventures, and virtual teams, this type of analysis may provide further insight into the reproduction and transformation of polyvocal cultural understandings.

It is important to note that Wilkins and Ouchi (1983) and Hofstede, Neuijen, Ohayv, and Sanders (1990) believed that national cultures and organizational cultures are constituted differently and that terminological care is needed when speaking of "culture" in this research genre. Hofstede et al.'s position was that culture is a different phenomenon at the national level than it is at the organizational level and that shared perceptions of daily practices were the core of an organization's culture, not shared values as other authors working off a national or ethnic model have maintained.

### Self-Identity

The idea of the self as a consistent integrated "thing" that confronts others in the world has been critiqued and the alternative argument advanced that what counts for "who you are" at any moment in time is constructed from those images that are currently available in the culture. Gergen (1991), for example, has been on the forefront in articulating a view of the self as fragmented. In postmodern conceptions of identity, the idea of a "bounded, interiorized self is a narrative convention" (Kondo, 1990, p. 25). Although his theorizing about self and identity differs somewhat, Giddens (1991) contended that self-identity is not a distinctive trait or even a collection of traits but is the "self as reflexively understood by the person in terms of her or his biography" (p. 53). In this sense, a person's identity is not found in behavior, or in the reactions of others (although this is part of the picture), but in the capacity to keep a particular narrative going (Giddens, 1991, p. 54). The "content" of self-identity varies much the ways stories do, in form and style, and socially and culturally. A key feature of this conceptualization is that the very core of identity—of choices we make about not only how to act but whom to be—is heavily influenced by our work and the choices available or not available to us.

Communication research has indicated that the choices for constructing identity in organizations are fraught with difficulties due to the myriad of situations that occur in organizational life (Cheney, 1991). By investigating the multiple roles and exigencies of members' lives in organizations, Cheney creatively explored both the constitutive role of communication in the managing of identity and varied responses to self-identity requirements in the cultural context of organizations. The problematizing of identity has included taking on fake or temporary identities (Scheibel, 1992). In his study of the communicative performances in "clubland" (the conventional communication practices of underage females and male gatekeepers in nightclubs), Scheibel finds faking an identity for entrance to an organization a challenging but commonly accomplished cultural performance. Although the larger implications for the reproduction of gendered organizations are clear, what is left unexplored is the impact on individual narratives.

Whether identity is considered a feature of historical geography—still important to those individuals not able or unwilling to join either the great diaspora or the tourist class—or a process of working on one's self as a mosaic of organizational, familial, and societal roles, the concept is a metaphor for our time, a struggle for coherence amid multiple discourses and optional organizational forms.

## Organizational Cognition

The discussion of self-identity reveals an interest in understanding the relationship between the social construction of the organization and the self-construction of individuals. One of the most commonly articulated views in the organizational culture literature is that this process is primarily cognitive. In other words, to understand the relationship between individuals and their organization one must investigate the cognitive frame that facilitates coordinated action. This approach to organizational culture is sometimes called the "ideational" perspective, and it defines culture as a pattern of shared assumptions, shared frame of reference, or a shared set of values and norms. While cognitive anthropologists have been the strongest proponents of this view (e.g., D'Andrade, 1984), this approach is evident in the literature on shared rules and cognitive patterns (see Barnett, 1988), in organization and management studies as shared values (Chatman & Jehn, 1994), and in studies of cognitive frames that dictate appropriate behavior (Thompson & Luthans, 1990).

When researchers analyze why organizational members behave as they do, they focus on what people say and take the response to be the reason for their behavior. Some scholars, such as Schein (1985), disagree:

> Yet, the underlying reasons for their behavior remain concealed or unconscious. To really understand a culture and to ascertain more completely the group's values and overt behavior, it

is imperative to delve into the underlying assumptions, which are typically unconscious but which actually determine how group members perceive, think, and feel. (p. 3)

Similarly, Barnett (1988) maintained that "culture consists of the habits and tendencies to act in certain ways, but *not* the actions themselves" (p. 102, emphasis ours). And D'Andrade (1984) believed that the most fruitful way to study culture is not through the examination of messages but rather with the study of individual "meaning systems."

In a study advancing the cognitive perspective, Shockley- Zalabak and Morley (1994) combined an emphasis on shared values with Schall's (1983) concerns about shared communication rules. They found that "management values during the formative years of an organization were closely related to the values of the employees initially hired into the organization. Additionally, management values were related over time to both management and employee perceptions of organizational rules" (p. 352).[1]

Mohan (1993) adopted a cognitive approach in her discussion of cultural vision, and in particular in her consideration of psychological, sociological, and historical "penetration." She centered on the degree to which a culture was shared in the organization as a cognitive conception. For example, psychological penetration was defined as the degree of consistency of shared meanings, sociological penetration surfaced as the pervasiveness of cultural assumptions, and historical penetration was the stability of cultural schemata (cognitive frames) over time. In a study of semantic networks in organizations, Contractor, Eisenberg, and Monge (1994) examined six organizations to determine both the degree and importance of consensus among employees on the meaning of the organization's vision, a key notion in organizational culture. They found that interpretations varied widely.

Other scholars in communication and organizational behavior have argued for a cognitive approach to culture. Sackmann (1991) asserted that "what makes a collection of people a cultural grouping is the fact that the people hold the same cognitions in common" (p. 40). Her fine-grained analysis divided cognitions into three types of knowledge: descriptive, or "dictionary" knowledge; causal-analytical, or "directory" knowledge; and causal normative, or "recipe" knowledge. All three are combined in cognitive maps that overlap to constitute an organization's culture. James, James, and Ashe (1990), in a work admittedly more directed at climate than culture, attacked social constructionism in claiming that no meaning ever resides even partially outside of individual cognitive systems. This is in sharp contrast to the views of Mead (1934) or Bakhtin (1981), both of whom have maintained that the meaning of any utterance is never the sole possession of an individual—that the meaning of any word always belongs, in part, to someone else (Holquist, 1990).

Other writers also take a cognitive approach to culture, only to describe their approaches in ways that display subtle yet important differences. For example, Louis (1990) came closest to "popular" understanding of culture when she stated that a common culture means that people recognize the same meanings for things, but do not necessarily agree on them. Myerson (1991) presented social work culture more problematically when she described it as a kind of "shared orientation" within which can exist multiple interpretations of specific concepts and behaviors. Hofstede (1991) maintained that it is the shared perceptions of daily work practices (and not shared values or beliefs per se) that are key to an organization's culture. Still others (e.g., Krackhardt & Kilduff, 1990) argued that effective coordinated action depends more on the quality of dyadic interpersonal relationships than on group or organization-wide consensus on interpretations. McCollom's (1993) definition blended a cognitively focused approach with the behavioral: "Culture is defined as the set of conscious and unconscious beliefs and values, *and* the patterns of behavior (including language and symbol use) that provide identity and form a framework of meaning for a group of people" (p. 84, emphasis ours).

In summary, one of the "black holes" of the culture conversation has been the locus of the meanings that constitute culture, mostly played out between proponents of the ideational and behavioral schools. At the same time, many have staked their definitions somewhere in the fuzzy middle, viewing culture as "redundancies of interpretation and practice" (Barley, 1983) or "configurations of interpretations, *and* the ways they are enacted" (Martin, 1992, emphasis ours). D'Andrade (1984) made the point that prior to 1957, culture was seen mainly in terms of observable behaviors, actions, and customs and that the movement from this position to an increased interest in cognition was to be celebrated. Yet Geertz reminds us that a countermovement took place at the same time, one whose purpose was to critique the twin myths of "inner reality" and private language. The key point of this countermovement (with which Geertz is sympathetic) was to define culture as a conceptual structure that is separate from individual psychology—that is, to assert that meaning is both public and social (Bakhtin, 1981; Gergen, 1991; Vygotsky, 1962). In an attempt at arbitration, Shweder (1991) suggested that the question of where meaning (or culture) resides may be irrelevant, like asking whether "redness" resides in a color chip or in a perceptual system.

Clearly, part of this debate is also methodological—the quantitative instrumentation developed to uncover individualistic perceptions are often static and unconnected with the generative mechanisms that produce them. It is clear to us that organizations are first and foremost action systems (Pilotta, Widman, & Jasco, 1988) and that little is gained in trying to separate enactment from interpretation. For this reason, the organizational cognition approach, to the extent that it is characterized by a mostly private view of language and an individualistic bias, will fall short. This is not to say that cognitions are unimportant, only that their importance depends entirely on their relationship to action and behavior and to ongoing conduct within a public conversation (Mead, 1934).

## *Culture as Climate*

There has always been a family resemblance between the culture as cognition research and climate studies in organizations, since much of the climate literature has been cognitively based. Those resemblances, however, have grown stronger during the past decade with an emphasis on the "acculturation" of climate. Perhaps no other research area has been so transfigured by the organizational culture metaphor as the umbrella concept of organizational climate.

The climate notion, adroitly described as an "attractive nuisance" (Bastien, McPhee, & Bolton, 1995), was a mélange of distinct research programs with competing theoretical orientations, different units of analysis, and nonequivalent measurement instruments loosely connected by the metaphor of the organization's atmosphere. Previous reviews on organizational climate (such as the one by Falcione, Sussman, & Herden, 1987, in the first edition of this handbook), written during or near the end when climate was an academic boom industry, typically divided the studies into three categories:

1. Climate as a set of attributes possessed by the organization—like an organizational personality—that was relatively enduring over time and persisted despite changes in individual members (e.g., Zohar, 1980)
2. Subgroup climates (e.g., Johnston, 1976)
3. The cognitive or psychological approach, which centered on individual summary perceptions (or the summary perceptions of subsystems) of the work environment rather than on organizational attributes (Hellriegel & Slocum, 1974; James & Jones, 1974)

Although a number of widely differing questionnaires and instruments were developed to measure climate, many used similar dimensions of autonomy, consideration, and reward orientation (Falcione et al., 1987).

The communication-related dimensions—such as supportiveness, trust, openness, participative decision making—most interested the organizational communication scholars and led to the concept of communication climate (e.g., Downs, 1979; Redding, 1972). Later, Poole and McPhee (1983) developed the argument that climate was actually intersubjective, related to specific organizational practices, and better understood as an ongoing process of structuration. This position was extended through Poole's (1985) notion of "kernel" climates that can be identified in an organization but are interpreted differently across subgroups and can change across time. Bastien et al. (1995) explicated how kernel themes were transformed into surface climates "in the course of reproducing the organization's culture and beliefs" (p. 87). Although their approach was not a culture study, it is indicative of the "regrounding" of much of the recent climate literature within the larger cultural metaphor.

With article titles such as "The Cultural Approach to the Formation of Organizational Climate" (Moran & Volkwein, 1992), "Climate and Culture Interaction and Qualitative Differences in Organizational Meanings" (Rentsch, 1990), and "Creating the Climate and Culture of Success" (Schneider, Gunnarson, & Niles-Jolly, 1994) and a book called *Organizational Climate and Culture* (Schneider, 1990), the shift in emphasis is quite apparent. Recent climate articles also display many practical concerns but little if any consideration of communication, for example, R&D project team climate (Youngbae & Lee, 1995), R&D marketing and interfunctional climates (Moenaert, Souder, Meyer, & DeSchoolmeester, 1994), sales-manager-salesperson solidarity (Strutton & Pelton, 1994), the relationship between climate and perceptions of personnel management practices (Toulson & Smith, 1994), looking for conducive climates (Turnipseed & Turnipseed, 1992), concern for customers and employees (Burke, Borucki, & Hurley, 1992), customer service (Schneider, Wheeler, & Cox, 1992), and the effects of climate on individual behavior and attitudes in organizations (Ostroff, 1993).

The growing fascination with culture management has also reconfigured, if not dominated, the research programs of organizational climate researchers. Early climate research was often descriptive in nature—calculating aggregate employee perceptions about such issues as goals and policies, supportive versus defensive atmosphere, and communication (Falcione & Kaplan, 1984). Although the number of climate studies undertaken has dropped significantly, most recent work positioned organizational climate in relation to culture and effectiveness (e.g., Schneider et al., 1994). The result is that most conceptions of organizational climate are best viewed as phenomena caused, changed, or managed by the organization's culture.

What promise does this acculturated form of climate hold for organizational communication? Perhaps if we refocus the research agenda and develop a core group of scholars to conduct research and provide critique its value could be significantly enhanced. While traditional communication climate studies are on the wane,[2] a revival of dynamic, intersubjective approaches to climate could bring alternative but complementary insights that would be superior to the more traditional attitude surveys that are so popular in large corporations today. These studies might explain how people feel about their organizations, and why, in ways that could engender ongoing dialogue between managers and employees—a precious activity in an era of massive restructurings, acquisitions and re-engineering.

### Culture as Effectiveness

The practical focus in the acculturated climate research is understandable when read alongside the large body of instrumental organizational culture research. The "effectiveness" or "corporate culture" perspective is perhaps best known in the management literature and the popular press. This approach treats culture as values or practices that account for an organization's success and that can be managed to produce better business outcomes. Ouchi and Wilkins (1985) observed that "the contemporary student of organizational culture often takes the organization not as a natural solution to deep and universal forces but as a rational instrument designed by top management to shape the behavior of the employees in purposive ways" (p. 462). Alvesson (1993b) restated this tendency, through the eyes of a critical theorist, as the dominance of instrumental values in service of the technical cognitive interest.

The corporate culture perspective clusters into three interrelated areas of study: (1) the influence of founders and leaders on the creation and maintenance and transformation of cultures, (2) the work on "strong" cultures and their values, and (3) organizational change and the management of cultures.

### Founders and Leaders

The corporate culture literature takes an activist stance toward the culture concept—culture is something to be created, shaped, and purposively transformed—and the studies that focus on founders and leaders are archetypal of this position. Primarily conducted by management and organizational studies researchers, these studies are not a mainstay of the communication discipline and as such, communication is not always the focus although it is clearly not ignored.

In Pettigrew's (1979) well-known essay on symbolic approaches to organizational cultures, using the founding and transformation of a British boarding school as its touchstone, his primary interest was in "how purpose, commitment, and order are generated in an or-

ganization both through the feelings and actions of its founder . . . man as a creator and manager of meaning" (p. 572). Attempting to redefine the prevailing organizational behavior interests away from the personality characteristics of leaders, Pettigrew stated that "the essential problem of entrepreneurship is the translation of individual drive into collective purpose and commitment. With this viewpoint the focus is not what makes the entrepreneur but rather what does the entrepreneur make" (p. 573). From this perspective, employee commitment is a requirement for a successful organization and this commitment must be earned by the founder or leader through vision, energy, sacrifice, and investment. Schein (1985) claimed that founders "teach" others through their actions and in this manner cultures are developed, learned, and embedded.

In one of the most vivid descriptions of the power of a founder to imagine an organization, McDonald (1991) described President Peter Ueberroth of the Los Angeles Olympic Organizing Committee. In her examination of such devices as the "Peter" test on Olympic knowledge, administered to all new employees by the president himself, the salience of the founder is codified. But it is in the description of the large staff gatherings—true rhetorical masterpieces with speakers like Jesse Jackson—where management's use of formal communication devices to create an organizational identity is clearly apparent. These devices are not without their dark side; McDonald also critiques their coercive nature. Smith and Eisenberg's (1987) exploration of Walt Disney's immortalization through "Disney University" and the "Disney philosophy" displayed a similar concern for the power of the formal communication devices and language surrounding the founder. And Siehl's (1985) examination of cultural influences "after the founder" looked for clues to the ongoing cultural routines in the residue of the founder's legacy in a variety of organizational enactments including language use and structured patterns of behavior.

## Strong Cultures

Many companies, such as the ones mentioned above, are famous for their self-conscious focus on corporate culture (e.g., McDonald's, Disney, Hyatt, Pepsi), and founders spend a great deal of time engaged in aligning values, systems, personalities, communication, and practices through ongoing socialization and monitoring. Moreover, some research reports claim to reveal a connection between corporate culture and organizational effectiveness/performance. Interestingly, all of the research that finds positive results operationalizes culture in terms of shared values. One example is Kotter and Heskett's (1992) study of 200 companies. Using a simple measure of corporate culture (perceived degree of value consensus), they observed that so-called strong cultures that exhibit a high degree of value consensus do not necessarily result in excellent performance and can even be destructive unless included among their norms and values is a focus on adaptation to a changing environment. Moreover, when "performance-enhancing" cultures emerge, they tended to exhibit two critical elements: (1) the presence of an entrepreneur with an adaptive business philosophy; and (2) an effective business strategy that succeeds and consequently adds credibility to the entrepreneur's position, as he or she engages in a constant dialogue that encourages challenges to received wisdom and invites ongoing adaptation and change. Chatman and Jehn (1994) took a similar approach in examining the relationships among industry norms, organizational culture (values), and individual employee fit using a measure of organizational culture called the OCP (O'Reilly, Chatman, & Caldwell, 1991). In applying this measurement tool to different organizations within and across industries, Chatman and Jehn noted significant differences in values across industries, as well as differences among organizations, even those within relatively homogeneous industries.

Other researchers are skeptical of the entire culture-effectiveness project. Siehl and Martin (1990) believed that studies like Kotter and Heskett's (1992) are methodologically flawed since attitudes and values seldom reliably predict behavior. In their critique, Siehl and Martin maintained that this research is also on the "wrong track" and deflects energy from more useful avenues of research that might focus on symbolism, ethics, diversity, and the uneven distribution of power at work. Saffold (1988) is even more specific in his critique and argues that overly simplistic studies of culture that employ monolithic, superficial conceptions and measurements of culture are unlikely to reveal clear culture-performance links. His proposal is to investigate issues of cultural dispersion, potency, and complex interactions that may exist between aspects of culture and organizational performance.

## Organizational Change and Managing Culture

The literature on organizational change and development acknowledges the role of culture in promoting, managing, or impeding change. The question, then, is whether managers or change agents can move cultures in specific directions to achieve certain organizational goals—for example, related to financial performance or issues like increased diversity. There is considerable debate about this subject, both with regard to techniques and to likelihood of success. In their attempt to enact planned culture change, many executives or leaders have found themselves in the awkward position of pushing an ideological stance that is at odds with the already established local culture. This dilemma has led to the conclusion that culture cannot be "managed" per se —although certain patterns of behavior can be encouraged and cultivated. Here we note a connection to the prior section on penetration. As long as organizational culture is approached cognitively in terms of shared meanings and assumptions, one is invariably tempted to try to alter these cognitions directly in a change effort and to be met with predictably high levels of resistance. Managers and consultants alike recognize that most improvement efforts of these kinds fail because they are "unnatural acts," incompatible with the local culture.

An alternative approach that treats "values" and "assumptions" as epiphenomena and aims instead to reshape practices—including communication practices—is less likely to be resisted, and paradoxically more likely to shape interpretations over time. Consequently, strategic change efforts are increasingly analyzing culture to maximize the chances of implementing new ways of doing business such as total quality management (TQM), self-managing work groups, and reengineering. With culture defined as present practices, many researchers argued that large-scale change efforts are impossible without, and as a result may constitute, widespread cultural change (e.g., Sashkin & Kiser, 1993; Spencer, 1994).

Alvesson (1993b) saw the instrumental view of culture—and the accompanying arguments about "good," "strong," or "ideal" cultures—as pervasive in the works of management theorists Schein (1985), Wilkins and Dyer (1988), and others (e.g., Baker, 1980; Trice & Beyer, 1984). He criticized these approaches as overly narrow and unlikely to reveal much about important, unplanned, organic changes initiated by employees, or by gradual changes in society. What passes for corporate culture, he maintained, is better referred to as management ideology: the norms and values that serve as ideals for a group. Corporate culture is bigger, less homogeneous, and more complex. Trying to extract a common set of values from an organization that employs a wide range of people, he argued, seems likely only to yield a superficial set of norms and values that may promote cohesiveness but have little impact on work behavior. Alvesson (1993b) also argued that in their attempts to identify culture as a "cause" of organizational performance, writers have systematically set up either an impoverished view of culture or a tautological theory. In other words, a broad view of culture, similar

to most anthropological definitions of the term, would include the process and outcomes of job performance as part of the corporate culture. When one author argued that a common culture promotes cohesion and communication, these positive "outcomes" seem part of the common culture. This suggests that the production of culture is a complex activity within which such concepts as cohesion and performance appear throughout the ongoing process of structuration.

Not all studies about organizational change, however, are conducted with a "management bias" or an impoverished view of culture, especially in the communication discipline. Howard and Geist's (1995) structurationist examination of organizational transformation is a prime example. Their examination of a merger was not undertaken to improve the results of the organizational change, nor do they underestimate the complexity of the situation. In fact, their study problematized the changes taking place and brought more voices into the discourse surrounding the changes. And not all descriptions of managing culture are solely designed to serve management's interests. For example, in his passionate account of life at W. L. Gore & Associates, Pacanowsky (1988) described the attitudes and practices of an "empowering" organization in which open, radically decentralized communication is the key feature of the culture. As a participant in the organization, Pacanowsky does not provide a detached account; rather, he offers an emotional argument for organizations that respect people, recognize maturity, and reward it. It serves as an argument for how this particular strong culture and its associated practices could be recreated elsewhere.

The motivations behind management's attempts to manipulate culture are well intentioned but are often naive. Usually, management begins with the hope of improving corporate performance by substituting a common vision and values for close supervision and autocratic management. While some scholars have argued that this practice is worse than overt domination (cf. Pilotta et al., 1988), many employees apparently see value-driven organizations as better places to work. Alvesson and Willmott (1992), however, argue that while it is easy to point out the forces of domination at work, life could be worse, and some emancipation from the abuses of power is better than none at all.

The corporate culture view engenders valuable conversations, particularly in the workplace, in that it encourages managers and employees to talk about their history, critique their activities, think in terms of processes, notice their interdependence, and take seriously human interaction. Its shortcomings stem from a monolithic view of culture, a superficial emphasis on norms and values, and a failure to consider the alternative cultures and countercultures that deserve attention and can also serve as sources of innovation and perhaps increased effectiveness.

This review of organizational culture themes has focused on the diversity of approaches and highlighted the difficulties and the vast terrain of this literature. This thematic display of culture as symbolism and performance and the approaches to texts, critique, identity, cognition, effectiveness, and climate force us to assess the congruences and disjunctures in this vast literature. As culture becomes the metaphor for all of our organizational lives, what seems salient in this work is its rapidly changing face, both as an academic concept and as a description of lived experiences. In the next section, we cover three issues that are grounds for future research investigations.

## FUTURE RESEARCH ON ORGANIZATIONAL CULTURE

The following discussion of self and community, diversity, globalization, and technology is driven by a communication orientation but is also shaped by the material conditions of our environment and the belief that those conditions need to be problematized and re-

flexively analyzed. This perspective does not rule out alternative approaches—indeed, we welcome poetry, fiction, film documentaries, and many other alternative windows into, or canvases over, performances of the concept we gingerly call organizational culture. These alternative approaches are not purely the domain of academics, since corporations such as Honeywell use plays and art to engage members in discussions about their culture. Our sense of the critical issues that need investigation are evoked by our experiences and our reading of the organizational culture metaphor.

### Self, Community, and Organizational Culture

Cultural practices—by any name—are inseparable from the stream of human life. The biological hallmark of our species, notably the presence of reflexive consciousness along with our comparatively low levels of instinct, requires the development of an elaborate social culture to guide human behavior (Geertz, 1973). The relationship between humans and their cultures, then, is a seamless and symbiotic one—human being and culture arise in relationship to one another, and cannot be separated in any meaningful way. "Being human" can thus make sense only in the context of culture(s), and the existence of any culture relies heavily on the thoughts and behavior of humans. As far as we know, humans are alone in their ability to say "I," and in so doing conceive of a "self" that is separate from an "other" or the "world." The self-other separation made possible by language and rationality is constantly under repair, as we seek identities that are simultaneously distinctive and aligned with social groups and organizations. Communication scholars thus need to investigate further the relationship between cultural phenomena in organizations such as gendered practices of team formation, the identity implications when families have multiple members employed in the same organization, or the continued strain on working parents trying to maintain positive identities in a mach-speed working world that does not leave enough time for the family.

If culture, then, provides generic cues to guide human behavior, then local cultures—organized along ethnic, gender, geographic, or organizational lines—serve as identity resources and exert powerful forces on human behavior. Academics in particular seem to want a renewed quest for community, to discover, resurrect, or invent places that seem like real places and can perhaps provide an enhanced sense of identification and support. In addition, much of this argument has to do with focusing less on the rights of individuals and more on their responsibilities to the local group (Etzioni, 1993). Deetz (e.g., 1985, 1992) has been one of the most articulate spokespersons for the importance of the relationship between organizational culture and communities. He argues that our dehumanizing, hierarchical, gendered discursive practices in organizations are indicative of a breakdown in community. As these practices are reproduced elsewhere in our lives, we need to recognize their wider power in society. Communication is at the forefront of this discussion because of its integral role in the structuring of both organizations and community. This is a call for communication scholars to focus on the "migration" of corporate practices into the community and family. For example, what values are at risk when educational institutions become "customer driven" or classrooms adopt TQM techniques? As faith in governments and political systems wanes, we also need to look toward new arenas of decision making such as immigrant support organizations, large networks of organizations like MADD (Mothers Against Drunk Driving), and activist groups like gay and lesbian legal action funds. We need to ask how the communicative practices of community organizations differ from more traditional/hierarchical organizations, if they do. For example, we know quite a bit about the culture-building activities of large-company

founders, but we know much less about those who started community-based organizations and what happened after they left.

These local cultures are the symbolic milieux, the "webs of significance" made famous by Weber and Geertz. But webs both provide easy travel and catch flies—culture always appears both as agency and constraint. At a theoretical level, understanding the role of culture as agency in both the production of self-identity and organizational change would be particularly illuminating. So, for example, can organizations that use concertive control also develop a reflexive dialogue about control? Research that examines the relationship between institutions and local organizations—for example, school boards, parents' groups, religious organizations—would be particularly salient. What do we really know about local community "power structures" (e.g., concerns about health or family) as they relate to disembedded practices brought directly from work? We need to investigate whether the decision-making practices are more open or participative, less gendered, or more moral.

## Globalization and Organizational Culture

Globalization is causing widespread changes in multiple constructions of culture both in and outside of organizations. The reality of a global marketplace is leading to homogenization of products and services worldwide and the increasing presence and influence of corporations in public and private life (Deetz, 1992). And the rise of a global economy has meant a rapid destabilization of the labor force, such that companies demonstrate no allegiance to place and seek the best value for their labor dollars worldwide (Barnet & Cavanaugh, 1994). In an even broader sense, our present situation might be characterized as reflecting a crisis of loyalty or identification. The actions of global corporations serve to undermine the relied-on allegiances and commitments made between workers and employees in every company worldwide. Even in Japan, which has for decades relied on lifetime employment, the system is eroding. Business deals that formerly relied on trust and relationships are increasingly going to the lowest bidder in a hypercompetitive worldwide labor market. The result is a widespread feeling among workers of fear, instability, and the absence of loyalty. Culture researchers need to observe how this "new social contract" with employees is enacted and how workers express alienation (graffiti on the walls?) or fear. Are organizations finding spaces for alternative voices, or have they developed cultural panopticons that silence deviants? Another question is, How will employees establish alternative loyalties to the firm? This phenomenon is similar to what Barnet and Cavanaugh (1994) call "globalization from below," which they say is on the rise—emergent networks of people at the grassroots level taking responsibility for developing meaningful relationships in the face of (and often in direct response to) corporate colonization and homogenization.

There are issues that tie questions of self and community to globalization. Giddens's (1993) analysis makes it clear that the issue is not just whether or not we invest ourselves in a job or company that could disappear tomorrow, or one that might continue to exist without us, but the role these work experiences play in the trajectory and transformation of self and identity. This is essentially an issue of the reflexive construction of self as organized in concert with the economic, moral, and practical features of organizational culture(s). Restated, how are we changing and how are organizational cultures changing simultaneously within this environment of persistent organizational reinvention (Eisenberg, in press)?

The rise of multinational, "imperial" corporations has many implications for researchers of organizational culture (Barnet & Cavanaugh, 1994; Eisenberg & Goodall, 2000). Globalization has made organizations pay at-tention to the contextual differences involved in doing business with consumers and employees originating in different cultures. More important, global capitalism and the accompanying decline of the political nation-state has led societies worldwide to be permeated by the substance of corporate culture, even in places where local or national cultures might better serve the interests of the people involved (Barnet & Cavanaugh, 1994). Scholars need to investigate the new relationships among employee groups of foreign national organizations and the adaptation, or diminution, of practices as corporate cultures intertwine with different national cultures. What are the implications for work effectiveness, solidarity, or decision making as "cultural enclaves" emerge within multiethnic organizations?

And the migratory nature of cultures is especially relevant given the close connection between large migrations, what Kotkin (1994) calls "diaspora by design," and the organizations that constitute the empire of these global tribes. For example, future organizational culture research might compare Taiwanese research and development organizations in the United States, which tend to be run by American-educated Chinese who are fluent in English, with Japanese research and development firms located in the States that are largely outposts manned by a rotating cadre of foreign executives. What are the local implications of that warning from the 1980s that "Chernobyl is everywhere"? In other words, how might we discuss the rising belief that there are no longer "others" only "us"? Since much of the focus concerning globalization is either on the media or the economy, we need to have a better understanding of the dominant cultural practices of those industries and institutions as well as the key organizations and leaders and a better understanding of the subcultures of professional groups such as economists and the fragmented lives of ex-patriots. A critical issue is our knowledge of the degree to which organizational culture is a mediated phenomenon. This is the question: What does culture mean in global organizations? Is it the constant structuring of local knowledge and practices within larger corporate systems?

Issues surrounding the mobility of the workforce have always been a societal concern, but they have not been a major feature of the organizational culture literature. Globalization is one of the drivers of growing workforce diversity in almost every industry, raising critical questions about ways of coordinating people of markedly different backgrounds to promote organizational and personal goals. Much of this challenge is communicative, but it is not just at the level of language translation. Key questions surround sensemaking in these environments; for example, are particular rhetorical forms developing that promote a sense of unity amid a diversity of interpretations? Training programs that deal with diversity or multicultural differences ought to be studied to determine the degree to which they are vehicles for personal growth and learning and/or hegemonic devices that attempt to impose cultural homogeneity in large organizations. This also suggests that we need to examine our related constructs culturally; for example, we would not be surprised to discover that our connotations of conflict resolution are overly parochial and that they may need expanding to explicate the tensions that arise from multiethnic cliques in the workplace. It appears that if we are to have a "cultured" organizational communication literature, then the cultural biases of our constructs and frameworks need to be more clearly articulated.

## *Technology*

Technology is changing the nature of work in organizations, as well as the nature of jobs. As the saying goes, technology applies only to things that were not around when you were young. To many children born since the late 1970s, for example, computers are not a technology, but a taken-for-granted part of the social fabric. This is true even for children who have never seen a computer, because the language of information networks and virtual reality and their underlying principles form the basis of children's television shows and toys (e.g., Power Rangers, "transformers," virtual reality games). Some research has occurred in this increasingly important area—for example, Barley (1986), who studied the adoption of CT scanners; Prasad (1993), who took a "symbolic interactionist" approach to work computerization in an HMO setting; and Aydin (1989), who showed that organizational culture and professional subcultures (e.g., doctors vs. nurses vs. pharmacists vs. social workers) have a strong impact on the ways in which technology is implemented. But the larger work of theorizing about the role of technology in creating and changing culture across different locales remains relatively unexplored.

We can expect the new technologies of today (groupware and other computer-mediated communication, virtual reality, biotechnology, multimedia, and the Internet) to have as powerful an impact on work cultures as their predecessors (telephones, e-mail, and voice mail). For example, electronic mail has made an enormous difference in the way many companies look with regard to paper flow, hallway talk, closeness of supervision, perceptions of privacy, speed of expected turnaround of work, and politeness norms. The reason it is so important for organizational culture researchers to pay attention to technology is that technology plays a key role in the structuring of behavior—of space, time, and interaction patterns. For instance, in the era of online newspapers, an organizational credo like "all the news fit to print" becomes almost quaint. In addition, the future of many organizations—and this will likely be the case across most industries and parts of the world—will thus be largely characterized by flexible learning through instantaneous communication. We ought to investigate the cultural practices that will be critical not just for organizational effectiveness but also the individual management of identity. What sources of resistance will appear in response to this pace, these expectations, and the associated reward structure, and how will they be interpreted?

Just as the idea of "job" is falling under scrutiny today, the idea of an organization as a place bounded in space and time is already problematic. This trend began with telecommuting and various forms of strategic alliances that linked "coworkers" electronically. In some cases, electronic communication augments other media, but in an increasing number of situations, employees' sole sources of contact are virtual; hence the idea of a virtual office or virtual team in which people report being "here," at work, when they are in effect connected via network in cyberspace. Even when there is a physical workplace, employers are beginning to replace stationary offices with "portable" ones. At the advertising firm Chiat Day, for example, employees check in when they arrive at work and are issued a computer and a cellular phone, then are encouraged to work anywhere in the company (depending on the specific needs of the project). These new patterns of work have implications for our theorizing about what it means to be "local." Our understanding of power and authority in organizations needs to change so that we can distinguish status even when no one is "home" or when the lines between work and home are so blurred that they become difficult to see. The question for cultural scholars may be less whether these events are good or bad but how are they interpreted and what moral lens is being used to discuss them. We need to be able to identify the communicative construction as well as the communication skill and components of these newly flexible jobs. We need to be sensitive to issues of ageism in firms where the oldest vice president is 27. We need to ask what are the cultural implications of leaving many people out of the information revolution as the technology gap grows ever wider.

## CONCLUSION

At one time, we considered titling this chapter "The Myth of Organizational Culture,"

suggesting that what passes for organizational culture is less distinctive and more reflective of larger societal groupings than most of us researchers would like to admit. In fact, the emphasis on benchmarking in business—evaluating oneself against other excellent companies—and the total quality movement led countless organizations to adopt eerily similar practices both within and outside of their industries (e.g., high-involvement management, shop floor control, capacity planning, future searches, strategic planning, reengineering, process improvement teams, learning organizations, knowledge management consultants, and training programs). None of this should be all that surprising, since the most significant information exchange among organizations has always occurred through personnel flows, where Company A hires a manager from Company B, or when workers in an industry (e.g., computers) move among companies following major developments and in pursuit of work. Nevertheless, the widespread acceleration of "cultural traffic" (Alvesson, 1993b) has led overall to reduced distinctiveness among companies and greater influence on the part of larger social groupings, such as gender, profession, class, and ethnicity, on organizational cultures. Arguably the most original contribution of Martin's (1992) book is her conceptualization of each organizational culture as a "nexus," a site at which cultural forces (practices, assumptions, values, interpretations) interact. The implication for communication research is that we must widen our lens in studying organizational culture and not assume that the reasons for organizational behavior are best found in or even near the organization. On the contrary, just as Geertz (1973) remarked that anthropologists "don't study villages, they study in villages," so too do organizational ethnographers study in organizations. As boundaries or organizations become less definite, it will make sense to worry less about "organizations" and more about the organizing and structuring of communicative relationships and our discursively produced environments. We need to push our conceptual development and the sophistication of our investigations. We need the resources to study large, networked organizations and the skills to delve into multiethnic cliques. We must adapt our theoretical frameworks so that we can use such concepts as complexity theory to investigate the myriad of cultural forces made manifest at an organizational nexus. We need to understand that our work becomes part of the cultural phenomena that we are studying and that we are, in part, reflexively creating the future of organizations.

## NOTES

1. It is important to note that Schall's (1993) conception of culture as shared communicative rules is not a strictly cognitive approach since the rules operate on behaviors and do not regulate thoughts and cognitions.

2. We uncovered several unpublished dissertations from the early 1990s conducted by education researchers interested in communication climates in schools.

## REFERENCES

Aktouf, 0. (1992). Management and theories of organizations in the 1990s: Toward a radical humanism. *Academy of Management Review, 17,* 407-432.

Alvesson, M. (1993a). Cultural-ideological modes of management control: A theory and a case study of a professional service company. In S. A. Deetz (Ed.), *Communication yearbook 16* (pp. 3-42). Newbury Park, CA: Sage.

Alvesson, M. (1993b). *Cultural perspectives on organizations.* New York: Cambridge University Press.

Alvesson, M., & Willmott, H. (1992). On the idea of emancipation in management and organizational studies. *Academy of Management Review, 17,* 432-465.

Aydin, C. (1989). Occupational adaptation to computerized medical information systems. *Journal of Health and Social Behavior, 30,* 163-179.

Baker, E. L. (1980). Managing organizational culture. *Management Review, 69,* 8-13.

Bakhtin, M. (1981). *The dialogic-imagination: Four essays by M. M. Bakhtin* (C. Emerson & M. Holquist, Trans.). Austin: University of Texas Press.

Banks, S., & Riley, P. (1993). Structuration theory as an ontology for communication research. In S. A. Deetz (Ed.), *Communication yearbook 16* (pp. 167-196). Newbury Park, CA: Sage.

Bantz, C. R. (1993). *Understanding organizations: Interpreting organizational communication cultures.* Columbia: University of South Carolina Press.

Barker, J. R., & Cheney, G. (1994). The concept and the practices of discipline in contemporary organizational life. *Communication Monographs, 61,* 19-43.

Barley, S. (1983). Semiotics and the study of occupational and organizational cultures. *Administrative Science Quarterly, 28,* 393-413.

Barley, S. (1986). Technology as an occasion for structuring: Evidence from observations of CT scanners and the social order of radiology departments. *Administrative Science Quarterly, 33,* 24-61.

Barley, S. (1990). The alignment of technology and structure through roles and networks. *Administrative Science Quarterly, 35,* 61-103.

Barnet, R. J., & Cavanaugh, J. (1994). Creating a level playing field. *Technology Review, 97,* 46-48.

Barnett, G. A. (1988). Communication and organizational culture. In G. M. Goldhaber & G. A. Barnett (Eds.), *Handbook of organizational communication* (pp. 101-130). Norwood, NJ: Ablex.

Bastien, D., McPhee, R. D., & Bolton, K. (1995). A study and extended theory of the structuration of climate. *Communication Monographs, 62,* 87-109.

Bennis, W. (1969). *Organizational development: Its nature, origins, and prospects.* Reading, MA: Addison-Wesley.

Boland, R., & Hoffman, R. (1983). Humor in a machine shop. In L. Pondy, P. Frost, G. Morgan, & T. Dandridge (Eds.), *Organizational symbolism* (pp. 187-198). Greenwich, CT: JAI.

Bormann, E. G. (1983). Symbolic convergence: Organizational communication and culture. In L. L. Putnam & M. E. Pacanowsky (Eds.), *Communication and organizations: An interpretive approach* (pp. 99-122). Beverly Hills, CA: Sage.

Brown, M. H. (1990a). Defining stories in organizations: Characteristics and functions. In J. A. Anderson (Ed.), *Communication yearbook 13* (pp. 162-190). Newbury Park, CA: Sage.

Brown, M. H. (1990b). "Reading" an organization's culture: An examination of stories in nursing homes. *Journal of Applied Communication Research, 18,* 64-75.

Brown, M. H., & McMillan, J. (1991). Culture as text: The development of an organizational narrative. *Southern Communication Journal, 49,* 27-42.

Burke, M. J., Borucki, C. C., & Hurley, A. (1992). Reconceptualizing psychological climate in a retail service environment: A multiple stakeholder perspective. *Journal of Applied Psychology, 7,* 717-730.

Carbaugh, D. (1988). Cultural terms and tensions in the speech at a television station. *Western Journal of Speech Communication, 52,* 216-237.

Chatman, J. A., & Jehn, K. A. (1994). Assessing the relationship between industry characteristics and organizational culture: How different can you be? *Academy of Management Journal, 37,* 522-553.

Cheney, G. (1991). *Rhetoric in organizational society: Managing multiple identities.* Columbia: University of South Carolina Press.

Cheney, G. (1995). Democracy in the workplace: Theory and practice from the communication perspective. *Journal of Applied Communication Research, 23,* 167-200.

Clair, R. (1993). The use of framing devices to sequester organizational narratives: Hegemony and harassment. *Communication Monographs, 60,* 113-136.

Clifford, J. (1983). On ethnographic authority. *Representations, 1,* 118-146.

Clifford, J., & Marcus, G. E. (1986). *Writing culture: The poetics and politics of ethnography.* Berkeley: University of California Press.

Conquergood, S. (1991). Rethinking ethnography: Towards a critical cultural politics. *Communication Monographs, 58,* 179-194.

Conrad, C. (1983). Organizational power: Faces and symbolic forms. In L. L. Putnam & M. E. Pacanowsky (Eds.), *Communication and organizations: An interpretive approach* (pp. 173-194). Beverly Hills, CA: Sage.

Contractor, N., Eisenberg, E. M., & Monge, P. (1994). Antecedents and outcomes of interpretive diversity in organizations. Paper presented at the annual meeting of the International Communication Association, May, Chicago.

D'Andrade, R. G. (1984). Cultural meaning systems. In R. A. Shweder & R. A. LeVine (Eds.), *Culture theory: Essays on mind, self, and emotion* (pp. 88-121). Cambridge, UK: Cambridge University Press.

Deal, T. E., & Kennedy, A. A. (1982). *Corporate cultures: The rites and rituals of corporate life.* Reading, MA: Addison-Wesley.

Deetz, S. A. (1985). Ethical considerations in cultural research in organizations. In P. J. Frost, L. F. Moore, M. R. Louis, C. C. Lundberg, & J. Martin (Eds.), *Organizational culture* (pp. 253-270). Beverly Hills, CA: Sage.

Deetz, S. A. (1992). *Democracy in an age of corporate colonization: Developments in communication and the politics of everyday life.* Albany: State University of New York Press.

Deetz, S. A., & Kersten, A. (1983). Critical models of interpretive research. In L. L. Putnam & M. E. Pacanowsky (Eds.), *Communication and organizations: An interpretive approach* (pp. 147-172). Beverly Hills, CA: Sage.

Downs, C. (1979). The relationship between communication and job satisfaction. In R. Houseman, C. Logue, & D. Freshley (Eds.). *Readings in interpersonal and organizational communication* (pp. 363-376). Boston: Allyn & Bacon.

Eisenberg, E. (In press). Building a mystery: Toward a new theory of communication and identity. *Journal of Communication.*

Eisenberg, E., & Goodall, H. L., Jr. (2000). *Organizational communication* (3rd ed.). New York: St. Martin's.

Eisenberg, E. M., Murphy, A., & Andrews, L. (1998). Openness and decision making in the search for a university provost. *Communication Monographs, 65,* 1-23.

Erez, M., & Earley, P. C. (1993). *Culture, self-identity, and work.* New York: Oxford University Press.

Etzioni, A. (1993). *The spirit of community: Rights, responsibilities, and the communitarian agenda.* New York: Crown.

Falcione, R. L., & Kaplan, E. A. (1984). Organizational climate, communication, and culture. In R. Bostrom (Ed.), *Communication yearbook 8* (pp. 285-309). Beverly Hills, CA: Sage.

Falcione, R. L., Sussman, L., & Herden, R. P. (1987). Communication climate in organizations. In F. M. Jablin, L. L. Putnam, K. H. Roberts, & L. W. Porter (Eds.), *Handbook of organizational communication: An interdisciplinary perspective* (pp. 195-227). Newbury Park, CA: Sage.

Farace, R. V., Monge, P. R., & Russell, H. M. (1977). *Communicating and organizing.* Reading, MA: Addison-Wesley.

Ferguson, K. (1984). *The feminist case against bureaucracy.* Philadelphia: Temple University Press.

French, W. L., & Bell, C. (1973). *Organizational development.* Englewood Cliffs, NJ: Prentice Hall.

Frost, P. J., Moore, L. F., Louis, M. R., Lundberg, C. C., & Martin, J. (Eds.). (1991). *Reframing organizational culture.* Newbury Park, CA: Sage.

Geertz, C. (1973). *The interpretation of cultures.* New York: Basic Books.

Geertz, C. (1988). *Works and lives: The anthropologist as author.* Stanford, CA: Stanford University Press.

Gergen, K. (1991). *The saturated self: Dilemmas of identity in contemporary life.* New York: Basic Books.

Giddens, A. (1991). *Modernity and self-identity: Self and society in the late modern age.* Stanford, CA: Stanford University Press.

Giddens, A. (1993). *New rules of sociological method* (2nd ed.). Stanford, CA: Stanford University Press.

Goffman, E. (1959). *The presentation of self in everyday life.* Garden City, NY: Anchor Doubleday.

Goodall, H. L. (1989). *Casing a promised land.* Carbondale: Southern Illinois University Press.

Goodall, H. L. (1991). *Living in the rock 'n roll mystery: Reading context, self, and others as clues.* Carbondale: Southern Illinois University Press.

Gronn, P. (1983). Talk as the work: The accomplishment of school administration. *Administrative Science Quarterly, 28,* 1-21.

Hellriegel, D., & Slocum, J. (1974). Organizational climate: Measures, research, and contingencies. *Academy of Management Journal, 17,* 255-280.

Hofstede, G. H. (1983). National cultures in four dimensions. *International Studies of Management and Organization, 13,* 46-74.

Hofstede, G. H. (1991). *Culture and organizations: Software of the mind.* New York: McGraw-Hill.

Hofstede, G. H., Neuijen, B., Ohayv, D. D., & Sanders, G. (1990). Measuring organizational cultures: A qualitative and quantitative study across twenty cases. *Administrative Science Quarterly, 35,* 286-316.

Holquist, M. (1990). *Dialogism: Bakhtin and his world.* London: Routledge.

Howard, L. A., & Geist, P. (1995). Ideological positioning in organizational change. *Communication Monographs, 62,* 110-131.

Jackson, M. (1989). *Paths toward a clearing.* Bloomington: Indiana University Press.

James, L. R., James, L. A., & Ashe, D. K. (1990). The meaning of organizations: The role of cognition and values. In B. Schneider (Ed.), *Organizational climate and culture* (pp. 40-84). San Francisco: Jossey-Bass.

James, L. R., & Jones, A. P. (1974). Organizational climate: A review of theory and research. *Psychological Bulletin, 16,* 74-113.

Jaques, E. (1951). *The changing culture of a factory: A study of authority and participation in an industrial setting.* London: Tavistock.

Jelinek, M., Smircich, L., & Hirsch, P. (Eds.). (1983). Organizational culture [Special issue]. *Administrative Science Quarterly, 28*(3).

Jermier, J. M. (1991). Critical epistemology and the study of organizational culture: Reflections on "Street Corner Society." In P. J. Frost, L. F. Moore, M. R. Louis, C. C. Lundberg, & J. Martin (Eds.), *Reframing organizational culture* (pp. 223-233). Newbury Park, CA: Sage.

Johnson, B. M. (1977). *Communication: The process of organizing.* Boston: Allyn & Bacon (Reprinted American Press, 1981)

Johnston, H. R., Jr. (1976). A new conceptualization of source of organizational climate. *Administrative Science Quarterly, 21,* 95-103.

Katz, D., & Kahn, R. L. (1978). *The social psychology of organizations* (2nd ed.). New York: John Wiley.

Knight, J. P. (1990). Literature as equipment for killing: Performance as rhetoric in military training camps. *Text and Performance Quarterly, 10,* 157-168.

Knuf, J. (1993). "Ritual" in organizational culture theory: Some theoretical reflections and a plea for terminological rigor. In S. A. Deetz (Ed.), *Communication yearbook 16* (pp. 112-121). Newbury Park, CA: Sage.

Kondo, D. (1990). *Crafting selves: Power, gender, and discourses of identity in a Japanese workplace.* Chicago: University of Chicago Press.

Kotkin, J. (1994). *Tribes: How race, religion, and identity determine success in the new global economy.* New York: Random House.

Kotter, J. P., & Heskett, J. L. (1992). *Corporate culture and performance.* New York: Free Press.

Krackhardt, D., & Kilduff, M. (1990). Friendship patterns and culture: The control of organizational diversity. *American Anthropologist, 91,* 142-155.

Kreiner, K., & Schultz, M. (1993). Informal collaboration in R&D: The formation of networks across organizations. *Organization Studies, 14,* 189-209.

Kunda, G. (1992). *Engineering culture: Control and commitment in a high-tech corporation.* Philadelphia: Temple University Press.

Linstead, S., & Grafton-Small, R. (1992). On reading organizational culture. *Organization Studies, 13,* 331-355.

Louis, M. R. (1990). Acculturation in the workplace: Newcomers as lay ethnographers. In B. Schneider (Ed.), *Organizational climate and culture* (pp. 85-129). San Francisco: Jossey-Bass.

Marcus, G. E., & Fischer, M. J. (Eds.). (1986). *Anthropology as cultural critique: An experimental moment in the human sciences.* Chicago: University of Chicago Press.

Martin, J. (1992). *Cultures in organizations: Three perspectives.* New York: Oxford University Press.

Martin, J., & Meyerson, D. (1988). Organizational culture and the denial, channeling and acknowledgement of ambiguity. In L. Pondy, R. Boland, Jr., & H. Thomas (Eds.), *Managing ambiguity and change* (pp. 93-125). New York: John Wiley.

McCollom, M. (1994). The cultures of work organizations. *Academy of Management Review, 19,* 836-839.

McDonald, P. (1991). The Los Angeles Olympic Organizing Committee: Developing organizational culture in the short run. In P. J. Frost, L. F. Moore, M. R. Louis, C. C. Lundberg, & J. Martin (Eds.), *Reframing organizational culture* (pp. 26-38). Newbury Park, CA: Sage.

Mead, G. H. (1934). *Mind, self and society.* Chicago: University of Chicago Press.

Moenaert, R., Souder, W. E., Meyer, A. D., & DeSchoolmeester, D. (1994). R and D marketing integration mechanisms, communication flows, and innovation success. *Journal of Product and Innovation Management, 7,* 31-46.

Mohan, M. (1993). *Organizational communication and cultural vision: Approaches for analysis.* Albany: State University of New York Press.

Moran, T., & Volkwein, J. F. (1992). The cultural approach to the formation of organizational climate. *Human Relations, 45,* 19-48.

Mumby, D. (1988). *Communication and power in organizations: Discourse, ideology and domination.* Norwood, NJ: Ablex.

Mumby, D. K., & Putnam, L. L. (1992). The politics of emotion: A feminist reading of bounded rationality. *Academy of Management Review, 17,* 465-486.

Mumby, D. K., & Stohl, C. (1991). Power and discourse in organization studies: Absence and the dialectic of control. *Discourse & Society, 2,* 313-332.

Myerson, D. (1991). Normal ambiguity? A glimpse of an occupational culture. In P. J. Frost, L. F. Moore, M. R. Louis, C. C. Lundberg, & J. Martin (Eds.), *Reframing organizational culture* (pp. 131-144). Newbury Park, CA: Sage.

O'Reilly, C., Chatman, J., & Caldwell, D. (1991). People and organizational culture: A Q-sort approach to assessing person-organization fit. *Academy of Management Journal, 34,* 487-516.

Ostroff, C. (1993). The effects of climate and personal influences on individual behavior and attitudes in organizations. *Organizational Behavior and Human Decision Processes, 56,* 56-91.

Ouchi, W., & Wilkins, A. (1985). Organizational culture. *Annual Review of Sociology, 11,* 457-483.

Pacanowsky, M. E. (1988). Communication and the empowering organization. In J. A. Anderson (Ed.), *Communication yearbook 11* (pp. 356-379). Newbury Park, CA: Sage.

Pacanowsky, M. E., & O'Donnell-Trujillo, N. (1983). Organizational communication as cultural performance. *Communication Monographs, 50,* 126-147.

Peters, T. J., & Waterman, R. J. (1982). *In search of excellence.* New York: Harper & Row.

Pettigrew, A. M. (1979). On studying organizational cultures. *Administrative Science Quarterly, 24,* 570-581.

Pfeffer, J. (1981). Management as symbolic action: The creation and maintenance of organization paradigms. In B. Staw & L. Cummings (Eds.), *Research in organizational behavior* (Vol. 3, pp. 1-52). Greenwich, CT: JAI.

Pilotta, J. J., Widman, T., & Jasco, S. A. (1988). Meaning and action in the organizational setting: An interpretive approach. In J. A. Anderson (Ed.), *Communication yearbook 11* (pp. 310-334). Newbury Park, CA: Sage.

Pondy, L. R., & Mitroff, I. (1979). Beyond open systems models of organizations. In B. M. Staw (Ed.), *Research in organizational behavior* (Vol. 1, pp. 3-39). Greenwich, CT: JAI.

Poole, M. S. (1985). Communication and organizational climates: Review, critique, and a new perspective. In R. McPhee & P. Tompkins (Eds.), *Organizational communication: Traditional themes and new directions* (pp. 79-108). Beverly Hills, CA: Sage.

Poole, M. S., & McPhee, R. D. (1983). A structurational analysis of organizational climate. In L. L. Putnam & M. E. Pacanowsky (Eds.), *Communication and organizations: An interpretive approach* (pp. 195-220). Beverly Hills, CA: Sage.

Prasad, P. (1993). Symbolic processes in the implementation of technological change: A symbolic interactionist study of work computerization. *Academy of Management Journal, 36,* 1400-1429.

Putnam, L. L., & Pacanowsky, M. E. (Eds.). (1983). *Communication and organizations: An interpretive approach.* Beverly Hills, CA: Sage.

Putnam, L. L., Phillips, N., & Chapman, P. (1996). Metaphors of communication and organization. In S. R. Clegg, C. Hardy, & W. R. Nord (Eds.), *Handbook of organization studies* (pp. 375-408). London: Sage.

Putnam, L. L., Van Hoeven, S. A., & Bullis, C. A. (1991). The role of rituals and fantasy themes in teachers' bargaining. *Western Journal of Speech Communication, 55,* 85-103.

Rabinow, P., & Sullivan, W. M. (1979). *Interpretive social science: A reader.* Berkeley: University of California Press.

Redding, C. (1972). *Communication within the organization: An interpretive review of theory and research.* New York: Industrial Communication Council.

Rentsch, J. R. (1990). Climate and culture interaction and qualitative differences in organizational meanings. *Journal of Applied Psychology, 75,* 668-682.

Ricoeur, P. (1971). The model of the text: Meaningful action considered as a text. *Social Research, 38,* 529-562.

Riley, P. (1983). A structurationist account of political cultures. *Administrative Science Quarterly, 28,* 414-437.

Riley, P. (1991). Cornerville as narration. In P. J. Frost, L. F. Moore, M. R. Louis, C. C. Lundberg, & J. Martin (Eds.), *Reframing organizational culture* (pp. 215-223). Newbury Park, CA: Sage.

Riley, P. (1993). Arguing for "ritualistic" pluralism: The tension between privilege and the mundane. In S. A. Deetz (Ed.), *Communication yearbook 16* (pp. 112-121). Newbury Park, CA: Sage.

Rogers, R. A. (1994). Rhythm and the performance of organization. *Text and Performance Quarterly, 14,* 222-237.

Rorty, R. (1989). *Contingency, irony, and solidarity.* Cambridge, UK: Cambridge University Press.

Sackmann, S. (1991). *Cultural knowledge in organizations.* Newbury Park, CA: Sage.

Saffold, G. (1988). Culture traits, strength, and organizational performance: Moving beyond strong culture. *Academy of Management Review, 13,* 546-559.

Sashkin, M., & Kiser, K. (1993). *Putting total quality management to work.* San Francisco: Berrett-Koehler.

Schall, M. S. (1983). A communication rules approach to organizational culture. *Administrative Science Quarterly, 28,* 557-587.

Scheibel, D. (1992). Faking identity in clubland: The communicative performance of "fake ID." *Text and Performance Quarterly, 12,* 160-175.

Scheibel, D. (1994). Graffiti and "film school" culture: Displaying alienation. *Communication Monographs, 61,* 1-18.

Schein, E. (1985). *Organizational culture and leadership.* San Francisco: Jossey-Bass.

Schneider, B. (Ed.). (1990). *Organizational climate and culture* (Frontiers of industrial and organizational psychology). San Francisco: Jossey-Bass.

Schneider, B., Gunnarson, S., & Niles-Jolly, K. (1994). Creating the climate and culture of success. *Organizational Dynamics, 23,* 17-30.

Schneider, B., Wheeler, J., & Cox, J. (1992). A passion for service: Using content analysis to explicate service climate themes. *Journal of Applied Psychology, 77,* 705-717.

Shockley-Zalabak, P., & Morley, D. D. (1994). Creating a culture: A longitudinal examination of the influence of management and employee values on communication rule stability and emergence. *Human Communication Research, 20,* 334-355.

Shweder, R. A. (1991). *Thinking through cultures: Expeditions in cultural psychology.* Cambridge, MA: Harvard University Press.

Shweder, R. A., & LeVine, R. A. (Eds.). (1984). *Cultural theory: Essays on mind, self, and emotion.* New York: Cambridge University Press.

Siehl, C. (1985). After the founder: An opportunity to manage culture. In P. J. Frost, L. F. Moore, M. R. Louis, C. C. Lundberg, & J. Martin (Eds.), *Organizational culture* (pp. 125-140). Beverly Hills, CA: Sage.

Siehl, C., & Martin, J. (1990). Organizational culture: A key to financial performance? In B. Schneider (Ed.), *Organizational climate and culture* (pp. 241-281). San Francisco: Jossey-Bass.

Smircich, L., & Calás, M. B. (1987). Organizational culture: A critical assessment. In F. M. Jablin, L. L. Putnam, K. H. Roberts, & L. W. Porter (Eds.), *Handbook of organizational communication: An interdisciplinary perspective* (pp. 228-263). Newbury Park, CA: Sage.

Smith, R. C., & Eisenberg, E. (1987). Conflict at Disneyland: A root-metaphor analysis. *Communication Monographs, 54,* 367-380.

Spencer, B. A. (1994). Models of organization and total quality management: A comparison and critical evaluation. *Academy of Management Review, 19,* 446-471.

Stoller, P. (1989). *The taste of ethnographic things.* Philadelphia: University of Pennsylvania Press.

Strutton, D., & Pelton, L. (1994). The relationship between psychological climate in sales organizations and sales manager-salesperson solidarity. *Mid-Atlantic Journal of Business, 30,* 153-175.

Taylor, B. C. (1990). Reminiscences of Los Alamos: Narrative, critical theory and the organizational subject. *Western Journal of Speech Communication, 54,* 395-419.

Taylor, B. C. (1993). Register of the repressed: Women's voice and body in the nuclear weapons organization. *Quarterly Journal of Speech, 79,* 267-285.

Thompson, K. R., & Luthans, F. (1990). Organizational culture: A behavioral perspective. In B. Schneider (Ed.), *Organizational climate and culture* (pp. 319-344). San Francisco: Jossey-Bass.

Tompkins, E. V. B., Tompkins, P. K., & Cheney, G. (1989). Organizations as arguments: Discovering, expressing, and analyzing the premises for decisions. *Journal of Management Systems, 1,* 35-48.

Tompkins, P. K. (1987). Translating organizational theory: Symbolism over substance. In F. M. Jablin, L. L. Putnam, K. H. Roberts, & L. W. Porter (Eds.), *Handbook of organizational communication: An interdisciplinary perspective* (pp. 70-96). Newbury Park, CA: Sage.

Tompkins, P. K., & Cheney, G. (1988). On the facts of the text as the basis of human communication research. In J. A. Anderson (Ed.), *Communication yearbook 11* (pp. 455-481). Newbury Park, CA: Sage.

Toulson, P., & Smith, M. (1994). The relationship between climate and employee perceptions of personnel management practices. *Public Personnel Management, 23,* 453-469.

Trice, H. M., & Beyer, J. M. (1984). Studying organizational cultures through rites and ceremonials. *Academy of Management Review, 9,* 653-669.

Trujillo, N. (1992). Interpreting (the work and talk of) baseball: Perspectives on baseball park culture. *Western Journal of Communication, 56,* 350-371.

Trujillo, N., & Dionisopoulos, G. (1987). Cop talk, police stories, and the social construction of organizational drama. *Central States Speech Journal, 38,* 196-209.

Turner, V. (1980). Social dramas and stories about them. *Critical Inquiry, 7,* 141-168.

Turnipseed, D., & Turnipseed, P. (1992). Assessing organizational climate: Exploratory results with a new diagnostic model. *Leadership and Organizational Development Journal, 13,* 7-15.

Van Maanen, J. (1988). *Tales of the field: On writing ethnography.* Chicago: University of Chicago Press.

Van Maanen, J. (1991). The smile factory: Work at Disneyland. In P. J. Frost, L. F. Moore, M. R. Louis, C. C. Lundberg, & J. Martin (Eds.), *Reframing organizational culture* (pp. 58-76). Newbury Park, CA: Sage.

Van Maanen, J., & Kunda, G. (1989). "Real feelings": Emotional expression and organizational culture. In L. L. Cummings & B. M. Staw (Eds.), *Research in organizational behavior* (Vol. 11, pp. 43-104). Greenwich, CT: JAI.

Vygotsky, L. S. (1962). Thought and language (E. Hanfmann & G. Vakar, Eds. and Trans.). Cambridge, MA: MIT Press.

Weick, K. E. (1979). *The social psychology of organizing* (2nd ed.). Reading, MA: Addison-Wesley.

Weick, K. E. (1991). The vulnerable system: An analysis of the Tenerife air disaster. In P. J. Frost, L. F. Moore, M. R. Louis, C. C. Lundberg, & J. Martin (Eds.), *Reframing organizational culture* (pp. 117-130). Newbury Park, CA: Sage.

Wentworth, W. (1980). *Context and understanding.* New York: Elsevier.

Whyte, W. F. (1943). *Street corner society.* Chicago: University of Chicago Press.

Wilkins, A., & Dyer, W. G. (1988). Toward culturally sensitive theories of culture change. *Academy of Management Review, 13,* 522-533.

Wilkins, A., & Ouchi, W. A. (1983). Efficient cultures: Exploring the relationship between culture and organizational performance. *Administrative Science Quarterly, 28,* 468-481.

Witmer, D. F. (1997). Communication and recovery: Structuration as an ontological approach to organizational culture. *Communication Monographs, 64,* 324-349.

Youngbae, K., & Lee, B. (1995). R and D project team climate and team performance in Korea: A multidimensional approach. *R&D Management, 25,* 179-197.

Zohar, D. (1980). Safety climate in industrial organizations: Theoretical and applied implications. *Journal of Applied Psychology, 65,* 96-102.

# 10

# Globalizing Organizational Communication

❖ CYNTHIA STOHL
*Purdue University*

*My grandfather was local, my father was national, and I have become European. . . .*
*It is no longer true that you can stay local and survive.*

—Antoine Ribald, chairman of the French manufacturer B.S.N.,
quoted in Magee (1989).

*Just being a European company would constrain us.*
*Like Socrates, we are citizens of the world, we converse with all.*

—Per Blanker, director of a large Danish can manufacturing plant,
personal interview, April 1989

*In today's global business community, there is no single best approach . . . each culture has*
*its own way of building relationships, motivating employees, negotiating, and working.*

—Fons Trompenaars (1994, p. 3)

On my office door at Purdue University there is a state map of Indiana showing the locations of over 315 organizations with significant international involvement.[1] Among the national flags scattered across the state we find a total of 95 Japanese-owned companies including Subaru-Isuzu Automotive; a corn-processing plant owned by the English company Lyle Stuart; a large German Health Diagnostics Corporation, Boerhinger-Mannein; the famous Irish paper company, Jefferson Smurfit; and literally hundreds of other companies with strong links in over 80 countries across five continents. And this map doesn't even feature the large number of voluntary/nonprofit organizations such as the YWCA, Amnesty International, and Greenpeace, which are part of a network of more than 18,000 international nongovernmental organizations that link individuals, families, and communities across the globe (Boulding, 1990). Nor does it include educational institutions such as Purdue University, which employs over 1,000 international faculty and scholars, enrolls over 4,100 international students, has faculty collaboration and exchange with more than 140 international institutions, and sends hundreds of students to study abroad every year (Office of International Programs, 1999).

Clearly, internationalization is ubiquitous. By the end of the 1980s, over two thirds of the American workforce was employed in organizations with international connections (Feld & Jordan, 1988). International business travel has become a burgeoning multibillion-dollar business, and every year hundreds of thousands of employees worldwide become "expatriates," moving around the globe, spending six weeks, six months, six years, or even longer on overseas assignments. Indeed, it is now virtually impossible to conceive of a completely domestic, unicultural organization or organizational communication practices that do not have intercultural dimensions. The Hudson report, *Workforce 2000*, highlights the increasing racial, gender, ethnic, cultural, lifestyle, and age mix of American organizations (Johnson & Packard, 1987); the open

borders of the European Union have diversified their workforces ("One to Us," 1994); the political upheavals across Europe, Asia, and Africa have increased immigration as well as global investments (Naik, 1993); and advances in transportation and communication technologies have minimized the saliency of geographic boundaries and national borders (Stohl, 1993).

Yet despite these trends, organizational communication scholarship has rarely addressed multinational and global organizing. Even in the extensive review chapter on cross-cultural perspectives in the *Handbook of Organizational Communication* published in 1987, only 15 of the 99 citations referenced articles in communication publications and 7 of those were in one volume edited by Gudykunst, Stewart, and Ting-Toomey (1985). Indeed, as late as 1994, when researchers in other fields had turned their attention to the importance of macrocultural issues in organizational studies (as evidenced, e.g., by special issues focusing on globalization in many of the major organizational journals[2]) communication scholars were still lamenting the lack of attention to communication issues in the multinational organization (MNO).

> Because the bulk of research on MNOs has been conducted by business scholars and social psychologists, it is not surprising that the literature on both organizational universals and national cultural influences infrequently focuses on communication issues. (Shuter & Wiseman, 1994, p. 7)

But now, driven by contemporary sociopolitical events, the increasing power of multinationals, pragmatic questions of how to manage a multicultural workplace, the internationalization of the labor movement, and our own professional and personal international experiences, there is growing recognition that organizational communication processes can no longer be viewed as bounded within a unicultural framework. For example, communication journals are beginning to publish a greater number of research articles on intercultural communication in multinational organizations (e.g., Lindsley, 1999; Stage, 1999) and globalization processes (e.g., DeSanctis & Monge, 1998), and the latest books on globalization written by scholars outside our field identify the centrality of organizational communication processes (e.g., Held, McGrew, Goldblatt, & Perraton, 1999; Scholte, 2000; Waters, 1995).[3] In terms of pedagogy, the same trend can be found. Graduate and undergraduate courses on global organizations and communicating in the global workplace are being developed across the discipline (see, e.g., the Web sites of courses jointly developed by Contractor, Monge, and Stohl: http://www. Spcomm. uiuc.edu:1000/global/index.html).

Concomitantly, recent theoretical and methodological challenges to the dominant epistemology and traditional social-scientific paradigm have made our discipline less parochial and more cognizant of, open to, and interested in alternative voices and interpretations (Mumby & Stohl, 1996). Moreover, because these "meaning-centered" perspectives focus on the constitutive role of communication in shaping organizational reality they have raised questions about the bounded nature, objectivity, generalizability, and universality of our constructs and theories, questions and tensions that resonate with the pressures inherent in and the study of transnational organizing. Multinational organizations are at the intersection of diverse communicative, cultural, and social practices. By definition they transcend the narrow perspective that treats organizations as isolated from the wider cultural patterns characterizing society.

This chapter examines organizational literature that addresses communicative processes associated with increasing globalization and cultural variability in multinational organizations. In this context, globalization refers to the interconnected nature of the global economy, the interpenetration of global and domestic organizations, and communication technologies that blur temporal and spatial boundaries (see Rice & Gattiker, Chapter 14 in this volume, and Fulk & Collins-Jarvis, Chapter 16, for further discussions of the relationship between technology and globalization). Cultural variability entails the attitudes, values, beliefs, and ways of knowing and doing that are associated with different cultural identities that may influence organizational and communicative systems.

Two distinct research trends characterize the research on globalization and cultural variability: *convergence* and *divergence*[4] (cf. Inkeles, 1998). The convergence literature refers to a set of imperatives embedded in the global economy that results in similar organizational structuring across nations. Historically rooted in contingency theory, this literature assumes that specific features of the global environment determine organizational form and concomitant communication practices. Thus, even when cultural differences are recognized, the research minimizes these differences and emphasizes the similarity of structural adaptation. The convergence literature addresses changing patterns of organizational communication as they relate to the demands of a global system that requires flexibility, responsiveness, speed, knowledge production, and knowledge dissemination. Convergence research operates within a framework of technical/instrumental rationality concerned predominantly with issues of organizational effectiveness. Communication is viewed as a conduit for the acquisition of resources, capital, information, and expertise, and structure is seen as a complex web of relationships designed to meet the survival needs of an organization. Rather than exploring organizational differences, this approach examines the mechanisms by which globalization produces alternative yet converging organizational forms.

In contrast, the divergence literature focuses primarily on issues of cultural difference. Despite similar environmental pressures on organizations throughout the world, research in this area highlights the communicative diversity found in organizations across the globe. Grounded in issues of practical rationality (Habermas, 1984), the focus is on human interpretation and experience of the world as meaningful and intersubjectively constructed.

The divergence perspective has its roots in two disciplinary traditions: social psychology and anthropology. Research from a social-psychological position sees culture as shaping organizational behavior and influencing communication because culture structures individuals' perceptions and ideas of the world. Work grounded in the anthropological tradition sees organizations as sites of sensemaking and interpretive activity strongly influenced by cultural affiliations. Communication is the essence of culture, inextricably and reciprocally bound together, and effectiveness is rooted in the ability of people from different cultures to work together. Whereas the convergence perspective assumes that similar actions, messages, and processes function in similar ways across cultures, the divergence perspective assumes that similar communicative actions may arise from differing interpretations and visions. Collective action is not necessarily predicated on shared meaning or shared goals but rather on interlocking behaviors (Erez & Earley, 1993; Weick, 1969). Sorge (1983) sums up this perspective succinctly: "There is no culture free context of organization" (p. 136).

Taken together, these approaches capture the dialectical tensions inherent in the globalization of organizational experience (what Barber, 1992, identifies in the political sphere as the forces of Jihad vs. McWorld). The environmental and technological pressures on contemporary organizations to become more and more similar clash with the proprietary pull of cultural identifications, traditional values, and conventional practices of social life. The position taken here is that neither the convergence nor divergence perspective alone can adequately account for the complex organizational processes of globalization. Communication is simultaneously a tool, a resource, a rational selection mode that facilitates or inhibits organizational survival and an interpre-

tive symbolic process that plays a constitutive role in shaping organizational reality.

Within the global workplace, communication embodies the dynamic unfolding of relations between actors and organizations embedded in a set of social and cultural constraints and opportunities that transforms individual and group action into organizational consequences. Because organizational communication scholarship generally (1) focuses on structure, process, and interpretation; (2) is sensitive to the interplay of micro- and macrolevel processes; and (3) acknowledges the permeable and socially constructed boundaries of organizations; it is centrally positioned to explicate the means by which organizations adhere to dominant cultural patterns while adapting those patterns and structures to accommodate differences in and pressures of the global system. As this chapter indicates, however, our contributions to this burgeoning field of global experience and scholarship are in its infancy.

The following section addresses the convergence perspective, exploring how communication functions as a primary mechanism for the production, reproduction, and transformation of organizational forms. First, the communicative imperatives embedded in the technologies of globalization are identified. Second, organizational transformations from domestic to global forms of organizing are described through a brief analysis of the various typologies found in the literature. These typologies are important insofar as they describe the incremental and systematic convergence of communicative processes and structures in the global environment. Third, there is a discussion of the mechanisms of convergence, focusing directly on the communicative activities associated with the increased isomorphism that undergirds the convergence approach.

Challenges to and limitations of the convergence perspective are then examined. Assumptions of generalizability, the culturally neutral character of organizations, and the culture-free nature of theoretical perspectives are questioned. It is argued that the dynamic structuring of globalization is a culturally saturated process that can be better understood by focusing not only on the constraints and demands of the global environment but also on the meanings, interpretations, and sensemaking activities that constitute multinational organizing.

The third section reviews the divergence literature and is organized around five interrelated themes: culture as a cerebral, aesthetic, or artifactual phenomenon; as a complex social pattern; or as communicative practice. Each theme represents a particular conceptualization of the relationship between culture and organizational communication. At the end of the section, several ironies that pervade the divergence literature are identified. Although the very foundation of the divergence perspective is grounded in the far-reaching importance of cultural difference, theoretical principles and the relationships among variables have typically been expected to be stable across cultural and national contexts. By ignoring the embedded nature of organizations, this approach also limits our ability to address the dialectic pressures inherent in the global environment.

The fourth section contains a detailed discussion of theoretical, methodological, and practical parochialisms that pervade both the convergence and divergence approaches to globalization. This discussion is designed to stimulate the development of creative and interdisciplinary research agendas that reflect the dynamic communicative processes of globalization and multiculturalism.

The final section of this chapter summarizes the ways in which organizational communication scholars are in a powerful position to explore globalization, not merely as a neutral phenomenon, but rather as a process fraught with ethical implications. Globalization has been conceived as both a threat to and the salvation of humanity. Economic integration, it has been argued, promotes prosperous stability and discordant stratification. Organizational convergence and divergence may help people to live their lives in more fruitful, peaceful, and satisfying ways or result in

forms of cultural/organizational imperialism that dwarf the powers of the state. The study of organizational communication can help us further understand the potential power, problems, and promise of globalization.

## THE CONVERGENCE APPROACH

---

Whether the culture is Asian or European or North American, a large organization with many employees improves efficiency by specializing its activities but also by increasing and coordinating specialties. (Hickson, Hinings, MacMillan, & Schwitter, 1974, p. 64)

The universal, deterministic, and rational assumptions embedded in the convergence perspective are exemplified in a series of classic cross-national studies that were part of the influential Aston program in Britain in the 1970s. Operating within a contingency/systems perspective, Hickson and his colleagues (Hickson et al., 1974; Hickson, MacMillan, Azumi, & Horvath, 1979) argued that there is a transnational and stable relation between variables of organizational "context" especially size, technology, and dependence on other organizations, on the one hand, and the structural/communicative characteristics of work organizations, such as specialization and decentralization, on the other. This work further assumed that all organizations will pass through similar stages of structural development as they grow and that strategic commitments will necessarily shape the structures of the organizations, which in turn mold and strongly constrain communication processes.

### Factors Influencing Convergence

#### Communicative Imperatives in the Global Environment

Despite critiques leveled at contingency theory in general, many contemporary scholars also suggest there are a set of imperatives embedded in the emerging communication technologies and the global economy that will result in the convergence of organizational structures and communicative practices across nations. "Common markets demand a common language, as well as a common currency, and they produce common behaviors ... culture and nationality can seem only marginal elements in a working identity" (Barber, 1992, p. 54). Theorists argue that as the socioeconomic bases of societies become the same, new communication technologies become readily available, international labor markets are opened, global competition expands, and environmental turbulence and uncertainty increase, social arrangements will converge and replace culturally specific structures (e.g., Clifford, 1988; Tichy, 1990). Across cultures, global organizations are expected to move from "centrally coordinated, multi-level hierarchies toward a variety of more flexible structures that closely resemble networks rather than traditional pyramids" (Miles & Snow, 1992, p. 53). The new arrangements or "global forms" necessary for organizational survival include radical decentralization, intensified interdependence, high-density connections, demanding expectations, transparent performance standards, dispersed leadership, alliance building, and interorganizational reciprocity (Hastings, 1993; Jarvenpaa & Leidner, 1998; Miles & Snow, 1986; Monge & Fulk, 1999; Nohria & Barkley, 1994).

## Typologies of Organizational Transformation

The transformation and convergence of domestic to global forms of organizing have been described in several ways. Typologies focus on the degree of internationalization of business and marketing functions (Ball & McCulloch, 1993); the primary orientation, strategy, managerial assumptions, and cultural sensitivity of the organization (Adler, 1991); the structural and communicative integration of business units across geographic boundaries (Varner & Beamer, 1995); the cultural mindset and orientation of upper management (Heenan & Perlmutter, 1979); the configuration of assets, capabilities, and operations; the role of overseas operations; and development and diffusion of knowledge (Bartlett & Ghoshal, 1986). Even the terms *multinational, international,* and *global* are used in different ways. For example, Bartlett and Ghoshal (1989) order the terms *multinational, global, international,* and *transnational* to describe the degree to which strategies, core competencies, and control are developed and maintained at centralized headquarters. Adler and Ghadar (1990), on the other hand, order the terms *domestic, international, multinational,* and *global* to describe the degree to which the organizing activities (both strategic and structural) incorporate a global perspective.

Despite these differences, however, each typology is based on similar responses to similar environmental constraints and contingencies. Table 10.1 presents a composite description/profile of each of five types of organizations typically described in the literature: domestic, multicultural, multinational, international, and global. These descriptions are based on the predominance of a single national/cultural identity, the perceived importance of an international orientation and perspective, the legitimacy of multiple voices and authority, the type of structure, the "ideal" management model, and the interconnected nature of interactions across a diversity of cultural groups.

Clearly, the convergence approach has within it an element of environmental determinism; that is, all organizations wish to survive and to do so they must adapt certain structures to the global environment. Moreover, communicative adaptation/convergence is considered a positive feature of organizations regardless of cultural differences and levels of economic development. Thus, the exploitative potential of certain global production practices regarding employment, displacement, factory development, outsourcing, and lean production tend to be ignored.

**TABLE 10.1** Typology of Organizations

| | Domestic | Multicultural | Multinational | International | Global |
|---|---|---|---|---|---|
| Predominant national orientation | Identification with one country and dominant culture; management recognition of only one culture within the workplace; internal and external linkages are perceived to be homogeneous | Identification with one country; some recognition by management of culturally diverse workforce; internal and external linkages, usually composed of subcultures within the dominant culture (e.g., African Americans, women) | Identification with one nationality while doing business in several countries; recognition by management of a multinational workforce, management, clientele, and environment; organization represents one national interest | Identification with two or more countries each of which has distinct cultural attributes; workforce, management, clients, suppliers, etc. are recognized to represent diverse national interests | Identification with the global system; transcend national borders; boundaryless organizations; within the workplace organizational membership takes precedence over national orientation; stateless corporation |
| Perceived importance of international orientation | None | Very little importance | Important | Extremely important | Dominant |
| Orientation toward subsidiaries and/or other cultural units | *Parochial:* There is no authoritative voice other than dominant culture | *Ethnocentric:* Authority is located with dominant cultural group; any accommodation to other cultures is at the micro/interpersonal level | *Polycentric:* Authority is vested in local nationals holding key positions in subsidiaries; managed from central headquarters, little communication between subsidiaries, communication with national headquarters | *Regiocentric:* Regional geographic basis for authority, personnel, and staffing development, interdependence across regions | *Geocentric:* Dispersed, interdependent, and specialized, differentiated contributions integrated into worldwide operations, development and sharing of knowledge worldwide; multinational flexibility and worldwide learning capability |

*(continued)*

Table 10.1 Continued

|  | Domestic | Multicultural | Multinational | International | Global |
|---|---|---|---|---|---|
| Structure | Hierarchical, traditional bureaucratic and matrix structures; one centrally located headquarters | Teamwork, flattening of hierarchy; one centrally located headquarters | Managed from a central location in an essentially hierarchical manner; national subsidiaries, miniature replicas teamwork employed; centralized and globally scaled, overseas operations implement parent company strategies, develop and maintain knowledge at headquarters level | Joint hierarchy; international divisions that integrate global activities, joint ventures; teamwork within subsidiaries but not across; some decentralized decision making | Decentralization of decision making and sharing of responsibilities; heterarchy; headquarters and subsidiaries see themselves as part of an organic worldwide entity; global strategy, dominant, global alliances; multicentric |
| Management models | Monocultural: Cultural differences are ignored, not recognized | Cultural dominance: Differences are expected to be accommodated through assimilation with dominant culture | Cultural compromise: Differences are recognized and somewhat accepted but dominant culture is typically enacted in task domain | Cultural synergy: Work together to try to build a third culture | Cultural integration: Recognition of diverse cultures and business conditions, cultural adaptation in the task realm, cultural integrity in the expressive realm |
| Level of international interaction | Import/export: Possibly send representatives abroad | Import/export: Possibly send representatives abroad; intercultural communication among workforce | Intercultural communication among workforce, management, clients, customers, government officials, international communication technology | Loosely coupled; intercultural communication among workforce, management, clients, customers, government officials, international communication technology | Global networks, integrative, tightly coupled; intercultural communication among workforce, management, clients, customers, government officials; international communication technology |

Unlike traditional contingency theory, however, where the organizational environment is conceived as a delineated set of contingencies emanating from the social, legal, political, economic, technological, and physical domains, the new convergence literature blurs the boundaries between an organization and the various sectors within the environment. Contemporary convergence literature transforms the view of organizations as bounded entities, separated in time and space from other parts of the environment to a position of permeability and flux, where there is no longer a clear distinction between the organization and its environment. Interorganizational networks are conceived as overlapping yet diffuse webs of interaction composed of suppliers, customers, unions, special interest groups, and competitors, as well as legal (e.g., rules, regulations, and obligations), political (treaties such as GATT), institutional (e.g., the International Monetary Fund), and cultural (e.g., ethnicity, religious affiliation) linkages that transcend what has typically been conceived of as relevant actors (Hatch, 1997). Communication is the means for bridging and bringing together the resources and contingencies that facilitate organizational transformation and survival in the global environment. The major question this literature addresses is, How do organizations adapt to the global environment?

### Mechanisms of Convergence

In a provocative article on the "new institutionalism," DiMaggio and Powell (1983) ask, "Why is there such startling homogeneity of organizational forms and practices?" (p. 148). They distinguish between *competitive isomorphism,* which assumes a rationality that emphasizes market competition, niche change, and fitness, and *institutional isomorphism,* change that occurs through three communicative mechanisms. The first mechanism of institutional isomorphism, *coercive,* stems from political in-

fluence and legitimacy. The pressures to conform may be felt as force, as persuasion, or as invitations to join in collusion. The second process, *mimetic,* results from standard responses to uncertainty. When environments and organizational technologies are ambiguous, volatile, and poorly understood, organizations model themselves on other organizations. The third mechanism of isomorphism, *normative,* is associated with professionalization. They claim that the similarity of the formal education of the managerial class across cultures and the development of an interconnected matrix of information flows and personnel movement across organizations result not only in what Kanter (1977) refers to as the "homosocial reproduction of management" but to the development of similar organizational structures across organizational fields. Although DiMaggio and Powell (1991) go on to say that "the ubiquity of certain kinds of structural arrangements can more likely be credited to the universality of mimetic processes rather than to any concrete evidence that the adopted models enhance efficiency" (p. 70), mimesis as a response to environmental uncertainty is rooted in rational efforts to enhance survival in the global arena.

### Communicative Convergence

Throughout this literature, the move toward global convergence is rooted in fundamental changes in organizational communication practices. If organizations are to flourish in the volatile global environment and meet the challenges of geographic dispersion, temporal asynchronicity, and cultural diversity (Monge, 1995), it is assumed that they must become more knowledge intensive, innovative, adaptive, flexible, efficient, and responsive to rapid change (Cushman & King, 1993; Kozminski & Cushman, 1993; Monge & Fulk, 1995, 1999; Taylor & Van Every, 1993). Cushman and King (1993) have developed "a new theory of organizational communication:

high-speed management" to address the "series of revolutions [that] have taken place within the global economy, transforming the theoretical basis for organizational coalignment, and thus all information and communication processes" (p. 209). They provide examples of how four dynamic communication processes—negotiated linking, New England town meetings, cross-functional teamwork, and best practices case studies—can enable organizations to improve effectiveness and gain competitive advantage. Negotiated linking, for example, is aimed at mobilizing external resources, and town meetings bring workers, suppliers, and customers together for intense discussions related to productivity, quality, and response time.

Likewise, at a University of Michigan symposium designed to set a global research and teaching agenda for American and European business schools in the 1990s (see Tichy, 1990), scholars and senior executives stressed communication issues related to coordination, integration, alliance building, network development, international team building, global leadership skills, and the development of a global managerial mindset. Weick and Van Orden (1990), for example, posit that the global organization will be an "organization without location" composed of fields of activities and systems of decision making rather than a single, static hierarchical entity. The new organizational form will "resemble temporary systems, federations, and project teams held together somewhat in the manner of the linking pins" (p. 56) and have a low degree of formalization, continual redefinition of task, low centralization, and ad hoc centers of authority located at critical but evolving locations. At the interpersonal level, they believe the global organization will encourage more complex and flexible strategies, greater participation and risk taking, and more open communication style and will experience more open management of conflict and more task orientation in the networks that emerge as a result of the conflict.

Overall, increasing experience with the processes of globalization has resulted in practitioners and scholars alike arguing for the inappropriateness of traditional hierarchical structuring and thinking and the development of alternative forms of organizing.

> Hierarchies do not contain the complexity in which society has to deal. . . . Neither a hierarchical organization nor a hierarchy of concepts can handle a network of environmental problems, for example, without leaving many dangerous gaps through which unforeseen problems may emerge and be uncontainable. (Lipnack & Stamps, 1986, pp. 162-163)

Empirically, the most dramatic changes can be seen in the Coca Cola Company, which in a move to make the company "more nimble" completely eliminated the very concepts of domestic and international. In a restructuring of business units on a regional but equal basis, the company eliminated the privileges and higher status of any one unit (Collins, 1996, p. 19). There are many other examples as well. The practitioner literature is filled with case studies of new organizational forms (e.g., Cusumano & Selby, 1995; Nonaka & Takeuchi, 1995), and scholars have begun addressing the theoretical implications of these new forms (e.g., Miles & Snow, 1986; Park & Ungson, 1997; Swan & Ettlie, 1997). Guterl (1989) documents how IBM, Corning, Apple Computer, and Philips, N.V. have moved from matrix hierarchical structures to less formal, "network" type organizations that will allow them to respond faster and more creatively in globally dispersed markets. Nonaka and Takeuchi (1995) illustrate how the highly successful "global organizational knowledge-creating" companies, such as Honda, Canon, Matsushita, and Nissan, have neither top-down nor bottom-up management systems but rather develop what they call "middle-up-down" management processes that "rely more on two-way communications such as dialogue, camp sessions, and drinking sessions" (p. 151).

Consider also the three components of "global network organizations" identified by Monge and Fulk (1995) "as a newly emerging organizational form" (p. 2) that transcends national boundaries and readily adapts to the volatile environment. Global network organizations,[5] which many view as the quintessential organizational form of the postindustrial global information society (see, e.g., Hastings, 1993; Miles & Snow, 1992; Mulgan, 1991), are

1. Built on flexible emergent communication networks, rather than traditional hierarchies
2. Develop highly flexible linkages that connect them to a changing, dynamic network of other organizations, transcending their local country-bound networks
3. Contain a highly sophisticated information technology structure that supports flexible emergent systems of communication

In their view, the global organization reflects communication relationships that transcend organizational levels and boundaries and "flexibility implies that these relationships wax and wane" (Monge & Fulk, 1995, p. 1).

Notwithstanding the technical and rational logic of this move toward the convergence of macrolevel/structural variables such as flattening hierarchies (Cleveland, 1985), global networking (Monge & Fulk, 1995), negotiated linking (Cushman & King, 1993), decentralization (Mitroff, 1987) and the increasing similarity of what Wiio (1989) refers to as hardware variables, that is, information sources, channels and their uses, number of messages, code systems, and communication networks, several limitations to these approaches have been identified. Some scholars suggest that "despite their contemporary framing," theories such as high-speed management still embody traditional managerial assumptions about linearity, continuity, and responsivity that are no longer appropriate (Seibold & Contractor, 1993). Poole (1993) further proposes that there are many alternatives to the demands, constraints, and opportunities of the global economy that are not considered in a theory such as high-speed management. Other scholars (e.g., Adler, Doktor, & Redding, 1986; Ady, 1994) argue

that despite what may seem to be convergence at the macrolevel, communication and sense-making activities are remaining culturally distinct and often undergoing increasing divergence. In this next section, we will address some of the challenges to the convergence perspective, paying particular attention to very recent developments in the organizational communication literature.

## Challenging the Assumptions of Universality and Organizational Convergence

> Intuitively, people have always assumed that bureaucratic structures and patterns of action differ in the different countries of the Western world and even more markedly between East and West. Men [sic] of action know it and never fail to take it into account. But contemporary social scientists . . . have not been concerned with such comparisons. (Crozier, 1964, p. 210)

More than 30 years ago, Michel Crozier, a French sociologist, highlighted the need to incorporate cultural variability into organizational research. His observations challenge three implicit assumptions, traditionally embedded in most organizational communication literature, and that still appear in most convergence literature: (1) research findings are generalizable across national contexts, (2) theories are culture free, and (3) organizations are culturally neutral.

### Issues of Generalizability

Even a cursory look at our journals reveals that most articles rarely include a discussion of the cultural/national identifications of the employee/managerial sample unless the study is focusing specifically on issues of cultural variability. Nor do we often find a caveat pertaining to the limited scope of the conclusions or our theories in terms of the national/cultural generalizability. For example, the management and communication principles elaborated by the classical organizational theorists and elucidated in our texts and handbooks (e.g., Daniels & Spiker, 1994; Krone, Jablin, & Putnam, 1987; Miller, 1995; Tompkins, 1984) are usually presented as culture-free theories with universal applicability. Yet these theories may be as culturally bounded as the actual processes of organizing and managing (Boyacigiller & Adler, 1991). Consider the congruence between German Max Weber's emphasis on impersonal relations and the importance of written communication in a bureaucracy and cultural descriptions of Germany as a low-context culture in which information is vested in explicit codes rather than in relationships and the context surrounding the messages (Hall, 1976). There is also great consistency between Henri Fayol's, France's first management theorist, emphasis on centralization and unity of command and the French culture's high degree of uncertainty avoidance and power distance (Hofstede, 1984). We can further contrast Fayol's views with Scandinavians' tolerance for ambiguity and low status differentiation, the cultural background of many of the sociotechnical theorists who emphasized the importance of semiautonomous work groups (Emery, Thorsrud, & Trist, 1969). Indeed, it is hard not to conclude that these theorists' conceptions of organizing were, in some large part, a product of their cultural heritage. Asante (1987) makes the point directly:

> The preponderant Eurocentric myths of universalism, objectivity, and classical traditions retain a provincial European cast. . . . The problem with this is that cultural analysis takes a back seat to galloping ethnocentric interpretations of phenomena. (p. 9)

A noteworthy exception to this charge can be found in a provocative paper by Mayer (1996). In a communicative analysis of Deming's early and later writings on the principles of quality control and management (1943-1986), Mayer persuasively illustrates how the evolution of his work can, in large part, be attributed to the waning influence of American's short-term, linear, detailed, and analytic mode of thinking and the increasing influence of Japanese culture and philosophy including synthetic, long-term, holistic, and configural thinking. For example, in the early stages Deming stressed complexity, variation, and the use of scientific method for learning and improvement, whereas in the later stages his approach became more holistic, including emphasis on leadership, cooperation, and trust. Interestingly, Mayer points out that after many years of immersion in Japanese culture, Deming (1986) identifies performance evaluation and annual merit reviews as incompatible with a company's effectiveness because these processes orient workers toward quick fixes and stress their replaceability. In Japanese thinking, no part of the whole can be replaced without damage to the whole (Yoshida, 1989).

### Cultural Differences

As the title of the following *New York Times* article, "It Takes More Than a Visa to Do Business in Mexico," suggests, understanding cultural differences is crucial for communicating and working in today's global environment. An excerpt from this article illustrates the types of cultural differences that are perceived to make a difference:

> In the Corning venture, the Mexicans sometimes saw the Americans as too direct, while the Vitro managers, in their dogged pursuit of politeness, sometimes seemed to the Americans unwilling to acknowledge problems and faults. . . . Another difference quite obvious from the beginning was the manner of making decisions. . . . The Mexicans sometimes thought Corning moved too fast; the Americans felt Vitro was too slow. (DePalma, 1994, pp. A16-A17)

The point is that, notwithstanding the increasing homogenization of organizational structures and technology discussed above, most empirical studies find that "cultural differences among nations do make a difference—often a substantial difference—in the way managers and workers behave in organizational settings" (Steers, Bischoff, & Higgins, 1992, p. 322). In a series of studies comparing Japanese and American managers' communication patterns, for example, although there were only minimal differences between the amount and direction of communication, there was a significant relationship between managers' national culture and the quality and the nature of the communication (Pascale & Athos, 1981). Inzerilli and Laurent (1983), comparing Western European cultures, also found communicative similarities with important differences. French managers had a more difficult time accepting subordinate roles than did English managers, even though hierarchy was perceived as necessary and appropriate under the same conditions by both cultural groups.

Thus, we can see that despite increased convergence of organizational structures at the macrolevel, the significance and meanings given to many of these features continues to diverge across cultural contexts. Fons Trompenaars (1994), one of the foremost proponents of the need for managers and scholars to develop a culturally based understanding of organizing, makes the point pragmatically. In addressing the technological and economic imperatives built into traditional organizational theory, he states:

> But the wrong questions have been asked. The issue is not whether a hierarchy in the Netherlands has six levels, as does a similar company in Singapore, but what hierarchy and those levels mean to the Dutch and Singaporeans. Where the meaning is totally different, for example a chain of command rather than a family, then human resource policies developed to implement the first will seriously miscommu-

nicate in the latter context. (Trompenaars, 1994, p. 7)

Embedded within Trompenaars's argument are two critical issues for the study of organizational communication in the global system that are not addressed by the convergence theorists. First, there is a comparative question (i.e., are there systematic differences in sensemaking activities among employees in different cultures?). Second, he raises questions related to intercultural interactions (i.e., what happens when people from various cultures interact with one another in an organizational setting?). In both cases, the answers can be found only in the study of communication.

Indeed, the focus on questions of meaning, interpretation, sensemaking, and interaction highlights further the contributions communication scholars can make to the study of multinational/multicultural organizing. Communication is the substance of global organizing in the sense that through everyday communication practices, organizational members collectively engage in the construction of a complex system of meanings that are intersubjectively shared and commonly misunderstood. This construction is strongly influenced by the cultural connections individuals bring into the system that transcend organizational boundaries (Stohl, 1995). Moreover, as organizations simultaneously become more integrated yet geographically dispersed, diverse, and homogenized, increasingly participative while heavily reliant on sophisticated information technologies, intercultural communication is no longer an "extranormal aspect of organizing nor a distinct kind of face-to-face communication that can be distinguished from other 'types' of communication. . . . Intercultural communication constitutes organizing processes that permeates all levels of activity and interpretation" (Stohl, 1993, p. 381).

Overall, then, communication scholarship can contribute to the understanding of global organizing at two levels: (1) the dynamic structuring of globalization, and (2) the culturally saturated processes of organizing and sensemaking. However, before examining the relationship among culture, communication, and organization it is first necessary to understand what is meant by culture and how it is associated with organizational divergence.

## THE DIVERGENCE APPROACH

Japanese and American management practices are 95% the same and differ in all important respects. (Takeo Fujisawa, cited in Adler et al., 1986, p. 295)

Fujisawa, cofounder of Honda Motor Company, is clearly suggesting there are important differences between the American and Japanese cultures that influence the processes of organizing in significant and systematic ways. His observations make a strong case for the divergence perspective, but he does not help us tackle one of the thorniest issues in social science: What do we mean by culture, and how is it related to collective action?

### Definitions and Themes of Culture

Indeed, Raymond Williams (1976) suggests that "culture is one of the two or three most complicated words in the English language" (p. 4). Geertz (1973) notes that in a 27-page chapter of *Mirror for Man*, Kluckhohn (1949) defined culture in at least 11 distinct ways ranging from "the total way of life" to culture as a map, a sieve, and a matrix. By the mid-1950s, Kroeber and Kluckhohn (1954) had already collected over 300 definitions of culture. And just as there is a plethora of definitions of culture, scholars have identified literally dozens of dimensions of cultural variability, that is, societal patterns of beliefs,

values, and practices that distinguish one group from another (Triandis, 1983).

Table 10.2 synthesizes this work and presents an overview of 12 dimensions of cultural variability that have been associated with important differences in organizational communication practices. These dimensions describe cultural orientations related to qualities of individuals, their relationships to nature, relationships with others, primary types of activities, and orientations toward time and space.[6]

But if we argue that pressures toward divergence are coterminous with a drive toward convergence, that is, even under similar global constraints and opportunities, the culturally saturated processes of communication and interpretation will likely result in different ways of organizing, we must have a sense not only of cultural dimensions but more specifically of how culture is conceptualized. Based on an exhaustive review of the meanings of culture in philosophy, critical aesthetics, literary criticism, anthropology, and sociology, Jenks (1993) develops a typology of cultural themes or categories that is quite useful (in an adapted form) for understanding the ways in which the relationship between culture and organizational communication practices has been studied. These adapted themes are labeled "culture as cerebral," "culture as aesthetic," "culture as artifact," "culture as a complex social pattern," and "culture as communicative practice."

Each theme provides a complementary pathway for exploring how, despite similar market and environmental pressures, cultural differences result in divergent forms of organizing activities. Within each set of literature, the focal features of culture, the topics most frequently studied, the role of communication, the dominant theoretical perspective, and the types of research and methods found across the literature are identified. Table 10.3 summarizes these conclusions. For example, when culture is viewed as a cerebral phenomenon, divergent meanings and structures are seen as a direct result of the different cognitions and values cultural groups have

**TABLE 10.2**   Dimensions of Cultural Variability

| Dimension | Constructs | Illustrative Impacts on Organizational Communication Practices |
|---|---|---|
| Orientation to nature | Control over/harmony with/ subjugation to (Triandis, 1983) | Degree of comfort and use of technology |
| Orientation to human nature | People are basically good/bad/ mixture (McGregor, 1960) | Degree of emphasis on control and surveillance |
| | Quality (social connections determine evaluation/performance; actions determine evaluation) (Parsons & Shils, 1951) | Degree of mobility, the importance of achievements (what person does) vs. ascribed status (who person is) |
| | Sex differences are innate/learned | Degree of integration of women into the workforce |
| Orientation to time | Monochronic/polychronic (Hall, 1976) | Degree to which schedules are adhered to; degree to which tasks are completed linearly |
| | Past/present/future (Kluckhohn & Strodtbeck, 1961) | Attitudes toward change and innovation; type of planning |
| Orientation to action | Being/being in becoming/doing (Kluckhohn & Strodtbeck, 1961) | Degree to which stress is placed on improvements and accomplishments; importance of job satisfaction |
| | Affectivity/affectivity neutral (Parsons & Shils, 1951) | Need for immediate gratification |
| Orientation to communication | Low context/high context (Hall, 1976) | Different emphasis on verbal or nonverbal messages; degree of communication directness; relative importance of relational networks |
| | Associative/abstractive (Glenn, 1981) | Context-dependent meanings; specific definitional requirements; type of information formally presented; types of arguments that are persuasive—emotionally based vs. data driven |
| Orientation to space | Private/public (Hall, 1966) | Requirements for personal space; office layout; private office vs. open office |
| Orientation to authority | High power distance (hierarchical)/ low power distance (equality) (Hofstede, 1984) | Levels of hierarchy; adherence to the chain of command; respect for titles and status; degree of worker participation |
| Orientation to community | Individualism/collectivism (Hofstede, 1984) | Motivational incentives; degree to which task is valued over relationships; basis of hiring and promotion; type of socialization practices; degree to which shame or guilt drives employees and managers |

*(continued)*

**TABLE 10.2** Continued

| Dimension | Constructs | Illustrative Impacts on Organizational Communication Practices |
|---|---|---|
| | Familialism (Redding, 1990) | Hiring practices; influence strategies |
| Orientation to goals | Instrumental (competitive)/ expressive (cooperative) | Degree of stress placed on quality of work life vs. attainment of materialistic goals; degree of gender differentiation; degree of assertiveness and nurturing value of specific motivators |
| | Masculine/feminine (Hofstede, 1984) | |
| | Process/goals (Glenn, 1981) | Emphasis on here and now |
| Orientation to structure | Simple/complex (Murdock & Provost, 1973) | Degree of hierarchical differentiation |
| | High uncertainty avoidance/ low uncertainty avoidance (Hofstede, 1984) | Degree of need for predictability and rules, both written and unwritten |
| | Tight/loose (Witkin & Berry, 1975) | Degree of pressure to conform to role definitions |
| | In-group/out-group (Triandis, 1983) | |
| Orientation to formality | Formal/informal | Adherence to traditions; attitudes toward change; importance of protocol; preponderance of rituals; emphasis on verbal and nonverbal appropriateness |
| Orientation to needs | Materialist/postmaterialist (Inglehart, 1977) | Degree to which employees focus on meeting physiological needs such as safety and sustenance as compared to meeting social and self-actualization needs such as belonging and self esteem |

about the way the world operates, issues of cause and effect, human nature, and so on. Rooted in the social psychological tradition, communication is portrayed as an outcome of the composite values and cognitions associated with a particular culture. There is a strong focus on training and the development of intercultural communicative competence, culture shock and assimilation, authority relations, and conflict and negotiation. Research tends to be managerially focused, quantitative, and comparative.

In contrast, when culture is viewed as an embodied and collective category that refers to the aesthetic pursuits of a group of people,

organizational arrangements are seen as extensions of societal principles of beauty and design. Communication is a way of knowing, a dynamic display of aesthetic qualities. This research tends to be more macro oriented and philosophically grounded, less focused on managerial prerogatives, and more concerned with the role of organizations in the larger society. Rooted in issues of practical rationality, each approach focuses on human interpretation and experience of the world as meaningful and intersubjectively constructed.

Clearly, these approaches are not mutually exclusive. To begin, culture enters organizations artfully, unself-consciously, and piece-

**TABLE 10.3** Typology of Culture and Its Relation With Organizational Communication

| | Culture us | | | | |
|---|---|---|---|---|---|
| | *Cerebral* | *Aesthetic* | *Artifact* | *A Complex Social Pattern* | *Communicative Practice* |
| Focus | Values, cognitions | Principles of beauty and design | Artifacts | Normative and routine patterns | Everyday interactions |
| Role of communication | An outcome | A way of knowing | A thing, a sedimented symbol | A transmitter | A constitutive element |
| | Communication is shaped by one's perceptions and ideas of the world | Communication reflects societal sense of beauty and balance | Communication is a manifestation and elaboration of culture | Communication is the enactment and reinforcement of cultural conditioning | Communication is quintessentially culture, an interpretive sensemaking process |
| Frequently studied topics | Communicative competence, culture shock; training and development; manager-worker relations; power, conflict; compliance gaining; and negotiation | Role of organization in society; organizational structure and design | Business letters, annual reports; handbooks; newsletters; business cards; gifts; logos | Gender and racial relations; class structure; power; role of economic/occupational institutions; identification of culture-specific constructs; communication ethics | Organizational identity; nonverbal communication; organizational messages; language issues; worker participation; organizational democracy |
| Dominant perspective | Microindividual and dyadic | Macrosocial | Micro-object | Macrosocietal | Interconnectedness between micro- and macrolevels of analysis |
| | Managerial | Societal | Managerial | Microinterpersonal | Worker and managerial |
| | Social-psychological tradition | Philosophical tradition | Social-psychological tradition | Anthropological tradition | Anthropological tradition |
| Types of research | Etic, empirical and theoretical, comparative, quantitative methods | Emic, theoretical, case studies | Etic/emic, empirical, discourse analytic techniques, semantic networks, quantitative methods | Etic/emic, empirical and theoretical, comparative case studies, ethnographies; interpretive, qualitative and quantitative methods | Emic, empirical and theoretical; interpretive, qualitative and quantitative methods |

meal through several avenues simultaneously (Sorge, 1983). Culture has been hypothesized to affect organizations through (1) political/ legal prescriptions and prohibitions, legal requirements, and regulations; (2) constraints and opportunities of the institutional environment; (3) preferences (values) and premises about what organizations can and should be; (4) rites, rituals, and other communicative practices; (5) the ways in which individuals perform their roles and relate to one another; (6) the mindsets of occupational communities; (7) the manner by which problems are solved; and (8) the instantiations of spatio/ temporal boundaries.

Second, across categories, definitions of culture share several assumptions. These include (1) culture is not innate, it is learned and passed on from one generation to another; (2) culture may change but transformation is slow; (3) individual aspects of culture are interrelated; (4) culture is shared and defines the boundaries of social groups; and (5) culture is simultaneously overt and covert, public and private, explicit and implicit, known and unknown.

Third, both culture-general and culture-specific approaches to communication are found across categories. In culture-specific research, scholars develop in-depth analyses of communication practices in a particular culture and may generalize about organizational communication practices in that specific cultural environment. In contrast, a culture-general approach identifies dimensions or ways in which cultures may vary across cultural contexts, using illustrations from particular cultures as examples of the more general concept (Victor, 1992).

Fourth, an important limitation has been noted by Child (1981):

> Although it is an oversimplification, the boundaries of culture are conventionally assumed to coincide with the boundaries of the nation-states. Culture is regarded as an expression of the values, norms, and habits which are deep rooted with the nation. (p. 304)

Indeed, across all these approaches we find that *nation* has been used as a proxy for *culture* for several reasons: (1) most theories of cultural variability use such a unit; (2) nationality has symbolic value—our identities are derived, in large part, by our affiliation to a nation-state; (3) nationality evokes a set of attributes, values, and stereotypes that becomes more conspicuous in a multinational environment; (4) organizational identity has traditionally been defined within national borders; and (5) globalization is conceptualized as a form of transcendence of the nation-state. Nonetheless, not everyone from a given country has the same culture. Ethnicity, race, age, gender, religion, sexual preference, region, and so forth comprise significant, often overlapping, cultural identifications. Every cultural context encompasses a multitude of individual patterns or modal types. Further, individuals do not necessarily conform to scripts written for them by a particular intersection of cultural identifications. But research has shown that national differences do exist in the variable distribution of individual types and in the social dynamics among these types. Within each macroculture, different patterns are reinforced, encouraged, and accepted, while others are ignored, marginalized, suppressed, or even punished (Maruyama, 1982). A serious challenge for both researchers and readers, then, is to maintain sensitivity to the potential dangers of stereotyping and remain cautious against minimizing or ignoring within-nation differences while simultaneously recognizing the value of the generalizations that are an inevitable consequence of cultural research.

Fifth, the relationship between national culture and organizational culture is neither simple nor straightforward. Most scholars agree that they are "phenomena of different orders; using the term 'culture' for both is . . . somewhat misleading" (Hofstede, Neuijen, Ohayr, & Sanders, 1990, p. 313). Even when two organizations are dominated by the same national-cultural affiliation, this does not necessarily mean the daily practices will be similar. Founder's values (Ashcraft & Pacanow-sky, 1995), type of industry (Maurice, Sorge, & Malcolm, 1981), and occupational communities (Van Maanen & Barley, 1984) are just a few of the features that contribute to the local culture of an organization (see Eisenberg & Riley, Chapter 9 in this volume, for an explication of organizational culture). Further, organizations are not simply passive recipients of culture. Organizational cultures simultaneously influence and are influenced by the larger cultures of which they are a part.

In summary, each cultural theme discussed below—culture as cerebral, culture as aesthetic, culture as artifact, culture as a complex social pattern, and culture as communicative practice—does not represent a mutually exclusive or inclusive representation of culture. Rather, the five themes are interrelated; each represents a specific conceptualization of the relationships among culture, communication, and organization. When taken together, this classification system provides a comprehensive guide for mapping the communicative dimensions of organizational divergence.

## Cultural Themes as a Typology for the Study of Organizational Communication

> My purpose here is to present . . . readers with a map of our existing territory, and a guide to that map in the form of a classification, or a morphology, of the central concepts and ideas in terms of their meanings, origins, and overlaps . . . if this work succeeds . . . it will also have shown this classification is itself a cultural practice involving critical reading, judgment, and discernment, and adherence to an intellectual discipline (a symbolic culture). (Jenks, 1993, p. 3)

### Culture as Cerebral

This approach to culture identifies it as a general state of mind, a cognitive phenomenon. Culture shapes behavior and influences communication because it structures one's perceptions and ideas of the world. Of central interest are systematic differences in (1) cognitive frames and (2) the strong association between cognition and values. The dimensions of cultural variability identified in Table 10.2 encapsulate the cultural "differences that make a difference" in communication studies. Friday (1989), for example, identifies specific differences between American and German managers' expectations regarding business relationships, personal needs, orientation to cooperation, status, confrontation, and common social intercourse and then predicts how these cognitive differences are manifest in contrasting styles of business discussions.

*Cognitive frames.* Triandis and Albert (1987) in the first edition of this handbook posit that culture reflects shared meanings, norms, and values and argue that the most important aspect of culture that affects organizational communication is "the cognitive frames societies provide their members for processing information that has been perceived" (p. 267). These cognitive frames reflect (1) the differing ways that cultures emphasize people, ideas, or actions; (2) the emphasis put on processes or goals; (3) differences in values; and (4) patterns of information processing and influence. Triandis (1983) illustrates how the classic management functions of defining goals, planning, and selecting, training, controlling, and motivating employees are facilitated and inhibited by the cognitive frames people bring to an organization.

The cognitive approach to culture undergirds most of the research on intercultural communicative competence in the workplace, intercultural training of managers and employees, and the experiences of culture shock and assimilation of expatriate employees. Models of culture shock are premised on the cognitive conflict, confusion, unpredictability, and frustration of uninterpretable cues that are created by the incongruence between what is expected from a particular cultural mindset and what actually happens in another culture (Storti, 1990; Tung, 1987). Cognitive differences are causally linked to cultural differences in decision making, negotiation, conflict, and management styles as well as organizational structures and authority relations (Cai & Drake, 1998; Hofstede, 1984; Laurent, 1983). Issues of selective perception, attributions, expectations, stereotyping, prejudice, ethnocentrism, and parochialism have all been explored as cognitive/cultural barriers to effective communication in the global workplace and the development of cultural synergy (see Adler, 1991; Brislin, 1989; Gudykunst, 1991; Harris & Moran, 1996; Moran & Harris, 1982).

Synergy, according to Moran and Harris (1982), is tied directly to organizational members' cognitions and is limited to immediate bounded interactions, neither transcending the particular nor generating systemic change. Cultural synergy "exists only in relation to a practical set of circumstances, and it occurs by necessity when two or possibly more culturally different groups come together" (p. 83). Cultural synergism creates groups that transcend any single culture, producing new and different systems of interaction. To enhance the synergistic potential of multinational groups, members are exhorted to recognize, empathize with, understand, and address cultural differences; develop a shared vision or superordinate goal; and develop mutual respect and provide feedback in culturally sensitive ways (Adler, 1991; Amir, 1969; Brislin, 1989). Success, always rooted in the dual processes of synthesis and accommodation, is determined by the dominant organizational interests.

Organizational training programs focused on the expatriate experience are also most often designed to sensitize individuals to their own cultural blinders and to increase awareness of cultural differences. Significantly, although some competency in the "other's" language is recognized as a significant contributor to the effective management of culture shock and successful interaction in the multinational workplace (Victor, 1992) the cognitively based research ignores, for the most part, language and/or translation issues in cross-cultural organizing. People are believed to become more open to cultural differences as they learn how their own culture influences perceptions, attitudes, values, and communication (Albert, 1983; Brislin, 1989; Gudykunst, 1991). In a study of managerial international competence, for example, Ratiu (1983) found that although the managers who were perceived as most international by their peers denied that "internationals" existed, they exhibited a different set of cognitive strategies for managing in a multicultural organization. International managers used a "blue loop strategy" (a microstrategy based on description, impression, private stereotypes, and modification) as compared to the less effective multicultural managers who used a "red loop strategy" (a macrostrategy rooted in explanation, theory, public stereotypes, and confirmation).

Culture conceived as a cerebral phenomenon that directly affects communication practices can also be seen in a set of studies conducted by Laurent and his colleagues (Inzerilli & Laurent, 1983; Laurent, 1983, 1986). Comparing the "implicit theories of management" of managers from ten European nations and the United States they concluded that the managers' sets of mental representations and preferences, and hence performance, were culturally determined. Managerial views of "proper management" and conceptions of structure as either instrumental (e.g., roles and positions are defined in terms of tasks and/or functions) or social (e.g., roles and positions are defined in terms of social status and authority) were associated with national origin. Significantly, Laurent (1986) found that cultural differences were not reduced when managers worked in the same multinational firm. "If anything there was slightly more divergence between the national groups within this multinational company than originally found in the INSEAD [an elite French business school] multinational study [i.e., where the international managerial sample came from different companies]."

*Cognitions and values.* Hofstede (1984), the most influential scholar in the area of culture and organizations today, defines culture as "the collective programming of the mind which distinguishes the members of one human group from another" (p. 210). Highlighting the information-processing aspects of organizations, he refers to the mental programs of employees as the "software of the mind" (Hofstede, 1991). Cultural values are of special significance in this approach. "The main cultural differences among nations lie in values" (Hofstede, 1991, p. 236) and nearly all our mental programs are affected by values that are reflected in our behavior. Basing his work on responses to questionnaires about work-related values of over 116,000 IBM employees in 50 countries, Hofstede (1984) originally identified four dimensions of cultural variability (power distance, uncertainty avoidance, masculinity, and individualism). In 1988, Hofstede and Bond added a fifth dimension, Confucian dynamism. The values associated with this dimension are rooted in Confucianism and the principles of stability, status, thrift, and shame.

Each of these dimensions reflects the differing values given to issues of equality, ambiguity, instrumentalism, and community in a particular country and are strongly associated with the ways in which individuals across the world perform roles and relate to one another. Chen and Chung (1994), for example, provide several examples of the ways in which four values of Confucianism, hierarchy, the family system, *jen* (benevolence), and the emphasis on education influence organizational communication processes such as the development of explicit rules, socialization activities, the elevated importance of socioemotional communication in the workplace, team development, and nonconfrontation conflict resolution. Stewart, Gudykunst, Ting-Toomey, and Nishida (1986) developed a questionnaire also based on Hofstede's (1984) decision-making style questionnaire and the ICA audit (Goldhaber & Rogers, 1979) to explore the influence of Japanese managerial decision-making style on Japanese employees' perceptions of communication openness and satisfaction.

Indeed, the communicative implications of Hofstede's dimensions are rich and provocative (see Teboul, Chen, & Fritz's [1994] set of speculative hypotheses based on these dimensions relating to formal organizational structure, informal networks, organizational assimilation, and new communication technologies). The individualism/collectivism dimension, for example, has been hypothesized to affect group dynamics such as social loafing (Earley, 1989) and decision shifts (Hong, 1978) both within unicultural groups (e.g., comparing Chinese managers interacting together with American managers interacting together) and multicultural settings (observing employees from different cultures as they interact together).

At times, we also find that Hofstede's work explicitly links values and communication. He argues, for example, that in high power distance countries such as Singapore, the Philippines, France, India, Venezuela, and Portugal, employers and employees are more likely to consider violating the chain of command as constituting serious insubordination. Low power distance countries such as Denmark, New Zealand, and Israel expect people to work around hierarchical chains and do not see hierarchy as an essential part of organizational life. When working in or with high power distance countries, Hofstede suggests, it is important to respect the authority structure and show deference to the formal hierarchy. In low power distance countries, organizations tend to be less formal and have more open communication across the social system (Hofstede, 1984).

Driskill (1995) substantiated these conclusions in a study of Euro-American and Asian Indian engineers. American and Indian coworkers identified situations involving authority, role duties, and supervision as the most salient contexts for the emergence of strong cultural differences. Asian Indians felt that competent supervisors should provide daily and direct surveillance, were very comfortable with an authoritarian decision-making style, and were accustomed to strict adherence to job descriptions and titles. In contrast,

Euro-American workers placed less emphasis on titles and were more comfortable with collaborative decision making and less direct supervision. The results of semantic network analyses also indicate that managerial interpretations of the term *participation* by Danish, Dutch, English, French, and German middle managers were systematically associated with the nationality of the manager and that these differences were consistent with country scores on Hofstede's dimensions of power distance, uncertainty avoidance, and masculinity (Stohl, 1993).

All five of Hofstede's dimensions have also been studied in relation to conflict and negotiation styles (Lee & Rogan, 1991; Ohbuchi & Takahashi, 1994; Ting-Toomey et al., 1991), compliance-gaining and influence strategies (Sanborn, 1993; Smith & Peterson, 1988), managerial decision making (Vitell, Nwachuku, & Barnes, 1993), job and communication satisfaction (Bochner & Hesketh, 1994), and leadership (Smith & Tayeb, 1988). Most of the work in this area supports comparative predictions based on cultural identification (e.g., managers from collectivist cultures are more likely to move toward a single effective leadership style whereas managers from individualistic cultures adapt their styles to situational demands; Smith & Tayeb, 1988): Chinese managers (collectivist culture) have highest performance under group conditions of shared responsibility, American managers perform best when individually responsible for the task (Earley, 1989), managers from collectivist cultures are less likely to use influence strategies based on ingratiation and more likely to use strategies rooted in a collective sharing of responsibility (Smith & Peterson, 1988). Despite this evidence, however, there are a number of studies where the hypotheses are not supported.

In a comprehensive review of the international business negotiation literature, Wilson, Cai, Campbell, Donohue, and Drake (1994) identify several studies whose findings do not fit this model. Lee and Rogan (1991) predicted that managers from collectivist cultures would "place more emphasis on maintaining interpersonal harmony than accomplishing tasks" and therefore would prefer nonconfrontational conflict styles, but their data indicate American managers were more likely to use nonconfrontational styles than their Korean counterparts. In a detailed analysis of bargaining, Graham and his colleagues (Graham, 1985; Graham, Evenko, & Rajan, 1992) did not find significant differences among Brazilian, Japanese, Russian, and U.S. managers' bargaining techniques, although they did find substantial differences in the nonverbal and discourse features of negotiation interaction. Belieav, Muller, and Punnett (1985), however, did find American managers' influence styles more individualistic, impatient, and time conscious than Soviet managers' styles.

Wilson et al. (1994) persuasively argue that these discrepancies are rooted in the far too simple and direct causal relationship that is posited in this literature between culture and communication. Individuals' cultural values and cognitions affect their interactions but only in conjunction and at times in conflict with other personal, situational, structural, and contextual factors. The issue, they suggest, is not whether cultural differences are associated with divergent forms of communicating but rather that the relationship among culture, communication, and organization is more complex than the culture-as-cerebral literature suggests. Specifically, the cognitive approach tends to isolate individuals from the social fabric within which organizations are embedded. However, the processes studied by these scholars, such as negotiating, compliance gaining, adhering to chains of command, and decision making, take place within intricately interwoven cultural tapestries that transcend individuals.

### Culture as Aesthetic

In contrast to the atomistic and microanalytic cognitive approach to culture, culture as aesthetic references the macroprocesses that constitute society. In this sense, culture invokes a state of intellectual and moral development in society and refers to the aesthetic, artistic, literary, musical, and intellectual pursuits of a group of people. Culture is associated with civilization, enlightenment, refinement, and polish (Jenks, 1993). Within this theme there are two major foci: (1) cultural principles of beauty and design and (2) communication activities and aesthetics. In general, this literature argues that organizational communication is a dynamic display of aesthetic qualities. Divergent communication processes and structures reflect and reproduce a collective aesthetic. Communication is a way of knowing. Communication activities and organizational forms are elaborated not as utilitarian responses to the challenges of a volatile global environment but rather as a form of knowledge and action that comprises a culture's pattern of sensibility to and appreciation of the value and beauty of forms (Kuhn, 1996).

*Cultural principles of beauty and design.* Although few scholars in communication have approached the study of organizational divergence from an aesthetic perspective, there are a few noteworthy exceptions in the organizational literature (see Clair & Kunkel, 1998). In one of the earliest references to aesthetics in global organizations, Mitroff (1987) examines the aesthetic principles embodied in a Japanese garden (e.g., nature is not conceived as an orderly precise machine, everything superfluous to the total effect of the garden is discarded, the gardener is concerned with the interaction of every part —shapes, colors, slopes, sounds). Mitroff argues that these represent the deepest expression of Japanese culture which can help us understand the success of Japanese organizational structures such as "just in time" inventory, the communication systems associated with decision making and quality control, and societal institutions such as the Ministry of International Trade and Industry. It is important to note that Mitroff is not claiming that the Japanese have explicitly or deliber-

ately used the concept of a garden in the design of their factories, compensation systems, treatment of employees, or the communication environment. "But," he writes, "there is an uncanny parallel. . . . Is it really any surprise to find a preoccupation with quality in a society that places such emphasis on the value of individual stones?" (p. 179).

More recently, in a series of essays on aesthetics and organizations (Calás & Smircich, 1996) several scholars take the position that (1) aesthetics is an important way of knowing the processual and everyday aspects of organizations (Kuhn, 1996; Ottensmeyer, 1996; White, 1996), and (2) theories of aesthetics help us understand the human artistry of organizational experience in the global marketplace (Buie, 1996). By involving scholars from several countries and disciplines, this special issue explicitly "sought to gain greater understanding of the relationships of cultural and social factors to aesthetics" (Ottensmeyer, 1996, p. 192) and thereby better describe, comprehend, and contend with the complexities of global organizations.

*Communication activities and aesthetics.* When culture is seen as aesthetic, the focus is not so much on organizational artifacts (for a fascinating exception, see Strati's [1996] discussion of chairs and the aesthetic dimension of organizations) but rather on communicative activity and the manner in which organizational life is approached and understood. Kuhn (1996), for example, forcefully argues that aesthetics are reflected in the processual/communicative aspects of organizations:

> The aesthetics of organizations will be displayed dynamically, since they are more akin to those of performing/conducting/directing/producing music, plays, dance, preaching, song, instruction, spectacles, sports, parades, ceremonies, dinners—even life itself. (p. 220)

Despite this resonance with a communicative perspective, few scholars have used aesthetics as a basis for exploring organizational divergence. Yet as the plethora of recent titles suggests (e.g., *Artful Work,* Richards, 1997; "Zen and the Art of Teamwork," Lieber, 1995; *Aesthetics and Economics,* Mossetto, 1993; "Aesthetic Components of Management Ethics," Brady, 1986), cultural principles and philosophies of aesthetics are beginning to infiltrate our understanding of organizational experience. At this time, however, artifacts are most often studied as a concrete embodiment of culture rather than as an interactive and dynamic process of aesthetic sensibility.

## Culture as Concrete Artifact

According to Jenks (1993), culture is often "viewed as the collective body of arts and intellectual work within one society. It includes a firmly established notion of culture as the realm of the produced and sedimented symbolism" (pp. 11-12). In this approach to culture, the emphasis is on the artifacts produced by human interaction. Communication is studied as a "thing" to be analyzed that physically embodies cultural differences. Two types of artifacts are distinguished: (1) communication artifacts (productions such as employee newsletters and corporate handbooks), and (2) objects intended for other uses (such as desks or gifts). All organizational artifacts are seen as communicative manifestations of culture.

*Communication artifacts.* Corporate handbooks, manuals, annual reports, and business letters are just some of the artifacts that may be examined as material manifestations of culture (Anderson & Imperia, 1992; Danowski & Huang, 1994; DeVries, 1994; Fiol, 1989; Varner, 1988a, 1988b). Jang and Barnett (1994) examined the impact of national culture on organizational culture by analyzing the full texts of 35 chief operating officers' letters from the annual reports of 18 American and 17 Japanese companies. The clusters derived from semantic network analysis indicated that the companies' businesses were not reflected in the texts but attributes

of national culture were strongly linked to the artifact. Varner's (1988a, 1988b) studies of German, American, and French business correspondence and DeVries's (1994) assessment of written artifacts throughout the world provide striking examples of the ways in which business cards, business letter format, stationery, and specific linguistic elements of the business letter such as salutations, closes, and forms of address organizationally reproduce and reinforce cultural preferences, values, and attitudes. Studies indicate, for example, that cultural ideas of directness and indirectness are firmly established in the business plans, reports, and other written documents of organizations. Varner and Beamer (1995) argue that the contrasts between direct and indirect interactive strategies often result in employees from each culture finding the others' messages tedious, equivocal, unfocused, inappropriate, incompetent, and at times, intentionally frustrating.

*Artifacts as cultural communication.* Reardon's (1981) study of gift giving provides an intriguing look at the way in which artifacts embody culture. Her interviews with multinational managers indicate that gift giving is a prevalent and important aspect of international business communication. Not only does the gift itself embody cultural meaning, but colors, shapes, and numbers are further instantiations of cultural standards of appropriateness. Goering (1991), in an eight-nation study of voluntary organizations related to a specific health problem, Rett syndrome, examined another type of artifact: organizational logos. Although all country groups used hands in their logos (a basic characteristic of Rett syndrome is compulsive hand gestures), she found systematic differences in the degree of intensity/gentleness and individualism/supportiveness portrayed in the logos that were consistent with country scores on Hofstede's dimensions of cultural variability.

Overall in this approach, researchers "find" culture in the empirical artifact and the object itself is endowed with cultural traces. The microanalytic focus provides compelling examples of how divergence "looks" in the workplace, but does little to help us understand the links between culture, communication, and organization. The next two approaches have a stronger focus on collective sensemaking activities and interpretative processes.

### Culture as a Complex Social Pattern

In this approach, culture is "regarded as the whole way of life of a people" (Jenks, 1993, p. 12). This perspective is the most general and pervasive. Rather than focusing on the ideational system, the focus is on culture as an adaptive system (Child & Tayeb, 1983). Culture is conceived as the "normative glue that holds a system together" (Smircich, 1983) and is composed of the "standards for deciding what is, what can be done, how one feels about 'it,' and how one goes about doing 'it' " (Goodenough, 1970). Organizations are seen as sociocultural entities placed in a particular society within a particular historical context; communicative processes are always grounded in the historical, political, institutional, and economic interstices of society (see, e.g., Kozminski & Obloj, 1993, and Gorski, 1993, for communicative analyses of organizing in the developing market economy in Eastern Europe). Communication transmits what is meaningful within a particular sociocultural context, enacting and reinforcing the distinctive patterns of a given culture. Research within this tradition highlights the ways in which organizations are positioned within society and the ways particular patterns, such as class, gender, and race, are enacted within the organization and identifies specific communicative constructs and concepts that have meaning only within a particular cultural pattern.

Papa, Auwal, and Singhal's (1995) study of the Grameen Bank's successful organizational mobilization and socioeconomic improvement of poor and landless Bangladeshi women serves as an exemplar of the way in which reciprocal relationships among the dominant organizations in society, subcultures of gender and class, and the structural/interactional features of organizations are embedded within this approach. Invoking coorientation theory, the theory of concertive control, and critical feminist theories, Papa et al. include a study of the broad social context of Bangladesh as well as a close analysis of the micropractices of daily organizing.

Their work illuminates how women and men relate to the means of production in an undeveloped economy and explores the ways in which organizational communication becomes the transmitter for empowering women (both in the organization and society) while simultaneously preserving male dominance. For example, because Bangladeshi women are confined to their homes, either in accordance with cultural practices or child care demands, the organization income-generating schemes (contrary to women's traditional role in the culture) were designed to allow women to stay close to home. The educational programs of the Grameen Bank challenged the men who wished to control the economic and social activities of women but were delivered to the women in a paternalistic manner. "Most of the women members are fed information that is intended to serve as a guide for their lives, rather than developing that guide for themselves" (Papa et al., 1995, p. 215). Organizational policies enabled women to relate equally to the means of production by giving them equal access to credit (further undermining the oppressive force of the traditional moneylenders) while coincidentally limiting the income-earning potential because they are restricted from selling their products themselves.

*The position of organizations in society.* When culture is seen as a complex social pattern, the position of economic/occupational institutions within the matrix becomes a fulcrum for understanding organizational communication. For example, some scholars put great significance on the fact that (1) the role of a Japanese business organization is not solely to gain wealth or to display strength but also to contribute to the progress of the community and the nation (see Mitroff, 1987); (2) German economic organizations are seen as a means toward the creation of social stability (Powell, 1995); (3) several cultures (including the United States) operate with efficiency and maximization of profit as the sine qua non of organizations (Thurow, 1983); and (4) in companies such as IRI in Italy, Unilever in Britain, and Belgium's Société Generale de Belgique, widespread societal employment is a primary function of the organization and efficiency is a secondary or tertiary goal (Victor, 1992). As a consequence, they suggest, "what is acceptable or prudent management practice in the United States is often seen as impractical —or even immoral—in other regions of the world" (Steers et al., 1992, p. 321).

These cultural patterns provide an interesting arena for communication research that has been relatively unexplored. For example, the differential manner in which General Motors and Honda faced production cuts in 1993 (GM laid off workers whereas Honda added training to their responsibilities, cut the hours of production per workers, and kept the workforce stable; Sanger, 1993) and AT&T's rationale and decision to lay off 40,000 workers even though the company was making a profit (Andrews, 1992) can help us understand the ways in which organizations rhetorically and instrumentally enact the cultural role of economic institutions.

This approach to culture and organizational communication is most evident in the myriad studies and books that examine distinguishing characteristics of Japanese practices based on political/economic history and institutions to understand their success in the global economy (e.g., Lincoln & Kalleberg, 1990; Mitroff, 1987; Ouchi, 1981; Van Wolferen, 1989). For example, Cole's (1989) insightful book *Strategies for Learning: Small Group Activities in American, Japanese, and*

*Swedish Industry* identifies cultural conditions that strongly influenced how particular organizational strategies related to teamwork were enacted in organizations across three countries. In particular, he notes that the private sector consultants associated with the implementation of quality circle programs in the United States were nonexistent in either Japanese or Swedish cultures and shows how the trajectory of quality circle implementations was affected by the different types of interactions, linkages, and organizational/institutional environments associated with each culture.

Victor (1992) further identifies nine types of cultural patterns that strongly influence organization communication processes across societies: kinship and family structure, educational systems and ties, class systems and economic stratification, gender roles, religion, occupational institutions, political and judicial systems, mobility and geographic attachment, and recreational institutions. His review links the cultural importance of family and kinship ties to hiring practices, investment opportunities, promotion, and organizational identification processes. Although institutional affiliations, such as where one attended college, are important in most societies, they have been shown to play a more critical role in the acquisition of knowledge, resources, and network linkages associated with power and control in some cultures than others (Wysocki, 1988; Zeldin, 1984). Religious and theological influences can be seen in anticipatory socialization practices, attitudes toward work, organizational rituals, and the role of women in organizations (Boulding, 1990).

*Class, gender, and racial issues.* The cultural patterns most often linked to multinational communication processes include class structure, economic stratification, gender roles, and racial identities. Feminist and critical organizational scholars commonly argue that gender relations, similar to class relations, are embedded within the larger culture and create an intraorganizational "relation of power which must be continually maintained, extended, and interactively recreated in the face of changing social conditions" (Walker, 1985, p. 72). Moody's (1997) comprehensive study of contemporary global labor relations and Ryder's (1997) plea that globalization must include social justice for all workers articulate today's concerns with multinational management strategies, international organizations such as the International Monetary Fund, and the ongoing transformation of global capitalism.

Several studies, based on community and organizational ethnographies (see Bossen, 1984), oral histories and interviews (Beneria & Roldan, 1987; Williams, 1990), network analyses (Rosen, 1982), participant observations (Rothstein, 1982), demographic analyses of work group distributions and occupational structure (Faulkner & Lawson, 1991), comparative analyses of the reorganization of production across neo-Fordist states (Gottfried, 1995), and data from UN publications, country-based data, and newsletters from women's organizations (Moghadam, 1999), have examined how changing global and economic conditions in Latin American, Indian, African, and Asian cultural contexts have affected issues of empowerment and employment for both men and women. Fuentes and Ehrenreich (1983), in a book-length study titled *Women in the Global Factory,* argue that multinational corporations in both Latin and Asian cultures exploit female workers by appealing to workers' "feminine sex roles through such organizational activities as beauty pageants and cooking classes; while on the other hand, these corporations resist unionization and repress collective protest" (p. 162). Fernandez-Kelly (1983) studies how working in the export-processing multinational plants in Mexico (*maquiladoras*) affects Mexican families and concludes that women enter factories not as autonomous individuals but as members of highly interconnected and dependent networks that contribute to women's continued structural and interpersonal oppression. Not surprisingly, research also shows that cultural inequities in gender roles permeate the communication ac-

tivities and policies of international unions (Cockburn, 1991) and global attempts at organizing workers (Lubin & Winslow, 1990).

Managerially oriented research has also looked at the communicative implications of cultural patterns of gender and race. Adler (1987) argues that although many of the constraints women face are similar across cultures, there are two distinct models of gender that are culturally based and influence the availability of jobs, strategies for organizational change, reward systems, and so on. One model, typically American, is the equity model, based on assumed similarity. The complementary model is based on assumed difference and is found in Scandinavian, Latin European, African, and Asian cultures. In the equity model, Adler argues, the primary change variables include legal prescriptions to open jobs to women and the training of women in management skills. Change strategies in the complementary model revolve around the creation of enabling conditions for both male and female contributions to be rewarded and combined.

Several books and articles have also explored issues of gender and race as they apply to cultural adjustment within a multinational environment. The difficulties and barriers international businesswomen face around the world have been well documented (e.g., Adler & Izraeli, 1988; Rossman, 1990), and studies are beginning to address the ethical dimensions of expatriate placement in relation to issues of gender and race (Adler, 1991). Although little communication research has yet addressed the pragmatic implications of cultural differences in what actions (if any) legally or experientially constitute sexual or racial harassment, the increasing number of women and minorities who work in multinational environments makes this an important area for future research (see Eyraud, 1993). Moreover, empirical data from international business surveys indicate that spousal involvement in the decision to relocate as well as his or her positive adjustment to the foreign country is critical to the expatriate employee's successful assimilation and work performance

(Berge, 1987; Thornburg, 1990), and research has begun to address the communicative dimensions of cultural adjustment for both the employee and the employee's family (see Stohl, 1995).

*Cultural constructs.* As suggested above, the focus on how distinctive patterns are transmitted through communication leads scholars to identify specific constructs or concepts that have meaning only within the patterned context. These concepts are believed to embody that particular social world and provide an avenue into understanding organizational phenomena. This research operates within an emic viewpoint; that is, the units of analysis are developed from within the culture and may not be comparable across cultures. Steers et al. (1992), for example, discuss the implications for equity theory and worker motivation of the African tradition of *ubuntu,* in which clan obligations make it natural for individuals routinely to share available resources and rewards regardless of who worked to obtain them. DeMente (1981) explicates the sociohistorical context of three Japanese terms, *wa,* which may be roughly translated as peace and harmony; *tatemae,* which implies face or facade; and *honne,* defined as honest voice, to illustrate the ethical principles that underlie Japanese organizational communication practices including what may seem to Western sensibilities their penchant for not being true to their word.[7]

Cultural constructs have also been identified as a way to understand the differences in communication ethics. What may be considered bribery, begging, or blackmail in Western culture, for example, may be *chai* or *zawadi* in eastern Africa, Swahili terms associated with gift giving, relational development, and traditional courtesy (Fadiman, 1986). Indeed, a great deal of research indicates that in many cultures, relational development, based on specific instrumental goals, is not only accepted but seen as a legitimate and appropriate way to do business and attain desirable resources. Hu and Grove (1991) explicate how the development of obligation networks called

*Guanxi* or *kuan-hsi* is central to influence and compliance-gaining attempts in Chinese organizations and Chinese society in general. These exchanges are not used in a cold or calculating manner, but are seen as the "grease" that makes daily life run smooth. In these cultures, those who do not grant special feeling or treatment to those who attempt to establish such instrumental connections may be blamed for "lacking human feeling" (Chang & Holt, 1991, p. 260).

Archer and Fitch (1994) similarly describe the Colombian concept of *palanca* (literally a lever, interpersonally, a connection) as the most purely instrumental form or aspect of an interpersonal relationship. "To move a palanca" or "to shake out a palanca" is to use a relationship like a tool to obtain some objective including getting a job or obtaining scarce resources, service, information, cooperation, or authorizations. They demonstrate how palanca involves transcending rules or scarcity and is inherently a hierarchical action. This ethnographic work is an excellent example of how basic beliefs about persons and relationships pervasive in a culture's interpersonal ideology may be present in organizational communication practices.

Clearly, ethnographic methods are especially appropriate in the study of divergence because "ethnography provides a system of analysis that allows its user to overcome stereotyping by understanding the logic of the way people communicate as a function of their culture" (Victor, 1992, p. 4). The assumptions embedded within an ethnographic approach are closely associated with the conceptualization of culture as communicative practice. These include

1. "Culture extends beyond the walls of organizations and involves in-depth examinations of cultural institutions such as schools, family, voluntary organization, and where possible successful native businesses."
2. "Language and culture are inextricably interwoven."
3. There are "systemic connections between cultural beliefs and the varied behaviors

they generate" (Archer & Fitch, 1994, pp. 88-89).

A distinguishing characteristic between conceptualizing culture as a complex social pattern and as communicative practice, however, is the latter's focus on the active, constitutive role of communication, language, and messages in the social construction of organizations. Within this last theme, communication does not represent culture; rather, discourse articulates identity and communication constitutes culture.

## Culture as Communicative Practice

When scholars approach culture as communicative practice, they are generally concerned with the constitutive role of communication in shaping organizational experience and action. Culture is grounded materially in day-to-day communication activity that cannot be separated from the organization. This perspective rejects the notion that organizations are reified structures; rather, organizations are ongoing products of communication practices that influence and are influenced by connections individuals bring into the system that transcend organizational boundaries. Organizations emerge from the collective, interactive processes of generating and interpreting messages and creating networks of understanding through a matrix of coordinated activities and the ongoing relationships among the subjective and emotional experiences of its members (Krone, Chen, Sloan, & Gallant, 1995; Stohl, 1995). Cultural identification thereby permeates, constrains, and facilitates organizational communication; organizations are the "nexus" of various, communicative, cultural, and social practices (Martin, 1992).

In this approach, communication and culture are inextricably and reciprocally bound. Culture becomes public in the meanings people construct in collective/communicative activity. Hall (1959), for example, "treats culture in its entirety as a form of communication" (p. 28) and goes so far to claim that "culture is

communication and communication is culture" (Hall, 1976, p. 169). Hall's framework distinguishes four communicative/cultural domains that help organize this disparate literature: (1) time (a "silent language" that "speaks more plainly than words"; Hall, 1959, p. 1); (2) context (the information that surrounds the interpretation of an event); (3) space (a "hidden dimension" that results in people of different cultures inhabiting different sensory worlds); and (4) message flow (how messages are constructed and communicated among individuals). Two other foci are (5) language (issues related to multilingualism and the possible choice of one working language) and (6) communication effectiveness (a construct isomorphic with cultural survival).

*Time.* Hall (1976; Hall & Hall, 1987, 1990) uses the terms *monochronic* and *polychronic* to capture the ways in which tempo, rhythm, synchrony, scheduling, lead time, and the rate of information flow become organizational instantiations of culture. In monochronic cultures, time is conceived as material, linear, and substantial, and hence organizations within these cultures (e.g., German, British) tend to compartmentalize functions and people, focus on punctuality and deadlines, and schedule the workday so that people deal with one thing at a time. In polychronic cultures (such as found in the Latin countries), time is nonlinear and insubstantial. Organizational schedules are not nearly as important nor rigidly adhered to, businesspeople do not sequence meetings or activities in a linear fashion, and people are involved with many things at once. In a series of interviews with Asian Indian and Euro-American coworkers, Driskill (1995) found that different perceptions and enactment of time were perceived to be a salient cultural difference during intercultural interactions. Both sets of employees discussed the influence of culture in relation to the perceived pressures associated with deadlines (flexible vs. rigid deadlines) and expectations for task completion (understanding vs. not understanding the time required for task accomplishment). Culture, we see, is embedded in the sensemaking activities of the organization.

*Context.* According to Hall (1976), "context-ing" reflects the types of messages employees create, desire, and understand. Some cultures are distinguished by highly interconnected and extensive communication networks and operate as high-context-message producers where information spreads rapidly and is fairly uncontrolled. A high-context communication or message is one in which most of the information is already in the person and the relationship while very little is in the coded, explicit part of the message. As a result, for most transactions within high-context organizations, people do not require nor do they expect much more background—the context is already very rich with information in which to carry on the transaction. However, when business associates do not know one another, a great deal of time must first be spent establishing the relationship and developing an elaborated context. Then, and only then, can business be conducted. Cultures with segmented networks are low-context-message producers; information is highly focused, compartmentalized, and controlled. Low-context cultures tend to separate personal relationships from work relationships; the mass of the information is vested in the explicit code not in the relationships. Consequently, each time people interact with others they expect and need detailed information.

*Space.* Space, as a hidden dimension of communication, instantiates the structure of experience as it is molded by culture. From this perspective, the spatial and social aspects of a phenomenon are inseparable; space is not just occupied, it is lived and imbued with meaning (Dear & Wolch, 1989; Harvey, 1989; Massey, 1984). For example, several discussions of the Chinese earth force *feng shui* capture the sense of culture as communicative practice (Adler, 1991; DeMente, 1989). Space with "bad feng shui" is believed to prevent an employee from being in har-

mony with nature and will bring failure to its occupants. Feng shui permeates Chinese business practices insofar as communication reproduces and reinforces activities affected by the layout, design, spatial arrangement, and orientation of worksites and houses. Culture is embedded in the communicative activities surrounding the assignment, choice, creation, design, and use of work space.

Hall's groundbreaking cross-cultural work on proxemics, including research on fixed-feature space (buildings, office layouts, functional/spatial segregation), semi-fixed-feature space (furniture arrangements, positions of material objects), and the use and definition of informal space, as basic ways of organizing the activities of people and groups, foreshadows the recent work of many critical, feminist, and postmodern theorists (e.g., Harvey, 1989; Soja, 1989; Spain, 1992). Although many of these scholars are not part of the organizational communication community, they take a meaning-centered approach focusing attention on how space is not only constructed and represented but how it reproduces meanings and power relations within organizations across cultural contexts. For these scholars, communication is not representational, it constitutes knowledge and truth; discourse articulates identity, communication constitutes culture.

Spain (1992), working within a feminist perspective, explores the social construction of domestic and organizational space across cultures ranging from nonindustrial cultures in Mongolia, South America, the Philippines, and the South Pacific to institutional and organizational arrangements in Indian, Algerian, and American societies. She hypothesizes that initial status differences between women and men create certain types of "gendered spaces" and that institutionalized gender segregation then reinforces prevailing cultural male advantage. Tracing workplace designs from the Panopticon through the home office, Spain reveals the common thread of reinforcement of cultural stratification systems through spatial arrangements.

*Message flow.* Studies that conceptualize culture as communicative practice not only compare and contrast the differences among the structural and interactional features of organizing as cultural production but also explore the significance and meaning organizational members attribute to the features of organizations. In this sense, the approach is quite similar to what Geertz (1973) describes as a "semiotic concept of culture" in which the focus is on meanings, interpretive frames, and action as public document or text. Organizational forms are culture's substance; organizations are viewed as symbolic activity.

Several studies indicate that managerial and employee interpretations of what is interpersonally appropriate are embodied in the communicative/cultural practices in the workplace. "Built right into the social arrangements of an organization . . . is a thoroughly embracing conception of the member and not merely a conception of him qua member, but, behind this is a conception of him qua human being" (Goffman, 1959, cited in Deetz, 1992, p. 45). For example, studies show that organizational face-saving practices reproduce and reinforce either high- or low-context cultures. Employees from high-context cultures pay much closer attention to the relationship, avoiding direct confrontation and negative interactions, enabling the maintenance and continued development of highly connected multiplex networks (Kras, 1988). In Japan, face-saving is so critical that managers and employees will use a "politeness strategy" composed of indirection and ambiguity so as to ensure that a person does not unintentionally lose face (Barnlund, 1989).

*Language.* Clearly, as the above examples illustrate, culture as communicative practice transcends issues of language differences in the workplace. Nonetheless, linguistic diversity in the workplace is a critical issue. Surveys of corporate leaders, for example, indicate the "new global aspirations and modern developments in management structures and styles depend even more heavily on good linguistic communication between all members of staff" (Lester, 1984, p. 42). In a series of interviews with corporate workers in several multinational corporations, American, German, and Japanese employees reported that the most serious source of difficulties in their everyday interactions was language (see http://webct.cc.purdue.edu/COM224 for the texts of these interviews). Hilton (1992) reports that although American employees were very critical of their international colleagues' misunderstanding of terminology, poor pronunciation, and inadequate grammar and believed language issues affected productivity, they made no attempt to learn even the most simple foreign phrases. Bantz (1993) notes that although cross-national research teams usually agree on a working language, differences in language competence, comfort in working in a nonnative tongue, and nontransferability of some abstract concepts sometimes minimized the contributions members could make to the team and strongly affected conflict management and the emergence of norms.

Studies outside the field of organizational communication indicate increasing dominance of English as the language of business (Berns, 1992; Grabe, 1988). English has even been adopted as the official company language in multinationals such as the Italian firm Olivetti, Dutch-owned Phillips Corporation, and the Japanese company Komatsu (Varner & Beamer, 1995). Rationales for a "one language" policy include arguments based on instrumental efficiency and interpersonal effectiveness. Having one official language, it is suggested, eliminates the need for costly and time-consuming translation in both written and oral communication, saves money on training and technology, and minimizes cycle time and awkwardness of interaction (Altman, 1989). The predominance of one language, it is argued, also builds social cohesion and trust, allows people to do their jobs better, and makes the work environment safer (Chan, 1995).

When culture is viewed as communicative practice, however, the importance of language choice in the workplace goes far beyond issues of productivity and effectiveness. "The meanings of culture are carried chiefly in symbolic conveyances, language being the most general and pervasive of symbolic system" (Nash, 1990). As communication scholars have so often demonstrated, language not only directs what we say but influences how we shape and frame experience, mediates the meanings we assign to action, helps define members of in- and out-groups, and confers status distinctions (e.g., Giles, 1977; Hymes, 1974; Milroy & Margraine, 1980; Whorf, 1952). When people are asked to comment on other languages, they most often comment on their perceptions of the other cultures (Flaitz, 1988).

Language and cultural identity are inextricably bound together, thus the linguistic context of organizational practices has meaning that transcends instrumentality. Studies show, for example, that in international governmental organizations such as the United Nations and the various commissions associated with the European Union, ministers and officials who are quite competent in English, French, or German, and will speak these languages during informal interactions, still insist on conducting business in their own language regardless of the time or immense cost involved in providing simultaneous translation (Tugendhat, 1988). "It is in our manner of communicating that we display our cultural uniqueness" (Barnlund, 1989, p. 33). Thus, we can see that from the perspective of culture as communicative practice, the pragmatic choice of an official organizational language not only has instrumental effects but enacts who and what is respected, validates certain types of knowledge claims, and creates expertise and privilege (Berns, 1992; Flaitz, 1988).

The French, of course, provide the best known examples of virulent opposition to the hegemony of the English language, but from many quarters there is concern that the increasing use of English as the common business language will lead to an erosion of national identity, the privileging of native English speakers within the workforce, and the encroachment of American values (Berns, 1992). Grabe (1988) writes:

> The English language users of information represent an information cartel: there is no reason to expect that a system which bestows such power upon its controllers would be altered or adapted by these controllers to allow a more democratic system of information management. (p. 68)

In the United States, where the number of employees who speak Tagalog, Spanish, Eastern European, and Asian languages has increased dramatically in the past ten years, several organizations, such as the Walt Disney Corporation, meat packing systems, insurance companies, and medical centers, have developed "English only" policies. Many of these policies have been shown to violate Title VII of the Civil Rights Act of 1964 insofar as they discriminate against specific classes of workers. The legal opinion thus far is that if English-only policies are initiated it must be a legitimate "business necessity" including productivity, quality, and safety; applied only during working hours, not lunch or breaks; and applied to all bilingual employees in the same manner (Chan, 1995). But the issues go much further than Chan's (1995) recommendation that there needs to be a balance among employees' right to communicate in ways in which they are most comfortable, the need for protection from harassment, and the organization's desire to promote a harmonious, cohesive, and safe work environment. Issues of identity, power, and control are tied to language.

One recent approach to the study of multilingualism or "overcoming Babel" in the workplace relates to the processes of translation as organizational practice (see Kölmel & Payne, 1989).[8] Scholars have addressed issues related to translation and the preservation of coherence in meaning (Kirk, 1986), the challenges of different argumentation styles (Hatim, 1989), barriers to effective translation (Brislin, 1989), and the cultural role of the interpreter within various contexts such as conferences, meetings, and negotiations (Altman, 1989). For example,

> in Anglo-Saxon negotiations, the translator is supposed to be neutral, like a black box through which words in one language enter and words in another language exit. The translator in more collectivist cultures will usually serve the national group, engaging them in lengthy asides and attempting to mediate misunderstandings arising from culture as well as language. Very often he or she may be the top negotiator in the group and an interpreter rather than a translator. (Trompenaars, 1994, p. 93)

Banks and Banks (1991), in one of the few organizational communication studies to address directly issues of language diversity in the workplace, demonstrate how the process of translation as mediation (Neubert, 1989), creation (Steiner, 1975), and domination (Glassgold, 1987) pose several other types of interactive problematics. The first type of translation is concerned only with the mechanisms of transferring meaning "accurately" from one language system to another. In the second formulation, translation is "conceived as a cultural transformation of texts," and the translator is viewed as an author/speaker whose sociocultural context, rather than the original sociocultural context, becomes central to the meanings generated by the process. The third process, translation as domination, addresses the political and ideological dimensions of discourse. Banks and Banks suggest that translators constrain meanings by their acts and hence "power relations are both encoded in and partially constituted in the discourse." Their discourse analysis of both the English and Spanish versions of a meeting between the general manager of a hotel and 75 workers whose dominant language is Spanish indicates that the three

problems involving translation in the workplace—inaccuracies, losses of common sociocultural contexts, and changes to power relationships—were all present. They argue that

> translation has the potential to degrade coincident meanings so that worker task accomplishment, productivity, commitment to programs and institution, and compliance are all vulnerable to erosion. The key practical issue is what can be done to mitigate the negative effects of translation. Although research is just beginning there appear to be two classes of remedies that can help the situation—procedural actions and attitudinal changes. . . . Long-term organizational ends will be fostered by an attitude of appreciation for language diversity while recognizing the impracticality of treating all languages identically or equally. (Banks & Banks, 1991, pp. 235-236)

*Communication effectiveness.* Taken together, the studies of linguistic diversity in an organizational setting establish how working together intensifies and highlights cultural differences. As suggested earlier, work on "cultural synergy" (Adler, 1980; Moran & Harris, 1982) and "third-culture building" (Casmir, 1993) also identifies the interactional features and competencies that best maximize the organizational advantages and minimize the disadvantages associated with cultural diversity. The strong managerial and cognitive perspective found in the synergy literature, however, is countered by researchers who view culture as communicative practice. While interested in global accommodation and organizational change, these communication scholars challenge notions of whose interests constitute and should provide measures of effectiveness. They problematize the very ground on which intercultural effectiveness is based.

Shuter (1993), for example, champions the practice of "culturalism" as an option to synergy, third-culture building, and multiculturalism. Like synergy, third-culture building

(Casmir, 1993) entails the commingling of cultural backgrounds to produce a new and different, blended culture, while multiculturalism is an enactment and celebration of cultural, racial, and ethnic differences. Shuter argues that in the contemporary workplace the retention and preservation of cultural identity is as important as the development of pragmatic and instrumental interdependence privileged in the synergy literature. Culturalism emphasizes interdependence, compromise, consensus, cultural adaptation, and development only in the task domain, that is, the performance of activities and behaviors by culturally diverse individuals for mutual gain; cultural integrity is maintained in the expressive realm. By viewing culture as communicative practice, Shuter gives voice to what is called for in multiculturalism (the retention of cultural identity and attitudinal, value, and behavioral differences) in the socioemotional domain while providing for the development of a new voice through communicative practices at the pragmatic level of task completion.

In a series of ethnographies that explore Japanese transplants in the United States, a set of industrial anthropologists goes even further and challenges the notion that multicultural interaction reflects a process of developing, generating, and perpetuating consensus. Rather, they address the processes by which intercultural organizational practices can fragment, mutilate, shrink, deform, and hollow out culture (Hamada & Yaguchi, 1994; Kleinburg, 1994; White & Rackerby, 1994). Hamada and Yaguchi, for example, explore how a corporate ideology, rooted in the paternalistic principles of the traditional Japanese household, begins to dissipate as a schism develops between the principles manifested in symbols (e.g., corporate manuals, ambiguous job descriptions) and the original logic (corporate familialism) of the practices. As Japanese management becomes sensitive to local conditions in the American Midwest, management tries to enhance and strengthen the "family" metaphor but the practices become incongruent with the intent. The culture loses interactive substance through "(1) the process

of growing dissonance between perceived social reality and underlying cultural assumptions, and (2) the process of growing dissonance between manifested symbols and their original meanings" (Hamada & Yaguchi, 1994, p. 194).

Recent studies of the communicative practices associated with worker participation and democracy also address the tensions that arise among individual and group identities, cultural integrity and accommodation, and the maintenance and enactment of traditional values and competitive performance in the global workplace (Alvesson, 1987; Cheney, 1995; Deetz, 1992; Giroux, 1992; Giroux & Fenocchi, 1995; Stohl, 1995). Studying the transition from local to global organizing in one of the oldest employee-owned cooperatives in the world, Mondragón, in the Basque region of Spain, Cheney (1995, 1999) looks at what it means to approach democracy, participation, and culture as self-critical, self-regenerating, and self-correcting communication processes. Giroux (1992) examines four decision-making cases in the Movement Desjardins in Quebec and addresses the ways in which "relations based on shared meaning" allow the cooperatives to maintain its sociocultural project, "relations based on use" form the economic project, and "relations based on property" give control over execution of the cooperative projects. In these studies, cultural values such as solidarity and equality are realized to a great extent through talk. Cheney finds participation and democracy are continually contested terms, and Stohl (1995) specifies the paradox of compatibility to describe the interactive pressures that evolve when cultural practices are incompatible with prescribed participative acts. Giroux's (1992) longitudinal study of participation of women in two cultural sector cooperatives in Quebec concludes that notwithstanding the democratic discourse maintained in cooperatives, actual practice by no means reflected gender equality in these organizations.

Overall, culture as communicative practice unveils the emergent and often contradictory relationships among the subjective experiences, multiple languages, behavioral patterns, and volatile structures inherent in multinational organizations. The consistent coupling of culture and communication puts meaning-centered interpretive processes at the center of the study of global organizing.

### Ironies Found in the Divergence Literature

In summary, across all conceptualizations of culture, the divergence literature provides strong evidence that the dynamic structures of contemporary organizations are produced and reproduced through the culturally saturated processes of organizing. Although some scholars suggest that culture is less significant to the web of rules and organizational structuring the further a country is along the road toward industrialization (Knudsen, 1995), cultural differences are blatantly obvious in organizational communication processes across both highly industrialized and less industrialized capitalistic nations. Systematic structural, processual, and interpretive distinctions are found across cultures despite environmental pressures toward organizational convergence. Culture enters organizations artfully, unself-consciously, and piecemeal through several avenues simultaneously. People create, enter, and leave organizations not as autonomous individuals but as members of highly interconnected and interdependent cultural networks.

However, what is not clear in this literature is the association between the mechanisms and processes of communicative convergence and divergence. That is, as provocative as the relationships among culture, communication, and organizing may be there is still little information about the conditions under which convergence or divergence takes precedence or explorations and explanations of the dynamic interplay among the two. Yet it is the continual management of these opposing forces that constitutes contemporary organizational experience. The imperatives of the global market, the availability of international resources,

the fluidity of a worldwide workforce, and the development and use of new communication/information technologies are making unprecedented demands on today's organizations while simultaneously people's cultural identities are becoming more salient both in and outside the workplace.

There are several ironies that pervade the divergence literature that contribute to this lack of coherence and integration across perspectives. To begin, much of the divergence literature is atheoretical, treating culture as a residual category or independent variable presumed to account for variations in organizing but with little explanation for how this happens. Tayeb (1992) cautions:

> Evoking national and cultural explanations for the existence of similarities or differences enables researchers to better understand their research only if the similarities and differences are an integrated aspect of their theoretical frameworks. (p. 133)

Second, despite the fundamental assumption that cultural differences significantly affect social practices, the theoretical principles and the relationships among variables are expected to be stable and unchanging across differing cultural milieux. Ironically, the presumption that relationships among constructs will be the same across cultures magnifies the possibility that researchers will interpret communication differences as meaningful when in fact the differences may be more apparent than real. By minimizing the possibility of finding evidence of convergence, the divergence literature possibly exaggerates the effects of culture and masks the synchronous homogenizing effects of globalization.

Third, a great deal of the divergence literature simply extends traditional topics into the global arena, conceptualizing questions, organizations, and communication in the same ways they have always been conceived. Without a radical reconfiguration of what constitutes relevant organizational boundaries, a decentering of organizational activities, and a reconsideration of communicative practices as the cause, medium, and outcome of fragmented organizational structures, the divergence research enacts "business as usual." We may continue to learn more about how organizations differ across cultures, yet the macro- and microlevel implications of the embedded nature of contemporary organizational communication will remain obscure.

In the next section, the implications of the theoretical, methodological, and practical parochialisms that imbue both the convergence and the divergence literature are further detailed. As we shall see, our typical ways of doing both types of research are challenged by the unsettled systems of cultured relations that permeate disciplinary practices.

## THEORETICAL, METHODOLOGICAL, AND PRACTICAL ISSUES IN GLOBALIZING ORGANIZATIONAL COMMUNICATION

Some prominent scholars in the field argue, in essence, that the academic establishment impedes or constrains the conduct and dissemination of international or cross-national efforts. This is done presumably through the use of parochial and culture-bound theories of management, through the insistence on traditional research methods as the criteria for journal acceptance, and through the downplaying of cross-cultural studies in our doctoral programs. (Steers et al., 1992, p. 322)

At first glance, the issues raised by Steers et al., writing about the management discipline, either do not seem to apply to the field of organizational communication or at most represent only a small fragment of our field. After all, we often self-consciously distinguish ourselves by the widely disparate methods, epistemologies, and theoretical assumptions that bind us together (e.g., Smith, 1993), and we collectively celebrate the plurality of voices in our field that give expres-

sion to various forms of knowledge, relations, and ways of organizing (Mumby & Stohl, 1996).

Nonetheless, Steers and his colleagues raise three important issues for our consideration. Each of these concerns, specified here as *theoretical, methodological,* and *pragmatic* parochialism, addresses issues of conception and praxis for the study of globalization and communication in multinational organizations. As suggested earlier, several of the theories they identified as "culture bound" have had a strong and continuing influence on organizational communication research. Yet rarely have we been concerned with the cross-cultural applicability of the theories we employ. Moreover, even though contemporary communication theories seem well suited to address the dynamic tensions embedded in the interpersonal, organizational, and community interfaces of global systems, these multilevel, interdependent, constraining, and enabling alignments are rarely studied together. Second, despite our field's acceptance of both interpretive and social-scientific methods, important methodological issues have not been resolved. Methodological parochialism refers to issues of transferability of research protocols, approaches to establishing construct validity and interpretive reliability, statistical appropriateness, and language into a culturally diverse, multilingual research environment.

Pragmatic parochialism encompasses the third concern. Although there has been recognition that it is counterproductive for our discipline to maintain a Maginot Line of scientific and scholarly isolationism (Jamieson & Cappella, 1996; Stohl, 1993), the subdivisions in our field and academic departments often resemble national borders in their capacity to limit knowledge, restrict cooperation, and impede collaboration. Arbitrary disciplinary boundaries not only create barriers for learning but also limit the types of questions researchers ask, the conceptualization of relevant constructs, the types of organizations we study, the ways we search for the answers, and the ethical stances we take. The issues faced by communication scholars as we try to understand, map, and reconcile the processes of divergence and convergence are paralleled in the debates contesting the efficacy of comparative politics and international relations scholars, and more generally, the relative value of area studies specialists and global experts. They too are struggling to find ways to study and "understand how the broad currents of social change are shaped, altered, and redefined as they come into contact with a variety of local circumstances" (Heginbotham, 1994, p. A68).

Most assuredly, issues of generalizability, interpretive reliability, methodological appropriateness, and disciplinary isolationism are not unique to global and multicultural organizational communication research. The relative newness and rapid burgeoning of this area of study, however, coupled with the increasing globalization of the production of knowledge, make these concerns particularly salient in this context. Each of these issues is designed to challenge and stimulate scholars to reconsider past practices and develop creative and collaborative solutions that reflect the dynamic and complex environment of contemporary organizations. (See Table 10.4 for a summary of the issues and strategies.)

## Theoretical Parochialism

A major premise of this chapter is that organizational communication takes place at the intersection of contexts, actors, relations, and activities that cannot be disassociated from one another. Theories therefore need to encompass the ways in which economic/organizational action is embedded in ongoing and overlapping systems of social relations constituting and reproducing trust/mistrust, power/control, and order/chaos in the global system. Yet despite the potential utility of structuration, postmodern, critical, chaos, and network/systems theories to address the multilevel and opposing forces of convergence and divergence, very little of our research has focused on communication efforts to organize

global transformation within a local system. Moreover, little consideration has been accorded the cultural biases of the theoretical perspectives we have used to study organizational convergence or divergence.

## Cross-Cultural Applicability

Several scholars have identified cultural biases embedded in the social-scientific and interpretive theories that have influenced organizational studies of convergence and divergence. From motivation, attribution, equity, and contingency theories to critical theory, postmodernism, and feminism, the Eurocentric foundations of these theories belie their universality and cross-cultural applicability (Asante, 1987; Boyacigiller & Adler, 1991; Hofstede, 1984; Sanborn, 1993).

Lee and Jablin (1992), in one of the few communication studies to address directly the issue of theoretical universalism (see Sullivan & Taylor's [1991] empirical test of compliance-gaining theory in international settings for another exception), found the transferability of Hirschman's (1970) theory of exit, voice, loyalty, and neglect to the East Asian cultural context was not straightforward. Their study, based on surveys and written responses to hypothetical scenarios, compared the communicative responses of Korean, Japanese, and American students to dissatisfying work conditions. The results supported the generalizability of Hirschman's model to Korean culture but the comparisons between cultures were quite provocative. Specifically, although they found that Korean and Japanese respondents were significantly more loyal in their communicative responses to dissatisfying work conditions than were the American respondents, a close examination of the probabilities, patterns, and meanings of the communicative responses underscored the importance of specific differences (in this case values of the family and individual competitiveness) even among workers from different

**TABLE 10.4**   Suggestions for Future Research

| Issue | Strategy |
|---|---|
| Theoretical parochialism | |
| Overgeneralized theoretical applications | Explicitly address the constraints and influence of our own cultural values on how we conceptualize organizational phenomena |
| | Study non-U.S. and non-Western organizations from both etic and emic perspectives |
| | Develop thick descriptions of organizational communication and the contexts in which organizations are embedded |
| Interpretive reliability and construct validity | Establish the equivalence of constructs and operationalizations prior to the interpretation of comparative results |
| Implicit universalism | Explication of the cultural and geographic domain of theory and research project |
| | Indicate the national and cultural aspects of the research sample |
| Methodological parochialism | |
| Method transferability | Triangulation of social-scientific and interpretive methods |
| | Integration of qualitative and quantitative approaches |
| Statistical appropriateness | Pretest measures on matching cultural sample |
| | Develop alternative procedures |
| | Use nonparametric statistics |
| Assumptions of homogeneity | Specify relevant subcultural identifications of sample |
| Language choice | Back translations |
| | Translation by mediation teams |
| | Multilingual research team |
| Practical parochialism | |
| Insularity of researchers | Create multinational, multicultural, interdisciplinary research teams |
| Limited models | Expand the organizational domain of our research (i.e., nonprofit, alternative organizations, governmental organizations, nongovernmental organizations) |
| Limited topics | Explore issues such as the impact of communication technologies, ethics from both convergence and divergence perspectives |

countries who share a common sociocultural heritage.

### Relationships Among Theoretical Concepts

Other studies that have looked at the cross-cultural applicability of communication constructs also suggest that posited theoretical relationships supported in one cultural context may not exist in the same form in another context. For example, Kleinburg's (1994) ethnography of a Japanese transplant notes markedly different interpretations of, and strong concern or lack of concern for, ambiguity expressed by American and Japanese employees in the same company. She concludes that the definition of organizational ambiguity itself is culturally constructed. Morley, Shockley-Zalabak, and Cesaria (1997), using a rule-based approach, found that the relationships among organizational rules, culture themes, founder values, hierarchical position, communication activities, and perceptions of a variety of organizational outcomes were similar in Italian and American high-technology companies although there was far less agreement on what constitutes value rules within the Italian companies. Ticehurst (1992) found that the communication satisfaction questionnaire tapped different functions of communication satisfaction for Australians as compared to Americans.

Clearly, issues of theoretical parochialism are complex, and there is a great need for more sophisticated and programmatic ethnographies, case studies, and comparative research that are consistent with the multivocal, equivocal, and embedded activities that comprise organizing. Increased awareness of the constraints and the efficacy of our theories, however, must also be coupled with a reconsideration of our own research agendas in light of our own "cultural baggage." That is, organizational communication scholars need to address explicitly the constraints and influence of our own cultured practices on how we

conceptualize and study organizational phenomena. For example, even the idea of searching for generalizable and universal theory is culture specific. Engaging in self-reflection and expanding our organizational horizons will not only help communication researchers learn more about the limits and the strengths of current theory, but it will enable us to develop new theory and insights into the processes of organizing. The disjunctures provide an opportunity to reexamine the assumptions underlying our theories and the posited relationships among theoretical concepts; the convergences enable us to build a strong foundation on which to address contemporary issues in the global workplace.

Moreover, concerns related to the transferability and comprehensiveness of theory in case and comparative studies must not only extend to theoretical foundations but also to the appropriateness of the statistical and methodological assumptions underlying the procedures and instruments developed to explore or test theory. Boyacigiller and Adler (1991) argue that "even when the applicability of these theories to other cultures is tested, researchers usually select methods that are most acceptable according to American norms, thereby rendering results that are culturally conditioned" (p. 272).

### Methodological Parochialism

Within the field of organizational communication, a number of widely used survey instruments such as the ICA audit, the Organizational Commitment Questionnaire, job satisfaction indexes, managerial style questionnaires, upward influence surveys, and participatory decision-making scales, developed in the United States and Western Europe, have been employed in cross-cultural comparative studies, and traditional univariate and multivariate statistical analyses have been undertaken (e.g., Barnett & Lee, 1995; Downs et al.,

1995; Hirokowa & Miyahara, 1986; Sanborn, 1993; Page & Wiseman, 1993; Stewart et al., 1986). Although each of these studies uses surveys that have been shown to be reliable and valid in the past, the heavy reliance on American and British workers to develop these questions, scales, and procedures raises questions about the appropriateness of the methods across cultural contexts.

## Equivalence of Measures

Lincoln and Kalleberg (1990) found that when confronted with Likert type questions to which there were no socially correct answers, American employees tended to respond with relatively extreme measures whereas the Japanese counterparts tended to respond more toward the middle of the scale. Barnett and Lee (1995), on the other hand, found that when Americans are asked to estimate the dissimilarity among pairs of symbols, they tend to use far smaller scales than their Japanese or Taiwanese counterparts. Adler, Campbell, and Laurent (1989) found that Chinese managers from the People's Republic of China produced bimodal distribution of responses to several questions on the Laurent Management Questionnaire, which had a normal distribution when given to managers from nine European countries and the United States. Thus, traditional techniques, such as rescaling mean values for purposes of statistical comparison, may mask the most important differences to be found in a cross-cultural study.

These examples raise the strong possibility that not only does culture influence how we feel, what we value, what things mean, how we organize, and how we communicate but also affects the ways in which people respond to research protocols. We must, then, remain skeptical of studies such as that of Downs et al. (1995), who conclude that communication with supervisors, top management, and colleagues as well as communication climate were consistent predictors of commitment across the United States, Australia, and Guatemala when they used the standard items on the Communication Satisfaction Questionnaire (Downs & Hazen, 1977) and Organizational Commitment Inventory (Cook & Wall, 1980). Items such as "I sometimes feel like leaving this organization for good" and "Even if the firm were not doing well financially, I would be reluctant to change to another employer" may not be scaled in the same manner nor tap the American-based construct "organizational loyalty" for respondents in countries like Guatemala where for 40 years (until late 1996) thousands of citizens had been killed annually by a series of military governments aligned with leading industrialists and the economic elite.

Indeed, similar results may have very different causal explanations. Universal responses to the same set of constraints and the similarity of responses and structures may be affirming the rapid rate of cultural diffusion and imitation that is indicative of the interpenetration of global communications, management training, and popular culture (Dogan & Pelassy, 1984). Or as Adler et al. (1989) found, differential reasoning may be associated with the same responses. For example, although over 66% of Italian and Japanese managers agreed with the statement "It is important for managers to have precise answers to most of the questions his [sic] subordinates may raise about their work" (only 10% of the Swedish managers agreed) the reasons they gave were quite different. Italians explained that managers should be experts, whereas Japanese respondents believed, "A Japanese would never ask his boss a question he could not answer" (p. 70).

Riordan and Vandenberg (1994), using covariance structure analytic procedures, ask the central question: "Do employees of different cultures interpret work-related measures in an equivalent manner?" (p. 643). Looking at three measures strongly associated with organizational communication processes (i.e., the Organizational Commitment Questionnaire, Mowday, Steers, & Porter, 1979; the Organization-Based Self-Esteem instrument, Pierce, Gardner, Cummings, & Dunham,

1989; and the Satisfaction With My Supervisor scale, Vandenberg & Scarpello, 1992), the answer is a resounding no. Clearly, then, there is a need to establish the equivalency of constructs and measures prior to interpreting differences on self-report variables between culturally diverse groups. A priori, we cannot know that the same conceptual frame of reference will be evoked across cultures, that interview questions will be interpreted similarly, that network linkages are comparable, or that diverse groups will calibrate the scores of an instrument in the same manner.

## *Appropriateness of Methods*

But it is not only the use of surveys and statistics alone that are of concern for researchers in a multicultural environment. The procedures and methods designed to collect both qualitative and quantitative data may be culturally inappropriate. For example, the use of hypothetical scenarios may not be a suitable methodology for cultures that typically engage in holistic thinking and circular patterns of thought and discourse, whereas they are quite useful in cultures characterized by linear, step-by-step cognitive patterns (Adler et al., 1989). Requests for certain types of organizational access may violate cultural norms, participatory observations may transgress cultural expectations, and interviewing techniques may compromise employees. Issues such as organizational entry, confidentiality, trust, social desirability, and informed consent are culturally constructed. Thus, regardless of whether we conduct ethnographies, interviews, participant observations, surveys, network analysis, or experiments, when researchers enter the global arena, cultural awareness, knowledge of others, and sensitivity are mandatory.

The sensibility that is needed is complicated by another potential form of methodological parochialism, the assumption of sample homogeneity. It is ironic that at a time when organizations and researchers are increasingly aware of, and sensitive to, issues of diversity in the American workplace (Cox, 1993; Fine, 1991) so much of the research assumes that organizations within other countries are composed of monocultural workforces. For example, despite what we know of the linguistic and regional diversity within Chinese society, studies of Chinese managers often treat them as one unicultural sample, middle-level managers from Hong Kong are often collapsed into one cultural unit for analysis, members of British and American corporate boards of directors are assumed to represent the national characteristics of the corporation's national origin, and workers in a Mexican company are often all labeled "Mexican" (e.g., Chen & Chung, 1994; Kras, 1988; Krone, Garrett, & Chen, 1992). This homogenization is especially troublesome when the basic goal of the research is to do some form of cultural description or comparison among groups. Just as it has become standard to describe demographic characteristics such as gender, age, and race, researchers need to investigate, adapt to, and if relevant, report the national, regional, and linguistic diversity within their sample groups. Cultural identity embodies a difference that makes a difference.

## *Language and Translation*

The interconnected nature of language and cultural identity also highlights the methodological significance of language choice in studies that cross national boundaries. We are faced with our own linguistic limitations in an environment in which the use of a particular language creates a system of relations that may be affirming or disconfirming, engaging or alienating participants in the research endeavor. Communication is, by its very nature, characterized by linguistic difference. Often there are no easy equivalents for terms or phrases (e.g., *manager* cannot be directly translated into either French or Italian, the English translation of the German term *papierkrieg* to red tape neutralizes a term that literally means paper war; see Victor, 1992), connotations and denotations are difficult for nonnative speakers to assess, the use of one language minimizes the diversity of the sampling frame and the comfort of the participants, and translation and interpretation are costly in terms of effort, time, and money. Nonetheless, with over 2,500 languages spoken around the world (Bryson, 1990) it is highly likely that research in contemporary organizations will take place in a multilingual environment.

Most cross-cultural researchers identify back translation as the most effective strategy for addressing issues of language diversity and equivalence (Varner & Beamer, 1995; Victor, 1992). Back translation is a two-step process. First, one translator (preferably a native speaker of one of the languages) puts the survey, interview questions, documents, and so forth into a second language, then the messages are translated back into the original language by a second translator. In this manner, blatant mistranslations as well as nuanced distortions can be identified. Adler et al. (1989), for example, express their dismay when they found that the item "Most conflicts in a company can be productive" on the Laurent management questionnaire became "Much physical violence in a company can be productive." on the Mandarin language questionnaire.

Wright, Lane, and Beamish (1988), however, identify several potential problems with back translations based on translators who (1) are unfamiliar with the technical vocabulary, (2) use a particular dialect that is inappropriate in the particular setting, and (3) are insensitive to political nuances and organizational constraints. Further, they indicate that there are often as many errors in back translations as there are in the original translations. In a comparative study of Thai and British organizations, Wright (1984) developed an alternative. She had a panel of four or five native speakers work through interview schedules and surveys (with the primary investigator providing input and explanation along the way), had another native speaker put their translations into graceful language, and then brought the translations back to the panel for a final evaluation.

Another approach designed to alleviate language problems and build on the strength embedded in linguistic diversity is to develop a multilingual research team who conceptualizes, develops, and collaboratively carries out the research project. Being able to move back and forth among relevant language groups enables scholars with multilingual skills to develop unique perspectives and insights at both the theoretical and praxis levels. Bantz (1993) provides a detailed look at his own experiences on a multilingual research team and as discussed earlier, gives many pragmatic suggestions for balancing issues of creativity and cohesiveness, effectiveness and efficiency, ethical responsibility and mutual respect within such groups. He describes the various tactics used to minimize the limitations of working in one language (English), including the legitimization and normalization of fast-spaced language switching during group discussion, which facilitated understanding, vigorous debate, and linguistic sensitivity.

### Pragmatic Parochialism

According to the "law of requisite variety" (Weick, 1969), organizations, to survive, must develop complexity equivalent to the diversity of their interactive environments. And in today's volatile and increasingly complex and interconnected global system, organizations are diffusing functions, diversifying structures, integrating units, and creating greater degrees of flexibility. Likewise, researchers who work in and study these complex and evolving systems require diverse sets of skills and expertise.

### Multidisciplinary and Multicultural Research

Organizational communication scholarship in the global environment requires at least an understanding of past and present economic, sociocultural, political, and business practices. It is no longer productive to isolate ourselves individually or wrap ourselves up collectively in the parochial cloth of our academic specialties. Multidisciplinary research teams can help facilitate requisite variety. Interdisciplinary research, however, without a multicultural component will not fully address the limiting consequences of traditional individualistic research programs. We need to develop more international collaborations, bringing together cultural insiders and outsiders, melding etic and emic perspectives. Just as the advantages of diverse work groups are well documented, anthropologists have long recognized that similarity, familiarity, and presumption (derived from a "native" perspective) may be impediments to analyses and descriptions that are not culture bound and trivial (Hamada & Yaguchi, 1994).

Pragmatic parochialism may also insinuate itself into the very fabric of our research in the most mundane manner yet have significant influence on our work. When choosing where to conduct our research, for example, "vacation empiricism," that is, choosing research sites based on availability and desirability of location, can severely limit the potential theoretical contributions of our work. Steers et al. (1992) urge that organizational researchers focus on "theory-based sampling, not sampling-based theory" (p. 328).

### Diversifying Organizational Types

To address the demands of this new research agenda, we also need to be less parochial in the types of organizations we study. As this review indicates, most of the research on cultural variability and organizational communication is concentrated in the profit-making, multinational sector. International labor unions, nonprofit organizations, worker collectives, international governmental agencies, and transnational voluntary associations are just a few of the types of organizations markedly absent from the organizational communication literature. By sheer numbers alone they should be included in our typologies and studies (there are over 18,000 such organiza-

tions reported in the *Yearbook of International Organizations*), but their importance goes far beyond their ubiquitous presence.

At a time when we are looking for solutions to our social and global problems in new partnerships among business and industry, education, government, and citizen groups, who, how, and what we study have powerful ethical implications. The old social contract has been broken and the community-organizational-individual relationship has been transformed. Globalization does not serve all interests equally. Looking at different types of organizations can provide us with alternative models, metaphors, ways of organizing and coming together that may be better suited for dealing with the complex, volatile, multicultural issues facing us today. The parochial view of what constitutes an organization worthy of study severely limits what we can learn about, who we can learn from, and who we will learn with.

## CONCLUSIONS

This is a world of complex connections. Joint ventures between McDonald's Restaurants of Canada and the Moscow city council (Vikhanski & Puffer, 1993) seem commonplace. Managerial decisions in a small savings and loan company in Ohio are tightly coupled with the value of British oil stocks (Boulding, 1990). Insensitivity to intercultural relationship formation by just a few members in an international work group can stymie years of sensitive negotiations and financial commitments to develop a cooperative joint venture (Seelye & Seelye-James, 1995). Power, influence, and financial resources of multinational corporations are far greater than those of many nations (Feld & Jordan, 1988). Employees can work closely together for the same company for years while remaining 12,000 miles and 12 time zones apart.

Thus, it is not surprising that in the years between the publication of the first and second editions of the *Handbook of Organizational Communication* the number of studies addressing communication processes and multinational organizing has dramatically increased. An essential part of contemporary organizational experience is communicating in a context of global interdependence and multiculturalism. Culture is not a thing that can be managed, controlled, or contained but rather a constitutive feature of organizing.

Certainly, the heightened interest in the dynamic tension between communication, culture, and organization invigorates traditional topics of study, giving them greater currency as well as opening up new sets of questions, issues, and concerns. A primary conclusion of this chapter is that organizations and individuals are simultaneously managing environmental, technological, and social pressures to become more similar while maintaining cultural differences. Influence attempts, compliance gaining, feedback, performance appraisals, and decision making take on greater complexity when individuals are trying to manage multiple and often conflicting identities in the global workplace. Organizational identification, team commitment, communication satisfaction, and communicative competence develop new meanings and new relations that transcend traditional organizational boundaries. Intercultural training, the involvement of the family in expatriate selection and adjustment, the role of organizations in community development, the introduction of new communication technologies, cultural conceptions of employee rights, and differing interpretations of harassment problematize concerns about communication ethics and definitions of responsible communication.

In other words, to understand and reconcile the processes of divergence and convergence, we need to continue to ask questions that focus on their interplay across cultural contexts. For example, uncertainty and ambiguity are constitutive features of the global environment. Does the management of ambiguity (as evidenced in mission statements, organizational symbols, and employee publications)

allow organizations to manage the tensions between processes of convergence and divergence? Do organizations use distinctive communication strategies to manage ambiguity as they move from domestic to global forms of organizing? How do organizational socialization experiences and programs reinforce the concurrent strengthening/weakening of organizational/cultural identifications? What sorts of framing devices are used in leader-member communication to enact global changes while maintaining the integrity of individual affiliations?

These sorts of questions resonate with the practical tensions that exist between processes of convergence and divergence in a multicultural environment. Not circumscribed by traditional organizational or disciplinary boundaries, the field of organizational communication is ideally suited to address the interpenetration of multiple spheres and interpretations of communicative activity. Explorations of the properties of emergent networks that help or hinder organizations and individuals to compensate for the cultural tensions inherent in the global workplace; explications of how communication outside the workplace (at the international, national, local, and interpersonal levels) reflects, reinforces, or retracts efforts toward cultural/organizational convergence; and identification of what and how specific communicative structures, processes, and message characteristics enable individuals and organizations to transcend, manage, or eliminate potential clashes between local and global practices will contribute greatly to our understanding of the substance and process of global organizing.

In summary, organizational communication scholars are well positioned to study the dynamic structuring of globalization and the culturally saturated processes of organizing and sensemaking. As a field, we are sensitized to the central problematics of voice and pluralistic understandings of what counts as rational, unified by a fundamental concern with messages, interpretations, symbols, and discourse, and grounded by an integrative communication orientation that at its most basic level recognizes meaning as internally experienced, subjective, embedded within larger systems, and socially constructed. Our participation and contributions to the scholarly discourse of globalization are just beginning.

## NOTES

1. The map is distributed by Public Service Indiana (PSI Energy, 1994).

2. See, for example, the introductions to special issues including those by Calás (1994), Earley and Singh (1995), and Tichy (1990).

3. Given the delay of the publication of this handbook, however, the majority of citations in this text are to articles published prior to 1997. Nonetheless, the conclusions drawn from this review are still representative. Organizational communication scholars continue to grapple with issues related to finding appropriate theoretical and methodological positions to enable us to participate fully and find our voice in the scholarly discourse of globalization.

4. Unlike communication adaptation theory where convergence is defined as the adjustment and accommodation of one's interpersonal communication style to match one's partner and divergence is narrowly construed as the adherence to cultural communication patterns in the face of difference (see Larkey, 1996, for a review of this literature), convergence here refers to the similar and mutual accommodation of organizational communication practices to external conditions. Divergence refers to the structural, processual, and interpretive distinctions within organizations that are a direct result of cultural differences that remain despite similar environmental pressures.

5. See the Monge and Contractor chapter in this volume for a discussion of global network organizations.

6. It is important to note that these dimensions do not refer to the values, behaviors, or communication of all people within any given culture; rather, they are generalized normative descriptions or stereotypes of large collectivities (Adler, 1991). Thus, these dimensions do not negate the existence of subcultures or individual differences. Indeed, throughout this literature scholars caution that knowledge of a person's culture cannot predict a particular individual's behavior (see Hofstede, 1984, pp. 24-25, for a discussion of the difference between ecological [between-culture] and within-society correlations).

7. See Goldman (1994) for a detailed review of another indigenous cultural precept, *ningensei*, that helps us understand Japanese organizational communication.

8. Another suggestion has been the use of an artificial or constructed language (Bryson, 1990). Indeed, over the past century several languages have been constructed, including Esperanto, Volapuk, Logolan, Frater, Anglic, and Sea speak, to neutralize linguistic difficulties and promote international understanding across contexts (Bryson, 1990). But despite the fervent arguments that "the unequal distribution of power between languages is a recipe for permanent language insecurity, or outright language oppression, for a large part of the world's population" (the 1996 Prague manifesto of the Movement for the International Language Esperanto; see www.esperanto.se), the practical, ideological, and social ramifications of this approach have doomed these efforts.

## REFERENCES

Adler, N. (1980). *Cultural synergy: The management of cross-cultural organizations*. San Diego, CA: University Associates.

Adler, N. (1987). Women in management worldwide. *International Studies of Management and Organization, 16*(3-4), 3-32.

Adler, N. (1991). *International dimensions of organizational behavior* (2nd ed.). Boston: PWS-Kent.

Adler, N., Campbell, N., & Laurent, A. (1989, Spring). In search of appropriate methodology: From outside the People's Republic of China looking in. *Journal of International Business Studies, 20*, 61-74.

Adler, N., Doktor, R., & Redding, S. (1986). From the Atlantic to the Pacific century: Cross-cultural management reviewed. *Journal of Management, 12*, 295-318.

Adler, N., & Ghadar, L. (1990). International strategy from the perspective of people and culture. In A. Rugman (Ed.), *Research in global strategic management* (pp. 179-205). Greenwich, CT: JAI.

Adler, N., & Israeli, D. (1988). *Women in management worldwide*. Armonk, NY: M. E. Sharpe.

Ady, J. (1994). *Minimizing threats to the validity of cross-cultural organizational research*. Thousand Oaks, CA: Sage.

Albert, R. (1983). The intercultural sensitizer or culture assimilator: A cognitive approach. In D. Landis & R. Brislin (Eds.), *Handbook of intercultural training: Issues in training methodology* (Vol. 2, pp. 186-217). New York: Pergamon.

Altman, J. (1989). Overcoming Babel: The role of the conference interpreter in the communication process. In R. Kölmel & J. Payne (Eds.), *Babel: The cultural and linguistic barriers between nations* (pp. 73-86). Aberdeen, Scotland: Aberdeen University Press.

Alvesson, M. (1987). Organization, culture, and ideology. *International Studies of Management and Organization, 17,* 4-18.

Amir, Y. (1969). Contact hypothesis in ethnic relations. *Psychological Bulletin, 71,* 319-341.

Anderson, C., & Imperia, G. (1992). The corporate annual report: A photo analysis of male and female portrayals. *Journal of Business Communication, 29,* 113-128.

Andrews, E. (1992, December 4). Job cuts at AT&T will total 40,000, 13% of its staff. *New York Times,* p. A1.

Archer, L., & Fitch, K. (1994). Communication in Latin American multinational organizations. In R. Wiseman & R. Shuter (Eds.), *Communicating in multinational organizations* (pp. 75-93). Thousand Oaks, CA: Sage.

Asante, M. (1987). *Afrocentric idea.* Philadelphia: Temple University Press.

Ashcraft, K., & Pacanowsky, M. (1995). *Beyond baby boom: An office dialogue of control.* Paper presented at the Top Three Panel, Organizational Communication Division, Speech Communication Association, San Antonio, TX.

Ball, D., & McCulloch, W. (1993). *International business: Introduction and essentials.* Plano, TX: Business Publications.

Banks, S., & Banks, A. (1991, November). Translation as problematic discourse in organizations. *Journal of Applied Communication Research,* 223-241.

Bantz, C. (1993). Cultural diversity and group cross-cultural team research. *Journal of Applied Communication Research, 20,* 1-19.

Barber, B. (1992, March). Jihad vs. McWorld. *Atlantic Monthly,* pp. 53-63.

Barnett, G., & Lee, M. (1995, May). *A symbols and meaning approach to organizational cultures of banks in the U.S., Japan and Taiwan.* Paper presented at the annual convention of the International Communication Association, Organizational Communication Division, Albuquerque, NM.

Barnlund, D. (1989, March-April). Public and private self in communicating in Japan. *Business Horizons,* pp. 32-40.

Bartlett, C., & Ghoshal, S. (1986, November-December). Tap your subsidiaries for global reach. *Harvard Business Review, 64,* 87-94.

Bartlett, C., & Ghoshal, S. (1989). *Managing across borders: The transnational solution.* Boston: Harvard Business School Press.

Belieav, E., Muller, T., & Punnett, B. (1985). Understanding the cultural environment: U.S. & USSR trade negotiations. *California Management Review, 27,* 100-112.

Beneria, L., & Roldan, M. (1987). *The crossroads of class and gender: Industrial homework, sub-contracting, and household dynamics in Mexico.* Chicago: University of Chicago Press.

Berge, M. (1987, July-August). Building bridges over the cultural rivers. *International Management, 42,* 61-62.

Berns, M. (1992). Sociolinguistics and the teaching of English in Europe beyond the 1990's. *World Englishes, 11*(1), 3-14.

Bochner, S., & Hesketh, B. (1994). Power distance, individualism, and job-related attitudes in a culturally diverse work group. *Journal of Cross-Cultural Psychology, 25,* 42-57.

Bossen, L. (1984). *The redivision of labor: Women and economic choice in four Guatemalan communities.* Albany: State University of New York Press.

Boulding, E. (1990). *Building a global-civic culture.* New York: Teachers College Press.

Boyacigiller, N., & Adler, N. (1991). The parochial dinosaur: Organizational science in a global context. *Academy of Management Review, 16,* 262-290.

Brady, F. (1986). Aesthetic components of management ethics. *Academy of Management Review, 11,* 337-344.

Brislin, R. (1989). Intercultural communication training. In M. K. Asante & W. Gudykunst (Eds.), *Handbook of international and intercultural communication* (pp. 441-457). Newbury Park, CA: Sage.

Bryson, B. (1990). *The mother tongue.* New York: William Morrow.

Buie, S. (1996). Market as Mandala: The erotic space of commerce. *Organization, 3,* 225-232.

Cai, D. & Drake, L. (1998). The business of business negotiation: Intercultural perspectives. In M. Roloff (Ed.), *Communication yearbook 21* (pp. 153-189). Thousand Oaks, CA: Sage.

Calás, M. (1994). Minerva's owl? *Organization, 1,* 243-248.

Calás, M., & Smircich, L. (Eds.). (1996). Essays on aesthetics and organization [Special section]. *Organization, 3*(2), 189-248.

Casmir, F. (1993). Third-culture building: A paradigm shift for international intercultural communication. In S. A. Deetz (Ed.), *Communication yearbook 16* (pp. 407-428). Newbury Park, CA: Sage.

Chan, B. (1995, Winter). Whose language is right? *The Diversity Factor,* pp. 28-30.

Chang, H., & Holt, G. (1991). More than relationship: Chinese interaction and the principle of kuan-hsi. *Communication Quarterly, 39,* 251-271.

Chen, G., & Chung, J. (1994). The impact of Confucianism on organizational communication. *Communication Quarterly, 42*(2), 93-105.

Cheney, G. (1995). Democracy in the workplace: Theory and practice from the perspective of communication. *Journal of Applied Communication Research, 23,* 1-34.

Cheney, G. (1999). *Values at work.* Ithaca, NY: Cornell University Press.

Child, J. (1981). Culture, contingency and capitalism in the cross-national study of organizations. In B. Shaw

& L. Cummings (Eds.), *Research in organizational behavior* (Vol. 3, pp. 303-356). Greenwich, CT: JAI.

Child, J., & Tayeb, M. (1983). Theoretical perspectives in cross-national organizational research. *International Studies of Management and Organization, 12,* 23-70.

Clair, R., & Kunkel, A. (1998). An organizational communication analysis of "unrealistic realities": Child abuse and the aesthetic resolution. *Communication Monographs, 65,* 24-46.

Cleveland, H. (1985). The twilight of hierarchy: Speculations on the global information society. *Public Administration Review, 45*(1), 185-195.

Clifford, J. (1988). *The predicament of culture.* Cambridge, MA: Harvard University Press.

Cockburn, D. (1991). *In the way of women: Men's resistance to sex equality in organizations.* Ithaca, NY: ILR.

Cole, R. (1989). *Strategies for learning: Small group activities in American, Japanese, and Swedish industry.* Berkeley: University of California Press.

Collins, G. (1996, January 13). Coke drops "domestic" and goes one world. *New York Times,* pp. 17, 19.

Cook, J., & Wall, T. (1980). New work attitude measures of trust, organizational commitment and personal need non-fulfillment. *Journal of Occupational Psychology, 53,* 39-52.

Cox, T. (1993). *Cultural diversity in organizations: Theory, research and practice.* San Francisco: Berrett-Koehler.

Crozier, M. (1964). *The bureaucratic phenomenon.* London: Tavistock.

Cushman, D., & King, S. (1993). High-speed management: A revolution in organizational communication in the 1990s. In S. A. Deetz (Ed.), *Communication yearbook 16* (pp. 209-236). Newbury Park, CA: Sage.

Cusumano, M., & Selby, W. (1995). *Microsoft secrets.* New York: Free Press.

Daniels, T., & Spiker, B. (1994). *Perspectives on organizational communication.* Dubuque, IA: William C. Brown.

Danowski, J., & Huang, H. (1994). *Organizational restructuring and changes in semantic networks in messages directed to external audiences.* Paper presented at the Organizational Communication Division of the International Communication Association, Sydney, Australia.

Dear, M., & Wolch, J. (1989). How territory shapes life. In J. Wolch & M. Dear (Eds.), *The power of geography* (pp. 3-18). Boston: Unwin Hyman.

Deetz, S. (1992). *Democracy in an age of corporate colonization.* Albany: State University of New York Press.

DeMente, B. (1981). *The Japanese way of doing business: The psychology of management in Japan.* Englewood Cliffs, NJ: Prentice Hall.

DeMente, B. (1989). *China's etiquette and ethics in business.* Lincolnwood, IL: NTC Business Books.

Deming, E. (1986). *Out of the crisis.* Cambridge, MA: MIT Press.

DePalma, A. (1994, June 26). It takes more than a visa to do business in Mexico. *New York Times,* pp. A16-A17.

DeSanctis, G., & Monge, P. (1998). Communication processes for virtual organizations. *Journal of Computer-Mediated Communication, 3*(4) (Introduction to special joint issue with *Organization Science:* Virtual Organizations, G. DeSanctis & P. Monge, Eds.) [Online]. Available: http://www.spcomm.uiuc.edu:1000/global/index/html.

DeVries, M. (1994). *Internationally yours: Writing and communicating successfully in today's global marketplace.* Boston: Houghton Mifflin.

DiMaggio, P., & Powell, W. (1983). The iron cage revisited: Institutional isomorphism and collective rationality in organizational fields. *American Sociological Review, 48,* 147-160.

DiMaggio, P., & Powell, W. (1991). *The new institutionalism in organizational analysis.* Chicago: University of Chicago Press.

Dogan, M., & Pelassy, D. (1990). *How to compare nations: Strategies in comparative politics.* Chatham, NJ: Chatham House.

Donaldson, T. (1989). *The ethics of international business.* New York: Oxford University Press.

Downs, C., & Hazen, M. (1977). A factor analytic study of communication satisfaction. *Journal of Business Communication, 14,* 63-74.

Downs, C., Downs, A., Potvin, T., Varona, F., Gribas, J., & Ticehurst, W. (1995, May). *A cross-cultural comparison of relationships between organizational commitment and organizational communication.* Paper presented at the annual convention of the International Communication Association, Organizational Communication Division, Albuquerque, NM.

Driskill, G. (1995). Managing cultural differences: A rules analysis in a bicultural organization. *Howard Journal of Communications, 5*(4), 353-372.

Earley, P. (1989). Social loafing and collectivism: A comparison of the United States and the People's Republic of China. *Administrative Science Quarterly, 34,* 565-581.

Earley, P. C., & Singh, H. (1995). International and intercultural management research: What's next? *Academy of Management Journal, 38,* 327-341.

Emery, F., Thorsrud, E., & Trist, E. (1969). *Form and content in industrial democracy.* London: Tavistock.

Erez, M., & Earley, P. C. (1995). *Culture, self-identity, and work.* Oxford, UK: Oxford University Press.

Eyraud, F. (1993). Equal pay and the value of work in industrialized countries. *International Labour Review, 1,* 33-48.

Fadiman, J. (1986). A traveler's guide to gifts and bribes. *Harvard Business Review, 64,* 122-136.

370 ◆ Context

Faulkner, A., & Lawson, V. (1991). Employment versus empowerment: A case study of the nature of women's work in Ecuador. *Journal of Development Studies, 27*(4), 16-47.

Feld, W., & Jordan, R. (1988). *International organization: A comparative approach.* New York: Praeger.

Fernandez-Kelly, M. (1983). *For we are sold, I and my people: Women and industry in Mexico's frontier.* Albany: State University of New York Press.

Fine, M. (1991). New voices in the workplace: Research directions in multicultural communication. *Journal of Business Communication, 28,* 259-275.

Fiol, C. (1989). A semiotic analysis of corporate language: Organizational boundaries and joint venturing. *Administrative Science Quarterly, 34,* 277-303.

Flaitz, J. (1988). *The ideology of English: French perceptions of English as a world language.* Berlin, Germany: Mouton de Gruyter.

Friday, R. (1989). Contrasts in discussion behaviors of German and American managers. *International Journal of Intercultural Relations, 13,* 429-446.

Fuentes, A., & Ehrenreich, B. (1983). *Women in the global factory.* Boston: South End.

Gattiker, U. (1990). *Technology management in organizations.* London: Sage.

Geertz, C. (1973). *The interpretation of cultures.* New York: Basic Books.

Giles, H. (1977). *Language, ethnicity, and intergroup relations.* London: Academic Press.

Giroux, N. (1992). Participation and strategic decision-making in a cooperative. *Annals of Public and Cooperative Economics, 63*(1), 5-24.

Giroux, N., & Fenocchi, V. (1995). *Women and cooperatives: Ten years later.* Paper presented at the Society for Co-operative Studies, Stockholm, Sweden.

Glassgold, P. (1987). Translation: Culture's driving wedge. *Translation Review, 23,* 18-21.

Glenn, E. (1981). *Man and mankind: Conflict and communication between cultures.* Norwood, NJ: Ablex.

Goering, E. (1991). *Hands in need: Cultural variability and institutionalization in Rett syndrome organizations in the United States and Europe.* Ph.D. dissertation, Purdue University, West Lafayette, IN.

Goldhaber, G. M., & Rogers, D. P. (1979). *Auditing organizational communication systems: The ICA communication audit.* Dubuque, IA: Kendall/Hunt.

Goldman, A. (1994). Communication in Japanese multinational organizations. In R. Wiseman & R. Shuter (Eds.), *Communicating in multinational organizations* (pp. 45-74). Thousand Oaks, CA: Sage.

Goodenough, W. (1970). *Description and comparison in cultural anthropology.* Chicago: Aldine.

Gorski, M. (1993). Hyperinflation and stabilization in Poland. In A. Kozminski & D. Cushman (Eds.), *Organizational communication and management: A global perspective* (pp. 168-182). Albany: State University of New York Press.

Gottfried, H. (1995). Developing neo-Fordism: A comparative perspective. *Critical Sociology, 21*(3), 39-70.

Grabe, W. (1988). English; information access, and technology transfer: A rationale for English as an international language. *World Englishes, 7,* 63-72.

Graham, J. L. (1985). The influence of culture on the process of business negotiations: An exploratory study. *Journal of International Business Studies, 16,* 79-94.

Graham, J., Evenko, L., & Rajan, M. (1992). An empirical comparison of Soviet and American business negotiations. *Journal of International Business Studies, 23,* 387-415.

Gudykunst, W. (1991). *Bridging differences: Effective intergroup communication.* Newbury Park, CA: Sage.

Gudykunst, W., Stewart, L., & Ting-Toomey, S. (1985). *Communication, culture, and organizational processes.* Beverly Hills, CA: Sage.

Guterl, F. (1989, February). Goodbye, old matrix. *Dun's Business Month,* pp. 32-38.

Habermas, J. (1984). *Theory of communicative action.* Boston: Beacon.

Hall, E. (1959). *The silent language.* New York: Doubleday.

Hall, E. (1966). *The hidden dimension.* New York: Doubleday.

Hall, E. (1976). *Beyond culture.* Garden City, NY: Doubleday.

Hall, E., & Hall, M. (1987). *Hidden differences: Doing business with the Japanese.* New York: Doubleday Anchor.

Hall, E., & Hall, M. (1990). *Understanding cultural differences.* Yarmouth, ME: Intercultural Press.

Hamada, T., & Yaguchi, Y. (1994). Hollowing of industrial ideology: Japanese corporate families in America. In T. Hamada & W. Sibley (Eds.), *Anthropological perspectives on organizational culture* (pp. 193-218). Lanham, MD: University Press of America.

Harris, P., & Moran, R. (1996). *Managing cultural differences.* Houston, TX: Gulf.

Hatch, M. (1996). *Organization theory: Modern, symbolic-interpretive and postmodern perspectives.* Oxford, UK: Oxford University Press.

Harvey, D. (1989). *The urban experience.* Oxford, UK: Oxford University Press.

Hastings, C. (1993). *The new organization: Growing the culture of organizational networking.* London: McGraw-Hill.

Hatim, B. (1989). Argumentative styles across cultures: Linguistic form as the realization of rhetorical function. In R. Kölmel & J. Payne (Eds.), *Babel: The cultural and linguistic barriers between nations* (pp. 25-32). Aberdeen, Scotland: Aberdeen University Press.

Heenan, D., & Perlmutter, H. (1979). *Management in the industrial world.* New York: McGraw-Hill.

Heginbotham, S. (1994, October 19). Shifting the focus of international programs. *Chronicle of Higher Education,* p. A68.

Held, D., McGrew, A., Goldblatt, D., & Perraton, J, (1999). *Global transformations: Politics, economics and culture.* Stanford, CA: Stanford University Press.

Hickson, D., Hinings, C., MacMillan, C., & Schwitter, J. (1974). The culture-free context of organisation structure: A tri-national comparison. *Sociology, 8,* 59-80.

Hickson, D., MacMillan, C., Azumi, K., & Horvath, D. (1979). The grounds for comparative organization theory. In C. Lammers & D. Hickson (Eds.), *Organizations alike and unalike* (pp. 153-189). London: Routledge and Kegan Paul.

Hilton, C. (1992). International business communication: The place of English. *Journal of Business Communication, 29*(3), 253-265.

Hirokowa, R., & Miyahara, A. (1986). A comparison of influence strategies utilized by managers in American and Japanese organizations. *Communication Quarterly, 34,* 250-265.

Hirschman, A. (1970). *Exit, voice and loyalty responses to decline in firms, organizations and states.* Cambridge, MA: Harvard University Press.

Hofstede, G. (1984). *Culture's consequences: International differences in work-related values.* Beverly Hills, CA: Sage.

Hofstede, G. (1991). *Cultures and organizations: Software of the mind.* London: McGraw-Hill.

Hofstede, G., & Bond, M. H. (1988). The Confucius connection: From cultural roots to economic growth. *Organizational Dynamics, 16*(4), 4-21.

Hofstede, G., Neuijen, B., Ohayr, D., & Sanders, G. (1990). Measuring organizational culture: A qualitative and quantitative study across twenty cases. *Administrative Science Quarterly, 35,* 286-316.

Hong, L. (1978). Risky shift and cautious shift: Some direct evidence on the culture-value theory. *Social Psychology, 41,* 342-346.

Hu, W., & Grove, C. (1991). *Encountering the Chinese: A guide for Americans.* Yarmouth, ME: Intercultural Press.

Hymes, D. (1974). *Foundations in sociolinguistics: An ethnographic approach.* Philadelphia: University of Pennsylvania Press.

Inglehart, R. (1977). *The silent revolution changing values and political styles among Western publics.* Princeton, NJ: Princeton University Press.

Inkeles, A. (1998). *One world emerging? Convergence and divergence in industrial societies.* Boulder, CO: Westview.

Inzerilli, G., & Laurent, A. (1983). Managerial views of organization structure in France and the USA. *International Studies of Management and Organization, 13*(1-2), 97-118.

Jamieson, K., & Cappella, J. (1996). Bridging the disciplinary divide. *Political Science and Politics, 29,* 13-16.

Jang, H., & Barnett, G. (1994). Cultural differences in organizational communication: A semantic network analysis. *Bulletin de Methodologic Sociologique, 4,* 31-59.

Jarvenpaa, S. L., & Leidner, D. E. (1998). Communication and trust in global virtual teams. *Journal of Computer-Mediated Communication, 3*(4) (Special joint issue with *Organization Science:* Virtual Organizations, G. DeSanctis & P. Monge, Eds.) [Online]. Available: http://www.spcomm.uiuc.edu:1000/global/index/html.

Jenks, C. (1993). *Culture.* London: Routledge and Kegan Paul.

Johnson, W., & Packard, A. (1987). *Workforce 2000: Work and workers for the 21st century.* Indianapolis, IN: Hudson Institute.

Kanter, R. M. (1977). *Men and women of the corporation.* New York: Basic Books.

Kirk, R. (1986). *Translation determined.* Oxford, UK: Clarendon.

Kleinburg, J. (1994). Working here is like walking blindly into a dense forest. In T. Hamada & W. Sibley (Eds.), *Anthropological perspectives on organizational culture* (pp. 153-192). Lanham, MD: University Press of America.

Kluckhohn, C. (1949). *Mirror for man: A survey of human behavior and social attitudes.* Greenwich, CT: Fawcett.

Kluckhohn, F., & Strodtbeck, F. L. (1961). *Variations in value orientations.* Westport, CT: Greenwood.

Knudsen, H. (1995). *Employee participation in Europe.* London: Sage.

Kölmel, R., & Payne, J. (Eds.). (1989). *Babel: The cultural and linguistic barriers between nations.* Aberdeen, Scotland: Aberdeen University Press.

Kozminski, A., & Cushman, D. (1993). The rise of global communication and global management: An overview. In A. Kozminski & D. Cushman (Eds.), *Organizational communication and management: A global perspective* (pp. 3-5). Albany: State University of New York Press.

Kozminski, A., & Obloj, K. (1993). A framework for understanding Eastern Europe's problems in integrating into the global economy. In A. Kozminski & D. Cushman (Eds.), *Organizational communication and management: A global perspective* (pp. 55-68). Albany: State University of New York Press.

Kras, E. (1988). *Management in two cultures: Bridging the gap between U.S. and Mexican managers.* Yarmouth, ME: Intercultural Press.

Kroeber, A., & Kluckhohn, C. (1954). *Culture: A critical review of concepts and definitions.* New York: Random House.

Krone, K., Chen, L., Sloan, D., & Gallant, L. (1995, May). *Managerial emotionality in Chinese factories.*

Paper presented at the annual convention of the International Communication Association, Organizational Communication Division, Albuquerque, NM.

Krone, K., Garrett, M., & Chen, L. (1992). Managerial practices in Chinese factories: A preliminary investigation. *Journal of Business Communication, 29*(3), 229-252.

Krone, K. J., Jablin, F. M., & Putnam, L. L. (1987). Communication theory and organizational communication: Multiple perspectives. In F. M. Jablin, L. L. Putnam, K. H. Roberts, & L. W. Porter (Eds.), *Handbook of organizational communication: An interdisciplinary perspective* (pp. 18-40). Newbury Park, CA: Sage.

Kuhn, J. W. (1996). The misfit between organizational theory and processual art: A comment on White and Strati. *Organization, 3,* 219-224.

Larkey, L. (1996). Toward a theory of communicative interaction in culturally diverse work groups. *Academy of Management Review, 21,* 463-491.

Laurent, A. (1983). The cultural diversity of Western conceptions of management. *International Studies of Management and Organizations, 13*(1-2), 79-96.

Laurent, A. (1986). The cross-cultural puzzle of international human resource management. *Human Resource Management, 25*(1), 91-102.

Lee, H., & Rogan, R. (1991). A cross-cultural comparison of organizational conflict management behavior. *International Journal of Conflict Management, 2,* 181-199.

Lee, J., & Jablin, F. (1992). A cross-cultural investigation of exit, voice, loyalty and neglect as responses to dissatisfying work conditions. *Journal of Business Communication, 29*(3), 203-228.

Lester, T. (1984, July-August). Pulling down the language barrier. *International Management,* pp. 42-44.

Lieber, R. (1995, December 25). Zen and the art of teamwork. *Fortune, 132,* 218.

Lincoln, J., & Kalleberg, A. (1990). *Culture, control and commitment: A study of work organizations in the United States and Japan.* Cambridge, MA: University of Cambridge Press.

Lindsley, S. (1999). A layered model of problematic intercultural communication in U.S.-owned maquiladoras in Mexico. *Communication Monographs, 33,* 145-167.

Lipnack, J., & Stamps, J. (1986). *The networking book: People connecting with people.* London: Routledge and Kegan Paul.

Lubin, C., & Winslow, A. (1990). *Social justice for women.* London: Duke University Press.

Magee, J. (1989). 1992: Moves Americans must make. *Harvard Business Review, 3,* 78-89.

Martin, M. (1992). *Culture in organizations: Three perspectives.* New York: Oxford University Press.

Maruyama, M. (1982). New mindscapes for future business policy and management. *Technology, Forecasting, and Social Change, 21,* 53-76.

Massey, D. (1984). *Spatial division of labor: Social structures and the geography of production.* London: Macmillan.

Maurice, M., Sorge, A., & Malcolm, R. (1981). Societal differences in organizing manufacturing units: A comparison of France, West Germany, and Great Britain. *International Studies of Management and Organization, 10*(4), 74-100.

Mayer, A. M. (1996). *The evolution of total quality: Japan's cultural influence on the teachings of Dr. W. Edwards Deming.* Paper presented at the Central States Speech Association Convention, St. Paul, MN.

McGregor, D. (1960). *The human side of enterprise.* New York: McGraw-Hill,

Miles, R., & Snow, C. (1986). Organizations: New concepts for new forms. *California Management Review, 28*(3), 62-73.

Miles, R., & Snow, C. (1992). Causes of failure in network organizations. *California Management Review, 32,* 53-72

Miller, K. (1995). *Organizational communication: Approaches and processes.* Belmont, NY: Wadsworth.

Milroy, L., & Margraine, S. (1980). Vernacular language loyalty and social networks, *Language and Society, 9*(1), 43-70.

Mitroff, I. (1987). *Business not as usual: Rethinking our individual, corporate, and industrial strategies for global competition.* San Francisco: Jossey-Bass.

Moghadam, V. (1999). Gender and globalization: Female labor and women's mobilization. *Journal of World-Systems Research, 5*(2), 367-390. (Special issue: Globalization, S. Manning, Ed.).

Monge, P. (1995). Global network organizations. In R. Cesaria & P. Shockley-Zalabak (Eds.), *Organization means communication: Making the organizational communication concept relevant to practice* (pp. 135-151). Rome: Servizio Italiano Pubblicazioni Internationali Srl.

Monge, P., & Fulk, J. (1995, May). *Global network organizations.* Paper presented at the annual convention of the International Communication Association, Albuquerque, NM.

Monge, P., & Fulk, J. (1999). Communication technologies for global network organizations. In G. DeSanctis & J. Fulk (Eds.), *Communication technologies and organizational form* (pp. 71-100). Thousand Oaks, CA: Sage.

Moody, K. (1997). *Workers in a lean world.* London: Verso.

Moran, R., & Harris, P. (1982). *Managing cultural synergy.* Houston, TX: Gulf.

Morley, D., Shockley-Zalabak, P., & Cesaria, R. (1997). Organizational communication and culture: A study of 10 Italian high-technology companies. *Journal of Business Communication, 34,* 253-268.

Mossetto, G. (1993). *Aesthetics and economics.* Dordrecht, Netherlands: Kluwer Academic.

Mowday, R., Steers, R., & Porter, L. (1979). The measurement of organizational communication. *Journal of Vocational Behavior, 14,* 224-247.

Mulgan, G. (1991). *Communication and control: Networks and the new economies of communication.* New York: Guilford.

Mumby, D., & Stohl, C. (1996). Disciplining organizational communication studies. *Management Communication Quarterly, 10*(1), 50-72.

Murdock, G., & Provost, C. (1973). Measurement of cultural complexity, *Ethnology, 12,* 379-392.

Naik, G. (1993, October 4). Western investment in Eastern Europe grew sharply during the recent period. *Wall Street Journal,* p. A7.

Nash, C. (1990). *Narrative in culture: The uses of storytelling in the sciences, philosophy, and literature.* London and New York: Routledge.

Neubert, A. (1989). Translation as mediation. In R. Kölmel & J. Payne (Eds.), *Babel: The cultural and linguistic barriers between nations* (pp. 5-12). Aberdeen, Scotland: Aberdeen University Press.

Nohria, N., & Barkley, J. (1994). The virtual organization: Bureaucracy, technology and the implosion of control. In C. Heckscher & A. Donnellon (Eds.), *The post-bureaucratic organization: New perspectives on organizational change* (pp. 108-128). Thousand Oaks, CA: Sage.

Nonaka, I., & Takeuchi, H. (1995). *The knowledge-creating company.* New York: Oxford University Press.

Office of International Programs [Online]. (1999). West Lafayette, IN: Purdue University. Available: http://www.ippu.purdue.edu/index.html-ssi.

Ohbuchi, K., & Takahashi, Y. (1994). Cultural styles of conflict management in Japanese and Americans: Pass, correctness and effectiveness of strategies. *Journal of Applied Social Psychology, 55,* 49-67.

One to us, closed to them. (1994). *The Economist,* pp. 43-45.

Ottensmeyer, E. (1996). Too strong to stop, too sweet to lose: Aesthetics as a way to know organizations. *Organization, 3,* 189-194.

Ouchi, W. (1981). *Theory Z: How American business can meet the Japanese challenge.* Reading, MA: Addison-Wesley.

Page, N., & Wiseman, R. (1993). Supervisory behavior and worker satisfaction in the United States, Mexico, and Spain. *Journal of Business Communication, 30,* 161-179.

Papa, M., Auwal, M., & Singhal, A. (1995). Dialectic of control and emancipation in organizing for social change: A multitheoretic study of the Grameen Bank in Bangladesh. *Communication Theory, 5,* 189-223.

Park, S. H., & Ungson, G. R. (1997). The effect of national culture, organizational complementarity, and economic motivation on joint venture dissolution. *Academy of Management Journal, 40,* 279-307.

Parsons, T., & Shils, E. (1951). *Toward a general theory of action.* Cambridge, MA: Harvard University Press.

Pascale, R., & Athos, A. (1981). *The art of Japanese management: Applications for American executives.* New York: Warner.

Pierce, J., Gardner, D., Cummings, L., & Dunham, R. (1989). Organization-based self-esteem. *Academy of Management Journal, 32,* 622-648.

Poole, M. S. (1993). On the joys and sorrows of predicting the future of organizational communication. In S. A. Deetz (Ed.), *Communication yearbook 16* (pp. 247-251). Newbury Park, CA: Sage.

Powell, B. (1995, November). Keep your profits. *Newsweek,* p. 98.

PSI Enegy. (1984). *International companies in Indiana map.* Indianapolis, IN: Author.

Ratiu, I. (1983). Thinking internationally: A comparison of how international executives learn. *International Studies of Management and Organization, 13,* 139-153.

Reardon, K. (1981). *International gift customs: A guide for American executives.* Janesville, WI: Parker Pen Company.

Redding, S. (1990). *The spirit of Chinese capitalism.* Berlin: Walter de Gruyter.

Richards, D. (1997). *Artful work.* New York: Berkley.

Riordan, C., & Vandenberg, R. (1994). A central question in cross-cultural research: Do employees of different cultures interpret work-related measures in an equivalent manner? *Journal of Management, 20,* 643-671.

Rosen, B. (1982). *The industrial connection: Achievement and the family in developing societies.* New York: Aldine.

Rossman, M. (1990). *The international businesswoman of the 1990s.* New York: Praeger.

Rothstein, F. (1982). *Three different worlds: Women, men and children in an industrializing community.* Westport, CT: Greenwood.

Ryder, G. (1997, July). Globalization must include social justice for all workers. *World of Work: The Magazine of the ILO, 20,* 15.

Sanborn, G. (1993). *Understanding cultural diversity: The relationship of differences in communication styles with career outcomes among white and Asian Americans.* Unpublished doctoral dissertation, Purdue University, West Lafayette, IN.

Sanger, D. (1993, March 21). Facing production cuts in two automotive plants. *New York Times,* p. C1.

Scholte, J. (2000). *Globalization: A critical introduction.* London: Macmillan.

Seelye, H., & Seelye-James, A. (1995). *Culture clash: Managing in a multicultural world.* Lincolnwood, IL: NTC Business Books.

Seibold, D., & Contractor, N. (1993). Issues for a theory of high-speed management. In S. A. Deetz (Ed.),

*Communication yearbook 16* (pp. 237-246). Newbury Park, CA: Sage.

Shuter, R. (1993). On third-culture building. In S. A. Deetz (Ed.), *Communication yearbook 16* (pp. 429-438). Newbury Park, CA: Sage.

Shuter, R., & Wiseman, R. L. (1994). Communication in multinational organizations: Conceptual, theoretical, and practical issues. In R. Wiseman & R. Shuter (Eds.), *Communicating in multinational organizations* (pp. 3-12). Thousand Oaks, CA: Sage.

Smircich, L. (1983). Concepts of culture and organizational analysis. *Administrative Science Quarterly, 28*, 339-358.

Smith, A., & Tayeb, M. (1988). Organizational structures and processes. In M. Bond (Ed.), *The cross-cultural challenge to social psychology* (pp. 116-127). Newbury Park, CA: Sage.

Smith, P., & Peterson, M. (1988). *Leadership, organizations and culture*. London: Sage.

Smith, R. (1993). *Organizational communication theorizing: Root-metaphors of the organization-communication relation*. Unpublished manuscript, Purdue University, West Lafayette, IN.

Soja, E. (1989). *Postmodern geographies: The reassertion of space in critical social theory*. London: Verso.

Sorge, A. (1983). Cultured organization. *International Studies of Management and Organization, 13*, 106-138.

Spain, D. (1992). *Gendered spaces*. Chapel Hill: University of North Carolina Press.

Stage, C. (1999). Negotiating organizational communication cultures in American subsidiaries doing business in Thailand. *Management Communication Quarterly, 13*, 245-280.

Steers, R., Bischoff, S., & Higgins, L. (1992). Cross-cultural management research: The fish and the fisherman. *Journal of Management Inquiry, 1*, 321-330.

Steiner, G. (1975). *After Babel: Aspects of language and translation*. London: Oxford University Press.

Stewart, L., Gudykunst, W., Ting-Toomey, S., & Nishida, T. (1986). The effects of decision making style on openness and satisfaction within Japanese organizations. *Communication Monographs, 53*, 236-251.

Stohl, C. (1993). International organizing and organizational communication. *Journal of Applied Communication Research, 21*(4), 377-390.

Stohl, C. (1995). *Organizational communication: Connectedness in action*. Thousand Oaks, CA: Sage.

Storti, C. (1990). *The art of crossing cultures*. Yarmouth, ME: Intercultural Press.

Strati, A. (1996). Organizations viewed through the lens of aesthetics. *Organization, 3*, 209-218.

Sullivan, J., & Taylor, S. (1991). A cross-cultural test of compliance gaining theory. *Management Communication Quarterly, 5*, 220-239.

Swan, P. F., & Ettlie, J. E. (1997). U.S.-Japanese manufacturing equity relationships. *Academy of Management Journal, 40*, 452-479.

Tayeb, M. (1992). *The global business environment: An introduction*. London: Sage.

Taylor, J., & Van Every, E. (1993). *The vulnerable fortress: Bureaucratic organization and management in the information age*. Toronto, Canada: University of Toronto Press.

Teboul, J., Chen, L., & Fritz, L. (1994). Communication in multinational organizations in the United States and Western Europe. In R. Wiseman & R. Shuter (Eds.), *Communicating in multinational organizations* (pp. 12-29). Thousand Oaks, CA: Sage.

Thornburg, L. (1990, September). Transfers need not mean dislocation. *Human Resources Magazine, 35*, 46-48.

Thurow, L. (1983). *Dangerous currents: The state of economics*. New York: Random House.

Tichy, N. (1990). The global challenge for business schools. *Human Resource Management, 29*, 1-4.

Ticehurst, W. (1992). *Organizational commitment in Australia, Japan and the United States*. Paper presented at the conference of the Australian and New Zealand Academy of Management, Sydney, Australia.

Ting-Toomey, S., Gao, G., Trubisky, P., Yang, Z., Kim, H., Lin, S., & Nishida, T. (1991). Culture, face maintenance, and styles of handling interpersonal conflict: A study of five cultures. *International Journal of Conflict Management, 2*, 275-292.

Tompkins, P. (1984). The functions of human communication in organization. In C. Arnold & J. Bowers (Eds.), *Handbook of rhetoric and communication theory* (pp. 659-713). Boston: Allyn & Bacon.

Triandis, H. (1983). Dimensions of cultural variation as parameters of organizational theories. *International Studies of Management and Organization, 12*, 139-169.

Triandis, H. C., & Albert, R. D. (1987). Cross-cultural perspectives. In F. M. Jablin, L. L. Putnam, K. H. Roberts, & L. W. Porter (Eds.), *Handbook of organizational communication: An interdisciplinary perspective* (pp. 264-296). Newbury Park, CA: Sage.

Trompenaars, F. (1994). *Riding the waves of culture: Understanding diversity in global business*. Chicago: Irwin.

Tugendhat, C. (1988). *Making sense of Europe*. New York: Columbia University Press.

Tung, R. (1987). Expatriate assignments: Enhancing success and minimizing failure. *Academy of Management Executive, 1*, 117-126.

Vandenberg, R., & Scarpello, V. (1992). A multitrait-multimethod assessment of the Satisfaction With My Supervisor scale. *Educational and Psychological Measurement, 52*, 203-212.

Van Maanen, J., & Barley, S. (1984). Occupational communities: Culture and control in organizations. In B.

Shaw & L. Cummings (Eds.), *Research in organizational behavior* (Vol. 6, pp. 287-365). Lanham, MD: University Press of America.

Van Wolferen, K. (1989). *The enigma of Japanese power: People and politics in a stateless nation.* New York: Knopf.

Varner, I. (1988a). A comparison of American and French business correspondence. *Journal of Business Communication 25*(4), 5-16.

Varner, I. (1988b). Cultural aspects of German and American business letters. *Journal of Language for International Business, 3*(1), 1-11.

Varner, I., & Beamer, L. (1995). *Intercultural communication: The global workplace.* Chicago: Irwin.

Victor, D. (1992). *International business communication.* New York: HarperCollins.

Vikhanski, O., & Puffer, S. (1993). Management evaluation and employee training at Moscow McDonald's. *European Management Journal, 11,* 102-107.

Vitell, S., Nwachuku, S., & Barnes, J. (1993). The effects of culture on ethical decision making: An application of Hofstede's typology. *Journal of Business Ethics, 12,* 753-760.

Walker, R. (1985). Class, division of labor, and employment in space. In D. Gregory & J. Ury (Eds.), *Social relations and spatial structures* (pp. 164-189). London: Macmillan.

Waters, M. (1995). *Globalization.* London: Routledge.

Weick, K. (1969). *The social psychology of organizing.* Reading, MA: Addison-Wesley.

Weick, K., & Van Orden, P. (1990). Organizing on a global scale: A research and teaching agenda. *Human Resource Management, 29,* 49-61.

White, D., & Rackerby, F. (1994). A regional perspective on the transfer of Japanese management practices to the United States. In T. Hamada & W. Sibley (Eds.), *Anthropological perspectives on organizational culture* (pp. 133-152). Lanham, MD: University Press of America.

White, D. (1996). It's working beautifully! Philosophical reflections on aesthetics and organizational theory. *Organization, 3,* 195-208.

Whorf, B. (1952). *Collected papers on metalinguistics.* Washington, DC: Department of State, Foreign Service Institute.

Wiio, O. (1989). *Intercultural and international issues and variables in comparative studies in organizational communication.* Paper presented at the meeting of the International Communication Association, San Francisco.

Williams, R. (1976). *Keywords.* London: Fontana.

Williams, W. (1990). Women and work in the third world: Indonesian women's oral histories. *Journal of Women's History, 2,* 183-189.

Wilson, S., Cai, D., Campbell, D., Donohue, W., & Drake, L. (1994). Cultural and communication processes in international business negotiations. In A. Nicotera (Ed.), *Conflict in organizations: Communicative processes* (pp. 169-188). Albany: State University of New York Press.

Witkin, H., & Berry, J. (1975). Psychological differences in cross-cultural perspectives. *Journal of Cross-Cultural Psychology, 6,* 4-87.

Wright, L. (1984). *Cross-cultural project negotiations in the service sector.* Unpublished doctoral dissertation, University of Western Ontario, London, Ontario, Canada.

Wright, L., Lane, N., & Beamish, P. (1988). International management research: Lessons from the field. *International Studies of Management and Organization, 18,* 55-71.

Wysocki, B. (1988). In Japan they even have cram schools for cram schools. *Wall Street Journal, 13,* pp. 1-16.

Yoshida, N. (1989). Deming management philosophy: Does it work in the U.S. as well as Japan? *Columbia Journal of World Business, 27,* 10-17.

Zeldin, T. (1984). *The French.* New York: Vintage.

# PART III

# Structure: Patterns of Organizational Interdependence

# 11

# Dualisms in Leadership Research

GAIL T. FAIRHURST
*University of Cincinnati*

There is evidence of several types of dualisms within the leadership communication literature. For example, in conceptualizing leadership researchers have been fond of contrasting leadership with managership (Bennis & Nanus, 1985; Zaleznik, 1977), transformational with transactional leaders (Bass, 1985; Burns, 1978), self-management with external or super-leadership (Manz & Sims, 1987, 1989), organic with mechanistic forms of authority (Burns & Stalker, 1961; Weick, 1987), consideration with initiating structure (Fleishman, 1953; Hemphill & Coons, 1957), participative with autocratic leadership styles (Bass, 1981; Tannenbaum & Schmidt, 1958), and formal with informal leaders (Levine, 1949) just to name a few. One of the most central dualisms in the leadership literature is the individual versus the collective. The history of leadership research has been very leader focused (Meindl, 1990), although interest in the collective is clearly growing. There also have been dual approaches to conceptualizing communication,

AUTHOR'S NOTE: I would like to thank Linda Putnam and Fred Jablin for their insightful editorial assistance. I am also indebted to Francois Cooren, George Graen, Steve Green, Bob Liden, Teresa Sabourin, Gary Yukl, and Ted Zorn for their helpful comments on earlier drafts of this chapter.

one approach focusing heavily on transmission and the other focusing on the formation of meaning (Putnam, 1983; Putnam, Phillips, & Chapman, 1996). Dualism is also apparent in the way leadership communication is studied. Some research focuses on what leaders and constituents see and experience in social interaction (e.g., Kipnis & Schmidt, 1988; Yukl & Tracey, 1992), while other research focuses on the accomplishment of mutually adjusting behaviors (e.g., Fairhurst, Green, & Courtright, 1995; Komaki & Citera, 1990). Finally, even social science inquiry itself forms a dual contrast between the "why" and "how do you know" questions of positivism versus the "how" and "why do you talk that way" questions of social constructionism (Putnam, 1983; Shotter, 1993).

Dualisms[1] are experienced as choice points within the research process; they are implicitly embedded in what and how we study. For example, extant theory usually favors one view of organizations, work, relationships, and truth over others. Like a camera angle, research methodologies offer a view of our subjects that inevitably precludes other angles and views. In both theory and methods, the buy-in process by researchers over time produces dominant versus marginal perspectives, mainstream versus emerging research, the *au couránt* versus the *passé*. Forced to choose among alternative views, the trade-offs of decision making often create dilemmas over the best way to proceed. For example, to focus on the exchange between leaders and constituents leaves questions about the role of vision, charisma, and language use in calculation of the exchange. To study surface structure power dynamics via influence tactics leaves unanswered questions about the deep structure linguistic influences that might prefigure the influence attempt. What communication scientists observe interactionally is accompanied by questions about what is experienced and vice versa. These dilemmas are constantly evolving as researchers come to grips with unanswered questions while discovering new ones.

The nature of the dualisms that leadership communication researchers confront ranges from the oppositional to the seemingly oppositional. For example, the individual versus the collective reflects a dualism between contradictory opposites (i.e., a dialectic). Too much focus on what leaders do bypasses the dynamics of the collective. Yet too much focus on the collective overlooks the individual's basis of action. A dualism can also reflect choices that are not necessarily mutually exclusive, but rely on conceptualizations that effectively set alternative views in opposition. Positivist versus critical-interpretive views of communication inquiry provide one such example. Finally, some dualisms reflect choices that are little more than rhetorical straw men. Difference turns into opposition only to highlight the features or relative advantages of one path over another (e.g., what is observed vs. experienced interactionally).

Dialectical theories of meaning suggest a reason why these various dualisms fuel our thinking about theory and research in leadership communication. Opposition is a bonding agent in our thought because we think by looking to the relation between things. We can know what something is by focusing on what it is not, although any number of "what it is not" ideas may be usefully contrasted with "what it is" (Rychlak, 1977). Derrida's (1976) *différance* attaches a similar fluidity to oppositional thinking.[2]

Since camps have been known to form around a given theory or research approach, dualisms may polarize researchers because of the tensions they create between alternate forms of research. However, on balance these tensions are healthy and energizing for a research community because of the debate they foster and the creative ideas they spawn (Pfeffer, 1981). This is a compelling reason, especially in a review essay, to refrain from choosing sides in these dualisms (assuming that no one approach garners the corner on truth) when each can provide a pragmatic means of understanding. In this respect, dualistic thinking is reminiscent of dialectical inquiry, which holds that both opposing poles of a dialectic are important regardless of how visible or dominant either pole might be. However, dialectical inquiry achieves its distinctive nature by going beyond the duality of a phenomenon to focus on the dynamic tension between unified opposites in a system and the possibility of resolution (Werner & Baxter, 1994).

Although important differences remain between a dualism and a dialectic (Baxter & Montgomery, 1996), a framework loosely modeled on a dialectical approach was selected to help make sense of this literature.[3] Although the dualisms marking leadership communication research are both oppositional and seemingly oppositional, their interplay over time is the subject of this chapter. With that in mind, four questions guide this effort. First, what are the dualisms and resulting tensions and dilemmas that characterize leadership communication research? Second, how do these dualisms currently intersect to form choice points in the literature? Third, how do these dualisms mark the evolution of leadership communication research in the past several years? To answer this question, I selected five fairly well-developed programs of research in leadership communication to document the dualisms that have surfaced in the past and present literature. Finally, how can these dualisms shape future leadership communication research? Following Kolb and Putnam's (1992) strategy, this chapter places particular emphasis on the understudied areas and choice points within the literature to suggest new directions for research.

The five research programs that are to be explored include the study of influence tactics, feedback, charisma and visionary leadership, leader-member exchange, and systems-interactional leadership research. While other important issues in leadership communication have been studied (e.g., gender, social support, empowerment, competence), the five programs reviewed have enough research to characterize the extant dualisms sufficiently and span the continuum of individual-

istic and systemic approaches. With some exceptions, most restrict their study of leadership to individuals who perform dyadically linked roles[4] in hierarchical organizations and who manifest relatively stable skills, styles, motives, expectancies, behaviors, and/or personalities in the performance of those roles.[5]

# THE DUALISMS OF LEADERSHIP COMMUNICATION

As Figure 11.1 reveals, this chapter poses three sets of dualisms that characterize the literature on leadership communication.[6] The first, the individual and the system, is the primary dualism because of its influence on the existence and development of the two secondary dualisms: cognitive outcomes and conversational practices, and transmission and meaning-centered views of communication. The primary versus secondary nature of these dualisms is explained further after each dualism is defined.

## Primary and Secondary Dualisms

### Primary Dualism: The Individual and the System

One of the strongest pulls in leadership research is that between the individual and the collective or system. The term *individual* refers to leaders or constituents by themselves. However, the term *system* refers to a dyad, group, culture or subculture, organization, industry, or any way a collective can be configured. This primary dualism is bipolar and oppositional, essentially dialectical in nature. It is similar to the centrality accorded to the individual-system dialectic in the therapy literature (Bopp & Weeks, 1984; Weeks, 1986), the individual-collective dialectic in cultural studies (Hofstede, 1981), and the independence-connection dialectic in the literature on personal relationships (Baxter, 1990; Rawlins, 1992).

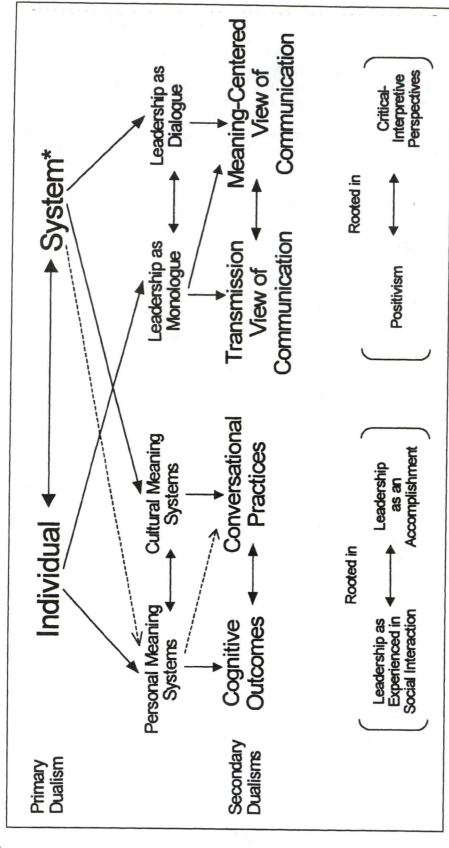

**Figure 11.1.** The Dualisms of Leadership Communication Research

*The arrow with the broken line indicates the combined influence of personal and cultural meaning systems on conversational practices.

There are definite patterns in the way researchers have managed the individual-system dualism in the leadership communication literature. Historically, dominant views of leadership have been shaped by a traditional psychological view of the world where in a figure-ground arrangement the individual is figure, the system is background, and communication is incidental or, at best, intervening. Over the past few decades, most of the ferment in leadership research occurred when the study of leadership traits gave way to the study of cognitions, acts, and meaning constructions (vs. coconstructions), all cut from the cloth of individualism. One implication of such an individualistic focus has been to romanticize and enhance the perceived role of the leader in effecting organizational outcomes (Meindl, Ehrlich, & Dukerich, 1985).

However, there are an increasing number of countervailing forces with a systems orientation. The literature within communication, leadership, and organizational development all illustrate this basic tendency. In communication research, Fisher (1985, 1986) reconceptualized leadership as an emergent property of group interaction. The locus of leadership is not the individual, but in the patterned sequential behavior of leaders and constituents who form an interactional system. A "systems-interactional" approach to leadership, to be discussed later, draws from general systems theory in emphasizing the properties of wholeness and interdependence and from information theory in emphasizing the redundancies in leader-constituent behavior.

A few years ago, the editor of *Leadership Quarterly* asked several leadership theorists to recast their theories at multiple levels of analysis. The upshot of this decision was to take many established theories beyond a focus on individuals and dyads to groups and organizations (Dansereau, 1995a, 1995b). Historically, leader-member exchange (LMX) has been one of the few leadership approaches to maintain an explicitly relationship focus almost from the outset. Interest in LMX research continues to be strong particularly in communication, LMX development, network applications, and intercultural studies.

In organizational development, relational concepts such as followership, empowerment, reciprocality, and leader accessibility are increasingly entering into the dialogue about leadership (Conger, 1989; Kouzes & Posner, 1993, 1995; Wheatley, 1992). Also in the organizational development literature, those who espouse such principles as systems theory (Senge, 1990), dialogue (Isaacs, 1993, 1999), and new science (Wheatley, 1992) are likewise eschewing an individualistic focus in favor of a systemic one. Senge and his colleagues now write about leadership communities where the leadership function is by necessity distributed to bring about organizational transformation (Senge et al., 1999). Thus, although an individualistic orientation has been the heavy favorite in leadership research, pressures are building to consider wider systems dynamics.

Finally, pressures are also building to treat individual-system tensions as problematic by focusing on how the tensions themselves are managed. The metaphors of leadership as jamming (Eisenberg, 1990) or jazz (DePree, 1993) are usually invoked in this regard because they simultaneously capture leadership's "improvisational nature and the need to mesh the competing voices of an ensemble into a coherent piece of music" (Barge, 1994b, p. 102).

Related to the individual-system dualism are two secondary dualisms that are not dialectical in nature. Before describing their interrelationships, each secondary dualism must first be defined.

## Secondary Dualism: Cognitive Outcomes and Conversational Practices

A secondary dualism in leadership communication research focuses on cognitive outcomes and conversational practices (Drecksel,

1991; Sypher, 1991). Cognitive outcomes are the thoughts and feelings experienced before, during, or after social interaction, but always as a response to it. As Figure 11.1 reveals, they are rooted in the experience of social interaction—the internal, psychological processes that individuals use in interpreting and producing messages and other social behavior. For example, social cognitive approaches capture individual experience through a focus on the differences in cognitive structures that lead to different message interpretations or plans of action (Hewes & Planalp, 1987). Observable behavior is never studied in isolation of ongoing interpretive and production processes. The emphasis is always on subjective reactions to so-called objective messages (Hewes & Planalp, 1987).

Cognitive models of leadership, especially those with a concern for communication, deal with such issues as perception and attention, schemata, attributions, salience processes, and motivated, programmed, and script-driven choice processes (e.g., Peterson & Sorenson, 1991; Smith & Peterson, 1988). These models suggest that the leader-constituent relationship is a context for communication.

As Figure 11.1 suggests, the study of conversational practices is rooted in the view that leadership is an accomplishment—interactionally constructed in the reciprocal behaviors of people who must continually adjust to one another (Fisher, 1986). Relational communication research and discourse analysis, two approaches that focus on the conversational practices of leadership, suggest that how leaders and constituents act in relation to one another constitutes the relationship. The relationship is synonymous with communication because redundancies in patterns of communicating define the form of the relationship (Bateson, 1972; Rogers, Millar, & Bavelas, 1985). As Drecksel (1991) observed, "Leadership is located, observed, and interpreted as a communicative process comprising externalized and directly observable behaviors" (p. 538).

The basis of cognitive outcomes, experience, and the roots of conversational practices, accomplishments, are also interdependent. While leaders and constituents bring to the organization unique purposes, personalities, past experiences, expectations, and opinions, the specific nature of their relationship at a given time is a product of their social interaction. Simultaneously, the relationship gives to leaders and constituents certain characteristics that would not exist otherwise. Thus, the context of any leadership encounter engenders a disposition of professionalism and role behavior in leaders and an expectation of resources, understanding, and/or direction in constituents.[7] Therefore, both experience and accomplishment form an interdependence; without accomplishment, there is nothing to experience and without experience, there is no ability to respond.

Those who see leadership as experience study it by collecting cognitive outcomes in the form of self-report data. Communication researchers in this area often study frequent, anticipated, or imagined interactions between leaders and constituents. The ease with which these studies can be designed typically leads to large samples. But as Knapp, Miller, and Fudge (1994) point out, many communication researchers have questioned the adequacy of their knowledge of communication when it is based solely on self-report data (e.g., Barge & Schleuter, 1991; Corman & Krizek, 1993; Rogers et al., 1985):

> Can people accurately recall or predict some aspects of their interpersonal communication behavior . . . ? Have we developed a body of knowledge that is limited to what people think they would do? Isn't there a need to supplement or seek validation of self-reports with observations of actual interaction behavior? Is it enough to know attitudes, opinions, and perceptions of one interaction partner often removed from any interaction context? How will the preferences expressed on the questionnaire manifest themselves in the presence of another person or persons governed by situational constraints? (p. 10)

Other leadership communication researchers answer these questions by focusing on conversational practices and naturally occurring talk. While subjective views of reality may answer questions about the self-conscious basis of social action, scholars argue that research practices should include the study of actual communication because that which is relational is social and between people. Montgomery (1992) noted that "social phenomena are defined by the relations among their characteristics—be they people, places, goals, or behaviors—not by the characteristics themselves" (p. 480); hence, the instantiation of relationships in communication. As Bateson (1972) observed, communication *is* the relationship.

Because of the difficulty of obtaining and transcribing actual organizational talk, most leadership communication research is based on a conception of messages that fails to take into account the actual interactive practices associated with message production. Nowhere will this be more evident than in the voluminous literature concerning leader and constituent influence tactics. However, Knapp et al. (1994) are quite correct in noting the inadequacy of overt behavior by itself:

> Even though we still have much to learn from the study of overt behavior, it is already clear that, first, what transpires during interpersonal transactions is more than mere responses to manifest signals. Communicator expectations, fantasies, plans, and the like may provide the basis for response; behaviors not shown by the interaction partner may provide the basis for response; behaviors shown in previous interactions (with and not with the current partner) may guide and direct reactions. (p. 10)

Cognitive outcomes and conversational practices specify different, but interdependent units of analysis. Cognitive outcomes is the study of "what people mean," while conversational practices study "how behavior means" (Scheflen, 1974). Without people, there is no meaning. Without messages, there can be no communication.

## Secondary Dualism: Transmission Views and Meaning-Centered Views of Communication

At the basis of the secondary dualism concerning transmission views and meaning-centered views of communication is the most basic tension facing social orders. As Figure 11.1 reveals, that tension lies between the constructed social world and the ongoing process of social construction (Benson, 1977). The reification of reality as a determinate influence on behavior forms a tension with reality in the making or its ongoing social construction. The interdependence between constructed and determinist views of reality surfaces from the knowledge that we make our own history, but not always under conditions of our choosing.

This fundamental tension is at the heart of social science inquiry. Positivist or determinist views of reality are associated with empirical and rational thought where reality is separate from the knower waiting to be discovered. In critical-interpretive views of reality, the individual takes an active, constructive role in creating knowledge through language and communication. Individuals are neither passive nor reactive, but intentional and reflexively self-aware. Taken to extremes, the upshot of the difference between the two views is that a determinist view essentially strips the individual of choice, while a socially constructed view may marginalize material constraints on behavior.

A transmission view of communication follows directly from the stance where reality is to be found or read (Morgan, 1986). The messages sent and received are assumed to have an objective reality about them. They exist independently of sender or receiver. By reifying messages in this way, communication becomes a tangible substance that flows through the organization conceived as a container. Putting content and meaning aside, the essence of a transmission view of communication lies more in transmission and channel effects: message directionality, frequency, and fidelity, blockages that inhibit transmission, and perceptual filters that hinder message reception (Fisher, 1978; Putnam, 1983).

In contrast to a transmission model, a meaning-centered view casts leaders and constituents as practical authors and coauthors. Practical authors exert choice over unchosen conditions whenever one linguistic formulation is chosen over possible others. According to Shotter (1993), an appropriate formulation of unchosen conditions creates

> (a) a "landscape" of enabling-constraints (Giddens, 1979) relevant for a range of next possible actions; (b) a network of "moral positions" or "commitments" (understood in terms of the rights and duties of the "players" on that landscape); and (c) [those who] are able to argue persuasively and authoritatively for this "landscape" amongst those who must work within it. (p. 149)

Authorship is contingent on understanding the formative power of language, which is the ability to create reality based on what may only be vaguely sensed intuitions or tendencies. An authorial view does not legitimate an "anything goes" view of authorship (Shotter, 1993), but neither does it place particular emphasis on the constraints on authorship. Thus, transmission and authorial views of communication appear to emphasize different, but complementary aspects of the communication process.

## Relationships Among Dualisms

In considering how these dualisms intersect with one another, I have argued that the individual-system dualism is primary because of its influence on both of the secondary dualisms. The dominance of the individual-system dualism can be seen in pronounced tendencies to emphasize different sides of the secondary dualisms. These are only pronounced tendencies and not absolutes as examples can certainly be found to the contrary. Nevertheless, they are strong enough to propose an overarching framework as described in Figure 11.1. I will first consider the influence of the individual-system dualism on cognitive outcomes and conversational practices followed by its influence on transmission views and meaning-centered views of communication.

### Links to Cognitive Outcomes and Conversational Practices

Based on the tendencies within the literature, an individualistic focus leads one to favor cognitive outcomes while a systemic focus tends to favor conversational practices.[8] However, Figure 11.1 reveals the personal versus cultural basis of meaning that links the individual-system and the cognitive outcomes-conversational practices dualisms together. An individualistic orientation often focuses on cognitive outcomes through the study of personal meaning systems. A systemic orientation leads to a focus on conversational practices through the study of cultural meaning systems or the interpenetration of cultural and personal meaning systems.

An individualistic focus places a heavy emphasis on the individual's idiosyncratic view of the world, a view shaped by the accumulation of unique life experiences. As the integration of one's experiences schematize, these schemas yield the dimensions along which aspects of new situations will be measured and assigned meaning (Fiske & Taylor, 1991). The meaning assigned is considered personal and idiosyncratic because no two individuals or life journeys are ever the same. Cognitive outcomes as measured through self-reports are the usual data of choice.

However, self-reports have a tendency to perpetuate the myth that meaning construction is mostly private and personal rather than subject to historical and sociocultural influences (Lannamann, 1991).[9] A focus on system functioning leads one to favor the study of conversational practices, which makes it apparent that meaning is not solely private. Meaning is also cultural because there must be some means by which members of a language community communicate with one another. For example, symbolic interactionists call the process whereby private meanings are transformed into collective, enduring, taken-for-granted realities the "sedimentation of meanings" (Berger & Luckmann, 1966; Fine, 1992; Prasad, 1993). Sedimented or conventionalized meanings yield a repertoire of strategies and linguistic resources that "are accessible by members of the speech community for sensemaking and useable as currency to signal to one's partner the state of affect, respect, intimacy, or power at that moment" (Fairhurst, 1993b, p. 323). In this way, conventional meaning assignments in a language community often precede and prefigure more personal and idiosyncratic meaning construction (Sigman, 1987, 1992).

Personal and cultural sources of meaning are often cast as oppositional forms (Berger & Luckmann, 1966; Leont'ev, 1978; Ricoeur, 1971). Huspek and Kendall (1991) argue that personal meanings grow out of a set of practices that "belong uniquely to the individual . . . to make sense of the inner life and its relation to the external world" (p. 1). In contrast, cultural meanings grow out of a set of social practices beyond any individual experience providing socially validated ways of seeing and representing the world. Thus, an individualistic orientation leads one to favor cognitive outcomes through personal meaning systems. A systems orientation leads one to favor conversational practices through the study of the cultural or the interpenetration of the cultural with personal meaning systems.

### Links to Transmission Views Versus Meaning-Centered Views of Communication

Figure 11.1 also reveals that leadership as a monologue versus leadership as a dialogue links the individual-system and the transmission-meaning dualisms together. Leadership as a monologue has its roots in two places. First, it hearkens back to transmission models of communication where the transfer of information goes from source to receiver where au-diences are often undifferentiated masses. This view prohibits treating meaning as contested or problematic. Second, a monologue approach also draws from the symbolic views of leadership as proposed by Pfeffer (1981), Pondy (1978), and Bennis and Nanus (1985). The blending of symbolic leadership with a transmission model casts leaders as the primary architects of meaning through such vehicles as an organizational vision, mission, and statement of values (e.g., Shamir, Arthur, & House, 1994). Bennis and Nanus (1985) write in this regard, "An essential factor in leadership is the capacity to influence and *organize meaning* for the members of the organization" (p. 39, emphasis in the original).

A monologic approach conceives of members as largely surrendering their right to make meanings by virtue of their employment contract within a hierarchical organization. Smircich and Morgan (1982) reflect this view when they state, "Leadership involves a dependency relationship in which individuals surrender their power to interpret and define reality to others" (p. 258). As such, meanings are created by the leader and remain largely uncontested by constituents. As will be shown, the study of charisma benefits from such a view.

Dialogic views of leadership merge interactional models of communication that stress feedback and mutual effects with transactional models that focus on holism and sharing (Littlejohn, 1983). Dialogic views tend toward a social constructionist orientation where emphasis is given to the coconstruction of meaning (Cooperrider, Barrett, & Srivastva, 1995; Gergen, 1985). Coconstruction presumes that talk is essentially contested where contestation is not just about what exists, but includes competing perspectives, future possibilities, and prescriptions for action (Shotter, 1993). For example, the literature on organizational visions increasingly reflects the view that shared visions require contestation, not a monologic transfer of vision from one person to the next. According to Senge (1990):

Visions that are truly shared take time to emerge. They grow as a by-product of interactions of individual visions. Experience suggests that visions that are genuinely shared require ongoing conversation where individuals not only feel free to express their dreams, but learn how to listen to each other's dreams. Out of this listening, new insights into what is possible gradually emerge. (pp. 217-218)

In the organizational development literature, a dialogic focus also tends to minimize hierarchical distinctions while simultaneously promoting the notion of community (Kouzes & Posner, 1993). Note the absence of hierarchical framing in the Senge quote. There is no leader or constituent, only individuals engaged in a dialogue of conversing and listening.

In summary, the dualism between leadership as monologue and dialogue ties the individual-system and the transmission-meaning dualisms together. An individualistic focus produces the tendency to see the leader's communication in monologic and transmission terms. A systems focus emphasizes meaning as a social construction through leader-constituent dialogue.

### Implications

The choice points or research dilemmas formed by these intersecting dualisms have enormous heuristic value. First, we can observe something of the nature of the conflict between scientists from different disciplines and theoretical orientations. For example, the pull away from the individual toward the system and its functioning for leadership researchers trained in psychology or a social cognitive orientation is often internal and, thus, nonantagonistic. The historical tendency to perceive communication as being incidental is counteracted by the observed effects of social interaction. These effects cannot be explained through the additive contribution of individuals and their perceptions.

However, communication scientists and others espousing a systems philosophy are much more likely to reject outright the individual as the exclusive orientation to leadership. Courtright, Fairhurst, and Rogers (1989) voice this position, "To understand social structure, however, knowing what people do individually is not sufficient. Rather, researchers must know what they do in conjunction with or in relationship to the other participants in an interaction" (p. 777); hence, their focus on the interact, two contiguous acts, as the minimally acceptable unit of analysis for leader-constituent communication.

In addition to providing an organizing framework for making sense of opposing views, a second heuristic associated with intersecting dualisms is that it opens up new directions for research. The reason for this is quite simple; most research programs manage the alternatives by favoring one approach over another for a given period of time (Werner & Baxter, 1994). Not all research programs favor the same approach, and the results can be used to pose questions from the understudied areas. In this way, future research may achieve a more complex view of the dualisms explored within this chapter.

To begin, we must characterize some specific points of departure. As previously indicated, I have selected five programs of leadership communication research where there has been enough study to characterize the dualisms and their resulting tensions. Their order of presentation corresponds to their orientation to the individual-system dualism. The study of influence tactics is the most individualistic of the programs because the influence process is largely conceived of as one-way. The study of feedback follows because organizational feedback research concentrates heavily on the individual's view of giving, seeking, or receiving feedback. Although the study of charisma historically has had strong individualistic leanings, individual-system tensions are increasingly articulated within this literature. By contrast, the study of visionary leadership is often more systemic than individual. Leader-member exchange, the fourth program of research, is more systemic than individual because it focuses on the leader-constituent relationship although typically from a social cognitive perspective. Finally, systems-interactional research is the most systemic of the approaches because of its emphasis on actual system functioning. As will become apparent, the systems approaches are as much in need of a counter-balancing individualistic focus as the individualistic approaches require attention to systemic concerns.

For each body of literature, I begin by characterizing some of the developments within the literature in the past several years in terms of the dualisms. I then use the understudied sides of the dualisms to identify new research directions.

# INFLUENCE TACTICS

The study of interpersonal influence between leaders and constituents takes many forms. While some research focuses on defensive strategies where influence is exerted to protect and manage an identity in the offering of an account for some type of failure event (Bies & Sitkin, 1992; Braaten, Cody, & DeTienne, 1993; Schonbach, 1990), most of the research focuses on more proactive means to goal achievement (Arkin & Sheppard, 1990; Schlenker, 1980; Tedeschi, 1990). The most dominant body of research in this regard is the study of compliance gaining or influence tactics. Dualisms and tensions exist within this voluminous body of literature.

## *The Individual-System Dualism and Other Tensions*

Although tensions around the individual-system dualism exist, the dominance of the individual has been significant. One person essentially asks another to do something with little or unspecified argument from the other; there is no parallel consideration of strategies for resisting another's influence attempts. Individuals have relational concerns (e.g., the relative status and power of the target, others' perceptions of interactional justice), but issues of relationship surface only as a context for the study of individual compliance-gaining behavior. Wider systems concerns are not of interest.

Most studies operate from a social cognitive perspective where cognitive outcomes are favored over conversational practices. The most popular measures are checklists that record global summary judgments recalled across all interactions. This method tends to obscure how strategy choice may combine with other strategies, may vary across situations, or may function within a sequence of reciprocal influence moves. Under this approach, the model of communication is "transmissional," and the social construction of meaning is taken for granted. Communication is strictly a medium for the self-conscious exercise of power based on some resource imbalance or dependency relationship.

The tendencies toward favoring the individual, cognitive outcomes, and a transmission view of communication reveal themselves in three questions dominating this type of research: (1) How can influence best be described? (2) What factors influence the production of tactics? and (3) What outcomes do the tactics produce? Table 11.1 summarizes a representative set of findings.

## *Describing Influence*

The most widely used influence tactic scheme is the one developed by Kipnis and his colleagues (Kipnis & Schmidt, 1988; Kipnis, Schmidt, & Wilkinson, 1980; Schriesheim & Hinkin, 1990), who inductively derived a set of tactics for upward, downward, and lateral communication. Each tactic (assertiveness, ingratiation, rationality, exchange of benefits,

**TABLE 11.1** Influence Tactic Research

| | |
|---|---|
| Description of tactics | |
| Influence message analysis | Case, Dosier, Murkison, & Keys, 1988; Dosier, Case, & Keys, 1988; Mainiero, 1986; Tjosvold, 1985 |
| Kipnis scheme | Kipnis & Schmidt, 1988; Kipnis, Schmidt, & Wilkinson, 1980; Schriesheim & Hinkin, 1990 |
| Rational, soft, and hard | Farmer, Maslyn, Fedor, & Goodman, 1997; Kipnis & Schmidt, 1985; Deluga, 1991a, 1991b |
| Yukl scheme | Falbe & Yukl, 1992; Yukl, Falbe, & Youn, 1993; Yukl, Guinan, & Sottolano, 1995; Yukl, Kim, & Chavez, 1999; Yukl & Tracey, 1992 |
| Influences on tactic use | |
| Agent versus target perspectives | Erez, Rim, & Keider, 1986; Xin & Tsui, 1996 |
| Attractiveness of constituents | Garko, 1992 |
| Authoritarian vs. participative leaders | Ansari & Kapoor, 1987 |
| Consideration and initiating structure | Chacko, 1990; Cheng, 1983 |
| Cross-cultural tactic use | Hirokawa & Miyahara, 1986; Sullivan & Taylor, 1991; Xin & Tsui, 1996 |
| Directional differences | Erez, Rim, & Keider, 1986; Kipnis et al., 1980; Xin & Tsui, 1996; Yukl & Falbe, 1990; Yukl, Falbe, & Youn, 1993; Yukl & Tracey, 1992 |
| Education | Farmer et al., 1997 |
| Expectations for success | Kipnis et al., 1984 |
| Expectations of constituent resistance | Sullivan, Albrecht, & Taylor, 1990 |

upward appeal, and coalition) has its own multi-item scale that is designed to assess retrospectively the frequency of tactic use for initial compliance gaining and then for follow-up attempts when resistance (unspecified) is encountered. In other research, tactics have been grouped into an alternative set of categories: rational (reason, exchange), soft (friendliness), and hard (assertiveness, higher authority, coalition) (e.g., Deluga, 1991a, 1991b; Farmer, Maslyn, Fedor, & Goodman, 1997; Kipnis & Schmidt, 1985).

While Kipnis and his colleagues used the agent's perspective to generate their influence tactics, Yukl and his colleagues (Falbe & Yukl, 1992; Yukl & Falbe, 1990; Yukl, Falbe,

& Youn, 1993; Yukl, Guinan, & Sottolano, 1995; Yukl & Tracey, 1992) also focus on the target's perspective. Several of Kipnis's tactics overlap the Yukl scheme. However, the latter adds the tactics "inspirational appeal to values and emotion" and "consultation" (Yukl & Falbe, 1990) and different forms of rational persuasion (Yukl, Kim, & Chavez, 1999).

Finally, other studies have chosen not to supply subjects with a preformulated checklist of strategies. Instead, these studies ask subjects to construct messages whose features are then coded for influence form. Using a critical incident or hypothetical scenario methodology, incidents are coded using strategies from previously developed checklists to

| Gender | Hirokawa, Kodama, & Harper, 1990; Lauterbach & Weiner, 1996; Yukl & Falbe, 1990; Yukl & Tracey, 1992 |
|---|---|
| Influence objectives | Ansari & Kapoor, 1987; Erez et al., 1986; Harper & Hirokawa, 1988; Kipnis et al., 1980; Schmidt & Kipnis, 1984; Yukl & Falbe, 1990; Yukl et al., 1995; Yukl et al., 1999 |
| Low vs. high power agents | Hirokawa et al., 1990; Mainiero, 1986; Schilit, 1987 |
| Leader-member exchange | Deluga & Perry, 1991 |
| Machiavellianism | Farmer et al., 1997; Vecchio & Sussman, 1991 |
| Mediators and outcomes of tactic use Commitment, compliance, or resistance | Falbe & Yukl, 1992; Tepper, 1993; Tepper, Eisenbach, Kirby, & Potter, 1998; Yukl et al., 1999 |
| Constituent earnings | Kipnis & Schmidt, 1988 |
| Constituent effectiveness | Case et al., 1988; Kipnis & Schmidt, 1988 |
| Constituent perceived interpersonal skills | Wayne, Liden, Graf, & Ferris, 1997 |
| Constituent promotability | Thacker & Wayne, 1995 |
| Constituent stress | Kipnis & Schmidt, 1988 |
| Justice perceptions | Dulebohn & Ferris, 1999; Tepper et al., 1998 |
| Leader effectiveness | Deluga, 1991b; Dosier et al., 1988; Falbe & Yukl, 1992; Yukl & Tracey, 1992 |
| Leader stress | Deluga, 1991b |
| Satisfaction | Deluga, 1991b |
| Task commitment | Yukl & Tracey, 1992 |

form a coding scheme (e.g., Falbe & Yukl, 1992; Hirokawa, Kodama, & Harper, 1990; Hirokawa & Miyahara, 1986) or based on emergent categories in the data (e.g., Case, Dosier, Murkison, & Keys, 1988; Dosier, Case, & Keys, 1988; Lauterbach & Weiner, 1996). Alternatively, other studies code for specific message features such as supportiveness, powerlessness, punitiveness, or threat (Mainiero, 1986; Tjosvold, 1985).

## *Factors Influencing Tactic Use*

As Table 11.1 reveals, a wide range of studies have looked at the influences on tactic use including directional differences, influ-

ence objectives, agent versus target perspectives, and a host of other relationship and individual variables.

Among the more notable findings are the various directional differences (upward, downward, and lateral) in tactic use. Research consistently shows that exchange of benefits is used in downward and lateral as opposed to upward influence, while assertiveness is favored in downward more than lateral or upward influence. Findings related to the other tactics remain inconsistent (e.g., Erez, Rim, & Keider, 1986; Kipnis et al., 1980; Yukl & Falbe, 1990; Yukl & Tracey, 1992).

Individuals also select influence tactics based on their objectives and goals. For example, pressure is often used to change the behavior of constituents (Erez et al., 1986; Harper & Hirokawa, 1988; Kipnis et al., 1980; Schmidt & Kipnis, 1984; Xin & Tsui, 1996; Yukl & Falbe, 1990). Rational persuasion and coalition tactics are often used with peers and leaders to win support for major changes in policies and programs (Erez et al., 1986; Kipnis et al., 1980; Schmidt & Kipnis, 1984; Xin & Tsui, 1996). But more than one study has reached the conclusion of Yukl et al. (1995), "Even though some tactics are used more often for particular objectives, the relationship between tactics and objectives was not a strong one . . . most of the tactics could be used for any objective" (p. 294).

Finally, hard influence tactics (e.g., assertiveness) are reportedly chosen more frequently when expectations for success are low versus high (Kipnis, Schmidt, Swaffin-Smith, & Wilkinson, 1984) and with authoritarian versus participative leaders (Ansari & Kapoor, 1987), high- versus low-power agents (Hirokawa et al., 1990), high versus low levels of Machiavellianism and education in agents (Farmer et al., 1997), low versus high levels of consideration and initiating structure in leaders (Chacko, 1990; Cheng, 1983), American versus Japanese leaders (Hirokawa & Miyahara, 1986), low versus high LMX relationships (Deluga & Perry, 1991), and unattractive versus attractive constituents (Garko, 1992).

### Outcomes of Tactic Use

A number of studies suggest that the use of hard influence tactics are associated with the most negative outcomes including constituent effectiveness ratings, leader stress levels, task commitment, and constituent promotability (Case et al., 1988; Deluga, 1991b; Kipnis & Schmidt, 1988; Thacker & Wayne, 1995; Yukl & Tracey, 1992). Studies also suggest that some form of rational persuasion yields the most positive outcomes (Case et al., 1988; Falbe & Yukl, 1992; Wayne, Liden, Graf, & Ferris, 1997; Yukl & Tracey, 1992).

Finally, there is a growing body of literature that focuses on constituents' use of influence tactics to influence the performance ratings they receive (e.g., Barry & Watson, 1996; Ferris, Judge, Rowland, & Fitzgibbons, 1994; Wayne & Ferris, 1990; Wayne et al., 1997). Soft supervisor-focused tactics have been associated with perceptions of procedural justice in this context (Dulebohn & Ferris, 1999). Also in this context, rational persuasion and hard tactics like assertiveness have been associated with leaders' perceptions of constituents' interpersonal skills (Wayne et al., 1997).

## New Directions: Conversational Practices, the Recovery of Meaning, and Systems Concerns

While the social cognitive basis of this work contributes to our understanding of social action, the influence process is more complex and more interesting than current research allows. However, we can recover some of this complexity by focusing on the understudied areas in this work: conversational practices, a meaning-centered view of communication, and system concerns.

### Conversational Practices

A focus on conversational practices should reveal more of the reciprocal nature of influence and the complexity of influence messages. A focus on the reciprocal nature of talk in the influence literature might call into question the usual emphasis on compliance gaining. Compliance resisting has not been explored in any systematic way in the organizational influence tactic literature, which may be more of a function of researchers' assumptions about its aberrance in reporting relationships. Empirical treatments of the subject, especially in organizations and/or relationships promoting empowerment, participation, and dialogue, will likely reveal that compliance resisting occurs with some frequency in both hierarchical and lateral relationships. Regardless of base rate, compliance resisting is worthy of study in the context of everyday influence. The study of empowerment with its emphasis on leader support for constituent autonomy may be the venue in which this emerges (e.g., Chiles & Zorn, 1995; Conger & Kanungo, 1988). The study of resistance is also prominent in critical theory approaches to organizations (e.g., Jermier, Knights, & Nord, 1994) because as Phillips (1997) observed, "upward influence is referred to as resistance and is understood to be a part of any asymmetrical power relation; where there is power, there is resistance, the two are mutually constituting and reinforcing" (p. 47).

A focus on conversational practices should also reveal more complexity in influence messages. In studying actual dialogue, as opposed to a self-reported strategy selection, specific message features that accompany a broad characterization of a strategy (e.g., "rationality," "exchange of benefits") are more difficult to ignore. For many organizational scientists who see communication only as a medium for the exercise of power, adding complexity to message schemes is not high yield (cf. Yukl et al., 1999). For example, variations on the tactic "exchange of benefits" may matter little if the comparison to other tactics is the primary concern.

Yet the introduction of status and power into interactional contexts frequently produces actors with multiple goals who want to pursue a task (task goal), usually without offending influential others (relationship goal), while promoting an image of competence (identity goal). In turn, multiple goals create multifunctional utterances. Typically, these utterances are marked by language that cloaks or moderates the influence attempt in order to address relational and identity aims while still achieving the task. Such language may include politeness strategies, semantic indirectness, language that triggers cognitive scripts, and the framing of intent (e.g., disclaimers, credentialling) (Brown & Levinson, 1978;

Drake & Moberg, 1986). All help the actor to position the self, assuage other's ego, reinforce relational ties, and/or trigger scripted behavior.

Despite promising recent efforts to examine episodic influence (Maslyn, Farmer, & Fedor, 1996), different versions of strategies (Yukl et al., 1999), and the combined use of tactics (Tepper, Eisenbach, Kirby, & Potter, 1998), survey studies tend to paint influence strategies in such broad strokes that the details of their instantiation are often lost. Yet the inconsistency across studies regarding tactic use and associated variables (e.g., directional differences, influence objectives) reminds us that the devil is in the details. To continue with my earlier "exchange of benefits" example, when this strategy is paired with linguistic palliatives or sedatives, it can suspend calculation of the exchange and win compliance in ways that "exchange of benefits" without these linguistic devices cannot. This is because the form of the influence attempt itself becomes an inducement (Drake & Moberg, 1986).

In a similar vein, Kellermann and Cole (1994) argue that we know very little about regularities in message behavior because most schemes neither cover an adequate range of influence strategies, nor do they identify theoretically relevant features of influence messages. Based on the notion that a strategy is conceived of a higher-order unit comprising other units, Kellermann and Cole state that the scheme advanced by Kipnis et al. (1980) contains strategies defined by form (e.g., sanctions), content (e.g., rationality), presentation (e.g., ingratiation, assertiveness), context (e.g., upward appeal, coalitions), and interactive use (e.g., exchange). From their perspective, the Kipnis scheme is a data-driven hodgepodge of elements that render nonsensical the study of "strategy use" as the variable of interest. As Kellermann and Cole (1994) observe, "The values 'strategy use' takes on are unknown (i.e., over what values does it vary?) and the one feature, quality, or characteristic of behavior that it tracks is not specified" (p. 45). They argue that the study of compliance-gaining message behavior requires a feature-based approach where researchers focus on theoretically driven and specific message features (i.e., the underlying dimensions of message variation such as target adaptiveness, prosocialness, politeness, threat, etc.) rather than on strategies (see also O'Keefe, 1994).

Kellermann and Cole's point is well taken. Most taxonomy approaches involve an overly general and simplistic characterization of the basic message strategy, thus would do well to incorporate more aspects of message features into their schemes. For example, Yukl and his colleagues increasingly use critical incident scenarios alongside checklist approaches and code for multiple strategy use (e.g., Falbe & Yukl, 1992). But if taxonomy approaches are lacking in depth (regarding the range of messages that forms dimensions of message behavior), their strength lies in their breadth. And if one's interest in communication is strictly as a medium for the self-conscious exercise of power, a taxonomy serves a useful role in setting forth a range of categorically distinct influence options available in typical organizational situations. However, the problem is that even with a sophisticated taxonomy, there is so much more to understanding power, influence, and communication between leaders and constituents.

## The Recovery of Meaning

Frost (1987) reminded us that communication is not just a medium for the exercise of power as a result of some resource imbalance or dependency relationship. Communication also is intricately involved in the formation of meaning. Communication is used to develop social consensus around labels and definitions of decisions and actions (Pfeffer, 1981; Shotter, 1993). Thus, getting others to do things rests as much on the framing and sensemaking of everyday life, which define the bounds of what is logical and sensible in a context of action. "Our situation here and

now," "the mistakes of the past," and "what we strive for" are just a few of the ongoing socially negotiated meanings that form the warrant for action including compliance gaining. When researchers are preoccupied with forcing influence forms into static typologies, meaning is taken for granted thereby stripping human communication of one of its most essential elements. In so doing, they artificially impose stability on power and influence processes obscuring both the complexity and fluidity of power dynamics as a result (Clegg, 1979; Conrad, 1983).

The recovery of meaning can begin by asking leaders and constituents not just to report their use of tactics, but by asking them to account for their strategy selection. When individuals are asked why they chose a particular tactic, social meanings emerge with respect to their own actions, the actions of others, or other aspects of the environment (Tompkins & Cheney, 1983).

## Wider Systems Concerns and Deep Structure

The argument for a more complex understanding of power and influence in leader-constituent relationships is further buttressed by the fact that communication as medium (vis-à-vis tactic use) and communication as meaning (vis-à-vis sensemaking and labeling) are surface manifestations of power that influence and are influenced by systemwide deep structures of power (Clegg, 1979; Conrad, 1983; Frost, 1987; Phillips, 1997). In seeking or resisting compliance, Conrad (1983) notes, "Organizational members will observe, interpret, and remember their choices and their presumed relationship to the structure of power which exists in the organization" (p. 178). At deep-structure levels, all choices are political in that some interests are served over others. Surface-level choices create structures of power that act back upon the choice-making process in taken-for-granted assumptions about what is real, what is fair, and what is legitimate in ways actors are scarcely aware of (Deetz, 1985) simultaneously reproducing and adjusting the structure of organizational power (Giddens, 1979).

Deep-structure systems of meaning are operative at wider systems levels (e.g., culture). These systems are a preconscious foundation for interpretation and action that limit the perception of choice and available options (Deetz & Kersten, 1983). But underlying tensions between surface-level tactics, surface-level meaning making, and deep structure can be observed. Examples include a focus on language, especially stories, and the myths and metaphors used to describe power relationships; behavior during conflict situations in which organizational constraints are most likely to be consciously violated and questioned; and organizational game playing in which surface-level political activities become intertwined with deep-level meanings (Conrad, 1983; Clegg, 1975, 1979; Frost, 1987). Unfortunately, deep-structure influences on surface-level tactic use have rarely emerged in the literature.

In summary, the understudied areas of the influence literature suggest that a focus on conversational practices, the recovery of meaning, and wider systems concerns may reveal more complexity in influence processes between leaders and constituents. Some of these same recommendations surface for the study of feedback.

# FEEDBACK

For most of this century, scholars have been interested in the link between feedback, motivation, and performance (Ammons, 1956; Kluger & DeNisi, 1996). Feedback research continues because of a possible performance-enhancing effect, although the literature increasingly suggests that the effects of feedback on performance and worker attitudes are quite variable and even damaging at times. Cybernetic theorist Wiener (1948) is credited with introducing the concept of

feedback into general usage defining it as "a method of controlling a system" (Wiener, 1954, p. 61). However, the following discussion reveals very strong pulls toward the individual that has lessened only slightly in the past several years.

## The Individual-System Dualism and Other Tensions

In his review of the feedback literature, Cusella (1987) correctly observed that despite the systemic origins of the feedback concept, almost all models of feedback and feedback research emphasized the internal psychological processes of feedback sending and receiving. Whether the emphasis was on feedback characteristics (goals, sources, types, functions) or its relationship to motivation and performance, the internal psychological state that formed the basis for feedback choices, rather than the actual feedback process, was the primary focus. Cusella's review was significant for communication scholars because his lone voice attempted to stem the tide of individualistic over systemic thinking: "From a communication perspective, feedback processes consist of an exchange of behaviors that emphasize the (1) symbolic; (2) relational; and (3) systemic aspects to feedback-motivation/performance relationships" (Cusella, 1987, p. 625).

Cusella's arguments centered on two chief points. First, patterns of control in feedback systems, sometimes characterized as "feedback loops," are frequently spoken of, but rarely operationalized in research. In operationalizing feedback loops, Cusella argued against the standard checklist approaches to selecting feedback messages. Instead, he focused on the conversational practices of feedback, practices that are best studied as an interconnected series of double interacts (Weick. 1969). Feedback is a process that takes place in "a circular closed loop of interaction" (Fisher, 1978, p. 298). Yet too often it is conceptualized as a mere response that ne-

**TABLE 11.2** Feedback Research

**Feedback sending and receiving**

| | |
|---|---|
| 360-degree feedback | Albright & Levy, 1995; Antonioni, 1994; Atwater, Rousch, & Fischthal, 1995; Atwater & Waldman, 1998; Barclay & Harland, 1995; Bernardin, Dahmus, & Redmon, 1993; Church & Bracken, 1997; Facteau, Facteau, Schoel, Russell, & Poteet, 1998; Funderburg & Levy, 1997; Hazucha, Hezlett, & Schneider, 1993; London, Smither, & Adsit, 1997; Smither, London, Vasilopoulos, Reilly, Millsap, & Salvemini, 1995; Smither, Wohlers, & London, 1995 |
| Feedback sign | Atwater et al., 1995; Fedor, 1991; Kluger & DeNisi, 1996; Louie, 1999; Martocchio & Webster, 1992; Podsakoff & Farh, 1989; Reilly, Smither, & Vasilopoulos, 1996 |
| Feedback sources | Becker & Klimoski, 1989; Fedor, 1991; Herold, Liden, & Leatherwood, 1987; Northcraft & Earley, 1989 |
| Feedback style | Korsgaard, Meglino, & Lester, 1997; Zhou, 1998 |
| Goal-setting and self-regulatory mechanisms | Earley, Northcraft, Lee, & Lituchy, 1989; Locke, Frederick, Lee, & Bobko, 1984; Latham & Locke, 1991; Locke & Latham, 1990; Mento, Steel, & Karren, 1987; Wood & Bandura, 1989 |
| Negative feedback effects | Baron, 1988, 1990; Geddes & Baron, 1997; Gioia & Longenecker, 1994; Kluger, Lewinsohn, & Aiello, 1994; Larson, 1989; Skarlicki & Folger, 1997 |

**Feedback seeking**

*Influences on feedback seeking*

| | |
|---|---|
| Feedback context (public vs. private) | Ashford, 1986; Ashford & Northcraft, 1992; Levy, Albright, Cawley, & Williams, 1995; Northcraft & Ashford, 1990; Walsh, Ashford, & Hill, 1985; Williams, Miller, Steelman, & Levy, 1999 |

glects the unfolding context in which feedback is administered and received. Moreover, contiguous feedback messages need to be analyzed to explicate the relational meaning or control function of feedback (Deci, 1975; Watzlawick, Beavin, & Jackson, 1967).

The second argument involving the systemic aspects of feedback concerns the cultural manifestations of consistent patterns of feedback. These patterns create feedback environments where cultural norms and values emerge around the sources of feedback and the types of information conveyed. Cusella (1987) argued that when the study of feedback is conceptualized in terms of feedback loops and feedback environments, the internal psychological (individual) and the external communicative (system) are jointly operative. He noted "a communication perspective to feedback processes, while representing a clear separation from cognitive models of feedback is, nevertheless, interdependent with them" (Cusella, 1987, p. 625). As Table 11.2 reveals, recent feedback research may be classified in terms of four general trends, the first two adhering to the traditional view of the concept.

### Feedback Sending and Receiving

The first trend reflects a strong interest in psychological views of sending and receiving feedback including the sources of feedback

| | |
|---|---|
| Feedback seeking costs/risks | Ashford, 1986; Fedor, Rensvold, & Adams, 1992 |
| Feedback source | Callister, Kramer, & Turban, 1999 |
| Goal orientation | VandeWalle & Cummings, 1997 |
| Performance | Ashford, 1986; Fedor et al., 1992; Northcraft & Ashford, 1990 |
| Role clarity | Callister et al., 1999 |
| Self-esteem | Ashford, 1986; Fedor et al., 1992; Northcraft & Ashford, 1990 |
| Source credibility | Fedor et al., 1992 |
| Tolerance for ambiguity | Bennett, Herold, & Ashford, 1990; Fedor, et al., 1992 |
| Uncertainty | Ashford, 1986; Fedor et al., 1992; Northcraft & Ashford, 1990 |
| *Outcomes of feedback seeking*<br>Amount of negative feedback | Larson, 1989 |
| Impression management | Ashford & Northcraft, 1992; Ashford & Tsui, 1991; Levy et al., 1995; Morrison & Bies, 1991 |
| Performance | Fedor et al., 1992 |
| Understanding | Ashford & Tsui, 1991 |
| **Feedback message analysis**<br>Attributional influences on feedback messages | Dugan, 1989; Gioia & Sims, 1986; Kim & Miller, 1990; Tjosvold, 1985 |
| Dimensionality | Geddes, 1993; Geddes & Linnehan, 1998; Larson, Glynn, Fleenor, & Scontrino, 1987 |
| Face support | Zorn & Leichty, 1991 |
| **Control chains** | Fairhurst, Green & Snavely, 1984a, 1984b; Gavin, Green, & Fairhurst, 1995; Green, Fairhurst, & Snavely, 1986; Morris, Gaveras, Baker, & Coursey, 1990 |

and their credibility, goal-setting and self-regulatory mechanisms, and feedback sign.

*Feedback sources.* Previous research on feedback sources (Greller & Herold, 1975; Hanser & Muchinsky, 1978; Herold & Greller, 1977) established differences in the perceived informativeness of five sources of performance feedback. In rank order, they are (1) oneself, (2) the task, (3) supervisors, (4) coworkers, and (5) the organization. Herold, Liden, and Leatherwood (1987) and Northcraft and Earley (1989) present confirmatory results. However, this order has been disputed (Becker & Klimoski, 1989), and there is some controversy over whether the self and task are distinct sources of feedback.

In his review of the literature, Fedor (1991) examines this conflict and the mitigating role of source credibility and relative power on recipient responses to different sources.

Finally, 360-degree feedback has been one of the most popular management innovations of the 1990s. This involves the systematic collection of feedback from a wide range of sources even those thought to be nontraditional or taboo such as internal and external customers or higher levels of management (Atwater & Waldman, 1998). Much attention has been paid to what 360-degree feedback is, how to implement it, and to the psychometric properties of ratings from various sources (e.g., Church & Bracken, 1997; Greguras & Robie, 1998). While less attention has been paid to outcomes, a few studies support a generally positive relationship between 360-degree feedback and leader performance (Atwater, Rousch, & Fischthal, 1995; Smither, London, Vasilopoulos, Reilly, Millsap, & Salvemini, 1995), although there are moderating factors like obtaining input on development plans from coworkers (Hazucha, Hezlett, & Schneider, 1993). Other studies focus on the characteristics of the feedback system that may garner a positive response by leaders. These include rater anonymity (Antonioni, 1994), rater accountability (London, Smither, & Adsit, 1997), multiple versus single sources (Bernardin, Dahmus, & Redmon, 1993), individual and normative data versus normative data alone (Smither, Wohlers, & London, 1995), rater competence (Barclay & Harland, 1995), source credibility (Albright & Levy, 1995), perceptions of organizational support (Facteau, Facteau, Schoel, Russell, & Poteet, 1998), and perceived social costs (Funderburg & Levy, 1997). The combined written and verbal aspects of 360-degree feedback is an understudied area.

*Self-regulatory mechanisms in goal setting.* In terms of goal-setting and self-regulatory mechanisms, Latham and Locke (1991) continue to assert that the effects of feedback are greatly misunderstood without acknowledging the goal-related processes that mediate the impact of feedback on performance (cf. Becker & Klimoski, 1989; Florin-Thuma & Boudreau, 1987). Put simply, in the absence of goal setting, feedback has no necessary relationship to performance. In the absence of feedback, goal setting is less effective. Locke and Latham (1990) reviewed 33 studies that compared the effects of goals plus feedback versus either goals or feedback alone. The vast majority supported the combined hypothesis (see also Mento, Steel, & Karren, 1987).

Self-regulatory processes are implicit in goal-setting theories; however, most goal-setting experiments have not emphasized them in their research designs (Latham & Locke, 1991). (Goals are typically assigned in these studies in order to manipulate goal level and type adequately.) However, developments in social learning theory suggest the means whereby feedback and goals combine to influence performance (Bandura, 1986, 1991; Bandura & Cervone, 1983). According to social learning theory, there are two cognitive regulatory mechanisms affecting how an individual will respond to performance feedback. The first is a self-evaluative mechanism where feedback helps gauge the extent to which prior behavior meets an internal goal standard. Negative feedback usually indicates a failure to achieve the goal, and if self-efficacy beliefs remain high, individuals should be motivated to set higher goals and increase their effort to achieve them. In contrast, positive feedback indicates that the performance is "on target" with few changes in performance required (Atwater et al., 1995; Podsakoff & Farh, 1989; Reilly, Smither, & Vasilopoulos, 1996).

The second process concerns self-efficacy, or individuals' assessments of their capabilities to undertake one or more courses of action successfully to achieve designated types of performance (Bandura, 1986). Self-efficacy information may come from both direct and mediated experiences (Bandura, 1982) including that of performance feedback (Bandura, 1986, 1991). Research on self-efficacy has shown it to be a significant predictor of performance (Locke, Frederick, Lee, & Bobko, 1984; Wood & Bandura, 1989). Moreover, combining self-evaluation and efficacy influences can predict the level of performance motivation (Bandura & Cervone, 1983).

*Feedback sign.* Latham and Locke (1991) note that the key to understanding performance improvement and feedback sign depends on the degree of dissatisfaction individuals have with their present performance as well as the confidence they have that their performance can be improved (i.e., self-efficacy remains high). Recent findings offer support for this view (Fedor, 1991; Martocchio & Webster, 1992; Podsakoff & Farh, 1989).

However, Kluger and DeNisi (1996) critique the feedback-standard discrepancy argument on which Latham and Locke's argument rests. In addition, in Kluger and DeNisi's (1996) meta-analysis of feedback research feedback sign did not emerge as a significant moderator of the feedback-performance relationship. Kluger and DeNisi (1996) note that "at present, there is no FI [feedback intervention]-related theory that can predict a priori the effects of all the important moderators that determine how feedback sign affects performance" (p. 276). Those moderators likely include a number of personality, cognitive processing, and task variables that direct attention more or less to the task or oneself with varying effects on the effort expended to alter task performance. Feedback sign is just one of several moderators of the feedback-performance relationship that Kluger and DeNisi (1996) investigate. They conclude generally that feedback affects performance through changes in locus of attention. The more attention is directed away from the self and toward the task, the stronger the benefit of feedback on performance. In addition, feedback's effects are moderated by the nature of the task, although the exact task properties that moderate feedback's effects are still poorly understood.

Finally, recent feedback sign research has also focused on its joint impact with feedback style (Korsgaard, Meglino, & Lester, 1997; Zhou, 1998) as well as the detrimental effect of negative feedback. Feedback that is perceived as destructive versus constructive can serve as the source of ego threat, defensiveness, conflict, and even aggression among organizational participants (Baron, 1988, 1990; Fedor, 1991; Geddes & Baron, 1997; Gioia & Longenecker, 1994; Kluger, Lewinsohn, & Aiello, 1994; Larson, 1989; Skarlicki & Folger, 1997). While "going postal" or other forms of active retaliation are less common re-

sponses to negative feedback, Geddes and Baron's (1997) work suggests a clear need to prepare leaders for potentially aggressive constituent responses. Feedback interventions that are conciliatory and attribution-shifting versus cathartic may counter the effects of destructive criticism (Baron, 1990), a potential antidote to the increasing spillover of violence into the workplace.

### Feedback Seeking

The second trend in feedback research involves a decided shift toward recasting workplaces as information environments (Ashford & Cummings, 1983). This recasting allows feedback recipients to become active monitors and information seekers rather than passive information receivers. The two primary strategies of seeking are monitoring and inquiry.

As Table 11.2 suggests, a number of individual and relational influences have been found either to thwart or encourage feedback inquiry. These influences include source of feedback and role clarity (Callister, Kramer, & Turban, 1999), supervisor unavailability (Walsh, Ashford, & Hill, 1985), goal orientation (VandeWalle & Cummings, 1997), self-esteem (Fedor, Rensvold, & Adams, 1992), uncertainty and fear of failure (Ashford, 1986), the presence of an audience or public context (Ashford & Northcraft, 1992; Northcraft & Ashford, 1990; Levy, Albright, Cawley, & Williams, 1995), and source supportiveness and peer reactions in a public context (Williams, Miller, Steelman, & Levy, 1999).

In terms of outcomes, Larson (1989) offered a theoretical account of the ways feedback seeking elicits less negative supervisory feedback than the unsolicited feedback a supervisor might otherwise give. Empirically, it has been shown that seeking positive feedback leads to more negative impressions by observers, while seeking negative feedback enhances impressions and produces more accurate understanding of the evaluations of others (Ashford & Northcraft, 1992; Ashford & Tsui,

1991). Finally, Fedor et al. (1992) found that performance was negatively related to feedback inquiry. This finding is important since this is one of the first studies to establish a link between feedback seeking and performance. However, they argue that different contextual conditions could also support a positive inquiry-performance relationship.

*Feedback Message Analysis*

A third general trend involves the increasing complexity recognized in the content of feedback messages. Larson, Glynn, Fleenor, and Scontrino (1987) raised concerns about treating the feedback message characteristics identified by Ilgen, Fisher, and Taylor (1979) (sign, timing, specificity, frequency, and sensitivity) as independent constructs. From feedback target and sender perspectives, Geddes (1993) analyzed the dimensionality of written feedback messages and found strong parallels with Larson et al. (1987). In Geddes's study, message valence (positive vs. negative) and message sensitivity were key dimensions. However, Geddes and Linnehan (1998) argue for the treatment of positive and negative feedback as distinct constructs each with its own dimensional structure.

Attributional influences on actual feedback message production have been studied by several scholars. Tjosvold (1985) coded the feedback messages of students role-playing supervisors of a low-performing worker. Messages were coded for supportiveness, assertions of power, and threat. Attributions associated with low effort elicited punitive and strong influence, while low-ability attributions generated attraction and a willingness to work together in the future. However, using a relational control coding scheme also in a laboratory simulation, Dugan (1989) found that a "tell and sell" approach was used to a greater degree when lack of ability was the attributed cause of poor performance and a more negotiative stance when lack of effort was the attributed cause.

Gioia and Sims (1986) studied attributional influences on the coded verbal behavior of both leaders and constituents. They discovered an attributional shift toward leniency as a result of constituents' ability to account for the leaders' behavior plausibly, a finding incorporated into Larson's (1989) arguments about the effects of feedback seeking. Gioia and Sims (1986) also found attribution-seeking "why" questions were asked of poor-performing constituents, while "what do you think" or "how" questions were asked of the more successful ones. Kim and Miller (1990) developed a coding scheme based on a combination of various influence tactic typologies to assess nurse managers' feedback messages. In contrast to Gioia and Sims (1986), attributions did not affect feedback message production. However, the research design appeared to preclude attributional effects.

Although Zorn and Leichty (1991) were not concerned with attributional effects, their study of face support in feedback messages revealed a positive relationship between leaders' use of autonomy and constituent job experience. As the following section reveals, the use of face support in feedback messages is also a concern in control chain studies.

*Control Chains*

A fourth and smaller trend is the study of poor performance as a chain of events and the impact of performance history on feedback message production. Fairhurst, Green, and Snavely (1984a, 1984b) argued that most research is based on single incidents of poor performance, but lacks veridicality because sequences of poor performance are more common than single incidents. While Gioia and Sims (1986) considered "effective" versus "ineffective" work history as a manipulated variable, Green, Fairhurst, and Snavely (1986) argued that the number, sequence, and relationship of a leader's actions to previous actions within a chain of poor-performance incidents has to be considered. Their study of bank branch managers showed that the use of formal disciplinary action was associated with less face support (positive face and autonomy) and greater escalation in harshness of actions within control chains.

Gavin, Green, and Fairhurst (1995) used a longitudinal lab design conducted in real time to simulate the dynamics of a chain phenomenon under more controlled conditions. They found evidence of both consistency and experimentation with leaders' punitive control strategies and verbal influence tactics over time. Constituents' perceptions of interactional justice were also related to the leaders' use of control tactics. Finally, Morris, Gaveras, Baker, and Coursey (1990) positioned their study of supervisory aligning actions at the problem-solving breakpoint in the model of supervisory control advanced by Fairhurst et al. (1984b). Aligning messages accompany messages of supervisory control, but are distinguished from them in that their goal is to enhance actor understanding of the situation. According to Morris et al. (1990), this could be done through explanation seeking, coorientation or alignment tests, accounts, or faultfinding.

### New Directions: Feedback Loops, the Recovery of Meaning, and Message Analysis

I began this section by noting that Cusella's (1987) review of the feedback literature attempted to shift the focus of feedback research to include feedback environments and a focus on conversational practices. To accomplish this, he called for the study of interactional patterns that are embedded within feedback systems, the content and relational dimensions of feedback messages, contextual influences on message production, and the cultural embeddedness of feedback messages. Recent research is beginning to address several of his recommendations. However, the numbers are not large, thus the understudied areas direct us to reinforce Cusella's call for systemic message-based research. In addition, a meaning-centered versus transmission view of communication also appears necessary.

Systemic concerns are addressed most prominently in research that operationalizes feedback loops.

### Feedback Loops

There are a few studies that have operationalized feedback loops (Dugan, 1989; Gavin et al., 1995; Gioia & Sims, 1986). Although these studies differ in their approaches, they capture the immediate feedback context by acknowledging the contested nature of constituents' performance. Previous feedback models and research capture several antecedent contextual influences or those influences that are present prior to a feedback encounter. However, they often fail to capture emergent influences including the discourse and the interaction between the discourse and perceptions of context (Haslett, 1987). Attributional shifts, leniency effects (Dugan, 1989; Gioia & Sims, 1986), and departures from progressive discipline policies (Gavin et al., 1995; Green et al., 1986) emerge because of discourse (most often, excuses and justifications) that triggers new attributions and behavioral responses.

Expanding the feedback process to include feedback seeking is important because of the potential to short-circuit the emotional build-up surrounding continued poor performance (Larson, 1989). This is clearly a different kind of feedback loop than when feedback is unsolicited and suggests a whole range of linguistic, emotional, cognitive, relational, and contextual processes that can be usefully contrasted with loops that begin with the leader. With its combined written and verbal components, the recent move to 360-degree feedback is also just beginning to be understood as a feedback mechanism of a different kind.

### The Recovery of Meaning

The mitigating role of the immediate context is not just a function of feedback loops. It is the interaction between the discourse and the perceptions of context in the sensemaking and meaning attributed to the unfolding encounter. However, most research tends to employ a transmission model of communication where issues of meaning are rarely made problematic. In his review of the feedback literature, Fedor (1991) argues that perceptions of feedback messages have rarely been studied. Recipient expectations should have a significant impact on feedback perceptions, potentially changing even the sign of feedback. For example, praise may not be favorably evaluated if laudatory comments were anticipated. Given his earlier research on the multiple sources of uncertainty that accompany feedback messages (Fedor, 1990, cited in Fedor, 1991), Fedor's arguments suggest that the sensemaking and interpretive requirements of most feedback encounters are neglected topics.

To understand the shift that must be made from a transmission view to a meaning-centered view of communication in feedback encounters, consider the subject of performance history. In the performance history research of Fairhurst, Green, and colleagues (Fairhurst et al., 1984a, 1984b; Gavin et al., 1995; Green et al., 1986), memory is seen as an internal property of managers, the unreliability of which could lead to distorted self-reports (Nisbett & Wilson, 1977). This effect holds even if leaders are aided by memory prompts such as documentation.

Rather than focusing on the way mental processes like memory construct action, a meaning-centered approach focuses on the way actions construct mental processes (Weick & Roberts, 1993). Under this approach, remembering and forgetting are seen as social constructions. Middleton and Edwards (1990) explain:

> The "truth" of the past is always, at least potentially, at issue. It is not to be found unambiguously deposited in some objective social record or archive, nor yet as infinitely malleable in the service of the present. It obtains neither as "fact" nor "invention," but an epistemological enterprise, created in dialectic and argument between those contrary positions. (p. 9)

Based on the social practice of commemoration, the act of leader and constituent remembering together opens up the potential for viewing history as problematic—not simply as an element of the interactional context, but as a ubiquitous, socially negotiated phenomena in its own right. History (like motives) is contestively established in talk each time feedback is given (Middleton & Edwards, 1990). The variation in the control chains reported by Green et al. (1986), which reflected a significant departure from progressive discipline policy, now makes a great deal more sense. It is not objective history that is considered when taking action. It is the intersubjective reconstruction of history within the moment that spurs action.

A potentially rich area of new research would ask about the functioning of conversational remembering as the basis for social action within the control chains. The work of Morris and Coursey (1989), although restricted to leaders' evaluations of poor performers' accounts, provides clues as to the nature of the inferences used to construct versions (real or imagined) of worker performance histories. The evaluations of accounts also draw on culture as a repository of acceptable and unacceptable explanations because, as Morris and Coursey (1989) suggest, accounts are never thrown into an explanatory vacuum. Thus, this approach also addresses Cusella's enjoinder to study the cultural embeddedness of feedback messages, an area that still remains largely unexplored.

### Message Analysis

Understanding the idea that feedback messages go beyond simple correction and feedback seeking goes beyond simple inquiry (in addition to monitoring) is also critical. Gioia and Sims's (1986) discovery of attribution-seeking "why" questions, Kim and Miller's (1990) discovery of counseling messages, Morris et al.'s (1990) focus on aligning actions, and Ashford and Tsui's (1991) and Larson's (1989) focus on identity management within feedback inquiry all point to the multifunctionality of feedback messages and the simultaneous management of multiple communication goals. At this early stage of exploring message analysis, variations in the conceptualization of feedback and the resulting coding schemes need to be expected. Echoing Cusella's (1987) idea, greater standardization is necessary to facilitate comparisons across studies. For example, it is not clear that Kim and Miller's (1990) "counseling" and Morris et al.'s (1990) "alignment" are conceptually distinct constructs. Finally, research on message analysis reveals the value of studying actual behavior as it occurs, a clearly positive trend. Unfortunately, it will likely increase an already strong tendency to use student samples in laboratory simulations where experimental conditions guarantee the monitoring of real-time behavior. However, external validity issues continue to loom large (Martocchio & Webster, 1992).

To summarize, this review of the feedback literature strongly supports Cusella's (1987) arguments to supplement psychologically oriented feedback research with a systemic focus on feedback environments, feedback loops, and the conversational practices of feedback. In addition, a meaning-centered view of communication in feedback encounters will add insight into its socially constructed aspects. I turn now to charisma and visionary leadership.

## CHARISMATIC AND VISIONARY LEADERSHIP

To understand the importance of charismatic and visionary leadership, one must understand the arguments of leadership's naysayers who, at various times, have either predicted its demise or weakened its utility as an explanatory construct (Hunt, 1999). For example, leadership purportedly makes little difference to the bottom line (Salancik & Pfeffer, 1977). There are substitutes that render leadership less necessary (Kerr & Jermier, 1978). Its impact gets overestimated, especially when cause-effect relationships are difficult to establish (Meindl et al., 1985). It puts too little emphasis on situational causes of behavior (Davis-Blake & Pfeffer, 1989). Finally, leaders may not affect culture in unique ways (Frost, Moore, Louis, Lundberg, & Martin, 1991; Martin, 1992). The most frequent response to these arguments is that leadership's true impact lies not in tangible outcomes, but in human sentiment and understanding: meaning, affect, belief, and commitment (Bennis & Nanus, 1985; Pondy, 1978; Pfeffer, 1981).

One of the cornerstones of charismatic and visionary leadership is symbolic leadership. Distinct from managership, symbolic leadership connotes (1) possession of a vision; (2) the ability to articulate it; and (3) a strategic use of slogans, symbols, rituals, ceremonies, and stories of success or heroism that amplify desirable values and promote identification with the organization (Bennis & Nanus, 1985; Conger, 1989, 1991; Gardner & Avolio, 1998; Rost, 1991; Shamir, House, & Arthur, 1993). Symbolic leaders' primary conversational goals are sensemaking and linking the conversation to organizational goal achievement (Barge, Downs, & Johnson, 1989).

Several recent reviews and critiques of this literature have appeared (Conger & Hunt, 1999; House & Aditya, 1997; Hunt & Conger, 1999; Jermier, 1993; Lowe, Kroeck, Sivasubramaniam, 1996).[10] This review focuses only on those aspects most relevant to communication. However, the individual-system dualism must first be explored because it occupies a central role in the literature on charisma and vision.

## The Individual-System Dualism

One of the strongest oppositions in the charisma literature is that between the individual and the system. This opposition first surfaced in a nonantagonistic pull away from the individual toward the relational, only to be followed by an antagonistic reframing of the individual and the relational as too micro in favor of meso and macro social system concerns. All of this movement can be traced to the ambiguity in Weber's theory of charisma.

Swayed by Weber's view that charismatic leaders were extraordinary, prophetic, and heroic, leadership scholars quickly psychologized charisma as they wrote about it (Calás, 1993). House's (1977) theory of charismatic leadership and Bass's (1985) theory of transformational leadership both have decided individualistic leanings. House's work was billed as "personal celebrity charisma" because of his focus on leaders' personality characteristics (Graham, 1991). Bass's theory of transformational leadership, based on the writing of Burns (1978) sans a moral component, focused on three key leader activities: charisma that included vision, intellectual stimulation, and individualized consideration. These were distinct from more transactional (contract-based) leader activities such as contingent reward and management-by-exception. However, the most blatant of the individualist charisma approaches is in the popular business press, which lionizes a familiar choir of CEOs and entrepreneurs and minimizes alternative explanations for firm success (Meindl et al., 1985).

But Weber was also ambiguous and somewhat contradictory about the relative emphasis of the individual over the relational. While writing about the extraordinary qualities of charismatic leaders, he also repeatedly stressed that constituents' collective beliefs in the wisdom and knowledge of the charismatic was the crucial test of charisma (Dow, 1969). Weber's relational emphasis led to the "social psychologizing" of the business charisma model. House extended his early work to focus on constituent characteristics and the means by which charismatic leaders are able to strike a chord in constituents to act in accordance with the mission (House & Howell, 1992; House, Spangler, & Woycke, 1991; Klein & House, 1995; Shamir et al., 1993). Bass's theory of transformational leadership adopted a relational focus most explicitly with its individualized consideration component (emphasizing meeting the personal needs of constituents), but also a measurement emphasis on constituent attributions of charisma.

House, Bass, Conger, and their colleagues accounted for most of the individual and relational research on business charisma focusing on personality correlates (House et al., 1991), reported behavioral factors and associated judgments of charisma (Bass, 1985; Bradford & Cohen, 1984; Conger, 1989; Conger & Kanungo, 1988), perceived differences between charismatic and noncharismatic leaders (Bass, 1985; Ehrlich, Meindl, & Viellieu, 1990; House, 1977; Howell & Frost, 1989; Yammarino & Bass, 1990; Yammarino, Spangler, & Bass, 1993), and the outcomes of charismatic leadership in both constituents and leaders (Avolio, Waldman, & Einstein, 1988; Bass, 1985; Hater & Bass, 1988; House et al., 1991; Howell & Frost, 1989; Yammarino & Bass, 1990; Howell & Higgins, 1990a, 1990b; Yammarino et al., 1993).

In 1993, a special issue of *Leadership Quarterly* was premised on an antagonistic reframing of individual and relational charisma research as too micro (Jermier, 1993). Many contributors to that volume argued that Weber's sociological leanings needed to be reclaimed because he situated charisma in a sociohistorical context (Weber, 1925/1968; see also Beyer, 1999). Among Weber's arguments were the following:

1. Difficult times were fertile grounds for the emergence of charisma.
2. Charismatic authority was a potential revolutionary force and a bridge between traditional and rational-legal forms of authority.

3. Charismatic authority was naturally unstable, an instability that could produce one of two outcomes for charismatic social movements and the development of charisma (Weber, 1925/1968). Charisma either dies out in the departure of the leader from the social scene or becomes institutionalized and incorporated into the routines of everyday life.

A number of contributors to this issue argued for reclaiming the meso and macro features of charisma through a renewed focus on its routinization, the instability and potential loss of charisma, the context surrounding the emergence of charisma, and the way charisma resides not in persons, but in the group processes of the community (e.g., Bryman, 1993; Calás, 1993; Conger, 1993; DiTomaso, 1993).

More recently, House, Bass, and Conger have extended their respective models beyond the individual and dyad to group and organizational levels (Avolio & Bass, 1995; Conger & Kanungo, 1998; Klein & House, 1995). There has also been more attention to context (Conger, 1999; House & Aditya, 1997; Hunt, Boal, & Dodge, 1999; Pawar & Eastman, 1997; Shamir & Howell, 1999; Shea & Howell, 1999). Finally, using a dramaturgical and interactive perspective, Gardner and Avolio (1998) examine the roles that context, actor (leader) and audience (constituents) play in jointly constructing a "charismatic relationship." The 1993 debate in *Leadership Quarterly* notwithstanding, this most recent work suggests movement away from the individual toward the system although emphasis on the dyadic relationship appears dominant.

## Charisma, Vision, and Communication

Communication and language have always been a concern of the charisma and vision literature (Awamleh & Gardner, 1999; Bass, 1988; Conger, 1991; Gardner & Avolio, 1998;

Howell & Frost, 1989; Kuhnert & Lewis, 1987; Riggio, 1987; Shamir et al., 1993; Zorn, 1991). As Table 11.3 reveals, studies generally fall into three categories. When reporting research testing Bass's (1985) model, the word *transformational* will be used instead of charisma to be consistent with his work.

### Charismatic Communication

The first category contains case studies of charismatic leaders (e.g., Conger, 1989, 1991; Seeger, 1994; Shamir et al., 1994; Trice & Beyer, 1986; Wendt & Fairhurst, 1994). This body of work, including much that is found in the popular press, is more suggestive than definitive in its approach to charismatic communication in business settings. It focuses heavily on charismatic political leaders, their style and vision in public communication settings, and the largely unacknowledged role that the media play in enhancing a charismatic persona. Work by Trice and Beyer (1986), Beyer and Browning (1999), and Fairhurst, Cooren, and Cahill (2000) are notable exceptions.

The second category consists of more traditional social scientific research on charismatic communication focusing on influence tactics and the outcomes associated with the delivery aspects of a charismatic's style. This research emphasizes the individual, cognitive outcomes, and a transmission view of communication. For example, in two studies of informal emergent leaders championing technological innovations, Howell and Higgins (1990a, 1990b) found that in comparison to champions, nonchampions displayed many of the qualities of charismatic leadership. Using Kipnis and Schmidt's (1982) typology, champions initiated more influence attempts; used a greater variety of influence strategies; and relied on coalition, reason, higher authority, and assertiveness more than nonchampions.

Using Yukl and Tracey's (1992) scheme, Tepper (1993) found that in routine influence attempts transactional leaders reportedly used more exchange and pressure tactics over

**TABLE 11.3** Charisma and Vision-Based Communication Research

| | |
|---|---|
| Case studies of charismatic leaders | Beyer & Browning, 1999; Conger, 1989, 1991; Fairhurst, Cooren, & Cahill, 2000; Shamir, Arthur, & House, 1994; Trice & Beyer, 1986; Wendt & Fairhurst, 1994 |
| Behavioral studies of charismatic leaders | |
|     Delivery style | Awamleh & Gardner, 1999; Avolio, Howell, & Sosik, 1999; Holladay & Coombs, 1993, 1994; Howell & Frost, 1989; Kirkpatrick & Locke, 1996 |
|     Influence strategies | Howell & Higgins, 1990a, 1990b; Tepper, 1993; Zorn, 1991 |
| Visionary leadership | |
|     Cultural consequences of a vision | Martin, 1992; Nadler, 1988; Pettigrew, 1979; Siehl, 1985; Siehl & Martin, 1984; Swanson & Ramiller, 1999; Tichy & DeVanna, 1986 |
|     Vision articulation | Conger & Kanungo, 1998; Den Hartog & Verburg, 1997; Fiol, Harris, & House, 1999; Gardner & Avolio, 1998; Shamir et al., 1994; Shamir, House, & Arthur, 1993 |
|     Vision content | Baum, Locke, & Kirkpatrick, 1998; Bennis & Nanus, 1985; Connell & Galasinski, 1996; Kotter, 1990; Larwood, Falbe, Kriger, & Miesing, 1995; Larwood, Kriger, & Falbe, 1993; Rogers & Swales, 1990; Swales & Rogers, 1995; Westley & Mintzberg, 1989 |
|     Vision implementation/routinization | Beyer & Browning, 1999; Fairhurst, 1993b; Fairhurst, Jordan, & Neuwirth, 1997; Trice & Beyer, 1986; Weierter, 1997 |

transformational leaders, who used more legitimating tactics. Tepper also found that transformational leaders engendered higher levels of identification and internalization in constituents than did transactional leaders. Zorn's (1991) research suggests that cognitive complexity and person-centered message production may explain the success of transformational leaders.

Cognitive outcomes associated with the delivery aspects of a charismatic's style such as eye contact, fluid rate, gestures, facial expressiveness, energy, eloquence, and voice tone variety (Bass, 1988; Conger & Kanungo, 1987; Holladay & Coombs, 1993; Howell & Frost, 1989) have also been studied. Howell and Frost (1989) conducted a laboratory experiment in which leaders were cast as either charismatic, considerate, or structuring. In the charismatic condition, the leader's use of the delivery features to communicate a vision yielded higher task performance, greater task satisfaction, and lower role conflict than did leaders in the other two conditions.

Because content (in the form of a vision) and delivery were confounded in this study, Holladay and Coombs (1993) isolated the effects of delivery on the communication of an organizational vision. Using the same delivery aspects described above, subjects in the "strong" delivery condition made stronger leader attributions of charisma than subjects in the "weak" delivery condition. Unexpectedly, the dramatic and animated communicator style constructs were not among the best predictors of charisma. However, the constructs of friendly, attentive, dominant, and open were. Avolio, Howell, and Sosik's (1999) research on transformational leaders suggests the addition of humor to that list.

Two studies examined the differential effects of vision content and delivery on perceptions of charisma. Both Holladay and Coombs (1994) and Awamleh and Gardner (1999) found that delivery contributes more strongly to perceptions of charisma than vision content. However, Kirkpatrick and Locke (1996) found just the opposite. Vision content was more strongly related to perceptions of charisma than stylistic features.

### Visionary Leadership

Very closely related to charisma, the third category of communication studies falls under the rubric of visionary leadership. The study of vision processes is an emerging area of research with a history in studies that focused on the consequences of senior leaders' visions on corporate cultures. Visions establish, maintain, or help cultures survive environmental fluctuations (Martin, 1992; Morgan, 1986; Nadler, 1988; Pettigrew, 1979; Schein, 1992; Siehl, 1985; Tichy & DeVanna, 1986; Trice & Beyer, 1991). They may also be the source of conflict and poor performance when discrepancies arise between the vision and some aspect of the environment (e.g., Beyer, 1999; Smircich, 1983; Smircich & Morgan, 1982).

Vision is central to the charisma literature. However, while charisma implies having a vision (Conger, 1999), the reverse is not necessarily true. Vision studies draw on the charisma and culture literatures quite often, but many neither explore the cultural consequences of a vision nor measure attributions of charisma. Instead, the focus is on actual vision content or its process aspects including development, articulation, and implementation (Larwood, Falbe, Kriger, & Miesing, 1995). For example, Swanson and Ramiller (1997) use the concept of an "organizing vision" to explain innovation surrounding new technologies. Such visions are thought to facilitate three important aspects of the information systems innovation process: interpretation, legitimation, and mobilization.

While vision is broadly defined as an envisioned future, this literature makes apparent several definitional issues related to visions (Bryman, 1992; Larwood et al., 1995; Larwood, Kriger, & Falbe, 1993). Of particular concern is a blurring of the lines between vision, mission, values, and the implementing programs. While conceptually distinct, they are often collectively referred to as "governing ideas" (Senge, 1990), a "corporate philosophy" (Ledford, Wendenhof, & Strahley, 1995), a "well-conceived vision" (Collins & Porras, 1996), or a "mission statement" (Rogers & Swales, 1990; Swales & Rogers, 1995). Despite confusing and unstable language, distinctions are typically drawn between a future direction (vision), a purpose (mission), a set of principles (values), and the initiatives intended to realize them (programs). However, a well-conceived future is almost always premised on a clear purpose and set of principles, and therein may lie the definitional confusion if writers fail to make this explicit. With these definitional caveats in mind, the reviewed literature focuses primarily on vision content and two aspects of vision process, articulation and implementation/routinization.

*Vision content.* Several studies on vision content may be found in case studies in the popular press (Bennis & Nanus, 1985; Doz & Prahalad, 1987; Conger, 1989; Fairhurst & Sarr, 1996; Kotter, 1990; Nanus, 1992; Nussbaum, Moskowitz, & Beam, 1985). However, empirical examples of vision content research are also beginning to surface. For example, Larwood et al. (1995; Larwood et al., 1993) studied a national sample of chief executives and business school deans to see how they defined their visions. Chief executives focused either on formulation, communication and implementation, or innovative realism. The group that was high on communication perceived more rapid changes in their organization, felt senior executives strongly accepted their vision, exercised a high degree of control over the business, and perceived that their visions extended farther into the future than did the other two groups. The analysis of business school deans was roughly comparable to that of the chief executives. In a longitudinal study, Baum, Locke, and Kirkpatrick (1998) examined the impact of vision content, vision attributes, and vision communication on venture growth in entrepreneurial firms. They found that both vision content (in the form of growth imagery) and vision attributes (such as quality or clarity) affected venture growth directly, but the indirect impact of these variables through vision communication was greater.

In contrast to the empirical methods of the previous studies, three studies used critical discourse analysis to study corporate philosophy statements (Connell & Galasinski, 1996; Rogers & Swales, 1990; Swales & Rogers, 1995). These studies examined recurring themes and tensions, differences in communicative purpose, authorial voice, and the rhetorical devices used to promote identification and affiliation (e.g., the assumed "we"). Corporate philosophy statements are significant for leadership communication study because their content predisposes leaders and constituents to communicate the vision/mission in particular ways. For example, work in the area of "soft missions" suggests that loosely formulated missions allow more flexibility in interpretation at local levels to capitalize on the opportunities of a turbulent environment (Bartlett & Ghoshal, 1994; Fairhurst, 1996).

*Vision articulation.* In vision articulation, Conger and Kanungo (1998) argue that the verbal aspects of a vision must focus on the negative aspects of the status quo and the positive aspects of the future path. Shamir et al. (1993) hold that charismatic leaders must target the self-concept of constituents in their communication. Leaders can promote frame breaking, frame alignment, and sensemaking for constituents by making references to (1) values and moral justifications, (2) the collective and its identity, (3) history, (4) constituents' positive worth and efficacy as individuals and a collective, (5) high expectations from collectives, and (6) distal over proximal goals. A rhetorical analysis of Jesse Jackson's 1988 speech to the Democratic convention supported several of their argu-

ments (Shamir et al., 1994). Also drawing from Shamir et al. (1993), Fiol, Harris, and House (1999) conducted a semiotic analysis of 42 speeches from all 20th-century presidents. They examined the differential use of three communication techniques (negation, abstraction, and inclusion) over the time span of the presidencies. Their findings showed that all three techniques peaked during the middle phase of the presidents' tenure. They also found support for the charismatic leaders' frequent use of the word *not* as an unfreezing technique.

The speeches of international business leaders were analyzed by Den Hartog and Verburg (1997) for rhetorical content dealing with international business and rhetorical devices such as contrast, lists, puzzle-solution, position taking, pursuit, and alliteration. Finally, unlike previous research that focused heavily on the charismatic leader, Gardner and Avolio's (1998) interactive and dramaturgical model of charisma focuses on impression management by charismatic leaders thought to be desirable by constituents. These impression management behaviors are grouped into four categories (framing, scripting, staging, and performing), which purportedly shape the content of the articulated vision.

*Vision implementation/routinization.* Fairhurst (1993a) used discourse analysis to study vision implementation in routine leadership communication. She found five framing devices (i.e., consistent themes in framing) in the routine work conversations of an organization charged with implementing Deming's total quality management (TQM) to achieve their vision. Out of the five framing devices (jargon use, positive spin, agenda setting, experienced predicaments, and possible futures), two stood out. Experienced predicaments, originating out of a perceived mismatch between the vision (or its programs) and local conditions, exposed the choice points around what and what not to adopt (Hosking & Morley, 1988). Possible futures for the vision were realized when steps were taken to resolve the predicament. Fairhurst,

Jordan, and Neuwirth (1997) created a "management of meaning" scale based on these framing devices. They found that organizational role and organizational commitment best predicted whether individuals managed the meaning of a company mission statement.

Trice and Beyer (1986) studied the charismatic leaders of two social movement organizations. They observed that the routinization of the leader's vision was critical to the success of that organization. Echoing many of their findings, Beyer and Browning (1999) found five elements marked the routinization of a charismatic leader in the semiconductor industry. These included an administration structure, the transference of charisma to constituents through cultural forms, incorporation of the charismatic mission into organizational traditions, the selection of a successor who resembles the charismatic, and continuity of the charismatic mission and continued coherence of members around it.

In contrast to the second group of studies on influence tactics and outcomes associated with the delivery aspects of a charismatic leader's style, the emerging research on visionary leadership is more balanced in its emphasis on communicative practices and cognitive outcomes as well as a transmission and a meaning-centered view of communication.

## New Directions: Conversational Practices, the Recovery of Meaning, and Wider Systems Concerns

The emerging vision communication research notwithstanding, an analysis of the charisma literature directs us to place additional emphasis on communicative practices, the recovery of meaning, and wider systems concerns. This focus should fill a great need to understand the dynamic nature of charisma and visionary leadership.

### Conversational Practices

Beyer (1999) recently noted how much the extant research on charisma is tied to the traits

and behaviors of leaders as measured by constituent self-reports. Indeed, in early charisma research much was made about "stripping the aura of mysticism" from charisma to deal with it only as a set of behaviors (Conger & Kanungo, 1987, p. 639, 1993). Yet we still know comparatively little about specific communication behaviors because of a propensity in the literature to measure metabehaviors and outcomes over behaviors. Riley (1988) described metabehaviors not as "descriptions of what these individuals actually do but categories and patterns of action that include evaluations of successful outcomes" (p. 81). Riley made this point of Sashkin and Fulmer's (1988) measure, but the same can be said of Conger and Kanungo's (1993) more popular behavioral attribute measure of charisma. Conger and Kanungo's scale includes items such as "exciting public speaker," "skillful performer when presenting to a group," "inspirational," and "able to motivate by articulating effectively the importance of what organizational members are doing." The specific behaviors or behavioral combinations under public speaking and inspirational deliveries are too numerous even to mention.

The charisma scale of Bass's (1985; Avolio & Bass, 1988) Multifacet Leadership Questionnaire (MLQ) is perhaps the most widely used measure of charisma. Lowe et al. (1996) report on some 75 studies using this scale. While the scale appears capable of measuring variance in charisma, it too does not measure specific charismatic leader behaviors (House & Aditya, 1997). Metabehaviors such as "provides a vision of what lies ahead" and "shows determination in pursuit of goals" and outcomes such as "makes others feel good," "generates respect," "instills confidence," and "transmits a sense of mission" typify this scale.

Although others would argue otherwise (Brown & Lord, 1999; Wofford, 1999), the variable analytic tradition may not be particularly well suited to the study of charisma and vision. Riley (1988) and other researchers (Westley & Mintzberg, 1989) offer a possible explanation:

The notions of charisma, vision, and culture all share a sense of the aesthetic—the art form of leadership (another Bennis term). This requires some forms of analysis that are sensitive to style, to the creation of meaning, and to the dramatic edge of leadership. Symbols like "leader" and "charismatic" have power in and of themselves because of their ability to evoke expressive and nonrational images and feelings. To use these terms as mere categories of behaviors runs the risk of stripping them of this power and moving them to the level of the mundane—plain-label symbols. (Riley, 1988, p. 82)

Riley's point is well taken. To anyone seeing a painting of Van Gogh, the labels "bold color" and "heavy brush stroke" do not even begin to capture the essence of his art. So, too, capturing the essence of charisma requires some attention to aesthetics, which variable analytic studies find difficult to capture. Apparently, Shamir et al. (1994) drew the same conclusion as they chose a rhetorical analysis for initial support of their theory.

### The Recovery of Meaning

To see the shift toward discursive practices and a meaning-centered approach fully realized, as well as to continue to explore the individual-system tensions in charisma, organizational scholars could turn to the study of rhetoric (Conger, 1991). Symbolic leadership has an unacknowledged rich history in the study of rhetoric dating back to Vico in the 18th century; Nietzsche in the late 19th century; and Richards, Burke, Perelman, and Foucault, to name a few, in the 20th century. All of these writers focus on the relationship between discourse and knowledge, communication and its effects, language and experience (Bizzell & Herzberg, 1990). Moreover, in speech communication the rhetorical studies of leadership at Purdue in the 1960s and interpersonal theories such as coordinated management of meaning (Cronen, Pearce, & Harris, 1982) also supply a rich heritage for leadership as symbolic management.

Using a theatrical model by Brook (1968), Westley and Mintzberg (1989) propose a very useful framework for the rhetorical study of charisma and vision. They conceive of leadership as a drama with the interaction of three concepts: repetition, representation, and assistance. In Westley and Mintzberg's interpretation of Brook's "repetition" concept, visionaries "practice" for the moment of a vision through the development of their craft just as actors practice for a performance (Mintzberg, 1987). In representation, the craft is turned into art with a variety of rhetorical devices. Finally, the audience must play a very active role in the performance, hence, "vision comes alive only when it is shared" (Westley & Mintzberg, 1989, p. 21).

Westley and Mintzberg go on to identify different visionary styles: creators, proselytizers, idealists, bricoleurs, and diviners. Visionaries' styles are distinguished on the basis of the external context, the vision's mental origin and evolution, and its strategic content, which the authors explain in terms of core and circumference. A vision's core defines its central theme. For example, creators focus on products, proselytizers on markets, idealists on ideals, bricoleurs on organizations, and diviners on services. A vision's circumference is composed of its symbolic aspects such as its rhetorical and metaphorical devices. A vision's contribution can be at the core, the circumference, or both.

With a few enhancements, Westley and Mintzberg's (1989) model can make an even greater contribution to the study of vision and charisma. For example, although they interpret repetition as the development of a craft to arrive at a vision, repetition may also be seen from the perspective of leaders' communicating a vision. For example, charismatic leaders are widely regarded as verbally skilled and often eloquent. However, Bass (1985) appeared in the minority in stating that these verbal skills can be learned and earned. Other scholars see charisma as personality and/or circumstance driven.

What is not well recognized is that the eloquence of charismatic or visionary leaders may be the result of priming themselves for spontaneity (Fairhurst & Sarr, 1996). Priming is a process through which concepts or information become activated or made readily accessible for recall (Bargh, 1989; Wyer & Srull, 1980, 1986). Priming typically centers on unobtrusive exposure to a stimulus that is later recalled in a spontaneous fashion. However, intentional exposure such as by leaders to their visions before and/or during repeated communication with constituents may enable them to be spontaneous, yet give very strategic performances with respect to the vision. For example, Shamir et al. (1994) noted columnist William Safire's comment about Jesse Jackson's 1988 speech to the Democratic National Convention. It suggests that priming played a prominent role in Jackson's success:

> This was a speech whose main elements have been shaped and honed on the road; we were listening to Jesse's Greatest Hits, the passages and metaphors that proved effective for months and years. . . . The speech was not written but grown (William Safire, *New York Times*, July 21, 1988). (p. 37)

Priming can occur through imagining the vision's relevance in the recurring contexts in which leaders and constituents find themselves, reviewing of the vision's core concepts, and/or reviewing its imagery and other symbolic aspects—all of which contribute to a script for spontaneous communication at a later time. In addition, the more communication with followers, the more the vision is permanently primed (Fiske & Taylor, 1991). Efficient and effective articulation of a vision to constituents occurs as long as overscripting is avoided so that leaders remain vigilant to distinctions that require the mindful adaptation of a message to a particular audience (Fairhurst & Sarr, 1996). By priming for spontaneity, Westley and Mintzberg's notion of "repetition" has a broader application than their original interpretation.

Westley and Mintzberg's representational concepts of core and circumference resemble Kenneth Burke's (1954, 1957, 1962; Weaver,

1953) work on ultimate terms, which describes in somewhat greater detail the nature of the symbols that leaders may employ in an engaging vision (Fairhurst & Sarr, 1996). According to Burke, an ultimate term is little more than an extreme good or bad form of a concept or theme out of which another more derivative set of terms may coincide. For example, a "god" term introduces a concept and infuses it with maximum value. There is a clear idea of what is good, what should be pursued, and why sacrifice in a material sense is required. A "devil" term does just the opposite. The adoption of ultimate terms like god terms can transcend disagreement among people with opposite views by identifying values or principles that nearly all people can agree upon. This was what Burke termed *transcendence.*

Ultimate terms correspond to the core of the vision, while the circumference corresponds to their frequency of use, strength, and clarity of the imagery, and the manner in which they may be linked with other key terms. As research is beginning to suggest, frequency, imagery, opposition, and association should thus provide some very specific clues as to the way charismatic and visionary leaders manage meaning from a vision (Den Hartog & Verburg, 1997; Fiol et al., 1999). Fairhurst and Sarr (1996) argue that this was the case with Deming's (1982) vision of TQM, although not all visions will be the sweeping, transformative philosophies of Deming's TQM. Visions may have fewer ultimate terms. They may also be modest and evolutionary rather than revolutionary, yet transformative because of the chord they strike in constituents and their ability to affect incremental change (Jermier, 1993).

Audience "assistance," the third part of the Westley and Mintzberg theatrical model, raises questions about the way visions get shared. Here is where the literature on charisma and vision parts company. Charisma researchers are much more likely to assume a monologic stance where constituents are believed to assent to the meanings of the charismatic (Conger, 1999). For example,

Wasielewski (1985) argues that the genesis of charisma lies in emotional interaction in which the leader articulates the feelings of constituents in an emotionally charged situation, challenges their appropriateness, and then reframes constituents' interpretations of their world and their emotional responses. The distinguishing features of charismatic leaders rest with the leaders' exceptional role-taking ability and emotional sincerity.

Shamir et al. (1993) suggest that constituents play a role in the emergence of charisma, but it appears to be one of heightening or lessening the charismatic impact based on whether the leader appeals to existing values and social identities. This view is supported by the analysis of speeches by charismatic leaders (Fiol et al., 1999; Shamir et al., 1994). Similarly, Gardner and Avolio (1998) and Weierter (1997) argue that it is the orientation of constituents that establishes the type of charismatic relationship (which, in turn, establishes the role of the charismatic message and personal charisma associated with the leader). It is a view of charisma that is more relational, yet the leader is still the primary symbolizing agent. On the monologic stance of much of the charisma literature, Jermier (1993) stated that

> charisma is not a one way influence process, as often imagined. It is a reciprocal relationship that is reproduced through interactions in which each participant exercises power. Of course, the charismatic relationship is not constituted by an equal balance of power among participants. Especially with mature, well-developed charismatic relationships, asymmetrical power can emerge and rapidly turn into tyranny (Couch, 1989). (p. 222)

In contrast to the monologic stance of charisma research, the organizational vision literature is much more likely to assume a dialogic focus. For example, Westley and Mintzberg (1989) argued against a one-way, hypodermic needle model of the vision communication process. They wrote, "Stripped to its essence, this model takes on a mechanical quality which surely robs the process of much of its evocative appeal" (p. 18). As argued at the start of the chapter, Senge (1990) suggests that the art of visionary leadership resides in shared visions constructed from personal visions and the creative tensions that arise from a lofty vision as it collides with local realities.

The more personal visions are encouraged in organizations, the more contested is the big picture. Recall contestation is not about something that already exists, but "what might be, what could be the case, or what something should be like" (Shotter, 1993, p. 154). "Our situation here and now," "our concept of purpose," and "our concept of the future" are all part of the *negotiated* politics of everyday life that may affect the ongoing frame alignment of visionary leaders as much as their constituents. Especially in more democratic and participative organizations, the role of the charismatic or visionary leader may be to initiate or trigger, rather than orchestrate, the symbolic management of the vision. This is not a subtle difference, but has major implications for vision content and process including implementation and routinization.

### Wider Systems Concerns

Beyer (1999) uses the term *charisma* rather than *charismatic leadership* so as to define charisma as a social process and emergent social structure that encompasses more than what leaders do. Similarly, the concept of audience also suggests that we may go beyond immediate constituent reactions to the ripple of interactions that constituents carry forth to implement and routinize the vision. Although discussions of the routinization of charisma are instructive in a broad sense (Bryman, 1992; Trice & Beyer, 1986), scholars know very little about vertical chains of communication in organizations (McPhee, 1988). This is particularly important for the study of charismatic leaders who may be socially distant versus close in the organizational hierarchy (Yagil, 1998). Even though these chains play an acknowledged role in endorsing or discounting new initiatives, there is much to learn about the way dyads use information relayed from higher-ups to affect innovation and routine production. Fairhurst's (1993a) study of framing devices in vision implementation suggests there are innumerable sites of audience assistance (i.e., opportunities for local usage of the vision and credible endorsements) and why the death knell sounds gradually when a vision is rejected. Much can be learned about vision implementation and routinization from analysis of the discourse and its silences within these chains. The vision's negotiated meanings will feed into and be fed by a cultural repository of vision-based understandings.

In summary, the following arguments prevail. First, in characterizing communication research on charisma, the focus until recently has been on cognitive outcomes and a transmission view of communication. Research on the understudied areas directs us to the recovery of meaning and different individual-system foci. Second, a theatrical model of visionary leadership by Westley and Mintzberg (1989), along with some enhancements, is a way to effect this change. Among the enhancements are priming for spontaneity, clarifying the symbolic aspects of the vision, and the role of vertical dyads in vision implementation and routinization. In the next section, I turn to leader-member exchange, which began with a leader-centered focus that quickly assumed a relational orientation.

## LEADER-MEMBER EXCHANGE

In the LMX model, leaders exchange their personal and positional resources for a member's performance (Graen & Scandura, 1987). The LMX model is based on Jacobs's (1971) distinction between leadership and authority. In this model, effective leadership is defined in terms of incremental influence, which is interpersonal influence earned beyond that which accompanies one's formal

position (Graen & Uhl-Bien, 1991; Katz & Kahn, 1978). In high-quality relationships (high LMXs) leader and member exert high levels of incremental influence. Mature "leadership" relationships develop because there is mutual trust, internalization of common goals, extra-contractual behavior and the exchange of social resources, support, and mutual influence. These relationships are also considered transformational in Bass's (1985) sense because members move beyond self-interests (Gerstner & Day, 1997; Graen & Uhl-Bien, 1995).

At the other extreme is "managership" where incremental influence is lacking and little more than the terms of the formal employment contract are fulfilled (Uhl-Bien & Graen, 1992). These low-quality relationships (low LMXs) are characterized by the use of formal authority, contractual behavior exchange, role-bound relations, low trust and support, and economic rewards.

Since its inception more than two decades ago, the research on LMX theory has been marked by four stages summarized in Table 11.4 (Graen & Uhl-Bien, 1995). However, Table 11.4 presents only those studies with an explicit communication focus. Gerstner and Day (1997), Graen and Uhl-Bien (1995), Liden, Sparrowe, and Wayne (1997), and Schriesheim, Castro, and Cogliser (1999) present more exhaustive reviews. As will become apparent, the interplay around the individual-system dualism defines the four stages.

### LMX Stages and the Individual-System Dualism

In Stage 1, initial LMX research was known as vertical dyad linkage (VDL). VDL successfully refuted leaders' use of an average leadership style finding instead that leaders differentiate among members. The term *in-group* was commonly used to describe high-quality exchanges, and *out-group* described low-quality exchanges. VDL research assumed that differentiated relationships emerged because a leader's time and re-

**TABLE 11.4** Stages of Leader-Member Exchange Research

Stage 1: Vertical dyad linkage

| | |
|---|---|
| Differentiated dyads vs. average leadership style | Cashman, Dansereau, Graen, & Haga, 1975; Graen & Cashman, 1975 |

Stage 2: Leader-member exchange (LMX)

Influences on LMX

| | |
|---|---|
| Affect | Dockery & Steiner, 1990; Liden, Wayne, & Stilwell, 1993; Wayne & Ferris, 1990 |
| Gender | Duchon, Green, & Taber, 1986; Fairhurst, 1993a; Wayne, Liden, & Sparrowe, 1994 |
| High LMX member characteristics | Graen, 1989; Graen, Scandura, & Graen, 1986 |
| Performance | Deluga & Perry, 1991; Liden et al., 1993; Wayne & Ferris, 1990 |
| Similarity | Bauer & Green, 1996; Liden et al., 1993 |

LMX communication and relationship maintenance

| | |
|---|---|
| Communication frequency | Baker & Ganster, 1985; Schiemann & Graen, 1984 |
| Control patterns in routine interaction | Borchgrevink & Donohue, 1991; Fairhurst, Rogers, & Sarr, 1987 |
| Coworker communication | Kramer, 1995; Sias, 1996; Sias & Jablin, 1995 |
| Impression management | Wayne & Ferris, 1990; Wayne & Green, 1993 |
| Influence | Deluga & Perry, 1991; Dockery & Steiner, 1990; Krone, 1991; Liden & Mitchell, 1989; Maslyn, Farmer, & Fedor, 1996; Wayne & Ferris, 1990 |
| Ingratiation | Deluga & Perry, 1994; Wayne et al., 1994 |
| Relationship maintenance | Lee & Jablin, 1995; Waldron, 1991; Waldron, Hunt, & Dsliva, 1993 |
| Social construction of LMX | Fairhurst, 1993a; Fairhurst & Chandler, 1989; Sias, 1996 |
| Cross-cultural LMXs | Graen & Wakabayashi, 1994; Graen, Wakabayashi, Graen, & Graen, 1990; Hui & Graen, 1997; Wakabayashi & Graen, 1984 |

Outcomes of LMX

| | |
|---|---|
| Career progress | Graen & Wakabayashi, 1994 |

sources were limited, and social exchanges were needed to accomplish the unstructured tasks of the work unit. In the history of LMX research, Stage 1 was the only one to focus exclusively on leaders. However, significant variance in member responses to queries about leaders during this stage led to casting the dyad as the unit of analysis in subsequent stages (Graen & Uhl-Bien, 1995).

In Stage 2, the nomenclature changed from vertical dyad linkage to leader-member exchange and the abandonment of references to

| Citizenship | Wayne & Green, 1993 |
| Commitment | Duchon et al., 1986; Schriesheim, Neider, Scandura, & Tepper, 1992 |
| Cooperative communication | Lee, 1997 |
| Decision influence | Duchon et al., 1986; Scandura, Graen, & Novak, 1986; Schriesheim et al., 1992 |
| Empowerment | Keller & Dansereau, 1995; Sparrowe, 1994 |
| Equity/fairness | Scandura, 1995 |
| Job enrichment | Duchon et al., 1986 |
| Job problems | Keller & Dansereau, 1995 |
| Performance | Graen et al., 1986; Keller & Dansereau, 1995; Schriesheim et al., 1992 |
| Satisfaction | Duchon et al., 1986; Schriesheim et al., 1992; Seers, 1989; Sparrowe, 1994 |
| Support | Keller & Dansereau, 1995 |
| Teamwork | Seers, 1989; Uhl-Bien & Graen, 1992, 1993 |
| Turnover | Kramer, 1995 |
| Measurement | Barge & Schleuter, 1991; Borchgrevink & Boster, 1994; Dienesch & Liden, 1986; Liden & Maslyn, 1998; Schriesheim et al., 1992 |

**Stage 3: Stages of LMX growth**

| High LMX training for all members | Graen, Novak, & Sommerkamp, 1982; Graen et al., 1986; Scandura & Graen, 1984 |
| Leadership making model | Graen & Uhl-Bien, 1991, 1995; Uhl-Bien & Graen, 1993 |
| Relationship development | Bauer & Green, 1996; Boyd & Taylor, 1998; Dienesch & Liden, 1986; Liden et al., 1993; Liden, Sparrowe, and Wayne, 1997; Sparrowe & Liden, 1997; Wayne et al., 1994; Zorn, 1995 |

| **Stage 4: Group and network levels of LMXs** | Graen & Uhl-Bien, 1995; Liden et al., 1997; Sparrowe & Liden, 1997; Uhl-Bien & Graen, 1992, 1993 |

"in-" and "out-groups" (Graen, Novak, & Sommerkamp, 1982). The research is voluminous and centers on the antecedents and determinants of LMX, communication and relationship maintenance, cross-cultural applicability, LMX outcomes, and measurement issues. In Stage 2, there is a greater recognition that both leaders and members influence the nature of the exchange and that the consequences of a high LMX could be significant.

Still focusing on the dyad, Stage 3 has the look of an emancipatory shift. In contrast to

VDL research that assumed a kind of natural selection model of high LMX members because of a leader's limited resources, Stage 3 drew on two longitudinal LMX studies that offered the promise of a high LMX relationship to any member who would take it (Graen et al., 1982; Scandura & Graen, 1984; Graen, Scandura, & Graen, 1986). Members who accepted the high LMX offer not only improved their performance, they enhanced overall unit functioning by increasing the percentage of high LMXs.

This work led to the development of the leadership making model, which describes the process through which relationships may become high quality. In this model, there are three proposed stages of LMX growth and development (Graen & Uhl-Bien, 1995; Uhl-Bien & Graen, 1992). The first stage, role finding, is an initial "stranger" phase in which members relate mostly on a formal basis with a "cash and carry" contractual economic exchange. If an offer for an improved working relationship is made (either implicitly or explicitly) and accepted, the dyads may mature into the second stage of relationship development, role making, also known as the "acquaintance" stage. This stage is marked by a testing period where both social and contractual exchanges are made. Not all dyads reach the final stage, role implementation, or the "mature partnership" stage. In this stage the exchange is highly developed; the exchanges made are "in kind" and marked by loyalty, support, and trust.

However, other researchers have contributed to our knowledge of LMX development. Bauer and Green (1996) recast role finding, role making, and role implementation in terms of trust development, arguing that high LMXs are the result of a successful series of member performance-leader delegation interacts. Liden and his colleagues (Dienesch & Liden, 1986; Liden, Wayne, & Stilwell, 1993) focused on leader-member expectancies and member performance as determining influences on relationship development. Sparrowe and Liden (1997) explored the effects of social networks on LMX development. Finally,

Boyd and Taylor (1998) and Zorn (1995) examined friendship development in the context of an LMX relationship.

Stage 4 expands the dyadic relationship to group and network levels. Higher-order system levels are cast in terms of "network assemblies" (Scandura, 1995) or systems of interdependent dyadic relationships (Liden et al., 1997; Sparrowe & Liden, 1997). Unlike the concept of charisma, which is held to change as one moves up system levels (e.g., Avolio & Bass, 1995), the basic nature of LMX does not change as one aggregates sets of dyadic relationships. LMX researchers have taken the network perspective in two directions.

First, Graen and Uhl-Bien's (1995) focus on network assemblies helps to explain the leadership structure of the organization. Using a network perspective, the leadership structure emerges both as a function of the task structure and the individual characteristics of leaders and members. The task structure is a particularly important moderating influence on the emergent structure of the organization. The primary research questions at the group level include examining the effects of mixed-quality relationships on unit functioning and task performance. Equity issues, peer influences, and optimum numbers of high, medium, low LMXs for different task structures also come into play. At organizational levels, questions include the dyadic enactment of critical task networks and the impact of relationships of varying quality on performance beyond the work unit both within the organization (e.g., with cross-functional work teams or hierarchically adjacent dyads) and with external stakeholders.

Second, Liden et al. (1997) use a network perspective to critique the emancipatory shift of Stage 3. Citing limitations on a leader's time and resources, they argue that a competitive advantage in information access will accrue only to those leaders who have nonredundant contacts in their networks. They write that "positive outcomes from differentiation may result when leaders invest time in nonredundant contacts with members who themselves are especially well connected with others beyond the boundaries of the work group" (Liden et al., 1997, p. 47). In contrast, social outcomes that are dependent on trust and cohesion will be enhanced by networks with strong ties (Sparrowe & Liden, 1997).

The primary research questions focus on (1) the sponsorship process through which newcomers are either assimilated into the leader's network or isolated from it; (2) the outcomes of differentiation on work group effectiveness especially when leader competence is taken into account; and (3) given the social networks of which leaders are a part, the likelihood that differentiation by them fosters homogeneity of high LMX constituent selection within social networks.

## Communication-Based LMX Research

The study of communication in LMX weighs in most heavily in Stage 2. Even though communication frequency has been linked to LMX (Baker & Ganster, 1985; Schiemann & Graen, 1984), more recent studies examine the interactive means by which members manage and maintain the quality of the exchange. Those studies that look at upward influence and relationship maintenance tactics emphasize cognitive outcomes and a transmission view of communication.

For example, upward influence tactics have been studied as impression management strategies designed to ingratiate and promote liking within the LMX. Wayne and Ferris (1990) report two studies where supervisor-focused tactics (as opposed to self- or job-focused tactics) affected supervisor's liking for members that, in turn, affected the quality of the exchange. Dockery and Steiner (1990) found three upward influence tactics (ingratiation, assertiveness, and rationality) used by members affected their rating of the quality of the exchange. Deluga and Perry (1991) found member-perceived high LMXs were significantly and inversely related to the reported use of coalition, higher authority, and

assertiveness. They also confirmed that high-quality LMXs were significantly related to member upward influence success. Finally, revisiting Likert's (1961) Pelz effect, Lee (1997) extended work by Cashman, Graen, and associates (Cashman, Dansereau, Graen, & Haga, 1976; Graen, Cashman, Ginsburg, & Schiemann, 1977) by demonstrating that work group members engage in more cooperative communication when they perceive their leaders' have high upward LMXs and when their relationship with their leaders was also high.

In the area of relationship maintenance, Waldron (1991) investigated the communication strategies that members reportedly used in maintaining upward influence. High LMX members reportedly used more personal and informal tactics, but they also displayed more contractual upward influence tactics. Low LMX members tended to report more regulative tactics (e.g., message distortion and avoidance) that are designed to avoid relational difficulties and aggressively manage impressions. However, Waldron, Hunt, and Dsilva (1993) found that contextual factors influenced the nature and size of LMX effects on influence behavior. Lee and Jablin (1995), to be discussed later, consider three types of LMX relational maintenance contexts: escalating, deteriorating, and routine relationship maintenance conditions.

In contrast to the study of reported communication tactics, a few LMX studies focus on the conversational practices of power and control. Researchers investigating interactional measures of power distance (Borchgrevink & Donohue, 1991), powerless speech forms (Fairhurst, 1991), relational control analysis of routine interaction (Fairhurst, Rogers, & Sarr, 1987), and culturally based language patterns (Fairhurst, 1993a; Fairhurst & Chandler, 1989) have shown how powerful/powerless language can vary across LMXs.

A few studies focus on the social construction of meaning. Two studies treat high, medium, and low LMX relationship labeling (as determined by members) as problematic. Fairhurst and Chandler (1989) found that choice framing, disconfirmation, topic control, and sustained challenges distinguished between a high, medium, and low LMX. Focusing on female-led LMXs, Fairhurst (1993b) found combinations of aligning, accommodating, and polarizing moves successfully discriminated between high, medium, and low LMXs. Aligning moves minimized power differences by including member extensions of the leader's view and spiraling agreement reflective of convergent thinking. Power and control issues were still being negotiated with accommodating moves such as role negotiation, choice framing, and polite disagreement. Polarizing moves such as performance monitoring, competitive conflict, and power games maximized power differences. Finally, based on work suggesting that members' perceptions of differential LMX treatment may influence coworker communication and relationships (Kramer, 1995; Sias & Jablin, 1995), Sias (1996) found that the social construction of differential treatment hung on frequent references to equity standards.

### New Directions: LMX Individual-Systems Concerns, Conversational Practices, and Relationship Dialectics

#### LMX Individual-Systems Concerns

Despite its popularity, LMX theory, research, and measurement have been widely criticized (Barge & Schleuter, 1991; Dienesch & Liden, 1986; Keller & Dansereau, 1995; Schriesheim et al., 1999; Schriesheim, Cogliser, & Neider, 1995; Yukl, 1994). In a special issue of *Leadership Quarterly* devoted to a multiple-levels approach, Dansereau, Yammarino, and Markham (1995) also took Graen and Uhl-Bien (1995) to task for marginalizing the role of the individual leader and member within current conceptualizations of

LMX. Similarly, House and Aditya (1997) call LMX a theory of dyadic relationships not leadership (in addition to suggesting that the empirical literature is less supportive of LMX theory than Graen and Uhl-Bien imply). However, Graen eschews an individualistic focus and calls the path of individualism a "failed paradigm" (personal communication, 1995) to draw attention to leadership as an inherently social phenomena. Nevertheless, a number of individual-level questions remain including the influence of communicative style, skills, and expectancies for the relationship on the negotiation of the exchange (Fairhurst & Chandler, 1989; Sparrowe & Liden, 1997).

If Graen and colleagues' stand against individualism is at least understandable given leadership's history, their stand on wider systems concerns is less so. Recall that group and organizational levels are reframed in dyadic terms as network assemblies. Dyadic functioning aside, organizations where high LMX opportunities are widely available would likely produce cultures of opportunity, while those that offered few such opportunities would produce cultures of difference. Cultures reflecting these themes would be apparent in the management systems, reward systems, value structures, cultural norms, and organizational identities, all forming intertwined systems of meaning quite apart from individual dyads. As cultural or subcultural understandings, they are part of the context for all dyadic interactions. They also provide the resources individuals draw on, but also occasionally reject, as they negotiate their individual relationships. Therefore, network assemblies are more than interconnected dyads; they also form cultures. The dyadic aspects of social networks emphasize leadership as a form of social influence; the cultural aspects emphasize leadership as a form of organizing.

As the following discussion suggests, there is also a corresponding need to understand the cultural and historical influences on LMX. This is done through a focus on conversational practices.

## Conversational Practices

Like the previously reviewed literature in this chapter, LMX shares a dominant epistemology rooted in psychology that stresses the role of individual perceptions (cognitive outcomes) and little attention to cultural or historical processes. A social cognition perspective is assumed when an individual's perceptions of the relationship operate within an information-processing model. When the focus is on an individual's perception of the relationship, explanation shifts to the psychological constructs of intention and planning rather than social processes (Baxter, 1988, 1992). Similarly, when the focus is on individuals' perception of their communicative practices, it privileges the belief that individuals are freely in control of their experience and marginalizes how the practices themselves influence interpretation. Lannamann (1991) noted that "these practices are concrete; they are not determined solely by the subjective state of individuals but rather by the grounded practices of subjects in interaction with other subjects, symbol systems, and social objects" (p. 191).

Therefore, in the study of leader-member relationships one must also ask, "What are the communication practices that shape interpretation of the relationship?" This question is analogous to Sigman's (1992) "micro-macro" issue, which examines the microcommunication practices that make relationships possible. To address this issue, one must acknowledge that interactional patterns are produced within relationships not only by drawing on private and restricted knowledge but also on shared cultural knowledge (societal and organizational) including that of language. By acknowledging the culturally recognized functions of language, individuals become members of language communities rather than distinct cognitive players (Baxter & Goldsmith, 1990; Hewes & Planalp, 1987; Sigman, 1987).

Therefore, the study of relationships should proceed on at least two levels. One

level of inquiry is to ask how leaders and members use the culturally recognized functions of language to enact a relationship that is culturally recognizable as a leader-member relationship (e.g., Fairhurst, 1991, 1993b; Fairhurst & Chandler, 1989). A second level of inquiry must proceed into how a unique relationship culture is simultaneously established through private message systems that may or may not adhere to public or cultural language rules (Baxter, 1992; Montgomery, 1992). Meanings are socially negotiated. Relationship partners may make use of standard meaning systems, but may also discard them as relationships accumulate history and uniqueness (Baxter, 1992; Montgomery, 1992; Watzlawick et al., 1967). As Montgomery (1992) puts it, the question is how can we study the interactive input of both culture and dyad?

## Relationship Dialectics

More than most leadership theories, LMX has been very concerned with -relationship development (Stage 3). An examination of Graen and Uhl-Bien's (1995) leadership making model, Liden and colleagues' expectancies model (Liden et al., 1993), Bauer and Green's (1996) trust model, Sparrowe and Liden's (1997) social network model, and Boyd and Taylor's (1998) friendship model reveals two similarities. First, all of these models represent traditional psychological views that treat communication in LMX development as incidental, implicit, or intervening. It must be quickly acknowledged that these views of LMX development are not necessarily incorrect; external causal influences on LMX development, influences of which the actors themselves may be unaware, must be studied along with the retrospective judgments of the actors concerning each other, the relationship, expectations, outcomes, and the like.

However, marginalizing communication leaves researchers unable to explain the effects of social interaction fully. Coconstructed relational dynamics, especially those that produce relational bonding, transformation, or fusion, are not easily explained by the additive contributions of individuals and their perceptions. This is because the process of relationship development is glossed and reified. The many contexts through which relationships evolve are summed over, and an artificial stability and order are imposed on a process that can be simultaneously orderly and disorderly, stable and unstable. In short, marginalizing communication comes at the expense of a more complex view of the relationship's dynamics.

Second, even though caveats about continual relationship evolution and change are usually offered (e.g., Bauer & Green, 1996; Boyd & Taylor, 1998), the models themselves reflect an assumption that successful LMXs follow a unidirectional and cumulative path toward increasing levels of closeness or fusion, openness, relational stability, and transformation beyond self-interests. Jablin (1987) argued that a focus on the communicative practices of leader-member role negotiation may lead to questioning the usual assumption of relational stability. Recent work in dialectical approaches to relationship development similarly calls this thinking into question. Instead, these approaches argue that healthy relationships are marked by dialectical oppositions that create simultaneous pulls to fuse with and differentiate from the other (Altman, Vinsel, & Brown, 1981; Baxter, 1988, 1992; Baxter & Montgomery, 1996; Montgomery, 1992; Rawlins, 1992). Relationship bonding not only implies fusion, closeness, and interdependence but also separation, distance, and independence.

Dialectics is defined as the copresence of two relational forces that are interdependent, but mutually negating. But in this case, the oppositions specify the contradictory tensions that forge the relationship. Several different types of dialectical oppositions have been named in the relationships literature (Altman et al., 1981; Baxter, 1988; Rawlins, 1992). The connection/autonomy dialectic has been named as the principal contradiction because connection is as central to a relationship's identity as autonomy is to an individual's identity. However, Baxter (1988) argued that openness/closedness and predictability/novelty form two secondary dialectical contradictions endemic to all interpersonal relationships. Openness is a prerequisite for bonding, yet creates vulnerability necessitating closedness. Relationships require predictability, but too much predictability leads to a rigidity that necessitates novelty or change (see also Altman et al., 1981).

However, it is the *strategic responses to contradiction* in message behavior that form the basis for understanding how relationships are forged. Baxter (1988, 1990) identified a number of communicative strategies through which the contradictions may be managed. These strategies include making one pole dominant (e.g., when closedness is consistently favored over openness); alternation of poles by time or by topic (e.g., when individuals choose to be open about some topics and closed about others); diluting or neutralizing the intensity of the poles (e.g., when ambiguity is favored over full disclosure or complete refusal to communicate); and reframing one pole as no longer the opposite of another.

Although Baxter was writing about social relationships in general, the three dialectics proposed and the strategies for managing them appear to have strong relevance for the leader-member relationship (Eisenberg, 1990; Zorn, 1995). Member latitude in decision making is a form of autonomy that has been reframed as connection in high LMX relationships (Graen & Scandura, 1987), but also in transformational relationships (Avolio & Bass, 1988) as well as within relationships with socialized as opposed to personalized charismatics (House & Howell, 1992). However, the management of the autonomy-connection dialectic over the life cycle of the leader-member relationship has rarely been viewed as an ever-evolving negotiated process between opposite poles. However, Phillips's (1996) study of LMX and friendship during "crunch times" in team functioning and Zorn's (1995) work on simultaneously hierarchical and friendship relationships offer a promising beginning.

Lee and Jablin's (1995) work provides strong evidence for the operation of the openness-closedness dialectic especially in the maintenance phase of the leader-member relationship. Arguing that the maintenance phase could be in flux (Jablin, 1987), they inductively derived a set of communication tactics for escalating, deteriorating, and routine relationship maintenance situations. In escalating situations where the relationship may be moving quickly to a higher level, high LMX members reportedly were less likely to avoid interaction or redirect the topic of conversation. In deteriorating situations where the relationship may be deteriorating to an unwanted level, low LMX members reported both more openness and deception and fewer attempts to create closeness. Finally, in routine situations where the parties are unconcerned about becoming more close or more distant, low LMX members reported using more avoidance and restrained expression and less supportiveness than high LMX members. Beginning with the premise of possible relational instability such as with Lee and Jablin's work is a novel approach that could greatly inform future work on LMX development.

Finally, leaders might manage the predictability-novelty dialectic for the low LMX member by selecting or favoring the predictability pole. This might be done through exaggerating knowledge of the member, reducing vigilance in keeping current with the member, and stereotyping the qualities of the member (Sillars & Scott, 1983). Although it may or may not seem scripted to members, leaders should initiate a much higher number of scripted episodes relative to unscripted episodes as a result (Fiske & Taylor, 1991). By contrast, leaders in high LMX relationships should initiate a larger number of unscripted episodes than in low LMX relationships because the former are expected to maintain a better balance in managing the predictability-novelty dialectic. Leaders would alternate scripted episodes with ones marked by information vigilance and perspective taking through active listening, more time spent with the other, and sharing information about one's

work and personal activities (Waldron, 1991). Increased monitoring of other enhances the chances for introducing more novelty and change in the relationship.

Indirect, neutralizing strategies are likely in the testing stage of leader-member relationships where leaders typically try to manage the predictability-novelty dialectic through secret tests of members (Baxter, 1988; Baxter & Willmott, 1984; Graen & Uhl-Bien, 1995). For example, endurance tests may emerge by making the relationship costly in order to determine the upper limits of commitment. Phillips's (1996) study of crunch times and LMX team functioning nicely illustrates this point. Separation tests may emerge to see what happens when the leader is away from the office. Loyalty tests surface when allegiances get divided, while knowledge tests are introduced to determine competency levels. Integrity tests surface within the presentation of moral dilemmas to determine a member's ability to do the right thing. Although the LMX literature suggests this testing period is relatively brief, a dialectical focus on message strategies or a situational orientation to relationship maintenance may call this assumption into question. Loyalty, integrity, endurance, and other tests may span the life cycle of the leader-member relationship.

As can be seen from the above discussion, a dialectical perspective provides a theoretical base for a communication-based view of relational development. Its chief distinguishing feature is that each contradictory pole is equally important in understanding relationships over time. Additionally, the study of conversational practices would add specificity and nuance to the identification and description of the coping strategies used to reconcile dialectical oppositions over the life cycle of the relationship (Baxter, 1988). In keeping with earlier concerns about cultural contributions to relationships, longitudinal language-in-use data also permit the study of interactive input to the relationship of both the culture and the dyad. Language analysis also characterizes systems-interactional research, the last area to be reviewed.

# SYSTEMS-INTERACTIONAL LEADERSHIP RESEARCH

A systems-interactional perspective on leadership seeks to understand the patterned sequential communication of leaders and constituents as part of an interactional system. Consistent with general systems theory, sequences of behavior are thought to define the system and are more salient than any one particular message. The minimum unit of analysis is the interact, a sequence of two contiguous messages, or the double interact, a sequence of three contiguous messages. Analysis of the data is usually stochastic in that the analysis examines the probabilities of a given state from an antecedent state. Finally, phasic analyses or recurring cycles of interaction may also be a subject of interest.

## The Individual-System Dualism and Other Tensions

Although not without its own limitations, this program of research provides a contrast from the previously reviewed research in this chapter. As the "systems-interactional" name implies, systemic over individual concerns dominate. Measurement and analysis focus heavily on relational systems, although a few studies in the area of relational control address wider systems concerns. Conversational practices are emphasized over cognitive outcomes. Meaning is either transmissional or derives from the structure of messages in evolving conversations. For example, relational control research distinguishes between the content and relational aspects of a message to focus exclusively on a definition of the relationship at the relational level as control patterns form.

## Relational Control Research

This line of research is based on the work of Edna Rogers and her colleagues (Courtright, Millar, & Rogers-Millar, 1979; Fairhurst et al., 1987; Rogers-Millar & Millar, 1979) and by Don Ellis (1979; Watson, 1982a, 1982b). This work is based on coding schemes that focus on control in relationships by assessing how people establish rights that define and direct relationships. Interactants reciprocally define their positions in terms of three specific types of control moves. "One-up" moves attempt to define a situation such as orders and instructions, while "one-down" moves accept or request another's definition of the situation. "One-across" moves are nondemanding, nonaccepting, leveling moves such as elaborations and extensions. Importantly, the Rogers and Farace (1975) and Ellis (1979) schemes differ in their treatment of the one-across category making comparisons across studies more difficult.

Using the Rogers and Farace (1975) relational control coding scheme, Fairhurst and colleagues have studied control patterns in routine work conversation in manufacturing settings. Fairhurst et al. (1987) found measures of leader dominance to be correlated with lower constituent performance ratings, leader understanding of constituents, and constituent desire for decision making as perceived by the leaders. Courtright et al. (1989) tested Burns and Stalker's (1961) theory of organic and mechanistic control. They compared the communication of leaders and constituents in a plant organized by an organic, self-managing team philosophy with a plant that had a mechanistic, authority-based philosophy. Consistent with Burns and Stalker's theory, they found that question-answer combinations initiated by the leader and conversational elaboration characterized the organic plant. The mechanistic plant was characterized by more hierarchical communication, nonsupport, and competitive interchanges.

A follow-up study conducted by Fairhurst et al. (1995) analyzed the potential effects of organizational inertia on the implementation of a sociotechnical systems (STS) philosophy in five manufacturing plants. Plant history (conversion from a hierarchical system, STS from start-up) and plant manager style (autocratic, participative) were posed as potential sources of inertia. When both counterproduc-